PRINCIPLES OF COMMUNITY PSYCHOLOGY

Principles of Community Psychology

PERSPECTIVES AND APPLICATIONS

Second Edition

Murray Levine

and David V. Perkins

New York   Oxford
OXFORD UNIVERSITY PRESS
1997

Oxford University Press

Oxford   New York

Athens   Auckland   Bangkok   Bogota   Bombay   Buenos Aires
Calcutta   Cape Town   Dar es Salaam   Delhi
Florence   Hong Kong   Istanbul   Karachi
Kuala Lumpur   Madras   Madrid   Melbourne
Mexico City   Nairobi   Paris   Singapore
Taipei   Tokyo   Toronto

and associated companies in
Berlin   Ibadan

Published by Oxford University Press, Inc.,
198 Madison Avenue, New York, New York 10016

Oxford is a registered trademark of Oxford University Press

Library of Congress Cataloging-in-Publication Data
Levine, Murray, 1928–
Principles of community psychology: perspectives and applications
Murray Levine and David V. Perkins. — 2nd ed.
p.   cm.
Thoroughly revised ed.
Includes bibliographical references and index.
ISBN 0-19-509844-7
1. Community psychology.   I. Perkins, David V.   II. Title.
RA790.55.L48   1996   362.2'2—dc20   95-46425
CIP

3 5 7 9 8 6 4

Printed in the United States of America
on acid-free paper

*To Seymour B. Sarason, and the spirit of the Psychoeducational Clinic—
ever since, I have been living off the intellectual capital I stored there;
to the memory of Susan L. Shackman, who left us all too soon; and to
Carolyn, Zach, and Ellen Sarah, who have brought us much joy.*

M.L.

*To Linda, my wife and partner, whose support and understanding made
my contributions to this book possible.*

D.V.P.

Foreword

This is less a second edition than it is a new book. To anyone entering, or considering to enter, the field of community psychology, the book is an unexcelled presentation of the origins of the field in relation to time and social era; its evolving theories and research base; its sharp differences from other approaches to the problems of people; its emphasis on social policy and social action; its commendably porous boundaries with other arenas of thought and action; its commitment to the preventive orientation over that of repair; its confronting of the inescapable issue of the "shoulds and oughts" of living in contemporary United States; and more, much more. Its contents are comprehensive, scholarly, and research-based; while at the same time it is eminently readable, free of jargon, intellectually provocative and compelling. The fact is that this is a book of importance for anyone interested in contemporary America. Of course this is a book about a relatively new field of questions and research, a field very much at odds with many aspects of psychology and other social sciences purporting to understand American individuals in American society. Of course this is a field whose intellectual, conceptual, and social roots are many and go back a long way in our national history. Of course this book deals with all this in a way that provides a student entering the field a basis for making decisions about where his or her talents or interests should lead. My point is that this is done in a way that *any* educated, socially concerned person will find instructive and rewarding. This is more than a book about the field of community psychology. It is about society, our society, a society in turmoil and change, acutely and agonizingly aware that problems seem infinite, resources are very limited, and past efforts to deal with them offer no basis for optimism.

There are texts, and there are texts. This is a very unusual text in that it forces you to rethink how we might better deal with the social problems our society confronts. This is a non-polemical book but the perspective that informs it is brought to bear on explosive issues. There is no hectoring but many readers will, upon reading it, feel a hectoring engendered from within because in its quiet way the book has forced them to rethink their customary or overlearned ways of defining and taking action in regard to social problems.

Seymour B. Sarason, Ph.D.
Professor Emeritus of Psychology
Yale University

Preface

This new edition differs from the first in several respects. First, we have updated the references and modified our presentation to take into account the results of new research. Many of the statistics in the chapter "Life Is a Soap Opera" are based on 1990 census data. The updated research also reflects the efforts of graduate students who took the community psychology course and who in response to an assignment found newer, better, or more critical studies they felt should be included. Second, we have added material on the history and background of the community psychology and community mental health movement. Levine's earlier book *The History and Politics of Community Mental Health* is now out of print, but the information is still relevant for our understanding of the community movement. Third, the chapter describing the Dohrenwend model has been expanded to illustrate its features better. Fourth, we have completely revised the chapter on prevention to take into account the profusion of research and newer thinking about this subject. Fifth, we have expanded the chapter on social and political action and have put the material on politics, research, and ethics into separate chapters. We include as an epilogue some comments about community psychology in a changing political climate. Sixth, we have added boxes that present longer discussions or case studies that illustrate issues in the chapters. Seventh, we omitted the chapter on consciousness raising because we felt it was outdated. Those interested can still refer to the first edition. Eighth, and most important, we have rewritten each chapter thoroughly to make it more readable. Any improvement is due to the editorial efforts of Adeline Levine, professor emeritas of sociology, SUNY Buffalo, who challenged every word in every line to improve readability. We thank her for her diligence and hard work and for her insistence on good style.

Acknowledgments

The following material was used with permission of the author and publisher.

Figure 3–1 from B. S. Dohrenwend (1978), Social stress and community psychology. *American Journal of Community Psychology*, 6, 1–14. Copyright 1978, Plenum Publishing Corporation. Reprinted with permission.

Figure 5–1 from C. Timko and R. H. Moos (1991), "A typology of social climates in group residential facilities for older people." *Journal of Gerontology*, 46, S160–169. Copyright 1991, The Gerontological Society of America. Reprinted with permission.

Table 5–1 from G. W. Fairweather, D.H. Sanders, H. Maynard, and D. Cressler (1969), *Community life for the mentally ill*. Chicago: Aldine. Reprinted with permission.

Figure 6–1 from T. J. Scheff (1984), *Being Mentally Ill: A sociological theory* (2nd ed.). New York: Aldine de Gruyter. Copyright 1984 by Thomas J. Scheff. Reprinted with permission.

Figure 7–1 from S. Cohen and T. A. Wills (1985), "Stress, social support, and the buffering hypothesis." *Psychological Bulletin*, 98, 310–357. Copyright 1985, American Psychological Association. Reprinted with permission.

Figure 8–1 from P. J. Mrazek and R. J. Haggerty (Eds.), *Reducing Risks for Mental Disorders: Frontiers for Preventive Intervention Research*. Copyright 1994 by the National Academy of Sciences. Courtesy of the National Academy Press, Washington, D.C. Reprinted with permission.

Table 8–2 from R. Caldwell, A. Bogat, and W. S. Davidson (1988). "The assessment of child abuse potential and the prevention of child abuse and neglect: A policy analysis." *American Journal of Community Psychology*, 16, 609–624. Copyright 1988, Plenum Publishing Corporation. Reprinted with permission.

Figure 8–2 from P. Aggleton, K. O'Reilly, G. Slutkin, and P. Davies (1994). "Risking everything? Risk behavior change, and AIDS." *Science*, 265, 341–345. Copyright 1994, American Association for the Advancement of Science. Reprinted with permission.

Contents

PRINCIPLES OF COMMUNITY PSYCHOLOGY

Introduction: An Overview of Community Psychology

This book is about community psychology, which is based on a way of thinking. Our intention in this book is to develop that way of thinking and to show how the perspective is applicable to a very wide range of contemporary problems.

A starting point for understanding community psychology is the community mental health movement. The community mental health movement is characterized by efforts to deliver services in the local community instead of in a hospital or clinic, to emphasize services other than long-term hospitalization, and to use outpatient services as much as possible. The community movement is also dedicated to the development of innovative services and working relationships with other agencies in the community for the client's benefit. Those adopting the community mental health perspective work to support people in the local community. We no longer follow the policy of isolating the repulsive deviant in pursuit of some chimerical goal of cure. When hospitalization does occur, the goal of treament is not to cure illness but to restore the individual's equilibrium so that he or she may be returned to the community as rapidly as possible.

This preference for community-based rather than institution-based treatment constitutes not only a perspective but also an ideology or a set of beliefs that characterizes community psychologists (Baker, 1974). In comparison to the clinical perspective, the community perspective directs more attention to the conditions of life for the person who is the client. The clinical perspective leads us to be concerned primarily with the person's inner life and perhaps with his or her relationships to family or close friends. The community mental health perspective may incorporate such concerns and interests, but it also leads the helping person to be concerned about living conditions—the availability of housing, employment, recreation, medical care, and transportation. Once the concerns extend far enough to examine the client's network of support, the community mental health worker is focusing on the community, a unit larger than the individual or the family.

Examining successes and failures of the community mental health thrust, we become even more aware of the extent to which our service system is embedded in the political structure. An understanding of funding streams is critical in understanding what happens to clients. Especially for the heaviest users of services, those who are seriously and persistently mentally ill, we find that many problems of living are related to welfare policies and laws. In adopting a community psychology perspective, we must use theoretical conceptions that extend beyond those that are useful in understanding an individual (e.g., diagnostic categories, psychodynamics, and traits) and incorporate larger units of analysis.

Several viewpoints or theories are incorporated in the community perspective. One important characteristic of the community field is an emphasis on the ecological viewpoint, or the study of the fit between persons and environments (Rappaport, 1977). The ecological viewpoint requires "a concern with the relationships of individuals to each other as a community; as a differentiated social grouping with elaborate systems of formal and informal relationships" (Mann, 1978, p. x). The community perspective includes a "focus on broader ecological levels than the level of the exclusive treatment of the individual" (Heller & Monahan, 1977, p. 16). An important difference between the community and the clinical orientation is the helping person's choice of point of intervention—individual, small group, organizational, community, or nation (Graziano & Mooney, 1984, pp. 371–373). This focus on the person-in-environment is also emphasized by community psychologists outside the United States (e.g., Orford, 1992; Thomas & Veno, 1992).

A paradigm shift in our understanding of social problems has occurred in that both the questions we must ask and the methods used to obtain answers have changed (Rappaport, 1977). It is necessary to develop research bases for informed intervention, but it is not sufficient. If psychology and social science are to be relevant and useful for the solution of social problems, then conceptual and research approaches will have to broaden to take into account the historical, social, economic, and political contexts within which policies are developed and implemented (Sarason, 1974, 1981, 1982a).

One can have less than radical aims and remain within the community orientation. Most psychologists following the community perspective accept the broader society as it is and see it as their mission to help create or change service organizations and other institutions. They work to achieve the goals of providing humane, effective care and less stigmatizing services to those in need while enhancing human psychological growth and development.

To make human service organizations more effective and more humane, community-oriented psychologists are interested in creating new services consistent with the ecological perspective. That perspective, and the actions that flow from it, differ from the medical model in which persons in need define their own problems and then seek out help from a professional helper, most often on a fee-for-service basis. The medical model is useful for many people and for many problems. However, the medical model, with its emphasis on highly trained professionals, is unable to provide for all in need. Moreover, certain forms of care may contribute to the perpetuation of problems because of the way problems are defined in the medical model as residing exclusively within the boundaries of an individual.

In the ecological perspective, human behavior is viewed in terms of the person's adaptation to resources and circumstances. From this perspective, one may correct unsuccessful adaptations by altering the availability of resources. Thus, new services may be created, or existing strengths in social networks may be discovered and conditions changed to enhance the use of resources. A good example is the way legal and cultural barriers to resources were eliminated in the United States as a result of antidiscrimination and voting rights legislation starting in the 1950s. The increased number of African Americans in professional, managerial, and technical occupations, the increase in income among middle- and upper-class African Americans, and the increased number of African American students in colleges and professional schools can be attributed to the civil rights movement. The increasing number of young, unemployed African American males, the correlated increase in absent-father families, and the concentration of social problems such as crime in certain urban areas can be attributed at least in part to a changing job market and to the loss of access to jobs, a critical resource for favorable adaptation (Wilson, 1987). From this perspective, solutions to problems in living do not require more professional therapists; instead community psychologists try to work through a variety of institutions and with people who may not have advanced training in the mental health professions to improve and develop resources. The ecological perspective encourages a search for resources instead of a search for psychopathology. It encourages us to view others as having strengths that may be put to good use in the service of their own development if resources are available. It may not be necessary to undo psychopathology first.

Crisis theory also provides a useful model that can be integrated with an ecological perspective. Crisis theory argues that as a result of either failures of past socialization or present circumstances, a person may experience transient distress. In attempting to deal with the circumstances and the feelings of distress, the person may return to a point of equilibrium, may worsen and need further care, or may come to terms with the distress and emerge strengthened. Crisis theory states that the difference in outcome is some function of the environmental supports and psychological mediators available to the person who is coping.

While the ecological viewpoint gives us different levels for intervention, crisis theory is helpful because it points to possibilities for intervention at different times during the process of coping with distress. It also directs attention to the necessity of resources, personal or social, in the coping process. Crisis theory focuses attention on the possibilities for improvement and leads us to view the potential for growth and development as more important than the underlying psychopathology. We should not overestimate the power of our theories, but neither should we underestimate it. Our concepts can serve as blinders or as guides. A combination of crisis theory and the ecological perspective directs us to explore new territory in ways that the psychopathological viewpoint and the medical model do not.

Community psychologists have also rallied around the theme of prevention. The concept of prevention comes from the field of public health. Public health professionals argue that the greatest advances result from preventing diseases instead of treating them after they occur. Deadly scourges have been all but wiped out by inoculations and modern sanitary methods. Our increased average length of life, and our better health throughout a longer fraction of that life span, are both attributable more to preventive than to therapeutic measures. The public health model leads us to seek out the causes of pathology and to act to prevent them by either modifying environmental conditions or strengthening the person. It is not clear that the public health model can be adopted wholly when we deal with social and mental health problems. However, it does provide a set of goals and a way of thinking that direct our attention to issues other than individual psychopathology and its treatment.

The concept of prevention offers different times and places for intervention. It asks us to think about whether it might be possible to take action before the undesirable behavior actually appears or, in the alternative, to position assistance—resources—so that problem resolution can occur very early in the history of a problem. As clinicians we are generally called in after an intolerable situation has developed for an individual or a family. In the preventive perspective, we are encouraged to think systematically about the beginnings of the process that results in people defining themselves or being defined by others, as "cases."

Preventive approaches also require us to function in new organizational settings. Historically, the setting for mental health professionals was the clinic, the hospital, or the private practice office. In preventive work using the community perspective, it becomes necessary to leave familiar settings and learn to live, work, and adapt in environments that are at best unfamiliar or uncongenial and at worst may be actively hostile to strangers and to change efforts, no matter how benignly intended. It is necessary to work with and through schools, welfare departments, recreation facilities, the mass media, the legislative and the political processes, and people representing many varied interests and values.

Community psychology directs attention to the larger context within which plans are developed and implemented. The possibilities for gaining resources must be carefully evaluated. The political climate supporting one type of programming at one time and another at another time must be understood. What is feasible at one time and under one set of political and economic conditions may often be approached only with great difficulty at another time or under other circumstances (Levine & Levine, 1992). Competition among agencies and groups for the same pool of limited resources becomes a crucial factor influencing what kinds and amounts of resources will be available and to whom. When we adopt the community perspective, our professional concerns necessarily broaden.

In this book we will examine some of the theories and programs in community psychology and some of the research related to them. We are interested in showing the interrelationships among problems and theories and in trying to develop as systematic a framework as we can for thinking about problems and their solutions. At this point in the development of the field, we can try to convey an orientation and a way of thinking. Hard knowledge is in short supply and may never be sufficient to satisfy the most hard-nosed critics. The problems of interest to this field will persist, however, and we will continue to develop better—if imperfect—ways of addressing them. When those of us working in this field in the early 1960s began, we were innocent of the questions as well as of the answers. Now at least we are developing an intellectual framework within which diverse experiences make some sense. We can at least ask questions that are more meaningful than ones we were able to ask thirty years ago.

The content of the book is organized as follows. The first two chapters establish a philosophical and temporal context for community psychology. Chapter 1 examines the nature and scope of issues and problems facing the field and discusses the implications of a view that asserts that the definition of a problem involves its situational context. Chapter 2 reviews the historical background of this perspective. Chapter 3 presents Barbara Dohrenwend's unified model of the community psychology field and the many activities it endorses. Much of the remainder of the book builds on Dohrenwend's model. Chapters 4 through 7 describe and assess the major conceptual foundations of community psychology, including principles of ecology, conceptions of behavior in a social context, labeling theory, and the increasingly useful concepts of stress and support. These concepts are also used to conceptualize programs designed to help those who need long-term assistance with chronic problems.

The remainder of the book focuses on applications of community psychology principles while maintaining the focus on concepts. Chapter 8 outlines and discusses community psychology's perspective on prevention.

This chapter pays particular attention to interventions intended to build individual competence and to reduce risks in important settings such as schools. Some of the ideas derived from prevention are applied in Chapter 9 to the condition of people who need help on a chronic, long-term basis. Self-help groups offer an important alternative to traditional clinical services in the way they conceptualize problems and the nature of their approach to overcoming a problem.

The remaining chapters elaborate on these issues. Chapter 10 considers the problem of change at the level of individual settings and organizations. Creating new settings and changing existing settings are both discussed, and two illustrative case studies are presented. Perspectives in community psychology also offer insights into the process of change at larger levels. School desegregation, for example, the focus in Chapter 11, was a change of nationwide proportions in which psychologists and other social scientists played a relatively important role. Chapter 12 examines the nature of problem definition in a community context and some of the alternative interventions that follow from different definitions. Chapter 13 completes the book by offering a community perspective on scientific research and the ethics and politics of intervention. We hope that everyone who reads this book will learn from it, but if we only stimulate the reader to think about the issues we raise, our most essential objective will have been accomplished.

I

ORIGINS
OF COMMUNITY
PSYCHOLOGY

1

Life Is a Soap Opera

In the 1950s there was a popular television program called *Queen for a Day*. Contestants competed by listing a catalog of personal miseries, tragedies, and catastrophes that they and their families had endured. The show was considered a vulgar display pandering to the morbid curiosity of the general public; its popularity was embarrassing if not puzzling. *Queen for a Day* was but one manifestation of the same deep interest in the plight of individuals and families who struggle with personal, familial, medical, psychiatric, legal, and economic problems that leads millions to read Ann Landers and to watch Oprah, Geraldo, and many others every day.

Such TV programs and newspaper features are like the ever popular soap operas but with real people as the actors. They chronicle for the American public the impact of death, disease, accident, divorce, crime, and sundry tragedies in the everyday lives of fictional characters. The popularity of soap operas is not explained by the loneliness of homemakers who fill their drab existences by experiencing vicariously the exciting lives of the beautiful, glamorous figures who populate televisionland. Soap operas do more than dispel boredom. The myths that are the staple fare of the soap opera touch on universal themes, provide an opportunity for catharsis, and teach, as all good myths do. Their lesson is that the tragedies of life are inevitable and, if not surmountable, at least to be endured with dignity.

We think that soap operas are popular not only because they are entertaining but precisely because they are a way of understanding life. Life itself is the soap opera. The popularity of the television versions simply reflects that fact. By looking at life as a soap opera, we can develop a better understanding of our cultural concern with psychological well-being, the demand for psychological services, the emphasis on crisis and coping in the contemporary professional literature, and the recent proliferation of self-help and social support groups. We may well come to a different view of what is "normal," in the sense of typical or not unusual.

An important theme of this book is that problem definitions themselves offer insights into social phenomena. For example, does a mental or emotional problem reside entirely inside a person, or does it also become tangled in the specific events and situations immediately surrounding the sufferer? The simple statistics that we will present suggest that multitudes are struggling with critical problems in living; struggle with life's problems is the rule, not the exception.

If struggles with critical problems are normative, then public services built on the assumption that serious problems in living are the exception have no chance of serving the full public need. Problems of living are not the exception at all; any such conception does a disservice to the people living through the events and is a definition of the problem that inevitably leads to ever increasing frustration. To understand why alternate forms of service, alternate personnel, and prevention are all necessary, we have only to turn to statistics describing the frequency of problems in living. It will help us to make sense of these statistics if we understand the concepts of prevalence and incidence. *Prevalence* refers to the number of new and old instances of some problem in the population at a given point in time (called "point prevalence") or, alternatively, the number active at any time during a specified interval ("period prevalence"). *Incidence* refers to the number of new cases coming into the population over a period of time, usually one year.

The Incidence and Prevalence of Problems in Living

In this section we present data from several sources, including statistics about people receiving psychiatric treatment and other prevalence estimates for mental disorders, epidemiological and survey estimates of certain maladaptive behavior patterns (e.g., alcohol abuse), disadvantaged social conditions (e.g., widowhood, poverty), and the implications for mental health of several contemporary social and cultural trends. Many items in this catalog of problems also appear on measures of "stressful life events." The prototype scale was developed by Holmes and Rahe (1967) (see Chapter 7). In the following presentation figures may not always add up exactly. Figures obtained from different sources vary from each other, and extrapolations from population figures may be taken from different bases in different years. However, that does not violate the picture of general trends which we want to present.

To appreciate fully the impact of the figures, keep in mind that the average household in the United States in 1992 consisted of 2.62 individuals (U.S. Bureau of the Census, 1993, Table 65[1]). Thus, for each individual affected by a given condition, nearly two other people were also affected to some degree. Research has, for example, documented the stresses and burdens of living with a depressed adult (Coyne et al., 1987) or a disabled sibling (Breslau & Prabucki, 1987).

Institutionalized Population

This population includes people in psychiatric hospitals and institutions for the retarded, the aged, youth in residential facilities, and the prison population. The size of the institutionalized population changes from time to time.

Psychiatric hospitals. With the growth of deinstitutionalization policies (see Chapter 2), the population of state and county psychiatric hospitals dropped from about 550,000 in the 1950s to about 152,400 in 1988. Table 1–1 shows that the average daily census, including patients in veterans hospitals and in psychiatric wards in general hospitals, is 227,900. Inpatient care for adolescents in private psychiatric hospitals has been increasing in recent years and is not reflected in the count of people in state and county hospitals (Weithorn, 1988).

Because of admissions and discharges during the year, the average daily census doesn't accurately reflect the number of people who receive psychiatric care. In 1988 there were 2,324,000 patient-care episodes in mental hospitals. In 1986 there were 1,400,574 additional psychiatric patient-care episodes in psychiatric wards of general hospitals (Kiesler & Simkins, 1991). Patient-care episodes are defined as the number of pa-

Table 1-1
Institutionalized Population of the United States

Population	Number of Persons in Institution	Year
Adult patients, federal, state, and county mental hospitals	227,900	1988[a]
Public facilities for the mentally retarded	281,542	1990[b]
Nursing homes for the elderly	1,772,032	1990[c]
Public and private juvenile justice facilities	96,148	1989[d]
Foster care	425,000	1991[e]
Correctional institutions, state and federal prisons	789,347	1991[f]
Jails	426,479	1991[g]
Total Institutionalized	4,018,448[j]	
Patient-care episodes in mental hospitals	2,324,000	1988[h]
Patient-care episodes in general hospitals	1,746,000	1986[i]
Patient-care episodes in outpatient facilities	5,970,000	1988[i]

[a]U.S. Bureau of the Census, 1992, Table 183. [b]U.S. Bureau of the Census, 1993, Table 193. [c]U.S. Bureau of the Census, 1993, Table 193. [d]U.S. Select Commitee, 1990. [e]U.S. General Accounting Office, 1993. [f]U.S. Bureau of the Census, 1993, Table 344. [g]U.S. Bureau of the Census, 1993, Table 342. [h]Kiesler & Simkins, 1991. [i]Redick et al., 1992. [j]Does not include group homes, halfway houses, or supervised independent living arrangements.

tients on the first day of the year, plus all admissions during the year; some are repeat admissions. If we consider both the patients and their families, we can say that up to 9.7 million persons (2.3 million inpatient episodes plus 1.4 million general hospital episodes times 2.62 persons in each household) are affected by an episode of psychiatric hospitalization during any given year. These sources do not count children treated for psychiatric problems in general hospitals or in other types of residential care or people who enter institutions because of mental retardation or developmental disabilities.

Facilities for the retarded. In 1990 there were 281,542 residents of facilities (e.g., institutions, group homes) that provided twenty-four-hour care for those with mental retardation (Table 193). There has been a decline of the census of those in state institutions due to the emphasis on community-based practice.

Facilities for the elderly. The institutionalized population includes 1,772,032 elderly persons living in nursing homes or similar residential facilities. People in nursing homes need varying amounts of supervision or personal help with bathing, eating, using toilet facilities, dressing, managing money, shopping, or walking (Table 85). Depending on the standards used, between 8 percent and 25 percent of the over-sixty-five population has some psychiatric disorder, and between 45 percent and 74 percent of those over age 65 in nursing homes have a mental disability of some consequence. Twenty percent of nursing home residents under age 65 are believed to be mentally retarded, and another 20 percent are mentally ill (Comptroller General of the United States, 1977).

Residential care. Many children and adolescents are also in residential care. In 1989 there were 96,148 youths in public and private juvenile justice facilities because they had been adjudicated as delinquents or as status offenders. A Select Committee of the U.S. House of Representatives (1990) projected that this number would reach 119,700 by 1995. In 1991 there were about 425,000 children in foster care (U.S. General Accounting Office, 1993). Many children were placed in foster care as a result of abuse or neglect.

Jails and prisons. The number of people in federal and state prisons and in jails (pretrial holding centers) has been increasing rapidly. In 1991 there were 789,347 inmates of federal and state prisons, and 426,479 more in jails (Tables 324, 344). There were about forty thousand female inmates in state prisons in 1991, an increase of about 75 percent since 1986. About two-thirds of the women and 56 percent of the men have children (Snell & Morton, 1994). Those children need care, and the extent of their difficulties that are directly related to having a parent in prison has not been documented.

Because of the "criminalization of the mentally ill" (Teplin, 1984; see Chapter 4), there is a large number of mentally ill people in prisons and jails. One report claimed that the Los Angeles city jail held more mentally ill inmates than the largest remaining mental hospital in California (Hilts, 1992). Conditions in many prisons and jails are very poor. In 1993 there were 647 deaths in jails, 36 percent of them suicides. Twenty-six percent of jurisdictions with jails holding more than one hundred inmates were under court order to improve conditions, which were found to be unacceptable (U.S. Bureau of Justice Statistics, 1990; Perkins, Stephan, & Beck, 1995).

Overall estimate. We arrive at an estimate of 4,018,448 institutionalized people. Using our multiplier of 2.62 for household size, we find that an additional 6,609,885 people are living with the fact that some household member has been institutionalized. This number does not take into account patient-care episodes and psychiatric care in general hospitals. If we reduce the number by 25 percent because of repeated admissions, we are still left with at least 5 million additional persons who are affected each year.

Outpatient Mental Health Care

We now examine estimates of the number of persons with problems treatable with formal mental health services provided on an outpatient (or "ambulatory") basis and the total number affected by each person's problem.

One index of the demand for services is the utilization rate as provided in standard reports to government agencies. In 1988 there were 5,970,000 episodes of outpatient care in outpatient facilities (Redick, Witkin, Amy, & Manderscheid, 1992). Using our multiplier of 2.62, we can state that the lives of nearly 10 million additional people were affected. These figures exclude people treated in private offices or in federal government facilities.

The nearly 6 million outpatient care episodes constitute 72 percent of all patient-care episodes in public mental health organizations. We can see the effect of the community mental health movement in these figures. In 1955 only 23 percent of all patient-care episodes took place in outpatient settings (Redick et al., 1992).

Outpatient mental health care is delivered across an array of overlapping but distinct sectors, and we obtain somewhat different figures on utilization by looking at data gathered with a different method. An ambitious study conducted in five representative communities in the early 1980s estimated that 22.8 million U.S. adults per year receive ambulatory help for a mental health problem. This figure includes those going to mental health specialists and those receiving help from their regular physicians. They made a total of 325.9 million visits for such help (Narrow, Regier, Rae, et al., 1993). An estimated 5.9 percent (9.4 million persons per year) receive treatment from a specialist in mental or addictive disorders, 6.4 percent (10 million) seek help for mental disorder from a general medical physician, 3 percent (4.8 million) consult other human service professionals (e.g., pastoral counselor, family services agency), and 4.1 percent (6.5 million) seek help from friends, family, and self-help groups (Regier, Narrow, Rae, et al., 1993).

Only part of the total utilization is accounted for by conditions significant enough to warrant a formal diagnosis using the *Diagnostic and Statistical Manual of Mental Disorders* (*DSM*; American Psychiatric Association, 1994). Narrow et al. (1993) report that 46 percent of those receiving ambulatory help do not have a current diagnosis, and about 9 percent also have no lifetime history of diagnosable mental disorder.

Utilization figures underestimate need because a great many persons do not seek help for their problems. When brief episodes are included, the annual prevalence of mental disorder in the United States rises to 28.1 percent, or 44.7 million persons, approximately twice the number who seek help from all sources combined (Regier et al., 1993). Using our multiplier, we can speculate that more than 100 million people are affected.

Looked at in this way, these data indicate that perhaps one-third to one-half of the noninstitutionalized population is affected by mental health problems. Is that large a percent of the population "sick"? We don't think so. We believe that the definition of subjective distress as a mental health problem or as a "diagnosable disorder" reflects the influence on the field of the medical model of care. This definition limits our vision because it directs us to think in terms of treating disorders instead of understanding what in fact are ubiquitous problems in living.

Substance Abuse

According to the U.S. Congress Office of Technology Assessment, between 10 and 15 million U.S. adults have serious problems related to alcohol, and 35 million Americans are indirectly affected by alcohol problems (Office of Technology Assessment, 1983a, Table 1–2). Regier et al. (1993) estimate the annual prevalence of any addictive disorder at 9.5 percent (15.1 million), of whom 7.4 percent have an alcohol disorder and 3.1 percent another drug use disorder (with 1 percent having both). In 1991 the U.S. Department of Health and Human Services said that about 18 percent of adults (32.7 million people) lived with an alcoholic when they were children, and about 9 percent of adults have been married to or have lived with an alcoholic (American Public Health Association, 1991). A substantial percent of youth and young adults are current users of marijuana, cocaine, and hallucinogens (Table 208). Not all have drug-related difficulties, but each one is potentially a problem user.[2] A survey of twenty-seven thousand randomly sampled high school students in New York (Barnes, 1984) indicates that 10 percent abuse alcohol at least once per week, 26 percent abuse alcohol six or more times per year, and 11 percent report being "hooked" (dependent) on beer, wine, or liquor.

Defined more narrowly, in 1991 there were 1,271,000 arrests on charges of driving while intoxicated and 625,000 arrests for drunkenness (Table 313). In 1991, 237,000 people were under treatment for drug abuse in the country (Table 207), and there were 763,000 arrests for drug law violations (Table 313). Again, we do not know the extent of overlap in these groups, and we have no idea of how many repeaters there are among those arrested. If we consider only those arrested and their families, we can say that the lives of about 7.5 million persons are affected by alcohol or drug abuse leading to some contact with the law.

Table 1–2
Substance Abuse

Condition	Prevalence	Year
Alcohol abuse and dependence	10–15,000,000	1983[a]
Percent who lived with an alcoholic as a child	18.0	1988[b]
Percent married to or lived with an alcoholic	9.0	1988[b]
Arrests, driving while intoxicated	1,271,000	1991[c]
Arrests, drunkenness	625,000	1991[c]
Arrests, violation of narcotics laws	763,000	1991[c]
Percent current users of marijuana		1991[d]
Youth, 12–17	4.3	
Young adults, 18–25	13.0	
Adults, 26+ years old	3.3	
Percent current users of cocaine		
Youth, 12–17	0.4	
Young adults, 18–25	2.0	
Adults, 26+ years old	0.8	
Percent current users of hallucinogens		
Youth 12–17	0.8	
Young adults, 18–25	1.2	
Adults, 26+ years old	0.1	
Clients, drug abuse treatment units	237,800	1991[e]

[a]Office of Technology Assessment, 1983a. [b]American Public Health Association, 1991. [c]U.S. Bureau of Census, 1993, Table 313. [d]U.S. Bureau of Census, 1993, Table 208. [e]U.S. Bureau of Census, 1993, Table 207.

Crime and Victims of Crime

Crime victims suffer distress that may last a long time. Our knowledge of the frequency of crimes also leads us to feel anxious that we may become victims. In 1991 police knew about 14,873,000 criminal offenses, of which 1,912,000 were for murder, forcible rape, robbery, or aggravated assault (Table 1–3). Victimization estimates based on house-to-house surveys show that thirty-one out of one thousand people over the age of twelve reported being the victim of a crime against their person (Table 309). Translated into 1991 population figures, 6,437,770 individuals experienced at least one episode as a victim of violent crime. Using our multiplier, these figures indicate that some 16.9 million Americans coped with an episode of violent crime in which some household member was a victim.

Interpersonal violence is a serious public health problem. The annual prevalence of partner violence against women is at least 2 to 3 million (Koss, Goodman, Browne, et al., 1994). One hundred seventy-three thousand people, mostly female, were the victims of rapes or attempted rapes in 1991. Almost half the attempted rapes were never reported to the police, and 40 percent of the completed rapes were not reported either. Twenty-nine percent of victims of attempted rape were physically injured, as were 58 percent of victims of completed rapes. Eleven percent of all rape victims were between the ages of twelve and fifteen, and another 25 percent were between sixteen and nineteen years of age (U.S. Bureau of Justice Statistics, 1985). According to another survey of crimes against youth, 11,880 females between the ages of twelve and fifteen were victims of rape, as were 32,884 between the ages of sixteen and nineteen (Whitaker & Bastian, 1991). A substantial percent of victims of sexual crimes suffer enduring psychological effects.

In addition, about 16 million individuals reported being the victim of a nonviolent crime in 1991. Probably 20 percent of the population, or well over 40 million persons, were affected by nonviolent crime directed at some household member. In 1992 some 23 percent of all U.S. households were victimized (U.S. Bureau of Justice Statistics, 1994). In

Table 1–3
Crimes and Victims of Crimes

Problem	Number of Persons	Year
Offenses known to police	14,873,000	1991[a]
Arrests—all causes	10,744,000	1991[b]
Arrests, sex offenses	82,000	1991[b]
Arrests, crimes against family	73,000	1991[b]
Victimization, over age 12		
Violent crime	6,437,770	1993[c]
Nonviolent crime	16,000,000	1993[c]
Rape and attempted		
rape victims	173,000	1991[d]
Percent rape attempts		
reported	50%	1985[e]
Percent rapes reported	60%	1985[e]
Rape victim age		
12–16	11,880	1990[f]
16–19	32,884	1990[f]

[a]U.S. Bureau of Census, 1993, Table 300.   [b]U.S. Bureau of Census, 1993, Table 314.   [c]U.S. Bureau of Census, 1993, Table 309.   [d]U.S. Bureau of Census, 1993, Table 308.   [e]U.S. Bureau of Justice Statistics, 1985.   [f]Whitaker & Bastian, 1991.

1977, 45 percent of the population said they feared walking around in neighborhoods within a mile of their homes (U.S. Bureau of the Census, 1981, Table 5–1). Fear of crime continues to be pervasive. In some ghetto neighborhoods where crime rates tend to be high, "fear has become a condition of life" (Moore & Trajonowicz, 1988).

The experience of criminal victimization can have important psychological consequences ranging from short-term discomfort to long-term posttraumatic stress disorders that may be disabling (APA Task Force on the Victims of Crime and Violence, 1984; Riger, 1985). A telephone survey of women eighteen years of age and older reported that 21 percent of respondents said that they had been victims of a completed or an attempted rape, sexual molestation, robbery, or aggravated assault. Victims experienced nervous breakdowns, thought of suicide, and made suicide attempts at a rate far higher than that for nonvictims. Those who were victims of a crime reported most often that their symptoms appeared after the episode of victimization, not before (Kilpatrick, Best, Veronen, et al., 1985). About a third of all victims of violent crime sustained physical injury and had some medical costs. Medical costs sometimes continue for a long period of time after the injury. About 8 percent of victims lost time from work, an average of 3.4 days per crime. The average economic loss of a crime in 1992 was well over $500 per victim (Klaus, 1994).

Arrests. A large number of people are arrested for crimes and experience stress for that reason. (Serving a term in jail is the fourth most stressful event on the Holmes and Rahe scale.) In 1991 some 10,157,000 persons were arrested for a crime (Table 313), and eighty-one thousand individuals were arrested for sex offenses and seventy-one thousand more for crimes against family or children (Table 313). Including household members, 26,611,340 persons are affected annually by an arrest for a crime. Assuming victims and perpetrators are nonoverlapping populations (not a wholly safe assumption), perhaps a third of the population is directly affected by crime each year.

Problems of Children and Adolescents

The problems of children and adolescents are not included in most of the figures cited earlier. Prevalence rates vary between 5 percent and 23 percent (Namir & Weinstein, 1982; Institute of Medicine, 1989). Using a conservative estimate of 12 percent, in 1991 about 7.8 million children under age 18 would be identified as having problems severe enough to warrant a psychiatric diagnosis (Table 1–4). The prevalence is probably higher among poorer and inner-city children than among those living in more well-to-do areas (Institute of Medicine, 1989). In addition, in 1991 22 percent of the 10.7 million people arrested and charged with crimes were under age 18 (Table 314). Juvenile courts handled 1,265,000 delinquency cases in 1990 (Table 337). That number does not include

Table 1–4
Problems of Children and Adolescents

Problem	Number of Persons	Year
Arrested under age 18	2,209,000	1991[a]
Juvenile court cases	1,265,000	1990[b]
Prevalence of disorder	7,800,000	1991[c]
Enrolled in public or private special-education facility	4,587,370	1989[d]
Mentally retarded, under 21	2,314,000	1991[e]
Child abuse and neglect		
Number of reports	1,670,000	1991[f]
Number of children	2,700,000	1991[f]

[a]U.S. Bureau of Census, 1993, Table 314.   [b]U.S. Bureau of Census, 1993, Table 337.   [c]Institute of Medicine, 1989.   [d]U.S. Department of Education, 1990.   [e]See text.   [f]U.S. Bureau of Census, 1993, Table 340.

tens of thousands of status offense cases (runaways, truants, incorrigible children), which may also be processed through juvenile or family courts and are often diverted to the service system.

Children's problems emerge in educational settings and involve issues of intellectual competence as well as of classroom adjustment. In 1988–1989, 4,587,370 children were enrolled in public special education facilities (U.S. Department of Education, 1990). The total includes almost half a million preschool children served under new amendments to the Individuals with Disabilities Education Act and the Elementary and Secondary Education Act. However, school-based programs for serious emotional disturbances are identifying and serving only a very small proportion of those in need (Knitzer, Steinberg, & Fleisch, 1990). In 1991 approximately 77,135,000 individuals were under age 21. By definition, some 3 percent of all children (or 2,314,000 children) are considered mentally retarded, and most of them are in need of special services. These numbers do not take into account children who are not sufficiently disturbed (or disturbing) to be classified as educationally handicapped or seriously emotionally disturbed but whose teachers may consider them maladjusted in some degree. Problems of delinquency and education are intimately intertwined. Perhaps 30 percent of all juvenile delinquents are learning disabled.

Children are victimized in familiar ways (e.g., assault) even more than adults. Children also experience relatively unique forms of victimization ranging from corporal punishment to abduction. While abduction is a rather rare event, it is much feared. About 750,000 incidents of corporal punishment occur each year in U.S. schools, with serious consequences for at least some children (Hyman, 1995). Sibling assault is experienced by more than 50 million children (Finkelhor & Dziuba-Leatherman, 1994).

Child abuse and neglect. The problem of child abuse and neglect first attracted public attention in the mid-1960s. States responded by passing legislation requiring professionals who work with teachers to report suspected child abuse and neglect to either child protection authorities or the police. After the passage of the Child Abuse Prevention and Treatment Act of 1974, all states created state central registries and hotlines that took calls from ordinary citizens as well as from mandated professionals. In 1991 there were 1.67 million reports involving 2.7 million children (Table 340). Half or more of the calls alleged neglect. Fortunately, serious physical abuse and fatalities attributable to maltreatment occur infrequently, although their importance should not be discounted.

Reports of sexual abuse have been increasing, constituting about 16 percent of all reports to child protection authorities. About 40 percent of all reports are substantiated upon investigation. A very high proportion of sex-abuse victims suffer short-term emotional upset, and a smaller number, perhaps 20 percent, suffer long-term damage (Browne and Finkelhor, 1985). Some research suggests that there are short-term and long-term emotional and developmental consequences for children who are the victims of child abuse or neglect. It is likely that as many as a third of abused children may in turn abuse their own children, become physically aggressive, or commit crimes (National Research Council, 1993; Widom, 1989).

The U.S. Advisory Board on Child Abuse and Neglect (1993) has said that the child protection system is in a state of crisis; the problem of abuse and neglect is a national emergency, and the foster care system is overwhelmed. The problem has been exacerbated by the number of "crack" and cocaine babies and babies who are infected with the human immunodeficiency virus (HIV). As a matter of policy, most child protective service agencies will not intervene when a baby is born with signs of drug addiction unless the parent is unable to care for the infant because of her drug problems. Only a small proportion of investigated cases receive any service. The Board has also recommended a complete overhaul of the existing system of child protection.

Number of child-related problems. If we use the 7.8 million prevalence estimate and our multiplier, there may be as many as 20.4 million individuals and their families who are coping with a serious problem related to a child. Without knowing the overlap in epidemiological sources and other reports estimating childhood distress, we can probably add another 20 percent to the overall figure without being too far wrong. That would bring the overall number to 24.5 million affected individuals and family members.

Medical Problems and Chronic Illness

Personal injury or illness, the sixth most stressful life event on the Holmes and Rahe list, is fairly common (Table 1–5). In 1991 there were 31.1 million hospital discharges, with an average stay of 6.4 days (Table 185). Obviously there were even more hospital admissions, since some patients died before leaving the hospital. Using our multiplier, we estimate that more than 80 million individuals and their families were affected by an illness requiring hospitalization. In 1990, researchers conducting a house-to-house survey found that 60.1 million individuals reported an injury sufficiently severe to lead the individual to cut down on usual activities for at least one entire day, including missing work or school and/or seeking medical attention for the injury (Table 196).

Examining the major killers and cripplers, we find that in 1990 19.1 million people had heart conditions; 1.13 million new cases of cancer were diagnosed in 1992;[3] 6.2 million people had diabetes in 1991; 27.1 million, high blood pressure; 6 million, asthma; 4 million, epilepsy; 750,000, cerebral palsy; 500,000, multiple sclerosis; and 200,000, muscular dystrophy. A total of 30.8 million persons required medical care for arthritis; 7.5 million were visually impaired, with 1.3 million so impaired that they could not read; 23.3 million had hearing impairments and about 15 million had birth defects of varying severity (Table 206).

In 1992 almost 15 million people between the ages of sixteen and sixty-four had work disabilities (Table 601). That estimate should probably be increased by some factor to account for those who had other limitations consequent to injuries, amputations, and other sources of chronic problems not specified in the selected group of disorders in the table. We may safely say that more than 70 million persons are coping with their own chronic physical limitations or those of a member of the household (Table 194; see Breslau & Pabrucki, 1987).

Sexually transmitted diseases (STD). Venereal disease may no longer be the social disgrace it once was, but it remains embarrassing at least, seriously disabling, or even lethal at worst. In 1991, 620,000 cases of gonorrhea and 129,000 new cases of syphilis were reported (Table 201). An estimated five hundred thousand to 1 million new cases of genital herpes are diagnosed annually, along with several million recurrences. Some fifty thousand women a year suffer from sterility resulting from pelvic inflammatory disorder, much of it caused by complications of sexually transmitted diseases, creating emotional distress for those who want to conceive but cannot (Department of Health, Education, and Welfare, 1979).

In 1992, 45,472 new cases of AIDS (acquired immune deficiency syndrome) were reported in the United States (Table 203). Many more persons have been exposed to HIV, the virus that causes AIDS. Because it is currently incurable and usually leads to death within a few years, AIDS is our newest plague. In 1992 alone, 22,675 persons in the United

Table 1–5
Medical Problems and Chronic Illness

Condition	Number of Persons	Year
Hospital discharges General medical	31,098,000	1991[a]
Injuries leading to one or more days of lost work or school	60,100,000	1990[b]
Arthritis	30,800,000	1990–92[c]
Visual impairment, can't read	1,306,000	
Cancer, incidence	1,130,000	
Cerebral palsy	750,000	
Hearing impairment	23,300,000	
Epilepsy	4,000,000	
Birth defects, varying severity	15,000,000 (estimate)	
High blood pressure	27,100,000	
Multiple sclerosis	500,000	
Muscular dystrophy	200,000	
Cardiac conditions	19,100,000	
Asthma	6,000,000	
Diabetes	6,200,000	
Limitation, major activity due to chronic illness	24,700,000	1979[d]
Work disability, ages 16–64	15,000,000	1992[e]
Venereal disease Gonorrhea, reported cases	620,000	1991[f]
Syphillis, reported cases	129,000	1991[f]
Genital herpes, new cases per year	500,000–1,000,000	1979[g]
HIV/AIDS per year Deaths	22,675	1992[h]
Reported cases	45,472	1992[i]

[a]U.S. Bureau of Census, 1993, Table 185. [b]U.S. Bureau of Census, 1993, Table 196. [c] U.S. Bureau of Census, 1993, Table 206. [d]U.S. Bureau of Census, 1981, Table 194. [e]U.S. Bureau of Census, 1993, Table 601. [f]U.S. Bureau of Census, 1993, Table 201. [g]Department of Health, Education, and Welfare, 1979, p. 31. [h]U.S. Bureau of Census, Table 131. [i]U.S. Bureau of Census, Table 203.

States died of AIDS (Table 131). AIDS was the second leading cause of death for males between 25 and 44 years of age in 1991 (Table 127). This devastating disorder is correlated with psychological distress and presents problems of adaptation to the millions who are afflicted, as well as to their families and friends. Moreover, in the absence of medical means of preventing the disorder, prevention depends on behavioral change and lifestyle change. Although the manifestations are primarily medical in nature, the problems of prevention and adaptation are social and psychological (Levine, Toro, & Perkins, 1993; interventions to prevent AIDS/HIV are discussed in Chapter 8).

Disasters

Hundreds of thousands of people each year are affected by natural disasters resulting at least in inconvenience and some degree of fear and at worst resulting in death (Table 381), severe injury, the necessity to change living arrangements or to start one's life anew, and in some cases enduring psychological distress (Zusman & Simon, 1983). While natural disasters do not take many lives in comparison to other causes of death, many individuals and communities are affected by them (see Table 1–6). In 1991 tornadoes, hurricanes, and floods took 119 lives, but sixty-four tornadoes each left property losses in excess of $500,000, while floods resulted in property losses totaling more than $1.4 billion (Table 381). Earthquakes can also result in devastating property damage. In 1991 there were 478,000 residential fires, which resulted in property losses totaling more than $5.5 billion (Table 353). Fire killed 3,575 persons and injured 21,850 in 1991. Nineteen percent of mass deaths in 1981 took place in hotels, boardinghouses, rooming houses, and facilities for the aged (Table 120).

Rescue workers risk death and injury and are affected as they work under grueling conditions coping with people who are injured or in pain or who have bloody, mangled, or burned bodies. Mental health workers

Table 1–6
Disasters

Condition	Episodes	Year
Residential fires, number	478,000	1991[a]
Dollar loss	$5.52 billion	1991[a]
Deaths	3,575	1991[b]
Tornado, flood, hurricane, deaths	119	1991[c]
Toxic-waste dump sites	80,000+	1983[d]

[a]U.S. Bureau of Census, 1993, Table 353. [b]U.S. Bureau of Census, 1993, Table 354. [c]U.S. Bureau of Census, 1993, Table 381. [d]U.S. Office of Technology Assessment, 1983b.

who volunteer in disasters can find themselves providing more support for the rescue workers than for the victims of disasters.

Technological advances have created the possibility of new technological disasters. Nuclear plant accidents at Three Mile Island, near Middletown, Pennsylvania, (Perrow, 1984) and at the Chernobyl plant near Kiev, Ukraine, made real the danger of an accidental nuclear disaster. There are a large number of nuclear plants in the nation, and fear of a possible nuclear accident, whether exaggerated or not, crosses the minds of many children and adults (Schwebel & Schwebel, 1981). The Love Canal episode (A. Levine, 1982; see also Chapter 12), in which a leaking, abandoned toxic-waste dump site threatened the safety of a residential area in upstate New York, brought that hazard to public attention. More than eighty thousand hazardous waste sites have been identified in the United States, 90 percent of which pose a threat of contamination to the water supply of nearby communities. Although a clear relationship between toxic waste and adverse health effects remains to be fully documented, untold thousands live with a threat to their health, safety, and economic well-being (Office of Technology Assessment, 1983b; Epstein, Brown, & Pope, 1982). The impact of technological disasters is as much psychological as it is physical (Wandersman & Hallman, 1993), but a community's problems are every bit as real in the technological as in the natural disaster (see Chapter 12).

Marriage and Parenting

Marriage and parenting are major life goals achieved by most people (see Table 1–7). However, marriage is the seventh most stressful of Holmes and Rahe's forty-three events, and parenthood is the fourteenth. Both events are major life transitions posing myriad problems of adjustment. In the United States, most people marry at least once; by age 40, 87 percent of women and 82 percent of men have married (Table 60). In 1991 there were 2,371,000 marriages involving 4,742,000 individuals (Table 91).

Many people who marry (and many who don't) have children, another important life transition. In 1991 there were 4,111,000 live births (Table 91). In 1990 about 28 percent of births occurred out of wedlock, 9 percent to unmarried mothers under nineteen years of age (Tables 91, 101). Births to unmarried mothers have increased steadily since 1970. Among white women out-of-wedlock births increased from 6 percent of all births in 1970 to 20 percent in 1990; among African American women out-of-wedlock births increased from 38 percent of all births in 1970 to 65 percent in 1990 (Table 101). A young mother who has a child out of wedlock will be coping with considerable stress. The chances that a young unmarried mother will complete high school are considerably lower than the chances of someone who postpones the birth of her first child until later. Young unmarried mothers are more likely to smoke and to

Table 1–7
Marriage and Parenthood

Condition	Number	Year
Marriages	2,371,000	1991[a]
Divorces	1,187,000	1991[a]
Live births	4,111,000	1991[a]
Out of wedlock	1,165,400	1990[b]
To mothers under 19	360,700	1990[c]
Fetal losses—miscarriages	840,000	1987[d]
Deaths of infants under 1 year	37,000	1991[e]
Births, retardation	123,000	1991[f]
Births, cerebral palsy	15,000	est.[g]
Births, genetic defect	158,000	est.[g]
Legal abortions	1,591,000	1988[h]
Percent to unmarried women	83.0%	1988[h]
Percent to under 19	26.0%	1988[h]
Abortions/Abortions with live births		
Under 15	.553	1988[h]
Under 19	.444	1988[h]
Adoptions	104,000	1986[i]
Foster care, total in care	425,000	1991[j]
Children involved in a divorce, each year	1,044,000	1988[k]
Percent "blended" households	24.0%	1990[l]

[a]U.S. Bureau of Census, 1993, Table 91. [b]U.S. Bureau of Census, 1993, Table 101. [c]U.S. Bureau of Census, 1993, Table 101. [d]U.S. Bureau of Census, 1993, Table 109. [e]U.S. Bureau of Census, 1993, Table 91. [f] Estimated 3% of births. [g]Health, United States, 1976. [h]U.S. Bureau of Census, 1993, Table 113. [i]U.S. Bureau of Census, 1991, Table 620. [j]U.S. General Accounting Office, 1993. [k]U.S. Bureau of Census, 1993, Table 144. [l]U.S. Bureau of Census, 1993, Table 77.

use drugs or alcohol during pregnancy, are less likely to receive good pre-natal care, and are more likely to have a low-birth-weight baby (Table 102). All of these factors presage a difficult future for the young mother and for her child.

Abortions. Not all pregnancies are desired. In 1988 there were 1,591,000 legal abortions; 83 percent involved unmarried women, and 26 percent of all abortions were obtained by women under nineteen years of age. The proportion of pregnancies terminated by abortion is highest among those under nineteen and lowest among those between thirty and forty; the rate rises again after age 40 (Table 113). U.S. Supreme Court decisions permitting states to legislate restrictions on obtaining abortions (e.g., waiting periods, parental consent) and the vigorous protest activities of right-to-life groups have undoubtedly made it more stressful to obtain an abortion. The effects of laws and of protest activities on the rate of abortions is unclear. If it is more difficult to obtain an abortion, will the rate of out-of-wedlock births go up, increasing problems associated with single-parent families, or will the restrictions result in decreased sexual activity or increased care in the use of contraception to avoid pregnancy? These are important questions for public policy and resources committed to ameliorating social problems.

Fetal and infant mortality. Not all pregnancies are healthy or happy events. In 1988 there were 840,000 miscarriages (Table 109). Those who wanted to be pregnant undoubtedly suffered emotional distress upon the loss, but bearing a child is no guarantee that the child will live and grow up. In 1991, thirty-seven thousand infants under one year of age died (Table 91). About 3.5 percent of these deaths may have been due to child abuse or neglect. The infant death rate has been going down since 1950 (Table 91), but as the death rate from other causes goes down the proportion of deaths due to maltreatment goes up.

Infant morbidity. For some sizable number of families, the birth of a child may signal the beginning of an enduring struggle with a chronic disorder, requiring an emotional adaptation on the part of the family and long-term planning for coping with the special problems that will inevitably arise. For example, about 5 percent of infants born alive have some genetic defect, and approximately 123,000 children born every year are diagnosed as retarded. About fifteen thousand infants, or roughly one per two hundred live births, are born with cerebral palsy, and about two hundred thousand persons, two-thirds of whom are children between the ages of three and thirteen, are afflicted with muscular dystrophy (U.S. Department of Health, Education, and Welfare, 1976).

Adoptions. Although the number of adoptions has declined since 1965, there were 104,000 adoptions in 1986, a little more than half of them by relatives (Table 620, 1991). The reason so few children were adopted by unrelated persons is that the foster care system, a source of children for adoption, is unable to place many abused and neglected children, even though parental rights have been terminated and the children are available for adoption. With the rate of children entering foster care greater than the rate leaving, the foster care population is growing (U.S. Select Committee, 1990).

Adoption solves the problem of childlessness for some couples—and increasingly for single parents who desire a child—and of parentlessness for the children who are adopted. The vast majority of adoptions work out well. Adoption, however, brings its own problems of adaptation.

While the total of adopted children is about 1 percent of the population of children, from 1.5 percent to 13 percent (an average of 4.8 percent) of children referred for psychiatric treatment are adopted (Kadushin, 1980).

Foster care. About 425,00 children were in foster care in 1991 (U.S. General Accounting Office, 1993). The courts removed most of them from their homes because their parents abused or neglected them or were unable to care for them. Extrapolating from current trends, the U.S. Select Committee on Children, Youth, and Families (1990) estimated that 553,600 children would be in foster care by 1995. Including adopted children, about six hundred thousand children a year enter new families, many after having endured stress or trauma in their birth families. A high proportion of these children have emotional problems, and few services are available for them (Horan, Kang, Levine, et al., 1993). Forming a relationship with such children provides new and special problems for adoptive or foster parents.

Divorce

In 1991 there were 1,187,000 divorces in the United States, with an average of one child per divorce (Tables 91, 144). Divorce and separation are the second and third, respectively, most stressful events on the Holmes and Rahe scale and are correlated with many physical and psychological difficulties (Bloom, Asher, & White, 1978). It is not clear whether there are long-term consequences for the psychological development of children of divorce, but divorce is a stressful life event; about 10 percent of divorces involve custody fights that may continue for years, involving repeated legal encounters (Clingempeel & Reppucci, 1982), and children's adjustment is poorer when former spouses are in conflict (Emery, 1982).

Many divorced people remarry. In 46 percent of all marriages, at least one of the spouses was previously married (Table 141). In 1990, 24 percent of married households with children were "blended families" or contained one or more adoptive children (Table 77). Thus, many people face the often difficult problem of becoming a parent of someone else's partially grown child.

This recital of dreary statistics is not meant to discourage marriage or parenthood. On the positive side, the overall prospects favor marriage and parenthood. We simply want to emphasize that problems in living associated with marriage and parenthood occur with great frequency in our society, affecting many millions of people each year.

Economics and Employment

Inadequate income. Poor people have more problems than those with more money. Socioeconomic status is consistently related to health outcomes (Adler, Boyce, Chesney, et al., 1994), and several events involving financial problems are in the top half of Holmes and Rahe's list. A great many people regularly struggle with inadequate incomes (Table 1–8). The Social Security Administration developed a poverty index[4] for individuals and families that is adjusted annually to account for changes in the cost of living. In 1991 the poverty line in the United States for a family of four was $13,924. In 1992 some 7.2 million families, 35.7 million people, had incomes below the poverty line (Table 740); an additional 3.5 million families had incomes below 125 percent of the poverty line (Table 744). The probability that an African American or Hispanic family will fall below the poverty line is about three times that for a white family (Table 744). In 1991, 16.1 percent of white, 46 percent of African American, and 40 percent of Hispanic children lived in families with incomes below the poverty line (Table 736).

The situation is especially difficult for families headed by women. In

Table 1–8
Economics and Employment

Condition	Number	Year
Income below poverty line		
Persons	35,700,000	1992[a]
Families	7,200,000	
Families with income below		
125% of poverty line	10,700,000	1992[b]
Number of persons		
in female–headed families		
below poverty line	18,600,000	1991[c]
Aid for dependent children		
recipients	13,489,800	1991[d]
children	9,126,000	
Supplemental Security Income		
for disability	5,118,000	1991[d]
Unemployed	9,400,000	1991[e]
Involved in strike	364,000	1991[f]
Business failures	96,587	1992[g]
In arrears on installment debt	18,000,000 (est.)	1991[h]
Bankruptcy petitions filed	972,490	1992[i]
Bankruptcy cases pending	264,867	1992[i]

[a]U.S Bureau of Census, 1993, Table 740. [b]U.S. Bureau of Census, 1993, Table 744. [c]U.S. Bureau of Census, 1993, Table 740. [d]U.S. Bureau of Census, 1993, Table 604. [e]U.S. Bureau of Census, 1993, Table 621. [f]U.S. Bureau of Census, 1993, Table 686. [g]U.S. Bureau of Census, 1993, Table 861. [h]U.S. Bureau of Census, 1993, Tables 816, 818 (see text). [i]U.S. Bureau of Census, 1993, Table 865.

1991, 34 percent of female-headed households, 18.6 million people, lived with incomes below the poverty line (Table 740). More than 47 percent of female-headed white families had incomes below the poverty line, as did 68 percent of African American female-headed families and 70 percent of Hispanic female-headed families (Table 744).

Poverty and divorce. Changing divorce laws have had strong, adverse economic consequences for many women (Weitzman, 1985; McLindon, 1987). Acknowledging that there are problems inherent in forcing couples to stay married when they do not wish to be married, that divorce based on "fault" can be based on fraudulent evidence, and that gender equality under the law is desirable, states have moved to no-fault divorce. Judges have been increasingly reluctant to grant alimony, partly as a consequence of the view that men and women stand on an equal footing after divorce and that sex-role stereotypes should not affect legal decision making. In addition, child-support payments can be a source of conflict in a divorce; a great many women receive no child support or receive it irregularly. In 1987 nearly a quarter of women who were awarded child support received nothing, while another quarter received sporadic payments. Only half received payments regularly (Table 616).

Women who are relatively younger at the time of divorce and do not have children may be less adversely affected (Jacob, 1989). However, many women go on welfare following a marital or relationship breakup (Harrington, 1984). There are new proposals to make it easier to collect child support, but for now many women go it alone, supporting their families on whatever they are able to earn. So many women and children whose family incomes are below the poverty line are in female-headed households that some have spoken of the "feminization" of poverty.

Welfare. Large numbers of people are on welfare or other forms of public support. In 1991 aid to families with dependent children (AFDC) went to 13,489,800 persons. Of those who received the aid, 9,126,000 were children. The mean monthly family allowance was $390, or about $135 per person (Table 604). In 1991 an additional 5,118,000 persons received Supplemental Security Income (SSI) payments because they were aged, indigent, blind, or otherwise disabled. Of this number, 3,569,000 were disabled. Many were former mental patients or individuals with retardation or developmental disabilities. Disabled persons received an average monthly payment of $321 (Table 604). Proposals to reform welfare will have profound effects on those families. Some recipients may benefit from reforms, but many others will experience distress as benefits are reduced or limited sharply by new legislation.

Homelessness. Homelessness is one result of poverty and is increasing among women and children (Shinn, 1992). Although the nature of homelessness makes it difficult to determine its prevalence, Levine and

Rog (1990) cite estimates that five hundred thousand to 1 million people in the United States are homeless on any given night, and up to 3 million experience homelessness at some point each year.

Even when they have homes, poor people live in less desirable residences than do wealthier people. Zahner, Kasl, White, and Will (1985) report a correlation between the presence of vermin in the home, particularly rats, and measures of psychological well-being in minority women. Those who reported a decrease in rat infestation in a repeat survey a year later reported a significant decrease in psychophysiological symptoms associated with anxiety—dizziness, sweating palms, headaches, and similar reactions. Conditions associated with poverty were associated with psychological symptoms of a kind that are measured only in epidemiological surveys. Had the research team measured only anxiety, they would have reported high levels, but in all likelihood the anxiety would have been interpreted as a disorder instead of as a response to unhealthy living conditions.

Unemployment. In 1992 about 9.4 million persons were unemployed (Table 621). Unemployment insurance cushions the economic shock for many, but for others unemployment triggers depressive reactions or feelings of worthlessness and requires some adaptation to unaccustomed free time. Some unemployed persons seek new positions, putting themselves under the stress of having their qualifications and competence evaluated by others, and some relocate to obtain work. Plant closings affecting entire communities present new problems of adaptation not only for those who lose jobs but also for those whose communities are affected because of new social problems or because people move away (Buss, Redburn, & Waldron, 1983). Other people lose time at work because of strikes or other work stoppages. In 1991, 364,000 workers were involved in a work stoppage or strike, for a median period of thirty-five days per worker (Table 686). In such cases a residue of bitterness and strained interpersonal relationships can persist for months and even years. The striking workers, even if covered by unemployment insurance or union benefits, lose money during the strike period.

Over and beyond unemployment and strikes, 96,857 businesses failed in 1992 (Table 861). Most were small businesses, but each one represented the dashed hopes of individuals and their families, affected their livelihoods, and forced some rethinking of a major life activity.

Debt. In 1989, 73 percent of all families had some form of debt (e.g., mortgage, credit cards, car loan). As might be expected from the numbers of people with low incomes and our credit economy, many have debts they cannot easily repay. In 1992, 972,490 bankruptcy petitions were filed in the federal courts, and an additional 264,867 cases were pending (Table 865). In 1992 U.S. consumers had installment debt in the amount of $741.1 billion (Table 816). Of the installment debt, 2.43

percent of loans were delinquent thirty days or more (Table 818). In other words, bills amounting to about $18 billion were chasing delinquent borrowers. If we assume that the average debt is $1,000, about 18 million persons are coping with bill collectors who are after them because they haven't paid the installment on a loan. Using our multiplier for household size, we estimate that 47.2 million people are affected by a delinquent debt.

Taking on mortgage debt is another item on the Holmes and Rahe scale. In 1991 some 48,260,000 mortgages were outstanding (Table 811). The median mortgage loan was in excess of $42,000 (Tables 1399, 1400). In 1980 the average monthly mortgage payment constituted 32 percent of income (Table 1395, 1981). High prices for homes and high mortgage interest rates may render many homeowners "house-poor," especially if real wages for middle class families decline.

Work, money, and family. We have been experiencing great changes in the nature of work and in the composition of the labor force. Women now make up 46 percent of the labor force (Table 635), and a majority of women with young children are now working (Table 633). The lack of affordable day care means that many "latchkey" children are unsupervised after school.

Married women contribute about 35 percent of family income. However, bringing in income and spending time working have consequences for family relationships. What constitutes appropriate sex-role behavior? How should authority and responsibility for the household and for children be shared (A. Levine, 1977)? Work and home responsibilities, including the care of elderly relatives, create stress for some. The high percentage of working mothers also underscores the need for affordable child care and for family leave policies that enable parents to take care of sick children. Implementing both of those social policies could go a long way toward relieving psychological and economic stress in many families. In addition, men and women who have lost high-paying jobs in factories and in middle management have been unable to find positions paying equally well; some work two or even three jobs, reducing the time they have available to be with children and family. Changing employment prospects, downsizing of large companies for economic efficiency, fewer well-paid jobs, and more part-time employment offering fewer benefits may well result in greater feelings of job insecurity, reduced optimism about future prospects, and more stress in families.

The changing nature of work and of work-related values. Since the end of World War II, the United States has been changing from an industrial to a service economy (Fuchs, 1968; Table 1–9). By 1992 only 3 percent of workers were employed in agriculture, 26 percent in manufacturing, and 71 percent in service industries (Table 644). These changes in the distribution of employment can have profound cultural and social

Table 1-9
Changing Work Force and Changing Values

Work force	1929%[a]	1975%[b]
Agriculture	20.0	3.2
Manufacturing	40.0	25.6
Services and other	40.0	71.2

Value	Number	Year
Dissatisfied with current employment		
Men	8,404,128	1980[c]
Women	7,011,122	

Leisure		
Service industries, average work week	28.8–35.8 hrs	1992[d]

Recreation Expenditures (constant 1987 dollars)	1960[e]	1991[e]
	$91.3 billion	$258.7 billion

Work Force Participation Ages 45–64	1960[f]	1992[f]
Males, married	93.7%	82.7%
single	80.1%	67.6%
divorced, widower	83.2%	74.7%
Females, married	36.0%	58.6%
single	79.8%	68.2%
divorced, widowed	60.0%	66.4%

Women and Work		
Labor force, percent female	45.5%	1992[g]
Percent women working with children under 6		
Single	48.5%	1992[h]
Married	59.9%	
Divorced, widowed	60.5%	
with children ages 6–17		
Single	67.2%	
Married	75.4%	
Divorced, widowed	80.0%	

[a]Fuchs (1968). [b]U.S. Bureau of Census, 1993, Table 644. [c]U.S. Bureau of Census, 1981, Table 649. [d]U.S. Bureau of Census, 1993, Table 660. [e]U.S. Bureau of Census, 1993 Table 398. [f]U.S. Bureau of Census, 1993, Table 631. [g]U.S. Bureau of Census, 1993, Table 635. [h]U.S. Bureau of Census, 1993, Table 633.

effects. They affect every individual (see Chapter 3) and will affect our educational system as well. As Fuchs (1968) put it:

> Changes in the industrial distribution of employment have implications for where and how men live, the education they need, and even the health hazards they face. Indeed it has been written that when man changes his tools and his techniques, his ways of producing and distributing the goods of life, he also changes his gods. (p. 184)

One example of the type of change Fuchs means can be found in gender relationships in the workplace. The nature of work in service industries—relating to other people—emphasizes interpersonal skills and makes demands on the ability to express and control emotions, demands different from those required of workers in manufacturing jobs. We now also recognize problems of sexual harassment in the workplace. Laws designed to redress a power imbalance between women who are subjected to harassment and men who have greater power in the workplace have led to a rethinking of workplace relationships. The process of working out new norms of conduct in the workplace between men and women creates stresses.

Leisure Time and Value Changes

In the United States, leisure time and industries catering to those with leisure are important (Table 14). From 1970 to 1991 population increased by 24 percent; recreational expenditures increased by 283 percent in the same period. People are spending much more of their personal resources on recreational and leisure activities. This change may have an effect on the work ethic. Shortening the workweek is a possible solution to chronic unemployment. The long-range trend may well move us toward greater leisure-time availability in the future. With shorter hours, increased vacation time, and a shorter lifetime work span, the average person today has an estimated forty-five thousand more free hours available during a lifetime than a counterpart one hundred years ago (DeGrazia, 1962).

These figures reflect a normative change that must be accompanied by a change in the value system. The call for a return to "family values" and the current political debate over whether there is a "cultural war" in U.S. society are manifestations of the problems attending changing values. Increasing leisure interests have already influenced, and will continue to influence, the school curriculum, to the consternation of "back-to-basics" advocates; our increasing emphasis on leisure will likely have long-range effects on other basic institutions as well. Change affecting basic institutions is invariably stressful as we seek to reach a new social equilibrium. The problem is how to develop a version of the good life that is well articulated, well internalized, and supported by other social and financial resources.

Summary. Having to cope and struggle with problems in living is more the rule than the exception. The problems documented in regularly kept statistics are similar to those that appear in stressful life-events scales (see Chapter 7). At any given moment, a large number of people are affected by acute and chronic illness and accidents, by disasters of one sort or another, or by problems related to crime, delinquency, drug addiction, and alcoholism. Marriage, divorce, and parenthood have their own special problems, and large numbers of Americans have serious financial problems as well. The work setting has introduced new problems and new opportunities, and increasing leisure also poses problems for adaptation.

We conclude that a large number of people regularly experience stressful events. That conclusion is an alternative to the view that there is a high prevalence of *DSM*-defined disorders. The ecological perspective leads us to examine the frequency and the distribution of the stressful life events in the population instead of examining the rate and distribution of psychopathology in individuals. Later in this book we will argue that the ecological perspective may provide us with a better basis for developing and implementing prevention programs.

Aloneness in American Society

Many Americans face their problems in relative isolation (cf. Slater, 1970; see Tables 1–10 and 1–11).

Table 1–10
Aloneness in American Society

Condition	Number	Year
Separations		
Deaths	2,165,000	1991[a]
Divorce	1,187,000[b]	1991[a]
Residential change within 5 years		
Percent changed residence	53.3	1990[c]
Percent moved to another		
state or county	19.1	
Live alone	23,974,000	1992[d]
Males, live alone	9,613,000	
Females, live alone	14,361,000	
Female-headed families	11,692,000	1992[d]
Male-headed families	3,025,000	

[a]U.S. Bureau of Census, 1993, Table 91.   [b]The number divorced does not include the number separated but not divorced.   [c]U.S. Bureau of Census, 1993, Tables 30, 34.   [d]U.S. Bureau of Census, 1993, Table 70.

Table 1–11
Number of Widowed Persons by Sex and Age, 1992[a]

	Male	*Female*	*Ratio Female/Male*
Total	2,529,000	11,325,000	4.48
By age:			
Under 24	2,000	11,000	5.50
25–29	13,000	26,000	2.00
30–34	10,000	83,000	8.30
35–44	108,000	303,000	2.81
45–54	128,000	642,000	5.02
55–64	351,000	1,659,000	4.73
65–74	841,000	3,648,000	4.34
75 and over	1,076,000	4,953,000	4.60

Number of Divorced Persons by Sex and Age[a]

	Male	*Female*	*Ratio Female/Male*
Total	6,752,000	9,505,000	1.42
By age:			
Under 24	119,000	222,000	1.87
25–29	485,000	811,000	1.67
30–34	837,000	1,200,000	1.43
35–44	2,205,000	2,793,000	1.27
45–54	1,606,000	2,285,000	1.42
55–64	877,000	1,271,000	1.45
65–74	506,000	681,000	1.35
75 and older	118,000	301,000	2.55

[a]U.S. Bureau of Census, 1993, Table 61.

Death and divorce. We noted that divorce and separation are among the most emotionally trying events, as measured on the Holmes and Rahe (1967) life-events scale. In 1991, there were about 1.2 million divorces, and probably more separations (Table 91). We have no comparable figures for emotionally trying breakups of relationships among those who are not married. In our own unpublished survey of life events in college students, we found that almost 20 percent were involved in the breakup of a heterosexual relationship each year.

The loss of a loved one also stands high on the scale of stressful events and is followed by consequences similar to those involved in the loss of a relationship in divorce or separation. On the Holmes and Rahe (1967) list of stressful events, death of one's spouse was the single most stressful event one could experience. Death of a family member was among the top five most stressful events, and death of a close friend was in the top half. These events are relatively common.

For most people bereavement is a fact of life. Only those who themselves die young escape the pain of losing someone they love through death. About 2.1 million persons die each year in the United States, affecting 3.4 million household members. Every year there are eight hundred thousand new widows and widowers. There are at least twenty-seven thousand suicides in this country annually, and probably many more, since suicide is underreported. Each year approximately four hundred thousand children under the age of twenty-five die. Just as each type of relationship has special meaning, so too each type of death carries with it a special kind of pain for those who are left behind (National Academy of Sciences, 1984, p. 4). There are many adverse health effects of bereavement, including increased mortality, depression, drug and alcohol abuse, cardiovascular disease, and accidents.

Residential mobility. Americans move frequently. Between 1985 and 1990, 47 percent of the population five years old and over moved at least once, and 19 percent of the moves were relatively long-distance (Table 30). Renters move more than homeowners, and college-age and younger middle-age people move more than other groups (Table 34). Geographic mobility in and of itself is not necessarily associated with increased risk of psychological disorder (Levine, 1966b), but moving disrupts existing networks of relationships and requires the development of new networks. Children who move even short distances face the problem of adapting to a new school (Felner, Ginter, & Primavera, 1982).

Living alone. In 1980 some 18,296,000 people lived alone. By 1992 that number had grown to 23,974,000 (Table 70). Of 95,669,000 households counted in 1992, 52,457,000 or 55 percent were husband-and-wife units with or without children, while 45 percent consisted of other living arrangements (Table 70). Of the remaining household units, 11,692,000 were female-headed families, and 3,025,000 were male-headed families (Table 70). More women than men lived alone (14,361,000 versus 9,613,000) (Table 70). The percent of persons living alone increases sharply with age. After age 65, 16 percent of males and 42 percent of females are living alone. Not all are necessarily isolated, but none is sharing the household with someone who could provide support in time of need.

The distribution of widowed and divorced adults differs by gender. In 1992 6.8 million men said they were divorced and were not remarried; 9.6 million women so characterized themselves. That year 2.5 million men characterized themselves as widowers, not remarried, as did 11.3 million women (Table 59).

At every age the odds that a widowed woman will find a widowed male to marry are poor. In 1992 women constituted 52 percent of the population eighteen years old and older. There were 7.9 million more adult women than men (Table 59). In 1992 there were more widows than widowers at every age range. The widow/widower ratio for those under forty years of age was 3.1; for those forty to sixty-four it was 4.64, and for those over 65 years of age it was 4.49 (Table 61).

Similar ratios hold true for the divorced population. The divorced female/divorced male ratio is 1.42 for those under forty, 1.39 for those between ages forty and sixty-four, and 1.57 for those over sixty-five (Table 61). There are more single males than single females at every age until one reaches age 65, but a substantial proportion of those males over thirty-five who have never married are probably not in the marriage market, for whatever reason. (The sex ratio may well have important implications for the way we live and for determining changes in relationships between the sexes [Guttentag & Secord, 1983]).

Because women live longer than men, women cannot count on developing another monogamous heterosexual relationship once having experienced a loss of relationship because of a death or a divorce that might have occurred when the woman was as young as 40. Divorced and widowed women may have friends, parents, relatives, and children on whom they can rely for emotional support, companionship, and other aid. These figures confirm, however, that the ideal image of a married couple coping with the problems of life together does not fit the picture for substantial numbers of Americans, and particularly for substantial numbers of women.

Some laws meant to support married women have not caught up with contemporary realities. The Social Security laws provide survivor benefits for minor children, but they provide no widows' pensions for women under age 60. Therefore, many women who were homemakers during a large portion of their adult lives may find themselves without any source of income after their children come of age and before they reach age 60. Because many have not had other work experience during the years they were homemakers, they will also find it hard to reenter the employment market. We now have some services for displaced homemakers to provide job training, placement, and counseling for women who are ineligible for existing health, retirement, or unemployment benefit programs.

Gender and psychological distress. There has been an ongoing debate in the United States about the relative rates of mental illness in males and females. It seems true that women are more often depressed and have higher rates of "neurotic" disorders than men. Men have higher rates of alcoholism, drug abuse, personality disorders, and transient situational and behavioral disorders (Gove, 1976; Guttentag et al., 1974; Myers, Weissman, Tischler et al., 1984; Benson, Milazzo-Sayre, Rosenstein et al., 1992).

We believe the gender difference is better described by ecological than by diagnostic considerations. Women live longer than men. In addition, they are likely to be struggling with problems in living (Mirowsky & Ross, 1989) and to be struggling with those problems alone (a conclusion whose implications will be explored further in Chapter 7). One consequence of aloneness may be a heightened tendency to reach for professional care when experiencing distress related to frequently occurring life events.

The Availability of Professional Care

In terms of stressful events, "normal" life is indeed a soap opera for most people who muddle through without formal help. But how much formal help is available to those who need it? Albee's (1959) pioneering work for the Joint Commission on Mental Health and Mental Illness alerted us to the problems of providing sufficient personnel if treatment is delivered by professionally trained staff through designated mental health organizations.

Our best estimate is that there are approximately fifty thousand doctoral-level clinical psychologists providing services, about fifty-three thousand M.S.W. social workers, and about thirty thousand psychiatrists. As a crude guess, we should add another twenty thousand marriage and family counselors, pastoral counselors, school psychologists in private practice, M.A. level psychiatric nurses, and assorted psychotherapists with varying training who may be unlicensed but are nonetheless practicing, for a total of about 153,000 professionally trained mental health practitioners (Torrey, Wolfe, & Flynn, 1988).

Assume a two thousand-hour work year (i.e., forty hours times fifty weeks). Assume further that 80 percent of that time is devoted to patient care, including record keeping and staff conferences but excluding in-service training, administrative meetings, and research that does not involve direct patient care. That is a generous estimate; in many facilities only 50 percent of time is devoted to direct patient contact. Multiplying the 153,000 full-time equivalent (FTE) positions by sixteen hundred hours (two thousand hours times .8) yields a liberal estimate of a total of 244,800,000 hours a year devoted to direct patient care by all professional mental health workers. If we looked just at the availability of psychiatrists, the number would be substantially lower.

If the entire number of patient-care hours was devoted to the care of the individuals involved in the 2,324,000 patient-care episodes in psychiatric hospitals, the 1,400,574 episodes in psychiatric wards of general hospitals, and the 5,970,000 outpatient-care episodes reported for the late 1980s, an average of about 25.25 hours of *some* professional's time was spent per patient-care episode. If we multiply the number of patient-care episodes by two to include only one of the household members who might have an interest in seeing a professional person during a patient-care episode, the time available is reduced to 12.12 hours per patient-care episode in an inpatient or outpatient mental health facility.

These hours are not available to all equally. There are important regional differences in the distribution of mental health services. Professional mental health workers are concentrated in urban and suburban areas where people have higher incomes, more education, and better insurance coverage. In addition, many psychiatrists in public mental health facilities are foreign-trained, speak English poorly, and are employed in state facilities because licensing requirements are modified for employees of public facilities. Many areas of the country are almost totally without specialized mental health services. The shortage of personnel trained to work with children and the elderly is also very great. In some places minority and bilingual personnel may go without treatment because insufficient numbers of trained personnel speak their language (Snowden, 1982), a problem that is relieved when such personnel are available (O'-Sullivan et al., 1989).

This construct allots no time at all for the 1.77 million residents of nursing homes, where up to 75 percent are estimated to have some degree of mental illness or for the more than 2 million persons who reside in other institutions (e.g., prisons, jails, juvenile justice facilities, institutions for the retarded).

Depending on the assumptions, we can arrive at figures of minutes or even seconds per week available to those who may be dealing with crises of living consequent to chronic and acute illness, employment and financial problems, or problems of death, divorce, and other separations. We have said nothing about the nearly 8 million children estimated to be in need, nor have we considered at all the problems in living consequent to transitions in adult life.

On numbers alone it is apparent that professionally trained personnel will never be available in sufficient numbers to meet even a fraction of the potential demand for psychological services. The actual demand, based on Regier et al.'s (1993) estimates of those with *DSM* diagnoses who actually sought help, is a third or less of the potential demand. That fact somewhat tempers our conclusion. We do not need to modify radically the basic point that we would have to increase professional personnel several times, an extremely unlikely occurrence, to provide adequate hours of treatment in the present mode of service delivery.

Problems of the Medical Model

Availability aside, the medical model of service delivery is also a problem (Zax & Spector, 1974). The fee-for-service medical model is built on the assumption that most problems can be handled by acute, episodic intervention that is limited in time and that has an enduring effect. Help provided with those assumptions will not serve the needs of the 27.5 million who suffer from chronic physical problems. Even when treatment for a physical disorder is stabilized, the patient and the family have to work out adaptations to the limitations imposed by the condition. If we add those people who are involved with the mental health, criminal justice, or welfare systems, we must concede that many problems are chronic and will not readily give way to acute, episodic interventions. In the words of Stanton Coit, one of the founders of the U.S. settlement house movement:

> If we consider the vast amount of personal attention and time needed to understand and deal effectively with the case of any one man or family that has fallen into vice, crime or pauperism, we shall see the impossibility of coping with even these evils alone, unless the helpers be both many and constantly at hand. (Coit, 1891, quoted in Levine & Levine, 1992, p. 61)

The medical model also implies a passive help giver who waits for the client to define his or her own need and then to request help. It assumes that people seeking help know the kind of help available and find that help culturally acceptable and that they are "acceptable clients" (e.g., can pay the fee, have the proper condition) to the help givers.

The medical model assumes that professionals are competent and that personal or social characteristics of the professional do not matter (Dawes, 1994). Cultural, racial, ethnic, and language characteristics of either the provider or the recipient can be barriers to help (Giordano & Giordano, 1976; Snowden, 1982).

A psychotherapist's productivity is improved by clients who are ready and willing to use psychotherapy. In the free-market system provided by the fee-for-service model, the YAVIS (young, attractive, verbal, intelligent, successful) client is preferred. Ryan's (1969) demonstration that a substantial proportion of the caseload of private psychiatrists in Boston consisted of college-educated women between the ages of twenty-five and thirty-five who lived in a few census tracts in Boston is a case in point. Contemporary services are not equally available to all who might need them, and some clients are better prepared than are others to use the services that are offered. Torrey et al. (1988) believe that mental health professionals have opted to deal with less serious problems in private settings. In their view, private-sector mental health services have skimmed off the easiest and most profitable patients and have left the more difficult problems to the public sector, which may have fewer and less-well-trained staff to treat them. Levine and Levine (1992) make a similar point about how services for children may not reach those in greatest need.

Health insurance and psychotherapy. With greater availability of health insurance coverage for mental health services, less-well-off people sought mental health care (Taube, Burns, & Kessler, 1984). Health care reform may be changing the picture. How much and what kinds of mental health services will be covered? If we move to a system of managed care in which services are carefully rationed, a number of changes may follow. If the amount of service is reduced and care is provided according to a protocol, then fewer doctoral-level and more M.A.-level personnel may be used in treating roles. With less service available, self-help may become more important. Consumers are organizing to see that managed care doesn't result in the rationing of care and in inadequate care (Malloy, 1995). Even with these changes, reliance on a public policy of trying to provide many more professional mental health workers will not come close to meeting public need. Alternatives are clearly necessary, and these will be considered throughout this book.

Disorders or problems in living? In the medical model, affective and behavioral responses to problems in living are called *disorders*, and professional services are *treatment* for those disorders. A subtle implication may be that because help is provided through professional services, the events that led the individual to seek help are unusual and should not have occurred. Higher recent estimates for the prevalence of mental disorders reflect a higher than expected incidence of relatively brief symptom episodes, especially anxiety and substance abuse (Regier et al., 1993), and we noted earlier that an estimated 46 percent of people who seek ambulatory help for mental health problems are not sufficiently impaired to warrant any current diagnosis (Narrow et al., 1993). For many of these people, the implication may be that feelings of anxiety, tenseness, or depression in relation to problems in living should not occur. Certainly that implication may exist for many of those Americans, two-thirds of them women, for whom 131 million prescriptions for psychotropic medications were written in 1984 (Baum, Kennedy, Knapp, et al., 1988). Given that 60 percent of the money spent on outpatient psychotropic medications in 1985 went for antianxiety and sedative-hypnotic (e.g., sleep aid) drugs (Zorc, Larson, Lyons, & Beardsly, 1991) and that such medications account for 11 percent of all prescriptions filled in U.S. drugstores (Baum et al., 1988), striking numbers of people have difficulty in living with the emotions that are generated day by day. For many, the widespread use of Prozac is a chemical solution for struggling with feelings related to problems in living. In 1991 the pharmaceutical industry shipped $7.82 billion worth of drugs affecting the central nervous system. This category of psychiatric pharmaceuticals outstripped the shipped value of drugs for infectious and parasitic diseases, for heart disease, or for digestive disorders. The existence of this help reinforces the belief that the event and the associated emotions are unusual, if not pathological.

Wilensky and Lebeaux (1965) described two conceptions of social welfare, the *residual* and the *institutional*. The residual concept holds that public welfare, or other helping services, should come into play only when the normal structures of supply—the family and the market—do not function adequately to meet a need. Because of their residual, temporary, substitute character, public helping services thus conceived carry with them the implication that if you cannot take care of your own and you have to resort to public assistance, it is your failure. Public assistance is provided grudgingly to exceptional cases. The *institutional* view, in contrast, recognizes the complexity of modern social life and accepts it as a legitimate function of modern society to provide aid to individuals to move toward self-fulfillment. This view recognizes that in today's interdependent society, institutional arrangements are necessary to help people solve problems of living; there is no implication that the distressing event should not have happened. A primary example is the social security system, in which aging leading to retirement or disability is treated as a to-be-expected event for which we have a formal institutional response for everyone meeting the age criteria. The institutional view is preferable because it minimizes any stigma or secondary reaction that one has failed because one has problems that need help.

An emphasis on professional assistance may undermine confidence in one's ability to cope, whether alone or with the assistance of a friend, neighbor, or relative. Furthermore, the conception that professional help should be available for problems in living may undermine the sense of responsibility one person feels for another or that a network or a face-to-face community might feel for one of its members; if a professional is available to take care of the problem, then send the problem to the professional who is paid to do the job.

Having said this, we want to back away from that position slightly, for we do not mean to give credence to some romantic notion that any nonprofessional is for that reason alone more effective than any professional or that professionals do not have valuable knowledge, experience, and special services to offer. Moreover, the essential aloneness of many people in U.S. society limits the utility of the idea that one can always rely on friends,[5] neighbors, or relatives, or even on the local bartender or hairdresser for help (cf. Cowen, 1982). As Jane Addams (1910) put it, too many seem to have "lost that simple and almost automatic reponse to the human appeal, that old healthful reaction resulting in activity from the mere presence of suffering or helplessness" (p. 71).

Some new helping forms are being built and will be built precisely out of the responsibility one person feels for another and the identification and sympathy one person feels for another. President George Bush's call for a thousand points of light and House Speaker Newt Gingrich's proposal that each church adopt a homeless person or a welfare client builds on that sentiment. That call may be deceptive if it is just an excuse for reducing institutional tax support for our helping services. Our history provides ample evidence that reliance on volunteers is not enough (Levine & Levine, 1992). There were never enough volunteers, and they didn't persist with the hard tasks. Volunteer help that lacks reciprocity, and that lacks safeguards against arbitrary demands from the giver of help, demeans the recipient of help. The self-help movement, so prominent today (see Chapter 9), is an example of a person-to-person, nonprofessional, nonstate-supplied service.[6] The U.S. Advisory Board on Child Abuse and Neglect (1993) has recommended a thorough review of the child protection system to make help more readily available in neighborhoods and to encourage neighbors to help neighbors. Its recommendation recognizes the inadequacy of the present system and the necessity to involve more of the community in solving individual problems of caring for children.

Even if most life crises and associated emotions are transient (Dohrenwend and Dohrenwend, 1969), the resources available to help mediate life crises can make the difference among an unfavorable outcome, an outcome that merely restores the individual's preexisting functioning, and an outcome that leaves the individual a better, stronger person for having coped successfully with distress.

Severe, chronic disorders exist in all countries and cultures. The causes of some disorders are consistent with a medical disease model (Dohrenwend, Levav, Shrout, et al., 1992). Many problems require highly specialized resources, trained personnel, and special facilities. We should distinguish, however, between problems that are amenable to one solution and those that require other solutions. The concept of mental disorder, implying a unitary phenomenon, is itself misleading. Although it is certainly true that a great many people have problems, it is not true that all of their problems are the same or that all problems will yield to or be ameliorated by the same solution. Even in the case of a chronic disorder with a physical cause, the degree of social disability will vary with the available solutions to the social problem and the modes of care provided.

Attitudes and Ideologies

We are not sure that we know in a cultural sense how to face the soap opera of life, that we have an appropriate belief system (ideology), or that appropriate social institutions have evolved to help us to do that as fully as we might wish. There is probably a substantial overlap between the functions professional psychotherapists fulfill and the functions our religious institutions fulfill. Professional psychotherapists are groping toward providing the ideology, but the professional therapist cannot provide the social institution within which an ideology is lived out day by day.

We probably do not prepare ourselves and our children well enough to cope with life's difficulties. Rossman (1976) points out that the best-selling self-help books are in those areas in which our socializing institutions have grossly failed us—marriage, giving birth, parenting, divorce, living with illness, and sexuality. There is a clue to prevention in this fact. Those who look to education and preparation for coping to provide individuals with the additional personal resources to reduce the worst consequences of life's stresses may have much to tell us. Graziano's (1977) work showing that parents can be taught to treat their children's problems offers a related method that suggests a change in role for professionals and a way of "giving away" psychology on a broad basis.

These particular directions—providing public resources in a way that empowers and does not undermine person-to-person responsibility and caring, encouraging face-to-face mutual assistance, teaching people to cope, helping to develop meaningful and satisfying life views that can be lived out in a supportive social organization—offer important possibilities for dealing with the soap opera of life beyond relying exclusively on specialized professional institutions.

Summary

To recapitulate, professional mental health personnel are not now, and never will be, available in sufficient numbers to provide assistance for the tens of millions who are daily coping with stressful problems in living. Moreover, our medical-model delivery system will be available in a psychological and social sense to relatively few people. Whatever position we take on the effectiveness of psychotherapy, and good arguments can be made that psychotherapeutic efforts are helpful (Lambert & Bergin, 1994), services provided in only that modality will be available in limited quantities. Psychoactive medications may relieve symptoms of anxiety and depression but do little to help individuals cope with ongoing problems in life. For some, relief from affective distress, or a reduction in pathological thinking consequent to the relief of distress, may be sufficient to enable them to adapt. For others, chemical relief of distress may be only a small step in dealing with day-to-day problems.

In any event, large numbers of people cope with significant problems in living on a daily basis. Many cope alone, living in relative isolation from others who might provide emotional support, an opportunity to see problems differently, or more concrete assistance. Furthermore, broad social and cultural changes continually add to the difficulties confronting many segments of the population. As we have noted, the problems in living discussed here appear on stressful-life-events scales and are correlated with psychiatric symptoms and physical illness (Rabkin & Streuning, 1976). We can arrive at similar estimates of the potential psychological need whether we use epidemiological studies of *DSM* diagnoses or a problems-in-living and stressful-life-events perspective. We have a different focus when we look at an epidemiology of "cases" as against an epidemiology of events. Cases lead us to treatment of individuals. An epidemiology of situations and events offers broader possibilities for thinking about helpful or preventive interventions. We obviously need to think our way through alternate analyses of the problems before us. In our opinion, an individual psychological orientation and the medical model seriously limit our thinking, while the view that life is a soap opera opens new vistas for the development of therapeutic and preventive services. In the following chapters we will examine some alternative models and service modalities and the concepts and the research related to them. As a group these topics constitute our view of what is called community psychology.

Notes

1. In citations throughout this chapter, if only a table number is given, the source is U.S. Bureau of the Census, 1993. Where a date is given along with the table number, the date refers to that year's statistical abstract.

2. The overall trend for using illegal substances and alcohol was down from 1974 to 1991 even as arrests went up (Table 208). The decline may be temporary and may not continue if budgets for prevention programs are substantially decreased. A recent national study reported that more youth are using marijuana and other illicit drugs since 1992 (Johnston, O'Malley, & Bachman, in preparation).

3. With improved treatment, more now survive for five years, but survivors, especially children, are faced with lifelong problems of adaptation.

4. The poverty index is based in large part on the amount of income necessary to provide a nutritionally adequate, economical diet. It is adjusted by family size and place of residence (farm versus nonfarm).

5. We know an apocryphal story about a famous experimental psychologist who attended a symposium considering the impact of psychoanalysis. The symposium was unusual in that it consisted of patients and their analysts. The experimental psychologist commented that he didn't think he had gotten much more out of his analysis than he would have gotten by spending the same time talking to a good friend. His analyst replied: "But Eddie, at the time you didn't have a friend!"

6. We agree with aspects of Kropotkin's (1902) position that the state's efforts undermine people's sense of mutual responsibility, and we believe that Sarason's (1976a) paper describing the anarchist insight says much of importance, but we also believe that public resources should be generously available to those in need. The problems of the aged, the mentally retarded, the chronically mentally ill, and many who are alone will not be dealt with satisfactorily, if at all, without the ample availability of public funds and resources. Our concern is with how the purposes of the funds are distorted when made available through the complex of fragmented governmental agencies and with how resources can be made to serve human rather than institutional needs.

2

The Origins of
Community Psychology
in the Community
Mental Health Movement

This chapter examines the seminal social and historical context for community psychology that was provided by the community mental health movement and the important place of community concepts in contemporary mental health practice. We review the history of mental health care to show how much our methods of providing care are embedded in our culture, in our political system, and in how we pay for the care.

Both community psychology and community mental health emerged in the mid-1960s during a period of great ferment not only in the mental health fields but in society at large. The successful civil rights movement of the 1950s and 1960s (Brooks, 1974) began with the Supreme Court's desegregation decision in *Brown* v. *Board of Education* (1954) and became a model for other groups to use in attacking social inequities in many areas of society. The Kennedy-Johnson War on Poverty (Levitan, 1969; Levitan & Taggart, 1971; Mann, 1978) stimulated assaults on a wide variety of social problems, including poverty, crime, delinquency, unemployment, poor education, mental retardation, welfare inequities, and troubles in prisons. In this period new questions were raised regarding social problems and their solutions.

President John F. Kennedy's address to Congress in 1963 in which he announced a bold, new approach to the care of the mentally ill and those with retardation was an important starting point. He advocated reducing the censuses of mental hospitals and reintegrating the mentally ill into the community; he also called for the prevention of personal misery and the promotion of mental health. Kennedy's new approach to mental health policy, quickly labeled community mental health, emerged as a direct consequence of post–World War II developments. However, there is always a "before-the-beginning" (Sarason, 1972), a distant and a more recent history that need to be examined to appreciate watershed policies like the Kennedy program.

The community mental health movement was a reform of the state hospital system, which had been the mainstay of the mental health system until the end of World War II. Having evolved from Seventeenth-century poorhouses and workhouses designed to care for chronically dependent people, state hospitals continued to provide refuge to various dependent populations well into the 1950s (Vogel, 1991). History helps us see matters which cannot be understood when we focus only on the psychopathology of those we label mentally ill. The following history shows how political, economic, social, welfare, professional, and legal issues affect mental health care.

Origins of Mental Health Care in the Welfare System

The welfare and the mental health systems are inextricably connected.[1] Many people served by the mental health system have a limited ability to care for themselves. The community mental health program was designed to support such people in the community rather than treat them in hospitals, where they had all of their needs met. A person discharged to the community may require housing, food, clothing, medical care, vocational training, recreation, transportation, and some degree of supervision, all of which cost money. If a person considered disabled because of mental illness is unable to work, under our current system the local, state, or federal government provides the needed funds. Although we may not want to characterize income provided to the mentally ill as welfare, such support does amount to providing for those who cannot entirely provide for themselves.

The Breakup of Feudalism and the Elizabethan Poor Laws

The mental health system in its modern form can be traced to the breakup of feudalism and the passage in 1601 of the Elizabethan Poor Laws, the grandmother of all welfare programs. The feudal system, which began with the Norman conquest of England in 1066, was built on a system of mutual obligation extending from noblemen to king, from lower-ranked noblemen to those of higher rank, and from villeins, peasants tied to the land they worked, to lower-ranked noblemen. In exchange for protection, people on a lower level of society paid taxes and pledged loyalty to those on a higher level. This loyalty pledge included the obligation to help raise troops and to serve in an army under the higher-ranked nobility or the king. Under this system of mutual obligation, the lord of the manor either took care of those who couldn't care for themselves or relegated those duties to the church. Economic dependence did not carry the stigma that it acquired in later times. The poor person provided an opportunity for the donor to perform an act of charity in fulfillment of a religious duty. Those in need had a right (entitlement, in modern terms) to receive aid, and those who were better off had a duty to provide it, as a matter of social justice (Coll, 1969).

The feudal system broke up beginning about the fourteenth century. The Black Death (bubonic plague) epidemic in 1348–1349 reduced the population of Europe by about one-quarter, creating a labor shortage. Workers with labor to sell moved from their homelands to other places in search of better-paid work, changing the economic system from one of mutual obligation to a "market economy" relying on wages. The employer owed his employee wages for time worked, but not much else. Those who couldn't earn wages or didn't earn enough to save for bad times "fell through the cracks." Over the next two hundred years, economic downturns and seasonal changes in the need for labor provoked restless movements of people from the country to the cities and from place to place. Local residents often feared and resented the migrants, who sometimes committed crimes or threatened to riot or even to revolt.

The Elizabethan Poor Laws, passed between 1597 and 1601, were the queen's and Parliament's answer to the question of who was responsible for the care of dependent persons. These laws placed first responsibility on the family for the care of its own but also established the principle of community responsibility for the poor if family members could not support them. Each parish was directed to appoint an overseer of the poor who was charged with building and maintaining almshouses ("indoor" relief), providing for relief in the home ("outdoor" relief), and establishing public works programs. Each parish was required to raise taxes for these purposes. Widows, orphans, the elderly, the retarded, the physically handicapped and disabled, and the mentally ill were all eligible for help. Once citizens were taxed to pay for these programs, however, the treatment of all poor people became harsher, and the reciprocity of mutual obligation was lost.

By the nineteenth century about 10 percent of the English population was housed in these institutions, despite the fact they were terrible places, designed to prevent the "welfare bums" of the day from taking advantage of the community's largesse. These institutions intermingled the poor with the mad and the bad. In addition, the overseers had financial incentives to spend a minimum on food and amenities and to pocket whatever was left from the funds appropriated for the care of the poor.

Mental Hospitals

The eighteenth century is called the Age of Enlightenment because of its triumphs in science. Although the poor and the mentally ill continued to live in almshouses and similar facilities, the middle class began providing for its own in private institutions. Lunatic hospitals, implying that mental illness was a disease that could be cured by scientific means, opened in England throughout the eighteenth century and supplemented the system of boarding the mentally ill in licensed private madhouses or private homes. William Tuke, a Quaker who operated a private institution, developed the "moral therapy" that was to become so influential in the United States later on.

In France at about this time, the philosophy of egalitarianism promoted by the French Revolution, as well as the scientific thinking of the day, provided a rationale for the physician Philippe Pinel to open the gates of two large institutions of confinement, the Bicêtre and the Salpêtrière, and to remove the chains from the mad men and women who were confined there with the poor. Pinel demonstrated that many inmates considered hopeless could be managed with a combination of kindness and firmness; some patients even improved.

George III, the king of England at the time of the American Revolution, suffered from a form of mental illness and was hospitalized several times. His care became a public issue when Parliament investigated his hospitalization. King George's physician claimed he could cure nine out of ten patients who had mental illness. Not to be outdone, other physicians made the same claims, producing "the cult of curability." Travelers carried this information along with Pinel's writings and news of Tukes's work from England to the United States, and eventually the information influenced the development of U.S. public policy.

Mental Hospitals and the Political System

The history of mental hospitals in the United States followed the pattern set in England. Colonists used the model of the Elizabethan Poor Laws and established some large, undifferentiated almshouses. They also relied on informal means of care for the mentally ill, although some private mental hospitals were established in the eighteenth century. In 1830 the Massachusetts legislature approved the construction of a publicly supported hospital exclusively for the care of the mentally ill, partly on the grounds that mental illness had been shown to be curable in England (the cult of curability) and in France (the work of Pinel). Legislators hoped to save money by opening a hospital that could cure the mentally ill and remove people from the welfare rolls.

Once created by state government, the mental hospital became embedded in our political system, and political values influenced its subsequent development. What happened with the first hospital was typical of what later happened elsewhere. That first hospital opened in 1833 in Worcester, a small town about a day's trip by horse and wagon from the population center of Boston. Given the prevailing belief that mental illness was caused by social stress related to the shift from an agricultural to a commercial and industrial economy, it made sense to establish the asylum in the peaceful countryside (Rothman, 1971).

Other factors may also have influenced the location of the hospital. The then governor of Massachusetts was a Worcester resident. Its town council voted money to purchase a site for the asylum, and the local area benefited from construction contracts, employment opportunities, and contracts to supply the hospital. To this day it is difficult to close unneeded state mental hospitals because local communities depend on them economically. Legislators regularly vote to keep state hospitals open, often against the recommendations of state mental health commissioners.

The Decline of Moral Treatment

Worcester State Hospital was designed architecturally to support the implementation of Tuke's and Pinel's moral therapy. When it opened, people had high hopes that patients could be cured of mental illness. Within a few years, however, that ideology gave way to the professional belief that insanity was incurable. These changes in ideology, practice, and beliefs about the fate of patients in institutions came about because the state mental hospital was now completely within the political system.

Politics changed ideology and practice. Proponents of moral treatment had sold the program to the legislature by overstating its effectiveness. A hospital discharging only 50 percent as cured instead of the expected 100 percent looked like a failure. Even if only a small percent of those who were admitted failed to improve to the point where they could be discharged, and if resources allocated to the hospital did not grow, inevitably the hospital would become swamped with chronic patients. With even a 90 percent cure rate each year, no cure of chronic patients after one year, no deaths, and no growth of facilities, the facility would fill with chronic patients rather quickly (see Table 2–1). A cure rate of less than 90 percent would swamp the facility much more rapidly. Although people who do not respond to treatment accumulate in every type of service, we make no real provision for them. As mental health professionals who

Table 2–1
Accumulation of Chronic Patients, Assuming a 90% Cure Rate

Year	Admissions	Discharged	Chronic/remain in hospital
1	100	90	10
2	90	81	19
3	81	73	27
4	73	64	36
5	64	58	42

have absorbed medical model ideology, we act surprised and chagrined that failures occur at all. Professionals tend to blame the consumer, saying that he or she is not appropriate for the treatment rather than admitting that the treatment may be inadequate.

The increasing number of chronic patients was an embarrassment to the developing profession of psychiatry. To conceal the patients' presence, hospital superintendents literally manipulated their institutions' statistics to show better success rates.[2]

Funding arrangements affected the population served in state hospitals. State law required local communities to pay hospital costs for their residents. Because it was cheaper for the local community to maintain a person in an almshouse, only the most difficult people were hospitalized, not necessarily those who could benefit from hospital care. The state legislature also withheld from hospital superintendents the power to control admissions; hospitals were required to admit "the furiously insane" and the criminally insane. Eventually the hospitals developed fearsome reputations as places where hopeless public menaces were incarcerated. Changing demographics also contributed to the loss of political support for the hospitals. In those years, for example, many poor, Irish immigrants were hospitalized at a time when Irish Catholic immigrants were looked down upon by the Anglo-American Protestant majority.

Because of the hospitals' reputations, middle-class people preferred to use private facilities if they could afford them. With the loss of middle-class patronage, state hospitals lost political support, and the legislative will to appropriate funds declined. Professional hospital administrators were not reformers. They managed as best they could with the resources they had. By the 1870s fiscal and managerial efficiency dominated practice in centralized state welfare bureaucracies. Cost and managerial efficiency became more important in evaluating hospitals than the quality of care.

Pliny Earle, a well-respected psychiatrist and hospital superintendent, concluded that insanity was incurable, an idea that came to dominate professional thinking. Even if a patient was adapting well with only residual symptoms and might have coped adequately in the community, hospital care continued because the patient not been cured. Critics claimed that patient labor was used to keep the hospitals going at low cost; hospitals had an incentive to keep good workers hospitalized to operate the hospital's farm, laundry, kitchens, grounds, and buildings, including the superintendents' palatial homes. (Pliny Earle's hospital actually turned a profit.)

Very large institutions housed a growing number of chronic patients and other social rejects. Few patients were discharged, because insanity was incurable. The large state hospital persisted as the major element of mental health care until well after World War II. A system of care that started out with high hopes had produced overcrowded "snake pits." It became the target of reform efforts that led to the community mental health approach.

Community Mental Health

The radical approach to mental health policy outlined in President Kennedy's 1963 address grew out of several post–World War II developments.

Military Psychiatry

During World War II, military psychiatrists demonstrated that with early treatment it was possible to restore a great many psychiatric casualties to full duty. The military claimed a high rate of cure (about 70 percent), in contrast to the very low rate of cure prevalent in civilian hospitals (5–20 percent). Community-based care in the new mental health centers was modeled conceptually after methods and approaches developed by the military.[3]

The military idea that help should be located close to the stressful situation and provided as quickly as possible was a forerunner of the current concept of social support (Mangellsdorf, 1985). In the military, psychologists, social workers, and nurses, as well as psychiatrists, had important roles in treatment, a consequence of "underpopulation" (see Chapter 5). The idea grew that other personnel in addition to psychiatrists could help treat mental illness, thus relieving the shortage of professional mental health workers uncovered in exposés of inadequate care in state hospitals. The military's success with crisis-oriented methods of intervention also sharply challenged the hopeless attitude toward mental illness that had prevailed since Pliny Earle's day.

Scientific Developments

The concept of stress as a physiological disorder and the possibility that science could solve hitherto insoluble problems came into public consciousness after World War II. Hans Selye and others made progress in understanding the psychophysiology of stress. If soldiers could succumb to the stresses of military life and show symptoms of mental illness, then mental illness among civilians might also be a response to life stresses. The definition of a mental disorder expanded to include "normal" distress in reaction to "abnormal" situations, such as combat. Later on we learned about the psychoactive drugs rauwolfia and thorazine, which seemed to be able to relieve depression, other anxiety, and psychiatric symptoms. Together with the public's belief, developed during World War II, in the power of science to produce, if not miracles, then certainly wonders such as atomic power, radar, sulfa, and penicillin, the time seemed right to make an all-out attack on mental illness, now recognized as an important public health issue. With psychoactive drugs in use by the mid-1950s, many patients could be maintained outside hospitals. If patients were to be maintained outside of hospitals, however, community-based services would be necessary.

Mental Health Reaches the Public Agenda

Public action occurs only after a problem has achieved a prominent place on the public agenda. The prevalence of mental health-related problems (see Chapter 1) was brought to public attention by World War II, when a distressingly high proportion of the men called up for service were rejected for neuropsychiatric reasons and neuropsychiatric conditions ranked high among medical reasons for discharge from service. In addition, conditions in state hospitals during the 1940s were exceedingly poor. Exposed in the media, these conditions became political liabilities for state governors. The governors, claiming they did not have the financial resources to improve conditions in the hospitals or to support training to meet the shortage of professional personnel, called for federal action. The political rhetoric of the 1990s calling for the return of our institutions to local control overlooks this history of failure of local control.

Community Mental Health and the Federal Government

In our political system, mental health care and welfare programs were traditionally local and state responsibilities. After World War II, federal policies and funds dominated mental health care. After passage of the Social Security Act of 1935, enacted to correct the inadequacy of state pensions for the elderly and for widowed mothers and their children, the federal government, through the mechanism of reimbursing the states for adopting federally approved programs, had a strong influence on each state's welfare policy. In the 1960s and 1990s new federal programs funding medical care (Medicaid, Medicare) and disability payments (SSI) were used to implement the deinstitutionalization policy.

Because mental illness was a prominent public health issue and because the government's partnership with science had been successful during World War II, postwar federal policy supported the development of a research and training capability in mental health. The National Institute of Mental Health (NIMH) was signed into law by President Harry S. Truman in 1946 to develop and support research and to produce trained clinical personnel in all the mental health professions. By 1955 NIMH had shown considerable success in carrying out its mission.

Community Psychology Grows from Community Mental Health

In a political climate favorable to reform, Americans began thinking beyond the problems of the severely mentally ill and the state hospital system and progressed to thought about prevention and alternative approaches to service delivery.

From State Hospital to Community Mental Health

The congressionally created Joint Commission on Mental Illness and Health (1955) was charged with developing a comprehensive mental health plan. The commission reported in 1961, just as Kennedy took office, that the existing patterns of care could provide for only a tiny fraction of those in need of help.[4] That report was the stimulus for Kennedy's 1963 address to Congress, in which the president went far beyond the commission's major recommmendations for revitalizing the state hospital system. The Community Mental Health Centers Act passed that same year.

Criticism of Conventional Mental Health Practice

The community mental health thrust was based on more than optimism that a new approach would help. Hope lived side by side with frustration (see Chapter 10). Critics asserted that mental hospitals created more problems than they solved (see Goffman, 1961). Aftercare facilities for adults released from mental hospitals were almost nonexistent, and institutions for the care of the retarded were in scandalous condition (Blatt & Kaplan, 1966). The new approach would solve these problems.

Szasz (1961) attacked the very concept of "mental illness," calling it a myth. He urged that we attend to the moral, legal, and social norms that produce our definitions of abnormal behavior and determine what kind of person becomes a patient. His argument directed attention away from the patient's "illness" and toward the social conditions under which illness and patienthood were defined. Epidemiological studies consistently showed that emotional problems were more frequent and more severe in low-income populations, especially in communities marked by social disorganization (Dohrenwend & Dohrenwend, 1969; Leighton et al., 1963; Srole et al., 1962).

Surveys of children's problems revealed much the same relationships (White & Harris, 1961). Low-income populations had higher rates of prematurity, problems associated with low birth weight, probable brain damage, and a variety of childhood disturbances, including behavior disorders and learning problems (Knobloch & Pasamanick, 1961). The Coleman et al. (1966) report confirmed on a national level that low-income children and adolescents had educational deficits that presaged a disastrous social and economic adjustment for many. Moynihan (1965) pointed to a state of disorganization in lower-class African American families that he believed would perpetuate social and psychological problems.[5] Considered as a whole, these data pointed to the need for social reform as well as better mental health care.

Hollingshead and Redlich (1958) showed that the existing system of service delivery provided one kind of care for middle- and upper-class individuals and another kind for lower-class people. Middle- and upper-class patients received less severe diagnoses and were treated with outpatient therapy more often. Lower-class patients had more severe diagnoses and were treated in a public system using custodial inpatient care, shock treatments, and lobotomies.

The effectiveness of mental health services was also questioned. Eysenck (1952, 1961) marshaled evidence challenging psychotherapists to show that their efforts produced more change than no special help over an equal length of time. Similar challenges were issued to those serving children (Levitt, 1957). Many dropped out of treatment (Tuckman & Lavell, 1959; Reiss & Brandt, 1965), raising the possibility that a great deal of clinical time was wasted.[6] The psychologist's testing functions also came under attack. Meehl (1954) argued that clinicians' predictive validity was no better, and often poorer, than that achieved by standard statistical prediction procedures. Diagnostic appraisal rarely influenced therapists' specific approaches to treatment.

Critics, citing sociological theories of deviance control, asserted that the mental health professions in general, and psychiatry in particular, contributed to the incidence of mental health problems by confirming and helping to enforce existing social norms (see Chapter 6). By defining mental illness in isolation from social conditions, these critics alleged, the profession distracted attention from social issues that were at the root of abnormal behavior in the first place. At a minimum, mental health professions needed to work more closely with the people staffing community agencies—schools, courts, welfare departments, churches, police departments—to encourage handling of problems by means other than referral to formal mental health agencies.

The Emphasis on Prevention

Kennedy's bold new approach went beyond the reintegration of former psychiatric inpatients into the community. He called for the prevention of disorders and the promotion of positive mental health. Positive mental health meant more than the absence of symptoms; it included the state of well-being that enables an individual to pursue personal fulfillment.

Once we target positive mental health as a goal, we necessarily study and attempt to influence social institutions that contribute to the creation, perpetuation, or exacerbation of personal misery. In a sense, all of the soap opera that is life becomes the mental health professional's concern. He or she retains an interest in the distressed individual but, as a helper, now tries to influence families, schools, social agencies, courts, industrial organizations, and perhaps even the overall economic order. The role model changes from that of physician and healer to that of educator, social critic, reformer, and social planner.

The Swampscott Conference on Community Psychology (Bennett et al., 1966) gave formal recognition to the emergence of a new field that needed appropriate training for its practitioners (Iscoe & Spielberger, 1970). The expansion in the scope of problems defined as mental health issues and the advocacy of social intervention by mental health workers were viewed by some articulate critics as a dangerous professional imperialism (Dunham, 1965).

The Influence of the War on Poverty

President Kennedy was assassinated in 1963. His successor, Lyndon B. Johnson, supported the community mental health movement. He also initiated a war on poverty that created a great variety of programs designed to ameliorate problems of the poor. Community action organization programs sponsored by the Office of Economic Opportunity (OEO) provided direct services, but they also intended to influence existing service systems (e.g., welfare, medical care, schools, clinics, employment services, police, housing authorities) to improve services to poorer populations (Levitan, 1969; Moynihan, 1969).

The War on Poverty had as a goal social change as well as the provision of direct assistance to the poor. It mandated the "maximum feasible participation" of those to be served by the programs, an idea that was translated into the concept of community control, which in turn led to a great deal of conflict between community organizations and local governments (Moynihan, 1969; Kellam, Branch, Agrawal, & Grabill, 1972; Zax & Specter, 1974). Community control as an ideology came to symbolize much more than making programs relevant to the people in the neighborhoods served.

The concept of community control had important economic implications. It meant the paid employment of neighborhood people. This strategy was justified on the grounds that middle-class professionals had little ability to understand people living in poverty. Community control was also a strategy to meet the labor shortage in the human services and to create permanent jobs for those who would otherwise not enter the middle class (Pearl & Reissman, 1965). The use of "paraprofessionals" proliferated (Sobey, 1970), and programs employing them were effective (Alley, Blanton, Feldman, Hunter, & Rolfson, 1979).

The climate of change encouraged experimentation in an effort to reach underserved and poorly served populations. Some mental health professionals became involved in the new community mental health center programs and in alternative service settings (Sarason, Levine, et al., 1966.) Given attacks on the validity of conventional professional practice, the reform-minded rhetoric of the time, and the accumulating evidence that alternative personnel and alternative services were viable, a great variety of programs emerged, both with and without the assistance of mental health professionals.

Activists, taking as their model the successful civil rights movement of the 1950s and 1960s, adopted similar ideologies, rhetoric, and strategies to achieve social and economic change. Their goals were not limited to material gains; they rejected the socially imposed view that a person in need was a deservedly despised deviant. Activists and the social groups they created provided socially shared bases for maintaining self-esteem and encouraging social action to change one's situation (Ryan, 1971; Goldenberg, 1978); activism in the social arena paralleled and was intertwined with the culturally profound antiwar movement and the sexual revolution, both of which distrusted constituted authority and tradition (Roszak, 1969; Reich, 1970; Slater, 1970).

Many programs were directed toward relieving psychological misery and enhancing self-esteem. Some mental health professionals believed that almost any social action legitimately fell within the province of mental health. Empowering the powerless was worthwhile in and of itself in the quest for a more perfect democracy through the attainment of political, social, and economic equality (e.g., Cloward & Piven, 1971). It could also be justified as treatment for, and prevention of, a range of mental health problems that were direct consequences of psychological apathy and helplessness (Rappaport, 1977).

The Need for New Theory and Concepts

The rapid expansion of the community mental health movement led to confusion. Community psychology covered everything from "showing Szondi plates [a then popular projective technique] to ghetto residents in an inner city storefront, to engineering new communities" (Cowen, 1973, p. 423). The new thrust went off in all directions at once, with little coherence and little conceptual clarity. Critics committed to traditional medical model practice looked askance at social activism. Those committed to "intrapsychic supremacy" (Levine, 1969)—the belief that problems in living result from people's internal psychological structures, which in turn dictate perceptions, feelings, and actions in everyday situations—viewed the activists as misguided romantics who had foolishly strayed from proper professional roles and activities.[7] Community-oriented critics of traditional practice were equally firm in their convictions but had little to offer by way of alternate theoretical conceptualizations.[8]

The new thrust developed along highly pragmatic lines. Emory Cowen, an early proponent of prevention programs and a practitioner skilled at delivering alternative services in the schools, operated by using what worked. His efforts were directed less by theory than by seat-of-the-pants experience, judged against research as thorough as circumstances would allow (Cowen, Trost, Izzo, Lorion, Dorr, & Isaacson, 1975; see Chapter 8). Levine (1973) justified novel activity on the basis of necessity, calling for a "responsible chutzpah," that is, doing the best one could even though the scientific base supporting novel activity was rather thin.

Seymour Sarason, a leader in the movement toward acting on the basis of "responsible chutzpah" (Sarason, Levine, et al., 1966; Sarason, 1982a), was well aware of the theoretical and empirical problems facing psychologists. He understood the limits to exploring new ground imposed by his own experience and thinking. Sarason asserted that traditional psychology and other social sciences were not prepared to offer much to policymakers (Sarason, 1981), a position that would have been well received by Moynihan (1969). Moynihan attributed the failures of the War on Poverty to the innocence of social scientists, whose theories were too simple to encompass the complexity of social action; they sent brave programs into hostile skies, naively unaware that many would be shot down by the flak of politics, limited resources, and cultural impatience with the pace and nature of change.

Arguing for more than relevance, Sarason (1981) urged us to go beyond the dominant person-centered psychology to an approach that recognizes history and social context to a greater degree. He said that the universe of alternatives in which problems are defined and solutions proposed can be severely constrained by cultural-theoretical blinders and narrow disciplinary perspectives.[9] Sarason argued that the social scientist's place and stake in the world is material. A problem doesn't just exist "out there." Social scientists, said Sarason, should consider how they define problems and propose solutions and from which value positions they operate.

Better science is not enough, Sarason argued. The nature of problem solving in social action is different from that in the physical sciences. Because social problems may be deeply rooted in the human condition, they may be intractable and will not yield to once-and-for-all solutions:

> [T]here will be no final solutions, only a constantly upsetting imbalance between values and action; the internal conflict will not be in the form of "Do I have the right answer?" but rather of "Am I being consistent with what I believe?"; satisfaction will come not from colleagues' consensus that your procedures, facts, and conclusions are independent of your feelings and values, but from your own conviction that you tried to be true to your values. (Sarason, 1978, p. 379)

We are developing theoretical perspectives and concepts that take us beyond individual psychology and beyond the limits imposed by psychology's reliance on experimental methods. Excursions into the community have opened our minds to new possibilities and pointed us in directions that may provide new insights into the human condition and the ability of the social sciences to illuminate that condition. We are now more aware than ever that we are inevitably dealing with matters of value and that action and research are inevitably intertwined with value considerations.

To summarize, community psychology emerged during the 1960s, a period of rapid social change. The field had a name, and to some extent an ideology, but it was unclear what community psychology encompassed and what its methods, goals or scientific theories were. Because one could justify so many diverse activities in the name of "community mental health," the concept appeared to have little real meaning and led to much soul-searching (Iscoe, Bloom, & Spielberger, 1977). A rough division emerged between rehabilitative and restorative efforts on the one hand and preventive-prophylactic efforts on the other (Cowen, 1973), a distinction others have called community mental health and community psychology, respectively (Rappaport, 1977).

The community movement had profound effects on the field of mental health and on our thinking about psychological issues. So many of community psychology's general concepts and programs have been taken over in clinical settings that in the 1990s the community perspective can no longer claim to be novel or innovative. In many areas, the community perspective has become the conventional wisdom. Furthermore, if indeed the past is prologue, then today's conventional wisdom provides the historical context for the next generation of perspectives and practices in psychology and mental health. The question of community psychology's scientific foundations is important, and we will return to it in coming chapters. In preparation for examining those issues, however, we first survey the contemporary situation in community mental health.

Current Issues in Community Mental Health

The community movement has had a far reaching impact on mental health services, well beyond the establishment of some 750 federally funded community mental health centers (CMHCs), about half the number originally envisioned under the 1963 Community Mental Health Centers Act. Community-based treatment requires a change in the mix of services. In this section we discuss current mental health practice, including the continuing movement to deinstitutionalize the mentally ill, community alternatives to inpatient care, mental health services for minority groups and other traditionally underserved populations, and mental health services for children.

Deinstitutionalization

The patient population in state and county mental hospitals has decreased from nearly 600,000 in the 1950s to less than 150,000 in 1995, while the number of persons in institutions for the retarded declined from more than 200,000 to less than 100,000 during the same period. These reductions in institutional populations fulfilled one goal of the CMHC program—to halve the institutional population within ten years of the program's inception. The decline is only partly attributable to treatment philosophy. It also reflects changes in funding and reimbursement practices and changes in law that make it more difficult to hospitalize or retain people in hospital involuntarily (Levine, 1981; see Chapter 4).

Not all commentators hold a benign view of the deinstitutionalization movement (Scull, 1977; Gralnick, 1985). Critics also argue that CMHCs have not really served the seriously mentally ill who were discharged from hospitals (Torrey et al., 1988). The problem of providing adequate community-based services for deinstitutionalized people continues to be an important challenge (Shinn & Felton, 1981; Torrey et al., 1988). Early in the deinstitutionalization process, patients were discharged from hospitals to single-room-occupancy hotels or to board-and-care homes in which the level of care was exceedingly poor. Elderly patients were simply discharged to nursing homes where, in too many instances, the care provided was scandalous. The scandals resulted in greater regulation, and conditions may have improved in recent years, but we would not be surprised if newspaper headlines were to expose continuing patient-care scandals in some of these facilities, especially if funds and regulatory standards are reduced with new legislation.

Deinstitutionalization policy has created new underserved populations of vulnerable individuals. We now have a new treatment category of mentally ill people whose substance abuse problems complicate the problem of providing care. Many are younger people, disinclined to use the formal mental health system, who resist the appellation "mental patient" (Segal and Baumohl, 1982; Bachrach, 1984).

The state hospital provided a full array of services from the time of entrance to the patient's discharge or death. The community mental health system cannot readily supply the same range of services. There is a large number of homeless street people, reflecting the unemployment rate and the conversion of former low-rent properties to high-rent properties. Roughly 15 to 30 percent of the homeless are seriously mentally ill, and many more have substance abuse problems (Fischer & Breakey, 1991; Toro & Wall, 1991). The odd behavior of some members of this minority offers visible signs of the problems in deinstitutionalization policy (Bachrach, 1984).

Many former patients will not use the formal system of care. The poor living conditions of many former inpatients (now called "consumers") and problems in dealing with some consumers now living in the community have led family advocates to try to change the laws to permit involuntary hospitalization on broader grounds than dangerousness to self or others (See the special issue of *Innovations & Research on Mental Illness and the Law*, 1993). Although some former patients acknowledge the need for involuntary hospitalization, and for involuntary medication, many still find the experience destructive and would prefer to avoid it (Garrett & Posey, 1993).[10]

In many cities, "service ghettos" (Dear & Wolch, 1987) have been created in which persons who are sick, poor, old, mad, or bad are concentrated, almost as they were in the poorhouses of old. The slogan "problem creation through problem solution" is very apt.

Deinstitutionalization has had many positive effects (Beiser et al., 1985). Studies rather uniformly report that consumers feel more satisfied in community settings than in the hospital. Many who might have spent a lifetime in a hospital now have more freedom and live safely in the community, although their lifestyles may be restricted. Some have formed consumer self-help and advocacy groups, while others have themselves become trained providers of case management and other mental health services (Nikkel et al., 1992; Sherman & Porter, 1991). The positive consequences of deinstitutionalization might well be enhanced if we could solve some of the challenges to the service system (Lamb, 1984; Thompson, 1985).

Care in the community. Since 1963 the ratio of inpatient-care episodes to outpatient episodes has changed drastically. Twenty years ago 75 percent of all patient-care episodes (patient admitted and discharged in a year) took place in state and county mental hospitals. In 1995 only 25 percent took place there. The change is reflected in data about where the 2 million persons with diagnoses of serious mental disorders (schizophrenia or bipolar disorder) live. Only a small percent live in state and county mental hospitals (see Table 2–2).

Resources designed to avoid hospitalization have not been adequately reallocated from state and county mental health budgets to community-

Table 2–2
Where the 2 Million Persons with Serious Mental Illness Reside

Residence	*Percent of Mentally Ill*
Hospital	8.0
Nursing homes	14.0
Foster homes, board-and-care homes, group homes, etc.	21.0
Live with families	40.0
Live alone	8.0
Homeless, public shelters	7.0
Jails or prisons	3.0

From Torrey, Wolfe and Flynn, 1988, p. 7

based services. Funds for inpatient care still absorb the lion's share of state mental health budgets. In Indiana, the state spent 60 percent of state-controlled mental health funds on just 3 percent of public mental health consumers (those cared for in state hospitals), leaving only 40 percent for the 97 percent of consumers served by state-supported community-based providers (Indiana Division of Mental Health, 1992). Savings from the reduced censuses of state hospitals do not go directly to community-based services but may be used to avoid deficits in the state's general budget.

One new development that has affected the service system is the growth of private-sector for-profit psychiatric hospital chains that take the easiest patients and keep them as long as insurance covers their care. These chains compete with public-sector agencies for the most qualified professional mental health workers, worsening the staffing problems of state hospitals and public-sector community-based agencies (Torrey et al., 1988).

Lengths of stay in mental hospitals have decreased drastically compared with those of thirty years ago. In 1969 the average length of stay in state and county mental hospitals was 421 days; in 1978 it was 189 days. The average length of stay for psychiatric conditions in general hospitals is only eight days. These shorter stays have produced a "revolving-door" phenomenon, with some patients in, out, and then in again (Kiesler, 1982).

A shortened length of stay reflects the community thrust of restoring the person's equilibrium as rapidly as possible and then returning him or her to the community. It may also reflect legal problems in holding people who are not dangerous to themselves or others (Levine, 1981). Considered alone, length-of-stay data do not tell us about the meaning of short stays to consumers and their families. If consumers improve as much in short stays as they do in longer ones, shorter stays have benefits for the consumer and for society. If consumers do not improve sufficiently to allow resumption of relatively peaceful and independent living, however, short stays may not be greeted with much enthusiasm, especially by families who felt relieved when hospitalization lifted a burden from their shoulders (Hatfield, 1993). Short hospital stays underscore the necessity of aftercare and of prepared environments, whether the consumer returns to the family or to some community residence. Unfortunately, private hospitals and general hospitals are less likely to provide case management and aftercare services than are public specialty hospitals (Kiesler et al., 1989; Dorwart & Hoover, 1994). The aftercare a consumer receives may depend on the facility in which he or she was hospitalized. A reallocation and reorientation of mental health resources is required to keep up with the ongoing changes in practice.

Community Alternatives to Hospitalization

Over the years, psychosocial rehabilitation models (Anthony et al., 1983), crisis and outreach programs (Cohen, 1990), intensive case management (Surles et al., 1992), and programs such as Assertive Community Treatment (Stein & Test, 1985; Test, 1991; see Box 2–1) have superseded medical models of care that depended on patients coming voluntarily to an outpatient clinic for aftercare. These more intensive outpatient services are often supplemented by day care programs or consumer organizations with their own clubhouses (See special issue on clubhouses, *Psychosocial Rehabilitation Journal*, 1992, *16*, No. 2, October). Some clubhouses are staffed and operated by former patients (Chamberlin, 1990).

Box 2–1. Assertive Community Supports

An important development in the formal system of care has been the increasing use of case managers to coordinate an array of diverse services for people in need. In newer versions these providers work from one or two hours per week up to many hours per week with the same individuals, delivering services in homes and other community settings. Two examples of this approach are Assertive Community Treatment for people with serious mental illness and the Homebuilders program for families at risk for having their children placed outside the home.

Assertive Community Treatment (ACT), also known as Training in Community Living or the Madison Model, provides intensive support to individuals with severe mental illness (SMI) to prevent or reduce hospitalization and to increase quality of life in the community. ACT provides practical services focusing directly on basic living skills, medications, finances, housing, and advocacy, helping the client obtain services from other providers. The ratio of staff to consumers is small (typically 1:10); staff members work as a team in an effort to increase consumer access to services (e.g., during evening and weekend hours) and to facilitate communication and support among staff (Stroul, 1986). Staff-consumer contacts occur almost exclusively in community settings rather than in clinic offices. The staff works to keep consumers enrolled in the program and promotes a mental health consumer's right to be fully integrated into community life.

ACT has been used successfully in rural and inner-city communities (Witheridge & Dincin, 1985). It is well suited to young adults with SMI (Stein & Test, 1985), who represent an especially challenging population (Iscoe & Harris, 1984). It has also been used among homeless mentally ill individuals and mentally ill substance abusers (Olfson, 1990).

As for its results, ACT consistently reduces hospital use and therefore costs of service (e.g., Bond et al., 1988; Bond et al., 1990; Dincin, 1990; Gilman & Diamond, 1985; Witheridge & Dincin, 1985). Other desirable effects such as symptom reduction and improved social relationships and subjective quality of life have been less easy to substantiate through research (Olfson, 1990). Although less costly than hospitalization, ACT is labor-intensive and thus relatively expensive compared to other forms of outpatient care. Lack of resources and some states' tendency to allocate resources to hospitals rather than to community programs limit its availability in many communities (Stein & Test, 1985; Torrey, 1990).

We may ask several questions about ACT. Are reductions in hospital use attributable simply to better compliance with medication under the intensive supports ACT provides (Taube et al., 1990)? What is ACT's optimum place in cost-conscious systems of "managed care"? Is ACT best used as an intense support during episodes of crisis, with less formal consumer-driven supports readily available at other times? Could ACT be blended with principles of mutual help by enrolling mental health consumers as ACT staff (Toro, 1990)?

Homebuilders (Kinney et al., 1991) is another assertive support program. It is an intensive, home-based program designed to prevent expensive and disruptive out-of-home placements for children at risk. Homebuilders limits worker caseloads to two families at a time. Workers spend as much as twenty hours a week in the family's home, providing concrete services, advocacy, counseling, and other treatment. Homebuilders' supporters claim that the vast majority of children who were at risk of out-of-home placement (a criterion for accepting the family into the program) stayed in the community for a year after the onset of treatment. Despite its labor-intensive approach, the program is believed cost-efficient because expensive out-of-home placements are avoided. Other programs that use intensive family-based interventions to change the behavior of youths in their natural environments (e.g., Henggeler et al., 1991) have also reported some success.

There are now many alternative community living facilities that serve former psychiatric inpatients, retarded persons, the elderly (Shinn & Felton, 1981), and delinquent or neglected youth who in the past were sent to large, isolated institutions. However, we know very little about how extensive these alternative programs are, exactly which segments of the population they serve, and how effective they are.

The many examples of new services provide conceptual and research challenges to the mental health community. Are they fads, or do they have substance? Are they therapeutically effective or simply designed to save money at the expense of consumers and their families? What are the mechanisms of their effectiveness? Do they have as yet unrecognized and unanticipated effects? Can we learn to measure humane values in care as well as outcomes such as rehospitalization or employment?

Kiesler (1982) reviewed a number of studies with reasonably good methodologies, comparing alternatives such as day hospitalization or the delivery of crisis services with hospitalization for mental illness. He concluded that "[a]lternative care always is as good or better than hospitalization regarding outcomes, and almost always is less expensive" (p.

1327). That conclusion holds for services provided within the formal system of mental health care and for consumers who would have been hospitalized. It cannot be generalized to cover all alternative services for all populations.

Alternative services operating outside the formal mental health care system have also increased in number. Many cities now have shelters for the homeless, for battered women, and for runaway youths. There are treatment and residential facilities for substance abusers, as well as peer counseling programs and street-worker projects. Facilities are staffed in whole or in part by people who themselves have suffered with the problem or who have a personal aptitude for the work instead of professional credentials. The staffs of alternative facilities believe that they offer different services than do traditional mental health services and serve clients who would not use traditional services (Gordon, 1978). The number of abortion clinics grew rapidly after *Roe* v. *Wade* (1973), and many of these facilities offer counseling along with abortion services. In addition to protesting abortion clinics, some antiabortion groups offer counseling and assist mothers to either place infants for adoption or to keep them. Rape counseling programs and victim assistance programs have also developed. Community action programs, first established during the War on Poverty, still provide neighborhood services, including counseling, training, advocacy for clients, and referral to other agencies.

Suicide prevention services developed during the 1960s and grew rapidly. Many now provide crisis services, broadly defined, using volunteers who are trained to staff telephone "hotlines" (McGee, 1974). This concept of anonymous services, readily available whenever a person feels the need, represents a different orientation from that reflected in weekly fifty-minute appointments at a service provider's office.

In some places church-affiliated or lay counseling centers have developed, staffed by volunteers trained in counseling methods and supervised by professionals. Volunteers, along with the paraprofessionals found widely in many mental health centers, have expanded the base of personnel available to deliver services (NIMH, 1970; Sobey, 1970). Self-help groups also have proliferated (see Chapter 9).

Our knowledge of alternative services is usually based on small-scale studies of programs that are probably unrepresentative, and the studies rarely include follow-ups. Who uses the services and who drops out? These questions remain for research if we are to understand which needs the community-based alternatives serve.

Outpatient psychotherapy. Outpatient psychotherapy providers have increased substantially in number. There are about 150,000 psychiatrists, psychologists, and psychiatric social workers in the United States, compared to about 9,000 in 1945 (Torrey et al., 1988). Services are also provided by psychiatric nurses trained at the M.A. level, marriage and family counselors, and pastoral counselors and clergy trained in psychotherapy or counseling, as well as by unlicensed "psychotherapists" with diverse and sometimes dubious credentials. This increase in professional psychotherapy is consistent with the extensive needs identified by epidemiological surveys (see Chapter 1). The psychotherapy market may be oversaturated in some metropolitan areas, but the shortage is still severe in rural areas and in less populated parts of the country.

Although many professional practitioners work in public clinics and agencies, a large number are in private practice (Taube et al., 1984). Insurance coverage for outpatient mental health services undergirded the growth of private practice. Because of insurance support, persons who could not otherwise afford psychotherapy can avail themselves of it (Taube et al., 1984).

The growth of managed care, limiting the number of visits, specifying treatment methods, and limiting the number of practitioners who may be reimbursed by insurance, is having profound effects on the field. The proliferation of outpatient providers has undoubtedly been beneficial for persons who can benefit from psychotherapy. Those who use outpatient services are not necessarily the severely mentally ill, and hospitalizations may not be avoided because of outpatient psychotherapy (Torrey et al., 1988).

Sex abuse memories recovered in psychotherapy. The publicity given to sexual abuse may have led more women to receive treatment for dysfunction associated with a history of sexual abuse than would otherwise have sought help (Wyatt & Powell, 1988). Referrals of child abuse victims and alleged perpetrators for treatment are becoming very common and present some unique legal problems (Levine & Doherty, 1991; Levine & Doueck, 1995). Some observers question whether certain therapy techniques cause mistaken accusations of sexual abuse based on faulty memories recovered in therapy (see *Newsletter of the False Memory Syndrome Foundation*, 1994; Coleman, 1990). Accusations of sexual abuse followed by confrontation of the parent who allegedly committed the abuse twenty or thirty years ago, as a matter of healing, may have other consequences. Lawsuits claiming psychological damages and seeking sizable monetary recoveries are often defended by insurance companies because claims are made against general liability clauses in homeowners insurance policies. The insurance companies may use their resources to try to limit legal actions. However, in deference to the claims of women's advocates about existing legal restrictions, a number of states have extended the statute of limitations so that an action may be brought many years after the alleged events occurred. Insurance companies and professionals who question some of the methods used to recover memories may seek more stringent licensing requirements for providers that may have an effect on the number of providers in practice in the future. This area is very controversial, but it raises intriguing questions about the nature of memory, the implications of treatment, and the role of the legal system (Bass & Davis, 1988; Loftus, 1993).

Bureaucratic obstacles. The community movement has undoubtedly had a strong impact on how we approach problems, but change doesn't come easily (see Chapter 10). Most mental health services offer primarily individual, group, and family therapy and psychotropic medications, and not always to those with the greatest need (Torrey et al., 1988). Furthermore, because most new services have developed piecemeal out of pragmatic considerations, the result has been a crazy-quilt pattern of funding and legislated eligibility requirements to receive services.

The New York Governor's Select Commission (Goldsmith, 1984) identified nineteen federal and state sources of funds for mental health programming, each with its own requirements. Before the community mental health centers program, 96 percent of funds for public mental health services came from state government. Now the federal government contributes 38 percent, local governments 9 percent, and state governments only 53 percent (Torrey et al., 1988). Program administrators must keep track of the different funding streams for treatment programs and the strings attached to each. Clinicians are also faced with keeping track of programs that help their clients individually—SSI, Social Security Disability, Medicaid, food stamps, state supplements, welfare, special housing programs, clothing allowances, and discounts for public transportation. Torrey et al. comment, "Since the professionals themselves have difficulty keeping all these programs straight, it is little wonder that individuals with serious mental illness are usually overwhelmed with them all" (p. 13).

The diverse funding streams have resulted in a "fiscal shell game" as officials sometimes working at cross-purposes try to shift fiscal responsibility from one level of government to another. Torrey et al. (1988) claim that the fiscal shell game, not patient care, is now the driving force behind public mental health decision making. This confusion has led to the anomaly of the state government participating as a plaintiff in a suit against the federal government to help those who have disabilities for mental disorders or mental retardation retain their federal disability status. If they were to lose that status, responsibility for income maintenance would fall on state welfare programs (Goldsmith, 1984).

Changes continue even as we write. The basic distinction between public and private care has begun to break down as states and counties realign themselves and begin collaborating with private organizations in an effort to meet consumers' needs (Snowden, 1993). Capitation systems, funded on the basis of eligible consumers rather than on fees for services, are being adopted in an effort to increase the efficiency and consumer-centeredness of services. Last, managed care, where services may be allocated in fixed amounts and purchased at competitive prices in the open marketplace, gives an uneasy glimpse of how far we've come from the ad lib support based on mutual obligation that was once provided during the Middle Ages. Block grants from the federal government to the states with few strings attached may be helpful in breaking down artificial barriers. However, financially hard-pressed states may simply divert funds to other functions to relieve pressures on state budgets, rather than improve mental health services.

New developments. In considering the future, we cannot pay attention to program ideas alone. At every step, our thinking must take into account the political, social, and economic contexts of ideas and the programs they inspire, just as political considerations and the conservative temper of the 1980s influenced the rhetoric and the allocation of funds for a "war on drugs" (Humphreys & Rappaport, 1993). We also need to consider alternatives to the medical model (see also Lorion & Ross, 1992). Kiesler (1992), moreover, arguing that medical model approaches are inherently flawed, concludes that unless alternative approaches to health policy in the provision of mental health care are devised, we can only expect more expensive and inappropriate care to emerge. If these ideas hold sway in the effort to reform health policy in the United States, the community approach will have continued significance in both mental health and substance abuse services.

This potential for still more diversity of service approaches challenges community psychology to articulate and test new concepts. This challenge was heightened by a renewed emphasis on preventive services attributable to the President's Commission on Mental Health (1978). Programs in prevention are the only mental health services that received new funding under the first Reagan administration and continued to receive support in the subsequent lean budget years. That may change as the "Contract with America" budget ax wielded by the conservative Republican congressional majority elected in 1994 falls on many social and health related programs. In the absence of a viable theoretical paradigm, however, community psychology's response to the challenge of prevention may fail. We will identify some promising theoretical concepts generated by the community thrust in Chapter 3. Before doing so, however, we will review the quality and availability of services available to racial and cultural minority groups and to children and adolescents.

Minorities and Other Underserved Groups

In 1978 the President's Commission on Mental Health identified rural populations and ethnic and racial minorities as unserved or underserved populations; following the commission's report, a new mental health policy was proposed to address that problem. Has the community thrust resulted in improved services to groups formerly less well served?

Blouch (1982) evaluated epidemiological studies of the mental health of persons in rural and urban areas. He found that mental health problems occurred frequently in rural areas but that rural populations continued to be underserved. Some other studies showed that underutilization of mental health services by Mexican Americans and Latinos had lessened

(Barrera, 1982; O'Sullivan, Peterson, Cox, & Kirkeby, 1989). Bilingual and bicultural therapists help in "marketing" services to ethnic populations. Hispanic adolescents were underrepresented on the rolls of a Los Angeles CMHC, compared to their numbers in the population of Los Angeles (Bui & Takeuchi, 1992). Service delivery to American Indian and Alaskan native communities has increased greatly in quantity, but not necessarily appropriateness (Manson & Trimble, 1982; O'Sullivan et al., 1989).

The increase in representation of minorities in the patient population of mental health centers reflects efforts to adapt services to the needs of different segments of the community. However, because of differences in "assumptions, experiences, beliefs, values, expectations, and goals" between service providers and many members of culturally diverse groups, underutilization may continue despite the availability of services. Similar conclusions hold for Asian American and Pacific American populations (Wong, 1982; Bui & Takeuchi, 1992).

Data on the utilization of services by African Americans are less well developed. Based on a national sampling survey, Neighbors (1985) found that African Americans tend not to use the formal mental health system in coping with stress. They are more likely to turn to informal networks, including their ministers. Shapiro et al. (1984) did not find racial differences in reported use of mental health services; another survey (Myers et al., 1984) found few racial differences in the prevalence of *DSM-III* diagnostic categories. However, African Americans have higher hospitalization rates than do whites (Task Panel, President's Commission on Mental Health, 1978). Bui and Takeuchi (1992) found that African American adolescents were overrepresented on the rolls of a Los Angeles CMHC, but they also had shorter lengths of stay in treatment than other groups. African Americans were significantly overrepresented on the rolls of a CMHC in Seattle (O'Sullivan et al., 1989).

From the viewpoint of some African American scholars, dealing with the many inequities in American society that may be related to the prevalence of mental health problems and stress in the African American population is a more important issue than utilization of mental health services: "What social changes are likely to promote the involvement and participation of black Americans as full and equal citizens?" (Moore, 1982, pp. 178–179). The question does not mean that we should ignore service delivery issues, but it suggests that other matters should be addressed as well.

Some scholars with minority backgrounds (Jones & Matsumoto, 1982; Zane, Sue, Castro, & George, 1982; Gordon, 1982) challenge the assumption that lower socioeconomic-level clients are not amenable to psychotherapy (O'Sullivan et al., 1989; Bui & Takeuchi, 1992). No formal outcome study shows lower psychotherapy success rates in economically disadvantaged groups; preparing clients for treatment may reduce dropout rates and improve treatment outcomes. According to these researchers, we need to design services that are more responsive to the needs of various populations. The suggestions they offer to help make service-delivery systems responsive to the needs of ethnic minorities are very consistent with the way community mental health programs have in fact developed (Zane et al., 1982). We may have learned something in the last twenty-five years. O'Sullivan et al. (1989) claim that utilization of services by minorities has improved substantially and attribute the improvement to changes in the pattern of service delivery:

> There were more ethnic-specific CMHCs located in their respective neighborhoods, more culturally unique and relevant treatment modalities being provided, and more ethnic and bilingual staff providing services. These developments were initiated within the ethnic communities and supported by local government. (p. 28)

Children and Adolescents

Mental health problems of children and adolescents received far less attention than adult problems, despite evidence of need.

The extent of need. The prevalence of diagnosable disorders among children and adolescents under age 18 ranges between 5 percent and 23 percent (Namir and Weinstein, 1982). The variation in estimates stems from different methods and sampling procedures. The National Advisory Mental Health Council (1990) estimated that about 12 percent (or about 7.6 million) of the 63 million young people under age 18 have some mental disorders, with half of them severely handicapped by them. The Institute of Medicine (1989), part of the National Research Council, speculated that the prevalence rate for all childhood disorders might fall between 17 percent and 22 percent but recommended adopting the more conservative estimate of 12 percent.

Among the poorest inner-city populations the prevalence of disorder may be as high as 20 percent. A number of groups have higher rates than the general population: children whose parents are mentally ill or substance abusers; children living in foster care; children with chronic medical illnesses; Native American children in some tribes with a high suicide rate; children living on welfare; homeless children; children separated from parents for prolonged periods; children suffering physical or sexual abuse; orphans; and children in unstable families or families characterized by marital discord. Children with low birth weights, developmental delays, brain damage, early temperamental difficulties, or mental retardation also tend to have prevalence rates of psychopathology in excess of that found in the general population (Institute of Medicine, 1989).

There are probably more than 2 million children and adolescents of school age who are not in school, many because they have been suspended or expelled for disciplinary reasons (Children's Defense Fund, 1974). The 350,000 to 400,000 adolescents who have out-of-wedlock children each year and their children constitute another population at risk; the adolescents tend not to finish high school, and their children are at risk for school failure. All these risk factors help us to identify characteristics of populations that should be targeted for services or for efforts.

Services. Children's services have been chronically neglected. Children from low-income populations have been underrepresented in child guidance clinics (Harrison et al., 1965), in clinics associated with the juvenile or family court (*In re Gault*, 1967), and in school-based services (Sexton, 1961). In the early 1960s, when the adult population of state hospitals was declining, the number of children between ages 10 and 14 entering state hospitals increased (American Psychiatric Association, 1964). Existing services were neither sufficient in quantity to meet childrens' need nor successful in reaching the populations at greatest risk.

In 1961 the Joint Commission on Mental Illness and Health documented the number and severity of children's problems, focusing on children on welfare, children in broken homes, the problems of foster care and adoption, and the increasing number of institutionalized children and adolescents. The Joint Commission's report called for an expansion of children's services, a recommendation that had little effect at the time.

In 1965 Congress appointed a Joint Commission on the Mental Health of Children (1969). This commission characterized services for children as grossly inadequate, poorly coordinated, and limited in scope. For a short period of time, special funds were made available to federally funded community mental health centers to develop services for children. When the Reagan administration took office after the 1980 election, however, block granting with no strings attached replaced the funding of specific mental health programs. The block grant program allowed each state to allocate the funds as it saw fit, and no special funds were designated for children and adolescents. The lag in children's services continued, and in 1983 the federal Child and Adolescent Service System Program (CASSP) was established to develop community-based care and to integrate fragmented community service systems (Friedman & Duchnowski, 1990).

In 1978 the President's Commission on Mental Health said that children and adolescents were "underserved." It pointed to the number of children who suffered from abuse, neglect, and indifference and whose families lacked access to prenatal, infant, and early childhood care. Too many troubled children, especially from minority backgrounds, were placed in residential or foster care. The commission documented increases in the use of drugs and alcohol and the rising suicide rate among adolescents, and noted that appropriate services and specially trained personnel were in short supply. The commission also decried the bureaucratic fragmentation that hampered the provision of services to children.

In 1990 the House of Representatives Select Committee on Children, Youth, and Families issued a report reviewing the impact of legislation passed in the previous decade to provide support for children and their families. They concluded that problems continue to mount:

> Chief among our findings is that today's social and economic conditions are hurting large numbers of American families in ways that our current child welfare, mental health and juvenile justice systems were not created and are ill-prepared to address. Mounting child poverty and rapid increases in child abuse reports are major contributors to the dramatic increase in placement of children outside their families. It is also impossible to ignore the devas-´ tating impact that drug and alcohol abuse are having on families, propelling children into out-of-home care at an escalating rate. (p. 2)

The congressional committee decried "uncoordinated, inefficient, and ultimately ineffective" services and they listed the following patchwork of federal programs that assisted children in need:

Abandoned Infants Assistance Act to help children and infants with AIDS (PL 100–505)

Adoption Assistance (Title IV-E, SSA)

Adoption Opportunities (Title II, Child Abuse Prevention and Treatment Act (CAPTA))

Alcohol, Drug Abuse, and Mental Health Block Grant, with a 10 percent set-aside for community-based mental health services for seriously emotionally disturbed children and youth (Title XIX, Part B, Public Health Service Act)

Child Abuse Challenge Grants to stimulate prevention-oriented programs (CAPTA)

Child Abuse Grants and Family Violence Grants (CAPTA)

Child Welfare (Title IV-B, SSA)

Foster Care and Independent Living (Title IV-E, SSA)

Runaway Youth Program (Title III, Juvenile Justice and Delinquency Prevention Act [JJDPA])

Juvenile Justice Program (JJDPA)

Social Services Block Grant (Title XX, Social Security Act [SSA])

Temporary Child Care for Handicapped Children and Crisis Nurseries Act

This listing does not include Aid to Families with Dependent Children (AFDC), nor does it include funds made available through the Education of Handicapped Children Act designed to serve infants, toddlers, preschool children, and school-age children with educational and related handicaps (U.S. Office of Special Education and Rehabilitative Services, 1990).

The various acts and programs are administered either by different federal agencies or by different divisions within the same agency. Sometimes the acts provide for direct grants to service providers for demonstrations and related programs that, if successful, are supposed to be picked up by state or local funding sources but rarely are, sometimes funds are given to state mental health or social services or youth authorities to be used in accordance with federal regulations. It is little wonder that critics complain of an ungainly, uncoordinated structure that delivers services inefficiently and ineffectively.

Despite the multitude of programs (or perhaps because of them), the problems in delivering services are so severe that the congressional report listed more than eighty lawsuits brought in twenty states asking the courts to order state child welfare, juvenile justice, mental health, or education authorities to live up to the requirements for service delivery that are written into law and for which the states received federal funds. A number of cases sought compensation for children who were maltreated or injured while in foster care or under the state's supervision.

Out of home placements. There are probably 450,000 children in foster care. Could the many out-of-home placements be avoided if other care was available? It is difficult to obtain accurate figures on the number of children and adolescents in need who actually receive services; estimates of the proportion receiving mental health services range from one in three (Knitzer, 1984) to one in ten (Namir & Weinstein, 1982). About 750,000 children receive services from mental health organizations (Sunshine, Witkin, Atay, & Manderscheid, 1991). About 13 percent received care in psychiatric hospitals, psychiatric wards in general hospitals (Kiesler, Simpkins, & Morton, 1989), or residential treatment centers. Children treated in psychiatric wards in general hospitals and in scattered beds in general hospitals constitute about 2 percent of children in need of mental health services (Kiesler et al., 1989). There are social-class, race, and ethnicity barriers in delivering services to children and adolescents (Namir & Weinstein, 1982). Although the CASSP initiative may have promoted interest in children's services, budget cutbacks may prevent any significant change from occurring.

While deinstitutionalization has reduced the census of adult mental hospitals, the number of children and youth in hospitals and residential centers has increased. Admissions of adolescents to state and county mental hospitals have declined, but admissions to private psychiatric hospitals have risen rapidly (Weithorn, 1988). Admissions to other residential treatment centers have also increased. Admissions to public and private facilities for those adjudicated as juvenile delinquents increased 12 percent between 1975 and 1985 (U.S. Department of Justice, 1989). Most youth who are admitted to private residential treatment centers are under age 18 (Sunshine et al., 1991). Newspapers have reported on allegations of fraudulent charges and unnecessary hospitalizations of youths in private for-profit psychiatric hospitals (Kerr, 1991). In response to funding considerations, many hospitals now offer outpatient and partial care services

(Sunshine et al., 1991). These may eventually have an effect in reducing residential admissions.

While the majority of children and adolescents in need of services are not receiving them, as many as 40 percent of people of this age who are hospitalized are there merely because more suitable alternatives are not available. While many problems are identified early enough to be amenable to treatment, appropriate services generally are not available (Knitzer, 1984).

The groups most likely to be inappropriately served or underserved are:

> [D]isturbed adolescents (particularly older adolescents with multiple prob-
> lems who are hospitalized or at risk of hospitalization); seriously disturbed
> children and adolescents who are in state custody under child welfare or ju-
> venile justice auspices (some states report that such children account for as
> many as 60 percent of the psychiatrically hospitalized population); and chil-
> dren from poor, disorganized, and troubled families who do not use or ben-
> efit from traditional mental health services. Despite research evidence of their
> vulnerability, children of mentally ill or substance-abusing parents are also
> likely to be poorly served. (Knitzer, 1984, p. 906)

Alternative services. Are children inappropriately served in inpatient and residential settings? Most children improve while in residential facil-ities, but improvement at the point of discharge has little predictive value for adaptation in the community or for recidivism. Moreover, those who were admitted with milder forms of psychopathology do better after dis-charge from residential care than those with more severe pathology. Post-discharge care appears to be important for successful postdischarge adap-tation (Levine, Toro, & Perkins, 1993). Taken together, these findings suggest that many who are placed in residential care could probably be maintained equally well if adequate community based services were avail-able. However, some youth undoubtedly need residential care.

Although more than 230 psychotherapeutic approaches were identi-fied by the Institute of Medicine (1989), most remain to be fully vali-dated. Innovations such as parent management training using behavior therapy principles may show particular benefits when used with children who have conduct disorders, although the problem of transferring gains made in the therapeutic milieu to other environments has not yet been solved (Graziano & Mooney, 1984). Aside from our limited knowledge of disorders of childhood and adolescence, then, our treatment tech-nologies leave much to be desired. The social and political problems com-plicating the picture might be easier to overcome if our treatment tech-nologies were more powerful.

There are good examples of responsive service systems (Knitzer, 1984; Namir & Weinstein, 1982; Institute of Medicine, 1989). Many follow the principles used in similar programs for adults (see, for example, Kriech-man, 1985). Services are delivered in alternative settings, using educational and rehabilitative as well as therapeutic modalities, and are staffed by traditional and nontraditional mental health personnel. In the future, we may see more school-based approaches and more efforts to use local schools as neighborhood community centers providing child-care and child-rearing aid to parents. These programs have potential value in preventing child abuse and neglect (U.S. Advisory Board on Child Abuse and Neglect, 1993; 1995). They appear to be cost-effective as well as clinically effective, but they require cooperation between independent agencies.

Despite their successes, programs that focus on one aspect of a child's life (e.g., the family) may have only limited impact on the child's school performance or interactions with peers in the community. In keeping with ecological principles developed in later chapters, we need to consider how we can increase generalization and maintenance of gains across settings and over time.

Integrating services in the community. New programs require cooperation among independent agencies. Political, social, and professional problems hamper the reform of children's services. Fragmented services, children's lack of political clout, and cultural attitudes emphasizing family responsibility for children limit reform (Knitzer, 1984; Namir & Weinstein, 1982).

Given block granting, which took effect in 1982, few states were responsive to initiatives like the CASSP program mentioned earlier. In 1986 Congress passed PL 99-660 requiring states to prepare service plans that included community-based psychosocial rehabilitation, case management, systems approaches, and input from consumers and families (Wohlford, 1990). The Robert Wood Johnson Foundation also provided demonstration funds to a few communities to develop integrated service programs (Beachler, 1990).

A comprehensive program requires cooperation and collaboration among diverse agencies responsible for child welfare, including school, health, and mental health services. For example, problems of sexual and physical abuse of children bring mental health workers into contact with police, prosecutors, judges, lawyers, and social service agencies. The problems in obtaining interagency cooperation are difficult to solve. A comprehensive plan for interagency cooperation requires coordination at the state and local levels and with local interagency planning groups. Financing coordinated outpatient services requires legal and regulatory changes to ensure that agencies asked to provide certain services can actually be paid to provide them. Agencies need "flexible service dollars" to provide individualized care. "Blended funds" from health, mental health, education, and social services should be used flexibly to avoid the restrictions of existing programs that focus on rigid diagnostic categories. Such an approach should probably include a case manager to mediate between the family's needs and the service system (Office of Mental Health, 1992).

How to integrate services and make the system both more attractive and more responsive to the needs of nontypical families (e.g., those with a single parent) and of families from different social classes and ethnic backgrounds is challenging. In the past, seemingly promising solutions have encountered insurmountable difficulties. It remains to be seen how the thrust to integration will fare given the drastic cutbacks in funds for social programs, prevention, welfare, and mental health approved by Congress in 1995.

Policy changes. Mental health services alone are not enough. Policies governing services to family in general, and specifically programs governing nutrition, health, prenatal care, day care, and help for single-parent families, all need reconsideration. Some very good studies of early childhood education programs such as the Head Start program have demonstrated the programs' remarkable success in preventing educational disability and later social disability (Zigler & Muenchow, 1992; see Chapter 8). With the exception of Head Start, however, large-scale programs holding out the promise of prevention have not received favorable political attention in recent years, and at this writing, Head Start may be in jeopardy as well. Given concerns over government budget deficits, the current political climate may not support innovative services and policy reforms. As Iscoe and Harris noted in 1984, "if the priorities of a nation are mirrored in its SCIs [social and community interventions], the welfare of children and youth are clearly not uppermost in the minds and intentions of policymakers" (p. 354).

Continued cooperation between citizen advocates and professionals and among agencies will be necessary to move ahead in solving critical problems and gaining new resources. Sarason et al. (1977) and Sarason and Lorentz (1979) described "resource exchange networks" designed to make more effective use of resources across diverse agencies. These ideas may be especially salient in the late 1990s. If anything, the community perspective is even more important when we consider programs for persons from culturally diverse groups and programs for children and adolescents.

Summary

Community psychology is connected to many social and historical developments, both distant and recent. The public's obligation to provide for the needs of chronically dependent persons descends from laws enacted hundreds of years ago in Elizabethan England. By the mid-nineteenth-century this responsibility was expressed in the form of the state mental hospital, the mainstay of mental health care in the United States for more than one hundred years. World War II, the struggle for civil rights in the 1960s, and other events have wrought great changes in U.S. society, to a point where a contrasting ideological and scientific perspective such as community psychology could gain credence. The community psychology concept emerged from the community mental health movement in the ferment of the 1960s and was in part a response to specific deficiencies in the traditional medical model of treatment for mental illness.

Community-based helping alternatives proliferated during the 1960s and 1970s as social change continued. The foundations of the community perspective in ideology, more than in well-validated scientific concepts, were not always recognized. Despite disappointments with the power of interventions or the pace of change, the community approach has brought considerable change in contemporary mental health practice. Community approaches now represent the conventional wisdom in such areas as long-term rehabilitation of the chronically mentally ill, programs for minorities and other underserved groups, and prevention of social problems in young children.

In the 1990s community life for people at risk is based less on a metaphor of "dependent care" than on the idea of supporting "normal" living for members of diverse groups. More relevant than the nature of specific mental health services provided may be the question of what social changes are likely to promote the community involvement and participation of all vulnerable persons as full and equal citizens.

In the next chapter we introduce several of community psychology's central concepts as we present a comprehensive framework in order to define community psychology and to distinguish it from clinical psychology.

Notes

1. The material in this section is based on Levine (1981) and sources cited in that book.

2. We will see in Chapter 13 that the use of research and statistics in politically charged contexts is always vulnerable to the claim that advocates are at worst manipulating the data and at best overemphasizing information that supports the advocate's position. This problem emerged early in the history of attempts to apply scientific methods to public policy issues.

3. The federal government had a role in mental health services since World War I, when the Veterans Administration (then the Veterans Bureau) served returning veterans who suffered from "shell shock," the term then used for posttraumatic stress disorder. After 1914 the Public Health Service had a responsibility for drug treatment and provided services for federal prisoners, many of whom had violated alcohol prohibition laws. The Public Health Service was also responsible for screening mentally ill or mentally deficient immigrants. After World War II, the Veterans Administration mounted a massive effort to provide mental health services to returning veterans.

4. During that period our economic high priests cast their statistical equivalents of dry bones and prophesied that growth in the gross national product (GNP), the sacred portent that the gods were looking favorably upon the nation, would depend on massive spending in the public sector. They argued that growth

depended on redistributing wealth and encouraging consumption of the goods and services produced in the private sector. Arguing further that public services and facilities required refurbishing, economists pressed for a policy of public spending for education, welfare, youth services, mental health, correctional services, and urban renewal and the construction of public buildings, roads, and other facilities (Galbraith, 1958). The Community Mental Health Centers Acts of 1963 and 1965, the Economic Opportunity Act of 1964, and subsequent legislation supporting community-oriented programs followed from this philosophy.

5. Critics of the Moynihan (1965) report attacked it impolitely by calling it racist and politely by asserting that it failed to consider the effect of racial prejudice on family structure and neglected the strengths of 75 percent of African American families in focusing on the 25 percent that were female-headed families (see Carper [1970], Payton [1970], and Tumin [1970] for commentary on the Moynihan study.) The Moynihan study may have stimulated African American scholars to redefine some of the research issues, enriching our understanding of black families and their needs (Special Populations Subpanel on Mental Health of Black Americans, 1978; Moore, 1982; Zane, Sue, Castro, & George, 1982). On the other hand, criticism of the Moynihan study may have created barriers to studying problems in black families. Cummings (1983) reported data showing that the proportion of African American female-headed households has nearly doubled since Moynihan's original report. Cummings indicated that leaders in the African American community were expressing more concern about the issue of female-headed households (see also Wilson, 1987, and Box 3–1). This episode provides an excellent case study of the interplay among research, social values, and political considerations.

6. Although many clinics have since streamlined their intake procedures, the dropout rate is still probably fairly high. Taube, Burns, and Kessler (1984) reported that the median number of visits to psychiatrists and psychologists in private practice was 4.0 and 5.0, respectively. They did not indicate what percentage of the cases were planned terminations. Bloom (1984) has summarized evidence indicating that clients may benefit from as few as one or two visits. As a problem the dropout rate may be more apparent than real.

7. Professional models for such activism existed in the settlement house movement of the late nineteenth and early twentieth centuries, but memory of those activities was lost (Levine & Levine, 1992).

8. Gerald Caplan's (1959, 1970) writings on consultation had become influential by this time. The theory of consultation, however, was simply an extension of clinical theory, and the practice was little different from the supervision of psychotherapy and perhaps not much more efficient (Levine, 1972). Consultation and education became a core service in community mental health centers and a major claimant on the imaginations, if not on the time, of professionals (D'Augelli, 1982). Consultation theory did not go very far in providing a guide to more general theory, strategy, or practice.

9. The division of universities into psychology, sociology, anthropology, economics, political science, law, philosophy, and English departments is no reason to believe that problems in the world are so divided. Unfortunately, those organizational divisions tend to compartmentalize knowledge in our minds as well. A personal incident is illustrative. Levine encountered Scheff's (1966) elegant, disarmingly simple, and persuasive book, *Being Mentally Ill*, shortly after publication. He was much taken with the presentation in propositional form of

labeling theory, a viewpoint not represented in clinical psychology. While preparing a reading list for his course, he found himself in a quandary about including Scheff's book, not because he doubted its value or its pertinence for his course but because the book's subtitle was *A Sociological Theory*. He debated with himself whether it was proper for a psychologist to include a sociological work as part of a course in psychology! Concluding that that way lay madness, he did include the book. The incident may reflect his concerns about criticism from colleagues within psychology or a misguided respect for intellectual turf. The critical point is that a conceptual label, the distinction between psychology and sociology (a meaningless distinction if we think about intervention in the social world), affected his thought process and his feelings and might have influenced the actions of someone supposedly attuned to the idea of "conceptual blinders."

10. It is possible in some states to commit patients to outpatient care and or to alternative treatment facilities such as day care or halfway houses (Mulvey, Geller, & Roth, 1987; Geller, 1993).

II

PERSPECTIVES IN COMMUNITY PSYCHOLOGY

3

A Conceptual Road Map of Community Psychology

Because of its rapid development, community psychology lacked a well-articulated, widely shared conceptual model, a set of theoretical principles that would help in making sense of the field's diversity and in guiding future development. The field recognized person-centered and environment-centered approaches. Some practitioners engaged in clinical work were moving toward developing preventive interventions. The field needed a conceptual framework to bring some order for its adherents.

In her presidential address to the Division of Community Psychology (later renamed the Society for Community Research and Action) of the American Psychological Association, Barbara Dohrenwend (1978) proposed a conceptual model to help answer two questions: "What do community psychologists do?" and "What's the difference between community psychology and clinical psychology?" These questions were pertinent because community psychology's diffuse activities, unified under the label *community psychology*, implied the existence of differences between it and other fields sufficient to warrant a separate professional identity.

The Dohrenwend model (Figure 3–1) is helpful for several reasons. First, it is based on a hypothesized connection between psychopathology and psychosocial stress (the kinds of problems we described in Chapter 1 as the soap opera of life). (As presented, it is a heuristic conceptual framework, not a tightly specified path analysis or other complex statistical model, although it might be developed in that direction.) The emphasis on psychosocial stress helps us to think about problems in terms other than diagnosis and illness.

Second, it shows how certain interventions might be helpful. Because the model includes a time dimension, it directs us to think about interventions that might be used *before* a person seeks treatment; we are not limited to thinking about what to do only after the client or patient shows up on the therapist's doorstep.

Third, it directs us to think about both person-centered and environment-centered issues within the same framework. That is, it directs us to consider mental health programs that create or strengthen the environmental resources available to persons at risk (upper row of boxes in Figure 3–1), as well as those that strengthen the individual resistance of people at risk (lower row of boxes).

The Dohrenwend Model

The field of community psychology has the very ambitious aim of reducing the prevalence of psychopathology in the population at large. Dohrenwend has a hypothesis about causation: The kind of life events discussed in Chapter 1 create psychosocial stress and, under some circumstances, can lead to psychopathology. The immediate emotional reaction to a stressful event is not pathological in and of itself. The aim is to understand the different points for and types of intervention that may undermine "the process whereby stress generates psychopathology" (Dohrenwend, 1978, p. 2).

Stressful Life Events

Under this model one looks at recent events in people's lives rather than at their early childhood experiences. Let us follow her argument. "The process . . . starts with . . . recent events in the life of an individual

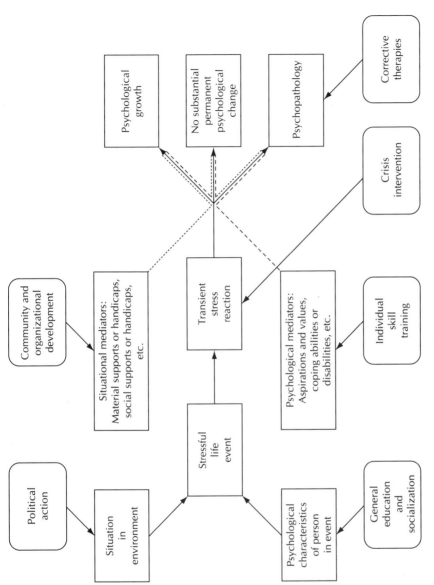

Figure 3–1. A model of the process whereby psychosocial stress induces psychopathology and some conceptions of how to counteract this process. (From Dohrenwend, 1978)

rather than with distant childhood experiences. It describes an episode that is initiated by the occurrence of one or more stressful life events, and is terminated by psychological change, for good or ill, or by return to the psychological *status quo ante* (pp. 2–3). A stressful life event challenges the person's previous state of adaptation and requires a new adaptation. If you lose your job, get a divorce, or discover, as people at Love Canal did, that your home is located near toxic chemicals that could seriously affect your family's health, you will have to do something different about your life. (Some researchers have extended this idea to include everyday hassles as a form of stressful life events.)

In the psychopathological framework, a person's feelings of depression and anxiety in response to a stressful life event are often understood as symptoms of illness. In the Dohrenwend framework these feelings of anxiety and depression are temporary signs that one's current adaptation is being challenged and that the psychological means to cope and the social supports available to deal with one's current situation may be insufficient.

Person and Environment

Dohrenwend's model takes into account both person and environment and allows us to focus on whichever aspect of a problem seems most salient: "Stressful life events vary in the extent to which they are determined by the environment or by psychological characteristics of the central person in the event" (p. 3). The model allows for the possibility "that an individual may take part in creating the very events that appear later to cause him to undergo psychological change" (p. 4). Thus, a stressful life event may be of the person's own making. A person may lose a job because a plant closes but also because he drinks heavily, is having a bad time in a relationship and neglects his work, or has poor attitudes about coming to work on time every day. Whether the job is lost for personal or circumstantial reasons, however, the person faces the need to adapt to a new situation. It is insufficient in this model to focus only on the person and to ignore all else, as the medical model of psychopathology leads us to do. The model doesn't exclude the possibility that biological vulnerability may contribute to the stress reactions. However, the outcomes may still depend on the processes suggested by the model.

Transient stress reactions. Transient stress reactions are self limiting. Regardless of the source of the stress response, "a common characteristic of all of these forms of stress reaction is that they are inherently transient or self-limiting. . . . What follows after the immediate, transient stress reaction depends on the mediation of situational and psychological factors that define the context in which this reaction occurs" (p. 4).

Transient stress reactions include feelings of anxiety, depression, confusion, helplessness, or rage and may include behaviors that resemble psychiatric symptoms, a person may develop headaches or muscle strain, for example, or lose sleep or seem very distracted. Usually these reactions are temporary, but should they persist for any length of time, they can themselves become troublesome as chronic reminders that one is feeling overwhelmed. Transient stress reactions are not considered psychopathological in and of themselves, however. In the normal course of events these reactions dissipate unless there is some reinforcement or secondary gain. Some claim, for example, that giving Supplemental Security Income (SSI) disability income to persons with mental illness may help to perpetuate the symptoms that qualified these persons for disability support, thus ensuring that they continue to receive payments indefinitely (See *NAMI Advocate*, 1993, p. 1). If symptoms get a person out of unpleasant circumstances or help to control the behavior of others, they may persist.

Situational and psychological mediators. By situational and psychological mediators, Dohrenwend is referring to resources a person may use that come from others in his or her support network and to the psychological strengths and attitudes with which the person copes with the demands of the stressful event. Both situational and psychological mediators of the stress-pathology relationship are important in Dohrenwend's model in determining the outcome:

> Other things being equal, an individual whose financial or other material resources are strained by the demands of a stressful life event is likely to have a worse outcome than a person with adequate material resources. Similarly, lack of social support is hypothesized to increase the likelihood of a negative outcome. . . . [Psychological] mediators . . . include "values" . . . and "coping abilities." (p. 5).

(See Chapter 7 for further discussion of these issues.)

Outcomes

Transient stress reactions and situational and psychological mediators interact in some complex fashion to produce one of three categories of outcomes. The person (a) may grow and change positively as a result of mastering the experience, (b) may essentially return to some state normal for that person, or (c) may develop psychopathology, defined by Dohrenwend as a persistent, apparently self-sustaining dysfunctional reaction. Dohrenwend uses that term to mean that the person is so affected that negative emotions predominate and interfere with the enjoyment of anything else or that functioning is so impaired that the person can't carry out the tasks expected given the person's age, gender, and general station in life. In other words, a waste of human potential results when the reaction continues past the events that precipitated it.

The usefulness of that definition of psychopathology aside, the model focuses attention on much more than the psychological and emotional reaction of the individual person. (In Chapter 7, we will contrast the concept of an acute neurotic reaction to the stressful-life-events or crisis model.) The concept of psychosocial stress requires attention to the individual's life circumstances and the resources—psychological, material, and social—available to meet the demands posed by events and circumstances.

The model accounts for the possibility that maladaptive psychological mediators (e.g., low self-efficacy, inadequate problem-solving skills, excessive "self-medication" using alcohol or drugs) may contribute to poorer outcomes and that adverse elements in the person's social environment can also contribute to poorer outcomes. By following the three outcomes (the boxes at the far right of the model in Figure 3–1) we see that the bulk of clinical efforts have been directed toward providing treatment at the *end* point of the process, the outcome labeled psychopathology.[1]

To summarize, Dohrenwend's model proposes that transient stress reactions often follow the occurrence of a stressful event. These reactions point to an elevated risk for maladaptive behavior. Factors involving the person and the environment affect whether a transient stress reaction occurs in response to a given event. If it does occur, then various outcomes are possible, depending on the strength and the effectiveness of personal and situational mediators that are present.

In the remainder of this chapter we discuss selected ways in which psychologists and others have intervened at various points specified by this model. Some interventions strive to limit the duration, intensity, or maladaptiveness of the transient stress reaction, while the purpose of others is to prevent a stressful event from even happening. The examples we review here are by no means exhaustive, and numerous others will be discussed or cited elsewhere in the book. In surveying these alternatives we will work backwards (in the model's hypothesized timeline) from the more treatment oriented elements on the right side of Figure 3–1 to the more preventive elements on the left.

Box 3–1. Poverty, Unemployment, and Social Problems

Problems are interconnected and intertwined at every ecological level (see Chapter 4). We will point out how the phenomena may be interpreted within the Dohrenwend framework.

Stressful life events are not randomly distributed in the population. Rates of crime, welfare dependence, out-of-wedlock pregnancies, and unemployment are especially high in a segment of the African American population that Wilson (1987) calls the "truly disadvantaged." There are "underclasses" in other ethnic groups, but Wilson wrote about African Americans.[2]

Applying Dohrenwend's model, we can interpret the data reviewed here in terms of changes in circumstances (environmental situation) that make stressful life events more or less likely and that may contribute to growth or to maladaptation (far right, Fig. 3–1). The quantity and type of stressful life events affecting an individual produce transient stress reactions. In the absence of social and situation supports (top center Fig. 3–1), and positive psychological mediators (bottom center, Fig. 3–1) adverse outcomes are more likely (bottom right, Fig. 3–1). Conversely, when barriers to access to resources are removed, the population that benefits from the relief will thrive (see Chapter 4).

Progress After Barriers Were Eliminated

African Americans have benefited from policy changes that protected against discrimination in education, housing, employment, public accommodations, and voting. The number of African Americans in professional, managerial, and technical occupations doubled from .97 million in 1973 to 1.95 million in 1991. The percent of African Americans earning more than $50,000 per year in constant 1990 dollars grew from 9.9 percent in 1970 to 14.5 percent in 1990. The median income of African Americans taken as a group, including many female-headed households with incomes below the poverty line, is substantially below that of the majority population. However, the income of married African American couples is now about 84 percent of that of majority married couples, a considerable improvement over the differential existing twenty years ago. In 1973, 2.6 million African American families owned their own homes. By 1991 that number had grown to 4.53 million. The rate of high school completion among African Americans increased from 31.4 percent in 1970 to 66.7 percent in 1991, and the percent of college graduates among African Americans increased from 4.4 percent to 11.5 percent. These figures also reflect improvements both in social supports available to African Americans and in the psychological mediators (education) used to cope with challenges of adapting to a changing occupational world. To the degree that income and occupational status are correlated with better mental health, the population that has benefited from supports or improved access to resources has also benefited psychologically.

Consequences of Widening Disparities within the African American Community

The gap between upper- and lower-income African Americans has grown. The most dramatic gains have come among those who entered professional, technical, and managerial occupations. Economic and social conditions have worsened since 1970 for those who were unable to take advantage of opportunity or who were affected by the loss of jobs in manufacturing and in urban centers. In 1970, 20.9 percent of African Americans earned less than $10,000 dollars. By 1990, that number had risen to 25.6 percent.

As middle-class professionals and skilled workers improved their situations, many moved out of the ghettos where restrictive housing and mortgage financing practices had kept them and into better homes in more desirable neighborhoods (Mincy, Sawhill, & Wolf, 1990; Taylor, 1990). Why is it desirable to move? For one, the rate of violent crime is much lower in suburban than in urban areas. For another, people believe that suburban schools are better. Moving thus reduces the likelihood of experiencing stressful life events related to violence or school failure. When the African American middle class moves out, the number of people left in the ghettos who have the clout and the know-how to demand better services from municipal officials is reduced. Public services may deteriorate in neighborhoods that lose middle class population; churches and other sources of community stability may decline. Situation mediators providing resources for coping are lost, increasing vulnerability. Taylor (1990) described the extensive network of "churches, neighborhood block clubs, community-based organizations, cultural groups, youth centers, civil rights organizations, social clubs, formal and informal political organizations, and educational and research institutions" (p. 14) in the Buffalo, New York, African American community:

> They [the organizations] stand on the front-line in the struggle against racism and in the fight to improve the quality of life in the black community. They serve as action groups that mobilize people around community problems and that articulate the needs of the black community to city government. This organizational network represents one of black Buffalo's greatest assets. It has helped African Americans stave off social catastrophes that have beset black communities in megacities. (Taylor, 1990, p. 14)

As the density of poorer people increases in a neighborhood, the likelihood that stressful life events will occur also increases; the lack of social supports and situation mediators and the presence of environmental handicaps combine to increase the likelihood that there will be adverse long-term effects for many people. The concentration in certain neighborhoods of those in poverty has increased in recent years (Mincy et al., 1990; Taylor, 1990). The poor are less scattered geographically than those who are better off. Those who could move out have done so, leaving a concentration of poorer people in particular neighborhoods. Although we have interpreted these data in terms used in the Dohrenwend model, the reader should also consider that similar data can be interpreted within the ecological analogy discussed in Chapter 4.

Youth, Crime and Unemployment

The African American population is younger than the majority population. The median age for majority populations living in inner cities is 30.3 years; for the African American population, it is 23.9. The concentration of young people increases the likelihood that people in the area will experience stressful life events. Younger people commit more crimes and are more often the victim of crimes. The risk of crime is higher in African American neighborhoods. Victimization rates are higher among African American males and females than in the majority group.

Members of the "truly disadvantaged" are also arrested and convicted of crimes disproportionately to their numbers in the population. Although African Americans are only 12 percent of the population, they constitute about 46 percent of the state prison population. If we also include federal prisons, local jails, and public residential treatment facilities, we find that about 4 percent of the African American male population is incarcerated at any moment in time. These men are not employed, and upon leaving prison they have histories that may close job opportunities for them. This problem requires political action to help create jobs and to create situation mediators to assist those leaving prison with the challenge of readapting in the outside world.

Female-headed Households

A high percent of all families are female-headed. However, 45.6 percent of African American households are female-headed, and in inner cities the figure is 60 percent. In 1970, 64 percent of the African American population was married; by 1991 only 43.6 percent were married. Moreover, 64.5 percent of births to African Americans are out of wedlock, with many infants born to teenagers.[3] Births to teenage mothers are events that seriously challenge the mothers' adaptation. If the births are accompanied by other stresses they may result in maternal drug use, in the birth of "crack babies," and in the neglect or abuse of the children, especially as pressures increase on the mothers.

The welfare system is a situation mediator for many young mothers. Some become welfare-dependent, a problem noted by Moynihan in 1965. Advocates of welfare reform argue that these situation supports should be considered negative in nature because they encourage out-of-wedlock births and welfare dependency. Welfare reform advocates have proposed policies that would change the negative situation supports that they claim promote maladaptation. Wilson discounts the argument that the welfare system discourages young women with poor job prospects from entering the labor force on economic grounds. Income from welfare in constant dollars has declined, but the number of welfare recipients has continued to rise. Proponents of welfare argue that children, who are the beneficiaries of the income and of their mother's care while she stays home, benefit from welfare as a support system.

No matter which side of the argument one takes, it can be stated in theoretical terms consistent with those used in the Dohrenwend model.

Job Market Changes

Marital status, birth rates of out-of-wedlock children, and crime rates are related to changes in the job market that create challenges to adaptation. Changes in the job market create circumstances in which stressful life events may arise for those who lose their jobs or who do not have the educational or other qualifications to pursue the new jobs. The great migration north of African Americans after World War II resulted from the mechanization of agriculture and the development of pesticides that reduced the need for farm labor in the South. Stressful life events related to unemployment have always been greater among African Americans. In 1970 the white unemployment rate was 4.5 percent; the African American rate was 9.4 percent. In 1991 the white unemployment rate was 6.0 percent, whereas the African American rate was 12.4 percent. Unemployment rates are particularly high among younger people. In 1991, 36 percent of African American youth between ages 16 and 19 were unemployed, as were 21 percent of those between ages 20 and 24. The comparable figures for the majority were 16 percent and 9 percent.

Other aspects of the job market have also changed, creating situation-based challenges to adaptation. Well-paid manufacturing jobs have declined greatly. From 1970 to 1991 the number of people working increased by 48.5 percent, but manufacturing jobs declined by 1.5 percent. Instead of jobs producing and distributing goods, today's work is information exchange, as more people now process paper or operate computer terminals. Employers require people with appropriate educational qualifications. In all population groups, the percent unemployed decreases with education.[4] Jobs that require less than a high school education are fewer, while those requiring higher levels of education have increased. The changed job market calls for people with different psychological mediators. People who have lost jobs require retraining. They may also need to develop appropriate psychological mediators. Older, displaced workers need situation resources to help develop those mediators—appropriate educational opportunities and income while attending school. Many may also need support to help develop more favorable psychological mediators—self-confidence about engaging in new learning and optimism about succeeding in a new and challenging venture. (We describe the Michigan Jobs Project in this chapter and in Chapter 8.)

The Male Marriageable Pool Index (MMPI)

Families provide important social support (see Chapter 7), and the rate of family formation is affected by the unemployment rate. Wilson developed the MMPI to illustrate the relationship between employment and family formation. The MMPI is the ratio of employed civilian males to women in the same age and ethnic grouping. Because of the large number of African American men who are unemployed, incarcerated, or dead due to street violence, the ratio of employed civilian African American males to African American females is quite unfavorable. For example, for ages 25 to 34, the ratio in 1982 was .60. Employment is presumably a minimum requirement for a desirable mate. The unfavorable MMPI, especially in the African American population, helps make the high rate of female-headed households understandable. If a two-parent family provides better support for the spouses and for their children, then the unfavorable MMPI suggests that fewer persons in the African American population have the benefit of those supports. Moreover, to the degree that a stable marital relationship provides psychological and financial advantages[5] for spouses and for their children, the reduced opportunity to develop that support system means that members of the African American population may be more vulnerable to stressful life events.

Policy Implications

The concentration of young, poor, single-parent homes in high-crime areas, with fewer middle-class people and social supports to promote stability, plus the demoralization and stigma associated with dependence on public welfare (negative support) reduces the number of persons who have the family and the neighborhood resources to be able to take advantage of the opportunities that do exist. According to Wilson, it is the truly disadvantaged group for which new solutions are necessary. From the 1950s to the 1970s the goal of the civil rights movement was to obtain and protect equal rights and to strike down legal barriers to equality. In part, these goals have been met, and there have been substantial improvements in the social and economic circumstances of middle-class African Americans. After its initial successes, the movement shifted its focus to affirmative action programs to ensure a more equitable distribution of employment opportunities. Affirmative action has resulted in controversy, objections, and resentment from those who believe that affirmative action created unfair competition for access to resources (see Chapter 4).

Wilson now argues that resources should be targeted to anyone who is truly disadvantaged irrespective of race to provide "equality of life chances." He would include anyone coming from a poverty background or from a low-income family, anyone who grew up in inadequate housing, and anyone whose cultural background and language are different from those of the majority. These "handicaps" cause a failure of preparation and support. Without adequate preparation, the likelihood is low that persons from those backgrounds can take advantage of existing opportunities.

Wilson sees a solution in an economic policy (upper right box in Fig. 3–1) that would sharply reduce the employment rate. He notes that during World War II employers faced with a labor shortage took on workers with lesser qualifications and either trained them or modified practices to make use of the workers' skills. Across-the-board income support such as a family allowance available to rich and poor alike may make it possible for persons to remain in the labor force, even at wages close the minimum wage level. Wilson is in tune with the ecological perspective when he suggests that resources be created and distributed to enhance adaptation.

Taylor, who studied similar problems in the African American community in Buffalo, concluded:

> The key to developing a plan to attack the problem of the inner city is to conceive of the black community in geographic terms and to formulate a territorial based strategy for dealing with economic and social problems facing African Americans. The strategic plan is to build a vibrant, economically prosperous, racially diverse, cross-class community where the middle-class, higher-paid workers, low-wage workers, and the poor and the underclass can live together in comfort and security. Logic says that if "bad neighborhoods" create an environment that makes the fight against economic and social dislocations more difficult, "good neighborhoods" will make the fight easier. (p. 21)

(We present similar concepts in Chapter 4 and in our discussion of community development strategies for change in Chapter 12.)

Opportunities for Intervention Based on Dohrenwend's Model

Crisis Intervention

Dohrenwend's model suggests that it is not necessary to wait until the stress reaction has run its course and produced long-term pathology to provide help. What if help could be available during the acute stress reaction via "crisis intervention" services? Dohrenwend has several criticisms of this strategy. Will enough people in need seek out the proffered help? Can crisis services be positioned to reach persons soon enough during acutely stressful episodes? Compared with the population that might be served, telephone crisis services tend not to be used very much, often drawing a large number of repeat callers. In our unpublished study of stressful life events in college students, we found that fewer than 1 percent used a hotline when they experienced a stressful life event.

One evaluation of crisis services supported Dohrenwend's judgment that crisis services might not be used as a support by members of the population at risk. Suicide prevention services illustrate her point. Although suicide prevention services may have an effect in reducing successful suicides among young white females, no statistically significant effect could be detected for other age and sex groups. Young white females are among the most frequent callers to crisis lines; however, the successful suicide rate is lowest in this age and sex group. Rates of completed suicide are twenty or more times higher among white males over age 65, and these men are not frequent callers to suicide prevention services (Miller et al., 1984). The crisis hotline seems to reach the group at lowest risk, albeit with some success, and fails to reach the group at highest risk. Crisis hotlines clearly have a "marketing" problem. (The Dohrenwend model doesn't deal with this type of problem.)

These limitations of crisis hotlines should not close the question; other methods for delivering services at times of crisis might prove more effective in reaching a target population. In recent natural disasters (hurricanes, floods, earthquakes), crisis teams have been sent to the locations to be available for psychological "first aid" to people who might have been overcome by their losses of property or of loved ones and to rescue workers who had to deal with maimed and burned bodies. These teams seem to benefit from debriefings with their leaders and members of their work groups in the period shortly after exposure to the dead (McCarroll et al., 1993). Support groups accessible to anyone in need, along with consistent and detailed information about coping shared communitywide by the media, have been credited with reducing the incidence of psychological casualties in response to disasters (see Gist & Stolz, 1982).

Reaching Target Populations

The life-stress concept provides certain advantages in guiding the positioning of services (e.g., in relation to predictable "milestone" events such as entering school, beginning a marriage, or taking a new job), and it suggests the possibility of prevention. However, recognizing that not everyone will use a particular service raises a number of questions: where, when, how, and to whom should a given service be offered? Developing a treatment technology to cope successfully with transient reactions is not the only concern.

We still need to learn how to "market" our services—to package, advertise, price, and sell—to different groups. A given service offered in a particular way will reach some in need, but characteristics of the service will likely result in a mismatch with the needs of others, effectively screening them out. If there is no convenient public transportation to a program, for example, people without automobiles are less likely to use the program than those who have them. A university psychological services center located on a campus in the suburbs with very little public transportation will not attract many clients from the poorer parts of the city. For another example, rescue workers who deal with dead bodies prefer to be debriefed not by mental health workers but rather by experienced members of their work group and by their leaders (McCarroll et al., 1993). How to tailor services, whether preventive or rehabilitative, to take into account the characteristics of the target consumer remains a problem for the mental health field. This problem, however, is not considered in the Dohrenwend model. We need other theoretical perspectives as well.

Intervention to Enhance Psychological Mediators

In theory, psychological mediators such as values or coping skills play an important role in determining the outcome of a transient stress reaction. Positive psychological mediators may aid in the adaptation required after exposure to a stressful life event. Just as there are negative situational supports (e.g., in the view of some, welfare), Dohrenwend's model makes provision for negative or handicapping psychological mediators. If one copes by abusing alcohol or drugs, throwing a temper tantrum, becoming highly dependent, or simply denying anything bad is happening and hoping it will just go away, the situation may well worsen. If you don't take care of business, so to speak, by the time you feel better so many new problems may have piled up so much that you will be overwhelmed with them.

Dohrenwend notes that strengthening a person's psychological mediators may help the person "develop a high level of ability to face and solve complex social and emotional problems" (p. 8). This may include early intervention to help children cope with emotional stresses or the challenges of growing up. The original child guidance clinics of the 1920s were based on a similar concept (Levine & Levine, 1992). Cowen's Primary Mental Health Project (Cowen et al., 1975) is an updated, school-based version of child guidance designed to help children who have already been identified as vulnerable in order to prevent the development of more serious problems later in life (see Chapter 8).

In an approach that deviates still more from traditional helping services, Spivack and Shure (1974) and Spivack, Platt, and Shure (1976) were among the first to demonstrate that social adjustment may be enhanced by programs explicitly designed to teach social and interpersonal problem-solving skills—that is, psychological mediators. These programs are offered not only to children in difficulty or even only to those at high risk. Instead, the programs are designed to be integrated directly into the educational curriculum to help children cope with day-to-day problems by teaching the skills needed to master or avoid interpersonal crises. Preschool programs designed to enhance children's abilities to adapt to elementary school are variants of this approach.

Some prevention programs are built on an analysis of the skills and attitudes one might use in dealing with problems should they arise. It is not clear how effective Nancy Reagan's "Just Say No" approach was in preventing substance abuse. However, it is an example of the idea that one should have a phrase available (a psychological mediator) to use when faced with the temptation to try drugs. The approach is similar in purpose to a fire drill. We engage in fire drills so that we will have cognitive mediators to guide our actions when an emergency arises. By rehearsing we make it more likely that we will be able to respond effectively if a fire ever does break out instead of just panicking or running and hurting others by trampling them.

Sex education within the school curriculum is another example, although it has been little studied in the context of prevention. Sex education has among its aims the provision of greater knowledge and healthier attitudes and values (psychological mediators) to help adolescents cope with sexuality and its demands (Valerio, 1985). In theory, increased comfort with sexuality in childhood and youth will have important ramifications for each individual's interpersonal relationships and personal satisfaction throughout life.

People differ about what constitutes appropriate sex education. Handing out condoms in schools to prevent disease and pregnancy is highly controversial. Some observers believe that sex education should emphasize abstinence as the best preventive and that, in addition to providing information about sexual anatomy and physiology, sex education should emphasize moral values. These critics assert that the psychological mediators taught in some contemporary sex education programs (e.g., encourage physical contact short of intercourse—a groping skill as a coping skill) promote maladaptation (Whitehead, 1994–1995). Preventive programs such as sex education that influence the general education and socialization of children and youth reach "back to the very origin of the stress process and have, therefore, moved as far as possible from the treatment of individual cases of psychopathology into the realm of primary prevention" (Dohrenwend, 1978, p. 9).

As a final example, consider loss of a job (see also Box 3–1). This event would precipitate a transient stress reaction in most people; unemployment can in fact have immediate negative effects on mental health and well-being (Warr, 1987), including reduced self-esteem and increased depression, anger, guilt, and boredom. However, as Dohrenwend's model would hypothesize, people differ in the likelihood they will respond to unemployment in these ways. Unemployment is more likely to elicit a transient stress response in middle-aged males than in other groups, such as teenagers, for example (Osipow & Fitzgerald, 1993).

Because financial strain is the single most stressful aspect of job loss (Kessler et al., 1987), rapid reemployment at adequate pay offers the best short-term intervention goal. However, many unemployed people lack the key psychological mediators of skills, confidence, and a positive or optimistic outlook when seeking reemployment (Kirk, 1995). Prompt intervention with recently unemployed people to help them find a job they will like may have especially valuable preventive effects.

The Michigan Jobs Project (Caplan et al., 1989) was a preventive intervention aimed at combatting the risk of poor mental health and low motivation to seek reemployment by providing job-seeking skills and supportive encouragement to the recently unemployed. Participants were randomly assigned to the training program or to a control condition that offered only a brief booklet of tips on job seeking. Initial results found that those receiving the intervention program were more likely to have become reemployed at one-month and four-month follow-ups and that people who became reemployed showed less anxiety, depression, and anger and higher self-esteem than those who did not. Within the intervention group, those who had not found reemployment were significantly less discouraged than were unemployed controls, suggesting an "inoculation" effect against future setbacks as one possible mediator provided by the intervention. By the 2.5-year follow-up intervention participants as a group had found jobs of higher quality, and found them more quickly, than did controls (Vinokur et al., 1991). Further analyses showed that the intervention was especially effective at reducing the risk of later depression in participants who were initially at risk for depression (Price et al., 1992).

Several features make the Michigan Jobs Project a good illustration of a preventive intervention to strengthen psychological mediators. People with diagnosable mental illness were screened from the sample. Participants were essentially ordinary people experiencing acute job loss (four months or less) and facing the rapid onset of problems that typically occur after job loss. Staff delivering the program were not professionals. They provided not "treatment" but rather instruction, practice, and support in the use of cognitive and behavioral coping skills. These skills were designed for use in coping with future setbacks as well as with current situations. The possibility of recurrent job loss in the future was fully recognized in the content of the intervention. Self-efficacy was the significant cognitive mediator of the intervention's effects on job-seeking behavior (van Ryn & Vinokur, 1992). Finally, as the Dohrenwend model would predict, the intervention succeeded in lowering the incidence of serious depressive symptoms in this risk group.

Intervention to Enhance Situational Mediators

The outcome of a transient stress reaction also depends on situation mediators, resources in the environment that an individual can call on when appraising the significance of a stressful life event. For most people, family and friends are their chief sources of social support (Caplan, 1976; Gottlieb, 1981; see Chapter 7). For many people and many purposes, however, the resources of family and friends are insufficient. One may not be able to share everything with family members. For example, rescue workers who handled dead bodies couldn't discuss their work very well with spouses, many of whom just weren't able to listen to the gory details (McCarroll et al., 1993).

When social supports are insufficient, situation moderators become more important. Public services are often necessary in lieu of family support. Levine (1982) points out that in the Love Canal emergency, blue-collar families simply did not have the financial resources to support a move away from the neighborhood threatened by toxic wastes. Government assistance, a form of situational mediator, was necessary. In many other problems, individual resources are insufficient, and collective resources are necessary. Some form of welfare (a situational mediator) is necessary for income maintenance for those who cannot provide for themselves. Unemployment insurance keeps many from despair when they lose their jobs. A women's shelter provides refuge to a woman trying to escape a batterer. Low-income loans after a flood or a hurricane are necessary to help businesses reopen and individuals rebuild their lives.

Public services are supports that aid in coping (Thoits, 1986). In their absence, community and organizational development efforts are needed to provide the necessary resources. As Kelly (1966) points out, one aim of the community movement is to produce the resources a community needs to cope with its problems. Thus, when community-oriented mental health professionals develop respite care for families with retarded children or help create a shelter for battered women or a service to help widows with no recent work histories reenter the labor force, they are helping to create situational mediators. As we noted in Chapter 2, Assertive Community Treatment teams provide support and coping assistance to people with serious mental illness and also work to strengthen directly the other supportive resources available to these persons. As a further example, increasing numbers of people at risk for maladaptive responses to bereavement, divorce, retirement, physical violence, and other life events now obtain some or all of the support they need from self-help groups (Jacobs & Goodman, 1989; see Chapter 9).

Not all social support is helpful, however. The wrong type of support, or other aspects of the situation, may simply add to the person's handicap. In Chapter 7 we will see that "negative" social support may be more important in creating distress following a stressful life event than is positive support in relieving the reaction. The availability of mediators, however, supplements and extends individual and family resources. In their absence, the outcomes of a stressful life event might be worse. Dohrenwend's model helps us see how such activity is comprehensible within a single conceptual framework.

Psychological Characteristics of the Person That Increase the Likelihood of a Stressful Life Event

In this section, we present several examples of sources of stressful life events that reflect individual vulnerabilities. These examples are not exhaustive, obviously, but they are meant to be illustrative.

Genetic or biological vulnerability. Some people may be more susceptible physiologically than others to the adverse effects of alcohol. Given the opportunity to drink at parties, such a person may be more vulnerable to the consequences of drinking. Here is a built-in limitation that enhances vulnerability to the maladaptive effects of drinking.

Having a schizophrenic parent may increase one's genetic vulnerability to stress. A child from such a genetic background, facing normal stresses—the demands of school, peer group rejection, developing sexuality, competitiveness—that another with less vulnerability might take in stride, may be more likely to experience a transient stress reaction that may persist. The Dohrenwend model asks us to consider whether some stresses can be avoided and whether we can help a potentially vulnerable child develop psychological mediators or social supports that can help the child cope with stressful life events.

Poor prenatal care, poor nutrition, and the use of tobacco, drugs, and alcohol by the pregnant woman can increase a child's likelihood of being born prematurely or with deficits that will affect later adjustment. Such children may develop poor self-control or have learning deficits. When faced with demands in school for discipline and learning, these children are more likely to fail and to become discipline problems. With failure they bond less to school. They are more likely to engage in delinquent activity and to make a poorer social and economic adaptation in the future. In other words, some inborn characteristics that make it more difficult to adapt to the challenges of a school program lead to a succession of stressful life events. In the absence of supportive school programs or other alternatives, these life events may result in failure and in a poor future adaptation.

There may also be environmental causes for vulnerability in school. Some children exposed to lead may lose IQ points, and thus be less effective in school compared to others not so exposed. If there is anything to the belief that dioxin may cause learning difficulties (see Gibbs & CCHW, 1995), then our understanding of the etiology of some learning disorders will change. Long-range prevention programs will be directed toward reducing exposure to harmful substances in the environment.

Insufficient preparation for school. Factors in the child's general education and socialization may contribute to increased vulnerability. In the late nineteenth and early twentieth centuries, when many of our great-grandparents came to the United States, many of them did not speak English. They were required to go to schools where English was the required language and the use of foreign tongues was discouraged. People with foreign accents were often made to feel ashamed of themselves. In those days, in different cities, anywhere from 20 to 50 percent of the children were two or more years behind in school because they had failed and were repeating a grade (Levine & Levine, 1992). Children who are left back are likely to drop out of school as soon as they can; their self-esteem may be impaired (Levine & Graziano, 1972).

Many Americans face similar circumstances today, especially Latinos and African Americans from homes where, for diverse reasons, children are not fully prepared to cope with school. If children do not respond to the usual school program, they are often identified as learning disabled or emotionally disturbed and given special education (U.S. Department of Education, 1990). Even though some children are helped, many are stigmatized by the labeling and the placement into special education programs. The initial insufficient preparation for school makes failure more likely and future adaptation less favorable.

The Head Start program for disadvantaged preschool children is an effort to provide something by way of preparation for school that the child's own education and socialization have not provided. In part Head Start can be seen as providing psychological mediators, that is, "coping" skills for school, and as a situation mediator that provides a great deal of support for parent and child in preparing for regular school. As we will see in Chapter 8 on prevention, Head Start may also help children and their family environments achieve long-term resistance to potentially stress-inducing events that occur with relatively high frequency in the lives of people in disadvantaged circumstances.

Alienation from family and community. Child-rearing practices and relationships within families may contribute to vulnerability in adolescence as well as in childhood. Some adolescents simply do not get along with their families; they lose ties to their families and may say they never have fun with their families and that their parent or parents do not know how they spend much of their time. Many of these adolescents lose interest in school and get poor grades. They tend not to be affiliated with church groups and come to see the future rather pessimistically. Young people with these characteristics tend to become risk takers; they hang out with other youth who share similar characteristics and are inclined to get into trouble. This pattern of alienation from family, school, church, and work and affiliation with other youth who get into trouble is associated with a higher rate of self-reported delinquency, drinking, drug use, and sexual activity (see Box 3–1). The probability of getting into difficulty in the community—being arrested, having an automobile accident involving drinking, or becoming pregnant—is increased by this pattern, and these stressful life events have important implications for later adaptation. Even though we can point to psychological mediators (e.g., attitudes toward school, risk-taking tendencies) that enhance vulnerability, efforts to increase youth bonding to school or to the community may help prevent the pattern of maladaptation.

Situations That Increase the Risk of Stressful Events

Some events can be so serious in themselves that for those who experience them, transient stress reactions (or worse) are almost inevitable, regardless of the available psychological, and supportive resources. Here we describe selected examples and comment on the roles available to psychologists for preventing distress related to such events.

Environmental threats. The Love Canal crisis that created substantial stress for so many families was a function of the growth of the chemical industry and its inadequate awareness of how to dispose of the toxic by-products of technology. The resulting damage included increases in the rates of miscarriage and congenital malformations in infants, fears about the health of children and adults, community strife, and eventually, for many, relocation to new homes (Levine, 1982; see Chapter 12).

Since the Love Canal episode many similar situations of environmental contamination threatening health have come to public attention all over the country and around the world, in Woburn, Massachusetts; Times Beach, Missouri; the Stringfellow Acid Pits in California; Tuscaloosa, Alabama; Bhopal, India; Three Mile Island, Pennsylvania; and Chernobyl, Ukraine. There have been concerns about atomic weapons testing in Nevada, PCB contamination at dairy farms in Michigan (Vyner, 1988), and water contamination in the Legler community in Jackson, New Jersey (Edelstein, 1988).

Regulations (upper left box in Figure 3–1) governing the safe disposal of toxic wastes and the proximity of such facilities to residences or schools can decrease the probability that people will be exposed to conditions that threaten life, health, and psychological well-being. Social and political action to develop appropriate laws and regulations can prevent the psychological distress that follows in the wake of the discovery of an environmental threat.

Social action to promote such laws is political in nature and preventive when it reduces the probability that a stressful event affecting the community will arise at all. Moreover, if people participating in community organizations share their problems, develop means for dealing with them, and teach each other, they develop psychological mediators to help deal with the transient stress reaction (Stone & Levine, 1985).

Divorce. Divorce is an event that transcends the problems of the individuals involved in the divorce. About half of marriages end in divorce, and many that do not involve significant distress and abuse (Vivian & O'Leary, 1990). Divorce is among the most stressful of life events as measured by the Holmes and Rahe type of scale. It is associated with increased use of psychological services, including hospitalization, increased use of alcohol, and increased risk of accidents, among other adverse consequences (Bloom et al., 1982; Bloom & Hodges, 1988). The distress and the increased risk for dysfunction may spread to children and family members. Failure to receive adequate child-support payments adds to the psychological distress of custodial parents and of parents who have support obligations but wish to start new families. No-fault divorce laws have increased the likelihood that some women will experience stressful life events due to inadequate income, and the plight of single, working mothers may be more acute because of the lack of affordable day care and other supports such as health insurance. These are situations in the environment that can best be corrected by political action to change certain features of the laws and to improve enforcement. On the individual level, groups such as Parents Without Partners, and programs to prepare and to teach adaptation to postdivorce problems for adults and children (Bloom et al., 1982; Pillow, Sandler et al., 1991) provide important preventive services.

Although psychotherapy for marital distress is increasingly common, prevention programs appear to have more powerful long-term effects (Jacobson & Addis, 1993). Given the high probability of marital dissolution, it is possible that individual skill training undertaken before marriage, to help cope both with the kind of issues that lead to divorce and separation and with the aftermath, would be reasonable preparation. Markman et al. (1993) report a longitudinal evaluation of a cognitive-behavioral program designed to improve communication and conflict-management skills in couples planning marriage. At the five-year follow-up, couples who received the intervention showed better communication skills and reported significantly less physical violence in their relationships than did control couples. While the rate of divorce of the experimental group was low after five years, however, it did not differ from that of the control group.

Unemployment. As we pointed out earlier, unemployment is a severe environmental stressor. The mental health risks of job loss are evident in the significant relationship between the onset of unemployment and later use of mental health services. Kiernan, Toro, Rappaport, and Seidman (1989) reviewed nineteen studies published between 1973 and 1986 that used time-series methods to relate changes in unemployment rates to variables such as admissions to mental hospitals, use of outpatient mental health facilities, suicide rates, and community surveys of depressed mood. These studies varied in their methods, some tracking changes on a month-by-month basis and some tracking annual changes over many years. Most (but not all) of these studies found that increased unemployment was associated with undesirable changes in behavior, even though some respondents sought to adapt by seeking mental health care.

Kiernan et al. (1989) conducted a similar time-series analysis of data for Illinois for the years 1970 to 1985. They assessed the lag between the time that unemployment rates increased and the time that the behavioral outcomes were measured. Their method took into account confounding variables such as population growth and seasonal variation. They also split the data into two time periods to provide a replication of any effects they found. In each case, particularly with manufacturing employment, they found that a decline in employment was followed one to six months later by increases in mental hospital admissions and in the number of cases opened at community outpatient facilities.

These are complicated results, and they suggest that a more marginal group with fewer economic resources and perhaps more individual vulnerability may react quickly to the loss of employment, while those with greater resources may take longer before their mental health deteriorates. Studies using aggregate data cannot show a direct relationship between loss of a job and mental hospital or community clinic admissions. People are not traced on an individual basis in this type of research.

Nonetheless, to take these data seriously suggests that anything that increases employment or reduces unemployment or, on the social support side of the model, anything that provides increased support, such as unemployment insurance, could reduce the incidence of psychological disorder and the necessity for treatment. Thus, social and political action to influence government policies would be a valid form of "preventive intervention" to reduce the prevalence of mental disorder in the population. As social support, we have seen the development of support groups such as the Michigan Jobs Project for unemployed people to provide mutual assistance and encouragement in seeking new employment.

Exposure to violence. People exposed to violence experience stress. Violence is more prevalent in the lives of some people because of the neighborhoods in which they live (see Box 3–1). When Garbarino and his colleagues (1991) studied children and youth living in neighborhoods characterized by violence, he found that many showed signs of a posttraumatic stress disorder in response to witnessing shootings, stabbings, and beatings and experiencing the death of friends, peers, or family members.

Living in an area characterized by violence also increases the risk of pregnancy complications. Women living in neighborhoods in Santiago, Chile, that were characterized by a high rate of violence and confrontation between citizens and police suffered from high rates of pregnancy complications compared to women living in the same city but in neighborhoods without high levels of violence. "A fivefold increase in the risk of pregnancy complications was associated with living in high-violence versus low-violence neighborhoods, after adjustments were made for lack of social support and perception of neighborhood milieu" (Zapata et al., 1992, p. 688). Even though the findings are correlational, the research workers used statistical techniques to rule out many confounding variables. These results may have some significance for pregnant mothers in neighborhoods that Garbarino and his colleagues characterized as "war zones." Reducing people's exposure to violence raises issues not always thought of as part of a mental health professional's work, and we discuss some of these concerns in the next section.

Preventing Stressful Life Events

Dohrenwend's model includes political and social activism in the mental health professional's repertoire of methods for working to reduce psychopathology. Some preventive programs aim to eliminate the circumstances that produce stressful life events in the first place; thus, programs to develop housing, recreation, and employment opportunities may prevent life events related to inadequate housing, inactivity or extreme boredom, and unemployment. Good nutrition and prenatal care may reduce the incidence of low-birth-weight babies at risk for several other disorders. Because the means necessary to attain such ends are political in nature, some have said that mental health professionals who wish to influence the political system should enter politics directly and run for office (Dunham, 1965). However, there are many means of influencing political action in addition to running for office. Harrington's (1962) book on poverty influenced John F. Kennedy's thinking about his political program and social objectives. President Bill Clinton mentioned Wilson's (1987) *The Truly Disadvantaged* as the best discussion he had seen of the problems in our inner cities. President George Bush was influenced by conservative writers such as Charles Murray and George Gilder. Speaker of the House Newt Gingrich frequently cites social scientists and historians as sources for his positions. Social scientists work as advisers to government, and some testify before congressional committees regarding their research and its implications. Some may help empower local community groups by providing expert advice and guidance.

There are thus many roles in addition to that of elected officeholder through which social scientists and mental health professionals can influence the political system. A living example of such activity was provided by the settlement house workers at the turn of the century. These early social workers were researchers, community organizers, lobbyists, and interpreters of the needs of poor immigrants to the middle class. Because of their knowledge, some were appointed to head governmental departments at state and federal levels. Later, some joined the Franklin D. Roosevelt administration and influenced many of its social policies. This tradition of social and political activism was forgotten because of the emphasis on individual psychology that began to permeate the social work field in the 1920s (Levine & Levine, 1992).

Professor Edward Zigler is a good contemporary example of an academic political activist. A Yale faculty member and a clinical and developmental psychologist, he was part of a group that worked with President Lyndon Johnson to develop the Head Start program (Zigler & Muenchow, 1992). Zigler later took a leave from Yale University and worked for two years in Washington, D.C., as the first head of the Office of Human Development. He has since headed Yale's Bush Center for policy studies in child welfare and has been a vigorous advocate for Head Start and other child welfare programs. However, he grounds his policy positions in thorough analyses of the appropriate literature or other databases.

A caution. The space we have devoted to Dohrenwend's model should not be taken to indicate that we endorse all of its propositions. The various situational contributions to stress and recovery are not described in detail in this model. The model fits discrete life events much better than more chronic, enduring stresses and is of limited help in understanding disorders having a strong biochemical base and an inexorable course over time. Such a course of illness may not be influenced very much by external factors, but the quality of life for the afflicted person and those around him or her may still be modified favorably by social support or enhanced coping techniques.

We believe that the model helps us get our bearings by asking us to view problems in a more holistic light. It tells us that we need to develop theories that take into account the "person-in-a-situation." The words "holistic" and "embedded in a total context" are nothing more than truisms unless developed in greater detail.

Summary

The model proposed by Barbara Dohrenwend provides a useful framework for integrating the disparate activities of community psychology and more traditional interventions such as psychotherapy and crisis intervention. This model directs attention to the relationship between stress and behavior, including processes very early in the sequence of events leading to pathology or to recovery. This view offers a greater variety of options, based on either person-centered or environment-centered interventions; particularly prominent in Dohrenwend's model are strategies aimed at prevention.

Dohrenwend's model is useful in several ways. It adds a time dimension to our thinking about intervening in problems. From this perspective the vast bulk of services following the medical model come into play at the end of a long sequence of events that culminates in what we are calling psychopathology. The Dohrenwend model directs our attention to earlier points in the sequence. The earlier in the sequence we intervene, whether to provide assistance or to prepare individuals by enhancing psychological mediators or to see that some supportive resources are available at convenient times and places for the person in difficulty, the more we are talking about prevention. If we can go back far enough in the sequence to do something to prevent the stressful life event from arising in the first place, we have something akin to what we will call primary prevention.

Moreover, the Dohrenwend model is useful because it helps us respond to life-as-soap-opera types of events. Recall that in discussing the prevalence of diagnosed disorder in the population, we noted that it is also possible to examine the prevalence of various stressful life events that many people face. The more one thinks about "disorder" or disease in the medical model, the more one is inclined to think about the cure of disease and the undoing of psychopathology. A diagnosis in and of itself provides few clues to preventive intervention unless the etiology, or the set of causative factors that lead to the disorder, is clear (Institute of Medicine, 1989). Moreover, diagnosis has proven to be somewhat unreliable, especially for disorders of childhood (Kirk & Kutchins, 1992).

Adherents of the life events perspective look at the circumstances in which different types of stressful life events arise and think about positioning helping resources at points when people experience transient stress reactions or where possible before stressful life events even take place. We will talk more about various strategies for prevention later on in the text, but for now we simply point out how this model alerts us to a much broader variety of helping and preventive strategies and guides us in using a much broader variety of helping persons or modalities for delivering help. A major advantage of the model is that it expands our thinking about the alternatives available across time, place, and approach.

As it stands, however, the Dohrenwend model is little more than a useful outline of a comprehensive field and its many activities. Considerably more theoretical detail is needed, as is empirical research. In the next four chapters we develop a number of theoretical and empirical details in preparation for a careful examination of prevention in mental health.

Notes

1. We cannot doubt that people in difficulty need, and in a caring society deserve, to receive help. Some (e.g., Scheff, 1966; Graziano & Fink, 1973) have argued, however, that the treatment of pathology may contribute to the problem of "secondary gain" that Dohrenwend mentions. For example, Hankin and Locke (1982) found that, contrary to expectations, initially depressed patients who continued to be depressed at follow-up were *more* likely to have had a psychiatry visit than were patients no longer depressed at follow-up. These differences were observed even after controlling for patients' initial levels of depression. Patients whose symptoms persisted also averaged more visits to psychiatrists than did patients whose symptoms remitted. (Of course, other interpretations are possible. Those who didn't improve might have been more seriously disturbed or had therapists who used less effective treatment methods. The idea that therapy may prolong symptom episodes is not the only plausible interpretation of these data.)

2. Race is often used as a variable in social science studies, but it is misleading. By no means are all members of a racial group beset with the problems exhibited by some members. The classification is overly broad and stigmatizes members of the group unnecessarily. Race is a sensitive area. Wilson, a distinguished African American sociologist, said that in the twenty-five years since Moynihan's (1965) controversial book (see Chapter 2) the problems of crime, poverty, single-mother households, out-of-wedlock births, and unemployment have increased. The uproar following publication of Moynihan's monograph did result in research and scholarship emphasizing the strengths of African American families, but Wilson believes that the criticism may have discouraged research workers and policymakers from giving problems careful attention; the intellectual climate of the time may have contributed to the problem by keeping it out of sight and off the public agenda.

3. The rate of out-of-wedlock births to majority women has been increasing. In 1970 there were 175,100 out-of-wedlock births to majority women. By 1991 that number had risen to 707,500. By comparison, there were 215,100 out-

of-wedlock births to African American women in 1970 and 463,800 in 1991. Although the rate is lower in majority than minority women, because the number of majority women is so much larger the number of births in that group is also very large.

4. It is debatable whether the U.S. economy is producing enough high-paid jobs even for those who have attained the appropriate educational qualifications. The job market for college graduates and even for people with graduate degrees has been very tight in recent years, leading to questions as to whether our institutions of higher education are overproducing people.

5. The median income of married African American couples is close to the median income of majority couples.

4

The Ecological Analogy

"Ecology" is a fundamental metaphor or analogy in community psychology, embodying both the structure of a scientific paradigm and a specific set of values (Slotnick, Jeger, & Trickett, 1980). By an analogy or a metaphor, we mean that we draw on concepts developed in another field, environmental biology, and apply them to the subject matter of community psychology. We assume that there are enough similarities between problems that concern community psychologists and those studied by biological ecologists that we may try to use the concepts to illuminate problems of interest to us. Analogies are always imperfect. Nevertheless, the principles may still be useful in helping us to understand and to conceptualize problems of concern to community psychologists.

By scientific paradigm, we refer to the pattern of research in use in an area of inquiry. A new paradigm means that we ask different questions, make different observations, and generally apply different research methods than those used in the experimental paradigm favored by conventional psychological research. The ecological paradigm includes a set of fundamental beliefs, among them the belief that environments exert significant effects on human behavior and that people can therefore explain and perhaps manage their behavior through greater understanding of specific environmental influences. A value held by many who adopt the ecological paradigm is that to the extent that understanding of these influences is achieved there is an obligation to apply the understanding in *actions* that improve people's lives.

When we act on the belief that environments exert significant effects, two further assumptions are involved. The first is that it is possible to change patterns of social and organizational relationships so that we can achieve programmatic, "wholesale" effects on the lives and adaptations of people, in contrast to the "retail" assistance provided to individuals when we use the medical model. On the other hand, this viewpoint does not say that anyone can become anything under ideal environmental circumstances. A person cannot become a tree, no matter the environment. If there are some inherent limitations due to biology (e.g., a person with mental retardation may have a damaged nervous system), changes in the environment may not compensate completely for that difference. However, two further points should be noted. First, even with certain limitations, different circumstances can still result in different adaptations, some more desirable than others. Second, the diversity among people in qualities or potentials is not necessarily a limitation or handicap to them or to society. Under the right conditions, diversity can be a catalyst or resource for social development and change.

A second assumption is that if we are to achieve programmatic effects, we must introduce change at some broader level of social organization than just the individual in need. Both assumptions mean that we need to know a lot more about the social environment, and we cannot find out what we need to know in the psychological laboratory. In the ecological perspective, we are directed to develop a greater variety of problem definitions and to examine a greater variety of solutions, one or another of which will serve the needs of different segments of the population (Rappaport, 1981).

Implications of the ecological analogy for scientific work are also important. Any intervention in the social environment is predicated on a particular understanding of what that environment is like, that is, a point of view. From a scientific standpoint, conceptualizing and measuring the environment of human behavior are relatively recent developments in psychology, and at present there is no single coherent and comprehensive theory. Several approaches offering a variety of heuristic constructs are regularly cited (e.g., Moos, 1973). In general, however, the empirical foundations of these conceptions are less thoroughly developed than are the theoretical proposals.

This chapter first presents the ecological analogy as a paradigm for thinking and research and then outlines four fundamental ecological principles to guide the community psychologist. These principles are illustrated by a number of examples. We also discuss principles of practice that follow from the ecological analogy and the values inherent in the position.

Ecology as a Paradigm

Ecology is the field of environmental biology. The term "ecology" derives from the Greek root *oikos*, meaning house. Ecology, then, is the study of "houses" within which organisms live or, more broadly, of their environments. The modifier "social," or human, is attached to indicate the specific interest in studying the environments in which people live.

In general, ecologists study units larger than individual organisms, including populations, communities, ecosystems, and the biosphere. A *population* is a group of similar individuals; *community* refers to the set of populations within a defined area. The community and the inanimate environment constitute the *ecosystem*, while *biosphere* refers to the larger inhabited environment. Although ecologists do not ignore the rest of biology, they believe that explanatory concepts should be appropriate to the level of organization studied. While concepts from another level can be helpful in understanding the phenomena under study, the more reductionist concepts can never fully account for phenomena at other levels of organization. In Odum's (1963) words, "to understand a tree, it is necessary to study both the forest of which it is a part as well as the cells and tissues that are part of a tree" (p. 4).

In a different use of the concepts of ecology, Bronfenbrenner (1979) developed an ecological model to interpret research in child development. He identified four levels that were important in understanding child development: the ontogenetic or individual level of development (e.g., age, sex, temperament); microsystem variables such as the family (e.g., father-absent families; dysfunctional families); the exosystem, or the community-environment level (e.g., medical, educational, recreational resources in the neighborhood to support family life), and the macrosystem or level of culture (e.g., attitudes toward children, toward violence).[1]

Most community psychologists who use the language of ecology have not adopted this perspective completely but rather find a useful analogy in its outline and general principles. In adopting the metaphor of ecology, proponents are trying to say both what they are for and what they are against. For example, they use the scientific language of ecology to assert that an individually oriented psychology is less than fully helpful in thinking about many problems, limits the range of options for intervention, and may distract attention from important issues. Proponents find ecological concepts attractive because they transcend individual psychology. Just as biological ecology directs attention to the intimate interrelationship between organisms and resources, the concept of the visible organism as a product of its built-in properties and its competitive adaptation to available or changing resources directs attention to more than the individual person.

A Paradigm Shift

Psychology is one of the few sciences that has no branch devoted to the observation of phenomena in their natural states. Psychology leaped from the armchair to the laboratory, omitting the study of people in natural settings.[2] Because of this leap, psychology's concepts are concerned with "inside" properties of organisms and treat the outside as alien. The emphasis in our clinical heritage on the measurement of individual differences and of stable personality traits whose expression transcends situations contributed to our tendency to ignore the natural environment. In the psychoanalytic perspective, which had such a strong influence on clinical theory and research, what mattered was the individual's perceptions and fantasies and the emotional reactions based on those fantasies or perceptions. All that needed to be done or to be understood could be accomplished within the confines of the consulting room. The assumption in psychological testing that one could measure an individual's characteristics by a test administered in one set of circumstances and then predict behavior in any number of other circumstances reflects the assumption that differences in social environments do not matter very much. Even Kurt Lewin (1935), the field theorist who developed the formula $B = f(P,E)$—Behavior is a function of Person and Environment—and the concept of a life space that incorporates an external world, primarily examined the responses of single organisms to the inner-defined life space. However, an individual's behavior may make little sense when viewed in isolation. One would understand little about a baseball game by observing the behavior of the first baseman alone, since his or her actions have meaning only as part of the surrounding game. In adhering to the idea that knowledge is best obtained through the momentary experiment, moreover, psychological research lost a time perspective and created the problem of ecological validity, that is, the questionable external validity or generalizability of its findings (Barker, 1965).

The markedly different nature of scientific research from the ecological viewpoint is described well by Trickett, Kelly, and Vincent (1985):

> Community research is an intervention into the ongoing flow of community life and should be approached as such. While community inquiry—like all research—is designed to generate knowledge, it also can serve as a primary vehicle for the development of a setting. By its very nature, it cannot help but have impact on the place where it occurs. (p. 284)

According to Trickett et al., research activities exemplify resource exchanges involving persons, settings, and events. The goal of research is to create products that benefit the community as a whole, not just the researcher or funding source. No distinction is made between setting and method. The method is part of the setting and vice versa (see the principle of interdependence, described later in this chapter). All those who are affected by research, including community residents who serve as subjects, are considered formal participants in it.[3]

Because it is part of the community and is affected by the community, ecological research is much more flexible and improvisational than is laboratory research. Unplanned events and "side effects" are expected and are accounted for in the research design (Tebes & Kraemer, 1991). Research inevitably changes the community and its residents in important ways, and so the whole enterprise of research must be understood *longitudinally* (over time). A longitudinal focus on research as a catalyst for creating and maintaining resources makes it more likely that any products of the research will endure over time. All research is in fact longitudinal, regardless of the stated design in a particular case, since there is always a preexisting context of relationships among participants and the research activity itself inevitably changes the subsequent nature of that context (e.g., for future research activities).

Box 4–1. *Community Research from an Ecological Perspective*

A project carried out over several years by Simon Singer, a sociologist and criminologist, and by Murray Levine, a psychologist, illustrates many aspects of ecological research. The New York State Youth Board, which provides funds to local agencies to support youth centers and recreational and other preventive services for young people, asked all of its agencies to develop plans for future services. The executive director of the Youth Board of Amherst, New York, Joseph Bachovchin, then asked the Research Center for Children and Youth at SUNY–Buffalo to work with his agency to develop a needs assessment for planning purposes. The Amherst Youth Board agreed that a survey of youth problems, including delinquency and drug and alcohol use, would be appropriate for its needs. However, because this was to be a communitywide survey in three school districts, the first step taken by the Amherst

Youth Board was to sponsor a community forum in cooperation with the parents' and teachers' organizations in each of the school districts. About seventy-five citizens, including parents, some adolescents, community leaders, and people who work with youth, attended. They were divided into groups to discuss specific problems that they felt were of concern in the community.

Their concerns were recorded by the research team and became basic source material for developing the survey instruments used with both parents and high school youth. The research team also included questions of theoretical interest to enhance the likelihood that the survey would produce findings that could be published in the professional literature. This aspect of the survey reflected the interests of the university-based research center; publication in professional journals is a matter of survival ("publish or perish") in a university setting.

The initial drafts of the survey instruments were reviewed by the citizen members of the agency's board of directors, who had been appointed by the town council to oversee all of the Youth Board's activities and programs. After the board members approved the drafts, the survey instruments were reviewed by representatives of the administration of each school district. The cooperation of the school districts was important in order to gain access to a list of names of students and parents, or a sampling frame, from which to draw a random sample of students for the survey and also to obtain the schools' mailing tapes to announce the study to parents. The school administrators also requested some modifications to see that their interests were adequately represented. Once the instrument was cleared in this way, the project was further reviewed by the SUNY–Buffalo Institutional Review Board for ethical propriety and to ensure that confidentiality was sufficiently safeguarded.

To take parental interests into account, the research team wrote to the parents of every high school student to let them know that a survey was to be conducted, that if their son or daughter was chosen to participate it would be because that name was selected at random, and that no high school student would be allowed to take the survey without written parental permission. To encourage participation, the research team offered participants a coupon valid for a record or tape at a local record store. The owner of the record store cooperated by providing the coupons at a wholesale price, reducing the costs of the survey to the Youth Board. Once the names were selected, parents and youth were again notified by mail and sent a parental permission slip. After the slips were returned, arrangements were made to administer the survey instrument in school during noninstructional time. The survey was administered successfully, and even though the survey contained some sensitive questions, no one complained. In fact, the Youth Board was widely praised for its concern for the community and for its efforts to communicate what it was doing.

Once the survey was complete, the research team prepared a preliminary report and reviewed the results with the Youth Board and the executive director of the agency. After receiving their comments, questions, and suggestions for additional analyses, the research team prepared a second report. Once this report was cleared by the Youth Board, the research team presented the results formally to the town council, the legislative body responsible for receiving state funds for the Youth Board's programs, and this meeting was attended by members of the press. The report was summarized in the metropolitan daily and in suburban newspapers, and a story featuring the executive director appeared on several of the local television news broadcasts. The study was also the subject of a favorable editorial in the metropolitan daily.

In the next several weeks, the report was fed back to citizen groups in open forums held in community centers and schools, and the executive director and the research team met with small groups of service providers, ministers, and youth workers to discuss the results of the study. On the basis of this information and feedback, the Youth Board made its plans for services for the next several years, a plan approved by its funding agency.

This process was repeated three years later. Community sentiment was sufficiently favorable that the second survey included questions about sexual activity, emotional distress, and suicidal inclinations. These topics had not been included earlier because some citizen leaders and some school district representatives felt that they were too sensitive. Three years later, however, the concerns were still there, but sufficient trust had developed so that the second survey could include these sensitive items. In keeping with national trends, the second survey showed a decline in alcohol and drug use over the three-year period. Although the decline could not be attributed specifically to Youth Board programs, it was certainly consistent with the goals of these programs.

The process continued. When the state legislature sought to reduce funds for Youth Board programs except to the most deprived communities, the results of the studies showing relatively high rates of delinquency and continued drug and alcohol use in this relatively affluent suburban community contributed to the legislative decision to continue funding for the program. The data have since been used by the Youth Board for planning purposes and have provided useful background data for community agencies that were themselves preparing grant applications for service programs. The Amherst school district, working in cooperation with the Youth Board, developed an application for a planning grant for a multiservice center to serve a neighborhood where scatter-site low income housing had attracted many minority children and children for whom English was a second language into one school's catchment area. The data collected earlier supported the project application. The Amherst school district and the Youth Board, in cooperation with Levine and Singer, conducted a needs assessment.

This study used census data, survey data from school children and open-ended interviews with students, parents, teachers, school officials, political leaders, low-income housing managers, and Youth Board authorities and resulted in a report showing the need for a community center serving a particular area in town. The report also suggested that the community center be built adjoining the school and use the school's gym, swimming pool, auditorium, and community room on weekends and after school hours. The report was presented to the school board and to the town council. The town council voted an appropriation of $100,000 for services in that area and authorized the Youth Board director to pursue other sources of funds for a community center. There have since been several community meetings to decide how best to spend the funds. The report prepared by Levine and Singer was influential in the appropriation of funds, and various community members continue to refer to the report in public meetings.

Implications for the Research Enterprise

Compared to the relative ease of conducting a laboratory experiment, ecological research is messy. It requires compromises and accommodations to the interests of persons other than the researchers. It is rare that one can establish a true random-assignment-of-subjects-to-conditions experiment in which challenges to internal validity and plausible rival hypotheses can be controlled or assessed. Furthermore, ecological psychologists typically rely on multiple measures, including unobtrusive techniques, to collect data in the field. These measures are designed to preserve the complexity of the phenomena under study and to maximize generalizability in the sense that the research seeks to understand phenomena as they are found "in nature." Ecological investigators prefer this kind of ecological validity to the tight control and internal precision of the laboratory experiment. Because ecological research frequently has an applied orientation, it is necessary to study natural, unarranged patterns of social relationships. When we speak of ecologically valid research, we want the methods to produce knowledge that will be valid in the natural situation of interest. Finally, given the longitudinal character of ecological research, we do not strive to understand human behavior as the linear effect of some single, isolatable cause. This "noncausal" way of understanding behavior marks a sharp break with the dominant traditions and philosophies in psychology built on the testing of causal hypotheses.

Given these alternative methods and assumptions, we may speak of ecological psychology as a paradigm shift, or revolution, in the Kuhnian sense (Kuhn, 1970). However, community psychologists using ecological concepts continue to use the language of science and in so doing confirm their endorsement of the values of science—objectivity, in the sense of requiring findings to be public and replicable, and empiricism, meaning that all concepts are open to modification in light of new evidence. Continuing identification with science is important in establishing certain boundaries for community psychology and ensuring that its intellectual products are not too discontinuous with other products of scientific endeavor. Identification with other sciences is important in another respect. Although the ecological critique of traditional individual psychology is intellectually grounded, it is also a political statement to the degree that it generates a basis for competing for resources necessary for the ecologist to thrive—research funds, jobs, and recognition within the community of science. In a sense, social ecologists can be viewed as a variant population competing for resources with existing populations in the same community.

The Youth Board example (see Box 4–1) illustrates how the research process itself may alter phenomena in the natural setting. As another example, a study of the civil commitment process in California reported that a 76 percent rate of commitment by judges in the month before the study fell to 43 percent during the course of the study (Miller, 1976). Assuming a direct relationship, the difference between 43 percent and 76 percent for civil commitments implies a substantial effect on the lives of many people and an instance where mere observation for purposes of research was far from neutral. Of what value is the obtained knowledge when measured against the impact of research on people's lives? Value problems arise that are not easily resolved. However, we believe that cooperative arrangements in which the research is undertaken on the basis of clear understandings and in accord with the varied interests of community populations is most likely to identify and come to terms with potentially conflicting values.

Given these many differences with the more familiar laboratory experiment, what standards of quality should we apply to ecological research? In particular, what implications follow from our assertion that the standards we strive to meet in the laboratory are less important for judging products in this new tradition? For one thing, we need standards of goodness if we are to assert entitlement to societal resources and to claim special status in society as professionals. If we relax our preference for control and internal precision, what standards will replace them? Sarason (1976b) struggled with this issue in trying to answer a student who asked how such research was anything more than "common sense." Sarason answered that such research was Everyman's common sense but, quoting the historian Becker, was "more consciously and expertly applied." Levine (1980a, 1982) has suggested that it is self-conscious discipline that distinguishes the professional worker from the layperson. Nonetheless, the standards of quality that are to be met if we or others are to rely on research findings emerging from such perspectives remain to be articulated. (See Levine, Reppucci, & Weinstein, 1990, for a discussion of epistemological considerations in community psychology.)

This issue of standards is not idle when viewed in relation to the competition for resources. To survive, a new population must have access to resources. One resource is a base within a university where research and scholarship may be conducted and the results disseminated by teaching. Standards for the goodness of research influence the award of grants and other funds and publication in journals, and those in turn influence tenure and appointment decisions—in a word, survival. New journals may proliferate because the standards of excellence as well as the substance of new work differ from the traditional. In other words, the effects of a given change radiate. Where and how one may obtain funds for research and where and how one might get work published strongly influence the thinking of researchers. Fortunately, the overall system does allow for diversity. A viable new population may find a niche and compete successfully for resources with other populations in the same community.

Principles of Ecology

James G. Kelly (1966) was an early proponent of the ecological analogy in community psychology. In the beginning of this chapter, we briefly defined four concepts that Kelly employed. Here we will elaborate on those concepts—population, community, ecosystem, and biosphere. *Population* refers to a group of similar individuals; for these purposes, they are individuals with similar "interests." Populations can be defined by social interests—age, gender, ethnicity, race, social class—and often by roles such as police officer, mental health professional, legislator, parent, or mental health consumer. By *interests* we mean a concern about resources needed for survival, for carrying out the obligations of one's role, for growth and development, or for the fulfillment of one's potential. The term "interest" includes the need to be free of barriers or social "toxins" that interfere with obtaining resources or that limit the growth and development of members of the population; thus, access to jobs on an equal footing and the equal commitment of money to education in different communities are examples of concerns about essential resources. Issues like this are important because we believe there is strong evidence that the lack of resources places many members of the population in poverty at risk of disorder. Homelessness, for example, is an obvious condition that places many children at risk of severe disorder and poor adaptation (Institute of Medicine, 1989).

By *community* we mean the populations sharing a defined area. For different purposes, the area that populations share will be different. Sometimes it will be a city, a county, a state, a neighborhood, a particular school or social organization, or, in the case of school desegregation (see Chapter 11), the entire nation. We cannot always be precise in specifying this unit of analysis, which differs for different purposes. The only constant is that any unit of analysis will always be composed of populations with differing, overlapping, and sometimes competing interests. Any effort to intervene or even to study a problem in a community must expect as a given to cope with the varied interests of members of different populations.

The *ecosystem* refers to both the community and the inanimate environment. For some problems, we do need to know something about the inanimate environment. How much lead is in the air, and how will the ingestion of lead affect children's intellectual growth? What kind of housing is available? The architectural design of some high-rise public housing developments makes it more difficult for residents to protect themselves against crime. The movement of jobs from the cities to the suburbs meant more unemployment among inner-city residents and eventually resulted in a high concentration of "the truly disadvantaged" in some neighborhoods, adding to the problems of disorganization (Wilson, 1987; see Box 3–1). Traffic rush hours are part of the ecosystem. For example, commuters who regularly drove through high traffic congestion reported that their general mood was poorer than those who had easier commutes. Perhaps because they had greater household and family responsibilities that made demands on their time, women were more sensitive than men (Novaco, Kliewer, & Broquet, 1991). In all these examples, the physical environment had important social effects. For our purposes, the ecosystem also includes social rules, customs and laws that govern access to resources, that might limit people's opportunities, that might restrict freedom, or that protect individual rights.

The *biosphere* includes the larger inhabited environment, or the whole planet. We have become familiar with worldwide environmental problems such as global warming, greenhouse effects, and the loss of protective ozone, each of which may have important behavioral effects. The analogue on the social level is large-scale movement of people due to changes in their own countries, e.g., the immigration of Latino and Asian populations to California. In 1970 about 80 percent of Californians were non-Hispanic whites. In 1992 this percent declined to about 55, and by the year 2020 the non-Hispanic white population is expected to be about 40 percent (Data Reference Book prepared by Robert Page for the California Commission on the Future of the Courts, 1992; see also Rogler, 1994).[4] Examining our own history, we know that immigrants often have severe problems in adapting to a new world with different language, customs and demands and with limits on the social supports—schools, churches, community organizations—that are normally available to assist people through difficulties. In the absence of these resources, or if helping agencies do not adapt to the culture and needs of the immigrants, the helping agencies may become part of the problem.[5]

Some changes have come about because we have a global economy with worldwide movement of capital. Multinational corporations take advantage of differentials in the price of labor and other costs of doing business and move industries to undeveloped countries. These changes often create new problems in the communities to which the industries move; they also create problems at home to the degree that they result in plant closings and a loss of employment in our communities (Buss, Redburn, & Waldron, 1983; Broman, Hamilton, & Hoffman, 1990). A great many steel workers in Lackawanna, New York, lost well-paying jobs in steel mills because of corporate decisions that it was more economical to build new plants elsewhere than to modernize in Lackawanna or that corporate interests were better served by trading with Korea or Japan. When the worker in Lackawanna loses his job, he may start drinking more and perhaps abusing his spouse because his major source of pride and self-esteem is gone. He may be demoralized because he is angry and frightened about the future, and his plight can be directly attributed to global processes.

In a very influential article, Kelly (1966) articulated four principles, adapted from ecology, that he believed were useful in approaching problems in community intervention. These are *interdependence, cycling of resources, adaptation,* and *succession.*

Interdependence

The first of these principles states that components within a social unit are *interdependent*; changes in one component of an ecosystem produce changes in other components of that system. For example, logging destroys trees and affects the habitat of other animals, such as the spotted owl, that may become extinct. As we will explain later in this chapter, the deinstitutionalization of patients from psychiatric hospitals had important effects on other systems besides mental health, such as justice and law enforcement.

Interdependence refers not only to the existence of mutual influence among community components but also to their dynamic interaction over time. In research, for example, the relationship between the investigator and the setting under study differentiates the community system in a particular way. Investigator and setting are assumed to have significant effects on each other during all stages of the research (Vincent & Trickett, 1983), as the Amherst Youth Board example (see Box 4–1) showed. Furthermore, because the populations making up a community interact and exert mutual influences, any change can have reverberating effects, and we should expect the unexpected when it comes to the consequences of change.

Plant geneticists find that they constantly have to adapt their techniques for creating insect-resistant plants because the insect populations become toxin-resistant over time due to selective breeding. They have to create plants with different toxins or even provide nontoxic plants so that susceptible populations will survive to breed with others, slowing down the rate of development of toxin-resistant pests (McGauhey & Whalon, 1992).

Another example of dynamic mutual influence requiring solutions to problems caused by earlier solutions is affirmative action, which was designed to redress the underrepresentation of women, African Americans, and other groups in desirable work settings. Affirmative action programs succeeded in opening up opportunity for members of those populations by improving access to those resources; members of the populations favored by the change in rules, the analogue to a change in the physical environment, could compete more favorably for resources after the barriers were removed. Because affirmative action changed the rules regarding competition for resources, those populations that believed they had lost out by its acceptance (e.g., white males) proposed changing the rules again, to reduce the effects of affirmative action or even eliminate it (Ezorsky, 1991; Taylor, 1991). In other words, change on behalf of one population affected other populations, which then responded to restore their access to resources.

By definition, interdependent populations exercise mutual influence. Deinstitutionalization policy returned many people with serious mental illness to the community, and back on the streets many of them became very visible. This visibility, and the feeling of many citizens (as expressed, for example, in newspaper editorials) that the former inpatients were not properly cared for, led to a discussion about changing the rules again to either serve these people more aggressively or make it easier to rehospitalize them. Consumer groups, representing a different population, tried to change the system by organizing patient advocacy and consumer-run alternative services (Chamberlin, 1990). Some members of the deinstitutionalized patients' families also organized to bring political pressure to improve services. Mental health officials, as a population, were influenced by the actions of other populations (consumers and their families) to work together in changing the system of care.

More examples of the manifestation of mutual influence will be apparent when we examine prevention programs. Arguments now going on among parent groups, educators, and others concerned with the spread of AIDS illustrate this mutual influence. Groups with different religious, political, and social interests are engaged in serious debate about sex education in schools and whether to issue condoms to high school students (Whitehead, 1994).

In Kelly's view, the principle of interdependence not only alerts us to the complexity of change but also directs us to deal with the community as the unit of analysis for some interventions. It directs our attention to a level of analysis other than the internal characteristics of an individual patient. A further implication of interdependence, moreover, is that mental health professionals intervening in the community-oriented mode will adopt different roles and work in environments different from those where professionals are normally found (their usual niches). It is one thing to see patients in a clinic, quite another to consult with teachers in a classroom, and still another to participate in a communitywide coordinating council. Should effective coordination require additional legislative authority, for example, then mental health professionals must know how to operate in the appropriate political environments. The principle of interdependence warns us in general that we should attend to the relationships that constitute the community system, but it does not tell us precisely to what we should attend in any specific case.

Cycling of Resources

Kelly's second principle, referred to as the *cycling of resources*, suggests that the transfer of energy in a biological system reveals the individual components that make up that system and also their relationship to each other. A larger animal feeding on a smaller one, feeding on a plant, deriving energy from the sun, leaves fertilizer for the plant. Energy is transferred throughout the cycle; one creature's waste is another's raw material. An intervention represents a change in the way resources are cycled; thus, this principle concerns the way resources are created and defined as well as how they are distributed. Furthermore, Kelly states that before intervening to change the distribution of resources (e.g., creating situational mediators that ameliorate crisis reactions), one ought to know how a community cycles resources on its own.

In a social system, the equivalent of energy is money, so basically we are talking about recycling money. Taxation results in income redistribution as money goes from one source, the individual earner or the corporate taxpayer, to other sources. These may be the beneficiaries of Social Security income, unemployment insurance, disability payments, food stamps, or Medicaid. They may also be human service providers who receive appropriations for providing services.

Publicly funded programs that are based on new policies require changes in the way resources are cycled. Unless we assume unlimited resources, whenever we develop a new program the resources for it have to be taken from somewhere else. If public policymakers decide that we need rape crisis programs, or programs for substance abusers, or programs to protect children against child abuse, then existing resources have to be allocated and reallocated. The difficulties encountered in transferring resources from the psychiatric hospital to the community at large in support of deinstitutionalization policy provide a good example of what happens to an intervention or policy undertaken without full cognizance of how communities distribute resources.

Without sufficient resources, the effort to help can create problems. For example, in the 1970s we thought it was a good idea to have child abuse reporting laws. Professionals who worked with children were required to report to child protection authorities any suspicion that a child they were seeing professionally was being maltreated. Legislators thought that sponsoring child abuse reporting hotlines would be a manageable resource reallocation, making it possible to help children at low cost (Nelson, 1984). However, the child protection system was quickly swamped with calls. In 1992, hot lines were expected to receive reports on 2.7 million children, and the child protection system is overwhelmed with cases.

In fact, the U.S Advisory Board on Child Abuse and Neglect (1990) stated that the whole child protection system was in a state of crisis, as we described in Chapter 1, in part because we do not have unlimited resources and are unable or unwilling to allocate sufficient resources to implement policy-driven solutions to problems. When we consider the cycling and recycling of resources, those issues have to be taken into account. Innovations can lead to significant increases in the resources available to persons at risk. As we will see in Chapter 9, for example, self-help groups represent significant innovations in the ecology of coping and support, in part because they are so much more efficient than professionals in their consumption of money and other resources.

Adaptation; Niche

Kelly's third principle is *adaptation.* No human environment is completely behavior-neutral; through the specific resources it provides, an environment effectively constrains some behaviors and facilitates others. Adaptation describes the process by which organisms vary their habits or characteristics to cope with available or changing resources. Consider the shape of a pine tree growing under different conditions. In a forest the tree may be straight and tall, its needles and branches bushy, while the same type of tree exposed to ocean winds on a Cape Cod sand dune will be scrubby, bent over, and close to the ground. Growing close to the low-oxygen line on a mountain, it will be shorter and have fewer needles. Without adaptation, changes in resources or the presence of toxins threaten survival.

Significant loss of resources is probably the most frequent trigger for adaptive responding. If one loses a job, unemployment insurance may help temporarily, but eventually it is necessary to find another job. If the new job doesn't pay as well, a family may have to move to a cheaper apartment or a less expensive home. Plans for children to attend an expensive private college may be replaced with a plan to send them to a less expensive state college. Some people may be demoralized by the change in status and lifestyle and employ less adaptive coping devices, such as drinking excessively or getting into marital arguments. Some may adopt entirely new lifestyles and move to different parts of the country. In Chapter 3 we noted that mental hospital admissions, suicides, and the overall level of pessimistic mood among people are all correlated with changes in the unemployment rate (Kiernan, Toro, Rappaport, & Seidman, 1989). The point is that the loss of a significant resource requires a variety of adaptations. Conversely, an increase in resources may also require adaptation. Because food is readily available many people eat too much, feel they are overweight, and go on diets to lose weight.

Sometimes adaptation is triggered by the presence (or recognition) of toxins in the environment. Consider crime as a community toxin. Residential burglary, for example, provokes significant psychological distress and may seriously disrupt the victim's supportive attachment to home and neighborhood (Brown & Perkins, 1992). With respect to ecosystem variables, crime is perceived as a bigger problem by people living in neighborhoods marked by physical incivilities, such as litter, graffiti, and run-down or vacant buildings (Perkins, Meeks, & Taylor, 1992). People living in such an environment may act defensively in terms of when and where they move about and the number of locks on their outside doors. However, if the levels of residential satisfaction and neighboring are sufficient, these same physical incivilities may serve as catalysts for increased participation in block organizations as an adaptive response (Perkins, Florin, Rich, Wandersman, & Chavis, 1990). Neighborhood differences in rates of child abuse are in part related to differences in good neighboring, even in the absence of socioeconomic differences. Children living in environments with high rates of violence learn to adapt by hiding in bathtubs when shooting breaks out, or by being sensitive to the appearance of teens or older youth who may begin to shoot at each other (Garbarino et al., 1991).

For some combinations of resource limits and toxins, adaptation may involve relinquishing attachments to specific places. Some say that homeless people who live on the streets adapt in that manner because they don't have the rent for a room and because they believe that the risk of being harmed in a shelter is greater than the risk of being harmed on the street. Living on the street is for them an adaptation to the available resources and to social toxins that stimulate avoidant behavior. The concept of adaptation directs us to look at more than the person and the diagnosis that can be applied to the person, although these may be important for some purposes. It directs us to look also at the person's resources, or lack of them, and to recognize the toxins and other negative influences in the person's environment to understand the person's behavior.

Changes in the availability of resources lead to new adaptations on the part of affected people. When the original Worcester state hospital grew overcrowded and the legislature didn't provide for growth in the staff, hospital personnel adapted by working out methods for managing patients as efficiently as they could (Levine, 1981). They kept patients minimally clean, fed them, and tried to keep them from hurting themselves or others or from running away. But the resources did not allow much else to happen beyond managing patients efficiently.

Modern-day professionals also adapt. When consumers who lived in the community refused to come to clinics for treatment, community mental health programs created outreach and crisis units that ventured out into the consumer's world. Professionals stopped insisting that consumers come to the clinic for appointments and started meeting them in restaurants for coffee, in the consumer's home, or in pool halls or other hangouts (Cohen, 1990; see Box 2–1). Consumers are a resource for mental health professionals in the sense that funding depends upon serving a certain number of persons, and professionals' self-esteem depends in part upon doing a good job. The concept of adaptation leads us to try to understand the other person's condition of life and to try to understand how that person's behavior reflects those conditions of life.

The concept of adaptation is related to the concepts of *niche* and *niche breadth*. Niche refers to a habitat within which a given creature can survive. The broader the range of habitats within which creatures of the same type are found, the greater the niche breadth. Niche can also refer to the contribution a given population makes to the community. Humans, by virtue of their great ability to adapt behaviorally and culturally, are found at the north pole and at the equator, in oxygenless space and underwater. In that sense, humans may be said to have a wide niche breadth.

We can see that populations are not randomly scattered throughout the community. There are ethnic and racial concentrations in different neighborhoods, and also gender concentrations in different occupations. Women are often found in nursing or in elementary school teaching, but less often in mathematics, engineering, or construction. For years the formal barriers of legal segregation and discriminatory customs kept African Americans from living or working in many niches. When those formal barriers were removed, African Americans could enter certain occupations, use public accommodations, and be admitted to schools, colleges, universities, and professional schools formerly closed to them. In other words, their niche breadth widened. The expansion of niche breadth is a continuing goal of advocates for groups such as women, gays, and minority group members. The argument about allowing gays into the military is essentially an argument about niche breadth.

Homeless people are more prevalent in some neighborhoods than others and in soup kitchens, missions and shelters more than in a town's premier restaurants. Before deinstitutionalization, the most important niche in which persons with serious mental illness could be found was the mental hospital. Now their niche breadth is enlarged, and mental health consumers are found in many different community settings.

Consider Geel, Belgium, a community with a seven hundred-year history as a religious shrine for mentally ill people. Although there is a psychiatric hospital located near Geel, hundreds of persons with mental illness live with families in Geel, which receive allowances for boarding them. Not everyone in town provides boarding. Most often it is working-class families and farm families, who welcome the extra income. If boarders go to the movie theater in town, they are herded into the balcony rather than being allowed to sit among the patrons in the orchestra. Although boarders are free to move around town, they are found only in certain bars and never in others. They sometimes attend church but are not found in all churches in town. Boarders are rarely observed at town meetings about governance, nor are they part of community groups planning charitable affairs or other community projects. In other words, they are not randomly distributed among town settings but are found instead in certain niches.

Similarly, in the United States group living arrangements for persons with serious mental illness or mental retardation are not found just anywhere. Initially, these homes were concentrated in neighborhoods where there was little community opposition. In Buffalo, New York, a great many group homes were initially established in the vicinity of a state hospital. However, so many former inpatients were wandering the streets and causing complaints from local businesses that a moratorium was declared on the placement of more homes in that area. Dear and Wolch (1987) described similar "service dependent ghettos" in other cities. Now laws generally allow the placing of homes in most communities, but opposition still arises in communities that are sufficiently stable that the neighborhood can organize to protest against a home coming into the area (Levine, 1981).

The concept of niche leads us to think about the development of functional roles within a new social organization (niche) and the provision of resources appropriate for characteristics of the population occupying this niche. Thus, some service systems employ former consumers but adapt the jobs to take into account any residual limitations. We can also contemplate teaching adaptive skills so that a population's niche breadth can be enlarged. Consider persons with severe and persistent mental illness who have lived for many years in psychiatric hospitals, for example. Their behavioral characteristics to some extent reflect limited situational resources and adaptation to the custodial nature of hospital care. By training such individuals in skills of daily living and providing other resources (e.g., group homes, income under the Supplemental Security Income program), we can widen their niche breadth and increase the likelihood that they will adapt to normal community life. Kruzich and Berg (1985) found that the self-sufficiency of chronic mentally ill clients was dependent upon the organizational characteristics of the long-term care facilities in which they were living. The attitudes of staff, and staff's willingness to allow some flexibility in patients' routines while maintaining a moderate degree of activity scheduling, predicted client self-sufficiency. Even within the hospital, Zusman (1967) reported changes in patient appearance when services adopted a therapeutic rather than a custodial orientation to care. Following discharge, moreover, persons with serious mental illness who live in communities giving them a wide niche (e.g., supportive arrangements for housing, employment, and recreation, plus a broad array of mental health services) are less likely to be rehospitalized. They are more likely to be employed and to report higher levels of well-being than are similar persons living in an otherwise comparable city providing a more limited niche (Beiser et al., 1985).

Many individuals labeled "mentally retarded" are impaired only with respect to their ability to cope with the intellectual demands of schools. Although many such individuals are limited to the special-class niche, follow-up studies indicate that, at least within the upper ranges of mental retardation, they fare no worse occupationally and socially than do other persons of similar social-class background when they leave school (see Sarason & Doris, 1969, pp. 86–89; Bloch, 1984). (If the job market changes and requires skills that those with mental retardation have difficulty acquiring, this picture may change and the niches become more limited.)

As another illustration, we note that the mobility of physically disabled people has been greatly improved by wheelchairs and other technological devices. Until well into the 1970s, however, the architecture of many buildings, including restroom facilities, made access by people in wheelchairs difficult or impossible. To a degree, one can say that the behavioral handicap of the person in the wheelchair is as much a function of the staircase or the curbstone as it is of the person's nonfunctional limbs. After the passage of regulations requiring wheelchair access ramps and restroom modifications, the adaptation of such individuals to key community settings improved, and they appeared in more niches.

The concepts of niche and adaptation are useful because they teach us to think about alternatives and about the resources necessary to provide an alternative. They also help us accept differences among individuals and, if necessary, consider political solutions, such as legal regulation, to problems of poor person-environment fit.

Succession

Kelly's fourth principle is *succession*. Environments are not static; they change. A change in the environment may create conditions more favorable to one population and less favorable to another. Eventually a more favored population will squeeze out the others, or at least dominate a given area, or some new level of homeostasis will develop among populations sharing the same area. While interdependence teaches us to understand the community before trying to change it, succession implies that change, both natural and human-made, can contribute to our understanding in the first place.

The history of immigration to the United States provides some excellent examples of this principle. As immigrants prospered, they moved out of poor neighborhoods into newer suburbs. The groups that later occupied the older housing were themselves moving up from what they had before. African Americans who moved to Chicago from unheated shacks with no running water in the rural, agricultural South found better quarters in the city tenements formerly occupied by other ethnic groups (Lemann, 1991). Urban ghettos developed over time, and when changes in civil rights laws opened new employment and housing opportunities for African Americans who had been denied them earlier, those who were able to take advantage of the opportunities moved out of the ghettos. These areas were left with high concentrations of poor, young people, who were more prone to crime and lacked both middle-class role models and peers who had the social clout and know-how to command services. Thus, the ghetto areas became progressively worse for those who lived there and could not get out (Wilson, 1987).

The deinstitutionalization of persons with serious mental illness provides another illustration of succession in urban neighborhoods. Psychiatric ghettos take root more readily in transient neighborhoods where anonymity is widespread, other populations have little rootedness, and there is little formal organization in the neighborhood. Such ghettos developed where properties were not profitable for other use, as in the old residential hotels on Manhattan's Upper West Side. As property values increased and tax benefits were made available to developers, "gentrification" took place, and these hotels were converted to condominiums. Many mental health consumers and welfare clients living in the hotels were evicted, sometimes ruthlessly, helping to create the troublesome phenomenon of homelessness. The economically and politically stronger middle class competed successfully with the poor for housing niches (Dear & Wolch, 1987).

Sometimes a neighborhood organization welcomes newcomers to the community because of resources the newcomers may bring. A YWCA residence with which we are familiar, dedicated to serving women but unable to attract young businesswomen as residents, opened its doors to women with serious mental illnesses. Its buildings were resources for these women, and their rental payments were resources to keep the building functioning and to pay for necessary staff. Convents in New York State, empty because of the declining number of persons entering religious life, were put to new use as group homes for retarded individuals deinstitutionalized under court order. Church organizations took in the deinstitutionalized persons, fulfilling the religious value of service, and received money for their care. Unused for their original purposes, convents became resources not only for the retarded living in them but also for administrators charged with carrying out the deinstitutionalization order. The church, with a stake in providing service, often used its influence to restrain neighborhood resistance (competition from still other populations) to the invasion of the new population (Rothman, 1982).

In addition to alerting us to some issues of change, the principle of succession teaches that some resources that would otherwise be discarded may be put to use by other populations. During much of the nineteenth century, railroad interests promoted the succession of midwestern prairies by farming, industry, and other intensive development (Cronon, 1991). A hundred years later many midwestern communities, now stuck with long stretches of abandoned railroad right-of-ways, have begun converting them to "linear parks" offering miles of uninterrupted hiking and biking trails for the recreational pursuits of twenty-first-century citizens. Similarly, from the self-help perspective, a "useless" individual, a drain on resources, becomes a therapeutic resource within the context of an organization such as Alcoholics Anonymous (see Chapter 9). Self-help movements, able to use different resources than those which professionals require, are to a certain extent succeeding the population of professional service providers. The literature on how self-help organizations and mental health professionals can relate to each other may be taken as an example of the development of a new homeostasis between populations, based on the possibility of exchanging resources to meet mutual needs.

Box 4–2. The Boom in Hong Kong's Elderly Home Industry

An interesting illustration of Kelly's ecological principles and the analytic insights they offer is provided by Cheng (1993). Between 1981 and 1990 the city of Hong Kong showed a dramatic rise in the number of private, for-profit residential facilities for elderly people. This change was not entirely attributable to growth in the elderly population as a whole. Rather, it reflected sharp increases in the number of dependent elderly caused in part by a decrease in the number of family caretakers (as more and more women took jobs outside the home) and an increase in the number of adults emigrating in advance of Hong Kong's return to Chinese control. Over the same time period Hong Kong's publicly funded and regulated residential homes for dependent elderly grew at an inadequate rate, creating long waiting lists. Social security income, allocated to the elderly directly to enable them to remain independent or under family care, was exploited by entrepreneurs as a means of funding profitable new private homes. Cheng suggests that many of these unregulated homes may have been substandard in quality.

Cheng used ecological principles to help explain why the rapid surge in numbers of dependent elderly had the effect that it did (i.e., an increase in private, for-profit residences). Following Kelly's principle of interdependence, for example, specific changes in one arena (Hong Kong's political relationship with China) provoked changes in other spheres of life (widespread emigration that disrupted family support systems and sharply increased the number of dependent elderly lacking adequate support). The cycling of resources is evident in the way money injected into the system at one point (elderly persons living in their own homes) ended up fueling the expansion of a new kind of setting elsewhere in the community. Adaptation is shown in the behavior of entrepreneurs who responded to rapid growth in demand for residential supports by creating profitable enterprises tied to guaranteed public commitments to social security funding. Adaptation is also illustrated in the rational selection of this private, for-profit housing option by many people facing challenging new circumstances and limited alternatives. Finally, succession is demonstrated in the process whereby the disappearance of family supports for elderly people due to emigration and to changes in the labor force, plus the slow response of public programs charged with meeting this need, created a social vacuum that rapidly came to be filled by a new kind of setting.

Cheng also points out how thinking ecologically helps us realize that solving the apparent problem of substandard homes is not simply a matter of enacting regulatory laws requiring private homes to meet certain rules, since other factors of importance would not be addressed directly by such laws and would continue to affect the situation, possibly making things worse. Costs resulting from regulation may shrink profit margins, causing private operators to quit the business and homelessness among the elderly to increase as an unintended consequence. Effective adaptations to changing conditions are more likely to evolve from the recognition that factors are interdependent and subject to modification by monetary and other resource considerations.

Mental Health and the Law

Kelly's principles of interdependence, cycling of resources, adaptation, and succession are well illustrated in the problem that Teplin (1983) called the criminalization of the mentally ill. As we have noted, the inpatient census of state mental hospitals has declined dramatically since the 1950s. Whatever the merits of the argument that incarcerating people in "total" institutions was harmful, unnecessary, and expensive, the fact is that federal policies, reflected in reimbursement formulae, made it advantageous to shift consumers from in-hospital niches to other niches—i.e., nursing homes, board and care homes, or other similar facilities. The consumer's adaptation to the community was to have been assisted by recycling resources in the form of supervised medication, day care, rehabilitation services, and outpatient psychotherapy. Those resources were not always forthcoming, however, nor were they forthcoming in forms many persons could use (Levine, 1981).

Levine (1981) described how litigation in the 1960s and 1970s, designed to correct abuses in the hospital system, led to a tightening of legal standards for involuntary commitment. To commit a person involuntarily to a mental facility for more than brief emergency care, it became necessary to show that the person was not just mentally ill but dangerous to himself or others or unable to survive even with assistance from family or friends. In many states these judicially imposed restrictions were translated into statutory standards affecting everyone concerned with the problem of deviant behavior. The person at risk for involuntary hospitalization was entitled to a number of procedural due process protections to ensure that the commitment and the loss of personal liberty occurred for good reason. It became more difficult to hospitalize someone involuntarily than it had been in years past. Relationships among the hospital as a resource, professional mental health workers as a population, and prospective consumers' families and other community agencies as populations changed.[6]

Although outpatient services have grown, it is not clear that those services have necessarily been directed to persons who formerly would have been served as inpatients. General hospital psychiatric services and outpatient clinics restrict the types of cases they believe are suitable for service in their facilities. A prospective consumer may be denied care because he or she doesn't have the financial resources and is not eligible for welfare or other insurance that will pay the costs of care. Other institutions may not have secure facilities to manage dangerous or suicidal persons. Teplin (1983, p. 60) reported that some mental hospitals will not accept a person who has any criminal charge pending, even if it is a minor one. Consumers can thus face barriers to gaining access to niches and the resources they contain.

These two sets of forces, mental health litigation and legislation regarding funding, made it more difficult to hospitalize people. The principle of interdependence leads us to predict that policies that keep patients out of the hospital will influence the working environments of two important populations in the community—those working in the criminal justice system and those working in the mental health system. The families of consumers will also be affected, and services may be altered to reflect characteristics of consumers to whom the services are targeted. If these changes are potent, then we can expect to see evidence of adaptation by members of these populations, and also some change in the niches in which they are found.

Law as a Factor in the Ecological Analogy

We noted earlier that the ecosystem includes the social rules, customs, and laws that govern access to resources, limit opportunities, protect rights, or restrict freedom. Changes in legal rules are changes in the ecosystem. These changes have had extremely important effects on the mental health system, on deinstitutionalization policy, and on the provision of services in the community, and they have now brought lawyers and judges as populations into the picture. Members of the legal system are now interacting more actively with members of other populations concerned with the care of mental health consumers, including mental health professionals and, as we shall see, police and corrections personnel in jails and prisons.

The larger community within which we live has a legal system that operates by rules designed to implement our highest values. Everyone in our society, at least after birth, is granted status as a person. The term persons includes children and adults, citizens and aliens, and the Fourteenth Amendment to the U.S. Constitution states basic protections for all persons:

> nor shall any State deprive any person of life, liberty, or property without due process of law; nor deny to any person within its jurisdiction the equal protection of the laws.

The Fourteenth Amendment preserves the rights and freedoms of individuals against the power of government to limit those rights and freedoms. Under the Fourteenth Amendment, every person is entitled to the equal protection of the laws. That means that even persons with *DSM-IV* diagnoses are persons under the law, entitled to the same legal protections of their basic rights to life, liberty, and property that every other person has.

Due process of law refers to those procedures that we recognize as necessary for the state to follow when the state acts to limit a person's rights. As a general rule, no right is absolute. All rights may be limited by state action if the state has sufficiently good reason and follows proper procedure. It is beyond our scope to deal with what constitutes due process under our Constitution. (The details of due process vary depending on the type of action and the interests at stake.) Suffice it to say that the state legislature must pass a law that authorizes involuntary commitment. The language of the law must be consistent with previous judicial interpretations of both the state's constitution and the U.S. Constitution. The law must also specify procedures to be followed if a person is to be committed involuntarily. If the person who is to be involuntarily committed has a hearing in front of a judge, and the hearing is carried out fairly—the judge is neutral and the person has been given notice of why the hearing was held and is given an opportunity to be heard, to be represented by an attorney, and to cross examine witnesses against him or her—then due process has been followed. If the person is committed involuntarily, we say that his or her liberty is restricted with due process of law. (Because of the nature of our federal system, with some functions reserved to the states, the precise form of the law differs from state to state, although all laws must be written so that they meet constitutional requirements.)

Until the 1960s there was a general belief that psychiatry could help a great many people, that professionals were benign and helpful, and that government, especially the courts, should not interfere with professional decisions. Involuntary treatment could be based on a professional judgment that a person needed treatment, with little court review of the order. Commitment could be for an unspecified time, and it was up to the hospital superintendent to decide when a person should be released. Patients in hospitals had very few civil rights. Patients had little privacy, and rights, such as those to marry, to make contracts, to write letters, to visit with friends or relatives, or even to see an attorney, were sharply limited. All of this, it was said, was being done for the patient's good.

Beginning in the 1960s and continuing into the 1970s, federal courts began to interpret individual constitutional rights to mean that a state could not involuntarily hospitalize someone solely because the person was diagnosed as having a mental illness or because some professional person said the person had a need for treatment. The courts began to insist that the state show that the person, in addition to having a mental illness, was dangerous to himself or herself or to others before involuntary commitment could be justified. The civil rights-oriented lawsuits were challenges to the professional and scientific authority of psychiatry and to the state's right to curtail individual freedom so sharply. The psychiatrist Thomas Szasz (1961) also challenged the role of psychiatry in limiting patient civil rights and freedoms, calling it a form of tyranny (see Chapter 6, p. 179).

These new viewpoints led to legal challenges to professional authority and to lax commitment laws. One important challenge to the scientific authority of psychiatry came in *Baxtrom* v. *Herold* (1966). Baxtrom was in prison because he had been convicted of assault. He was transferred to a state institution used for the confinement of prisoners who became mentally ill while serving their time. When Baxtrom's time was up, the authorities continued to hold him because they said he was mentally ill. Baxtrom brought suit requesting that he be released or committed to a civilian hospital for treatment.

When Baxtrom's case reached the U.S. Supreme Court, the Court said that Baxtrom could not be held arbitrarily and was entitled to the same procedures used to commit anyone involuntarily. The Court ordered the same review for everyone else who had been confined under the same conditions. One result was that a large number of prisoners in New York and other states were either released outright or transferred to civilian hospitals after a judicial hearing to determine the necessity for continued hospitalization.

In this situation, people who had been convicted of committing crimes and who were also allegedly mentally ill, were placed in less secure state hospitals or released to the community. Follow-up studies of those who were both mentally ill and "dangerous" showed that over a four-year period about 14 percent were known to have committed an act injurious to another person either while in a civilian state hospital or after release to the community. If we say that by history (based on diagnosis and history of conviction for a criminal offense) 100 percent were expected to act out, then the follow-up study showed that prediction was wrong in 86 percent of the cases, casting serious doubt on the professional expertise and authority of mental health professionals (see Monahan, 1976).

The legal cases exposing abuses in legal process and abusive situations within institutions contributed to reform (see Chapters 2 and 10). The legal rules changed the ecosystem by making it more difficult to hospitalize patients and to keep them hospitalized. Along with the changes in the way federal government reimbursed state governments for patient care and for disability pensions (see Chapter 2), psychiatric patients could no longer be restricted to the psychiatric hospital niche. And once patients occupy niches in the community in addition to hospitals, the principle of interdependence tells us that other populations in the community will also be affected.

Adapting to Legal Change

Mental health professionals. Jacoby (1983) studied the implementation of a 1976 statute reforming Pennsylvania mental health law (Mental Health Procedures Act, 1976). This act, similar to many passed by other states in those years, had as its purpose to decrease long-term mental hospitalization, provide greater procedural due process in commitment proceedings, provide for periodic judicial review of commitment, and encourage appropriate treatment in the least restrictive setting. Although the formal leadership of the state psychiatric association favored the new law, Jacoby noted that a great many frontline mental health professionals were not at all happy with its provisions. One source of opposition was the substitution of a legal standard—dangerousness to self or others—for a professional judgment of the need for treatment. As Jacoby put it, bureaucratic norms were set in opposition to professional norms of making judgments about what is or is not in a patient's best interests.

Mental health professionals reacted to the new law and related developments. Responding to the vigorous advocacy of the public defender in Philadelphia who specialized in mental health work, they used the legal definition to exclude some who would have been hospitalized in an earlier time. In addition, the high visibility of people with obvious mental illness, "bag ladies" and others on the streets, resulted in the perception that it was difficult to have people committed in Philadelphia. Patients were being committed with great regularity, although something like a plea-bargaining process went on, with mental health professionals adapting by releasing some patients because they feared they would not be able to get a court order to continue holding them. (Gupta, 1971, described a similar process of negotiated "out-of-court settlements" when attorneys became a part of the work environment of mental health professionals.) Jacoby described the adaptation of mental health workers to a change in their community, or their ecosystem, assuming that the statutory provisions for due process are considered part of the inanimate environment.

The police. The police represent another population in this community faced with the problem of adapting to changes in its work environment. Police act under a complex set of rules designed to protect citizens against the abuse of police power. They can take into emergency custody people involved in a disturbance, but they cannot take a person into custody without having an arrest warrant based on a complaint from someone that the person has done something wrong or, in the absence of a warrant, witnessing the infraction themselves or having other probable cause to act.

In general, police have a great deal of authority to take into custody people who are overtly dangerous to themselves or others. Police are called to the scene of many disturbances, and, generally speaking, they cannot refuse to come when called. The police have authority to arrest someone who is committing a crime or disturbing the peace. They have less authority, however, to detain someone who is apparently unable to care for his or her own basic needs (and whose life or health is in danger for that reason) or who seems disoriented and confused but is sufficiently alert to decide that he or she does not wish to receive care. About 8 percent of all police encounters with citizens involve mentally ill persons (Teplin, 1984). As the ABA standards note, police must make an "on the spot" determination in such cases, weighing the state's interest in protecting an individual from harm against the individual's constitutionally based interest in being free to manage his or her own affairs. A moment's reflection on the inherent complexity of this decision helps to explain why police may be reluctant to become involved in noncriminal situations.

Both the availability of facilities in the community and the policies and attitudes of mental health workers affect police willingness to take someone into custody for mental health-related purposes. The ABA standards (p. 7–37) cite research indicating that police become cynical about mental health services if the admission procedure is tedious or uncertain. On occasion the mental health worker may refuse admission to someone who later attempts suicide or engages in violence. A police officer may have to defer other important duties for several hours while waiting with a patient in an emergency room, only to have the admitting doctor decide that the person doesn't meet the legal criteria for admission and should be back on the street. Such episodes may enter into folklore, not as the exceptional case but rather as the general rule, helping to shape police attitudes toward the use of mental health facilities as an alternative disposition in cases where the police have discretion in taking the person to a lockup or a hospital.

It is not that police view symptoms of mental disorder with indifference. Based on observations of police-citizen encounters, Teplin (1984) found that if there was some indication of mental disorder, independent of the severity of the episode, the police were twice as likely to make an arrest as when such indication was absent. Most prospective patients who come to police attention have probably committed at least a violation, if not a more serious crime. Even if the violation is disorderly conduct, once convicted the person can receive a jail sentence of up to fifteen days. If the charge is sufficiently serious, the arraigning magistrate can set bail at a level the accused person may not be able to meet, requiring him or her to be held in custody until trial. If someone raises a good-faith doubt as to the accused person's mental or emotional competence to stand trial, he or she may be held for an examination to determine competency or be admitted to a hospital for that purpose (ABA, Part IV).[7] This combination of factors, including police preference for the criminal justice rather than mental health system, leads to the hypothesis that many people formerly confined to mental hospitals during an era of less rigid standards for admission and more rigid standards for discharge now will be found in new niches, jails and prisons.

The National Alliance for the Mentally Ill (NAMI), a self-help and advocacy group (see Chapter 9) composed of family members of persons with mental illness and consumers of mental health services, released a 1992 report (National Alliance for the Mentally Ill Staff & Public Citizen's Health Research Group Staff, 1992) on the mentally ill and jails. They estimate that there are approximately thirty thousand persons with mental illness in jails (generally pretrial lockups, or facilities where short-term sentences are served). The report claims that there are more mentally ill persons in the Los Angeles County jail than in any psychiatric hospital in Los Angeles County. NAMI claims that although most seriously mentally ill individuals are charged criminally when arrested, most of the charges are for relatively trivial offenses that are more the manifestation of their mental illnesses than of any intent to commit a criminal act. The report also claims that 29 percent of jail officials admitted that they held seriously mentally ill individuals who had no criminal charges levied against them.

If more disturbed persons are now found in jails and holding centers, and in prisons after sentencing on criminal charges, we are faced with a societal problem of reallocating or redistributing professional resources to new institutional settings. For one thing, any right to treatment probably extends to a person with a history of mental or emotional disturbance who is being held on criminal charges. That issue aside, arrest and jailing constitutes a distinctively stressful experience, often triggering fear, anxiety, and depression. The suicide rate among inmates in county jails is sixteen times greater than among adults of comparable age in the population at large. For youth held in adult jails, the rate is three to five times higher than the rate in the general population (Hayes, 1983). A heightened state of arousal may precipitate excited aggressive acts toward both custodial personnel and other prisoners, especially in individuals prone to such behavior. The NAMI report states that in 84 percent of jails, corrections officers receive either no training or less than three hours of training in dealing with the problems of mentally ill inmates. Custodial personnel in holding centers and short-term correctional facilities need training in the day-to-day management of disturbed persons and, if medication is used, to understand the nature and side effects of such drugs (see ABA, Standard 7–2.8). NAMI has proposed some fundamental reforms of the public mental health system to guarantee mentally ill detainees both fundamental legal rights and humane treatment.

It is difficult to answer the question of whether, as a result of deinstitutionalization policies, more people with mental and emotional disorders are being cared for now in the criminal justice system and in correctional facilities than was the case before such policies became widespread (Teplin, 1983). Certainly very disturbed individuals are being arrested, arraigned, and jailed. The NAMI survey found that 69 percent of jail officials reported that they were seeing far more mentally ill individuals than they had ten years earlier.

One hypothesis that seems to have solid support in the research literature is that formerly hospitalized persons have higher arrest rates than those without such histories (Teplin, 1983, p. 57). A NAMI study reported that 40 percent of mentally ill relatives of NAMI members had been arrested at least once. However, Teplin notes that interpreting the existing data is complicated and that a simple "hydraulic" hypothesis, i.e., that overflow from the mental hospitals due to deinstitutionalization accounts for the increase in the prison population, cannot be sustained.

If police do prefer the criminal justice route, however, then there should now be more disturbed persons in jails (presentencing holding facilities) than was formerly the case. Although the epidemiology is difficult, Teplin reads the evidence to conclude that jail has indeed become the poor person's mental health facility as a consequence of changes in the admission of persons to mental hospitals. It would indeed be ironic if that was the case, for Dorothea Dix's mid-nineteenth-century crusade to build mental hospitals in part grew out of her observations that too many mentally ill people were being held in jails (Levine, 1981, p. 24).

This excursion into the complex interrelationships among systems and the rules that govern their operation should adequately illustrate the implications of interdependence when community change occurs. Change requires adaptations on the part of existing populations in the ecosystem, in this instance police, mental health workers, jailors, and court personnel. Adaptation by some populations can force another population (persons with mental illness) into new niches (jails). Furthermore, such changes require reallocation of resources to populations and niches with mental health personnel more active in criminal justice niches. Erie County, New York, added a fifty-bed infirmary to its jail to care for the mentally ill now in the facility. The principle of succession reminds us that opportunities will open up for new populations to enter and influence the mental health and the corrections system.

None of these events can be understood in terms of individual psychopathology or by examining clinical treatment or diagnostic processes. An understanding of behaviors that enter into a determination of diagnosis under the categories of *DSM*-IV will not explain the decisions mental health workers make. Similarly, examining the formal rules under which such workers operate will not fully explain the behavior and attitudes of police in exercising discretion when arresting and charging persons they encounter. Moreover, Jacoby's and Teplin's research required field study and an analysis of data that could not possibly have been generated in a laboratory. This complex example indicates that mental health workers cannot fully appreciate their own behavior and the behavior of their clients without stepping back and looking at the system of which they are a part. Very similar processes have been observed in the deinstitutionalization of persons with mental retardation (Willer & Intagliata, 1984). The concepts of ecology, crude as they may be when applied in this context, are useful because they direct our attention to important issues that affect us every day and that we cannot understand without examining the larger system around us.

Box 4–3. *Unforeseen Consequences of a Change in Child Protection Laws*

The death of a child touches everyone deeply. We are especially outraged when we learn that the child protection system knew about a high-risk case and wasn't able to protect the child from a brutal death or when a judge returns to his or her family a child taken into foster care because of abuse and the child is then injured or killed. These stories receive wide publicity and prompt demands to punish officials and ·change the law.

Child protection workers try to keep children with their families, and judges try to return children to their families, because of the family preservation policy established in 1980 (PL 96–272). This preference for keeping children in their own homes and returning them quickly from the custody of social services was designed to reduce the rapidly growing number of foster home placements that occurred in response to a rising tide of reports of child abuse and neglect. The policy favoring custody in the family home is under attack as citizens and legislators react to the death of children reported in the media.

Ecological principles tell us that a change in any one part of a system affects other parts and that actors in the system adapt to changes in the environment. The Joseph Wallace case in Chicago resulted in widespread publicity, calls for a judge to resign or be relieved of his duties, and calls for a child protection worker to be prosecuted criminally. As a result of the publicity, the law in Illinois changed, but, as happens all too often, changes in laws that take place in an emotionally charged context are not well thought through and have unintended consequences.

Joseph Wallace was born while his mother was in a mental hospital. Her doctors did not believe that his mother, Amanda, was able to care for him, and on their recommendation Joseph was placed in foster care. As the law required, social services workers tried to help the mother prepare to take care of her child. Amanda, who was never clearly psychotic, wanted her child back, and in fact the child was returned to her. After she had a second child and was hospitalized again, both children were taken into temporary care. Amanda entered treatment, and once again social services workers worked with her so that she could have her children back. Amanda also hired a private attorney who argued her case. However, the workers helping her turned over rapidly, the judges and legal guardians appointed to represent Joseph's interests were all overburdened with cases, and the case records were kept in another court. The upshot was that no one really knew Amanda's history, and a judge returned her children to her. Two months later, Amanda was arrested and accused of killing her three-year-old son. At this writing she was in prison awaiting trial on the homicide charge.

The press is also an element in the community. Events such as the Joseph Wallace case may be viewed as a "resource" for the press. Depending on the position the press takes, its news columns and editorials may be a resource for some actors and a toxin for others. In any event, a sustained story in the press creates turbulence in the environment, provoking new adaptations by other actors.

The Joseph Wallace case inspired many stories, editorials, and influential newspaper columns. One columnist called for a judge's resignation. The public defender, who had not objected to returning Joseph to his mother, called for the criminal prosecution of the caseworker because he believed she was derelict in not having assembled all the relevant information about Amanda. The social services department appointed a person to review what went wrong, and other investigations took place. The public defender argued that the culprit was the family preservation policy that encouraged the unwarranted return of children to unfit parents. He called for a change in the law from the family preservation policy to a "child's best interest" standard, arguing that this approach would give the judge more discretion and would result in better placements. The state legislature changed the law in Illinois.

The change in law grew out of emotional outrage over a child's death, but the new policy was not well conceived. First, it was not the standard that was at fault but rather the overburdened child protection system that imposed huge caseloads on child protection workers, lawyers, and judges. Second, the death of a child due to maltreatment remains a relatively rare event, with the incidence of deaths related to maltreatment estimated to be 1.94 per 100,000 of child population (McCurdy & Daro, 1993), and the change in law overlooked the problem of accurately predicting such low-frequency events. Knowing that child fatalities due to maltreatment are rare occurrences, simply on statistical grounds we can predict there will be a large number of inaccurate predictions. Thus, in trying to ensure the safety of a child, the decision maker will inevitably remove from their homes a great many children who could safely remain there and will be unwilling to return home a great number who will end up in foster care for longer periods than necessary.

The ecological view tells us that actors adapt to a new element in their environment, in this case a law that presumably offers greater discretion to the judge as decision maker. Judges are elected and are sensitive to public opinion, and the primary purpose of child protection workers is ensuring the safety of children. What new calculations in the mind of a judge or child protection worker result from the change in law? If either one allows a maltreated child to remain in the home and the child is harmed, he or she will come under great criticism, whether or not that is fair. However, anyone who recommends that the child be placed out of the home will not be subject to criticism. Similarly, if a judge or child protection worker recommends that a child in foster care be returned to the parent and the child is harmed, he or she will be criticized harshly, but if that person recommends that the child remain in the foster home, there is little chance of criticism.

This process of playing it safe was noted immediately after the law giving judges greater discretion to consider the child's best interests went into effect. The director of child welfare services in Chicago was quoted as saying, "Clearly, children are safer, because we're electing to take them into custody in more situations than we were before." However, child advocates in Chicago claimed that the system was becoming increasingly clogged with cases because judges appeared more reluctant to send children home from foster care.

Although the research hasn't yet been done, it is predictible that the net result of a policy adopted in response to emotional pressure will be to recreate the situation that led to the development of the earlier policy it replaced. In the present example, the new law will increase pressure on an already overburdened foster care system to absorb still more children.[8] Under pressure to provide for more children, social service officials will take less care in selecting, training, and supervising foster parents, with deleterious consequences for some children. Moreover, there is already considerable pressure on the child welfare system to find permanent adoptive homes for children when parental rights have been terminated and the children have been released for adoption. The change in law may make that problem worse. Although the "child's best interests" policy may allow legislators to express moral disapproval of the system's previous mistakes, in the absence of committing adequate resources to permit proper care of children the ecological analogy gives us some confidence in predicting that a symbolic gesture of this sort may well end up making things worse.

It is easy to offer examples of concepts. Such an exercise should not be mistaken for solid evidence of the validity of the concepts or of their utility in providing predictive guidelines. However, new concepts enable us to depart from conceptual ruts and to explore the universe of alternatives more thoroughly by encouraging us to roam over many different terrains in search of resources.

New concepts also ask us to view our research problems in a different way. The ecological viewpoint tells us that the behavior we observe may be at least in part an adaptation to a specific situation and thus that the behavior we see in the clinic or the laboratory may work itself out in quite a different fashion in another setting.

The ecological perspective poses different questions: How do members of different populations adapt to their environments? When a deviant (variant) individual comes to our clinical attention, is that an isolated aberration, or are we perforce directed toward examining the environment to see what other populations share the same space, and what nutrients are missing, and what toxins are present that might be removed? In this perspective, each variant case represents a class of phenomena that challenges our current level of understanding.

Ecology and Values

The ecological perspective asks us to examine the researcher's (or intervenor's) social values and perspective as well as his or her methods and concepts. Textbook writers in community psychology clearly believe the field's purpose is to serve the underdog. This desire reflects compassion and a sense of social justice. Rappaport (1977) wrote that the professional work of community psychology is directed toward the implementation of "a more equitable, just and fair society."

Those aims are frankly political. Viewing mental health issues in terms of the redistribution of power and money provides congruence between those writers' scientific interests and their personal and political values, and is also congruent with community psychology's origins in the Kennedy-Johnson War on Poverty. When public resources were allocated for the benefit of the underdog, the social justice concept attracted many social scientists whose values resonated with that idea. They saw an opportunity to fulfill, in professional roles, their personal social and political values.

Environmental explanations for the causes of social misery were then prominent (see Levine & Levine, 1992). It was easy to accept the argument that poverty and the evils attendant upon poverty were associated with lack of opportunity and the failure of social agencies to serve those in the poverty group. According to this viewpoint, schools, welfare agencies, employers, landlords, and police acted in concert to deny or to minimize opportunity. Chronic mental illness was attributed, at least in part, to hospitals that were inadequate to their task of healing and structured in a manner designed to perpetuate maladaptation. Goffman (1961), calling hospitals "total institutions," saw patient behavior as not entirely the result of psychosis but instead as an adaptation to life in the oppressive hospital. Szasz's (1963) attack on psychiatry as a threat to civil liberties added to the climate of the time. Championing social justice and the cause of the underdog could be accomplished through applications of science and enabled social scientists to fulfill in professional roles the values they held as persons and citizens.

The ecological analogy is consistent with the values of democracy and equality, for it directs us to value diversity (Rappaport, 1977). It asserts that while populations may look different from each other, culturally speaking, they are not different when viewed as products of adaptation.

The concept of adaptation to available resources leads us to think not of inferior persons but of persons whose characteristics must be understood in relation to the resources available in a niche, to their ability to extend niche breadth by adapting, and to the barriers to extending niche breadth due to competition from members of other populations. The ecological perspective stands in contrast to a hereditarian position that attributes variance in human behavior primarily to unchangeable genetic characteristics of individual organisms. Social ecology accepts that organismic characteristics set certain limits for development. Within those limits, however, the variance among organisms is strongly related to available resources and to necessary adaptations.

Just as a potted houseplant may be small while its brother in a tropical rain forest is huge, the ecological analogy suggests that the person in one setting, nurtured in one way and competing for resources, might have been different in another setting if nurtured differently or if given different cultural tools for adaptation. The problems and limitations we face reside not in people but in the ability of our imaginations to envision and create new settings. Scientific principles thus blend with personal values in a political argument for resource redistribution, and with an ideology that at once does not blame the victim (Ryan, 1971) and expresses hope for a brighter future.

Ecology and Practice

The ecological analogy led Levine (1969) to propose five principles of practice in community psychology:

1. *A problem arises in a setting or in a situation; factors in the situation cause, trigger, exacerbate, and/or maintain the problem.* This principle indicates that we cannot direct our "diagnostic" efforts exclusively toward describing the characteristics of the individual person. We have to understand the characteristics of settings as well. We need to look for a lack of fit between persons and environments, for environmental "toxins," and for the possibility that with different resources the individual's behavioral adaptation might be different. The principle also implies that we must leave our offices and learn to appreciate how problems are actually manifested in a given setting.

2. *A problem arises because the problem-resolving (i.e., adaptive) capacity of the social setting is blocked.* The ecological notion of interdependence implies that persons and settings function as parts of the same integrated system. A second principle implies that the adaptive capacity of people in a setting is limited in some ways by the nature of its social organization or its access to resources. If we ask workers in any human service setting to describe the problems they face in providing service to their clients, they will describe a number of problems. If we then ask for solutions to the problems, they will suggest a number of creative ones. If we ask further why

the solutions are not implemented, system problems will emerge. In effect, the principle states that a problem is that for which one does not have a solution. When one has a solution, adaptation will occur. Problems are thus understood differently from an ecological perspective. Because a problem requires adaptation, it is essentially an opportunity for short- and long-term change in the system.

3. *To be effective, help has to be located strategically to the manifestation of the problem.* This principle emphasizes the situational approach inherent in the ecological analogy. It suggests that we should alter our view of how help is to be delivered. Rather than send the person to the help, the principle suggests that we should bring help to the person or, more precisely, to the setting in which the person is defined as a problem. The term "strategically" can have temporal as well as spatial referents, which helps us to think of *when* in the course of the development of a problem it is useful to deliver assistance. The ecological analogy suggests that we examine environmental circumstances, while Dohrenwend's model (Chapter 3) introduces the dimension of time. This principle suggests that the design of helping services should make use of both the spatial and the temporal dimensions of a problem.

   Modern-day crisis intervention programs for the seriously and persistently mentally ill operate on this principle. Homebuilders (see Box 2-1) is a popular program for intervening in families where a child is at serious risk of being placed out of the home because of child abuse or neglect. The Homebuilder workers are on call twenty-four hours a day and go out to the family as necessary. Evaluation research shows that Homebuilders is successful in maintaining children in their own homes, even on follow-up a year later (Kinney, Haapala, & Booth, 1991).

   Kraft and DeMaio (1982) describe a program built on ecological principles and designed to work with adolescents from low-income families. The program offers family counseling, individual counseling, a group experience involving counseling and recreational activities, and consultation on a regular basis with social agency and school personnel. In other words, the intervention seeks to have a presence in each of the systems affecting the youth—home and family, neighborhood, and school. The various interventions support one another because the workers know what is happening in each setting where intervention occurs. Moreover, when the program ends, an aftercare arrangment can be developed that may include periodic family or group sessions, with the primary counselor continuously available to deal with periodic crises. Although no full evaluation was published, the group claims that after twenty-five months the participants in the program maintained consistent school attendance and appeared in court fewer times and that few of them had been institutionalized.

4. *The goals and values of the helping agent or service must be consistent with the goals and values of the setting.* Settings have both latent and manifest purposes. If the goals of change are consistent with the latent and the manifest purposes of the setting, the change process will not stimulate re-

sistance on those grounds. If the essential values of the change agent conflict with values in the setting, then the agent can expect opposition, including efforts to block the change or to extrude the agent. For example, a change agent may be able to justify on mental health and prevention grounds a course on sex education and the art of love, including supervised laboratory experiences. However, no high school in the country would allow such a program because of the conflict in values and goals that would be introduced. A change agent proposing such a project would undoubtedly be extruded from the setting, if not worse.

Some argue that conflict is essential to change and that conflict should be used consciously to induce change. That may be so. The error is in not anticipating conflict or in misunderstanding its basis. This principle cautions us to expect conflict with change.

The principle also requires the change agent to confront the potential conflict between his or her values and the values of those in a setting. Suppose, for example, that the Ku Klux Klan (KKK) wants help in improving communications among its own members so that it can more efficiently carry out attempts to terrorize or to intimidate various minority groups. It approaches a university center for help. Staff members might have the technical skills to help the KKK improve communication and develop as an organization. Should the center accept the assignment? Essentially the same problem is posed if the change agent is asked to help improve the adjustment of prisoners to an oppressive institution or of school children to a rigid or sterile school program or to help develop methods to uncover welfare mothers who may earn some extra money doing housework without reporting the income to the welfare worker. Change may be accomplished using knowledge and methods that appear to be value-free, but not all changes are equally desirable, and a request for help in achieving change may force the change agent to confront his or her own values (Sarason, 1978).

5. *The form of help should have potential for being established on a systematic basis, using the natural resources of the setting or by introducing resources that can become institutionalized as part of the setting.* This principle suggests that one should strive to understand the nature of resources and how a community cycles its resources. It implies that one would prefer to introduce a change that will endure and continue to help resolve problems in a particular setting. Using the ideas of interdependence and succession is the key to achieving truly long-term preventive effects through programs. Head Start is a good example of a program that became a permanent niche in its community, enabling parents and other citizens to become full participants (see Chapter 8).

These principles establish a framework for conceptualization and action in community psychology. They foreshadow a number of important issues that will be taken up in the chapters that follow, including assessment, intervention, community change, and research.

Summary

Community psychology is founded on a point of view perhaps best represented by the ecological analogy. This analogy is explicit in its endorsement of certain values and raises important implications regarding the conduct of scientific research. As a conceptual paradigm, ecology deals with units larger than the single individual, emphasizes natural settings rather than laboratories or clinics as the most valid and appropriate locus of intervention and research, and conceptualizes research as an ongoing, longitudinal collaboration between the researcher and the residents and settings of the community.

Four principles are fundamental to the ecological perspective. The first is that, because the people and settings within a community are interdependent, change occurs in a social system, not just an individual, and thus a variety of different problem definitions and solutions are possible in any situation. Second, community systems are defined by resource exchanges among persons and settings involving commodities such as time, money, and political power. Third, the behavior we observe in a particular individual always reflects a continuous process of adaptation between that individual, and his or her level of competence, and the environment, with the nature and range of competence it supports. Adaptation can thus proceed by changing the environment as well as the person. Fourth, change occurs naturally in a community, as well as by intentional design, and that change represents an opportunity to redefine and reallocate resources in ways that facilitate adaptation by all populations in the community.

We offered an extended illustration of these principles in describing how the deinstitutionalization of mental health consumers from hospitals to community settings forced law enforcement and justice officials to work alongside mental health professionals in unexpected ways and with unanticipated results. All parties concerned were affected, including the consumers and their families. The generality of the principles was suggested by a second detailed illustration concerning the consequences that followed the adoption of a new law affecting the placement of children at risk for maltreatment. The chapter closed by summarizing the values embodied in the ecological analogy and presenting five principles of practice derived from the metaphor of ecology.

We conclude on the point that the ultimate usefulness of the ecological analogy for theory, research, or intervention remains to be demonstrated. It is an analogy useful only at the most general level, and it has not yet been employed in rigorous study, even within its own terms. Not much has been done as yet in designing interventions using ecological principles, although some research (e.g., Kelly, 1979) has been reported on issues relevant to general questions in this field. Other conceptions and the research associated with them are examined in Chapter 5. Although in sum ecology remains largely a metaphor, it is a metaphor that may yet open our minds to new approaches to variety of problems.

Notes

1. See also Belsky (1980) and National Research Council (1993) for a discussion of the use of these concepts to guide research on child maltreatment.

2. Psychology broke away from philosophy in the late nineteenth century after the natural sciences had succeeded theology and the humanities as the dominant populations in the university community. The victory was so complete that the ideology of science and its language were adopted by traditional fields, even law (Auerbach, 1976). The justification for separating psychology from philosophy was that its mission, methods, and needs for laboratory space and scientific equipment differed from those of philosophy. By going into the laboratory and modeling their field on the physical sciences, psychologists concentrated on the individual and failed to study the individual in context.

3. Wandersman and Florin (1990) have published a set of insightful articles on how citizens may be empowered through cooperation and partnership with research workers.

4. The reaction against immigrants and affirmative action in California may well reflect the white majority's concerns about the changing composition of the population.

5. See also Lemann's (1991) history of the migration of southern African Americans to northern citiies in search of employment after agriculture was mechanized and the discussion in Box 4–2.

6. Arnhoff (1975) suggested a number of other unintended ecological consequences of mental health policies supporting care in the community. These include the effects on children of being reared by a psychotic parent in varying degrees of remission controlled by drugs. He also noted that persons who are hospitalized have low rates of reproduction and cited evidence that the policy of deinstitutionalization has resulted in an increase in both the in- and out-of-wedlock birth rates among mentally ill people. Moreover, if one accepts the concept of genetic risk, then the overall risk of mental illness is increased by having a larger number of individuals with a predisposition to mental illness reproducing. Arnhoff cited studies indicating that the policy of deinstitutionalization increases the amount of stress experienced by family members who are forced to cope with a disturbed person.

7. The courts have an obligation to determine a defendant's competence to stand trial any time the defense counsel, the prosecutor, or the judge raises a good faith doubt about such competence (ABA, Standard 7–4.2). There is no recent evidence on the point, but in the past the process of ascertaining competence was used as an alternative disposition to criminal charges. Some critics believed that prosecutors used incompetence as a pretext to hold against their will persons on whom the evidence to convict was weak (see *Jackson* v. *Indiana*, 1972).

8. In a period of eight days, in Connecticut, three small children were killed by their caretakers. The deaths "rocked the state." Within one month of these episodes the Social Service Department removed one hundred children from their parents' care, and between March and June, the number of children in foster care rose from 14,500 to 16,700. The Social Service Department appointed an investigation panel and conducted an internal review of five thousand cases. Several child protection caseworkers and their supervisors were disciplined or demoted for "sloppy work." Some observers claim that because of cautiousness workers are slower in processing cases and that the severe shortage of foster care homes has been made worse. One judge believed that more cases were coming in with insufficient evidence to warrant taking a child into custody (McLarin, 1995).

5

Three Psychological Conceptions of the Environment

Perceived Social Climates

Behavior Settings

Social Roles

    Box 5-1. The Fairweather Lodge

Postscript: What Role Remains for Individual Differences?

Summary

In Chapter 4 we concluded that the ecological perspective on human behavior has important theoretical and political implications for community
psychologists. The five principles of intervention we used in summarizing the ecological analogy, however, are more abstract than specific. The
metaphor of ecology tells us to recognize and attend to alternatives, for
example, without directly helping us identify what those alternatives are.
Scientific advances and effective practical applications will require sharper
conceptualization of the operational units making up human environments than was provided by Kelly's pioneering work.

    What details are left out of the orientation provided by the five prin-
ciples of intervention? Principles I and II (Chapter 4) propose that problems and their solutions be defined in situational terms. This implies a
need to identify explicitly the specific characteristics of situations that are
relevant to problems of adaptation. By what mechanisms do settings facilitate changes in behavior? By what processes does a person adapt to a

setting (or vice versa)? Theoretical conceptions are needed that offer more detailed descriptions of these effects.

Our classification schemes for settings are crude. Labels such as "foster home" or "group home" tell us little about size, staffing, rehabilitative focus, or quality of care. They also reveal little about the program or about how the program facilitates or impedes the development of helpful relationships between staff and resident. Such settings as schools (Sarason & Klaber, 1985) or Head Start preschools are not uniform by any means. If settings of a similar kind produce different outcomes for children, what characteristics of settings account for the difference? If we believe in the concept of a person-environment fit, then how can we characterize settings so that we can evaluate who would do better in one setting than in another? Settings are also occupied by people who have a different relationship to it. Leader, members, children, teachers, and research workers all have different relationships, different objectives for participating, and, very likely, different views of what goes on in the setting. Settings also change from time to time. How can we understand, track, and evaluate changes in the characteristics of settings?

These questions are useful in setting the stage for a review of some current conceptions of the psychological environment. The present chapter focuses on three of the best-known conceptions—Moos's "perceived social climate" approach, Roger Barker's "behavior-setting theory," and Theodore Sarbin's "role theory." Each perspective is reviewed, after which the community lodge program developed by George W. Fairweather and his associates is presented and used to illustrate the perspectives in practical terms.

Perceived Social Climates

Henry Murray's seminal work on personality theory (Murray, 1938) presented a model of behavior based on relative degrees of fit between what he called individual *needs*, for example the need to achieve or to affiliate with others, and environmental *presses*. Presses refer to characteristics of a setting that make it more likely that a need will be facilitated or impeded. Considerable effort has gone into developing instruments, such as the Personality Research Form (Jackson, 1965), that measure the individual personality needs identified by Murray. It remained to Moos and his associates (Moos, 1976), however, to develop a corresponding set of scales assessing the behavioral presses of key community environments.

The underlying assumptions of Moos's approach are that (1) we can think of environments as having "personalities," such as achievement-oriented, interpersonally supportive, or controlling, and (2) these setting personalities can be measured using the same methods used to assess the personalities of people. In Moos's approach one simply asks the participants in a given setting to respond "true" or "false" to a set of declarative statements describing what it is like to be in that setting. The responses of all participants are then averaged to obtain a single profile (generally presented in terms of standard scores) describing the "perceived social climate" of the setting. These measures are a way of objectifying the characteristic responses people make to that environment (Kiritz & Moos, 1974).

Recognizing that such quantitative information would be useful for a broad range of natural community settings, Moos and his colleagues have developed specific social climate scales for psychiatric wards, community-oriented programs, family environments, work settings, classrooms, residence halls, military organizations, correctional facilities, and sheltered care settings for the elderly.

Moos believes that the key psychological aspects of any human environment are represented in three dimensions in all perceived social climate measures: *relationship-oriented dimensions, personal-development dimensions*, and *system-maintenance and change dimensions*. The specific subscales, or dimensions of environmental press, vary somewhat in the instruments used to measure perceived social climate in a family, in a work setting, or in a psychiatric ward. In the Family Environment Scale, for example, the specific relationship dimensions include *cohesiveness* (e.g., "Family members really help and support one another") and *conflict* ("We fight a lot in our family"); the personal development dimensions include *independence* ("Family members almost always rely on themselves when a problem comes up") and *achievement* ("We feel it is important to be the best at whatever you do"); the system dimensions are *organization* ("Activities in our family are pretty carefully planned") and *control* ("There is a strong emphasis on following rules in our family").

Considerable data have been accumulated on the construct validity of Moos's scales (see Moos, 1976, 1987). Occupants of settings high in relationship-oriented dimensions, for example, show high satisfaction and self-esteem, low anxiety, depression, and irritability (Moos, 1976), and low amounts of physical complaints (Moos & Van Dort, 1979). Members of settings high in personal-development dimensions have more positive attitudes and higher skill acquisition, but in some cases they also exhibit greater tension (Trickett & Moos, 1974). A complex stimulus such as a school classroom can have unwanted as well as wanted effects. In schools, high order and clarity on the systems and maintenance dimension is associated with high satisfaction, while high degrees on the control dimension are associated with dissatisfaction and other negative outcomes.

Moos's social-climate scales have several useful applications in community psychology. One of these is to clearly describe and compare settings. For example, although mutual help groups are believed by their advocates to serve some of the same functions as professionally led therapy groups, do these groups differ from each other? Toro, Rappaport, and Seidman (1987) compared profiles from Moos's Group Environment Scale for thirty-three mutual help groups in the GROW organization (see Chapter 9) with those of twenty-five insight-oriented, professionally led therapy groups serving the same general clientele. GROW groups were perceived as more structured, task-oriented, and cohesive than professionally led therapy groups, while the latter were more flexible and more tolerant of members' expressions of anger and other intense emotions. Clarifying such differences in focus between helping alternatives can assist our understanding and may facilitate more appropriate referrals.

As an example of classification, consider the increasing visibility and importance of sheltered care settings (nursing homes, congregate apartments) for the elderly. Because sheltered care settings differ in relevant social climate characteristics, Lemke and Moos (1987) developed the Sheltered Care Environment Scale as a practical, efficient method of assessing relationships, personal growth, and system maintenance and change dimensions in such settings. Timko and Moos (1991) analyzed Sheltered Care Environment Scale profiles from a national sample of 235 nursing homes, residential care facilities, and congregate apartments, identifying six distinct types of social climate in these settings. Two of these climates, both labeled "supportive," differed primarily in how much resident influence existed; two other types of climates emphasized "conflict" (one allowed open conflict and one tended to suppress conflict). Figure 5–1

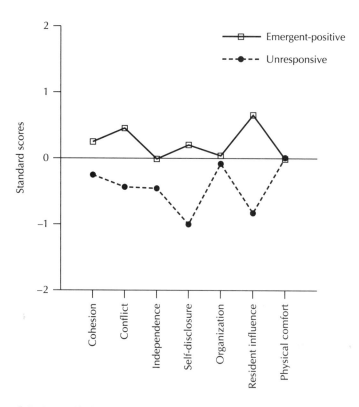

Figure 5–1. Mean Sheltered Care Environment profiles for emergent-positive and unresponsive facility clusters. (From Timko & Moos, 1991)

compares the profiles for the remaining two types of settings, identified by Timko and Moos as "emergent-positive" and "unresponsive."

The climate in the emergent-positive settings is high in resident influence and emphasizes cohesion, conflict, and open disclosure of personal feelings. By comparison, the climate of unresponsive settings puts relatively little emphasis on resident influence, independence, and self-disclosure and thus is low in responsiveness to residents' preferences. Emergent-positive and unresponsive facilities were both more likely to be nursing homes than less intensive kinds of care providers, did not differ in either typical size or nature of ownership, and were perceived by residents as average in degree of organization and physical comfort. However, residents in emergent-positive facilities scored higher on measures of well-being than did residents in unresponsive settings. These findings support the importance of factors such as resident self-direction. They also show the advantage of using comprehensive profiles rather than relying on single dimensions (such as physical comfort) to assess programs.

Another intriguing implication of the Timko and Moos (1991) findings is that the psychological environments of thousands of different sheltered care settings all over the country are meaningfully reducible to six general types. Investigators studying new programs or supportive interventions, for example, can control for important psychological characteristics of the residential milieu in which the programs are tested simply by sampling representatively from each type of setting.

A second practical application of the perceived social climate approach is in evaluating the effects of consultation services or other interventions. A useful tactic at the outset of consultation, for example, is to have setting participants complete the relevant social climate scale twice, once as they currently perceive the setting and again as they would ideally like it to be. The two profiles can then be compared. Any disparities between them indicate characteristics of the psychological environment that deserve attention. Consultation sessions can then be devoted to discovering what influences the disparities and how change might be achieved. Later the scale can be readministered as a method of evaluating the outcome of consultation. If both real and ideal forms are again used, any remaining real-ideal discrepancies can form the basis for further consultation.

DeYoung (1977), for example, administered real and ideal forms of the Classroom Environment Scale (CES) to an undergraduate social science class. Discrepancies between the real and the ideal profiles indicated that students wanted to be more involved in the class, experience more innovative teaching methods, and understand more clearly the organization of the course and the instructor's expectations. The next term DeYoung modified the course to include more individual contact with students, a more explicit grading policy, and group projects and other innovative forms of classroom participation by students. He readministered the real and the ideal forms of the CES to evaluate the effect of the changes. Although the ideal climate did not change noticeably from one term to the next, students' perceptions of the actual classroom environment more closely resembled the ideal profile on each of the specific dimensions targeted for intervention. Furthermore, the changes during the second term were associated with greater student interest, participation, and attendance.

A third use of Moos's scales is in setting selection to maximize person-environment fit, for example, when deciding on a residential placement for someone with special needs. People who have serious mental illness represent a diverse population, but the community-based group homes are not standardized by any means. Differences in size, structure, programming, and social climate may have significant implications for the levels and sources of stress and support experienced by people living in them.

Downs and Fox (1993) obtained responses to Moos's Community-Oriented Programs Environment Scale (COPES) from staff members at forty-nine diverse group homes for adults with mental illness. They used a statistical technique called cluster analysis to categorize the forty-nine homes into four groups on the basis of differences among the COPES profiles. On these measures, the first group, or cluster, of homes provided little support, structure, and staff involvement to individual residents, while those in the second cluster tended to be stimulating and goal-oriented for residents. Cluster 3 homes supported spontaneous expressions of feeling among residents without granting them a great deal of autonomy, and Cluster 4 homes were highly structured but did not provide programs for the personal development of residents.

Given these systematic variations among homes in social climates, choice of a group home placement might usefully be based on the fit between a prospective resident's needs and the social climates of available homes. For example, a goal-oriented person tolerant of high levels of stimulation would probably respond better to a Cluster 2 home than a Cluster 1 home, while an outspoken resident who had difficulty dealing with structure would adapt more easily to a Cluster 3 home than a Cluster 4 home. Similarly, a setting high on the personal development dimension might appeal to a young college student recovering from mental illness but might distress a much older person who wished to be left alone. Measurement using the COPES makes it possible to base a residential placement on the fit between a resident's personality and a home's social climate, as well as on relevant physical characteristics such as the home's size and location.

Last, perceived social-climate scales can be used in the planning and creation of new settings in the community. Those responsible for developing a new mental health center program, for example, could use the COPES to develop a shared conception of what the optimum social climate in the new setting would be. The ecological prescription that all points of view be represented in the data used to understand a setting could be addressed by obtaining separate profiles from line workers, supervisors, members of the administrative support staff, and other workers.

Settings can be designed to accomplish certain purposes by thinking through the desirable organization according to the COPES dimensions. If staff "burnout" is likely to be a problem, for example, a high degree of interpersonal support among staff members will be desirable. Regular meetings of a peer support group made up of program staff to enhance the relationship aspects of the setting might be planned for the program right from the start. Once the new program is under way, the COPES might then be readministered as a means of evaluating the social climate present in the setting and guiding adjustments in the program as necessary.

Moos's perceived social climate concept has many practical applications. Its chief advantage over other approaches is probably the ease with which the relevant information can be collected and interpreted (the ninety-item full-length scales require only about twenty minutes to complete). However, to answer the items meaningfully, the respondents must have regular face-to-face contact, and the number of respondents must not be too large (no more than twenty to twenty-five) so that the group profile is not attenuated by excess error variance. Of course, the profiles generated by these instruments are not objective descriptions of the environment. They are products of specific circumstances and events, respondents' roles or positions in the setting, and respondents' personal beliefs and values (Lemke & Moos, 1987).

Setting taxonomies are being developed using this concept, although the focus thus far has been on types of settings such as psychiatric wards (Price & Moos, 1975), high school classrooms (Trickett, 1978), and special residential programs, instead of on the spatial and temporal distribution of setting climates as they occur in people's lives. In general, this view presents one of the clearest illustrations available of how psychologists can take seriously the need to assess and understand characteristics of key community environments as well as of the people inhabiting them. It assists people in "tuning in" to the social climates surrounding them (Moos, 1979). From an ecological perspective, it takes seriously the perceptions and experiences of rank-and-file participants in a setting or program and helps empower people to participate more widely in the process of community assessment and change (Vincent & Trickett, 1983).

Behavior Settings

If Moos conceives of the psychological environment much as a personality theorist does, Roger Barker might be said to have viewed it more as a behavioral psychologist does—that is, with an emphasis on physical and behavioral characteristics that are directly observable and objectively definable. Barker (1968) realized that most human behavior is not randomly distributed across space and time but instead occurs in consistent patterns of regularly scheduled activities that he called "behavior settings." Everyday examples of such settings include school classrooms, stores, government offices, playgrounds, and even sidewalks. For Barker, an important characteristic of every setting is the set of "standing" behavior patterns that define the nature and meaning of that setting regardless of its occupants (e.g., singing hymns in a church, sunbathing at the beach). In fact, the essence of any behavior setting resides in the relationship between these behaviors and the characteristics of the setting's physical and temporal milieu (Barker, 1968). In most classrooms, for example, the chairs, desks, blackboards, and open spaces are uniquely constructed and arranged to facilitate performance of the standing behaviors in that setting—speaking, listening, sitting, and writing.

Behavior-setting theory includes two key assumptions. First, the individuals who perform in a given setting are thought to be more or less interchangeable. Even a complete turnover in participants does not change the activities one would see in that setting. In Barker's conception, then, the psychological environment is defined independent of the people in it, which is not the case in Moos's approach.

Second, it is a key assumption that settings themselves generate the forces necessary for their own maintenance and survival (Barker, 1968). Behavior settings are seen to possess "forces" that, in the interest of keeping the setting going (homeostasis), impel their occupants to perform the standing behavior patterns and conform to setting programs. These homeostatic forces are organized into several formats, including:

1. *Program circuits*, which represent the agenda connecting people to the required sequence of behavior patterns. In a church service, for example, the congregation stands or sits in unison at the appropriate times (e.g., for singing or prayer), as indicated by the organized ceremony of worship. In a classroom children do seat work and recite when called upon, while in gym class they play games organized in terms of specific programs of actions and rules. Even long-term patients in mental hospitals will eat when brought to a dining room.

2. *Goal circuits*, which represent the confluence of participants' individual needs with specific experiences or products provided by the setting. The motivations of those attending a church service, for example, are typically congruent with the specific kinds of social and spiritual satisfactions such a setting provides. Similarly, the effectiveness of a school is partly based on the assumption that children are motivated to learn what the school is teaching. Problems can arise when a child is "unmotivated," i.e., does not actively engage the program circuits provided by school settings.

3. *Deviation-countering circuits*, which reduce or eliminate behavior that deviates from the program. A baby crying loudly during a wedding ceremony elicits prompt efforts by those nearby to quiet the child. A child who ignores assigned seat work to get up and wander about the classroom brings an admonishment from the teacher to rejoin the setting program. A person who eats in a library will be asked to stop. Even a celebrity

who hires a prostitute to participate in an "obscene act" will be stopped and arrested when the act is performed in public, as was the British actor Hugh Grant.

4. *Veto circuits*, which result in the ejection of a nonconforming occupant from the setting. The crying baby who cannot be quieted during a solemn ceremony will usually be ushered quickly away from the setting; a child who repeatedly refuses a teacher's direct admonition may find himself banished to the principal's office, suspended, or, in an extreme case, expelled from school (see Barker, 1968, pp. 167–185). Willie Bosket, who was very young when he was convicted of murder, is serving a life sentence and cannot be ejected from the maximum security prison in which he resides. However, because he continues to be dangerous and attacks corrections officers, he is kept in isolation, a form of ejection in that setting.

Roosens's (1979) description of the community experiences of people with chronic mental illness living in Geel, Belgium, offers many examples of these homeostatic setting forces. Geel has a long-standing practice of paying local families to board people with serious mental illness, who are called "boarders." Recognizing boarders' aspirations to be as normal as possible and the benefits that come from participating in community settings (goal circuits), townspeople have allowed boarders a reasonable degree of integration into everyday town life. Given many boarders' limitations, however, integration is most evident in settings having programs that require only a few simple responses of participants (e.g., parades, church worship services). In general, integration is accomplished through "trial and error"—behavior that deviates from the setting program (e.g., playing a radio and pelting others in the audience with popcorn while at a movie theater) is tolerated up to a point but sanctioned via correction or removal if it becomes too disruptive to the setting program.

Given the uniformity of behavior expected within most settings, the Geel example illustrates why people find it so easy to attribute noticeable deviations from a setting's program to significant person-centered deficits such as mental illness, drunkenness, or mental retardation. This active, even coercive influence of settings on behavior is known as "behavior-environment congruence." The concept has important practical and theoretical implications for eliciting and maintaining specific changes in human behavior (Barker, 1968; Wicker, 1972).

People establish settings and the norms of behavior in settings. When we speak of settings, we assume human agency. The processes or mechanisms by which settings coercively influence participants' behavior are not well understood, although one kind of internal homeostatic mechanism operating within program circuits is thought to be the degree of "underpopulation" present (Schoggen, 1989). Underpopulation concerns the effects of various numbers of occupants in a setting relative to the optimal number for that setting; it grew out of Barker and Wright's (1955) behavior-setting survey of a town in Kansas (pseudonym "Midwest"). Barker and Schoggen (1973) subsequently extended the survey to a town in Yorkshire, England (pseudonym "Yoredale"). In 1953–1954, they identified 884 settings in the town of Midwest (population 830). Yoredale (population 1,310) contained only 758 settings.

Barker's theory assumes that people want to continue settings. Barker and Schoggen (1973) interpreted these differences in settings compared to population size to indicate that settings in Midwest, the smaller community, faced greater overall threats to their continued existence. Using their theoretical language, they said that people in the smaller community strengthened their program and goal circuits, relaxed their deviation-countering and veto circuits, and in the process effectively "pulled" more behavior from their occupants than did the settings in Yoredale. What this means is that with more settings, the smaller number of people residing in Midwest of necessity participated more often and for longer lengths of time in the town's public activities. Barker and Schoggen also believed that because of the greater importance and responsibility given each resident of Midwest, social distinctions were less sharp than in Yoredale.

Subsequent comparisons among small, "underpopulated" and larger, "overpopulated" high schools in Kansas showed that, on the average, students from small schools participated in more school settings, assumed more positions of responsibility, and expressed a greater "sense of obligation" to their schools than did students from large schools (Barker & Gump, 1964). Other research supported the predictions in churches of different sizes (Wicker, 1979) and in several laboratory-based experiments (e.g., Perkins, 1982; Wicker, 1979).

This dimension of underpopulation may provide new insights into how environments can be described and their effects on behavior understood. One study concluded that no relationship exists between size of residence and resident outcome. However, as a measure, the number of residents is too crude to be useful. From Barker's viewpoint, the relevant characteristic is not number of residents but the number of residents per setting or activity (Perkins & Baker, 1991). The lower this ratio (i.e., the more underpopulated the settings are), the higher will be the average level of satisfaction reported by residents.

We can think about deliberately creating underpopulated settings to widen the niche breadth (see Chapter 4) of at-risk populations. People in underpopulated settings may welcome participation by a wider range of persons. Sarason et al. (1977) argue that, in theory, participants in underpopulated settings develop a psychological sense of community. We apply this concept and other aspects of behavior setting theory in our discussion of mutual help groups (Chapter 9).

Some observations are inconsistent with the theoretical expectations derived from the concept of underpopulation. For some settings, fewer than the optimal number of occupants apparently does not produce greater satisfaction. Whyte (1980), for example, found that certain public settings in smaller communities (i.e., those considered more underpopulated by Barker) are generally less successful psychologically than similar settings in large cities. The best solution is for the smaller communities to "compress" or "concentrate" public spaces and the people in them to a much greater degree (p. 92)—that is, to make them more *over*populated. The physical arrangements are also important. Whyte's (1980) observations of urban plazas pointed to the importance of easy access, movable seating, good lighting, and opportunities to eat and drink and also to the aesthetic value of trees and water (e.g., a fountain) for creating satisfied users. Successful community central points serve to foster participation by the largest number of different community groups. Unstructured, informal contact among people (i.e., visual and/or verbal, with no particular commitment to any strictly defined setting program) facilitates communication (e.g., news, gossip), social support, and, ultimately, the establishment and maintenance of a strong sense of community.

The importance of the number of participants may have more to do with the overall purpose of the setting for its occupants. For some settings (e.g., parades, political conventions), whose purpose is to bring together large numbers of people, the optimal number of participants may be quite large, regardless of the number of different roles available. Consider that the purpose of a bar is to sell drinks. A lone person sitting at a bar is in an "underpopulated" setting. The person may nurse the drink for a long time. When the bar is filled (overpopulated), the customers will call for more drinks. Thus, people fulfill the purpose of the setting more when it is crowded than when it is not. At least one other dimension is necessary to understand how the over- or underpopulation concept predicts behavior.

Behavior-setting theory has made two fundamental contributions to community psychology. First, it provides an environmental "unit of analysis" for the description and assessment of human behavior on situational and community levels. The behavior setting is a naturally occurring unit in the environment. Behavior settings are discrete, relatively stable, and "objective in the sense that they exist independent of anyone's perception of them" (Barker & Schoggen, 1973, p. 9). People live their lives in behavior settings (Wicker, 1979), and in this sense they are important to our understanding of what influences people's actions and feelings.

Furthermore, although any individual setting may have only limited impact on a given person or community, Barker and Schoggen (1973) showed how settings can be aggregated systematically to measure the psychological character of a community. These concepts are complex and are expressed in the researchers' special language. One, the habitat concept, is rather broad, but by using it the community psychologist can accomplish the behavioral assessment of an entire community by cataloging its settings. The methods of behavior-setting theory thus make possible a systematic, comprehensive assessment of the specific behavioral opportunities provided in a given community. Furthermore, the settings available to particular subgroups, such as children, the elderly, and deinstitutionalized mental health consumers, can be compared with the specific behavioral needs of these groups (e.g., for health care or social services) in order to provide sharper and more detailed assessments of how habitable a given community is for specific groups. Behavior-setting theory thus provides a range of progressively inclusive units of analysis, from a single activity (setting), a specific kind of activity (genotype), and a general sphere of community life (habitat) to an entire community (a collection of habitats). Aggregates of communities and even larger units are also possible in theory, providing a basis for systems of social and behavioral accounting on a macroeconomic scale (Schoggen, 1989).

Second, the behavior-setting theory concepts of behavior-environment congruence and underpopulation provide a way of thinking about how environmental settings may affect changes in behavior across different settings in the person's life (Levine & Perkins, 1980b). Because behavior is a property of settings as well as of people, it provides a basis for direct examinations of person-environment fit, including the process by which people acquire new behaviors when participating in new settings. For example, preschool children develop preventive "interpersonal cognitive problem solving skills" by actively participating in gamelike settings where the specific behavior pattern emphasizes *how* to think, not *what* to think, in solving interpersonal problems (Spivack & Shure, 1974; see Chapter 8). Similarly, the mechanism of underpopulation is exploited when mutual help groups are replicated in a target area using a procedure Zimmerman and others (1991) call the "Johnny Appleseed" approach (i.e., convening the minimum number of participants required to fill necessary positions and letting the benefits of underpopulation—flexible roles, sense of importance, and so on—accrue; see Chapter 9).

Practical applications of the behavior-setting approach have focused on such problems as (1) assessing the range of therapeutic behavioral opportunities available to high-risk populations, such as persons with serious mental illness (Perkins & Baker, 1991; Perkins & Perry, 1985; Dewart & Hoover, 1994) and the residents of inner-city housing projects (Bechtel, 1977); (2) intervening to reduce problems of overcrowding in popular national parks (Wicker, 1979); and (3) evaluating the behavioral and environmental effects on a community of creating an artificial lake nearby (Harloff, Gump, & Campbell, 1981). With respect to behavior settings for persons with mental illness, Perkins and Baker (1991) developed a simplified behavior-setting assessment procedure that they validated on large samples of supervised community residences and program activities for mental health consumers. Perkins and Baker then evaluated these settings in terms of their appropriateness for client needs, especially self-care skills and other functional competencies.

Barker's comprehensive community focus also helps us recognize important settings that may not be available to mental health consumers, such as paid employment or opportunities to live in housing that is fully integrated with that of nondisabled people. Like anyone else, people with special needs should have access to neighborhoods or work sites that include public gathering places (e.g., parks, public libraries, break areas) to facilitate their participation in community life and neighbors' or coworkers' awareness and acceptance of them.

Behavior-setting theory offers an approach to the evaluation of the concept of the "least restrictive setting," an important idea when assessing the legal rights of mental health consumers. In practice the determination of restrictiveness rests on rather crude distinctions, such as living in the community rather than in a hospital or in one's own apartment rather than in a supervised group home. A group home, however, while often less restrictive than a hospital, may still be rather "institutional" in the behavior patterns it requires of staff and residents (Mowbray, Greenfield, & Freddolino, 1992). An apartment may lack restrictiveness but provide little stimulation or support. Behavior-setting theory allows for a more specific and substantive determination of behavioral restrictiveness and focuses our attention on such questions as, What is it like to live in this residence? in this neighborhood? How do people here spend their time? What are they learning? Implicit in this view is the belief that, with the right resources, natural settings should offer sufficient supports to help consumers acquire and maintain the living and working skills needed for a satisfying life in the community.

Focusing on specific subpopulations raises the issue of diversity. One basis for dealing with diversity descriptively is Barker and Schoggen's (1973) concept of "habitat-inhabitant bias" (pp. 381–397). The concept is a way of quantifying the observation that people are not distributed randomly among community settings. The degree of bias for any population subgroup in the community (e.g., infants, African Americans, women) is the extent to which the mean occupancy time of that subgroup in a given habitat varies from that of the population as a whole. This latter value is arbitrarily taken to be 100, and subgroup bias is expressed as a percentage of 100. Thus the bias for females in Midwest's "primary business habitat" was 87 in 1963–1964, while that for males was 103 (Barker & Schoggen, 1973, p. 387). Although systematic and quantitative, this concept implies nothing about the process of person-environment selection or the psychological significance of such a difference. As a result, behavior-setting theory has yet to integrate meaningfully any individual difference factors, even those based solely on overt behavior, into a working model of the community.

Behavior-setting theory is limited in another way. It has no terms that allow one to predict or explain changes in setting. The theory is *ahistorical.* Starting, stopping, and maintaining a setting cannot even be fully described, let alone understood, without reference to factors external to it and without formal consideration of the purposes that setting serves.

One theme of this chapter, and the preceding one, is that preventive and therapeutic changes in individual behavior reflect processes of person-setting interaction and fit. What may prove more useful for community psychology than Barker's descriptive concept of habitat-inhabitant bias may be looking for ways to link persons and settings systematically, using dimensions that are directly comparable to each other, such as the behavioral repertoire of the person and the set of standing behaviors required of that person by key community settings. Perkins and Perry (1985), for example, empirically derive several dimensions of behavioral "demandingness" for use in assessing the settings of a community residence for mental health consumers. (Among the high-demand settings in this residence were playing bridge and holding a business meeting, while gardening and attending a speaker's lecture were relatively low-demand settings.) When combined with similar information on the behavioral capacities and skills of the residents themselves, such information allows psychologists to estimate the fit or lack of fit between patients and settings, with significant implications for patients' long-term adaptation to community life (Anthony, Cohen, & Vitalo, 1978).

Barker also overlooked characteristics of the setting program. A setting is not just "out there" in the environment; its program also resides inside the heads of its occupants (Schoggen, 1989). Moreover, maladaptive behavior at work and in other public settings by persons with serious mental illness or retardation might be understood and dealt with in terms of their lack of relevant cognitive scripts. You have to know how to participate and be motivated to do so. Some settings, for example, such as fast-food restaurants, have programs that are so straightforward or familiar that almost everyone behaves appropriately, while others, such as working efficiently with a complicated new computer system, require considerably more preparation. Understanding the interaction of setting characteristics with the cognitive scripts or schemas held by occupants may help to shed light on the process of setting creation and change.

Behavior-setting research is evolving away from the study of entire communities toward more in-depth investigation of single genotypes (Sommer & Wicker, 1991), such as mutual help groups, block organizations, and prevention programs. Why do some settings thrive while other, similar settings struggle and fail? Luke, Rappaport, and Seidman (1991) suggested that a better understanding of setting "phenotypes" (i.e., differences in the pattern of "behavioral regularities" characteristic of different settings within a type) would increase behavior setting theory's usefulness in answering such questions. To illustrate this point, they studied thirteen different GROW mutual help groups (see Chapter 9), all derived from the same genotype, and found that they exhibited significant variation in the frequencies with which important behavior patterns occurred. This elaboration has the potential to enrich our functional understanding of settings to the point where effective community interventions (e.g., mutual help group phenotypes tailored specifically to currently underserved populations) can be developed and disseminated more reliably and efficiently.

Barker's work is ecological in its emphasis on the interdependence of environments and their human participants. It is also ecological in method (see Chapter 4). Barker's example of nonintrusive, empirical, community-based research strongly influenced later community psychologists such as Kelly (1990) and Price (1990). Although its potential usefulness to community psychology is thus considerable, behavior-setting theory remains in need of further development (Perkins, Burns, Perry, & Nielsen, 1988). Especially needed at this point are units of analysis that fit both the individual and the surrounding social context. Such a unit is the basis of role theory, the concept we consider next.

Social Roles

The concept of role provides another heuristic basis for defining the relationship between an individual person and his or her social environment. The concept may be more useful in diagnosing problems of adaptation and in designing interventions than concepts centered on individuals (Sarbin, 1970). Role theory is also a useful bridge between the discussion of the basic ecological analogy in community psychology and our analysis of labeling theory in Chapter 6.

Sarbin introduces his version of role theory by arguing that *environment* is too vague a construct to be useful for community psychologists. The concept of *setting* is somewhat more defined but lacks a social dimension. In Sarbin's view the environment is a set of differentiated "ecologies" within which people must correctly locate themselves to survive and to thrive. He identifies four ecologies: *self-maintenance*, *social* (or the role system), *normative*, and *transcendental*.

To survive as a biosocial organism, an individual must recognize the difference between friend and foe, between the edible and the poisonous, between potentially hostile and potentially benign circumstances. Upon encountering a new object or person, an individual quickly runs through such questions as: Should I run from, attack, or ignore this new object? Can I play with it, eat it, have sex with it, or make use of it in some other fashion? In addition to cognitive and perceptual reality testing, social reality testing is also necessary. Are the social conditions appropriate for the activity I would like to select? Am I the appropriate person to engage in such activities in this situation? Incorrect answers to these questions result in dysfunctional conduct and, if sufficiently severe, some segregation of the individual—to a mental hospital, an institution for the retarded, or a prison. We believe that correct answers to these questions depend on appropriate socialization and education and on an intact, or at least not too severely impaired, organism.

The second ecology, related to the first, is the social ecology, or role system. The question to be answered is, "Who am I in relation to you, in this situation?" A man is king if others bow down and recognize his authority. If he calls himself king and others do not recognize his authority, under many circumstances he is considered a madman. Role relationships are reciprocal. Answers to the question "Who am I in relation to you?" or to the question, asked by another, "Who are you?" define one's social identity. Failures (in terms of one's behavior) to answer these questions properly (that is, in accord with mutual expectations) lead to conflict and breakdown in social relationships. When Alfred Kinsey and his colleagues were interviewing thousands of Americans about their sex histories, one of Kinsey's interviewers appeared in a young psychology intern's office when the intern expected a psychotherapy client. This particular "client" turned the normal therapy relationship upside down by interrogating the therapist about intimate details of the therapist's sex life, an experience that reportedly sent this novice therapist screaming from the office.

Entrance into and recognition of appropriate roles depend on adequate socialization and also on adequate opportunity. Social rules—gender, racial discrimination, or stigma—may prevent some individuals from entering some roles or from receiving acceptance in those roles. Changing social rules, by changing laws, by engaging in conflict and confrontation, or by changing incentives, can open up a greater variety of roles for those who were formerly denied them. In addition to examining the socialization of people for particular roles, Sarbin's position allows us to examine the opportunities for entering into given roles as well and to work to change those rules.

. The third ecology is the normative. Here one asks how *well* one is meeting the particular requirements of a given role. The answer "Not too well" is often accompanied by low self-esteem, and the answer "Pretty good" by a more positive sense of satisfaction. The answers to these questions are based partly on self-evaluations and partly on the feedback received from others. For example, even experienced college teachers sometimes feel, on the basis of their own expectations or the behavior and attitudes shown by their students, that a course or a particular lecture is not going well. A perception that such difficulties are occurring more and more frequently may encourage the instructor to avoid that material or that course in the future or may even cause the professor to consider retirement.

Attributions for the "cause" of failure may vary. Under some circumstances people engage in self-blame; under others they see cause of failure residing in factors beyond their control. At one and the same time, an individual may believe that the cause of failure (or success) resides in his or her own efforts, even while an external observer views the cause as situational in nature. The reverse may also be true, of course. We must recognize the implications of different perspectives, for the solution chosen will depend on how the problem is defined. How we perceive and value our accomplishments or devalue ourselves for real or perceived failures depends in part on the normative framework we adopt. It may also depend on the system of values we hold, and that system of values in turn depends in substantial part on our participation in social relationships with others who share those values. We shall see how those issues work themselves out when we examine self-help groups in Chapter 9.

Sarbin's fourth ecology, called transcendental ecology, consists of abstractions that give meaning to life. For some people, the important abstraction is the relationship to a deity. For others, it may be existential issues: Given that death is inevitable, how am I spending my life? For still others at different ages, the question may be one of integrity, to use Erikson's (1950) term—the acceptance of one's lifestyle and the willingness to defend it against attack by others or by the vicissitudes of life. In other words, we need to achieve and maintain a sense of order, meaning, and continuity to our experiences. We gain that sense through a set of beliefs that help us come to terms with ourselves and with events in the world. One of the important outcomes of participating in a mutual assistance group is the development of a way of thinking about one's condition (that is, an ideology) and a concrete program for coping with everyday problems (e.g., a twelve-step program). Such beliefs are best developed and maintained by our participation in social groups, and to be part of a group means one has a role within that group. One may be born into the role, as a family member, one may choose to participate in it, as a member of a political party; or one may earn a position within a group through accomplishment and effort.

People continually strive to locate themselves within the four ecologies. Everyone has many roles and participates in many different social groups. Furthermore, the nature of most behavior in social settings is much more a function of the given roles being performed than of the individuals performing them (Katz & Kahn, 1966). Over the sum of their behavior as members of a given psychology class, for example, individual students are much more alike than they are different; each goes through the complicated process of registering for the course within the time specified, buying the required books, reading and studying the various assignments, attending class meetings, and completing tests, papers, and any other requirements for the course (i.e., roles can involve multiple settings). The instructor's role has a similarly constraining effect on the nature and range of his or her behavior. The most efficient way to describe any person's behavior in the context of this course is thus based on the role he or she occupies, not on individual characteristics.

Earlier we discussed the concept of behavior-environment congruence. Roles are similarly coercive in their influence on behavior, because people exert considerable behavioral effort in many cases to maintain their eligibility for certain roles (e.g., medical students study hard, athletes spend long hours training). Loss of roles is a serious threat to people, because most communities require their members to maintain stable role performance or run the risk of being labeled some sort of deviant. Minor criminal offenses such as loitering and vagrancy and psychiatric diagnoses such as depression and mental retardation are applied at least in part on the basis of the individual's failure to perform adequately a sufficient number of socially required roles.

In practice every adult is called on to perform many different roles, not all of them necessarily compatible. Roles conflict with each other when they limit the person's behavioral choices in a mutually exclusive way. For a woman who is strongly career-oriented, for example, the birth of a first child, with its intense and anxiety-producing demands, can seriously divide her attention and lead to strongly mixed emotions. If performance of a given role limits choices in some cases, however, it also protects them in many others. People whose roles bring them substantial incomes, for example, can qualify for mortgages and loans to purchase homes and other expensive possessions even when they have little or no money currently on hand.

One issue for the community psychologist is thus the availability of adequate numbers of roles and settings in a community, given the number of people who live there. Beyond mere availability, however, the ecological perspective directs us to examine the degree of fit between the available roles and each individual's behavioral propensities, social aspiration, beliefs, and other role-related characteristics. Does a small college town have a sufficient number of suitable jobs for the professionally trained spouses of new faculty? Does an inner-city neighborhood have an adequate number of organized athletic programs for the interested young people there? Does a community have enough organized opportunities for newcomers to meet other residents and learn about the community?

Not all roles have equal importance, either to the individual holding them or to others. Sarbin proposes that the relative contribution of different roles to an individual's social identity can be determined by examining each role along three dimensions: status, value, and involvement. *Status* refers to one's position in a social structure, such as parent or child, student or instructor, army general or private. *Value* concerns the positive or negative evaluations attached to performance, or failure to perform, in a role. When you complete a course evaluation form, for example, you are "grading" the instructor just as he or she graded your work in the course. *Involvement* refers to the degree of participation in the role as measured both by time spent in it and by energy expended in performing it. For example, a police officer may always be on duty, carrying a firearm, and obligated to arrest anyone he or she finds using an illegal drug. (A news story once told of a police captain who arrested his own daughter for drug dealing.)

Sarbin further differentiated the status dimension into two types, *ascribed* and *achieved*. *Ascribed* statuses are those that are biosocial in nature. We enter those statuses with little contribution on our parts, and we can do little about changing them (e.g., age, kinship, or race). *Achieved* statuses are those about which we have some degree of choice, often a great deal. For most people the most important achieved status is their occupation.

At a minimum, each individual is granted the status of a person, which entitles the individual to certain minimum rights no matter what his or her circumstances are. People in prisons or in mental hospitals, no matter how disturbed, are granted certain minimum rights regarding the way others may treat them. They can't be beaten, starved, or killed by official action. They should have minimum basic food and shelter. With achieved statuses, on the other hand, the individual is granted a great deal of power and social esteem. The president of the United States or the board chairperson of a major corporation exercises a great deal of power and receives much esteem from others.

Sarbin points out that we receive little positive valuation for minimally adequate performance in ascribed roles such as mother or father, male or female, for such performance is expected. To fail in such roles brings considerable social opprobrium, however. A neglectful mother may have her children taken away from her and under some circumstances may be prosecuted for criminal behavior. A good mother may be lucky to receive a Mother's Day card in some families. In contrast, no matter how poorly it is performed, an achieved role constitutes a basis for some esteem. Accepting a U.S. president's denigration of the accomplishments of his predecessor, for example, might lead us to consider the predecessor a complete failure in his role as president. Yet a former president receives many "perks" and is accorded the greatest respect when he arrives at a public gathering. The same is true for almost any occupation. Having had an occupational title earns some social points, almost no matter what else is true of your performance in that occupation. If you have a job, you are someone. If you don't and you should (i.e., you are not disabled, the beneficiary of a trust fund, or excused in some other fashion), you are considered a loafer or a bum. Sarbin also says that the degree of involvement varies with the type of status. We are always involved in our ascribed statuses, whereas we can more easily step in and out of other statuses. However, we may have great difficulty escaping from some achieved roles, such as prisoner or "bag lady," even for brief periods.

Sarbin argues that persons with degraded social identities are those with few opportunities to enact roles that are entered by choice. The best such a person can hope for is to attain a neutral valued social identity if he or she meets all the expectations for whatever makes up his or her predominant ascribed status. In a sense, one can say that the best an individual with a degraded social identity can expect is to be ignored. The social relationships of persons with degraded social identities are often limited to those with similar identities, and in many cases their networks include a large proportion of persons who are paid to take care of them— doctors, nurses, social workers, jailers.

Sarbin's analysis is interesting, for it suggests additional avenues for diagnosis and intervention. In treating persons with degraded social identities, for example, role theory suggests increasing the variety of roles and social relationships available to such persons and working to promote positive social esteem and value for all roles, including ascribed ones (e.g., "old" people). Behavior-setting theory offers useful methods for identifying roles and describing their behavioral content. Given that achieved roles are typically enacted as part of specific behavior settings, the Johnny Appleseed approach to fostering the proliferation of underpopulated settings (described earlier in this chapter) offers one practical strategy for increasing the pool of achieved roles. Creating jobs, for example, even within sheltered settings, may be an important means of helping to undo a degraded social identity. For some persons (e.g., those with serious mental illness or retardation) who find the work or volunteer roles available to them in the community ambiguous or unsettling, individualized training and support can help clarify the obligations and behavioral expectations necessary to achieve and maintain these roles. Organizing support and advocacy groups or clubs, with roles such as president, secretary, or committee chairperson, also helps to upgrade social identities. Such clubs may even provide, if not a full ideology, at least a partial ideology to serve as a guide to behavioral conduct, to articulate some values, and to support the individual's self-esteem. Participation in self-help groups that admit to membership persons who are otherwise isolated helps to undo social degradation. Some people are able to find important positions of leadership in such organizations and can, to some extent, rebuild their social identities around participation in them (see Chapter 9). All these efforts have as their goal an increase in the number of role choices available to community residents and a decrease in the amount of role conflict taking place.

Role theory implies a mechanism of "role congruence" (presumably analogous to Barker's concept of behavior-environment congruence) in explaining how an individual's behavior, cognitions, and identity change and how these changes are maintained over time. Some recognition of the importance of person-environment fit (the need for available roles to match the individual's goals and values) is also present. Like Barker, however, Sarbin's conception makes little use of person-centered factors. It does not explain, for example (if the position stated by Alcoholics Anonymous is correct), why the alcohol abuser begins the process of recovery at the very moment he or she accepts what is otherwise an extremely ascribed and degraded role: that of alcoholic (see Chapter 9).

Role theory also leaves unanswered the question of how a community psychologist participates directly in the creation of jobs and other achieved roles. Role theory suggests a problem for the community psychologist: In what types of roles and in which settings can the community psychologist participate in creating roles for others? Role theory offers a conception complementary to those of Moos and Barker, however, in defining a unit commensurate with the individual person that can also encompass many different settings at the community level.

Box 5–1. The Fairweather Lodge

An excellent example of the application of social ecology to community intervention is the lodge program developed by Fairweather and his associates (Fairweather et al., 1969, 1974; Fairweather, 1980; Fairweather & Fergus, 1993). Beginning as a "milieu treatment" program inside the walls of a psychiatric hospital, this intervention involved small, self-governing patient groups operating under an unusually limited degree of staff authority. Within the hospital this program was highly successful in helping patients recover from acute psychiatric episodes. The major difficulty encountered was that once patients were discharged from the program and away from the daily support of their peers, they had difficulty assuming or maintaining the kinds of roles and responsibilities that would help ensure their adaptation to the community.

Clinically, the traditional explanation for this kind of problem focuses on the characteristics of persons with chronic mental illness and attributes their failure to adapt to independent living to the behavioral deficits that are perceived to set them apart from other people. As we noted in Chapter 4, however, adaptation is not a person-centered trait but a process of fit involving both person and environment. Maladaptive responses usually occur episodically over time (see Morell, Levine, & Perkins, 1982) and tend to involve certain situations more often than others. Fairweather's explanation for the poor adaptation shown by patients focuses on the community, particularly its intolerance of patients' psychotic symptomatology (e.g., delusions and hallucinations).

Table 5–1, taken from Fairweather et al. (1969), elaborates this explanation in some detail. The bottom row indicates the essential problem. Prior to Fairweather's development of the community lodge concept, the two psychiatric statuses available to individuals were "sick person," entailing supervised living in an institution with limited rights and duties, and "well person," requiring completely independent living with full adult rights and obligations.[1] The lightly supervised group work-living situation in the community, described in the right center column, initially was not available to patients at release from the hospital.

Reasoning, much as Kelly did, that adaptation to the community needs to occur in the community instead of inside patients' heads (in some metaphorical sense, anyway), Fairweather worked with a group of consumers to develop a new kind of community setting. This "small-group" unit was designed to be a transitional step bridging the successful inpatient treatment program and the less receptive community set-

Table 5-1
Autonomy of Mental Patients' Social Status

	Dimension of Autonomy				
	None			Partially autonomous individual status	Complete
Social situation	Supervised institutional situation mental hospital				Autonomous individual status
	Closed locked ward	Open unlocked ward			
		Living situations (home care, day care centers, day hospitals)			
	Supervised community situations	Work situations (sheltered workshops)	Unsupervised community group situations		No treatment
		Combination of work-living situations	Discharged former-patient-led group work-living situations—work in reference groups	Counseling or psychotherapy	
Status situation	Very limited adult rights and duties	Some adult rights and duties	Otherwise, full adult rights and duties	Otherwise, full adult rights and duties	Full adult rights and duties
Available social statuses		Sick person	(Unavailable)	Well person	

Reprinted with permission from G. Fairweather et al., *Community Life for the Mentally Ill* (Chicago: Aldine), 1969.

tings outside. Its goal was to help the community assimilate diversity in the form of former hospital patients with serious mental illness. Fairweather draws an analogy between the lodge concept and the "melting pot" role attributed to ethnic ghettos—both were intended to be protective and tolerant of the in-group's characteristic behavioral idiosyncrasies, while at the same time providing an important and challenging interface with the larger society.

A guiding value of Fairweather's approach was that "any program that attempts to empower the mentally ill must have as its ultimate goal improving their social status so that they can make binding decisions for themselves" (Fairweather & Fergus, 1993, p. 3). The consumers themselves therefore decided who would be members of the lodge, and those chosen were assisted in developing small commercial enterprises (i.e., gardening and janitorial services). Mental health professionals designed the lodge program and initially took a great deal of responsibility for it. These professionals later reduced their participation to consulting roles and eventually turned over full responsibility for the operation of the residence and businesses to the residents.

Once they expressed a preference for the lodge lifestyle, how did prospective members prepare for its challenges? In Fairweather's original model, group support and skill acquisition were initiated inside the hospital prior to discharge. (Given the increased emphasis on community care in recent years, the lodge movement now includes "training" lodges where consumers who have spent little or no time together in mental hospitals learn these preparatory skills; once in the community, members of the lodge continue to attend regular meetings designed to handle problems, review procedures, plan activities, and maintain the group-oriented focus of the lodge program.) Many positions of responsibility came with the residential and commercial operations of the lodge. Each of the two businesses had three levels of responsibility— crew chief, worker, and "marginal" worker (the latter sometimes affectionately referred to as "the nebbish")—and support services at the lodge residence required a cook, dishwasher, housekeeper, medication distributor, bookkeeper, and truck driver. In what Fairweather (1980) describes as a "principle of substitution," every resident performing a given job was backed up and could be replaced by another resident with little or no notice.

Several principles of Barker's behavior setting theory are clearly evident in the Fairweather lodge. For example, participation in the meetings, commercial activities, and other settings helped patients to recognize, model, and rehearse key behavioral skills necessary to community life. As Fairweather (1980) described it,

> Each member of the crew had a particular task; the usual composition of such a crew was a leader (crew chief), worker, and a marginal worker. It was the marginal worker whose work was constantly brought up to acceptable

standards by the working example of the supervisor and the worker. Without the framework of the group and the supervision and help of the crew chief, the marginal worker often failed. (p. 29)

Lodge members thus carefully managed the "program," with "deviation-countering" and "veto" circuits operating as part of its settings. That these circuits sometimes operated differently here than in other settings is illustrated in another passage from Fairweather (1980):

It is difficult, if not impossible, for individuals who have been hospitalized continuously to discard aberrant behaviors immediately upon entry into a community if, indeed, such behavior can be totally extinguished at all. The members of the subsystem must be tolerant of these behaviors. In the Lodge, for example, members often hallucinated while talking with other members within the confines of the Lodge itself. To take an extreme example of such tolerance, one member who openly hallucinated within the Lodge and on the way to work was informed by his crew chief upon arrival at the work site that no talking was permitted on the job. Usually he was silent during work hours, but upon entry into the truck for the trip back to the lodge he began hallucinating again—an acceptable behavior to his peers. (p. 27)

Movement back and forth between jobs and levels of authority was used to assist a member in reaching the maximum level of participation he was capable of during a given period of time. Barker's principle of behavior-environment congruence, which focuses attention on the spatial and temporal regularities of behavior and not on the internal state of a specific performer (and assumes that individual performers are in fact interchangeable), was clearly a useful mechanism of therapeutic change here.

From Sarbin's viewpoint, the Fairweather lodge worked because it entailed roles other than that of "mental patient." Two key characteristics were that the new roles were (1) achieved instead of ascribed and (2) flexible in the degrees of involvement they entailed. Both of these characteristics served to increase the value or esteem given residents and enhance their social identities. Indeed, Fairweather believes that a key effect of the lodge intervention was the way it changed role expectations in both directions; people with serious mental illness earned new respect from their neighbors and customers as they worked in recognizable ways to earn a basic living, while members of the lodge (especially those assigned to prepare written bids for job contracts) learned much about what is expected of people who wish to be taken seriously in the world of competitive work.

Moos's interest would be drawn to the social-group format of the lodge and to characteristics of the social climate that residents provided to one another on a day-to-day basis. From Fairweather's description, this climate appears high in such "relationship-oriented" dimensions as support, cohesiveness, and involvement and also in "personal development" dimensions such as autonomy and responsibility. Also consistent with Moos's conception, Fairweather suggests that the program not exceed a certain overall size to keep it on a human scale. The maximum size ever reached by the lodge was thirty-three members.

Fairweather did a careful experimental evaluation of the initial lodge program (Fairweather et al., 1969). Among the results were that over a forty-month follow-up period lodge members spent more time living in the community (rather than the hospital), and more time working, than did a control group that received traditional aftercare services. However, lodge members did not fare better than other consumers in their psychosocial adjustment and symptomatology, and many of those who left the lodge later became unemployed. Thus, compared with the hospital, the lodge was an economical source of support and gainful work, although it was not a cure for mental illness and was not really directed toward changing individuals per se. Instead, a setting was created that promoted some degree of social and vocational rehabilitation—if not for all, at least for many. Residents who were unable to adapt to the setting demands simply left or returned to the hospital.

Fairweather and his associates (Fairweather et al., 1974) also demonstrated that the lodge program could be replicated in other communities. In keeping with the experience that introducing change is not easy (see Chapter 10), however, they reported that considerable effort was necessary to interest other hospitals in adopting their program. It may also be relevant that many consumers and providers have other options now, including publicly funded alternatives such as Assertive Community Treatment (discussed in Chapter 2) and programs that provide supported housing and employment.

Postscript: What Role Remains for Individual Differences?

The strong emphasis in this chapter on environmental influences on behavior may seem unsettling to some readers in light of the widely held assumption that personality traits and other individual characteristics are important precisely because they dominate behavioral responding across time and place. Personality traits have received increased attention in recent years, with some agreement among authorities that dimensions such as extroversion, conscientiousness, and negative affect (sometimes called "neuroticism") consistently account for differences among people (Goldberg, 1993), and may reflect genetic factors to a significant degree (Bouchard, 1994). It has also become increasingly apparent in recent years that biological factors play a significant role in the behavioral symptoms of major mental illnesses such as schizophrenia and bipolar mood disorder (Torrey et al., 1994).

How can our almost exclusive focus on settings in the present chapter be applied in light of these other influential views? Recall from our

discussion of Dohrenwend's model (Chapter 3) that individual characteristics of persons may increase or decrease the likelihood that a stressful event will happen and also the nature and success of the person's coping efforts in response to that event. What are these individual
characteristics?

Mischel (1973) discussed two person-centered variables that help us
anticipate the concepts of coping, support, and prevention, all discussed
in later chapters. One of these Mischel calls "cognitive and behavioral
construction competencies," which refers to differences in the efficiency
with which people process information about the environment to come
up with adaptive, effective coping responses to specific situations. Aside
from the fact that the new settings and the responses they require may
be unfamiliar, a person with serious mental illness may not automatically
thrive when moved from an intense hospital-based program directly to
the community if he or she has chronic difficulty in attending and responding to new stimuli or is heavily medicated. More generally, Mischel
suggests that competence in cognitive and behavioral responding is related to such familiar constructs as intelligence, cognitive and social ma-
turity, ego strength, and social and intellectual achievements. It thus
points the way toward possible person-centered interventions that would
build competence and foster positive mental health by explicitly facilitating the development of cognitive and behavioral competencies in high-
risk individuals (see Chapter 8).

A second relevant person-centered characteristic is one that Mischel
called "encoding strategies and personal constructs." These include ideological beliefs about oneself and the meaning of one's experiences. Such
constructs have important implications for actions such as attributing
blame for one's problems and evaluating the relative desirability of different solutions to problems (e.g., psychotherapy versus self-help).
Changes in people's personal constructs or encoding strategies may help
them maintain their adaptive responses across different situations precisely
because this characteristic is generally so resistant to change. For example, Recovery, Inc., a self-help group for persons with chronic mental illness, encourages a belief by its members in their own individual power
to make choices and to reject emotionally arousing stimuli. Members are
taught to use a specific term, "spotting," to identify certain risky situations (e.g., "angry temper") and then to use a specific coping device (e.g.,
"deliberately smile") to deal with those situations. Last, personality factors may influence a person's choice of situations. One implication of environmentally oriented theories is that ideal communities provide a rich
and varied set of opportunities from which a person can choose. In order to evaluate the opportunities, we need concepts and methods for assessing settings and their characteristics.

Once a community's richness of opportunities has been evaluated,
self-determination requires that the consumer have opportunities to exert his or her preference and choice among those settings. Some years

ago, for example, problems following the massive deinstitutionalization of people with serious mental illness led authorities to propose creating and funding a continuum of residential services running from hospital through nursing home and group home to supervised apartment and eventually independence, with consumers steadily moving through the continuum over time to increasingly less restrictive and more independent residences. There were two problems with this conception; first, it was not always the case that all steps in the continuum were actually available in a given community, and second, where it did exist the continuum did not foster movement and progress by consumers toward greater independence but functioned simply as a static array of alternative long-term placements (Geller & Fisher, 1993). Today, we try to start with the consumer and his or her aspirations and preferences, rather than with a hypothetically derived continuum or taxonomy of settings. That is, a diverse set of alternatives should be available, but consumers themselves choose where among these alternatives they wish to live, with the helping agency providing the supports needed for each consumer to succeed in the chosen residential situation (Carling, 1990, 1993).

In spite of a resurgent emphasis on the importance of personality characteristics and biological influences on behavior, we believe that the relevant perspective for the community psychologist is still the "person-in-context." Consideration of both components, person and situation, opens up a much wider avenue of potential solutions to problems of adaptation, including environmentally facilitated changes alone, individual competence building alone, and strategies that unite both components in the pursuit of stable change, such as helping people with special needs recognize and select personally optimal environments (Levine & Perkins, 1980). In summary, community psychologists believe that solutions should be divergent rather than convergent (Rappaport, 1981), with the kind of understanding of settings we developed in this chapter used to promote change and adaptation through individual choice and empowerment.

Summary

This chapter began by raising a number of potential limitations to the ecological metaphor in psychology. For example, what specific mechanisms of behavior change does this analogy provide? How are changes in behavior maintained over time? To what extent have taxonomies of environmental settings been developed, particularly with respect to the often overlooked spatial and temporal dimensions of behavior? What place is given by specific ecological concepts to individual differences in the expression of values, goals, and purposes using environmental settings? Moos's concept of perceived social climates, Barker's behavior-setting theory, and Sarbin's role theory were reviewed in some detail as important theoretical systems community psychologists have used in developing answers to these questions.

Each of these concepts is essentially descriptive and ahistorical. The mechanism of behavior change each articulates is more intuitive than it is precise and complete. Moos's notion of fit between individual needs and environmental presses, for example, depends on a concrete behavioral prescription to achieve and maintain individual change. The complexity of environmental influences, which often produce unwanted as well as wanted effects, has not been fully examined using these concepts. Furthermore, the issues of how current environmental conditions came to be and what conditions are likely to follow them are not readily answerable. Relatively little research using these concepts has been longitudinal or otherwise focused on long-term changes.

We illustrated some of the ideas generated by these concepts in our discussion of Fairweather's community lodge program for persons with serious mental illness. Interpreted from the vantage of the three concepts reviewed here, membership in the lodge community provided patients with a supportive network of relationships, gave them regular opportunities to rehearse adaptive behavioral responses to key community settings, and created respectable roles for them that helped to compensate for their erstwhile status as psychiatric inpatients. We closed the chapter by concluding that a place remains for individual differences in the community psychology field, especially when applied in helping empower individuals to recognize and control important aspects of their environment.

In conclusion, the social context of behavior helps to define its nature. In so doing, it gives us an important perspective on individual and community change. There are limits to what a single individual acting alone can do, however. Important restrictions can be imposed by others in the social context, as we will see in Chapter 6.

Note

1. The person in the mental hospital loses many rights associated with personal liberty when committed by a court. After discharge, the person in the community has all the rights that every other person has, including the right to refuse to participate in any aftercare program. The problem of treating people with serious mental illness in the community stems in part from their right to refuse treatment. Patients who are merely on a temporary furlough from the hospital can be rehospitalized readily, but those who are discharged have full liberty to decide for themselves about treatment. In some jurisdictions it is possible to "commit" a person to outpatient treatment, thus creating an intermediate legal status between those of sick person and well person. The roles are a function not only of custom but also of legal regulation.

6

Labeling Theory:
An Alternative to the
Illness Model

In Chapters 4 and 5 we examined the idea that behavior is best understood not as a specific sign of health or disease but as the product of human adaptation to specific situations. The basic ecological analogy (see Chapter 4), however, is rather abstract and thus difficult to use in specific predictive applications. The conceptions offered by Moos, Barker, and Sarbin (discussed in Chapter 5) are more concrete and practical for many problems but do not explicitly integrate a view of human individual differences into the perspective they provide on behavior. In this chapter we examine a theoretical perspective that does make an effort to explain behavior in terms of a dynamic interaction between the person and his or her social context.

This perspective is known as "labeling theory." Developed during the 1960s, labeling theory was a product of new thinking about abnormal behavior and of criticism directed at traditional mental health diagnosis and treatment. An important tenet of labeling theory is that what gets formally diagnosed as psychopathology is not all the deviant behavior that occurs but merely the behavior that is officially *noticed*. Whether or not a deviant episode is noticed is determined by factors other than the behavior itself, such as the individual's social identity and position and the discretionary actions of professionals engaged in diagnostic and treatment activities. Like role congruence, labeling theory postulates a process in which other people actively interpret and respond to a person's behavior by imposing and maintaining the boundaries defined by a role.

Labeling theory was developed by sociologists. It is an interpersonal theory of deviance that places abnormal behavior in a social context and shows how a systems approach illuminates issues in mental health. In this theory, deviance is a property of an individual's actions and is also "in the eye of the beholder," beholders being all those who interact with the person who exhibits deviant behavior, including those who are in professional helping roles. The deviance perspective, as developed by sociologists Lemert, Becker, and others (see Gove, 1980), was refined by Scheff (1966, 1984) into an elegant alternative to the illness model. Scheff's presentation of deviance theory in propositional form set the terms of debate for the decade following its appearance.[1]

This chapter begins with a review of social and historical factors that attended the development of labeling theory and then presents its central concepts. We continue by examining the issue of stigma in abnormal behavior.

The Social Context for the Development of Labeling Theory

The labeling position took hold at a time when many people were seeking alternatives to the medical model. During the 1950s and 1960s the reality of the terrible conditions that prevailed in many mental health institutions became an impetus for reform. Goffman's (1961) widely acclaimed book *Asylums* argued persuasively that mental hospitals were inherently oppressive and acted to disable patients as as much or more than did the conditions that brought them to the hospital in the first place.

This attack on "an oppressive social institution" came during the same period as the Kennedy-Johnson reforms and at a time when the ideals of social justice and the plight of the underdog were moving our society to action. Moreover, an alternative to institutional care had emerged from experience in military psychiatry during World War II (Levine, 1981). The labeling viewpoint fit well with the thrust toward deinstitutionalization and provided an intellectual rationale for that policy (see Bachrach, 1975).

Szasz (1961, 1963), using strong language, added to the criticism of hospitals and mental health professionals by stating that mental illness was a myth and that psychiatrists working in the mental hospital were not healers. Most of the legal and social applications of psychiatry, undertaken in the name of psychiatric liberalism, he said, were actually instances of despotism. To be sure, it was despotism based on health values, but it was despotism nonetheless. Why? Because the promoters of mental health did not refuse to use coercive methods but, on the contrary, eagerly embraced them, creating a danger of tyranny by therapy (Szasz, 1963, pp. vii–viii).

Szasz (1961) worked independently of labeling theorists. He asserted that problematic behavior was not a medical illness based on known physical pathology but instead was simply behavior that violated social, ethical, moral, and legal norms. Deviance was not an illness but a social status created in response to our demands for social conformity. If deviant behavior was defined by acts violating social norms, moreover, psychiatrists and, by implication, other mental health professionals with formal responsibility for certifying that norms had been violated were as much agents of social control as agents of healing. Morse (1978) arrived at a similar conclusion after a careful review and analysis of the legal, psychiatric, psychological, and sociological literature.

Szasz's attack fit well with several other trends of that day. First, because Szasz's position implied that "illness" was a culturally relative concept, it supported by implication the criticisms of existing social norms. His position attracted those who felt disaffected with the state of life in the United States, for it fed into the distrust of constituted authority, including psychiatric authority, that was to become so prominent later in the decade (Sedgwick, 1982).

Second, his attack on the medical aspect of mental health was welcomed by groups competing with the medical establishment for dominion in the delivery of mental health services. The mental health revolution, as Klerman (1982) called it, was just beginning. We were fast becoming aware of the size of the market for mental health services. Professional battles about who would be included and who would be regulated out of that market were just heating up. World War II had shown that psychologists, social workers, nurses, and paraprofessionals could provide competent services. If mental illnesses and similar disorders were determined socially and psychologically, not medically, other nonmedical professional groups could argue that it was not necessary to have medical training to provide psychotherapeutic services in the private sector or to hold positions of authority within public-sector institutions.

In addition to the effort to reform inferior mental hospitals, the modes of psychiatric practice prevalent in the 1950s came under scientific attack as well. Hollingshead and Redlich (1958) showed that both diagnoses and treatment rendered were correlated with social class, a point initially disputed bitterly by clinicians. Hollingshead and Redlich's data challenged the social neutrality of the practice of psychiatry. Psychologists began developing their own versions of behavior modification, based on psychology's long suit at that time—learning theory (Graziano & Mooney, 1984). The ability to modify behavior therapeutically without first undoing complex psychodynamic and unconscious problems undermined the authority of psychoanalysis, in that day practiced largely by medically trained psychiatrists. This assault on the medical model opened the field to new thinking.

Principles of Labeling Theory

Labeling theory is designed to account for the presumed "amplification" of acts of *primary* deviance (violations of norms) into *secondary* or "career" deviance. Labeling theory seeks to answer this question: If deviant behavior is merely a norm violation, why do so many deviants become chronic mental patients, unable to assume other than ascribed roles?

Primary and Secondary Deviance

Scheff, following other theorists of his school, differentiates *primary* and *secondary* deviance. Primary deviance is the specific act that violates one or more social norms. Labeling theory does not address the *cause* of the act of primary deviance in any explicit way. Primary deviance may originate from four sources—an organic deficit, psychological dynamics, external stress, or volitional acts in defiance of social rules. The theory implies that an intact person is capable of producing a much greater variety of behavior than we ordinarily believe, especially when we consider the labeling theory assumption that most pathological behavior is transitory in nature. In this view, less behavior is genuinely "abnormal" or "sick" than most of us believe. In the absence of public attention, the act of primary deviance is transitory, and, if it goes unrecorded, that is the end of it.

Secondary deviance is a term applied to the role of a career deviant or chronic patient. Following an act of primary deviance, the single most important event in determining entrance into the role of career deviant is the societal response to the primary deviance. Depending on the class of rules broken, the individual will be referred to and processed by a specialized agency of social control (i.e., oriented to helping, punishing, containing, or isolating). People who have broken rules affecting property or who have harmed others "normally" are handled by the criminal justice system. Children who cannot function adequately in school may be characterized as mentally retarded and treated by the special education system, or they may be admitted to an institution for the retarded.

Juveniles are treated differently, depending on their offense. Status offenses are acts that would not be criminal if committed by an adult (e.g., running away, incorrigibility, sexual activity, truancy) but that subject the juvenile to the court's jurisdiction. They are less serious in society's view than delinquent acts, which would be crimes if committed by adults. Juveniles who have committed delinquent acts are less often referred for psychiatric and social services than are juveniles who commit status offenses. Status offenders are more likely to be referred to a social service agency under diversion programs, while juvenile delinquents receive probation or are sent to secure facilities (Murray, 1983; Handler & Satz, 1982).

People who are processed through the psychiatric system have broken what Scheff calls "residual rules." These are the remaining social norms, so taken for granted that the violation of "goes-without-saying" assumptions regarding proper and decent conduct or the nature of social reality immediately leads to a perception of the individual as bizarre, strange, and perhaps frightening. An individual biting his nails in public might strike an observer as tense or nervous but would elicit little other reaction. A person who bit his hand, sucked his fingers, nervously twisted his hair into braids, and then chewed the braids might seem bizarre to the observer. Ordinarily we do not expect an individual to walk down the street smiling vacantly, gesticulating, talking to himself, apparently tuned to inner space (unless the person is carrying a Sony Walkman). Smiling at no one in particular, talking aloud to one's self, and gesticulating with no one to receive the communication are acts that so violate our assumptions about how people ought to act socially that we immediately question the person's sanity.

Because labeling theory postulates that residual rule breaking is transitory, it assumes that a healthy person is capable of a great variety of behaviors and this variety is not necessarily abnormal. Moreover, what are taken as symptoms of mental illness can be interpreted as violations of culturally particular norms. Thus interpreted, the "symptoms" should be studied by methods designed to analyze behavior in social contexts, not by methods suitable for the study of individual psychopathology.

The norm-violating behavior alone does not elicit the effort at social control, Scheff argues. Social control is exerted whenever a "socially unqualified person" engages in the norm-violating act. In this viewpoint, who is behaving where, when, and in whose presence are more important questions than what behavior was actually performed. A soldier on the battlefield killing an enemy is not committing murder, but one civilian shooting another is. A mime in a store window holds his body in an awkward position for a long time, completely unresponsive to those around him who may try to make him flinch or smile, but no one would consider him a catatonic. A medium may talk to spirits or claim to be influenced by unearthly forces, yet is not considered a paranoid schizophrenic. A patient in a psychiatric hospital claims she is possessed by a devil; yet the priest who tries to exorcise the devil will not be committed.[2] A person who isolates himself or herself, refuses to speak, practices

self-flagellation, dresses in a strange costume, refuses to eat for long periods, keeps odd hours, arises at dawn, and goes to bed at a child's hour
might well compel the anxious attention of friends or relatives—but not
if that person belongs to a religious order. In short, the overt acts and
expressed thoughts or feelings are not the only determinants of the outcome. The reactions of others to the actor are critical.[3]

In labeling theory the reactions of others may determine whether or
not the individual enters into a career deviant role. In particular, the public labeling of the individual as mentally ill is critical. Labeling theory asserts that the individual is culturally prepared to accept a self-definition
of mental illness, first, because the individual can apply the label of "crazy"
to his or her own behavior, and, second, because the definition of self as
mentally ill is reinforced by powerful others in the hospital. Once the person is released, after having been in the role of "good patient," the stigma
associated with the mental illness label will keep the person in the role of
mental patient.

On the other hand, consider the example of becoming a shaman or
healer. Murphy (1964) describes the process as one in which the candidates for shamanship "go crazy" for a period of time. The person might
wander alone, go without sleep or food, suffer physical hardship, and exhibit severe agitation, all of which are instances of primary deviance.
Shamans report that they feel "sick and perplexed" during this period.
Not all prove to be acceptable candidates, but once the acute phase of
distress passes, those who do enter the shaman's role are received with
honor and enrolled in the profession for further training. One could argue that entry into shamanship represents a favorable outcome of some
unknown stressful life event, with the favorable outcome determined by
the reactions and support of the prospective shaman's community. This
scenario seems plausible; yet Murphy claims that few of the shamans enter that role after having been considered mentally ill by their fellows, although she cites other scholarly opinion that shamans may be recruited
differentially from among the mentally ill.

Murphy's (1982) informants distinguish the shaman's behavior from
mental illness. "When the shaman is healing, he is out of his mind, but
he is not crazy" (p. 64). The fact that he is not crazy afterward (Murphy,
1976) does not contradict the possibility that had his crisis been treated
differently, he might not have come through so well.

Murphy (1982), an anthropologist, advocates the illness model of deviance especially for conditions such as schizophrenia. She notes that all
groups have members who do not function normally and that some are
considered crazy. The symptoms considered crazy are similar from one
group to another. Some of those considered crazy respond to native treatment, to Western treatment, or to a combination of therapies, and some
become chronically disabled whether or not they receive care. Murphy's
observations suggest that labeling theory has distinct limits. In her view,
entry into career deviance occurs for certain people without regard to the
care they received. The process of entry into shamanship, however, re-

veals that a socially *qualified* individual who exhibits deviant behavior will not necessarily be labeled a deviant and will not perforce enter a deviant career.

Cultural Stereotypes and Labeling

In labeling theory, both the agent of social control and the rule breaker have to be able to recognize the manifestations of mental illness. Members of the public are one component of the agents of social control, but so are police and mental health workers. In labeling theory, the person who commits the rule-breaking act as a participant in the culture also has internally incorporated images of mental illness and may apply those images to him or herself.

These issues have led to one body of research to determine the public's stereotypes about mental illness. Scheff and Gove disagree about the nature of the stereotypes of mental illness held by the public and whether societal and individual reactions to acts of primary deviance are in keeping with cultural stereotypes of mental illness. The argument between them depends in part on whether cultural stereotypes are measurable using the survey instruments we have available. Tebes (1983) points out that results of studies using survey instruments are so method-bound (that is, the results differ greatly depending on the wording and presentation in the survey instrument) that generalization is difficult.

We believe that the argument about stereotypes has been too narrowly conceived. Today a whole range of behaviors other than serious mental illness has fallen within the domain of the mental health professions. Mental health services have been used for purposes of social control of a wide range of behaviors for a long time. Oltman and Friedman (1965) reviewed first-admission data over a twenty-year period in a state mental hospital that had had little turnover in senior psychiatric staff. First-admission diagnoses of alcoholism, neuroses, character disorders, and addictions were proportionately much higher among patients admitted later in the period under study than among those admitted earlier, and the numbers increased at a rate faster than could be accounted for by the increase in population in their catchment area. First admissions for schizophrenia and other major mental disorders remained relatively constant compared to the increase in population. In other words, a greater number of people were being hospitalized in the mid-1960s than could be accounted for by the overall increase in population, and the increase was in categories other than major mental disorders. Writing from another perspective, Kittrie (1971) discussed the growth of the "therapeutic state." As alcohol and drug problems, sex offenses, and the behavior problems of juveniles were more and more treated as mental health problems rather than as criminal offenses, responsibility for controlling and regulating a large variety of deviant behavior shifted from the criminal justice system to the mental health system.

Because the behavior patterns now coming to the mental health system are so diverse, the argument over public stereotypes of serious mental illness is less relevant. Just about every day, advice columnists tell us that persons with a great variety of personal idiosyncrasies ought to be referred to some professional agency for care. It is very easy for present-day observers of deviant behavior (including self-observers) to apply the label of "sick" and for individuals to be psychologically ready to receive confirmation of that judgment from professionals who, as Scheff pointed out, are only too ready to find pathology.

Gove (1980, 1982) also argues that the increasing proportion of voluntary-to-involuntary admissions to mental hospitals and the fact that most referrals for service are voluntary in all types of mental health agencies are difficult for labeling theory to explain. There has been an increase in the proportion of mental hospital admissions that are classified as voluntary, in part due to changes in mental health law (Levine, 1981). The numbers don't tell the full story. Lewis et al. (1984) systematically observed negotiations between public defenders and mental health personnel about whether a patient should be admitted involuntarily or released after an emergency commitment. They observed that a great many people accepted voluntary commitment under conditions that could only be considered coercive: "If you don't sign yourself in, you will be committed." Rogers (1993) found that approximately half of patients who admitted themselves to a psychiatric hospital felt coerced, and the psychiatrist was mentioned most often as the professional responsible for the coercion. Hoge, Lidz, Mulvey, et al. (1993) and Lidz, Mulvey, et al. (1993) reported similar findings on the basis of observations in an emergency room and on an admissions service. Invountary commitment may have changed in name only.

Moreover, understanding and acceptance of services are now more widespread. Attitudes toward seeking and accepting mental health services may have relaxed. Gordon (1982) reports that the attitudes toward mental illness and mental health services of lower-class African Americans and lower-class whites are not very different, nor do they differ from attitudes reported as characteristic of middle-class individuals. Although it may be easier to *accept* treatment now, it does not follow that the consequences of having been labeled are different.

Instead of being an argument against labeling theory, the increase in voluntary help seeking can be seen as an argument for extending the premises of labeling theory to a broad range of problems in living. Encouragement in the media to seek help, the sympathetic portrayal of mental illness on the screen (Gove, 1982), the availability of ordinary health insurance for psychotherapeutic and psychiatric care, and the wide prevalence of care providers in contemporary society are evidence of social support for seeking help. Those same social structures encourage self-definitions that include a "sick" part, having "unresolved issues," or being in need of help. For some, that aspect of self-definition may come to play a central part in their lives (Kaminer, 1992).

If people continue to define all kinds of problems in living as mental health problems, there may eventually result a normalization of such conditions and some degree of destigmatization. The argument about cultural stereotypes may be much more irrelevant today. The question should be the types of behavior and the conditions under which behavior patterns create sufficient social concern to elicit coerced intervention or the conditions under which people self-define as in need of mental health services.

When Is Residual Rule Breaking Labeled?

Scheff states that most instances of residual rule breaking are ignored, denied, or rationalized away. Lacking a societal reaction, these episodes do not lead to illness but just fade away. Scheff's position assumes that illness does not exist unless the illness has social consequences.[4] If most primary deviance is ignored, making the episode transitory, unrecorded, and of no particular social consequence, why in other cases does the same behavior lead to social control and public labeling? The outcome is essentially determined by five sets of variables (see Figure 6–1):

1. Irrespective of cause, the degree, amount, and visibility of the rule breaking are determinants of whether there will be any public reaction and efforts at social control. As an extreme illustration, if an individual was capable of exhibiting crazy behavior but engaged in it only when alone, that behavior would never come to the attention of others, would pass, and would not be recorded as illness. Those who work with chronic mental patients understand this principle when they encourage clients to suppress symptoms when in public. Thus, patient members of Fairweather's community lodge (see Chapter 5) were told they were not allowed to act crazy while interacting with customers of their janitorial and gardening service, and most were able to suppress norm-violating behavior (Fairweather et al., 1969). Patients were allowed to act crazy while at home in the lodge. This form of treatment recognizes that societal reaction has consequences for continued living in the community. In Scheff's view, to the degree that symptoms are "invisible," there is no illness.

   Many people suffer from anxiety, depression, strange thoughts, or bizarre, frightening, or embarrassing fantasies but are able to meet everyday responsibilities and conceal their symptoms from all but themselves. Their conditions may wax and wane without attracting the notice of others; without public notice, there is no illness.

   The intensity, frequency, and duration of the rule-breaking episode may present primary conditions for the initiation of treatment and efforts at social control. Gove (1980, 1982) cites literature indicating that those who enter treatment have more severe symptoms than those who do not. Gove notes that families tolerate a great deal of disturbed behavior before they act to hospitalize a member of the family. Whitt and Meile

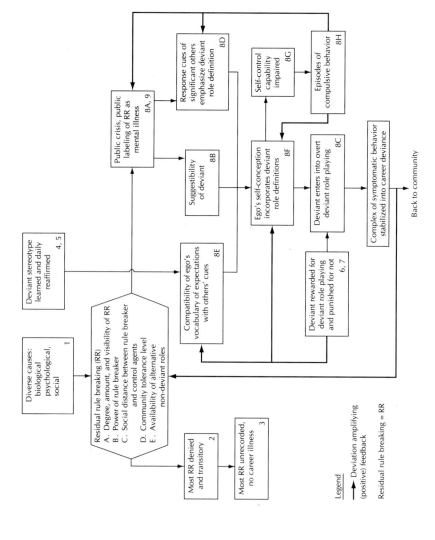

Figure 6–1. Flowchart–stabilization of deviance in a social system. (From Scheff, 1984)

(1985) find that people are not likely to label behavior as mental illness even when the label is suggested to them. Herz and Melville (1980) report that the overwhelming majority of patients and their families were aware of changes in thoughts, behavior, and feelings for at least one week, and in many cases for more than one month, before rehospitalization occurred. Morrell, Levine, and Perkins (1982) reviewed the daily logs kept by staff in a proprietary home for adult mental patients located in a city neighborhood. Those patients who were later rehospitalized had many more episodes that brought the residents to the attention of staff as recorded in the log book than did comparable patients who were not rehospitalized. This difference in number of behavioral incidents was noticeable for many weeks before rehospitalization. Because both groups comprised chronic patients, these data suggest that greater frequency and visibility of disturbed behavior is associated with rehospitalization and not just the episode of "rule breaking."

2. Scheff's second variable deals with the power of the rule breaker vis-à-vis the agent of social control. If the power differential favors the rule breaker, he or she may not be readily subject to social control. During his last days as president, Richard M. Nixon is said to have exhibited some bizarre behavior (Woodward & Bernstein, 1976). Although many expressed concern over the state of his mind, no one did anything to bring the president to the attention of a mental health professional. Taking another example closer to the everyday experience of people in the mental health field, we note that untold numbers of neophyte psychotherapists have been urged if not ordered by therapy supervisors to work out some personal problem that is interfering with their work by entering treatment. Although any number of neophyte therapists may well have entertained serious doubts about the mental health of some of their supervisors, it is a rare student or intern who would have the courage to urge the supervisor to seek treatment. The student certainly could not order the supervisor to enter treatment and enforce the order with a threat of dismissal or a poor recommendation or letter of reference.

Gove criticizes the argument that lower-class individuals, a relatively powerless group, draw more serious diagnoses and tend to be treated in state facilities with more drastic therapies because of their powerlessness. A task panel of the President's Commission on Mental Health reported that nonwhites were admitted to psychiatric facilities at a rate approximately 1.3 times greater than that for whites (Task Panel, 1978a). We can assume that nonwhites as a group are more powerless and of lower social class than are whites as a group. Gove agrees that African Americans and individuals in lower social classes have a higher rate of hospitalization, but he believes that this reflects the higher degree of stress in the lives of lower-class people. Although Gove (1980) acknowledges that well-controlled studies do not appear in the literature, he believes the available evidence indicates that controlling for social class washes out nonwhite-white differences in hospitalization rates.

Another explanation

Looking at still another index of social power, Gove notes that people who occupy central roles in families and who presumably have greater social power are hospitalized sooner than those occupying more peripheral roles. If a mother is unable to meet her obligations, the household soon falls apart, and others will seek help for her. If grandmother wanders and is forgetful or incoherent, however, she may not be hospitalized for a much longer time after symptoms have been noted.

Gove (1980) points to other relationships between social class and aspects of mental illness that do not support predictions from labeling theory. For example, members of the lower social classes tend to define indices of mental illness much more narrowly in terms of aggressive or antisocial behavior. Much that would be recognized as "sick" in people of higher social class would be ignored in lower social classes, thus reducing the vulnerability to labeling in a relatively powerless group. In fact, Gove believes that the theory of labeling should postulate *greater* vulnerability to the effects of labeling among the upper classes (the more powerful group), which views a wider range of behaviors and expression of feelings as indicative of mental illness. The vulnerability to labeling may work itself out in a different fashion among the middle and upper social classes. If lower-class individuals turn out to be more subject to pejorative public labeling, the difference in attitude toward mental illness held by members of different social classes may not be relevant to labeling theory.

3. The social distance between the rule breaker and the agent of social control may also be a factor in determining whether the agent of social control will act in relation to an episode of primary deviance. Keil et al. (1983) found that people of higher socioeconomic status were better able to avoid rehospitalization for excessive drinking than were those of lower status, even when drinking patterns were controlled. Consider the following example. A police officer seeing a drunk who is obviously a homeless street person may arrest the person or consider emergency hospitalization. The same officer seeing a disheveled but well-dressed drunk vomiting and staggering down the street may find a cab and send him home.

Gove (1980), however, claims that the scenario is not accurate for mental disorder. He believes that police are quite discerning in selecting the circumstances in which to intervene and are more likely to ignore primary deviance among lower-class citizens, intervening only when violence threatens or at the behest of a relative of a prospective patient. In Gove's view, the facts do not support predictions from the social distance factor of labeling theory. Teplin (1984) observed that police are more likely to arrest a person who is showing signs of psychological disturbance than a person who has come to police attention and is not showing signs of disturbance. Her data do not provide a test of labeling theory except to indicate that the violation of some norms is more likely to call forth police acts of social control than are violations of other norms.

4. Scheff's fourth factor is the level of tolerance for deviance within a community. A psychiatrist on an admitting service of a large urban receiving

hospital reported a conversation with a newly arrived, itinerant, streetwise patient who desired to be admitted to the psychiatric facility in a city unfamiliar to him. The patient inquired seriously about what he had to do to be admitted—break a window or run down the street with his clothes off. In that particular city, the better choice would have been nudity. Yet in San Francisco's Golden Gate Park it would not have been unusual during the height of the "flower child" years of the 1960s to see an adult male, stark naked, happily listening to a concert in the park. That community's tolerance for personal oddity was much greater.

Citizens of Geel, Belgium, a haven for mental patients for more than seven hundred years (Roosens, 1979), have unusual tolerance for deviant behavior. The patients wander the streets freely, and other residents quietly but effectively engage anyone who is disruptive and stop the disruptiveness; everyone in the city accepts it as an obligation to work with patients. More overtly troubled and troublesome patients are returned to the hospital, of course, but the citizens of Geel accept a great deal of oddity without special notice. Patients find appropriate niches in Geel. In some of the Geel community settings, patients are segregated. They are seated in the balcony of the movie theater, patients are accepted in some bars but not in all, and in many community settings no patients are present. Apparently the level of tolerance may be enhanced by a tacit understanding of whose turf is whose (Roosens, 1979).

Geel is an important example; there are understood limits to the integration of people with deviant characteristics into the community. Even where there is great tolerance and substantial integration, by no means is either tolerance or integration complete.

5. Scheff's fifth factor regarding the labeling of residual rule breaking is the availability of alternative nondeviant roles. He describes several examples of primary deviance interpreted in such a fashion that the person's status was elevated. One example is the entrance into shamanship following a period of agitation. A related example is that of religious prophets who report extraordinary extrasensory communications but normalize that communication by putting it into a religious context. Such people sometimes emerge as respected members of a community. John Humphrey Noyes, founder of the religiously based Oneida commune, went through a "dark night of the soul" and emerged strengthened from the experience after his friends assisted him and continued to accept him as their spiritual leader (Levine & Bunker, 1975). A third example Scheff offers is a woman who experienced hallucinations while in church at a time when her personal problems seemed overwhelming. Although she was startled by her hallucinations, her chance encounter with a stranger who identified herself as a psychic helped the woman to reinterpret her hallucinations as manifestations of psychic powers. The encounter led her into a career as a psychic.

The best-known example of the creation of niches and roles for mental patients as forms of treatment is the Fairweather et al. (1969) creation of roles for patients as managers of residential lodges and businesses (see Chapter 5). In contemporary society, an alternative nondeviant role is often provided to those who participate in various self-help groups and become deeply involved as senior members or as more formal leaders. In these cases, it is necessary to have experienced the primary deviance (the alcoholism or the "nervous breakdown") and to have overcome it by active participation in the self-help group. Krizan (1982) describes a small religious sect that evidently had success with some disturbed individuals who found personal havens and missions for themselves by joining the congregation and proselytizing for it. In these examples, people entered existing social organizations while under great stress. Whether prepared niches can be created as therapeutic devices for people who are experiencing great personal problems and who are acutely disturbed remains to be seen. In a later section we will discuss how deviant behavior may be managed to avoid the undesirable effects of the labeling process and of social control.

Diagnosis and Labeling Theory

The diagnostic process is an important element within labeling theory. After a person goes (or is brought by someone else) for care, a mental health professional uses a diagnostic process to certify whether or not the person has a disorder suitable for treatment in that particular facility. The U.S. Supreme Court based its decision in *Parham v. J. and J.R.* (1979) on the assumption that a child's personal rights when brought for hospitalization by a parent are sufficiently safeguarded by the integrity of the diagnostic process that additional safeguards of due process are unnecessary.[5] However, we must still ask whether we can depend on the validity and integrity of the diagnostic process to identify and label only those who are ill and in need of care.

Scheff notes that the diagnostic process itself occurs within a social context that has implications for the outcome. In the cultural attitudes of physicians, it is more important to avoid failing to diagnose pathology when it exists than to suspect pathology when it doesn't exist. It is more harmful to miss a diagnosis and fail to institute treatment than to continue to observe and test in order to rule out pathology. The medical assumption that it does less harm to observe further than to miss illness may not be appropriate for mental illness, because the *social* costs for the prospective patient of hospitalization to diagnose mental illness are greater than the social costs of hospitalization for diagnosing physical illness. Admission to a hospital for laboratory tests and x-rays doesn't have the same implication for the person's social identity as admission to a psychiatric service.

Scheff believes that mental health professionals, by virtue of their positions in the social system providing care, are biased toward finding pathology and holding people for care. His argument is important for the "deviance amplification" position of labeling theory in that any behavior pattern is potentially subject to labeling. Mental health professionals have to be able to differentiate between those whose problems are best characterized as manifestations of illness and those who have other problems in living.

This problem turns on two issues: the social context within which mental health professionals make professional judgments and the inherent unreliability of the diagnostic procedures and systems in use. Scheff shows that in the commitment context, psychiatric interviews were often brief, legal hearings were often perfunctory, and the necessary evidence regarding the criteria for commitment, posing a danger to self or others, was often not clearly brought out in the record or the psychiatric testimony (see also Albers et al., 1976; Warren, 1977; and Hiday, 1977.)

Scheff argues that the commitment system encourages findings of illness because mental health professionals who are not well paid for public work of this sort often increase their incomes by reducing the amount of time they spend per case. Moreover, judges facing dispositions for troubled people brought to public attention also face possible political repercussions if they release someone who then harms him- or herself or others. They are therefore inclined to favor commitment. Judges may encourage mental health professionals in subtle and not so subtle fashion to produce findings supporting commitment. Ennis and Litwack (1974) note that mental health personnel are at risk for liability in a civil suit if they release someone who harms another, but they are far less likely to be found liable if they hold someone in a hospital for further treatment.[6]

In part, the issue is the reliability of psychiatric diagnosis. Spitzer and Williams (1982) agree that in the past such reliability left much to be desired. They claim that the situation improved substantially with the development of *DSM*-III. However, Kirk and Kutchins (1992) claim that the reliability of the *DSM* system is no better than it was under the earlier system. Be that as it may, the weakness of psychiatric diagnosis and clinical methods has been exposed in many adversary hearings, such as the trial of John Hinckley, who attempted to assassinate President Ronald Reagan. Levine (1985) has summarized evidence showing that psychiatric judgments are highly unreliable, especially within the adversary process. The degree of reliability that may emerge in research tests of the diagnostic system may not hold for other contexts. Moreover, psychiatric judgments are difficult to support when they are subject to question. Theoretical abstractions applied with minimal rules of inference from shaky evidence are easy to dispute. The evidence that patients who are represented by attorneys more often win dismissal of petitions to retain them than do unrepresented patients underscores the point (Wenger & Fletcher, 1969).

The nature and degree of the patient's presenting condition are not the only (and may not even be the primary) considerations in the decision to hospitalize and thus to assign a diagnostic label for the record.

Many other variables affect the decision to admit. On admission services, the family's desire for the individual to be hospitalized tends to be a stronger factor in the admission decision than is the clinician's judgment of degree of disorder, although some parents who have unsuccessfully sought the hospitalization of a spouse or adult child may dispute that conclusion. Many factors beyond the patient's presenting condition influence admission decisions, including fear of being manipulated by a patient, research needs for a certain kind of patient, or the need for certain cases for teaching or training purposes (Baxter et al., 1968; Hogarty et al., 1968; Richart & Milner, 1968; Tischler, 1966).

Those who are selected for labeling may have some social or clinical characteristics that make it easier for some labels to stick. Lindsay (1982) demonstrates that his research subjects could readily detect first-admission persons with schizophrenia from nonpatients when observing interviews on the topic of schooling, even when given false labels. Apparently, in some patients, disturbance is obvious.

However, the stringency of the decision-making process leaves much to be desired under ordinary working conditions, as Rosenhan's (1973) classic study demonstrates. Rosenhan showed that pseudopatients (researchers who presented themselves to a mental hospital admitting service as ill but who demonstrated only the most minimal symptoms) were readily admitted on their own application, and their deception went undetected. The diagnostic process is sufficently unreliable under ordinary working conditions that labels can readily be misapplied (Kirk & Kutchins, 1992). This body of evidence supports one component of the labeling theory model, although it by no means confirms the major proposition of labeling theory that anyone thus mislabeled could be made a career deviant.

Behavior Is Assimilated to the Label

Few rules govern observation and inference in the psychiatric setting. Many clinicians are unaware of the limits of inferences drawn from clinical observations (Dawes, 1994). Any behavior observed in the hospital may be readily interpreted in light of the initial diagnosis or the patient's status as a patient. Patients are observed and diagnosed on the basis of an important unstated assumption of the clinical enterprise that stems from the pervasive influence of Freudian thinking on clinical workers. In the Freudian system, surface appearances are distrusted and situational factors are discounted. The important factor is not what is apparent but what lies underneath the apparent. Because there are no or few explicit rules relating observed behavior to the unobserved construct, anything can be related to anything else. One can accept the surface behavior or reinterpret it to fit whatever construct the worker has in mind.

Observing psychiatric residents in training, Light (1982) notes that they were often bewildered by the intangible nature of psychiatric symptoms and complaints. He believes they were subject to doctrinaire instruction, with little review of the research literature to foster an appreciation of the weakness of the methods and theories they were being taught. He argues that the process of psychiatric interviewing leads to accentuating the neurotic characteristics of everyone concerned, including the psychiatric interviewer. Consequently, interviewers feel a need to distance and to differentiate themselves from patients.[7] Light argues that all of the uncertainties lead to quick assimilation of the psychiatric culture, including uncritical use of diagnostic labels. We have no reason to believe that clinical psychologists or psychiatric social workers training in medical settings are any more immune to this culture than are psychiatric residents. We have some evidence that psychologists trained in behavioral approaches may be less inclined to resort to inferences about unobservable causes and may be more immune to labeling effects in observing patients (Langer & Abelson, 1974).

Once a tentative diagnosis is developed, many aspects of patient behavior are assimilated to the diagnosis. Rosenhan (1973) reports that perfectly normal behavior of his pseudopatients was recorded as symptoms of disturbance. Light (1982) also reports that the psychiatrists he observed were unaware of the degree to which their own personal styles in dealing with patients contributed to patient reactions. There was an uncritical assumption that the way the patient appeared in the clinical interview with that doctor was predictive of the patient's behavior in all other circumstances and that all behavior was a function of the patient's psychopathology.

Psychiatric training, centering as it does on the classification of disorders into mutually exclusive categories and on the assumption that environmental circumstances do not matter very much, fails to sensitize practitioners to the situationally determined character of much behavior. Braginsky, Braginsky, and Ring (1969) demonstrated that patients can manipulate their presentation of themselves in psychiatric interviews depending on their goals. Blind ratings of psychopathology from tape recordings of interviews showed that when patients wanted to achieve a valued goal (e.g., move to a more desirable ward), less psychopathology was found than when patients believed the interview would have a result they wished to avoid (e.g., for these chronic patients, discharge from the hospital).

Many studies have shown the limited predictability of clinical assessments to behavior in other settings. Ratings of psychopathology based on psychiatric interviews, for example, do not predict work competence (Lipton & Kadin, 1965; Olshansky, 1968). Quite a number of studies have shown that professional prediction of adjustment in the community, based on knowledge of behavior in the institution, is poor (Ellsworth et al., 1968; Stack, Lannon, & Miley, 1983). Tuckman and Lavell (1962) showed that patients discharged against medical advice did just as well in the community as those discharged with medical approval. The only difference was that patients discharged against medical advice had somewhat shorter hospital stays. Even if the use of *DSM*-IV criteria results in more reliable application of clinical labels, we have no reason to believe that judgments predicated on those labels will have any greater validity. The mental health world view simply does not take situational influences sufficiently into account, and so it is all too easy to assume that any behavior that is observed is related to pathology.

In labeling theory, staff within institutions assimilate patient behavior to patient diagnosis and find reasons that the patient is "sick." Patient complaints and objections are likely to be treated as manifestations of resistance or as part of the patient's illness. The patient's suggestibility during a period of crisis and the patient's distress at treatment in the hospital may lead to behavior that appears out of control both to the observer and to the patient.

A patient may refuse medication for any number of reasons, for example, including the fear that medication will produce untoward side effects. Yet hospital personnel may label the patient's resistance to taking the medication "paranoid" and insist that the patient accept it. If the patient continues to refuse and loses his or her temper or cries when pressed, the patient may be considered to be hostile and aggressive or in a labile emotional state. The patient, noting the emotional behavior in himself or herself, may feel out of control. At that point, self-observation coupled with reinforcement from powerful others feeds into the formation of the person's identity as "sick."

Once the self is viewed as "sick," the next step is to accept the role of good patient and to play it out until discharge. During a hospital stay, much of a patient's life is regimented. Patients lose a great deal of autonomy and are encouraged to rely on the advice and direction of treating personnel. A "good" patient accepts the therapeutic regime without question. One who disputes the professional's view of his or her intentions, motives, feelings, or behavior is judged resistant. Rosenhan (1973) reports that a pseudopatient who was bored by the lack of activity in the hospital paced the dayroom. When questioned by a nurse, the pseudopatient said that he was bored. The nurse insisted that the pseudopatient was anxious and persisted in getting the pseudopatient to accept the "true" nature of his "symptom" of pacing. If the pseudopatient expressed annoyance at the nurse, in all likelihood he would have been characterized as resistant and hostile. If he accepted her interpretation of his state, he would have been characterized as having "gained insight" and thus improving. In other words, powerful social forces are at work to encourage the patient to accept and to internalize the hospital's and the professional's views of the patient's condition and capabilities.

Gove is willing to admit that in bygone days, chronicity may have been fostered in total institutions that kept patients for long periods. He believes the situation has changed drastically in recent years, however (see Kiesler, 1982). Given modern clinical practices, most patients are released relatively quickly, with little time for chronicity to set in. In addition, the removal of a patient from a stressful life setting has ameliorative effects in and of itself. The hospital experience provides a retreat during which the person may recover. Moreover, active therapy does help a great many individuals. Gove argues that far from keeping patients in the patient role, adequate treatment frees patients. He points out that in the absence of treatment, many deinstitutionalized patients quickly deteriorate.

In sum, methods of diagnosis and observation are probably not very good. We do not have powerful theories and constructs that allow us to predict accurately to new circumstances (see Chapter 5). We can too easily assume that once sick, always sick, or that everything we observe in a person reflects his or her sickness. Mental health personnel probably convey such attitudes to their patients, and to some degree patients tend to accept those views of themselves. Present-day conditions of treatment surely are not sufficient to produce the kind of chronic condition that is implied in the concept of a career deviant. Nonetheless, labeling theory's emphasis on the undesirable side effects of care should be taken seriously, if only to cause us to reexamine our attitudes and practices with an eye toward understanding their consequences and limitations. Not all that is done in the name of doing good in fact does good.

Stigma

The final factor aiding in the formation of a deviant career is the stigma attached to the role of mental patient or former mental patient (see Goffman, 1963). In Scheff's view, once the patient returns to the community, the stigma of having been a mental patient continues to follow him or her. Opportunities for employment may be affected, and, equally important, other people will tend to interpret the individual's behavior in light of the history of mental illness. The person may also feel more uncomfortable knowing that his or her status is suspect, and that discomfort may leak, providing others with data to confirm their suspicions. It may be easier for the individual to be rehospitalized because he or she has never been fully rid of the taint to social identity. The stigma attached to mental illness serves to keep the released patient in the tainted role, thus creating the role of career deviant or chronic mental patient. The disagreement between Scheff and Gove revolves around the role of stigma in creating chronic mental patients. Labeling theory places a great deal of emphasis on this issue, while Gove claims that the primary determinant of any social reaction to a former mental patient is the person's current behavior.

In an earlier day, in addition to whatever informal social sanctions followed commitment, the individual was placed under a number of formal constraints. His or her liberty to engage in a great many activities was restricted. A committed mental patient, regardless of competence, might lose a driver's license, be unable to contract for goods and services, be disqualified from marrying, or be barred from military service. In recent times, however, the rights of mental patients have been better protected (Ennis & Siegel, 1973). In addition to formal disabilities, former mental patients also carried occupational and social stigma. The President's Commission on Mental Health (Task Panel, 1978a) indicated that in its view, stigma was still a critical factor in the contemporary mental health scene.

In labeling theory, stigma helps to keep the person in the patient role. Significant others may interpret the individual's behavior in light of their knowledge of the person's history. Anger, dislikes, disagreements, moods, or failure to achieve may all be read as continued manifestations of disorder or as prodromal to another episode, even after a period of normality. Recall Rosenhan's (1973) report that the normal behavior of his pseudopatients was interpreted as pathological by nurses and attendants and recorded in case files as symptoms of disorder; pacing out of boredom was characterized as anxiety, and note taking for purposes of research became compulsive writing. Even after discharge, the diagnosis was not changed, and the person continued to carry the label—Schizophrenia, Chronic Undifferentiated Type, in Remission. To use Goffman's (1963) term, the patient's social identity was "spoiled."

If we have any question concerning the power of stigmatization, we need only look at Senator Thomas Eagleton, who was forced to withdraw from candidacy for the vice presidency in the 1972 election campaign after it was revealed that he had been treated for a depressive disorder many years before. Even though he had functioned visibly and responsibly in positions of public leadership for many years following the episode, the stigma of mental disorder was sufficient to disqualify him from running for that office.

Not only public figures suffer. One of the authors was psychotherapist for a boy of about fourteen who had been having more than the usual share of growing-up difficulties. Several years later the young man joined the navy. He completed basic and specialist training successfully and performed competently in the navy. Despite the navy's experience with him over several years, when his promotion required an additional security clearance, a naval intelligence officer contacted his therapist, wanting to know about the nature of problems for which the boy had been treated several years earlier.

The ordinary person is also concerned about stigma. During the initial days of the Love Canal crisis, blue-collar families actively avoided the eager mental health worker on the scene. They avoided the table labeled Mental Health, not because they were not under emotional strain but because they feared their neighbors' reactions if they openly accepted help. "I'm not crazy!" they would say (Gibbs, 1983).

Is stigma a potent factor in producing career deviants? One body of studies using surveys and questionnaires suggests that Americans have become more tolerant of mental illness over the years. The research procedure often makes use of vignettes portraying various types of disorders; it measures social distance in terms of a scale that asks questions such as: Would you accept such a person in your community? Would you work with such a person? Would you rent a room in your home to such a person? Would you want such a person to marry into your family?

Studies using these methods have reported very mixed results (Socall & Holtgraves, 1992). Most of the studies used one of two different methods of collecting data. In one group of studies, subjects completed paper-and-pencil social-distance scales using vignettes describing patients. The second group of studies employed face-to-face interviews and asked about a hypothetical mental patient. Researchers coming from medical backgrounds and institutions tended to use the face-to-face interview, using the hypothetical mental patient as the stimulus, and found that public attitudes toward the mentally ill were improving. Social science researchers preferred to use self-response questionnaires and vignettes as the stimulus material. Their studies consistently reported negative attitudes toward mental patients (Socall & Holtgraves, 1992). Results reporting the degree of optimism or pessimism attributed to the public may thus be a function of method and discipline of the investigator more than of the public's real attitude (Brockman, D'Arcy, & Edmonds, 1979).

At an attitudinal level, at least as measured by scales and self-report, the stigma attached to having a history of mental illness may have been reduced from the level of earlier times (Skinner et al., 1995). Public education campaigns to reduce the stigma of mental illness conducted by the American Psychiatric Association (Regier et al., 1988) and the National Alliance for the Mentally Ill (see Chapter 9) may be helping in this regard. We really know very little about the relationship between expressed attitudes and behavior. Public education on questions of mental illness may have influenced what people are willing to say on questionnaires, but it does not necessarily follow that people always act in complete consistency with their expressed attitudes.

Some studies, however, show that families of mentally ill people are more tolerant toward the mentally ill than is the general public. Family members report experiencing little stigma despite their expectation that stigma would be great (Clausen, 1981). Family members do report concealing to some degree the family member's history of hospitalization for their own social comfort. A body of literature summarized in Tebes (1983) suggests that family members often reduce the frequency of their visits to mentally ill persons and that many are reluctant to accept the person back into the home. Distinguishing between rejection that results from stigma and rejection that results from the strain of dealing with a mentally ill person is difficult. Tebes believes the explanation that family members reject the mental patient because of the physical, economic, and psychological burdens of care is more plausible than the theory that rejection is based on stigma.

The situation of family members may differ from that of potential neighbors, employers, landlords, and others dealing with the former mental patient. Many court cases have challenged zoning ordinances that exclude group homes for the mentally ill and the mentally retarded from residential neighborhoods. (The U.S. Supreme Court decided such a case in 1985: *City of Cleburne, Texas* v. *Cleburne Living Center*, 1985.) The existence of zoning ordinances reflects community attitudes. People fear being harmed or they fear property values will decrease. Both of those fears appear to be exaggerated.

In the case of the mentally retarded, studies show that the presence of a group home has little or no impact on any measurable aspect of neighborhood property value (Dolan & Wolpert, 1982). Studies also show that mentally retarded individuals living in group homes in the community have a far lower rate of contact with the police than do average citizens in that community (Lubin, Janicki, Zigman, & Ross, 1982; Uhl & Levine, 1990). When a group home is proposed for a neighborhood, there is often vocal community opposition, and plans to open some group homes may have been changed because of local opposition. If such a home does open, however, follow-up studies show that neighbors become positive or indifferent toward it after a while. We assume that if undesirable consequences actually had followed the opening of a group home, neighborhood opposition would have increased with time. The initial attitude thus appears to be prejudiced and based on stigma, not on the actual events that follow the opening of a group home.

Employers may stigmatize persons with a history of mental illness, making it difficult for the former mental patients to obtain employment. Brand and Claiborn (1976) sent four undergraduates and two graduate students to answer ads for job openings in retail sales. Each student participated in six interviews. In two they gave histories as former tuberculosis patients, in two they said they were former convicts, and in two they described themselves as former mental patients. They were coached to dress and to act the same in each role. In the role of former tuberculosis patient, 75 percent received job offers. Those who said they were former convicts and former mental patients drew job offers 58 percent of the time. These results indicate that although employers will hire former patients for some jobs, former patients are still at some handicap when being considered for employment. That this handicap is no worse than that facing former convicts does not change the conclusion. These were entry-level jobs. We don't know what would happen if the experiment were to be repeated with positions requiring more responsibility. Note also that Scheff's model should apply to any form of deviance.

Once the former mental patient has a job, the degree of disability associated with a history of hospitalization is relatively small. Ratings by work supervisors were somewhat poorer for those who had had a schizophrenic diagnosis than for those who had had a neurotic diagnosis, but the latter were rated much the same as those who had no psychiatric history. People with diagnoses of schizophrenia showed lower rates of promotion and higher rates of demotion and job leaving, but the majority (78 percent) had no such difficulties. It was not clear in the study (Cole, McDonald, & Branch, 1968) whether work supervisors were aware of the former patients' histories of treatment. If they were blind to the histories, differences between patients and others can be attributed to patient behavior and not to the label.

Gebhard and Levine (1985) constructed résumés of people already employed and asked management students to say whether they would promote the people described to a more responsible position. The résumés were identical, except that in one the individual had lost time from work three years earlier due to a gall bladder operation; in the second, the person was described as having lost time from work due to alcoholism; in the third, the person was described as having lost time from work due to alcoholism and was a member of Alcoholics Anonymous. The label of alcoholism significantly reduced the person's chances of being considered for promotion, even though the résumés all indicated very good job performance and no indication of alcohol problems for the preceding three years. The study was designed to test the hypothesis that membership in Alcoholics Anonymous would be destigmatizing. That hypothesis could not be confirmed.

Former patients are probably subject to labeling effects in social relationships. Page (1977, 1983) called landlords who had advertised the availability of rental units in the classified section of a daily newspaper. If the person calling identified himself as having been a mental patient, the response from the landlord was immediately less positive. In one study, the simple fact that the caller stuttered was sufficient to reduce the number of positive responses to the call (a positive response being that the rental quarters were still available and the person was encouraged to make an appointment to see them). In other words, any deviant condition may be sufficiently stigmatizing to reduce opportunities for the person so stigmatized.

The courts have noted that stigma can be a problem. It is not necessary that a claimant for disability under Social Security or under the Supplemental Security Income (SSI) program be represented by an attorney. In *Cullison* v. *Califano* (1980), however, the court noted that claims for disability on the basis of mental or psychological symptoms are likely to lead to highly prejudiced determinations by the administrative officials who review these claims. The court stopped short of requiring that counsel be provided to ensure that these claims are reviewed thoroughly and impartially. The claimant's credibility is at stake in such instances, and persons with histories of mental disorder, having spoiled identities, may be much less able to speak for themselves because their identities lead others to discount what they say. In speaking as it did, the court was recognizing a consistent problem in the cases that had been reviewed on appeal.

Tebes (1983) reviewed a large number of field and laboratory studies testing the effects of stigmatization. He concluded:

> The results from studies of labeling effects reveal that, in social interactions, both the perceptions and behaviors of persons carrying a mental disorder label and those responding to them are significantly affected by the pejorative impact of the label. This impact predisposes the labeled person to feel and be rejected by others. On the one hand, there is the situation where the non-labeled social participant is aware of the person's deviant history. In many such cases, the labeled person can expect social responses of rejection and/or avoidance especially if the labeled participant is male. On the other hand, if the former patient believes his deviant history is known to others in his immediate social situation, the problem is further compounded by the likelihood that he will act in a way which alienates those around him, thus predisposing him to rejection. Clearly, the former mental patient would do well to conceal his status if at all possible, a practice which, ironically in itself requires considerable social agility, as Goffman (1963) has described. (pp. 70–71)

The question of whether stigma is sufficiently powerful to prevent a person who is otherwise behaving normally from reentering normal life must be restated. For some people, some occupations, and some relationships, stigma may operate forcefully, while in other cases it will not. The available evidence does support labeling theory's emphasis on the force of stigma in maintaining a person in a deviant role, but the proposition as stated is oversimplified.

Some Cautions

The usefulness and attractiveness of labeling theory as an analytic device do not imply that its every detail is accurate. Whatever the validity of its specific propositions, however, labeling theory is useful as an analytic device, provided one does not overlook the fact that the behavior of many who do come to the attention of some system of social control may indeed be difficult to tolerate, burdensome, repulsive, or dangerous. A flaw of labeling theory is that it feeds too neatly into an antiauthority stance in favor of any underdog. Nonetheless, the theory points out areas of interest for research, service, and prevention. As a model, it helps us pay attention to a broader set of variables than individual psychology includes.

Our first caution is that the labeling position in its strong version (i.e., that under given conditions, a chronic mental patient can be created out of nothing more than the violation of a social norm) is almost certainly wrong, as Gove (1980, 1982) has diligently and persuasively shown. The reader should thus take Scheff (1966, 1975, 1984) along with a full dose of Gove (1980, 1982), a proponent of the medical model and labeling theory's chief critic. The weaker version, that social disability (i.e., career deviance) based on an initial episode of rule breaking may vary depending on treatment, is a more viable position (Killian & Killian, 1990). Even that version is unable to account for variations in outcomes after the initial deviant episode, however. Not all who are treated become chronic patients, and diagnosis does have some predictive significance for long-term outcomes. People diagnosed as schizophrenic, for example, are more likely to become chronic patients than those who receive diagnoses of depressive reactions. Since all patients are affected by the same diagnostic and treatment system, labeling theory must account for the fact that outcomes differ systematically by diagnostic category.

Outcomes also vary by initial symptom picture and diagnosis. Not all who are publicly labeled become career deviants, a fact that labeling theory does not explain. Nor does it explain why some who have not been labeled also have symptoms that persist or develop chronic conditions. Moreover, other longitudinal studies have revealed perplexing problems for labeling theory. Robins (1974) showed that antisocial behavior in childhood predicts antisocial behavior in adult life among those who were treated (labeled) in a child guidance clinic. Yet most children with antisocial behavior patterns do not grow up into antisocial adults, whether or not they receive treatment. Moreover, those children who presented neurotic complaints and were treated (labeled) were no different at follow-up than were untreated controls. Studies of these two categories of behavior show that outcome does vary by initial symptom picture, and labeling theory cannot account for that fact. Labeling theory is at best incomplete, and at worst wrong.

A second caution is also in order. Because labeling theory pays less attention to the behavior triggering the labeling process and more to the labeling process and its consequences, its adherents may well overlook the fact that difficult behavior does exist, and not only in the eyes of the beholder. Because labeling theory argues that the social reaction is critical does not mean that the behavior that triggers the labeling process is objectively harmless. Rule-breaking behavior can be difficult to bear, both for the person exhibiting it and for those around him or her. Such behavior may understandably elicit reactions of fear, anger, loathing, helplessness, or weariness.

Scheff's (1966, 1984) exposition depicts deviance as a social status or role within the larger culture, but a role whose characteristics are closely related to the way in which mental hospitals and mental health professionals work. Perforce, labeling theory extended our vision to include among the variables of interest the individual's social position and the professional care system. Even if wrong in its details, and if it did nothing else, labeling theory has made it more difficult for us to think about psychopathology in isolation from the social context and the system of care.

Summary

We have emphasized that labeling theory is to be valued more for the analytic perspective it offers than for the correctness of its details. We cannot overlook the reality that some of its predictions have not been verified. However, a scientific conception that leads us to seek out observations that will test its propositions is valuable for that reason alone. Labeling theory has done exactly that. It has asked us to look at data that we would have overlooked had we adopted the perspective that psychopathology resides solely within an individual's skin.

Labeling theory encompasses individual differences in behavior. It does not say that any behavior or person is equally subject to labeling or to developing a deviant career. The theory does direct our attention to the social setting within which the particular behavior pattern is manifested, however, and asks us to look at the relationships among individuals in their roles, the agents of social control, and the therapeutic system. If we recall the ecological lessons of Chapter 4, labeling theory alerts us to the consequences of diversity in status, values, and goals among different groups that happen to share the same community settings. It explains more thoroughly than did Sarbin's role theory how the behavior of others can limit one's opportunities in ways that cut across multiple situations and endure over time.

A weakness of labeling theory is that it does not distinguish among the initial causes of abnormal behavior and thus provides no new insights into this aspect of the problem. Unlike the conceptions presented in Chapters 4 and 5, however, labeling theory does consider the individual's contribution to the process. The theory provides a conceptual corrective for our exclusive reliance on the psychology of the individual.

Labeling theory has something in common with the Dohrenwend position discussed in Chapter 3 (and considered further in Chapter 7). Both are systems theories that emphasize the context within which behavior is studied. Both viewpoints also emphasize the transient nature of the initial deviant episode. Labeling theory focuses on the undesirable and unanticipated effects of the existing treatment system, which might be understood as society's effort to supply social support to the individual in need. Dohrenwend's position calls attention to the positive effects of existing social and personal resources for helping when an individual is experiencing a stressful life event.

The reader should reflect on the similarities between the concepts of adaptation, crisis, coping, and social support and labeling theory. Primary deviance, for example, may be thought of as the initial emotional and behavioral reaction to a stressful life event. One may also draw a parallel between the social support available to a person and the system of care provided for mental health problems. In addition, one may consider how the societal reaction to an emotional response produced by acute stress (whether or not the person's problem comes to public attention) is influenced by the psychological mediators the person uses as well as the so-cial support that is available.

Last, when we propose alternative methods of providing assistance to the individual in distress, the reader should keep labeling theory in mind. Especially in its emphasis on the stigma associated with treatment under some conditions, labeling theory reminds us that interventions generally have multiple effects. It directs us to examine the possibility that the newer forms of assistance, designed to assist the processes of coping and adaptation following a stressful event, may also have unintended consequences. Having noted the complementary features of the Dohrenwend and the labeling viewpoints, we turn now to an elaboration of the Dohrenwend discussion and some concepts and research associated with it.

Notes

1. Although Scheff's model and the present discussion center on the problem of chronic mental illness, the model is applicable to any form of deviance.

2. We are indebted to attorney Sheila Graziano for this example drawn from her practice.

3. This position has something in common with Dohrenwend's model (see Chapter 3). In neither Scheff's nor Dohrenwend's models does the stressful experience inevitably proceed to a pathological reaction.

4. This position is related to Bishop Berkeley's famous philosophical question about whether a tree falling in the forest makes a sound if no one hears it.

5. Melton's (1984) critique of the U.S. Supreme Court opinion in Parham is based on empirical data assessing the validity and reliability of diagnosis. Berger (1985) raises many questions about the due process implications of giving as much decision-making authority to mental health workers as Parham does.

6. In *O'Connor* v. *Donaldson* (1975), the U.S. Supreme Court upheld the civil liability of a hospital superintendent who refused to discharge a patient who was not dangerous to himself or others. The legal decision adds to the problem a psychiatric decision maker faces. If a patient is released prematurely and injures someone, the decision maker may be held liable; if the patient is held unnecessarily, liability may also accrue.

7. As a personal anecdote, Levine notes that when he worked in a mental hospital he often found himself fingering the keys that differentiated him from the patients. These keys served as a security blanket.

7

Adaptation, Crisis,
Coping, and Support

In Chapter 3 we introduced Barbara Dohrenwend's (1978) useful perspective on stress and disorder as a more comprehensive model of mental health than that provided by traditional clinical conceptions, and one offering alternative solutions to mental health problems. The present chapter elaborates Dohrenwend's overall model. We begin by examining the concepts of adaptation and crisis in light of the traditional psychoanalytic conception of disorder, extend the idea of a psychological crisis to recent research on stressful life events, and then reevaluate the person-environment approach using what has come to be called the "vulnerability" model. This model paves the way for a discussion of coping and social support.

One issue is how individuals avoid developing psychopathology or, more positively, move to restore psychological equilibrium, and even achieve psychological growth, as a result of exposure to and mastery of a stressful life event.

Adaptation

Dohrenwend (1978) defines the aim of community psychology as "undermining the process whereby stress generates psychopathology" (p. 2).[1] A useful starting point in understanding this process is the concept of "adaptation." Adaptation refers to improvements in the fit between an individual's behavior and the specific demands and constraints imposed by the settings that make up his or her environment. Adaptation is facilitated by widening the niche provided in the environment and/or increasing the behavioral competence of the resident person—that is, strengthening his or her "niche breadth." Recall that in Fairweather's lodge for people with chronic mental illness (see Chapter 5), residents' living and working conditions were modified somewhat to compensate for their lack of full autonomy and employability, and residents also worked to develop useful social and job-related skills as employees of their own businesses. Dohrenwend's model implies that change in the environment is an ongoing stimulus to behavior and that any given state of adaptation is therefore episodic and time-limited, always subject to challenge by the next stressful event.

In addition to meaning the modification of one's behavior in response to altered conditions, adaptation has additional (dictionary) meanings that refer to conformity or adjustment. From a humanistic, "self-actualizing" perspective, the concept of adapting or adjusting oneself to external conditions can be anathema. If one sees the social environment as oppressive, then encouraging adaptation to it is to act as an agent of oppression. Should disadvantaged, poverty-stricken, stigmatized, and other relatively powerless groups play the game of adaptation to the social world as it is, or are their interests sometimes better served by methods that raise consciousness and demand change in the environment?

Raising this question may alert us to a problem that has no absolute solution, because it is impossible to think of a criterion of mental health that does not refer to a social order of some kind. Freud, for example, defined the normal, healthy person as one who can love, work, and play. These seem like individual goals, but as soon as one says love, work, or play, one is necessarily involved with other people in some kind of social order. Inevitably, even those change strategies that Goldenberg (1978,

p. 17) terms fundamental or basic and that meet his criteria for social intervention (i.e., "collective action, an institutional focus, and an orientation toward altering existing practices and priorities") have as their end result the adaptation of individuals to some social order. Although the term *social adaptation* seems to imply that individuals must adjust to a fixed social order and thus appears conservative, in fact every individual adapts to some social order. Furthermore, nothing in the concept precludes adapting by acting to change social conditions.

Social adaptations imply socially structured transactions between person and environment. A stressful event may threaten the availability of resources, disrupt ongoing transactions, and require an adaptive response. The range of possible disruptions is broad, and the adaptive change required may be quite significant. To survive as a biosocial organism in the "self-maintenance" ecology (see Chapter 5), one must correctly identify objects and events and define oneself in relation to those objects and events; one must correctly identify one's own need for food, oxygen, shelter, and the like and have the wherewithal to obtain those necessities (Hansell, 1974). To have money, or purchasing power, is one form of attachment to the social order; in the absence of the means to participate in the exchange of goods and services, the individual is in serious difficulty. Health risks, for example, are linearly related to socioeconomic status. It is no surprise that you can expect to live a longer and healthier life if you have more money (Adler, Boyce, Chesney, et al., 1994).

Sarbin (1970) speaks also of the "social" ecology, where through a variety of social roles one achieves a sense of self-worth and belongingness. Failure to locate oneself correctly within the social ecology violates others' expectations and leads to corresponding efforts to have expectations fulfilled. The threatened loss of an important achieved role may well put a person under stress. A recently retired judge, for example, accustomed to receiving deference from others, may be distressed by the experience of being treated like any other anonymous older person.

Failure and disappointment with oneself and the reactions of others to oneself are critical to locating oneself within the "normative" ecology (i.e., to answering the question "How well am I doing?"). If the answer is "Not very well," the person may be forced to seek some other form of adaptation.

Finally, the individual must locate himself or herself in what Sarbin calls the "transcendental" ecology, where the questions have to do with values. Hansell (1974) also recognizes the necessity for a comprehensive system of meanings that help clarify current experience and help define ambiguity in events and relationships. When one's gods fail and a state of meaninglessness threatens, one is greatly troubled and may seek new sources of meaning or a new kind of adaptation.

To summarize, adaptation can involve biological, social, self-referent, or value-laden dimensions. A given state of adaptation is also situation-specific and temporary, not sweeping and permanent. It may be disrupted

by new stressors and other changes in the external environment, with periods of adaptation inevitably alternating with transient periods of disequilibrium. How can we conceptualize the disruptive state that signals
the need for adaptation?

Crisis and Neurosis

Just as the individual deprived of oxygen or food experiences a physiological crisis or emergency, so too does the individual whose attachments
(in Hansell's terms) or locations in the several ecologies (in Sarbin's terms)
are disrupted enter a state of crisis. Crisis is defined here as any rapid
change or encounter that provides an individual with a "no-exit" challenge, no choice but to alter his or her conduct in some manner (Hansell,
1974).

The concept of crisis was very influential in the development of community mental health and preventive modalities of care. Crisis theory began with Erich Lindemann's (1944) follow-up study of relatives of victims of a Boston nightclub fire. Each survivor had to carry out "grief
work" by detaching from the relationship with the deceased person,
readapting to an environment no longer including the deceased, and then
forming new attachments and relationships. Lindemann concluded that
stressful events in the life cycle require adaptation, a shift in emphasis from
the dominant thinking in mental health at that time.

To understand fully the shift in orientation signaled by the crisis concept, we will contrast it with the psychoanalytic theory of neurosis. The
person-centered model of psychoanalysis postulated that behavioral problems were the result of unresolved conflicts left over from earlier phases
of development. These conflicts were repressed or otherwise defended
against psychologically. As long as the defenses worked effectively, enabling the individual to avoid anxiety, all was reasonably well, except that
the individual's lifestyle would be constructed to maintain the defensive
pattern. At some point, however, something might happen to interfere
with the effectiveness of the defense. If the underlying repressed impulse
became too strong, the defense would fail, and repressed energy would
return in the form of great anxiety.

For psychoanalysis, "symptoms" are a means of controlling the intense anxiety associated with the return of a formerly repressed impulse.
At times the individual debilitated by a symptom (e.g., repetitive, compulsive hand washing) achieves "secondary gain"—that is, others may organize their lives about the sick person, take care of him or her, or otherwise allow the symptom to control their relationships. The symptom is
reinforced because it creates other benefits, but further disability may result. Other life tasks may not be accomplished, leading to further problems in adaptation.

The classical Freudian model recognizes as a precipitating event whatever it is that strengthens a drive or weakens a defense and results in anxiety. The compulsive hand washer feels compelled; any attempt to limit the hand washing elicits strong fear. The earlier "arrest" in psychological development returns to disable or at least badly disturb the individual. Thus, the focus is on the individual instead of on the precipitating event.

Psychoanalytic theory dealt with clinical observations of people who had already become disabled. Freud, who was a physician, accepted the disease model. Because his theory postulated that the basic cause of a present disorder took place long ago, little could be done in the present until the "original" problems were worked through. This psychoanalytic conception limits the possibilities for intervention. Furthermore, the specific precipitating events are not important because their meaning derives from the individual's unconscious interpretation. If a panic state is precipitated by taking a new job, that event would have psychopathological significance only if the individual viewed the new position of authority as a displacement of his father, with the rearousal of Oedipal fears that father will castrate the upstart challenger.

In crisis theory, accepting a new job is viewed as a challenge to the previous state of adaptation, thus requiring a new adaptation. Accepting a new position of authority may call for new, yet to be learned, or unpracticed coping skills. Entering a position of authority also changes the individual's adaptation within a network of supportive relationships. After all, one can hardly get together with the boys to knock the boss when one *is* the boss.

The crisis concept is similar to that of "neurosis," except that crisis does not imply disease. The terms themselves express a difference in outlook. *Neurosis* comes from a Greek word meaning "sinew" or "tendon." The term also referred to the condition of an object, its strength, vigor, or energy—for example, a taut bowstring. By Freud's time, neurosis meant a functional disorder of the nervous system, unaccompanied by organic change. In the medical model, the underlying concept of "nervous" means that the nerves themselves are not functioning properly.

Crisis comes from a Greek root meaning "to decide." It describes a point in the course of a disease that is decisive for either recovery or death. More generally, the term means a critical turning point in the progress of some state of affairs in which a decisive change, for better or for worse, is imminent. The idea that change can be for the better and not just for the worse leads us to think and act differently; it implies a reserve of strength, a capacity to deal or cope with or master the distress.

While neurosis is defined as a failure of the defenses, a crisis occurs when an individual faces seemingly insurmountable obstacles to important life goals and the customary methods of resolving problems don't seem suitable. We may say the individual is dislocated in one of the four ecologies or that some vital attachments have been disrupted and a new response is required. Anyone can experience a state of crisis, not only those with some previous "fixation." A state of crisis should be expected whenever some external event requires a change in one's customary ways of dealing with a problem.

Crisis theorists (Ewing, 1978; Golan, 1978; Parad, 1965; Slaikeu, 1984) postulate several essential features of a crisis. First is a stressful or hazardous event or events requiring change. The event presents a new problem which the person may perceive as unsolvable in the present or the immediate future.

Hazardous or stressful life events are classified as *anticipated* or *unanticipated*. *Unanticipated* events are losses beyond the individual's control (e.g., death in the family, lost job, illness resulting in disability or disfigurement) or threats (e.g., physical disaster, assault, rape, or assault to one's personal integrity, as in the case of a woman in a concentration camp who had to make a choice between her life and her mother's life). Although unanticipated events are those whose timing cannot be predicted, in some cases (such as the death of a family member) the general class of events may be predictable. *Anticipated* events generally refer to role transitions, changes in a way of life, new responsibilities, or the necessity to develop new social relationships. Entering school, getting married, retiring, becoming a parent, or moving to a new location are all examples. Because these events are predictable, we can devise preventive actions or position assistance so that it is available when and where it is needed.

A second characteristic of a crisis is that the new problem taxes the material, physical, or psychological resources of the individual, his or her family, or others in the individual's social support network. Experiencing a bereavement, losing a parent or a spouse, having a premature child born into the family, becoming a parent for the first time, or becoming the boss all require people to take action, experience new emotions, and make unfamiliar decisions. A crisis arises when one's methods of dealing with one's own emotions and the external problems are inadequate. A person in crisis may feel helpless, ineffective, anxious, fearful, and guilty, with the result that his or her behavior is less efficient than usual.

The crisis situation may awaken old personal problems as well. For example, a person rejected by all the graduate schools to which he or she has applied faces two problems. The person must decide what else to do, a task that may bring back ambivalence and uncertainty about making choices or about growing up. Second, he or she usually feels rejected, frustrated, and a failure, which may reawaken old feelings about rejection or helplessness when someone else decides one's fate. (From a psychoanalytic viewpoint, this concept that the new problem may revive old problems is similar to the idea of the return of the repressed.) Once the individual is vulnerable, memories and feelings from the past may return, adding to the problem of coping in the present.

The acute phase of the state of upset must last more than a day or two to qualify as a crisis. Some say that the acute phase rarely lasts longer than six weeks,[2] although other evidence questions this claim (e.g., Lewis, Gottesman, & Gutstein, 1979). Data on this point are not plentiful, but as a matter of definition we do not call the episode a crisis unless the state of upset persists for more than a relatively brief period. The acute phase is sometimes referred to as a state of heightened vulnerability and is further divisible into two periods, one of initial impact and one of rising tension.

Initial impact refers to the recognition that the individual faces a situation that demands some response. Sometimes the initial phase is accompanied by a state of shock or numbness, but shortly thereafter tension rises rapidly as one recognizes the need to act. With the rise in tension the individual initiates his or her habitual problem-solving responses, which can be as varied as depending on someone else to solve the problem, retreating, or actively seeking information or alternatives.

Tension dissipates once the problem is solved. If the problem-solving device used was a new one, the person can be said to have grown or developed new knowledge or skills and now can command additional personal resources for dealing with the world.[3]

Box 7-1. Research on Stressful Life Events

Not all crises are resolved successfully. One hypothesis is that environmental factors and personal characteristics are both involved in adjusting to stress. Lindemann's seminal study of nightclub-fire survivors marked the beginning of a broad shift in attention away from pathological characteristics of certain individuals and toward the pathology-inducing aspects of stressful events. Similar investigations of otherwise ordinary people undergoing situational crises followed. Evidence accumulated showing a higher than expected incidence of disorders following highly traumatic experiences such as marital disruption (Bloom, Asher, & White, 1978) and economic distress (Kiernan, Toro, Rappaport, & Seidman, 1989; Dooley, Catalano, & Wilson, 1994). Selye's (1956) description of the "general adaptation syndrome" theorized that any significant change in a person's life upsets his or her equilibrium, creates stress, and thus requires a compensating, adaptive response. Large changes such as divorce or job loss, but also a series of smaller events in close succession, can overtax the individual's coping resources, threatening his or her physical or psychological well-being.

Subsequent investigators systematically pursued the idea that discrete, time-limited events requiring change or adaptation increase risk for a wide range of human disorders. An early list compiled by the psychiatrists Thomas Holmes and Richard Rahe (1967), called the Schedule of Recent Experiences (SRE), contained forty-three human events (e.g., marriage, change in residence, major personal injury or illness). An individual's life-stress score was simply the number of events he or she reported experiencing during some recent interval of time (usually between six and twenty-four months). Holmes and Rahe soon recognized that some of these events (e.g., death of spouse) required considerably more change and adaptation than did others (e.g., vacation), and so was born the Social Readjustment Rating Scale (SRRS), which weighted each event for the amount of change or readjustment the event required. The estimate of total life stress experienced by a person thus became the sum of the weights, or "life-change units," for the events reported. Events representing both positive experiences (e.g., Christmas) and those that are clearly negative (e.g., being fired from one's job) may make adaptive demands and thus produce stress.

Despite their limitations, life-events scales have become a standard measure of stress in surveys and have been used with many populations. Lazarus (1990) believes that stressful life events as defined in the Holmes and Rahe scales occur too infrequently to be useful. He believes that that measures of daily stressful encounters are better. The massive empirical literature leaves little doubt that a significant relationship exists between the cumulative experience of stress, as assessed by life-events scales,[4] and a host of adverse medical and psychological conditions (see Bloom, 1984, for a review).

Critical reviews, however, have pointed to the modest size of stress-disorder correlations (typically .30 or less, accounting for less than 10 percent of variance) (Rabkin & Streuning, 1976; Lazarus, 1990). Monroe and Steiner (1986) argue that because of overlap in language and meaning on life-events or "hassles" scales and measures of disorder, the reported relationships may be partly artifactual. Lazarus et al. (1985), on the other hand, do not believe that the apparent confounding of stress measurement and measures of disorder is sufficient to account for the relationships reported between stress and outcome.

This debate appears to turn on how stress is measured. Does the scale simply ask whether the event happened, or does it also determine whether the person perceived the event as stressful? Lazarus (1990) believes that confounding is inevitable because his theory requires that the event be appraised in terms of its harmfulness. The appraisal and the subsequent response are also measured subjectively. A significant correlation between a hassles measure and a self-report of the experience of stress may be influenced by "negative affectivity," a style of responding to self-report scales with a readiness to appraise situations as traumatic.

To what extent are the results "method-bound"? French, Knox, and Gekoski (1992) identified health-related items on a stressful life-events scale (e.g., hospitalization) that overlapped with outcome items (e.g., perceived health, total number of illnesses). These confounded stress and outcome items showed significant correlations in both males and females that decreased substantially when general health status was taken into account. French et al. concluded that "when a relation between life events and health status measures in elderly samples is observed, much of it is due to health-related item confounding" (p. 249).

Confounding is not an issue in all studies. For example, Chilean women who lived in areas characterized by a great deal of social and political violence experienced more frequent pregnancy complications than women living in less disruptive areas even when a variety of other social factors were controlled statistically. Stressful life events included the presence of armed forces and police, political arrests in the neighborhood, and knowledge that political prisoners were being kidnapped, executed, and subjected to torture. In this instance, the independent and dependent variables were not affected by confounds (Zapata, Rebolledo, Atalah, et al., 1992). Rowlinson and Felner (1988) reported that a measure of hassles did correlate with self-report of adjustment, but it also correlated with teacher ratings of adjustment. The two ratings were made independently, so a confound based on something like negative affectivity could not have occurred.

This debate notwithstanding, the degree of risk for virtually all outcomes, as measured by life-events scales, appears to fall short of the expectation created by the early studies, and several conceptual and methodological issues are worth raising. The quantification of life events as a measure of stress was a methodological breakthrough in what was previously a qualitative area of study. The empirical limits to stress-disorder prediction may to some extent reflect construct validity problems in the life-events scales, such as the implicit assumption that the stress-disorder relationship is linear: Catastrophic events elicit much stress and high risk for disorder, everyday events also entail some stress and some risk, and some stress is always riskier than no stress. On the other hand, it is also plausible that the absence of life events may itself be stressful and that exposure to some degree of stress is necessary for developing coping skills.

In Holmes and Rahe's work, moreover, life events are nonspecific stimuli having no differential impacts. No significant role is played by the individual's cognitive appraisal of events or the degree of social support available to him or her. The original idea now seems oversimplified, and an alternative approach emphasizes not life change per se but the psychological and emotional aspects of adapting to events. This alternative differentiates events in terms of the degree of undesirability or threat they entail and the individual's ability to predict or control them. Life events interact with characteristics of the individual (e.g., cognitive appraisal) and the situation (e.g., social support) in producing stress.

Furthermore, any single life-events list presents items that may or may not be relevant to a specific target population. Many Holmes and Rahe items (e.g., retiring from work, facing foreclosure on a mortgage or loan, having a son or daughter leave home) would have little direct relevance for a population of college students, for whom the experience of many events not on that list (e.g., having academic difficulties, relating to parents) would more closely reflect their exposure to stress. Investigators now tailor events lists for specific populations by asking representatives of the target group to nominate events on the basis of what has happened to them or to people like them (Levine & Perkins, 1980a). Lazarus (1990) now believes that research workers should pay much more attention to the content of stressful life-event and hassles scales; the events that impinge on males and females, or younger and older people, or those of higher and lower status and power are quite different.

Dohrenwend's general view that various personal and situational factors interact with characteristics of life events to produce stress and influence outcome is widely accepted (Perkins, 1982). Surveys at three contrasting colleges (Perkins et al., 1982) found that the students at greatest risk for both number of stressful events and total amount of stress were the freshman or sophomore women who lived off campus. Other research has shown that younger, better educated, or separated/divorced persons were at increased risk for experiencing life events (Goldberg & Comstock, 1980). Younger people, those going to college or graduate school away from home and family, and those experiencing marital disruption have opportunities to make changes in school or work activities or in their places of residence. Sometimes it is difficult to separate personal from situational factors in identifying conditions of risk.

Mirowsky and Ross (1989) strongly criticize both the life-events and the hassles approaches to studying adaptation because these methods focus attention on individuals and overlook the socioeconomic correlates of distress. They suggest that "both the idea of daily hassles and that of life change trivialize the social causes of psychological distress. . . . The link [to distress] is the undesirable events, losses, failures, and ongoing stressors that flow from inequality, inequity, and lack of opportunity" (p. 130).

Dimensions of personality have also been linked with life events and distress. Such processes as individual perception, ego defense, psychophysiological responsiveness, "sensation seeking" (Smith, Johnson, & Sarason, 1978), and coping ability have all been hypothesized to mediate the effects of life events. Luthar and Zigler (1991) reviewed the literature on children who were described as "resilient" or "stress-resistant" because they have adapted well even though they had serious stressors in their lives. Infant temperament, gender, humor, social problem-solving skills, a sense of personal control, and support from the family have been identified in various studies as characteristic of children considered resilient. A combination of temperament, coping styles, and social support apparently moderates the relationship between stressful life events and later adaptation.

To summarize, measures of recent stressful events do not predict with great accuracy a person's future level of well-being. Progress on this problem will require a return to interest in the qualitative aspects of life stress, in the details of how events are experienced, and in what people actually do to cope with specific stressors. Research will have to

focus more explicitly on the individual, situational, and life-event correlates of specific outcomes.

Vulnerability: An Integrative Perspective

Dohrenwend's model suggests three possible outcomes following a
transient stress reaction: The person can return to the previous level of
functioning, become a case of psychopathology, or resolve the experience
and grow stronger. Stress is ubiquitous in contemporary life (see Chapter 1), yet clearly not everyone succumbs. While stressful events seem to
increase a person's overall risk for disorder in a nonspecific way, no given
external stressor is likely to be etiologically specific for any particular medical or psychological dysfunction.

Another tenet of Dohrenwend's model is that stress-related disorders,
such as depression, alcohol abuse, and even schizophrenia, are usually
episodic at least to some degree; their symptomatic manifestations come
and go over time, alternating with periods of more adaptive functioning.
People suffering from those conditions tend to seek relief in a variety of
ways, including formal treatment and self-directed "natural healing" and
mutual support (see Chapter 9). Their efforts are frequently successful in
the short run but in the long run may be followed by recurring episodes
of difficulty. A simple dichotomy between health and illness may be misleading. Individuals who at a particular moment are dysfunctional will
eventually recover to a greater or lesser degree and for some period of
time. Individuals who are currently healthy could conceivably become
stressed to the point of succumbing to an episode of disorder. A study
of children from abusive families who were characterized as resilient in
the earlier school years, for example, found that these children were not
necessarily high functioning in later adolescence. Those who were subject to chronic abuse in the family and who came from dysfunctional
homes with frequent changes in the caretaking figures often did not do
well in adolescence (Herrenkohl, Herrenkohl, & Egolf, 1994).

It is useful to distinguish between an individual's degree of predisposition to disorder on the one hand and the onset and course of a given
episode of disorder on the other. Stated another way, everyone is en-
dowed with a specific degree of vulnerability to such episodes (somewhere
from high to low) that under certain conditions will express itself in a
time-limited crisis of adaptation. No one has zero vulnerability, and vulnerability represents the potential for disorder, not the manifest disorder
or symptomatology itself. One's degree of vulnerability is determined partially by inborn or other "predisposing" factors such as genetic inheritance and prior coping competence and may be offset by protective factors such as social support. An episode of disorder occurs when the degree
of disequilibrium initiated by recent stressful experiences exceeds the
threshold imposed by the individual's level of vulnerability.

Our bland phrase "recent stressful experiences" understates the complexity of some situations. Genetic factors may contribute substantially to the vulnerability faced by children of people with schizophrenia, but in addition the display of schizophrenic behavior in a mother or father may be chronically and unpredictably stressful. Vulnerability is intertwined with genetic predispositions over two generations, repetitive life stresses stemming from the parent's disorder, and inadequate or even harmful intervention into family life (Dunn, 1993; Grunbaum & Gammeltoft, 1993). The same may hold true for parental depression as a risk factor for a child's depression (Hammen, 1992).

This vulnerability perspective has advantages over the older person-centered view of psychopathology. Like Dohrenwend's model and the ecological analogy (see Chapter 4), it relates both person-centered and environmental factors to time-limited episodes of health and dysfunction. Even with a relatively stable degree of initial vulnerability, one's levels of acute stress and environmental support may fluctuate over time. In addition, while short-term improvement may result from a reduction in the level of external stress, more stable improvement may result from reduced vulnerability (e.g., developing better coping skills, making a permanent change in one's environment). The model is consistent with the observation that while nearly everyone experiences the soap opera that is life, most people do not develop diagnosable pathology. Finally, "vulnerability" is a less stigmatizing concept than "disease" (because everyone is vulnerable to some extent), yet it is compatible with evidence for stable individual differences in the risk of illness. Those at greatest risk share a high degree of vulnerability, not a uniform pattern of environmental experience.

We now turn to a review of ideas and research on individual coping and social support, two important protective factors in Dohrenwend's model.

Coping

In theory, coping ability reduces vulnerability to stress (Dohrenwend, 1978). Coping can be defined as "cognitive and behavioral effort made to master, tolerate, or reduce demands that tax or exceed a person's resources" (Kessler et al., 1985, p. 550). In this section we describe the general nature of coping and the evidence for important individual and situational differences in coping.

General Characteristics of Coping

The individual facing a stressful event has two problems. One is how to manage the internal stress, anxiety, tension, depression, anger, restlessness, difficulty in concentrating, sleeplessness, and fatigue and the associated thought content, self-doubt, and self-blame. Efforts to manage such feelings are called *emotion-focused* coping. The second problem is deciding what specific action to take. This response is called *problem-focused* coping. A third kind of response, *perception-focused* coping, uses altered cognitions to reduce the threatening nature of an event (Folkman & Lazarus, 1988; Thoits, 1986).

In the Dohrenwend model, having adequate psychological mediators implies a reduced vulnerability to stress. Risk reduction may result from managing feelings, managing the situation, or altering an event's meaning, and the wherewithal to manage effectively may come from resources in the support network. Given that both coping and interpersonal support may be emotion-focused, problem-focused, perception-focused, or all three of these, Thoits (1986) proposes conceptualizing social support as the provision of coping assistance. Strategies for the treatment or prevention of stress-related problems might then be organized along two dimensions: the nature of the individual's adaptive response (emotional, problem-oriented, and/or cognitive) and the focus of intervention on either "psychological mediators" (e.g., education) or "situational mediators" (e.g., increasing support resources).

Lazarus (1966) and Folkman (1984) originally defined two phases in the cognitive appraisal of stressors. The first phase includes *primary* and *secondary* appraisal. *Primary appraisal,* which is biologically designed to provide sufficient energy to respond to the problem at hand, involves making an individual judgment about whether the situation is harmful or potentially harmful (some people may find the situation potentially harmful but also challenging). The person then engages in *secondary appraisal,* deciding whether he or she has the resources to cope or can gain access to them. In the first phase, the individual "decides," on the basis of the nature of the event and his or her personal history, whether adaptation is threatened and whether personal and social resources are adequate for coping. In other words, is the person "vulnerable"? In the second phase, if the person has adequate resources, he or she deals with the situation. A person with resources or with access to resources is less vulnerable than someone without the resources. Some people recognize the potentially difficult situation but do not feel vulnerable because they feel up to the challenge and may even enjoy testing themselves in the new situation. If the person does not feel that he or she has the resources to deal with the situation, further strain follows. If the event-induced arousal is interpreted through self-statements as bad, wrong, sick, or a sign of weakness or incompetence, the person may not be up to coping and may worry about worrying, adding tension to the emotional mix.

As a cognitive means of coping with emotions, education may help one to understand, identify, and tolerate a range of feelings and thus to prevent the secondary reaction to primary arousal. Some preventive efforts consist of little more than preparation and warning. If the dentist tells you that you will feel pain or the surgeon tells you that you will have a certain kind of discomfort following surgery, when the pain occurs later you tend not to worry about it because it was expected. Here discomfort is not a sign that something has gone wrong; it indicates that one's condition is "normal under the circumstances." Simple preparation and warnings prior to surgery can have a measurable effect on the postsurgical course of recovery. One study, based on an extensive review of the literature, concluded that hospital patients who received information and emotional support in rather brief preoperative sessions had shorter lengths of stay than untreated controls. The effect may be enhanced when the intervention is matched to the patient's coping style; patients who cope with stress by denial (under some circumstances a negative psychological mediator) may get little benefit from preoperative explanation and warning, while those who cope by seeking information and mastery derive more benefit from such preparation. These interventions are inexpensive compared with the cost of a hospital day and are thus highly effective from a benefit-cost viewpoint (Mumford, Schlesinger, and Glass, 1982).

Many people have learned how to mediate their feelings by talking to themselves, distracting themselves, or suppressing their feelings by using substances (alcohol, tranquilizers) or other means (e.g., relaxation) that may temporarily reduce arousal. Thoits (1986) characterizes these methods as altering physiological sensations of stress cognitively or behaviorally. Folkman and Lazarus (1988) studied how coping styles may influence emotions during stressful encounters. The eight coping styles they examined included two that were problem-focused—confrontive coping (e.g., standing one's ground and requiring the other person to change) and planful problem solving (planning a response in advance and carrying it out)—and several that were emotion-focused (e.g., distancing, or ignoring the stressful event; positive reappraisal, or changing oneself positively in response to the event). Interviews with young adults and retirement-age adults found that planful problem solving, confrontive coping, positive reappraisal, and distancing were strongly associated with emotional changes following stressful events. In particular, planful problem solving as a coping style was associated with both increases in positive emotions (pleasure, confidence) and decreases in negative emotions (anger, worry). Keefe, Caldwell, Queen, et al. (1987) evaluated six cognitive styles of coping in patients with painful osteoarthritis: diverting attention, reinterpreting pain sensation, ignoring pain sensations, coping self-statements (e.g., "I can do it"), praying or hoping, and "catastrophizing" (seeing events in the worst light). Controlling for participants' demographic background and medical condition, those who did not catastrophize and who believed they could control or decrease their pain reported less pain and less physical and psychological disability.

Findings like these are encouraging, and the teaching of techniques to mediate stress-related feelings is becoming an important area for research. Teaching these skills to everyone may provide the basis for a preventive program. Individual training and workshops to teach stress management offer one approach; participants may be exposed to "graded" doses of stress under conditions in which they can rehearse effective responses (Meichenbaum & Jaremko, 1983). Systematic desensitization is another example; in this method phobic clients imagine increasingly more anxiety-arousing experiences while sustaining the calming response of deep muscle relaxation. Coping-skills interventions may help people anticipate and prepare for possible failure and learn that specific techniques can be applied in new situations.

People facing certain stressors may benefit from coping responses specifically tailored to the problems posed by those events. Telch and Telch (1986) developed a training program of cognitive, behavioral, and emotional coping skills to help patients adapt to cancer. Groups of patients learned techniques for relaxation and stress management, effective communication and assertiveness, problem solving and constructive thinking, feelings management, and planning pleasant activities. Behavioral components included homework, goal setting, self-monitoring, behavioral rehearsal and role playing, and feedback and coaching. After six weeks patients in these coping-skills groups had improved significantly in their moods and self-efficacy and were having fewer problems related to their illness. They were superior in these outcomes to patients randomly assigned to loosely structured support groups. The support group intervention may also have been beneficial, however, since other patients randomly assigned to a no-treatment control group actually deteriorated on these measures over the same period and were significantly worse off than those in the support groups. It is important to note that because coping-skills training also occurred in groups, it is possible that some form of mutual support was a significant component of that intervention as well.

Others have reported similar results in teaching people to cope with continuing stressors. People with multiple sclerosis (MS) have functional losses and develop a great deal of uncertainty about themselves and their future. Schwartz and Rogers (1994) devised an intervention to increase individuals' flexibility in choosing a better means of coping. The intervention was both supportive and educational and was designed to help participants express their feelings about their illness, become aware of the metaphors they were using in describing themselves and their conditions, and set goals that would take into account realistic limitations. They were taught to recognize and to compensate for cognitive problems by learning to talk to themselves to keep on target for a task or to use organizer notebooks to compensate for disorganization consequent to some cognitive loss. They were also taught to communicate with caregivers and to understand their own role in the helper-helped relationship. At the end of the course, participants were assigned partners and encouraged to call each other to troubleshoot and to obtain a different perspective on problems they were having. The intervention was designed to increase the repertoire of coping skills and thus to provide more flexibility in coping. Although this intervention was evaluated only informally, the authors believed that it was effective in relieving both psychological and physical problems.

Kirkby (1994) used a coping skills treatment with women who identified themselves as having "serious premenstrual problems." The participants were taught cognitive restructuring approaches and self-efficacy. They also learned some relaxation techniques, practiced assertiveness, and were exposed to some stress inoculation. The classes concentrated not on premenstrual problems but on coping with life's problems in general. Compared to controls, the women taught these coping approaches showed significant reductions in menstrual distress at the end of the course, as well as at follow-up nine months later. They also showed reductions in "irrational thinking" and in depression as a result of the intervention.

Once the acute stress is under control, the second major task is that of taking appropriate action to cope with the situation. One coping task is emotional; it involves the arousal of hope or a sense that one may indeed be able to do something about one's situation. After an initial psychotherapy interview clients often feel that something good may come of it—there is some hope that a desperate situation will be relieved. Consider as an example a woman with a new baby who moves to a new community and hasn't yet made any friends. Her husband is busy in a new and demanding job and doesn't have much time or energy to help at home. Finances are tight, and they can't afford household help. Their families live far away and cannot be counted on too much, for there are often petty squabbles when mother and daughter or son and mother-in-law are together for too long a time. One day the woman's husband disappoints her badly, and she considers leaving him to go home to her mother. She is greatly distressed, crying one moment and raging the next, and can't get over the episode, remaining tense and depressed. Finally she calls a therapist who helps her work out a plan of action. After a few days she calls back to report that she is following through and that she is hopeful something good will happen. That feeling of hope represents an important aspect of her belief that she will be able to deal with her circumstances.

We know very little about hope. In his encyclopedic work on emotions, Lazarus (1991, p. 282) says: "Far less has been written about hope . . . than about other emotions. . . . [H]ope is so important in the psychological economy of people as antidote to despair." Under what circumstances is hope aroused? Does it require some support from another person? Can hope be generated from within by recalling other occasions when one has succeeded in overcoming adversity? Is the ability to generate hope an indication that one has been strengthened by overcoming earlier adversity? Is the emotion of hope a necessary part of determination? Are there comparable motives such as a desire for revenge or a desire to prove something to another that can stimulate effort to overcome adversity? These last motives may be less praiseworthy, but they nonetheless can be quite powerful. Many survivors of Nazi concentration camps managed to develop a transcendent goal—to tell the world about the experience or to finish some unfinished work—that aided them in coping with extreme adversity and helped them avoid surrendering to seemingly insurmountable difficulties (Frankl, 1963). Some studies of resilient children note that the determination to be different from one's parent and an overriding goal of achieving something can be important in overcoming severe adversity (Dunn, 1993; Herrenkohl et al., 1993). Because much of our knowledge of personality derives from the study of persons who may be said to have succumbed to difficulty, we know all too little about those who have mastered difficulty and have become stronger for it.

Coming to terms with a crisis is in part an emotional task. Solving problems requires additional thought and action. Consider a widow in her late forties or early fifties with grown children, who is not yet eligible for a Social Security pension, has only minimum resources from her husband's insurance for financial support, and has not been in the labor market for twenty or twenty-five years. She can expect to live another thirty or more years. In addition to living with the complex emotion of grief following the loss of her husband, the widow faces the problem of supporting herself. She may have little experience in managing finances or investments and now has to decide what to do about what money she does have. She has to assess her own resources, her assets on the job market. She may take an entry-level job with other workers much younger than herself. She may have to find opportunities for training or education. Having decided on a program, she may then have new experiences of studying, taking (and worrying about) examinations, and relating in an unaccustomed role again to people much younger than herself. She may have to make new friends, especially if she finds herself uncomfortable as a single person among friends who are married couples. She may have to cope with problems of dating, should she decide that she wants to develop an intimate relationship. She will also face many other problems, including how to maintain or repair the house if she continues to live in it or how to find and manage workers who will do the work. Beyond home and social relationships, she has to decide how to spend her time. Similar problems confront widowers and divorced men and women. Little wonder, when we review all of the adaptations that are necessary, that the death of a spouse and divorce are heavily weighted on life-events scales.

The widow's situation can be conceptualized in problem-solving terms: She must examine each problem, develop alternative strategies for solving it, assess the resources each solution requires, and then risk failure by acting in uncertain and unfamiliar territory. Psychologists have developed techniques and approaches to problem solving that, when taught to people, become psychological mediators (Spivack & Shure, 1974, 1985). Whenever a person has taken new risks, engaged in new experiences, or mastered some new approach to living, he or she may be said

to have grown psychologically. The crisis model directs us to work to enhance the individual's ability to solve problems. If the technique is taught
before the problem arises, we have a preventive approach in which the
psychological mediator, the problem-solving approach, is made available
in advance of the crisis.

Stages in Crisis Resolution

The crisis model offers an analytic advantage for understanding the
individual's situation and for providing appropriate services. It postulates
stages in the resolution of crises that change over time. Kubler-Ross
(1969) made an important contribution to the field of death and dying
by specifying the stages that people go through in coming to terms with
death. Lindemann (1944) had earlier specified stages in working though
loss on the basis of the reactions of people grieving over family members
lost in a fire. The resolution of other crises may also progress in stages.
It is important to understand this point because the types of coping and
support appropriate at one stage may not be appropriate at another stage.

Resolving a crisis in the short term does not necessarily result in the
assimilation of the event into the personality. If the event arouses strong
feelings of fear, anger, or guilt, memory of the event may haunt the person from time to time. Thus, men with combat-related anxiety states
sometimes report bad dreams and feelings of estrangement from other
people for years after being in battle (Atkinson et al., 1984). These recurrences, flashbacks, and intrusions of experiences are part of what is
called posttraumatic stress disorder (PTSD).

Women who have been raped seem to go through three stages of recovery (Sutherland & Scherl, 1970; Burgess & Holmstrom, 1979). The
first stage centers on simply getting through the trauma, fear, shame, and
related concerns. The second phase includes making efforts to return to
normal and to control or minimize the significance of the event for one's
life. In the third phase, occurring weeks or sometimes months later, the
experience returns to conscious attention, and the individual is once again
faced with integrating and resolving it. This phase is often marked by depressive feelings or anxiety (Kilpatrick, Veronen, & Resick, 1979). In this
last phase, the person works to integrate the experience into the self, to
incorporate or assimilate within the general self-concept a view of oneself
as one who was once assaulted, violated, and subjected to sexual abuse.
Rape counselors encourage their clients to think of themselves not as victims but as survivors. Even though self-blame may reflect the introjection
of cultural values or experiences with insensitive police, prosecutors, medical personnel, relatives, lovers, or friends, many survivors of rape blame
themselves: "I shouldn't have been out at night alone," "I shouldn't have
been hitchhiking," "I shouldn't have gone to his apartment," or "I should
have screamed louder or fought harder." The truth of the matter is sub-
ordinated to the process of self-blame (Libow & Doty, 1979). There may

be some adaptive value to this self-blame in that the person may be say-ing, "If I had something to do with causing the event, perhaps I can pre-vent a repetition in the future."

At a later time, to master the experience, rape survivors sometimes become involved in social or political action to offer escort services or rape crisis services or to seek greater police protection, more vigorous prosecution, or more sensitive handling of people injured by a rape. Such efforts can also work to change culturally determined attitudes of some males that place a woman at risk simply because of her sex.

Anger is among the complex emotions a woman who was raped may experience. In the early phases of recovery, the woman may suppress or deny the anger, viewing the rape impersonally as a social fault. In the third phase, however, her anger can become more personalized and, in a sense, more real: "That SOB! He used me! I could kill him!" Such feel-ings of rage after the event need to be worked through. We have not considered the complications a rape introduces into relationships with lovers or husbands and the often frustrating, if not humiliating, encoun-ters with the legal process (Silverman, 1978; Burgess & Holmstrom, 1979).

Reliving the experience may not occur with all challenges to adapta-tion and may be more likely when the strongest emotions—fear, rage, and guilt—are engaged. However, characterizing the emotional experi-ence as a phase in the restorative process recasts the experience as a tran-sient emotional state appropriate to the kind of event one has been through. The emotions and thoughts can be interpreted not as manifes-tations of a neurotic illness but as something more like the postsurgical discomfort one had been warned about. This may make it easier to live through the experience and even turn it to personal advantage.

Individual and Situational Differences in Coping

Any life event may have positive or negative effects. Negative aspects are nearly always apparent almost immediately, while positive effects may take some time to emerge. Not everyone is able to benefit in a positive way from stress. What accounts for this difference? In the vulnerability perspective, the notion of protective factors enables us to shift the focus from personal and situational processes that damage a person's mental health to those that strengthen it. Here the question is not what accounts for disorder in response to stress but what accounts for strength.

Finkel (1974, 1975; Finkel & Jacobsen, 1977) had people describe significant life experiences that had strengthened their personalities (which he called "strens") or that had been traumatic, harmful for personal de-velopment. Unexpectedly, many people spontaneously described *three* kinds of experiences: negative events, positive events, and events that started out as negative but later became positive in their overall effect. Finkel called these last experiences trauma-stren conversions. They began with a sudden insight or "flash" that enabled the person to reinterpret the traumatic event in a more positive light. The previous debilitating construction produced by the event was replaced by a new construction that emphasized the individual's ability to cope, adapt, and learn from the trauma. Conversion was not simply a defensive distortion of the experience, since the person fully acknowledged feelings of pain, regret, and anger during the initial period of trauma. Only in hindsight was the event construed to have had positive value.

For most converters the first conversion produced a significant change in their subsequent experience of life events. Before their first conversion, converters did not differ from nonconverters in the proportions of traumas and growth-promoting experiences they reported. After the first conversion, however, converters reported only half the proportion of traumas and 50 percent more positive events than did nonconverters, as well as additional conversion experiences (Finkel & Jacobson, 1977). Thus, from a preventive standpoint, achieving one's first conversion may represent a kind of "protective factor" that helps reduce the negative impact of subsequent life events and perhaps lowers the risk of stress-related psychopathology as well.

Is the conversion of life events generalizable? Can even severe psychological trauma be converted? What are the psychological correlates of converting stressful life experiences? About 4 percent of college students experience a parent's death during a given academic year. Parental death is among the most stressful of student life events (Levine & Perkins, 1980a), yet from four to twenty-two months following a parent's death about half of students convert the severe stress into positive change (Tebes & Perkins, 1984). What is the specific nature of a life-event conversion? Can we learn to facilitate trauma-stren conversions in individuals who would fail to do so on their own as a method for the primary prevention of stress-related problems? What roles are played by the individual's prior competence and current levels of social support and life stress? How do these factors interact over time to influence cognitive appraisal? Is conversion an intuitive cognitive skill, as Finkel maintains? If so, why aren't converters able to convert all the stressful events they experience? From an ecological viewpoint, is conversion a fortuitous adaptation assisted in important ways by specific situational resources? For example, is the Alcoholics Anonymous program's twelfth step—helping others—a means of converting the terrible alcoholic experiences to something positive?

Taylor (1983) provided another view of conversion experiences. She described a process of self-enhancement by means of social comparisons that allowed the person experiencing a stressful life event to feel better off than someone else and illustrated the concepts in her study of women adapting to breast cancer. Women who make positive adaptations to breast cancer use what Taylor calls "beneficial illusions." Beneficial illusions are not denials; they are constructions of reality that permit one to function with a degree of optimism and a sense of control over events. Do these cognitive mechanisms help our understanding of the potential in stress-ful experiences for enhancing growth and self-esteem under difficult cir-cumstances?

Other researchers have taken the position that stable, trait-like psy-chological mediators play a central role in coping with a stressful experi-ence. Kobasa (1979) identified a "hardy" personality style. Individuals with hardy personalities easily *commit* themselves to what they are doing, believe themselves to be in *control* of events, and consider life change a *challenging* and necessary impetus to development. People low in hardi-ness often feel alienated, powerless, and threatened by change. Kobasa worked with middle- and upper-level executives with especially high lev-els of life stress who were divided into groups high and low on symptoms of illness. The high-stress/low-illness group showed significantly greater personality hardiness than did high-stress/high-illness subjects. Hardiness was particularly effective in reducing the risk of illness during high-stress periods.

From the perspective of crisis theory and Dohrenwend's model, adap-tation is determined not by these personal characteristics alone but by the relationship between psychological mediators and specific factors in the environment. We do not know how to produce hardiness or other indi-vidual difference characteristics. If hardiness and other traits are inborn, then as a preventive strategy we might look to approaches that help peo-ple enhance their personal fits with key environments (Levine & Perkins, 1980b).

In contrast to the emphasis on trait-like psychological mediators, strategies for effective coping may be situation-specific, rather than global. Not all coping responses are equally effective across all life situations; re-sponses that are effective in resolving marital conflict, for example, are not necessarily successful in handling conflict at work (Pearlin & Schooler, 1978). That no single coping response has been found to be universally effective suggests that we should be as careful in describing the specific stressful situation as in delineating successful or unsuccessful coping strate-gies.

Folkman and Lazarus (1980) attempted to answer directly the ques-tion of how consistently people use specific coping behaviors across a sam-ple of everyday situations. Middle-aged men and women reported the spe-cific thoughts and actions they used in coping with recent stressful events. Both problem-focused and emotion-focused coping were used extensively; contrary to cultural stereotype, women did not use emotion-focused cop-ing more than men. The situation and how it was appraised were the strongest determinants of the coping response. Work-related events, where an effective concrete response was often possible, elicited more problem-focused coping. Health-related problems, which may offer fewer opportunities for constructive action, were more likely to elicit emotion-focused coping. Lazarus (1990) called on research workers to pay more attention to the nature of the stressor than they had in the past. The results of the studies support Dohrenwend's (1978) idea that the relationship between the person's individual appraisal of an event and its situational context determines the coping response.

Even when people are coping with similar problems, their experiences and circumstances may dictate different coping efforts. Components of a group program designed to assist family members caring for frail, elderly patients were differentially effective with the patients' spouses and with their middle-aged children. The spouses made less use of information about what to do because most knew what to do, but they did need the advice to take care of themselves and to find support in the form of approval and praise from others for their often heroic efforts. On the other hand, middle-aged relatives responsible for care needed more information about what to do and how to find resources (Labrecque, Peak, & Toseland, 1992).

An individual's developmental needs may be a factor in determining how best to intervene to enhance coping. Hoffman and Mastrianni (1992) describe a program of integrating college classes with psychiatric treatment for hospitalized young adults. The young people were assisted in accomplishing tasks appropriate to their developmental stages, so when the acute state of vulnerability passed, they were able to go forward and accomplish appropriate tasks. Here again, a specific approach seemed to be more useful than a general one.

Theory and research on coping remain in a relatively primitive state (Kessler et al., 1985). Few researchers have examined "natural" coping by ordinary people in response to commonplace events. The role of religion in coping in particular has been neglected. Millions participate in organized religious services and consider themselves religious people; millions more rely on their religious beliefs to bring them through crises or other troubles. Trust in God, praying, confessing sins, or finding a lesson from God in the life event are examples of religious coping. One's religiosity can affect one's likelihood of experiencing some adverse events; stress will be reduced if one develops a healthier lifestyle and on religious grounds doesn't use drugs or engage in extramarital affairs. Religious beliefs may also affect one's appraisal of those events that do occur and one's choice of coping strategies. Religious communities can also be significant sources of social support. Religious beliefs and methods of coping appear to have important implications for mental health and for the prevention of psychological problems (Pargament et al., 1990; Hathaway & Pargament, 1991).

Sermabeikian (1994) believes that professional relationships involve a spiritual dimension that she characterizes as "an exchange of ideas, feelings, beliefs and values" that deal with the "meaning of life" and with looking at the "inspirational" and the "meaningful" in experience as well as the pathological aspects (p. 178). She argues for greater respect for and inclusion of the spiritual dimension of life in therapy. Therapists, uncomfortable with the nonmaterial, may not be aware of the spiritual dimension and may not "facilitate spiritual solutions in keeping with the client's belief system" (p. 182).

Important questions remain. To what extent are variations in coping strategies (e.g., direct action, cognitive reappraisal) consistently associated with a particular outcome achieved in response to a stressful event? Because coping and appraisal probably exert a reciprocal influence on each other over time, longitudinal studies examining the dynamic aspects of coping need to be done. As we come to understand the coping process better, we may learn how to teach coping skills in a timely fashion to prevent crises and maladaptations.

Social Support

A person enters a state of crisis when adaptation is threatened *and* he or she lacks the immediate resources to cope. Some coping resources may come from the person's social network (Thoits, 1986). Consider the example of a young woman who goes to a new city with a man she does not know very well. Far from home, he suddenly and unexpectedly tells her he is tired of their relationship, and he leaves her there alone. She is shocked, frightened, and too ashamed to call home. Fortunately, she remembers an old friend of the family who lives nearby. This person takes her in, allows her to stay, and asks no unwanted questions until she is able to make plans to return home.

An individual in crisis may also require material resources, emotional support, and guidance. As a second example, suppose a college woman becomes pregnant, decides to terminate the pregnancy, and does not have the money to pay for an abortion. She tells friends in her residence hall of her plight. They raise the money from among their friends, arrange for the abortion at a clinic, arrange for her to stay in another city with a college friend while she recovers from the abortion, and then have other friends meet her at the airport in her home city and take her to her parents' home. The involvement of her social network might be exactly the same if she decides to continue the pregnancy to term.

The women in our examples obtained something they needed from their respective social networks. How typical is this? Like stress, support is sometimes assumed to be ubiquitous in people's lives. Gottlieb (1983) includes among his types of supportive networks one's family and friends, "natural caregivers" such as family physicians, lawyers, and clergy, organized neighborhood associations, and self-help groups. In spite of these widespread sources of support, some people are still isolated, and isolated people may be restricted to seeking support only from formal agencies—welfare or the police—and bearing all the social costs of accepting such aid. Furthermore, people who are able to make use of the resources available through friends and relatives may have the social skills to develop good relationships in the first place (Heller & Swindle, 1983).

In both examples the women felt free to ask for help and judged correctly who could provide assistance. Thirty or forty years ago stigma would have attached to each woman's conduct. Each might have been reluctant to reveal her plight, in consequence cutting herself off from possible aid. Even today an individual may feel so guilty, have so little self-esteem, or feel so hopeless that he or she does not use available support. People embedded in a close and supportive social network have committed suicide despite the best efforts of friends, relatives, and professional therapists. Their difficulties in using support may reflect a maladaptive coping style that reduces their ability to see or to generate alternatives (Ellis, 1986).

In both examples those asked were willing to help. Sometimes a person's needs are so great, and he or she has "gone to the well" so often, that the well turns up dry. Some people may be isolated precisely because they have exhausted others' goodwill and other interpersonal "credits." Tebes (1983) showed that families of people with chronic schizophrenia tended to reject them, not so much because of the stigma but because of the burden of caring for someone with a serious and chronic illness. Under circumstances of chronic stress, support can erode, and that erosion can add to the distress of all concerned.

The social networks of people with serious mental illness often consist of workers in agencies—case managers, vocational counselors, welfare workers, or police officers (Holmes-Eber & Riger, 1990). In sharp contrast, most other people can look to spouses, lovers, family, and friends, or they can afford to hire private-sector professional helpers—doctors, lawyers, or tax accountants—whose help is not stigmatizing. Both those who use a social network of public helpers and those who use a private and personal network must possess certain skills and qualifications to gain access to the network's resources; those who rely on a public network may need to have "bureaucratic competence," while those who rely on their families and the private marketplace utilize other skills. We should not confuse the skills necessary to function in one network with those necessary to function in another. It is one thing to be a good client and another to be a good friend.

Even among those who give help willingly over a long period of time, new concerns can arise. Parents of retarded or mentally ill individuals worry about what will happen to their adult children as the parents "age out." "We are getting on in age, and there will be no one to look after our mentally ill son." "My son is terrified of what will happen to him when I die. So am I." "I hope and pray that one day there will be special housing." (Grosser & Vine, 1991, p. 288).

We have very little information about the effects of giving support in the long term on the one who gives support. After eight months, college students living in crowded apartments experienced reduced social support and increased levels of psychological distress. Over time, roommates can get on each others nerves, with resultant loss of the sense of support from roommates and an increase in distress (Lepore, Evans, & Schneider,

1991). Women who had cared for frail elderly spouses for a long time apparently needed support to enable them to take time off, to take care of their own needs, and to receive recognition for what they had been doing. Younger women who were beginning to care for frail elderly relatives had more need for information about resources and about what to do in specific circumstances than they had for emotional support (Labrecque, Peak, & Toseland, 1992). Giving support is as important to understand as receiving support.

Knowing when and whom to ask for help and not going to the well too often may be matters of judgment or interpersonal skill. If they are interpersonal skills, those skills might be teachable. If the skills are teachable and are aids in adapting during a crisis or avoiding a crisis altogether, we can think about the possibility of prevention (see Chapter 8).

In both examples the individuals from whom help was sought did things that were helpful. Some people in a network of relationships might not be helpful and, if approached, might either not provide the support required or act in such a way as to make the problem worse. Middle-aged adults who were caring for their elderly parents were deeply disappointed at not receiving the support of someone from whom support was expected; this made the total experience more stressful as the person providing the care struggled with feelings of anger and disappointment as well as with providing the care (Perrotta, 1982).

Just as we should think about teaching skills of seeking and using support, we should also think about providing support to those who are giving support, especially when dealing with chronic problems that have periodic exacerbations. Especially with the current emphasis on home care over institutional care, we should consider the help provider's needs as well as those of the person in need of assistance.

Sometimes well-meaning but inappropriate support can compound a problem by creating sources of distress in a supportive network. For example, in trying to protect a grandmother from the knowledge that her beloved granddaughter had committed suicide, other relatives told her nothing until she arrived in the city where the funeral was to be held. The grandmother had no opportunity to prepare herself for the loss and was emotionally devastated on hearing the news; she was quite angry with those who had failed to respect her by telling her what had happened.

Negative interactions within a support network correlate significantly with increased psychological distress and diminished well-being, and these harmful relationships tend to be stronger than those involving positive network interactions (Finch et al., 1989; Schuster, Kessler, & Aseltine, 1990). Rape victims often must deal with unsupportive behaviors from people in their network. Davis, Brickman, and Baker (1991) studied post-rape adjustment among young women and found that positive support from a significant other ("encouraged me to see a doctor," "took over some of my responsibilities temporarily") was outweighed by unsupportive behaviors ("has indicated I should have fought back more during the crime," "has criticized me for not being more careful"), thus making adaptation more difficult.

Distress in the family network after divorce can also be a problem. Luepnitz (1978) found that children in divorced families were more maladjusted when their divorced parents continued to be in conflict. Children in divorcing families who get little positive support from family adults and other adults are more vulnerable to the stresses of divorce and have poorer adjustments than those with better support (Wolchik, Ruehlman, Braver, & Sandler, 1989). Support may come from chums, although the effects can differ depending on the age of the child (Lustig, Wolchik, & Braver, 1992).

Distress in the family network may have negative repercussions for other problems as well. D'Augelli and Hershberger (1993) found that suicidal ideation and depression in gay and lesbian youth was associated with fears about the reactions of parents and others in their social network to the discovery of their sexual orientation.

Social support is more than unconditional positive regard. Clinical interventions for obesity, smoking or substance abuse, and lack of assertiveness are often effective initially, yet "backsliding" is common once therapist support is withdrawn at the end of treatment (Janis, 1983). What is the nature of therapeutic support for stressful changes such as stopping smoking or dieting to lose weight? Janis (1983) identifies three sets of support variables. The first set is building referent power, by which he means that the helping person becomes a significant other, one whose approval or disapproval exerts influence on the client. The second set refers to the use of referent power to enhance the client's commitment to change by rewarding actions that promote the desired goals and expressing *mild* disapproval of actions contrary to these goals. The third set includes those actions that help retain referent power after treatment ends by promoting internalization of the commitment and the rewards. These techniques are designed to help the client shift from other-directed to self-directed approval.

Thus, an effective therapist does more than just listen empathically. Janis points out that successful treatment requires unconditional acceptance most of the time. Once established, however, referent power is used to express mild criticism when the client departs from the agreed course of action. (See our discussion of Caplan's description of social support in the next section.)

Support is a complex concept. The words, actions, and feelings that constitute support can differ depending on the persons, problems, and circumstances, and the approach Janis describes may not be useful for all problems. Taylor (1983) described cognitive approaches developed by women adapting to mastectomies. These women may need help in developing and sustaining "illusions," such as seeing a setback as a temporary frustration and not as evidence of impending disaster. Taylor's approach resembles the use of cognitive "antidotes" by members of self-help groups (see Chapter 9).

Isolated individuals, those who by definition are not part of a social network, may be highly vulnerable for that reason alone (D'Augelli, 1983; Leavy, 1983). Isolation and loneliness may even be lethal (Blazer, 1982; House, Landis, & Umberson, 1988). A fifty-year study of cardiac disease in a close-knit supportive community revealed that when the social cohesiveness of the community eroded, rates of cardiac disease increased (Egolf, Lasker, Wolf, & Potvin, 1992). There is some evidence that effective prenatal support can reduce the difficulty a woman experiences in labor and is also positively correlated with babies who are heavier at birth and appear healthier on delivery. Support is also related to a reduced risk of postpartum depression, although the statistical relationships are complex (Collins, Dunkel-Schetter, Lobel, & Scrimshaw, 1993).

Theory and Research Concerning Social Support

Social support acts to increase or decrease, in some nonspecific way, a person's vulnerability to or resistance to stress. In crisis theory social support changes the situational context of stress. Not everyone who experiences high levels of stress is equally at risk for disorder. The active role of social support illustrates the conceptual alternatives provided by Kelly's ecological principle of "adaptation" (see Chapter 4) and its analysis of behavior in terms of person-environment fit. Instead of being labeled "withdrawn" as a stable individual trait, for example, a person with chronic schizophrenia can be described as someone who lacks a social support network (Leavy, 1983). In this way the search for specific medications and other person-centered treatments for withdrawal can be supplemented by strategies to connect the person with schizophrenia to a network of other people (see Box 7–3).

Social support and the model of a family. Gerald Caplan has used the family as a prototypic model of social support. Caplan (1976) maintains that an *idealized* family fulfills several functions for its members (he does not assert that *every* family functions in such a supportive fashion.)

First, the family collects and disseminates information about the world. Just as parents share their knowledge of the outside world with children, providing the basis for learning, even if vicariously, about various roles one might play in the world (e.g., parent, worker), so, too, people in supportive relationships share information with each other about characteristics of the world. Self-help groups disseminate information for members who suffer with a disease or share information about the service system and how to negotiate it. Information receipt is one of the components in many scales measuring social support.

Second, the family serves as a feedback and guidance system to help its members understand their reactions to others and the reactions of others to them. Caplan notes how family members almost ritually discuss with each other the day's events. During these discussions family members help each other evaluate the significance of others' reactions and evaluate the family member's behavior in relation to the family's beliefs and values. This aspect is not directly represented on social support scales, although having someone who listens is.

Third, Caplan notes that the family group is the major source for developing "the belief systems, value systems, and codes of behavior that determine an individual's understanding of the nature and meaning of the universe, of his place in it, and of the paths he should strive to travel in his life" (p. 23). These "encoding strategies and personal constructs" (see Chapter 5) come from direct teaching within the family, from a deep—even if unverbalized—learning of the family's culture, and from the day-by-day living out of these values. By applying the tenets of the ideology to everyday problems, the ideology provides, as Caplan puts it, "prescriptions for wise conduct." Support groups or supportive persons may help to provide or articulate an ideology helpful with a particular problem. This component of support is also not directly represented on social support scales.

A fourth family function is serving as a guide and mediator in problem solving. Family members share one another's problems, offer advice and guidance, assist in finding external sources of aid, and may even make arrangements for such assistance. It is in the nature of family life for members to assist one another in dealing with the emotional and cognitive difficulties attendant upon role changes—entering school, becoming an adult, getting married, becoming a parent, experiencing loss, and facing the change in status that comes when a spouse dies or a divorce takes place. Older members have gone through the changes and serve as models or transmit experience, and certain ceremonies mark role transitions and help make the changes less ambiguous. Families share both joys and sorrows and find emotional sustenance in the shared experiences; Thoits (1986) says that it is easier to accept assistance from one with whom the recipient can identify. Giving advice is represented on social support scales, but such scales don't usually deal with the relationship within which support is offered or received. As Stanton Coit, one of the originators of the settlement house movement of the late nineteenth century, put it: "It is terrible when men draw together only in suffering; whereas those who have laughed and thought together, and joined in ideal aims, can so enter into one another's sorrow as to steal much of its bitterness away" (quoted in Levine & Levine, 1992, p. 61).

A fifth function that family members perform is to provide material aid and concrete services to one another. Gifts, help with specific tasks, housing, financial aid, and dozens of other exchanges take place on a daily basis. This aspect of support is represented on social support scales, which we will discuss later.

As a sixth function, the family offers a haven for rest and recuperation. One can go home and lick one's wounds from the day, knowing
that in the idealized family others will understand the need for peace and
quiet. One can relax and be one's self within the family. There is no need
to conceal or to explain the problem to anyone. All understand because
all have experienced similar needs and emotions. Some children of parents with schizophrenia described how they sought out "normal" families with whom they could just spend time, free from the strife and disorder that characterized their own homes. A refuge was an important
support (Dunn, 1993). This aspect of support is not directly represented
on social support scales.

A seventh function of the family is to serve as a reference and control group. Family members are highly sensitive to one another's opinions about attitudes and behavior reflecting family values. As Caplan notes,
family members are likely to be judgmental. Success in meeting the family's expectations is rewarded, and failing to live up to the family's expectations is punished in some fashion. The family's standards are thus
enforced, helping to maintain behavior in conformity with family standards. Whether or not the individual family member lives up to family
ideals, he or she is still a family member and entitled to call on the family for assistance as a matter of right. This aspect of support is also not
directly represented on social support scales.

An eighth function of the family is to provide the foundation for
personal identity. As Caplan puts it: "During the frustration and confusion of struggling with an at-present insurmountable problem, most individuals feel weak and impotent and tend to forget their continuing
strengths. At such times, their family reminds them of their past achievements and validates their precrisis self-image of competence and ability
to stand firm" (p. 30). This function is not directly represented on social support scales.

As a ninth function, family members assist each other with the task
of emotional mastery. Family members ideally offer love, affection, and
comfort to a member in need. By their constancy of support, family members help to counter feelings of despair or helplessness and thus kindle
hope that difficult situations will be resolved. Moreover, in a time of crisis family members shore up the sense of personal worth by continuing
to treat the individual with love and respect and, if a loss is involved, providing an alternative source of satisfaction. This aspect may be represented
in social support scales in items asking about whether the person has one
or more people who are considered intimates.

The set of functions that Caplan specifies for the family may be
thought of as dimensions of support that can be evaluated when studying support networks. His model may lead us to a more sophisticated and
complex understanding of support than we have managed to achieve so
far. It is also useful in understanding self-help groups, as we will see in
Chapter 9.

Empirical research on social support. Reviews of the literature (Cohen & Wills, 1985; Kessler et al., 1985) conclude that the presence of social support has consistently been associated with lower risk for psychological problems. People with depression, for example, receive less support than do normal individuals. In addition, normal people experiencing high levels of stress are apparently at lower risk for disorder if they enjoy high levels of support than if they do not (the so-called buffering hypothesis).

The hypothesized mechanism here is that lack of support in the face of acute stress engenders negative psychological states such as anxiety, helplessness, and depression. These psychological states in turn affect physical health, either by directly influencing susceptibility to disease (involving the neuroendocrine or immune systems), or by provoking certain behavioral responses (such as smoking, drinking, or failing to seek needed medical care) that actually increase risk of disease or mortality (Cohen & Wills, 1985). An important question is whether the amount of support and the degree of health are related in a direct monotonic fashion (i.e., with one variable increasing smoothly and steadily as the other does across all of their respective values) or whether there is instead simply a "threshold" effect in which only those people with the least amount of support (those who are truly isolated) have a significantly elevated risk for disease or death.

As with coping, the relationship between high levels of support and successful adaptation to stressful circumstances is a two-way one. Marital stability and a large circle of positive friendships may produce high self-esteem and competent coping, but these qualities may also explain why a particular person is able to attract and maintain many supportive relationships in the first place (Heller & Swindle, 1983; Monroe & Steiner, 1986).

Investigators differ in their conceptual and operational definitions of social support, making it difficult to compare the outcomes of different studies. Support has both quantitative and qualitative dimensions that are distinguishable empirically as well as conceptually and that correlate only modestly with each other (Cohen & Wills, 1985). When studies report different results, it may be because the measures differ in detail even when they are called by the same or a similar name. Coping strategies and types of social support may be differentially useful with different problems and at different times in the resolution of a problem. In one study, different coping strategies and different types of support were related to measures of adaptation to HIV infection depending in part on the stage of the illness (Pakenham et al., 1994). Collins et al. (1993) similarly found that different aspects of their social support measure were related to different outcomes in pregnancy. These complex relationships mean that we must develop a more complex theory of social support and coping that takes into account more of the context within which people are struggling with problems in living and within which they give and receive support.

"Structural" or quantitative measures of social support supplement measures that deal with the quality of support. Social support has been operationalized quantitatively as the *number of people* in the person's "network" (i.e., family and friends with whom the person is frequently in contact), the *frequency of contact* with members in the network, the *degree of demographic homogeneity of members* (the similarities among members of the network in terms of factors such as age, race, sex, and social class), the number of people in the network who know each other, sometimes called the *density* of the network, and/or the *degree of reciprocity* in supportive transactions among members (i.e., as givers as well as receivers of support). Qualitatively, social support has been defined by the nature of the resources provided by one person to another, by the specific content of social interactions (e.g., emotionally warm versus hostile and destructive), and by perceptions of whether network members are helpful in times of need.

Barrera (1986) reconciled some diverse findings by differentiating among types, conceptual definitions, and measures of support and associating the resulting patterns of correlation with various outcomes. He noted the importance of findings involving *perceived support*, in contrast to *enacted or received support*. This latter development puts an interesting cast on the concept of support, since it implies that one's expectations about help from others are more important for managing stress than is the coping assistance actually received. It also opens up new questions, such as which factors affect the perceived adequacy of support. It also leads to the question of artifactual relationships. Do correlations between measures of social support and criterion measures of adaptation reflect a "real" effect, or are they based on something like response styles ("negative affectivity") or overlapping meanings between dependent and independent variables? The problem of artifacts is not present when the dependent variable is measured completely independently of the measure of social support (e.g., teachers' ratings versus self-ratings or objective measures of health such as infant birth weight). However, artifacts have not been evaluated for measures of social support in the way they have been for stressful life-events measures.

Cohen and Wills (1985) conclude that support appears to influence well-being in two ways: (1) by fostering structural embeddedness in a network of human relationships, which may engender feelings of stability and predictability regarding one's social world, and (2) by providing the specific resources required to cope effectively with stressful situations. The general model presented by Cohen and Wills (1985) and depicted in Figure 7–1 suggests that stress results when one appraises an event or situation as demanding a response that one is unable to make.

Support mitigates the effects of stress in one of two ways. First, the presence of social support may reduce the probability that the event will be appraised as stressful in the first place. That is, the threat implied by an event, such as changing jobs, may be reduced or eliminated by the perception that others can and will provide the resources necessary to adapt to this change. A second possibility is that even if the event is ap-

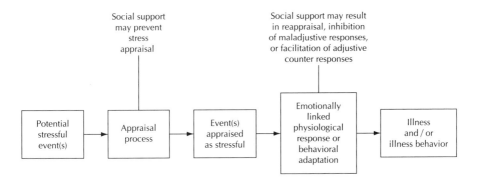

Figure 7-1. Social support and the buffering hypothesis. (From Cohen & Wills, 1985)

praised as stressful, perceived or enacted support may attenuate the stress reaction by offsetting the transient stress response (e.g., through restoring self-esteem), by directly facilitating healthy coping (e.g., through material assistance), or by influencing the individual's self-perceptions (e.g., regarding self-efficacy—"You can do it!") in a way that leads to more persistent coping efforts.

Box 7-2. Coping and Support in the Context of Culture

William Dressler (1991) has produced a conceptually and methodologically sophisticated study of the stress/coping/social support model as adapted to deal with issues of history, culture, and social structure. Dressler studied the distribution of symptoms of "depression" or "demoralization" (which he justified as a measure of disease) in an African American community in the rural south, as well as the availability of social supports (which he characterized as sources of resistance to disease). He took as a starting point his belief that the civil rights movement had profound effects in American society, not only in terms of race relations but also in effecting social stratification and differentiation in the African American community.

In part, Dressler was interested in understanding the role and strengths of the African American family. However, he went beyond that issue, introducing an important historical and social-structural perspective to the study of the relationship among stressful life events, social support, coping, and disease. In addition, his research group engaged in a large number of open-ended interviews to identify the issues as perceived by members of the community. The formal measures were selected, modified, or created to be meaningful in this community.

The civil rights movement had as a major effect the creation of a more differentiated socioeconomic structure in the African American community. With the lifting of formal legal barriers to participation in

American life, and with the enforcement of antidiscrimination legislation, many more African Americans were able to achieve higher occupational statuses and incomes. At the same time, the gap between the top and bottom of the socioeconomic scale within the African American community widened (Wilson, 1987). Dressler took this social change into account, for he hypothesized that the meaning of stressors, or threats to an individual's social and personal identity, would differ by class and by history, as would the meaning of social supports that might serve to mitigate the adverse effects of stressful life events.

The older generation, especially in communities like the small southern rural one he studied, grew up within a rigid segregation system that limited opportunity for education or employment and, viewed from the outside, created a relatively homogeneous socioeconomic community. There was a small middle and upper class, but most people had low-paid, low-prestige, low-skill jobs and had little chance for advancement. For most people, the extended family, others who were "near kin," and the church provided the important constants, the social reference groups, and, therefore, the important sources of support. If a person had little opportunity to advance economically and to accumulate the visible signs of success, then the sources for maintaining and enhancing self-esteem had to be found within the limits provided by the social structure as it existed. People developed their social identities (e.g., father, worker, churchgoer, "good person") as the culture and social structure allowed; within this framework people looked to others for help when it was needed to cope with life's vicissitudes. In this community, stressors were those factors that threatened people's social identities or their links to others.

The older generation worked for and saw the changes wrought by the civil rights movement, and their efforts resulted in an historic achievement that rightly made many feel proud. However, for members of this age group, the changes in opportunity to advance economically and socially may have come too late; for them, Dressler hypothesized, stressors would continue to be those factors that threatened their linkages to the community or their social identities. Moreover, their sources of support would continue to be those provided by the extended family and by the church. For older members of the community, Dressler believed, continuity would be important in helping to sustain identity, whereas younger members would be more likely to strive for material success. Salient stressors would differ depending on the person's social position.

Dressler drew a further distinction between those in the older generation who were relatively well off and those who were more economically limited. The social stressors (life events) related to illness (depression) and the sources of resistance to illness (social support and coping assets) would necessarily differ for those who were better off and those who were less well off, even within this generation. He therefore predicted that different statistical models would relate stressor, resistance

to stressor, and illness, both within generations (depending on socioeconomic status) and between generations.

The younger generation did not experience the rigid limitations of
segregation and had greater opportunities (albeit still limited by racism)
for education, employment, and social and economic advancement.
These greater opportunities encouraged younger people to identify
with the larger American culture and to adopt for themselves the standards of success and social interaction prevalent in the larger culture.
However, Dressler hypothesized, the desire to obtain the possessions
that reflect a successful material lifestyle (car, clothes, home, furnishings, vacations) might be discrepant with economic realities.

The discrepancy between accepting certain ideals of success and
having the wherewithal to attain those ideals, Dressler thought, would
probably be greater in the less successful younger person than in the
more successful person. The less successful person would be concerned
with whether or not he or she could enter and keep valued roles (obtain a job, keep a job, afford to get married)—to use Sarbin's term,
with developing and maintaining an achieved identity. The better-off
younger person, who had obtained an education, a job, and a spouse,
in contrast, would have an achieved identity in several roles and would
be more concerned with locating himself or herself in the normative
ecology. Using Sarbin's terminology, How well am I doing in the several achieved roles? would become the pertinent question. Stressors that
affect a person's sense of control and mastery would be more likely to
affect the more successful younger person. In other words, the
younger, less well-off person would be concerned about entering or
keeping roles, while the better-off younger person would be concerned
with performing well in his or her roles.

In addition, Dressler argued that for younger people, unlike older
people, nonkin support would be more important than kin support in
ameliorating distress related to stressors. He argued, as did Thoits
(1986), that support would be best provided by someone who shared
the same values and goals and understood the problems from firsthand
experience. Support would be better accepted or more useful if it came
from someone with whom the younger person could identify.

Dressler tested these propositions by adminstering a survey to a
randomly selected sample of adults in the community. He then supplemented the quantitative surveys with a series of open-ended interviews
to obtain members' perceptions of the key issues. Dressler illustrated
the quantitative findings by presenting eight case studies of people who
represent the different life circumstances he deemed important.

A sampling of the quantitative results illustrates the power of his
conceptual scheme. For example, he found a significant relationship between lifestyle incongruity (discrepancy between one's lifestyle and the
means to support it) and depression in younger persons, but the effect
was reduced in middle-aged persons. Economic stressors were more
closely related to depression scores for young and middle-aged people

than for older people. The relationship between unemployment and depression was much stronger among the less well off than it was among the better off. The occurrence of one or more stressful life events in the lives of those of lower-class background was more closely associated with depression than it was among those of middle-class or higher class status. When combined stressors (including those that stemmed from perceptions of living in a bad neighborhood, having problems on the job, or having problems in one's marriage and in the parenting role, as well as economic problems and unemployment) were considered, the analysis showed different risk factors for depression depending on the respondent's age and economic class. For example, unemployment was unrelated to depression among those age forty and over who were in a higher economic class, whereas it was related to depression among those who were age forty and older but in a lower economic class. Depression was, however, more closely related to problems in the marital relationship, problems with children, stresses on the job, and concerns about retirement among those better off economically than it was among those less well off in the same age group.

Dressler was also able to isolate "buffers" for the relationship between depression and lifestyle incongruity and between depression and life events. Among those in the younger, lower economic class, the greater the availability of resources, the lower the level of depression when confronted with stressful life events or with lifestyle incongruity. When he examined the perceived availability of social support for those in the younger group, he found that depressive symptoms in the face of stressful life events was high in those with low social support from friends and low in those with high support from friends. On the other hand, kin support was relatively more important in reducing depression in the older group. These complex results are illustrated by a series of case studies based on brief life histories.

The importance of this work is in the interactions showing that the variables related to depression, and the degree of their effect in buffering the effects of stressors, are different in defined social groups. This study tells us that we must elaborate our models of the stress/coping/social support field to an order of complexity that takes into account the nature of a community, its stratification, and the culture of the people. It also tells us that our methods need to be adapted to the nature of the problem in a specific community and must consider the historical flow of events affecting people in that community.

New Directions in Research on Social Support

Our present understanding of social support, its power, and its limits are based largely on the results of correlational studies. Experimental methods can help determine whether supportive friendships can be established as a protective factor for persons at risk and whether such supplements actually enhance people's supportive resources and mental health. An experiment allows us to make "causal" statements about phenomena. An experiment by Heller et al. (1991) raised a number of useful issues about social support.

Heller et al. (1991) arranged for regular telephone conversations between assigned pairs of isolated, low-income, elderly women. Participants were acclimated by ten weeks of regular phone contacts with research staff and were then divided into one of two treatment groups. The women in one group carried on regular phone contacts with an assigned peer, while those in the other continued telephone contacts with research staff. There was also a control group that received no contacts over the same period of time. At the end of the study, measures of mental health and perceived friend support showed that the two intervention groups were not significantly different from each other or from the control group.

Given that the participants were all strangers to each other initially and that all contact was by telephone, Heller et al. suggest that the intervention was too weak to establish significant new friendships. They speculate that a different intervention, such as one that increased the participation of these women in meaningful activities involving mutual interests and face-to-face contact, would have had more significant effects. Interestingly, research and theorizing about social support has so far paid relatively little attention to support derived from participation in a variety of nontherapeutic groups in community settings (Felton & Shinn, 1992).

Heller et al. raised other useful questions. Are there substantive differences in the support coming from different sources (e.g., family member, friend, coworker)? Heller et al. speculated that attention and support from family members, particularly adult children, might have been more important to the women in their study than attention from friends. Having a role in the family and achieving self-esteem by performing this role cannot be duplicated in a friendship. Elderly persons may miss the satisfaction that comes from having their wisdom respected by younger people. Parents may also feel that they have sacrificed for their children and feel disappointed when there is no reciprocity. These unmet expectations may not be resolved very easily by substitute activities, and sources of support may not be interchangeable.

The failure of an intervention like this one does not add much to our understanding of the nature and process of social support. For example, do the types of support provided need to be specific for particular psychological situations? Does the ability to provide support have to be distributed symmetrically, or can different functions be "bartered" among the members of a network (e.g., informational support from one person exchanged for material aid from another)? Furthermore, the optimal nature and amount of support may vary during a given stressful experience. In the case of bereavement, a small, dense network may be more effective during the initial traumatic reaction, whereas for subsequent periods of transition to new roles a broader, looser network of relationships and sources of information is probably more helpful (Walker, MacBride, & Vachon, 1977).

Most research has focused on the recipient of support. Much less is known about the costs and benefits of providing support for someone else. What would Heller et al. have learned had they interviewed the children who, according to their parents, were not paying sufficient attention to their aged parents? People involved in caring for elderly or ill relatives may invest hundreds of hours in this activity, with significant detrimental effects on other aspects of their lives (Perrotta, 1982).

More sophisticated conceptualizations of support will be required to improve our level of theoretical understanding. The possibility that support is situation-specific and source-specific also suggests that more than one aspect or component of support should be measured (see Blazer, 1982). Can we specify the circumstances in which each component is useful? Work by Kobasa and Puccetti (1983), Pakenham et al. (1994), Collins et al. (1993) and Dressler's work (see Box 7–2) all suggest that different components of support correlate with different measures of distress or physical disorder at different times.

The specific nature of support may differ depending on whether we are speaking of the home setting or the work setting. It may also differ by problem. How much should the support fit the needs elicited by the particular stressful event? Material aid may be the most useful form of support in response to a loss of income, but will informational support or self-esteem support be equally effective in maintaining well-being? The source of the aid also matters. It is one thing to obtain support from unemployment insurance ("deserved," "earned," "nonstigmatizing"), another to obtain it from welfare ("undeserved," "stigmatizing"), and still another to obtain it from parents ("guilt-producing" "obligations created").

Some studies (such as Kraus, 1981) suggest that there is a degree of generality in the way people use support in different situations. Is there some general trait of "support use," or do the results reflect the methods employed? Method-specific results present distinct problems for our understanding of process in this and in other areas of psychology. Future research that takes these issues into account may help clarify our understanding of the specific mechanisms of support. However, the more complex the interactions, the more difficult it is to do the research. Support scales could also benefit from incorporating some of the features of Caplan's construct of the family as a support system.

Most of the attention has been devoted to social support as an independent variable (i.e., support hypothetically has direct causal effects on a measured dependent variable such as feelings of self-esteem). Support as a dependent variable has not been so extensively studied. Broadhead et al. (1983) suggest that community characteristics, social roles, and coping skills be investigated prospectively for their potential contributions to the development of social support networks. We may add that there is probably a distinct advantage in studying these variables in relation to common stressors such as the death of a parent, rather than examining them globally. We have much to learn at a phenomenon level before we leap to a higher order of generality.

Box 7–3. Support Interventions for People with Disabilities

In Chapter 2 we noted that the deinstitutionalization movement put back into their communities large numbers of mentally ill and retarded persons. Because many of their families are unable to provide adequate care and support, people with special needs have been targeted in recent years for extra social support. We reviewed Assertive Community Treatment (ACT) in Chapter 2. Here we describe programs of supported living, supported employment, and supported education that form part of a movement known as Psychosocial Rehabilitation (Farkas & Anthony, 1989).

Supported living or supported housing is normal, fully integrated living for people with special needs, including housing no different from that available to the general public (Carling, 1990). The major difference between consumers of supported housing services and other community residents is that case managers or other service providers offer flexible support to consumers tailored to their individual needs. Case management may involve help locating appropriate choices of housing, advocacy, crisis intervention, and other services as needed and can range in intensity from an occasional phone call to full-time, live-in assistance during times of intense crisis.

Supported employment is paid work that a person with special needs chooses and undertakes as part of a fully integrated, competitively obtained job (Bond, 1992). Here much of the support is provided by a "job coach," who assists to the extent necessary with all aspects of the consumer's work career from job development and interviewing to help on the job site (a form of support that typically fades away within a few weeks) to advocacy and education of employers and coworkers to reduce stigma (see Chapter 6) and who offers advice about quitting or changing jobs.

Supported education helps disabled people pursue the social and career advantages of postsecondary education (Moxley, Mowbray, & Brown, 1993). Support services help the person at risk obtain information about school and course offerings, contact school-related services such as academic advising, obtain financial aid, and cope with the stresses of school life.

Some programs offer all three kinds of supports. Rhoda Zusman, the founder and director of Operation Return in Tampa, Florida, operates a twenty-four-unit apartment complex in connection with a community center for consumers who were formerly patients in the mental health system in Florida. Residents, all former patients, pay a subsidized rent that is sufficient to enable Project Return to maintain the mortgage on the property. The center offers courses in computer skills, prepares participants for general education high school diplomas, offers some college-level courses through a community college, operates a business (a thrift shop), teaches arts and crafts, puts on arts and craft shows, and exhibits and sells consumers' work. The center has a drama group that puts on plays.

There is a range of social activities, including a weekend recreational program, social events, field trips, parties, and community meetings. The center also engages in extensive fund-raising efforts that involve the community. Some of the paid employees are consumers, and the program makes use of many volunteers. The center services as many as a thousand consumers per month. Zusman has been instrumental in stimulating a statewide network of thirty-five centers and clubs, and she has been in demand as a consultant in several other states and overseas.

Two recent developments in these services include the creation of organized teams of support providers and the recruiting and training of peers (that is, people with similar special needs) to fill the provider roles. Supportive services are provided in the actual settings where the people at risk live, work, or go to school. These supports assume that people with special needs are similar to other people in the adaptive challenges they face—where to live, how to get money—and that the best way to meet those challenges is through fully integrated, competitively obtained housing, work, and schooling. Successful adaptation will help to transform the person's identity from that summarized by a stigmatizing label like "mental patient" to one of neighbor, coworker, or college student.

To critics it may appear that social support from a paid staff is even more artificial and contrived than what was attempted in the Heller et al. (1991) study reviewed earlier. Advocates of the interventions described here acknowledge that the support they provide is not adequate by itself and that it is always better to have and use family, friends, and other natural, spontaneous sources of support. However, for many people with disabilities such natural supports are inadequate or nonexistent. The question is not "Are program supports as good as natural supports?" but instead "Are program supports better than no support at all?" It may be useful to see these services as analogous to the Employee Assistance Programs (EAPs) that are increasingly available to nondisabled people. EAPs are designed to give workers at risk for maladaptive outcomes second chances and extra supports to improve their chances of coping successfully.

The support services described here are not panaceas. The typical homes or jobs of these consumers are modest or "entry-level," similar to those of other people with comparable incomes, education, or skills. As a result, average or above-average home- or job-related stressors such as safety concerns, low pay, and lack of control can be expected to complicate the consumers' coping efforts. In addition, fully integrated residences and jobs may be widely dispersed throughout a community, hampering access to support from other consumers. Community psychologists can help address this by assisting in the development of self-help groups for consumers (see Chapter 9).

Summary

The specific concepts of adaptation, crisis, coping, and support are very useful when we consider the daily "soap opera" affecting a significant number of Americans of all ages and in all walks of life. The concepts of crisis and vulnerability open up a wider range of possible interventions and allow us to consider the possibility that a large proportion of human misery can be alleviated, even though we do not yet know whether the most serious and disabling mental illnesses can be prevented in this fashion.

We reviewed the process of coping and the state of crisis that ensues when a person's state of adaptation is disrupted in the absence of the psychological, social, or material resources necessary to produce a new adaptive response. Nearly everyone is assumed to be at risk for such experiences. The ensuing affective state is not a sign of illness but a natural response to a specific set of circumstances. Dysphoric feelings are a signal that the individual is in a situation calling for some change in customary ways of dealing with demands or solving problems. The crisis concept directs us to separate the issues into two parts: managing affect (emotion-focused coping) and solving the problem (problem-focused coping). Learning to manage or modulate feelings and learning to solve problems more effectively are important both therapeutically and preventively.

There are two classes of crises, anticipated and unanticipated. We speak of anticipated changes when the network of relationships, the tasks to be accomplished, and the roles the individual occupies will change predictably. Crises following anticipated changes are situational-transitional in nature, or developmental. If changes are anticipated, we can devise preventive strategies. Preparation, rehearsal, anticipation of feelings, warnings, advance preparation of resources, and practice with techniques for dealing with new problems all may be helpful in meeting anticipated challenges. Sex education in high school or training for parenting might similarly prepare individuals for new relationships and new challenges. In addition to preparing the individual to cope when crises can be anticipated, help can also be positioned so as to be available when the event occurs, or soon afterward.

If general problem-solving skills exist, we can teach those skills as part of the regular school curriculum. As we learn how people handle problems on an everyday basis, we can translate that learning into curricula and methods for teaching everyone. Spivack and Shure (1974), in fact, did precisely that when they created a curriculum in interpersonal problem solving that could be employed by nursery school teachers with preschool children (see Chapter 8).

The concept that crises have phases and that each phase is different is useful in devising helping strategies, because what constitutes useful assistance may vary with different phases in the crisis. If people are able on their own to convert traumatic events into growth-promoting experiences, perhaps assistance can be provided in advance to help that process. Alternatively, the crisis stages may themselves be understandable as adaptive responses to specific situations.

Much of what we have said about managing feelings and solving problems involves "psychological mediators." Individuals call on members of social networks to obtain coping assistance, to find the psychological, social, or material resources useful in achieving a new state of adaptation. The individual's ability to find and to call on members of a social network may depend on that person's understanding of reciprocity in social relationships. It may also depend on having the social skills necessary to function in a social network. In this sense we have been discussing the interaction between psychological and situational mediators. While apparently separable at a conceptual level, they are in reality intimately intertwined (Folkman & Lazarus, 1980; Heller & Swindle, 1983; Lazarus, 1990).

Research on natural coping by ordinary people places emphasis on action-oriented, problem-solving responses in dealing with stress. Of course, some people, under some conditions, by virtue of their experiences and their biological and psychological makeups, would find the types of interventions we point to here inadequate and insufficient to help them cope with their problems. The psychoanalyst Herbert Herskovitz used to distinguish between those clients who, he said, came by their problems "honestly" (i.e., had sufficient adversity in their backgrounds to account for their present state) and those whose problems could not be readily understood by examining their histories. The crisis concept and associated interventions may be meaningful only for those who come by their problems honestly. Our theoretical doubts, however, and the broad gaps in our knowledge should not prevent us from experimenting with different approaches when a reasonably interesting theory points the way.

Notes

1. Although some community psychologists (e.g., Bloom, 1984) draw a distinction between the concepts of crisis and stress, one strength of Dohrenwend's model is that it examines these two constructs using the same conceptual framework.

2. The six-week period calls to mind the number forty associated with crises in the Bible (e.g., Noah on the waters for forty days, Christ in the desert for forty

days, Moses wandering for forty years). It also parallels the forty-week period of human gestation normally required to create and deliver, in a literal sense, a "new life."

3. A problem may be resolved by redefining it. Members of Al-Anon, the organization for families of alcoholics, may join out of desperation over their inability to stop their spouses from drinking. Al-Anon teaches that one can control only one's own behavior so that all the dysphoric feelings related to one's inability to stop the other from drinking may fade. Another possible response to some crises is "need resignation." The person not admitted to graduate school, for example, may decide that he or she never really wanted to go anyway, thus divorcing the stressful event from one or more of the individual's ecologies or need states.

4. Initially researchers hypothesized that any life change, positive or negative, would be sufficient to produce stress. The evidence clearly showed, however, that only negative life events predict later disorder. Positive life events do not offset the effects of negative life events or correlate on their own with disorder.

III

APPLICATIONS OF COMMUNITY PSYCHOLOGY

8

Prevention

The history of efforts to reduce the prevalence of mental and emotional problems in the United States is largely one of treating problems in individuals after they have arisen. However, from time to time various authorities have argued that proactive, preventive efforts should be given more emphasis. Levine and Levine (1992) discuss the work of Clifford Beers and the mental hygiene movement and the child guidance clinics of the 1920s and 1930s as examples of earlier efforts with a preventive thrust. Crisis theory as developed by Lindemann and others as early as the 1940s (see Chapter 7) provided a beginning for contemporary thinking about prevention. In the years after World War II prevention was a focus of those who saw psychiatry as an instrument of social change (Grob, 1994), and the Joint Commission on Mental Illness and Health (1961) discussed the desirability, if not the necessity, for programs in prevention. Both the 1963 Community Mental Health Centers Act (Bloom, 1977) and the President's Commission on Mental Health (1978) highlighted prevention as a major strategy for dealing with mental health problems in the United States. More recently, the Institute of Medicine (IOM) of the National Academy of Sciences summarized the existing knowledge base regarding prevention (Mrazek & Haggerty, 1994). We refer to those ideas in this chapter.

Healthy People 2000 is a federal government policy document outlining prevention goals to be achieved by the year 2000. It describes the present state of the U.S. population with respect to many preventable illnesses, sets specific goals for preventive efforts, and suggests directions for those efforts. *Healthy People 2000* reflects a federal interest in emphasizing prevention that goes back to 1979 and the presidency of Jimmy Carter. Carter's initiative was expanded when Ronald Reagan took office in 1981, and even though many other initiatives in social services and mental health were soon sharply curtailed during the Reagan administration, policies promoting preventive interventions were preserved (Levine, 1981). *Healthy People 2000* was written and published during the presidency of George Bush and continues to be cited in public health sources today, showing the continuity of the policy through several national administrations.

Those interested in pursuing prevention programs will find the document worth examining, although many of its specific proposals may be on hold given the political climate of the mid-1990s, which discourages more "government interference" in the lives of individuals and protests the commitment of more money to anything that can be labeled a "social program" (see Chapter 13). *Healthy People 2000* considers neither the problem of finding resources to achieve the percent change objectives it recommends nor the time necessary. The embeddedness of prevention programs in our economic, political, and social structures is readily apparent, a point we emphasize throughout this book. The complexity of problems is no excuse for not trying to develop solutions, but understanding the complexity should give us pause for thought and a sense of humility about the time and resources necessary to achieve these objectives.[1]

A moment's reflection may suggest why prevention is appealing. One reason is certainly the "numbers" problem we examined in Chapter 1. Given the way psychological problems have traditionally been defined, there are not now and presumably never will be enough trained professionals to meet the mental health needs of most communities. Prevention of mental disorders would also improve the efficiency of the health care system in the United States by reducing costs related to long-term disabilities and the inappropriate use of medical services to treat psychosocial problems (Mrazek & Haggerty, 1994).

A second impetus for prevention, mentioned in Chapter 2, is dissatisfaction with the effectiveness of traditional helping interventions, especially given the restrictive policies of managed care and other limitations in the service system. Lack of eligibility for mental health services and other barriers keep many potential clients from receiving treatment at all. For problems like antisocial personality disorder that resist the known forms of psychological treatment, prevention at a *prior* stage of individual development (e.g., prevention of conduct disorder in childhood) may be more promising than treatment (Mrazek & Haggerty, 1994).

A third compelling impetus toward prevention is that prevention may be much more cost-effective than treatment. The Michigan Jobs Project (see Chapter 3) was designed to prevent depression and anxiety in unemployed adults and to enhance their motivation to seek new employment. A follow-up after two and a half years found that people who had received the intervention had higher rates of reemployment and earnings, fewer job changes, and reduced anxiety and depression compared to those who had been randomly assigned to a control condition. For the average person in the intervention condition the program cost $286 but generated more than $5,000 in additional earnings and more than $1,000 in additional federal and state tax revenue. The average participant's additional earnings were projected to reach $50,000 over the years remaining until his or her retirement (Vinokur, van Ryn, Gramlich, & Price, 1991). Large financial benefits have also been reported in a twenty-five-year follow-up of Head Start participants (Barnett, 1993).

Why, then, has prevention enjoyed only sporadic popularity among mental health professionals? Some critics take the position that the existing knowledge base is inadequate for effective prevention. They believe that we are obligated to provide care for those in need; resources devoted to uncertain efforts at prevention would take away from the limited pool of resources currently available for treatment (Lamb & Zusman, 1979). A more precise understanding of disorders and interventions would undoubtedly be helpful to prevention efforts. However, making an effort at prevention is worthwhile despite the uncertainty of the knowledge base. Our understanding of the biological nature of serious mental illnesses and of the risk factors and support resources affecting those and other disorders has steadily improved in recent years. The empirical support undergirding prevention programs for depression, alcohol abuse, and certain other disorders is comparable to what existed concerning cardiovascular disease at the time prevention efforts were initiated in that area (Mrazek & Haggerty, 1994).

Another constraint is the lack of formal training in prevention

(Cowen, 1977). Without the decisions made following World War II to train psychologists in Veterans Administration hospitals and other medical settings, professional clinical psychology might have looked more like education than medicine and specialized more in prevention than in treatment (Sarason, 1981b). Psychology's roots in the study of learning, cognition, social behavior, and normal development give its subject matter much more relevance to positive, growth-producing changes than to the treatment of "diseases" through a medical model.

Prevention has not been popular among professionals and the public because its benefits are less immediate and because it requires us to confront social and political factors in defining the solutions to social problems (Levine, 1981). A strategy of prevention implies environmental explanations for the causes of psychological problems and a firm belief in the value of large-scale, active intervention using public resources over more passive efforts by smaller private interests (Albee, 1986). Implementing preventive programs may require professionals to take social and political action designed to achieve change. Although we have a historical precedent for an activist role in the settlement house movement (Levine & Levine, 1992), in times of social and economic conservatism most professionals want to avoid "biting the hand that feeds them" (Rappaport, 1992).

Basic Concepts in Prevention

The core idea of prevention is that action taken now can limit or avoid an undesirable consequence or state of affairs in the future. While the undesirable state of affairs does not necessarily have to be an illness, prevention concepts are rooted in the nineteenth-century public health movement (Bloom, 1979). While the disease model is not fully applicable to the problems of living that occupy our attention, we will review concepts borrowed from it and will also explain some recently proposed alternatives.

Two terms are important, and we therefore define them a second time. The incidence (I) of a disorder is the number of new cases that arise in the population of interest during a specified interval of time, usually one year. Prevalence (P) is the number of cases in existence at a specified point in time; it reflects both the incidence rate and the duration (D) of the disorder. Note that prevalence (P) will be reduced if incidence (I) is reduced; P will also be reduced if treatment reduces the duration (D) of an episode of disorder. The formula $P = I \times D$ summarizes the concepts.

Gerald Caplan (1964) introduced the distinctions among primary, secondary, and tertiary prevention strategies in mental health. *Tertiary prevention* does not reduce the prevalence of a disorder; tertiary prevention efforts are directed toward ameliorating the disorder's long-term symptoms and preventing further ramifications. Supported living and supported employment programs, for example, help people with serious mental illness live and work in fully integrated community settings. These opportunities help to reduce the social disability associated with mental illness even though the consumers are still counted as cases of mental illness in an epidemiological survey.

Secondary prevention is the reduction in the prevalence of a disorder achieved by drastically curtailing the disorder's duration, typically through early case finding and prompt intervention. Crisis intervention, juvenile delinquency diversion, employee assistance programs, and psychological screening of elementary school children (e.g., Cowen et al., 1975) are examples of secondary prevention efforts. These programs are "preventive" in the sense that P is reduced if a case is successfully treated early and the duration (D) of the disorder is shortened. The rate of new cases (incidence, or I), presumably is not affected.

When an intervention actually reduces the incidence of a disorder (I), the program is referred to as *primary prevention*. By definition, after the primary prevention intervention, the program's targets must show no detectable signs of the disorder. Social support groups for the newly widowed to prevent depression and training in cognitive problem solving to prevent school failure are examples of primary prevention. The goal of such programs is to act before an undesirable end-state becomes manifest to prevent its appearance.

Public health concepts do not apply readily to the prevention of mental disorders (Mrazek & Haggerty, 1994). The "primary/secondary" distinction assumes a clear demarcation between states of health and states of incipient disorder. In mental health we typically lack valid definitions or signs for making such distinctions. Instead, we emphasize a *continuum of risk* for disorder that is based on multiple factors. In addition, "secondary" connotes a less direct and perhaps less significant effort than one designated "primary," yet depending on the intervention's focus and cost-effectiveness this may not be the case. "Tertiary" efforts are preventive in an indirect fashion. They assist in the long-term support and rehabilitation of persons with special needs.

In light of these conceptual problems, prevention in mental health is developing its own language and concepts. In the current terminology, *indicated prevention* is an intervention aimed at individuals who already possess detectable signs or biological markers of disorder even though they are not yet diagnosable. A man prone to depressed moods would not be diagnosable if his episodes were always brief (less than two weeks), for example, but the eventual likelihood of serious mood disorder is such that medication or other interventions might be worth considering immediately as a way of reducing the risk of diagnosable disorder. Indicated prevention involves the identification (and thus the labeling) of specific individuals. It is not appropriate unless a cost-effective intervention is available.

When the target person faces above-average risk but as yet shows no indications of disorder, the program involves *selective prevention*. For example, a pregnant woman should minimize her use of alcohol and other drugs to prevent harm to her fetus. Although the targeted individuals are at elevated risk, they do not yet show any indications of disorder, making the program equivalent to primary prevention. Deciding whether a given psychological or behavioral characteristic is better understood as a "marker" or a "risk factor" (and thus subject to indicated or selective prevention, respectively) is difficult (Mrazek & Haggerty, 1994).

An intervention provided to everyone without regard to relative risk is called *universal prevention*; an example is ads urging people not to start smoking. Universal prevention programs can reach large numbers of people, but since relatively few people are likely to be at imminent risk, the programs can be inefficient and thus low in cost-effectiveness. If they are relatively inexpensive financially and carry few social costs compared to the costs of having even a few cases develop, intervention may still be worthwhile. Figure 8–1 locates these preventive activities on a spectrum of interventions for mental disorders. Aside from prevention, this spectrum includes active *treatment* for individuals who meet or approximate formal diagnostic criteria for mental disorder and *maintenance* strategies to support adaptation and coping and to reduce the likelihood of relapse or deterioration.

Historically, indicated (or secondary) prevention has appealed to mental health professionals, even though it rests on certain assumptions and typically reveals some of the pitfalls of prevention efforts. We therefore will discuss an important example of indicated prevention before reviewing examples of selective and universal prevention.

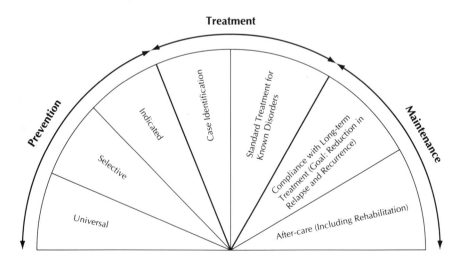

Figure 8–1. The mental health intervention spectrum for mental disorders. (From Mrazek & Haggerty, 1994)

Indicated (Secondary) Prevention

The Primary Mental Health Project

The best-known indicated prevention program in mental health is the Primary Mental Health Project (PMHP) conducted since the 1950s by Emory Cowen and his associates at the University of Rochester. The program has been widely praised because of its innovativeness, durability, and devotion to documenting its effects and has been adopted successfully by school systems all over the United States. Because its developers have studied it carefully, their experience sheds considerable light on the practice of indicated prevention. This review is based on information from Cowen, et al. (1975) and Cowen and Hightower (1989).

Cowen, having observed that many children with behavioral problems show milder degrees of difficulty early in their school careers and reasoned that effective intervention might be possible during elementary school years, prior to the onset of full-fledged disorder, began PMHP as an early detection and intervention program for children in the primary grades of a Rochester elementary school. After classroom observations, psychological tests, and parent interviews, the PMHP team rendered a clinical judgment classifying each child into one of two groups: those showing signs of psychological problems or potential problems (overall, about 33 percent) and those showing no problems and no indication of future problems (about 67 percent). The project was thus an example of indicated prevention because the children selected were already showing some signs of problems. The initial intervention included informal conferences, meetings, and educational efforts for parents and teacher-led after-school groups. Two comparison schools, demographically similar to the target school, were selected for later use in evaluating long-term preventive effects on children in the target school. PMHP staff provided no preassessment or intervention in the two comparison schools.

An evaluation of this early phase (Cowen et al., 1963) found few significant differences overall between the children in the target school and those in the two control schools. Children identified as having problems remained below the others in average achievement, teacher behavior rating, peer and self sociometric ratings, and overall adjustment as assessed by the PMHP team. These results indicated that (1) it was possible to differentiate children who would later have adjustment difficulties as early as the first grade at better than a chance level, and (2) the intervention program as then implemented had not succeeded in eliminating this deficit.

PMHP's staff then revised the intervention program, using alternative mental health resources such as homemakers and college students and making it possible to provide much more direct help inexpensively to children in the experimental school on a 1:1 or small-group basis. By the next evaluation of PMHP (Cowen, et al., 1966), the children in the target school were doing significantly better on average than the children in the control schools on about half the outcomes measured, including grades, achievement test scores, teacher ratings, and self-reported anxiety. On the other hand, within the experimental school the high-risk children continued to fare more poorly than the other group on nearly all measures. Despite having been identified early, they continued to have problems. One possible explanation is that labeling affected teachers' sensitivity to the children's difficulties (Levine & Graziano, 1972).

How well did PMHP's classification of children in the first grade predict the incidence of *treated* psychological disorder later? Cowen and his colleagues (1973) determined which of the children in all groups ended up receiving psychiatric treatment in local clinics up to thirteen years after finishing first grade. The proportions of children from the target and the control schools who later received treatment did not differ significantly (7–8 percent in each), indicating that PMHP did not noticeably prevent the occurrence of treated psychiatric conditions in the target school as a whole. Only 19 percent of the identified children turned up in the treatment group, which means that 81 percent of those predicted to have problems were not found to have received treatment. The predictions for these children were erroneous; more precisely, the children were "false positives" if we take their identification to be a "prediction" that they would have to be treated in the future (see Box 8–1).

In sum, PMHP demonstrated statistically significant success in predicting level of risk for later maladjustment in children as young as the first grade of elementary school. The effectiveness of its various intervention programs at reducing the degree of maladjustment shown by the high-risk children is more open to debate. On a positive note, PMHP has evolved in keeping up with advances in mental health intervention practices. It has adopted programs for training young children in social problem-solving skills (Gesten et al., 1982) and for helping children of divorce (Wolchik et al., 1993). Obviously, a period of research and development is necessary. We cannot expect that the initial efforts will be instantly effective. The voluminous publications by Cowen and his associates have clarified important issues in the practice of indicated prevention. We now examine these more closely.

8–1: *The Problem of False Positives*

Indicated and selective prevention strategies require accurate information about the risk of later disorder in populations targeted for preventive intervention. Accuracy of prediction can be judged in terms of the rates of two types of errors in classification, "false positives" and "false negatives." A false positive occurs when an individual is predicted to develop a disorder when in fact he or she will not. Conversely, a false negative represents the *failure* to predict later disorder in a case where the individual will eventually show it.

These prediction errors are ever-present challenges to cost-effective prevention. Consider the following example. Violence is a serious problem of increasing concern in the United States, and among those prone to commit violence a significant proportion are people described as having antisocial personality disorder (APD). APD is notoriously resistant to psychological treatment. However, because abuse and neglect during childhood are implicated in the development of APD in adulthood (American Psychiatric Association, 1994), some observers have asked whether we can prevent APD and violence against others by reducing the number of children who are abused or neglected.

How accurate are predictions of adult APD diagnoses based on documented experience of abuse or neglect in childhood? Luntz and Widom (1994) identified 416 adults in a single metropolitan area whose histories included documented evidence of physical and sexual abuse and/or neglect occurring approximately twenty years earlier (when they were eleven years of age or younger). Luntz and Widom identified a comparison group of 283 young adults who had not experienced abuse or neglect as children but who were matched with the abused group on the basis of sex, race, approximate date of birth, and home neighborhood. All members of each group were located and interviewed; they were all evaluated according to the diagnostic criteria for APD. Table 8–1 summarizes the researchers' findings, which showed that more of those in the group that had been abused or neglected as children met the diagnostic criteria for APD than in the comparison group. Note, however, that the false positive rate for this widely accepted predictor variable was a whopping 87 percent! That is, among individuals who were abused or neglected as children, the number who met the diagnostic criteria for APD as adults was less than one sixth the number of those who did not meet the diagnostic criteria. Although the prediction was "accurate" in a statistical sense relative to the comparison group, it included many more errors than correct identifications.

This particular false positive rate is specific to the prediction of APD and in no way undermines the moral need to reduce child abuse

Table 8–1
Prediction of Adult Antisocial Personality Disorder (APD) Based on History of Abuse or Neglect in Childhood*

| | | Diagnosed with APD as Adult? frequency (row %) | | |
		No	Yes	Total
Abused or neglected	No	263 (93%)	20 (7%)	283
as a child?	Yes	360 (87%)	56 (13%)	416
	Total	623	76	

*χ^2 (1) = 7.11, $p < .01$ (From Luntz & Widom, 1994, p. 671)

and neglect. However, we must consider the social cost to an already victimized child of being erroneously placed in a program targeted at individuals who are considered likely to become perpetrators of antisocial behavior as adults. More accurate predictions based on a thorough consideration of all known risk and protective factors might reduce the false positive rate to an acceptable level. Otherwise it would not be far-fetched to see the prediction and targeting of abused children for "violence prevention programs" as yet another form of abuse.

Preventing child maltreatment. In Chapter 4 we discussed the tragic death of Joseph Wallace, a three-year-old who was murdered by his mother. A judge had restored custody to this mother on the recommendation of a child protection worker and of professional therapists who had presumably treated her. How does the problem of false positives hamper efforts to prevent such tragedies?

Recall that one estimate is that maltreatment-related child fatalities occur with an incidence of about 1.94 per 100,000 children. Several "risk factors" may be related to prevention. First, the vast majority (80–90 percent) of children who die because of maltreatment or neglect are under age 5, and a high percent of those are infants and children under age 2. These very young children are also at the highest risk of receiving injuries severe enough to warrant hospitalization.

Second, the deaths are probably concentrated among low-income and ethnic minority families. Third, perhaps 75 percent of fatalities related to *physical* abuse involve a male (father, stepfather, boyfriend) acting either alone or together with (usually) the child's mother. Very few maltreatment deaths of very young children can be attributed to strangers. Almost all are committed by caretakers.

Fourth, it is difficult to tell how many maltreatment-related deaths are due to neglect (e.g., the child who is left alone and drowns in a bath tub or who plays with matches and is fatally burned) and how many to abuse (physical assault). However, our best estimate is that between one third and one half of maltreatment-related fatalities are related to neglect rather than abuse.

Fifth, although the number varies in different studies, perhaps a third of the cases involving abuse-related deaths have had some prior Child Protective Services (CPS) involvement. Sixth, a sizable proportion of abuse-related fatalities are due to "blunt trauma" to the head or body, and another significant percent are due to "shaken baby syndrome" in which an adult holds a baby and shakes the child vigorously, injuring the infant's brain. Other deaths result from medical neglect, inadequate parental supervision, drowning, and suffocation.

Seventh, at least some theory and some data support the view that infanticide and less severe forms of abuse are discontinuous in nature. That is, people who commit lesser degrees of abuse or neglect are not particularly likely to kill a child. If this is true, then prevention efforts directed at the greater number of people who perpetrate mild abuse may have no effect on incidence of child homicide (Levine, Compaan, & Freeman, 1994; U.S. Advisory Board on Child Abuse and Neglect, 1995).

It is difficult to predict low-base-rate events without making a large number of false positive errors unless the predictive instrument is perfect or near perfect (see Caldwell, Bogat, & Davidson, 1988). We will have to commit a great many resources to intervene in the lives of many people in order to reach the few who are identified correctly as potential child killers.

Two additional concepts are useful. *Sensitivity* refers to the ability of a predictive instrument to identify the target or high-risk population correctly. The correct predictions of outcomes we wish to prevent are the true positives. Instances of these target outcomes that we fail to predict are called false negatives. Sensitivity therefore equals true positives over true positives plus false negatives. *Specificity* refers to the ability to screen out the nontarget group, that is, to identify correctly those who are in the nontarget population. These are the true negatives. The cases that would be misidentified are called false positives. Specificity thus equals true negatives over true negatives plus false positives.

Table 8–2 (from Caldwell et al., 1988) shows the percent of errors for instruments with different sensitivities and specificities. We can use the table to illustrate the issues. Pianta, Egeland, and Erickson (1989) conducted a six-year longitudinal study of mothers who were all considered at high risk of maltreating their children. After one year, thirty-two of 267 mothers were classified as having "seriously maltreated" their children. After two years, forty-four of 267 mothers had maltreated their children in one or more ways, a base rate of 16 percent. Since all the moth-

Table 8–2
Percentage of Population Assigned to High-Risk Status Who Are Misclassified by Assessment Procedures of Indicated Sensitivity and Specificity[a]

Sensitivity	Specificity						
	.70	.75	.80	.85	.90	.95	.99
.70	97.7	97.2	96.6	95.5	93.4	87.6	58.6
.75	97.5	97.1	96.4	95.2	93.0	86.8	56.9
.80	97.4	96.9	96.1	94.9	92.5	86.1	55.2
.85	97.2	96.7	95.9	94.6	92.1	85.3	53.8
.90	97.1	96.5	95.7	94.3	91.7	84.6	52.4
.95	96.9	96.3	95.4	94.0	91.2	83.9	51.0
.99	96.8	96.2	95.2	93.8	90.9	83.3	50.0

[a]Assumes actual annual incidence rate of 1%   (From Caldwell et al., 1988)

ers were classified as high-risk initially, the false positive rate was 84 per-cent. After six years, forty-seven of the two hundred mothers remaining in the study were determined to have maltreated their children in one or more ways for a true positive rate of 23.5 percent. The false positive rate was thus 76.5 percent.

For study purposes, Pianta et al. (1989) examined data about the maltreating group (N = 20) and a nonmaltreating group (N = 38). Com-plete data were available only for these fifty-eight cases. Under these cir-cumstances, and using seven variables known to differentiate the groups, Pianta et al. achieved a sensitivity rate of 75 percent and a specificity of about 87 percent. The false positive rate was 13 percent and the false neg-ative rate 25 percent.

Assuming that it is feasible to obtain the relevant information, we can apply Pianta et al.'s sensitivity and specificity figures to prediction in the general population. Using an annual incidence rate for maltreatment in the general population of 1 percent, 97 percent of the cases predicted to be at high risk would be misclassified. If we intervened on the basis of cutoff scores, we would serve 3 percent who needed to be served and 97 percent who didn't need the service. Given that the annual incidence of maltreatment-related fatalities is closer to two per one hundred thousand, the errors of classification would be magnified accordingly.

Can we improve our predictions? K. Browne (1993) used a screen-ing instrument completed by British home health visitors in England who visited 14,252 children born in 1985 and 1986. About 7 percent, or 964 cases, were classified as being at high risk for abuse or neglect. All the families were followed for five years. At the end of that time, 106 of 14,252 cases, or 0.7 percent, had been officially reported for suspected or actual maltreatment. The screening instrument had a sensitivity rate of 68 percent, since it correctly identified 72 of the 106 maltreating cases, and a specificity rate of 94 percent. The screening instrument *incorrectly* identified only 6 percent of the nonmaltreating cases; however, the ac-tual number of errors was very large because of the low base rate of mal-treatment. The screening instrument identified a rate of false positives that was ten times the actual rate (7 percent predicted versus .7 percent ac-tual). If we had intervened on the basis of the high-risk scores, 90 per-cent of the intervention costs would have been unnecessary. Moreover, we would still have missed a small number of false negatives (34 of 13,288 cases identified as not at risk, or 0.25 percent).

Prediction could have been improved by studying the 964 identified families more closely, using additional risk factors, perhaps having a sec-ond round of screening using measures similar to those used by Pianta et al. (K. Browne, 1993). What could we expect from a second round of screening? Using the sensitivity rate of 75 percent, we would correctly identify fifty-four cases (.75 × 72 true positives = 54). Using the speci-ficity rate of 87 percent, we would correctly identify 776 cases (.87 × 892 true negatives = 776) but misidentify 116 cases as false positives. Predictive accuracy would improve, but we would still be treating 116 false positive cases unnecessarily in order to reach the fifty-four true positives, and we would still be surprised by the thirty-four false negative cases that we missed in the original screening. Keep in mind that the false positive problem would be much worse if we were trying to predict the much rarer fatalities due to maltreatment.

Implications for prevention. Using data and theory, we can set some parameters for a program to prevent maltreatment fatalities. Targeting high-risk populations, even using a two-stage screening process, will not overcome the false positive problem. Even under a favorable two-stage screening scenario, we would still be spending two dollars on false positive cases for every dollar we spent on true positives, and we would still miss the false negatives. That's just the dollar cost. What of the political, cultural, and psychological cost of intervening in a situation with a high false positive rate? How would the intervention be explained to the recipient in a way that would avoid the stigma of having the family or some family member labeled as a potential killer and the child labeled as a victim? Moreover, unless the high-risk parent voluntarily accepts services, under present law the state has no power to intervene coercively simply because of a predicted risk at some time in the indefinite future (Levine, Doueck, & associates, 1995).

An individual-level preventive strategy is bound to be inefficient. Because it is inefficient, it will be effective only if members of the high-risk population and the public accept the intervention. Home visiting for infants is a potential intervention to prevent maltreatment fatalities because the children most at risk are infants and preschoolers. The home visitor can do more than simply observe to prevent fatality. The visitor can provide other valued services and call for further intervention when it appears the family is in difficulty. Fatalities due to neglect occur as often as those due to abuse (Levine, Compaan, & Freeman, 1994). If neglect and abuse are qualitatively different phenomena, each with its own risk factors and dynamics, then a single program emphasizing either cannot be fully effective. More than one program is necessary.

We cannot depend on Child Protective Services to prevent all or even most child fatalities. Although cases known to CPS are at higher risk for child fatalities, the rate of fatalities is very low, and we would still have to deal with the false positive problem in an already overburdened system.

Partial solutions may be possible. For example, a high proportion of maltreatment-related fatalities result from shaken baby syndrome. Many people are unaware of the dangers of shaking babies. A simple video warning all new mothers of the danger would be easy to develop and to use. If the video also were to contain information about coping when a baby won't stop crying, it would be useful generally, inexpensive, and culturally unobjectionable. The video might also warn viewers against assuming that a young child is willfully disobedient when a mishap occurs during toilet training or some other activity. Another example of a partial solution pertains to the incidence of injury from scalding water. Many children each year are injured severely by hot water and require intensive medical care, sometimes lasting over many years. A simple governor that shuts off tap water when it gets too hot can prevent many of the burns (U.S. Advisory Board on Child Abuse and Neglect, 1995).

A more difficult prevention problem is posed by the finding that perhaps 75 percent of abuse-related deaths involve a man. What kind of prevention program can teach a mother how to deal with a potentially abusing man? What if the man isn't the child's father and doesn't come into the picture until after the mother returns home from the hospital? Can a mother be expected to deal effectively with a potentially abusive man (Levine, Compaan, & Freeman, 1994)?

Warnings about the dangers of leaving infants alone may be useful, especially if reinforced by frequent reminders. Assuming that parents sometimes reach the limits of their tolerance, advance preparation such as finding a neighbor or a relative who will provide some respite for a parent might help. However, abusive or neglectful families may be socially isolated and/or live in neighborhoods where not much neighboring goes on, in which case that solution may be difficult to implement. Greater availability of nurseries, day care, and preschools would bring more young children into situations in which they can be observed. That route is expensive, however, and also requires some mechanism to identify potentially high-risk situations and to intervene early.

No single approach will be uniformly successful in preventing fatalities. One message and one program are not enough. Multiple approaches based on an ecological understanding of the conditions under which maltreatment-related fatalities occur are necessary.

Limitations of Indicated Prevention in Mental Health

Indicated prevention requires both early detection and effective intervention. Problems with the accuracy of detection and the efficiency of early intervention raise important concerns about the cost-effectiveness of indicated prevention efforts in mental health. Screening procedures may rely on incomplete knowledge about risk factors and ignore compensating protective factors. Normal individuals may be mislabeled as cases of "incipient" pathology, and we may miss important early problems in others. We often do not understand the natural course of a disorder over time well enough to identify its incipient stage, yet the incipient stage, assuming there is one, is the crucial period for indicated prevention. What we think of as an incipient stage may actually be a normal variation in behavior. Is an adolescent who stays in his room for much of the time and always wears a hat showing signs of early schizophrenia, or is it just adolescence? If the latter, then intervention may be wasted, or worse. On the other hand, by the time we are able to identify an "early" case the problem may already exist in a more entrenched and resistant stage, making effective intervention more difficult.

Because target group status is based on *probabilities* of future disorder that are less than 100 percent (and usually not known precisely), the costs of being wrong in some number of individual cases cannot be overlooked in evaluating the overall effectiveness of an indicated prevention program. Many highly regarded prevention programs are not intended to enhance the overall mental health of populations but focus much more narrowly on preventing specific disorders such as alcohol abuse or schizophrenia (Mrazek & Haggerty, 1994). However, a specific disorder like schizophrenia may occur in only 1 percent of the population, and controlling costs by minimizing the rate of false positives can be very difficult when the base rate of a disorder is less than the rate of cases the identification procedure can reliably detect.

A similar problem arises with suicide. The rate of successful suicide is 71.9 per 100,000 for men over 65; the rate for adolescent males is 19.4 per 100,000 (Garland & Zigler, 1993). The rate of suicide in those hospitalized for a suicide attempt is about 2 percent in the year following hospitalization and 10 percent within ten years. No detection procedure would improve the error rate (false positives plus false negatives) over simply predicting that no one would ever commit suicide, and there would be enormous financial, psychological, and social costs associated with hospitalizing everyone we believed was at risk. Our inability to predict accurately creates important dilemmas, not only for prevention but for clinical decision making in contexts where predictions are important.

The social costs of false positives and false negatives depend on the particular disorder. A person would presumably rather be told he might have cancer when in fact he does not (i.e., be a false positive), for example, than *not* be told he might have cancer when in fact he does (false negative). Tests for the presence of cancer can be carried out with little social cost to the individual; a missed diagnosis on the other hand, may cause the person to lose the opportunity for effective treatment. However, a diagnosis of mental illness carries with it stigma and other disadvantages. The action of holding a person for further study of mental illness carries with it social costs that are not present with other medical diagnoses.

There are also several requirements if we are to justify indicated prevention. Few, if any, behavioral or pharmacological interventions are universally effective; for disorders involving poor impulse control or violent antisocial behavior there may be no effective intervention program. What if we can detect a serious disorder but can do nothing about it? Do ethics require that we inform the person (or parent) and thereby increase anxiety even if we have no treatment to offer? Is it better to ignore the signs of incipient disorder and let nature take its course? One justifiable option is intervention to reduce the *current risk* of later disorder. For example, we might work to improve the quality of peer relationships in adolescents at risk for schizophrenia and target peer relationship quality (rather than schizophrenia) as the primary outcome of interest. Whether such a program is truly preventive, of course, remains an empirical question. We might not see a lower than expected rate of schizophrenia among treated individuals later in adulthood.

Even a highly effective intervention has to meet two further requirements. First, because the *timing* of the intervention is crucial to indicated prevention (the target may show precursor features for only a limited time before more entrenched pathology sets in), the intervention must be aggressively delivered to reach enough cases to have a measurable effect on prevalence. Although some authorities assert that crisis intervention has a secondary preventive effect, such a program requires additional backup mental health services to be fully effective. In addition, the typically "passive" format of intervention (persons in need must locate the service provider, rather than vice versa) effectively keeps crisis intervention from having an impact on very many people. Fewer than 1 percent of college students in one study who experienced stressful life events used a hotline or a crisis service (Levine & Perkins, 1980a). Many indicated prevention efforts referring alcohol abusers to employee assistance programs are delivered too late in the development of the disorder to test the benefits postulated for early intervention.

Second, the intervention must be deliverable *economically* and in *quantity* if it is to produce a significant reduction in the prevalence of disorder. The limits of lengthy, costly one-to-one interventions should be obvious by now—there are simply too many potential cases in existence for any kind of 1:1 approach to deliver a cost-effective indicated prevention service. Bloom's (1984) assertion that brief one- or two-session psychotherapy has positive lasting effects is interesting in this context, but we have no evidence of its preventive efficacy. Indicated prevention suffers from some of the same conceptual and practical problems that limit the social utility of psychotherapy and other variants on the medical model (see Chapter 1).

The reduction of misery is a valid humanitarian argument, and there are others, for making treatment readily available as soon as it becomes evident that someone is having difficulties. But the promise of a systematic decrease in the prevalence of disorder is not one of the stronger arguments. Selective and universal prevention strategies avoid some of these problems, as we will see in the next section.

Selective and Universal (Primary) Prevention

Historically, medical disorders have been brought under control by the pursuit of primary prevention strategies that reduced the number of cases arising in the first place. Public health has accomplished the primary prevention of physical diseases through such specific measures as the development of vaccines, and through nonspecific measures such as improved sanitation and purified drinking water. Reasoning by analogy, authorities on prevention in mental health suggested that extensive, lasting benefits might be expected from large-scale social system changes and improvements in the quality of life, even though such efforts are not specifically targeted at reducing the incidence of a specific disorder (Albee, 1986). However, the scope of possible targets and interventions is exceedingly broad, as Kessler and Albee (1975) found:

> [W]e found ourselves constantly writing references and ideas on scraps of paper and emptying our pockets each day of notes on the primary prevention relevance of children's group homes, titanium paint, parent-effectiveness training, consciousness raising, Zoom, Sesame Street, the guaranteed annual wage, legalized abortion, school integration, limits on international cartels, unpolished rice, free prenatal clinics, antipollution laws, a yoghurt and vegetable diet, free VD clinics, and a host of other topics. Nearly everything, it appears, has implications for primary prevention, for reducing emotional disturbance, for strengthening and fostering mental health. (p. 560)

"Prevention" is a very loosely defined construct. Cowen (1983) would restrict the term *primary prevention* to programs that (1) are directed at groups, not at individuals, who are (2) well, not disordered, and who (3) receive an intervention that rests on a knowledge base sufficient to allow for the evaluation of well-articulated, specific goals.

Useful proposals such as Cowen's do not take into account the problems inherent in prevention. Any deliberate intervention into the lives of normal, healthy people raises questions about priorities and values. Resources are not limitless; money spent on preventing future problems is by definition not available to help people already in difficulty. The counterargument asserts that diverting resources to prevention is worthwhile because of the potential for great savings in human misery and in dollars.

What of the values of privacy and freedom? Some problems involve voluntary individual choices (cancer caused by smoking, HIV infection from unsafe sexual practices). What business do we have trying to influence such choices, and, when we do try, what precedents are we setting for trying to dictate other voluntary choices (Leichter, 1991)? How long would it be before any arbitrarily defined condition of "risk" could qualify a person for "preventive" correction? The following "high-risk" groups were targeted for preventive interventions in the 1880s: "children of the insane, isolated persons, dark-haired persons, and the idle rich" (Spaulding & Balch, 1983, p. 60). Assessments of risk can be influenced by social and political factors as much as by physiological and behavioral ones (see Chapter 6). How far do we wish to go in abrogating individual freedom or privacy by intervening in people's lives in the name of public mental health?

Furthermore, since no intervention is risk-free, what we do may well have unintended negative consequences. That is, procedures we believe to be powerful enough to change permanently a person's behavior in one direction are presumably capable of having significant harmful effects as well. Consider the well-known Cambridge-Somerville Youth Study (CSYS), for example, in which boys at risk for delinquency were randomly chosen to receive regular family counseling, academic tutoring, and membership in community-based activities such as Boy Scouts for five years. After thirty years, those who had participated in the program were compared with controls who had not with respect to adult criminal behavior, mortality, disease, and vocational history. Most comparisons revealed no significant differences, but those differences that were significant all favored the control group. Men who had been chosen at random to participate in the CSYS thirty years earlier were significantly *more* likely to (1) have committed multiple crimes, (2) shown signs of alcoholism, serious mental illness, or heart disease, (3) died at a young age, or (4) have worked in lower-status occupations (McCord, 1978).

The reasons for the apparent negative impact of the CSYS intervention are not clear. The choice and use of "supportive guidance" as the preventive intervention was based on professional judgments at that time instead of on solid empirical evidence that such help would provide an antidote to later antisocial behavior. Perhaps the labeling of the boys in the intervention group as delinquency-prone became a self-fulfilling prophecy. Perhaps the socially and economically disadvantaged boys in the intervention group became dependent on the support and attention the program provided, so that ending the program after five years had a negative effect on them. (Keep in mind that stopping a long-term program is itself another "intervention" in the lives of participants.)

Another example helps make this last point. Schulz and Hanusa (1978) describe the results of a preventive intervention designed to counteract the isolation and loss of control that elderly people may experience while institutionalized. Groups of elderly people living in an institution received regular social visits from college students. In one condition the frequency and duration of the visits were under the elderly person's control, while in another the visits were not under the elderly person's control. Members of an additional control group received no visits. Immediately after the intervention, the residents who had controlled the visits they received were rated higher in health status and zest for life than were the other groups. By forty-two months after the end of the intervention, however, this same group was significantly lower than the others on both dimensions, and more people in this group had died. If increasing the amount and degree of control over social contacts was a positive intervention, then abruptly ending this program appears to have been a potent negative intervention.

Iatrogenic (physician- or treatment-induced) effects have been recognized in psychotherapy for some time (e.g., Bergin, 1971), and they are of even greater ethical concern in prevention. Psychotherapy clients have initiated help seeking voluntarily; participants in prevention programs enter in a healthy condition and therefore stand to be worse off if the program is harmful. The specific risks and benefits of participating in a prevention program whose effects are presumed to endure for the rest of one's life are not always predictible. If we adopt a preventive intervention on a large scale, we risk magnifying any negative effects. Universal interventions for very low base-rate problems such as teen suicide are of questionable value if these interventions have any side effects at all—for example, if the curriculum is emotionally upsetting to some recipients—since such interventions may do much more harm than good. Clearly, participation in prevention programs should be voluntary and with fully informed consent.

There are two major approaches to selective and universal (primary) prevention. First is a set of methods directed at strengthening the organism, using inoculation as a model. The second group of strategies is directed at changing the social environment; metaphorically, we may call this approach "cleaning out the swamps." A variant may be termed "accident prevention" (Peterson & Mori, 1985).

Risk and protective factors. We can't really afford to deliver interventions to everyone. Currently healthy individuals may have different relative risks (genetic, prenatal, developmental, and experiential variables) for disorders. Although the risk that any randomly selected member of the population will develop schizophrenia is about 1 percent, for example, the risk for the child of a person with schizophrenia is about 13 percent (Gottesman, 1991). Keeping in mind the false positive problem, programs to prevent schizophrenia could be delivered more efficiently if they were aimed selectively at these children rather than administered to all children. Implementation of a prevention program can be difficult with this population. Schizophrenic parents who have custody of their children are often not amenable to intervention. Some parents may deny their difficulties, may fail to cooperate, or may flee to avoid involvement, even when legal action is threatened involvement (Grunbaum & Gammeltoft, 1993).

In a typical example, a cohort of individuals who are initially at risk (e.g., because all are children of persons with schizophrenia) is followed prospectively until the period of risk for the disorder has passed (age 50 or so). By that time those who will develop schizophrenia have done so; any factors differentiating them from those who do not develop schizophrenia provide a basis for improving estimates of risk. These additional factors, above and beyond being the child of someone with schizophrenia, may suggest additional preventive interventions. If stress during adolescence compounds the risk of being the child of a person with schizophrenia, we can try to reduce the stress for those at risk or increase their ability to cope.

This "high-risk" design has its own difficulties. The cohort at risk does not necessarily split into two "clean" groups (cases versus normals) by the end of the risk period. Instead, it can fragment into several sub-groups (e.g., borderline cases, those with other kinds of disorders). Another complication is that the time interval of interest is very long. Primary prevention of schizophrenia means a reduction in the incidence of the disorder over the entire duration of the period of risk, until every member of the cohort is at least forty-five or fifty years of age. The expanded time perspective complicates our problem. The significance of risk and intervention may change with maturation and development across the life span. The vulnerability model suggests there may be no person- or situation-oriented *early* intervention that has the power to overcome all possible future stressors or losses of support. There are also practical problems in evaluating preventive interventions when their effects must span a lengthy period of time (Heller, Price, & Sher, 1980).

Strategies aimed at high-risk individuals may nonetheless be very effective if the risk factors predict a high incidence of disorder among the identified population. They may be still more effective if research pinpoints specific points of vulnerability later in life that may yield to additional timely intervention. But we cannot depend on a one-time, forever-effective intervention in psychology. Most problems have complex etiologies and are affected by many variables that change with time.

Prevention research and intervention is becoming more sophisticated. Interest in hypothesized "protective" factors arose following the observation that some children at-risk show resilience and develop normally. Protective factors are not just normal advantages like high socioeconomic status but include specific resources and characteristics that modify the individual's responses to conditions of risk (Mrazek & Haggerty, 1994). Because a given factor (e.g., ability to delay gratification) can affect the likelihood of developing more than one disorder, and because many disorders have low base rates, prevention now focuses on reducing the incidence of disorders by intervening to moderate risk factors and/or strengthen protective factors (Coie et al., 1993).

Risk and protective factors present a challenge. There may be many factors, not all equally important. Some may be incidental correlates of disorder, while others may be causal in nature. Furthermore, most problems are associated with more than one risk factor, most risk factors are associated with more than one problem, and individuals can be exposed to risk factors in more than one way (Coie et al., 1993). Most important are risk factors that play a direct causal role in the disorder.

We should try to specify precisely the vulnerable group, the targeted risk and protective factors, and the expected outcomes. These requirements are easier to meet when we work with a well-validated theory of how the given intervention should change the targeted factors to produce the desired outcomes. In the absence of a solid theory, however, the risk and protective factors may be vague and nonspecific.

The increased risk for schizophrenia because one is the child of a schizophrenic parent could be due to genetic factors, environmental factors, or the interaction of both. Children of schizophrenic parents are at risk for other disorders besides schizophrenia. Growing up with a schizophrenic mother can be psychologically difficult, if not actually damaging to personality development (Dunn, 1993). The coefficient of prediction (efficiency of prediction) for any single risk factor is small. Eighty-nine percent of people who develop schizophrenia do not have a parent with schizophrenia, and 63 percent have no family history of schizophrenia at all (Gottesman, 1991). Moreover, Coie et al. (1993) cite evidence that 74 percent of the children of people with schizophrenia are entirely normal.

Developmental theory is a starting point for a theoretical analysis of risk and protective factors. The importance of a given risk factor for a given disorder is different at different ages and with cumulative risk exposure (Coie et al., 1993). Peer influences, for example, may be especially powerful in early adolescence and less significant at other times. One can pinpoint individuals about to enter a developmental period of heightened risk.

We can also consider alternative intervention goals. In many disorders (e.g., juvenile delinquency, alcohol abuse) later-onset cases tend to be less severe. An alternative to outright elimination of the disorder is intervention to delay its onset in a highly vulnerable group. Helping young people hospitalized with schizophrenia to continue their college educations helps them stay on target developmentally (Hoffman & Mastrianni, 1992). Also, postponing age at first intercourse is a central goal of sex education programs (e.g., Howard & McCabe, 1990) designed to reduce the incidence of unwanted pregnancies and of sexually transmitted diseases.

Multifactorial etiologies. The health problems for which effective treatment and prevention efforts have lagged (e.g., heart disease, cancer, the common cold, and mental illnesses) all can be characterized as having multiple rather than single causes. They all include behavioral factors (e.g., habits, lifestyles, coping responses) among the contributing causes (Bloom, 1979). Multifactorial etiology may account for the observation that any single factor is usually not sufficient to produce a case of disorder. In some cases the symptomatic manifestation of a disorder can occur long after the individual risk factors are present and active. For example, many people exposed to HIV progress rapidly to AIDS, whereas others remain infected for years without showing symptoms, and some do not become infected at all.

The complexity of the interaction of multiple causes may explain why progress in treating and preventing these disorders is so slow. Few interventions deal directly with more than one risk factor. Few investigators can follow their subjects for the number of years required to demonstrate conclusively that prevention was achieved. Multifactorial etiologies may complicate our conceptual understanding of cause and effect. However, some part of the risk and the incidence of the disorder can be reduced by intervening in relation to one contributing etiological factor. In theory, reducing one risk to zero may also influence all the other risk factors with which the eliminated risk would have had to interact to produce the adverse effect. We might reduce the incidence of serious child abuse by providing supportive respite care for overstressed parents. That won't reduce all child abuse, but it may have an effect on those episodes related to parental overstress.

Precipitating vs. predisposing factors. The vulnerability concept (see Chapter 7) distinguishes between *predisposing* and *precipitating* factors. *Predisposing* factors may be genetic in nature or may reflect the individual's history and experiences. A predisposing factor for committing child abuse, for example, may be the person's experience of having been abused as a child (Rosenberg & Reppucci, 1985). *Precipitating* factors occur close to the point when an episode of disorder begins. Exposure to severe combat may be a precipitating factor in the development of a stress-trauma syndrome, for example; being isolated with a crying child for a long period of time may precipitate an episode of child abuse (Rosenberg & Reppucci, 1985). Stressful life events (see Chapter 7) can be conceptualized as precipitating factors.

On the assumption that predisposing factors are discernible in children's lives and are more important than anything that happens later in life for the development of disorder, primary prevention efforts have been directed more at children than at any other age group (Spaulding & Balch, 1983). Our emphasis on predisposing factors has not met with much success, whether in treatment or with respect to prevention (Bloom, 1979). It might prove more fruitful to focus instead on proximal, precipitating factors such as stressful life events.

The natural history of many psychological disorders is not well understood. Over time, there are discontinuities in behavior. Herrenkohl, Herrenkohl, and Egolf (1994) followed children whom they had identified as "resilient" in elementary school. These were children who came from abusive backgrounds but who were doing well in elementary school. In adolescence, about a third of those previously high-functioning students had dropped out of high school. Those who had a poorer outcome had less support, and had been subject to more abuse after elementary school. However, some managed to survive, if not thrive, under similar circumstances; somehow they developed the ability to hope for a different future for themselves and to work toward it.

Ecological conceptions of behavior (Chapters 4–6) and the vulnerability model (see Chapter 7) teach us that an individual's vulnerability varies with circumstances throughout life. Primary prevention should be effective at later life stages—adolescence, middle age, or even old age—as well as during early childhood. Excessive emphasis on interventions in infancy and early childhood, in the absence of compelling evidence on their long-term benefits, may needlessly hamper the practice of prevention at other milestones.

A focus on precipitating factors (see Chapter 3) directs us to think about reducing the occurrence of stressful life events (e.g., lowering unemployment) or creating resources that are well positioned in time and place to reduce vulnerability (e.g. the Michigan Jobs Project). The stressful-life-events model directs our attention to here-and-now events that are predictable and can be modified to prevent difficulties. We may also be able to prepare individuals to cope with such events.

Research on preventive interventions. Prevention research may be different from other psychological research. The Institute of Medicine (IOM) report (Mrazek & Haggerty, 1994) presents a framework called the "preventive intervention research cycle." The initial steps in this cycle include defining the disorder or problem to be prevented, gathering information concerning specific risk and protective factors associated with that disorder, and studying the existing literature regarding effective interventions for that problem. Only after understanding this context for the problem is it appropriate to design and conduct intervention studies. Initially these should take the form of pilot studies to refine the program, determine the magnitudes of its likely effects, and test the research instruments and procedures. Promising results at this stage justify large-scale field trials and, if the program's effectiveness is confirmed, its later dissemination to other sites. Throughout this process, the investigator should be working collaboratively with other stakeholders, including policymakers, community leaders, and representatives of the population targeted to receive the intervention.

The IOM model for prevention research is useful for its attention to basic and epidemiological research as well as to the literature on interventions. The model also requires that policymakers have a tolerance for experimentation and redesign. If an intervention doesn't produce its intended effects on the first effort, prevention researchers should have the leeway to make false starts and to learn from them. The first drug that was successful in treating syphillis was called 606 because its discoverer had tried 605 previous compounds unsuccessfully. Few prevention research programs have had the same opportunity to redesign interventions based on the results of experimental trials.

Prevention research also needs to be theoretically based. Psychological and behavioral problems are complex. The bare finding that an intervention group does better (or worse) than a control group may provide little insight into why this happened. Research should include process measures that document that the intervention worked as planned and that can be used to disseminate it to other sites. (There is a dispute about whether intervention programs can or should be faithfully duplicated in each new setting or whether the intervention needs to be adapted for each new situation, such as rural versus urban). Having a solid theory behind the intervention presumably makes it easier to implement the essential aspect of a successful intervention in a new situation (Bauman, Stein, & Ireys, 1991).

The point(s) at which short-term and long-term outcomes are assessed is also determined by their theoretical relevance. Recall that Schulz and Hanusa (1978) found that the results three years after terminating their intervention with institutionalized elderly were the exact opposite of the results obtained when the study first ended. A program to prevent delinquency in adolescents by intervening with primary-school children, for example, might initially look at whether those who received the intervention showed improved peer relationships and school performance. Some years later, it would be important to determine the incidence rates of delinquency in the intervention and nonintervention groups. A single postintervention measurement is not sufficient in prevention research.

Promoting positive mental health. Methods for improving the health of people in general (e.g., improving nutrition and exercise) are directed toward producing a higher prevalence of generally healthy people. An analogous strategy in mental health is to increase the prevalence of positive mental health rather than to reduce the prevalence of psychopathology (Albee, 1986). The aim of such interventions is to increase the overall level of well-being and thus reduce the potential for undesirable outcomes. Improvements in prenatal care, dissemination of information regarding effective child rearing, neighborhood-based family life development centers, and the creation of mutual support systems are all methods we have mentioned.

Efforts to promote positive mental health rest on a weaker scientific foundation than do efforts to prevent specific diseases. It is difficult to identify and measure outcomes of mental health promotion efforts and to estimate their specific costs and benefits. The superior clarity and substance of the existing literature on interventions to prevent specific physical disorders is only a matter of degree, however. Since individual factors make a person at risk for multiple disorders, there is still some reason to pursue overall increases in positive mental health at the same time that we work to reduce the incidence of specific disorders.

What person-centered protective factors may be stable across situations and over time and may have some role in promoting positive mental health? Recall the discussion in Chapter 5 concerning "cognitive and behavioral construction competencies" of the sort identified by Mischel (1973). In the following section we examine the theory and research on "teachable" protective factors in primary prevention in mental health.

Competence Building

By the early 1970s several streams of thought had come together to form a primary prevention strategy known as "competence building" (Cowen, 1973; Task Panel on Prevention, 1978). Its roots can be found in psychoanalytic, cognitive, behavioral, humanistic, developmental, and evolutionary perspectives on behavior (Masterpasqua, 1989). Ultimately, the zeitgeist of the 1960s supported competence building. As an intervention, it was based squarely on the then popular assumption of the "plasticity" of intellectual and psychological structures (Hunt, 1968). Competence building is best exemplified by the Head Start program (reviewed later in this chapter).

The competence-building paradigm starts with a theoretically or empirically based assumption that high-risk individuals within a given population differ from low-risk individuals in the same population in their lack of some basic psychosocial skill or skills and that individuals who lack these competencies can acquire them under the right conditions. These skills are then taught directly to the groups at risk. In theory, their acquisition eliminates the fundamental discrepancy between the high-risk and the low-risk members of the population, thus reducing or eliminating the added risk.

Spivack and Shure (1974, 1989) pioneered in developing competence-building programs as a preventive intervention. Their initial research showed that about half the inner-city children in day care and kindergarten displayed behavioral problems, including impatience, overemotionality, aggression, or excessive shyness and fear. Studies of hundreds of four- and five-year-old children revealed that those with behavior problems were often distinguishable from those without by their lack of certain "interpersonal cognitive problem-solving" (ICPS) skills, including:

1. *Alternative thinking:* the ability to conceptualize alternative solutions to problems involving peers or adults
2. *Consequential thinking:* the ability to foresee accurately the consequences of one's own actions
3. *Causal thinking:* an appreciation of the role of antecedent events as causes of other events
4. *Sensitivity:* an awareness of the interpersonal nature of their problems
5. *Means/ends thinking:* the ability to plan a course of action in pursuit of a goal, one that can involve several different steps.

The Spivack and Shure prevention program consists of some forty or more "game" activities, each taking about twenty minutes, designed to be used by preschool teachers in regular preschool classrooms or by parents at home to teach preschoolers the following kinds of skills: (1) *understanding word concepts*, such as "not" or "same-different," which prepare children to understand the meaning of "*not* a good idea, try something *different*"; (2) *developing interpersonal skills*, such as listening, watching, and understanding the other person's feelings; and (3) *generating alternative solutions* to a problem situation, including conceptualizing the potential consequences of actions and analyzing the relationship between cause and effect.

Spivack and Shure try to teach the child *how* to think, not *what* to think, and instruct parents and teachers to avoid making evaluative judgments about a child's responses during the games. They claim that the *process* of thinking is what is important, not its content. The games teach the process of thinking by posing interpersonal problems, not by using the puzzles studied in the laboratory. Spivack and Shure believe that once children learn to predict the likely consequences of their actions for themselves, short-sighted, ineffective responses will naturally drop out. Another skill taught to both teachers and mothers is "dialoging," or solving a problem interpersonally when it occurs in real relationships. When an interpersonal problem arises, the adult is taught to ask what the child's thinking is about the nature of the problem, what his or her feelings about it are, what he or she can do about it, what might happen if that particular response is tried, and whether any alternative responses might be more effective.

The results of this brief, focused training program were quite positive. Nearly all children gained in measured ICPS skills; those rated initially as more maladjusted gained more than those who were better adjusted initially. Improvement in ICPS skills was related to behavioral improvement. The most important ICPS skills seemed to be alternative and consequential thinking. At a two-year follow-up assessment, training effects had been maintained; children who had received the program were rated as better adjusted than control children during the next two years of elementary school. In some of the studies, the later teachers who rated the children's adjustment were "blind" to the training the children received. The program's positive effects were not related to the children's IQs or socioeconomic status, and mothers and teachers were about equally effective as trainers.

This program is useful not only as an illustration of the competence-building paradigm but also as a demonstration of how successful mental health interventions can be carried out in ordinary community settings by natural caregivers. The program has been widely disseminated; teachers and parents have been consistently positive about their experience with the ICPS intervention. Spivack and Shure and their colleagues continue to study ICPS skills and the response-specific preventive impact of ICPS training on violence, substance use, teen pregnancy, and suicide.

Concerned that the ICPS paradigm was being misused in some settings, Spivack and Shure (1989) cautioned that ICPS training was not a treatment intervention for children or adults already exhibiting disorder and that brief excerpts from the program cannot be substituted for the full package if the same effectiveness is desired. Furthermore, research by other investigators indicates that the relationship between learning specific ICPS skills and later reductions in the incidence of psychopathology may not be as simple as we had hoped (Durlak, 1983). The positive impact of ICPS training is clearer for preschool children than for children older than five, and the specific links between skills and outcomes may vary among children of different ages and different sociodemographic groups (Gesten et al., 1982).

Spivack and Shure (1989) caution that regular practice of the various ICPS skills through "dialoging" in problem situations as they arise is necessary to maintain the skills and preserve their link to adjustment. Additional training, or booster sessions, are also very helpful, not only because learned responses may fade over time but also because new situations and challenges continually arise.

Recent competence-building interventions. Spivack and Shure's ideas have been adapted for older school children. Schools are a key setting for prevention efforts because they maintain sustained, intensive contact with nearly all children throughout childhood and adolescence. School provides important cognitive, social, and interpersonal challenges, and the cognitive and social aspects of competence-building interventions make them very compatible with educational settings.

The most widely known school-based competence-building interventions have focused on normative transitions. One program (Improving Social Awareness–Social Problem Solving/ISA–SPS) for elementary school children is designed to facilitate their adjustment to middle school. The program teaches social decision making and problem solving in three phases: (1) readiness, which focuses on self-control, group participation, and social awareness; (2) instruction, which involves intensive work on means-ends thinking and other ICPS-inspired skills; and (3) application, which emphasizes guided use of the skills in new situations to promote maintenance and generalization (Elias et al., 1986).

Compared with control children, middle-school children who had received the intervention showed greater sensitivity to others' feelings, greater ability to analyze and understand interpersonal behaviors and situations, and more positive self-concepts. Intervention children were also rated as better adjusted by their teachers and were sought out for help more often by their peers than were control children. Children who lacked SPS skills were more likely to report intense stressors, suggesting that SPS skills mediated or were responsible for the positive effects of the intervention on overall adjustment (Elias et al., 1986). Follow-ups five and six years after the intervention found modest differences in academic achievement and psychological adjustment (especially the levels of depression, delinquency, and self-efficacy) that favored the intervention group (Elias et al., 1991).

Another important milestone is the transition to high school. During mid-adolescence, with its increased stress and vulnerability, some students loosen their ties to school (Kazdin, 1993). At the same time, however, many young people acquire key coping skills that help them adjust to the ever increasing demands of school and young adult life. Reducing the number of students who drop out of school would lower the risk of substance abuse, unwanted childbirths, and conduct problems. Dropping out of school is usually not sudden or unpredictable; changes in peer relationships and increasing alienation from school precede dropping out (Srebnik & Elias, 1993). Warning signs of impending dropout include declines in academic performance and increases in absenteeism and substance use. The most useful approach to preventing this would be to intervene during middle school, while most adolescents still have some attachment to school.

Competence can increase in ways other than through cognitive intervention with individuals. Aspects of the social and physical environment can be modified to promote growth-enhancing experiences and to avoid some potentially destructive life events. The STEP (School Transitional Environment Program) intervention is a one-year program designed to ease the transition from middle school to high school (Felner & Adan, 1988). Both personal and environmental characteristics can constitute risk factors for dropping out and other adverse outcomes whose probability of occurring is increased when risk factors are present. Personal factors include a history of frequent changes in schools, socioeconomic disadvantage, low family support for schooling, and membership in an ethnic minority. Environmental risk factors include a complex school environment with high student turnover, haphazard scheduling, and inattentiveness to student needs, as shown by the amount of time teachers take to get to know students individually.

The goals of STEP were to increase (1) the social support available to students undergoing such transitions, (2) students' access to information and their ability to use it effectively, (3) students' sense of accountability while reducing their sense of anonymity, and (4) teachers' familiarity with students. STEP works to increase these coping and support resources in two ways: by reducing the complexity of a school's environment by simplifying new students' schedules (e.g., by having a group of new students take most or all classes together in rooms located near one another), and by redefining the role of homeroom teachers to facilitate more active involvement with students (e.g., by having homeroom teachers provide students with some of the counseling and guidance support normally provided only by school guidance staff and contact students' families to develop a relationship when school begins and, later, whenever absences occur).

In contrast to ISA-SPS and other school-based programs, STEP does not use a new curriculum or other modification of instruction. It entails a strategic change in how settings are organized. STEP reduces the scale of the learning environment and simplifies the new student's task of forming a support network. In behavior-setting terms, the multiple settings that challenge a new student are organized in such a way that they have many elements in common, making it possible to learn the various setting programs more quickly and easily. Homeroom is a multipurpose setting whose program includes built-in mechanisms for developing teacher-student relationships. In terms of Moos's social climate perspective, STEP is clearly directed at helping schools meet students' "relationship-oriented" needs (e.g., for social support) as well as those involving "personal development" for which schools are more traditionally responsible. By controlling the location of STEP classrooms within the building and the movement of students through the building, the program also minimizes contact with older children who might exploit the younger ones.

After one year, students in a predominantly minority school who had been randomly assigned to STEP had higher grades, better attendance, and more stable self-concepts than did control students (Felner, Ginter, & Primavera, 1982). Several years later those who had been STEP students had only half the dropout rate of control students. Teachers also expressed satisfaction with the STEP program. The program was implemented at relatively little cost, since it entailed a reorganization of existing resources rather than the allocation of new resources. Its positive effects were replicated in another setting: student well-being and teacher-rated adjustment were improved among students making the transition from elementary to junior high school (Felner et al., 1993).

Conclusions regarding competence building. We share the widespread enthusiasm for competence building as an approach to primary prevention. However, there are cautions. Although many high-quality programs devoted to building cognitive and behavioral competencies in young people have shown promising results, one-shot interventions are probably not sufficient to produce permanent reductions in risk for most who receive them. Programs that provide opportunities to rehearse and apply these skills in ecologically relevant situations are likely to have more lasting effects. Because risks are ongoing, competence-building programs for children and adolescents should be included in comprehensive health education efforts for children from preschool through high school or beyond (Weissberg & Elias, 1993).

Furthermore, successful dissemination of innovative programs cannot be taken for granted. School systems have their own agendas, and resistance to change on an organizational and system basis can be expected. An ambitious new program will have to fit into the existing curriculum and values of a target school and will also require additional training and ongoing supervision of teachers and other participants (Elias & Weissberg, 1990).

Thorough use of this paradigm depends on a clear definition of "competence." To what extent is competence a global, all-purpose "skill" or a type of cognitive and behavioral construction competency (see Chapter 5; Mischel,1973)? To what extent might it be better conceptualized as a situation-specific skill? In practice it has been taken both ways. The Spivack and Shure (1974) method and Finkel's (1975) concept of the "trauma-stren conversion" (see Chapter 7) represent attempts to induce or study widely generalizable and durable cognitive changes.

Much of the preventive work with stressful life events (e.g., Bloom,

Hodges, & Caldwell, 1982) takes a more situation-specific approach. This perspective is also illustrated in a study by Sarason and Sarason (1981), who found that training inner-city ninth-graders in specific skills related to finding employment led not only to more and better problem-solving solutions in a test situation, but also to better performance in actual job-seeking interviews. These results suggest that it may be more useful to teach specific competencies to deal with particular events rather than to concentrate on general skills. The demonstration that many findings using ICPS type of interventions are difficult to replicate suggests that we need to examine the issue of specificity more carefully (Durlak, 1983).

To the extent that competence turns out to involve a specific set of skills whose value varies from one risk-group/outcome context to another, however, more work is clearly necessary to identify the specific skills in all of the relevant contexts. The generalizability of any one set may not be broad. From the ecological vantage point, the problem is one of adaptation (see also Trickett et al., 1985). Adaptation is not just an individual feat but an ongoing process of person-environment fit. Do the relevant ICPS skills differ or even conflict with each other in key settings such as school, home, workplace, or street? Conditions of adaptation change over time as well, and the relationship between an individual's ICPS performance in childhood and his or her psychological adjustment as an adult has yet to be established.

Both global and situation-specific skills may develop out of competence building. Global competencies may reduce the risk related to predisposing causes (e.g., poverty, constitutional vulnerability), while task-specific skills may reduce the risks associated with precipitating causes (e.g., unemployment and other stressful life events). The competencies can in fact be learned. However, will the new skills be used after inevitable changes in time and situation? Will cognitive skills taught in a relatively low state of emotional arousal be available and effective in a state of high emotional arousal? More information is needed regarding the nature of behavior-environment continuities across time and place. One day we may wish to teach the ability to assess environments behaviorally and either modify them according to one's needs or select those that naturally provide the best fit (Levine & Perkins, 1980b). The work we described using Barker's behavior-setting concepts to evaluate person-environment fits for mental health consumers is a case in point.

As practiced, the approach of individual competence building intentionally or unintentionally engages in what some critics (e.g., Albee, 1986, 1995; Ryan, 1971) have called "blaming the victim"; the "problem" is ultimately seen to reside in the existence of specific individual differences between high-risk and low-risk individuals. The inevitable implication is that the only way to rectify the problem is to *change* the high-risk individuals to make them "normal," or acceptable. This leads ultimately to *blaming* the high-risk individual for the predicament (Caplan & Nelson, 1973). Iscoe (1974) and Rappaport (1981) point out that competence building at the community level escapes this moral and political dilemma to a significant degree.

To summarize, the competence-building approach to primary prevention arose out of interest in whether acquiring and using certain cognitive behavioral skills improved psychological adaptation. The empirical literature on competence building, while encouraging overall, has nevertheless left us with a complicated picture. From an ecological vantage point, it is important to remember that behavioral skills are not solely the property of individual people but rather attach to settings and their "programs" (see Chapter 5). These vary over time and place. Still needed are conceptual advances that relate persons and situations in behavioral terms and therefore make it possible to develop competent settings and communities as well as competent individuals. In the next section we present a general environmental strategy relevant to prevention.

Prevention through Stepwise Risk Reduction

A different approach to prevention is based on a metaphor of "accident prevention." An "accident" does not imply something random or unpredictable; accident prevention also does not depend on a disease concept. Rather, this approach applies to undesirable end-states, including mental or physical problems or lifestyle predicaments, for which there are specific known risks. Often these risks are of different kinds. Some may involve personal characteristics and others environmental conditions, and these may occur independent of each other. Vulnerability is partly a function of exposure to risks. The goal in the accident-prevention approach is to reduce the incidence of maladaptive episodes by reducing individual vulnerability or the degree of risk added by "traumatic accidents."

Risks may occur sequentially, an idea expressed in the distinction between proximal (near in time), or precipitating, and distal (removed in time), or predisposing. The sequential relationship can be depicted by a Markov chain. Any given outcome is the end result of a particular sequence of steps. Each step has a dichotomous alternative—"yes" or "no" answers to a specific question. One may prevent accidents, or the injury associated with accidents, in any number of ways. Using the accident-prevention model, we examine the sequence of events that precede the undesirable end-state. We may identify promising points of intervention anywhere along the chain. In this view, if an event earlier in the chain is prevented from occurring, then an event later in the chain is less likely to occur.

Consider unwed teenage pregnancy. Children born to teenagers are more likely to have physical and behavioral problems, and their mothers also face maladaptive outcomes. They are more likely to drop out of school, to become welfare dependent, and to suffer from depression. Pregnancy is not a disease; thinking of this complex social and psychological problem in biological terms leaves only a few limited options available for preventing its occurrence—abstinence, contraception, and abortion. Taking the longitudinal view depicted in the Markov chain allows us to consider other possibilities as well.

The sequence of steps that can produce maladaptive behavior as a result of unwanted pregnancy is depicted in Table 8–3 using a Markov chain. Depending on the answer to each of a series of questions, the risk of poor adaptation is either high or low. Aside from the biological statuses of pregnancy and abortion, there are alternative behavioral responses concerning amount of sexual activity, use of contraception, and compensating responses made after the child is born (such as placing the child for adoption or making some other arrangement that prevents the mother from dropping out of school and other high-risk conditions). The important point is that choosing *any* one of the alternatives leading to the low-risk condition is sufficient to break the chain leading to poor adaptation. Prevention is the result of interventions that increase the number of teenagers who change their trajectory in the more adaptive direction at any point in the sequence. For example, Furstenberg et al. (1985) show that fifteen- and sixteen-year-olds exposed to sex education delay their initiation of sexual activity. Byrne, Kelley, and Fisher (1993) discuss programs specifically designed to increase motivation for contraception and decrease situational factors that inhibit contraception.

To summarize, teenage pregnancy is complicated and difficult to control. It is not just one condition but the culmination of social and behavioral events, as well as biological ones. The stepwise risk-reduction approach uses the idea of multifactorial etiologies and proximal versus distal steps in the causal chain to increase the number of different opportunities for prevention. Some of these opportunities occur much earlier in

Table 8–3
Markov Chain for Problems Associated with Teenage Pregnancy

High-Risk Condition	*Low-Risk Condition*
Chaste?	
↓ No	$\overrightarrow{\text{Yes}}$
Contraception?	
↓ No	$\overrightarrow{\text{Yes}}$
Pregnant?	
↓ Yes	$\overrightarrow{\text{No}}$
Abortion?	
↓ No	$\overrightarrow{\text{Yes}}$
Compensating abilities?	
↓ No	$\overrightarrow{\text{Yes}}$
Poor adaptation	
School dropout	
Child abuse	

time than the target condition itself. When delivered on a community-wide or milestone basis, for example, through sex education or through creating a social climate supporting abstinence, they have a potentially wide impact. Furthermore, in this view nearly everyone is subject to at least a slight degree of risk for most kinds of problems, because risk is a function of events and circumstances as well as of people. Universal prevention programs that assume everyone is at risk may be politically and socially acceptable and less stigmatizing than programs that focus on people singled out as already being at high risk.

Box 8–2: Influencing Auto Safety Legislation

The broadest preventive impact occurs when large segments of the population perform behaviors consistent with maintaining a low-risk status. Education is one approach used to induce large numbers of people to modify their behavior in a low-risk direction, although it is not always successful by itself. Use of seat belts and child safety restraints in automobiles is widely credited with preventing deaths and injuries, for example, yet under completely voluntary conditions many people do not consistently use seat belts or child restraints. On the other hand, evidence suggests that most adults will adopt such behaviors once they are legally prescribed, especially if the laws are actively enforced by police.

A study by Jason and Rose (1984) provides an interesting example of the interplay in the legal system of activism, prevention, and social science research. Jason and Rose noted that many of the sixty thousand injuries and one thousand deaths in children under age 5 that occur annually because of car accidents could be prevented if parents used appropriate car safety seats. Working in cooperation with an advocacy group, they undertook a research project to provide data to help influence the passage of legislation in Illinois that would mandate the use of safety seats for children under age 4. The researchers selected two intersections to observe whether children in cars were in safety seats. Over a nineteen-month period they observed that, on average, fewer than 50 percent of infants under one year of age were in appropriate restraints. Approximately 10 percent of children between ages 1 and 4 were in proper safety seats. A telephone survey of randomly sampled citizens in the area found that about half the respondents regularly transported children in automobiles. Nearly 80 percent of those surveyed agreed that using safety restraints was important, and 78 percent indicated that they would support state legislation mandating the use of proper car safety restraints for children.

The Illinois legislature had failed to pass a law mandating seat belts during the previous legislative session. Knowledgeable observers predicted that the Illinois House would pass the legislation in the next session, which in fact did happen. In the researchers' judgment, however, the vote in the state Senate was much more doubtful, and the investigators had the opportunity to test whether legislators would be influenced by scientific data. Nine days before the critical vote in the state Senate, the investigators sent a personal letter to half of the state senators, selected at random. The letters described the data on seat restraint usage and the results of the citizen survey. The letter included Illinois statistics on deaths and injuries over a five-year period and estimates of the lifetime dollar costs of rehabilitating a child who had sustained a serious injury. Written on university stationery and identifying the authors as faculty members, the letter asked the senators to consider the data when deciding how to vote on the pending bill. Of twenty-nine senators who received the letter, twenty-three or 79 percent voted yes. Of the thirty who were not sent the letter, sixteen or 53 percent voted yes. The difference was statistically significant.

Special conditions were undoubtedly involved in this case. The legislation would probably have passed anyway (but perhaps by a smaller margin), judging from the number of positive votes in the unsolicited half of the Senate. Perhaps the information contained in a single letter was influential because there was little active controversy about the legislation. It would probably have been more difficult to demonstrate the effect of the letters if there had been opposition to the proposed legislation or an effort to present data disputing the findings of the one study.

Some research supports the preventive benefits of safety seat legislation, however. Guerin and MacKinnon (1985) did a sophisticated time-series analysis of accidents in California that resulted in injury to children under age 3 and between ages 4 and 7. California's statute required that children under age 3 use safety seats, but there was no such requirement for children between ages 4 and 7. The data clearly showed a statistically significant *reduction* of 8.4 percent in injuries to children under age 3 and a nonsignificant *increase* in injuries in the older group in the twelve months following passage of the legislation. In Texas, which had no legislation requiring safety seats, there was a nonsignificant increase in injuries in children of the same ages as those in California over the same time.

Persuasive as this particular result may be, we can't be completely sure that passage of the law and subsequent increases in the use of child safety seats were the critical factors responsible for the reduction in injuries. More recent research by Seekins et al. (1988) examined pre/postlegislation changes in motorists' use of car safety seats for children as laws mandating their use went into effect in different states. Following passage of such legislation there were increases in the use of safety seats for children in three states and decreases in two other states. Thus, legislation by itself is not always completely effective in changing behavior.

A Markov chain analysis suggests several additional steps where useful intervention can occur. One factor associated with higher compliance with the new law was a higher rate of citations for noncompliance issued by the police. Another step in the chain would entail intervention to change police behavior regarding citations. Lavelle et al. (1992) report that an educational intervention for police concerning the importance of enforcing the use of child safety seats produced a forty-four-fold increase in the number of police citations issued for noncompliance.

Enhancing the effectiveness of car seat laws can be accomplished by selective as well as universal prevention approaches, such as targeting the parents of newborns before there is an opportunity not to obey the law. Alvarez and Jason (1993) took such an approach in targeting the newborn child's first ride home from the hospital in a sample of low-income Hispanic parents. An instructional intervention building upon the Illinois law and based on education, modeling, and loan of a car safety seat increased the percentage of newborns who took their first ride in a safety seat.

A Markov chain approach alerts us to the fact that there are several steps that affect final outcomes in addition to simply passing a state law mandating a desired change in behavior. It encourages us to think about the intermediate processes involved in changing behavior instead of focusing just on outcomes, and it suggests that different programs working simultaneously at independent points in the causal sequence can have cumulative effects greater than those produced by a massive effort at only one point in the chain.

Parenthetically, we may note that this brief example of the relationship between law and social science research indicates a mode of cooperation that will continue to develop. Legislatures often review pertinent facts in developing policy and when writing legislation to implement policy. Social scientists can provide some of the legislative facts not only by sending letters to legislators but also by testifying before committees and by publicizing research in other forums in order to influence public opinion. Social science research can influence legal process in the interests of prevention or the amelioration of harm. (The relationship between science and politics is discussed further in Chapter 13.) The research in our example shows that intervention at a distal point—the state legislature—had effects at a proximal point—in the car involved in an accident—that prevented physical injuries.

Preventing Partner Violence

Interpersonal violence offers another example of the usefulness of a Markov chain analysis of prevention alternatives.[2] The lifetime incidence of partner violence against women is estimated at 25 to 33 percent, with an annual prevalence of at least 2 to 3 million (Koss et al., 1994). Over half of murdered women in the United States are victims of partner homicide. The consequences of partner violence can include physical injuries requiring medical treatment, posttraumatic stress disorder, depression, substance abuse, and suicide. Children who witness partner violence are themselves more likely to be perpetrators or victims of violence as adults (Tomkins et al., 1992).

Violence is self-perpetuating. It is unlikely to stop in the absence of intervention. In the psychological tradition, the first research workers studied victimized women who sought help. These studies emphasized victim characteristics and psychiatric symptomatology (A. Browne, 1993). Prevention efforts based on that set of risk factors would target victims to change their behavior. Perpetrator characteristics, however, are better predictors of violence than victim characteristics (Hotaling & Sugarman, 1986); therefore, another target group could be those most likely to perpetrate partner violence. However, Koss et al. (1994) argue that a focus on individual psychology alone will not effect large, permanent reductions in male violence against women. The Markov chain concept lets us think about alternatives to a person-centered approach and tells us instead to attend to proximal risks and to examine personal, situational, and community factors.

The risk of partner violence is higher when there is ongoing physical aggression in the home (e.g., corporal punishment of children), the woman is socially isolated and economically disadvantaged, a handgun is readily available, and/or alcohol is used to excess. These are all factors in the situation, and we could intervene preventively by teaching parenting skills and limited use of alcohol. Couples-oriented intervention may be helpful early in a relationship if partners are unable to handle conflict constructively (Holtzworth-Munroe, Markman, O'Leary, et al., 1995). Couples who participated in a premarital communication and conflict-management program later reported significantly fewer instances of physical violence than did couples randomly assigned to a no-intervention control group (Markman et al., 1993).

Partner violence is more likely to occur if the woman lacks knowledge of the available community resources (e.g., shelters), lacks skills sufficient to formulate a plan for responding to a threat of violence, and/or is pregnant. Information about community resources and other alternatives presented to women as part of routine prenatal classes could have a preventive effect to the degree that information and knowledge improve personal competence. Risk is higher when shelter and other services are not readily available in a community, so helping to create resources in a community can have a preventive effect. The police are another potential community and situational resource; many advocates believe that the risk of partner violence is higher when law enforcement policies do not actively inhibit such behavior.

As a link in the chain, effective antiviolence policies enforced communitywide by the police could have a comprehensive preventive impact. In a widely discussed study known as the Minneapolis Domestic Violence Experiment (MDVE), Sherman and Berk (1984) had police resolve misdemeanor domestic violence (i.e., assault that was not aggravated or life-threatening) with one of three randomly selected interventions: immediate arrest, on-the-spot advice and mediation, or an order that the perpetrator leave the premises for at least eight hours. Offenders who were arrested were the least likely of the three groups to commit another partner assault over the next six months (based on police records and victim interviews). The MDVE was followed by a substantial increase in arrests and the enactment of laws in many states mandating the arrest of misdemeanor offenders as a way of preventing future domestic violence.

Later studies in other communities did not all replicate the basic MDVE finding that mandatory arrest deters repeat violence, and the data also showed that with follow-ups done later than six months after the reported incident the proportion of repeat violence could be *higher* among arrested than among nonarrested abusers. Perpetrators who are most likely to reduce their subsequent violence after arrest are those who have a stake in conforming to the system, i.e., those who are employed and married and those who live in cities with higher proportions of white and Hispanic residents (Sherman, 1992). One complication of an immediate arrest policy is that in about half of domestic violence reported to the police, the offender has fled by the time police arrive. Interestingly, a study in Omaha found that, among perpetrators who had fled, those selected at random to be served with arrest warrants were only about half as likely as those not served to injure their partners or be rearrested over the subsequent six months (Dunford, 1990). The finding may underscore the effectiveness of police intervention under some conditions.

Sherman (1992) is cautious about the evidence on interventions to prevent partner violence. The fact that many states changed their laws to mandate immediate arrest on the basis of one study (MDVE) illustrates that the results of community research are always interpreted within a social and political context (see Chapter 13). Sherman suggests that future research focus on high-risk couples who exhibit repeated episodes of violence. The intervention should include a range of alternatives to mandatory arrest, such as letting the victim or the police decide whether to have the perpetrator arrested or relocating the victim to a protective shelter. Providing a choice would answer some feminist critics who complain that mandatory arrest policies treat women as incapable of making decisions about prosecution.

Although preventing partner homicide is an important concern, this most serious consequence of domestic violence fortunately occurs rarely; that is, it has a low base rate. Recall our earlier discussions about the problem of a high false positive rate when predicting adult antisocial personality disorder or child maltreatment. Sherman (1992) presents data showing that, while the rate of partner homicide at residences that made one or more calls to the police was several times higher than the rate at residences making no domestic calls, the highest such rate over a five-year period was still only one-twentieth of one percent. This makes partner homicide even less common than suicide, and we have already discussed how the problem of false positives affects suicide prevention.[3]

Dramatic reductions in the incidence of partner violence may be difficult to achieve soon. The right to privacy inhibits many opportunities for research and intervention with high-risk couples. However, an accident prevention approach can still assist those working in a challenging area to identify additional causal steps in the chain, better understand the processes leading to different outcomes, and test the alternative interventions that result from this analysis.

Implications of an accident-prevention model. The paradigm of accident prevention directs our attention to different issues for research and intervention than does a disease model. Research using the accident model focuses on the conditions under which undesirable events occur, the factors that lead to those conditions, and the reaction to the undesirable event. An ecological analogy is highly appropriate in an accident prevention orientation.

An additional example may help in making the point. When parents with children divorce, a formal agreement is reached settling the custody of the children and the noncustodial parent's visitation rights. In most cases, the custody settlement is satisfactory, and problems that arise are resolved informally between the parties. In perhaps 10 percent of the cases, however, continuing conflict between the divorced spouses centers on their relationships with the children. The primary occasion for contact and for face-to-face conflict between divorced spouses occurs when one spouse arrives at the home of the other to pick up or deliver a child for a visit. The reasons for the conflict are complex and need not detain us here, but they often result in the parents returning to court to seek modification or enforcement of the visitation order.

Stott, Gaier, and Thomas (1984) describe a program of court-ordered, supervised, neutral-site visitation conceived and funded as part of a delinquency-prevention program. The sponsors reasoned that intervention in disrupted families would reduce the "negativity and trauma" associated with the visit and therefore reduce the child's potential for future acting out. Supervised visitation was ordered by the court in families with multiple problems and long histories of involvement with the courts, social services, and mental health agencies.

After an interview, a schedule was established for weekly one- to two-hour visits at a neutral site. Both parents signed a contract specifying the conditions of visitation. The custodial parent dropped the child off at the neutral site and left the child with a worker. Fifteen minutes later, the noncustodial parent arrived to pick up the child, thus avoiding the opportunity for face-to-face conflict with the former spouse. The worker participated actively in the visit if there was reason to suspect abuse or if a parent exhibited poor parenting skills. Records were kept on each visit, and the worker sent recommendations for future visitation based on these reports to the referring court.

No formal evaluation of this program has been conducted. According to Stott et al. (1984), however, the program had "the enthusiastic support of the family court judges, who are relieved of many hours of counterproductive courtroom time with noncompliant parents" (p. 216). The program provided safe visits for parents and children, when in the past there had been no visits or the visits had been stressful. It provided an opportunity for the noncustodial parent to continue a relationship with the child, and it offered both parties the opportunity to document allegations that the other was breaking agreements concerning visitation. Some parents worked out satisfactory arrangements with each other, if only because the court-imposed visitation was inconvenient.

The intervention was independent of any measurement or evaluation of the personalities or any analysis of the relationship between the parents that resulted in the continuing conflict. The intervention depended on an analysis of the situation in which conflict emerged. The circumstances were modified to prevent overt conflict. Just as a safety seat prevents injury to a child in an accident, so this intervention reduced the sum total of overt conflict, and presumably the undesirable sequelae of the conflict as well. The accident prevention model may have much to recommend it in preventing such phenomena as child abuse or driving while drunk. The success of Head Start in preventing social problems also yields to analysis with an event avoidance model (see Box 8–3).

Research on a variety of social problems undertaken from an ecological perspective may help us to define the chain of events leading to undesirable end states and may offer us new and different strategies for intervention. Creation of the original Holmes and Rahe (1967) stressful-life-events scale was stimulated by the observation that stressful life events occurred frequently in the histories of those treated for psychiatric disorder. An analysis built on the Markov chain concept may well demonstrate that many behavior patterns that we now consider manifestations of illness can instead be understood as the outcome of a potentially breakable chain of events.

One complication is that the accident prevention model may require its own approach to evaluation, for the primary initial goal is to control specified target behaviors, not final end states. In addition, the history of overall improvements to health and longevity resulting from environmental modifications suggests that simply changing the environment (e.g., making condoms more readily available to sexually active young people) may not be very effective unless at the same time people are educated about the risk and protective factors involved (Sagan, 1987). If we do not limit ourselves to the disease model, we may open other opportunities for prevention.

Box 8–3: *Head Start: An Experiment in Selective Prevention*

Head Start, a federally funded program for preschool children, has been called "the nation's most successful educational and social experiment" (Zigler & Muenchow, 1992, p. 244). It has clearly been the most popular and enduring of the 1960s' War on Poverty (WP) programs. Head Start was based on a belief that more could be accomplished by taking preventive action and attempting to affect very young children than by just dealing with youth and adults already enmeshed in poverty.

Head Start's original goals were quite broad. They included (1) improving the child's physical health, (2) fostering emotional and social development, (3) improving mental processes and skills; (4) raising positive expectations for the child in creating a climate of confidence for subsequent learning efforts; (5) increasing the child's capacity to relate positively to family members and others; (6) developing a responsible attitude toward society; and (7) increasing the sense of dignity and self-worth within the child and his or her family. Head Start serves children from any racial or ethnic background. Eligibility is limited only by family income (Richmond, Stipek, & Zigler, 1979; Zigler & Styfco, 1993). From the outset, sponsors of Head Start programs were given great discretion in tailoring the programs, which made it easier to obtain local support but hampered the replicability of Head Start interventions. As a result, Head Start was never a static intervention program but an "evolving concept" (Zigler & Muenchow, 1992).

Initiated in 1966 on a crash basis because political leaders believed that continued political support for the overall antipoverty program required rapid results that were popular and visible, Head Start grew, but with little direction. The Office of Economic Opportunity (OEO), the agency designated to carry out the War on Poverty, required community participation and insisted on parental involvement.

Parents were offered classes in child care; other parents took jobs as teacher aides, cooks, or playground supervisors. Programs began in public school buildings, in church basements, and in other makeshift facilities. Issues regarding the qualifications of teachers, standards for facilities, equipment, curriculum, and quality control soon arose. As the price tag grew, moreover, and the riots of the late 1960s struck many inner cities, demands for evaluation increased.

An early evaluation known as the Westinghouse study (Cicirelli, 1969) created a stir by reporting that no lasting effect of participation in Head Start programs could be measured: IQs of Head Start children rose immediately following participation in the program, but any differences in cognitive ability between children who had been in the Head Start program and those who had not disappeared within three to four years after the children entered public schools. Nevertheless, Head Start has remained popular with the public, presidents, and Congress. It is worth keeping in mind that while IQ was easier to assess than children's health, parents' involvement in the program, or family mobility, a gain in measured IQ was not the definitive outcome goal in the minds of Head Start's developers (Zigler & Muenchow, 1992).

Why has Head Start survived? Many explanations exist. Its nation-wide implementation and the deliberate involvement of parents helped politically in building a broad grassroots constituency. More relevant to our focus here is the possibility that professionals, sponsors, parents, and others connected to Head Start have recognized the tangible benefits it provides to children, their families, and society.

Many investigations of Head Start and other preschool programs have been undertaken, a number of them reasonably well-designed studies, many with follow-up evaluations. At some sites it has been possible to mount true experiments, with random assignment of children to preschool programs. In other places quasi-experimental designs were used because ethical and field conditions made it difficult to initiate or sustain random assignment studies.

In order to overcome some of the limitations of field studies, social scientists conducting twelve longitudinal studies formed a Consortium for Longitudinal Studies to pool their data and subject them to the most rigorous analysis. These pooled data contained information on approximately three thousand low-income children. In 1976 and 1977, members of the Consortium collected similar data on as many children as they were able to follow. These children ranged in age from nine to nineteen at time of follow-up (Darlington, Royce, Snipper, Murray, & Lazar, 1980; Lazar et al., 1978).

One of the best-designed studies, and the one that has been most successful in following all of the children in both the preschool-educated and the nonpreschool-educated groups, was conducted in Ypsilanti, Michigan (Schweinhart & Weikart, 1988). The Ypsilanti study was not funded through Head Start. Called the Perry Preschool study, it was initiated between 1962 and 1967 and followed a cohort of fifty-eight children who had preschool education and sixty-five who did not, to age 25. (Data on some variables from eleven other studies are available to provide adequate replication.) All the children came from a single pool of families who had indicated an interest in preschool education at the outset. All were African American, and all were from lower socioeconomic backgrounds as measured by parents' education, father's or single parent's occupation, and the ratio of rooms in the residence to number of family members. The children's IQs ranged from 60 to 90, and none showed evidence of organic damage. The groups were assigned randomly at the outset, and the research team ensured that there were no pretest differences between the two groups on critical variables so that any differences that emerged later would be apparently attributable to the difference in the groups' access to preschool education.

The Perry project, and others like it, have consistently reported that the preschool experience results in improved performance on IQ tests in the early grades. The early increase in IQ score represents more than simply improved cognitive performance. It reflects greater ability to concentrate on school-like tasks and better ability to communicate verbally and to adapt more successfully to the demands imposed by adults and structured settings. Although the advantage in IQ scores disappears within two or three years (Darlington et al., 1980), teachers working with preschool educated children consistently rate them as better adjusted and more mature than similar children who have not been exposed to preschool education.

One remarkable finding from the Perry project was the difference in the number of children from the two groups to be classified at some point as mentally retarded. Thirty-five percent of those without preschool education received such a classification, compared with only 15 percent of those with preschool education. Darlington et al. (1980) reported a similar finding in the large group of studies they analyzed. Whereas 45 percent of children without preschool education had spent some time in special classes, that was true for only 24 percent of the preschool educated subjects across all the studies.

Although not all studies found this discrepancy, in the Perry project consistent superiority in performance on academic achievement tests was still apparent at age 14 for those who had been exposed to preschool education. The Perry project also reported higher high school grade-point averages for the preschool-educated group, and more favorable attitudes toward high school. Not surprisingly, a significantly higher number of the preschool group graduated from high school (67 percent versus 49 percent) and went on to obtain postsecondary academic or vocational training. Perhaps as a consequence of their better performance in school, by age 19 subjects from the preschool group were more likely to be working and had higher median earnings than did their nonpreschool-educated counterparts. In keeping with their greater academic and vocational success, fewer were receiving public assistance.

The effects of preschool education, such as greater bonding to the school setting as a result of better performance, also showed up in better performance in the community. Fewer of the preschool-educated group had been arrested, either as a juvenile or as an adult (31 percent versus 51 percent), as indicated in records from the juvenile courts and state police. Females in the preschool educated group reported seventeen pregancies or births by age 19, while those not in the preschool group reported twenty-eight. Using standard methods of economic analysis, measuring short-term costs and benefits and projecting those to lifetime benefits, the Perry Project reported an economic benefit-to-cost ratio of 7.01 for one year of preschooling and 3.56 for two years. The net projected saving to society was $25,000 per child: "The estimated present value of net benefit is positive for both taxpayers (especially potential crime victims) and program participants. No one loses; taxpayers and participants are both better off with early education than without it" (Berrueta-Clement et al., 1984, p. 92). Barnett (1993) has since provided a cost-benefit analysis for the children followed to age 25. The large dollar savings continue to grow.

Head Start and related programs made varying efforts to involve parents in the preschool as volunteers or in paid positions. The Perry preschool program included weekly home visits with the mothers. While helping parents to learn to teach their children was not essential to the success of the preschool programs (Lazar et al., 1978), increased contact with preschool staff may have taught parents a great deal about schools and how they work, making these parents more sophisticated in interacting with school personnel, more adept at seeking educational advantages and opportunities for their children, and more alert to possible pernicious placements for their children. That the good outcomes we have described may simply have resulted from increased sophistication about schools is not a failure but an unexpected consequence, a benefical side effect.

Because of Head Start eligibility requirements, the first children to participate in the program were selected from clearly disadvantaged groups, such as African Americans from poverty backgrounds; most had below-average IQs. Later Head Start programs recruited disadvantaged children from all ethnic and racial groups. The significant effects of preschool education on later life outcomes shown for these children may not be generalizable to children from different or more advantaged backgrounds. It is also apparent that Head Start children as a group do not fully catch up to middle-class children in their subsequent school achievement (Zigler & Muenchow, 1992).

Although no single program is sufficient to "vaccinate" children against all future problems, preschool education may indeed have considerable effectiveness as a preventive program for the misery that befalls some who fail to do well in school. Head Start's comprehensiveness and degree of family involvement, the development of important cognitive competencies, and the repeated successes experienced by preschool-educated children are responsible for their superior "social competence" later in life.

Recent efforts have focused on improving program quality and expanding eligibility for Head Start and related programs to include infants and toddlers and elementary school children and low-income families above the poverty line (Zigler & Muenchow, 1992; Zigler & Styfco, 1993). Head Start's advocates see the program as much more than simply an educational boost. It is intended to help parents have an impact on other agencies as well as on the children. It would be useful to study the role Head Start might play in affecting other agencies with which participants must interact, such as those providing welfare assistance, health care, nutritional guidance, or dental care.

Prevention of AIDS/HIV

From 1981 through the end of 1994, nearly half a million Americans were diagnosed with Acquired Immune Deficiency Syndrome (AIDS) (Centers for Disease Control, 1995) following infection by its precursor, the human immunodeficiency virus (HIV). Tens of thousands had died of AIDS, and AIDS was the leading cause of death among persons ages 25 to 44 years (CDC, 1995). Each case of AIDS prevented saves a life and an estimated $100,000 in direct health care costs (Kelly, Murphy, Sikkema, & Kalichman, 1993), making prevention of HIV infection a top priority. Until a fully effective vaccine is discovered, behavior change is the most effective strategy for lowering the incidence of HIV infection. (Behavior change would also help prevent the spread of other sexually transmitted diseases, which a vaccine against HIV would not do.) Prevention programs based on changing behavior thus constitute an important opportunity for psychologists. Interventions to prevent HIV infection include media campaigns, small-group educational and skill-building programs, and social changes to promote new behavioral norms.

Media Campaigns

Media campaigns are universal, and designed to increase knowledge and understanding about AIDS, because all people are potentially at risk if they engage in unsafe behaviors. Universal targeting is cost-effective. Some media-driven programs, however, take a selective approach, targeting specific populations. Crawford et al. (1990) developed a media-based intervention designed to facilitate communication about HIV within urban families in which eighth-grade students in Chicago schools were given copies of a newspaper supplement about AIDS and encouraged to watch a series of television news segments on AIDS. Children in the intervention group viewed more of the broadcasts, learned more about AIDS, and talked more with their parents about AIDS than did children in the control group.

Reaching the African American community. HIV education programs targeted to the African American community may have special problems. The notorious Tuskegee syphillis study, which began in 1929 and continued until public disclosure of the study in 1972 forced its discontinuation, continues to have repercussions. In the Tuskegee study, 399

African American men who had contracted syphillis were followed to "end point" (autopsy). They were not given treatment; in fact, they were discouraged from obtaining treatment, even after penicillin became available, in order to protect the scientific purpose of the study, which was to determine the "natural course" of untreated syphilis. Members of the African American community believed that this study was evidence of a genocidal conspiracy by a white government against blacks. Recent surveys of the African American community show that a third believe that AIDS is a form of genocide, 44 percent believe the government is not telling the truth about AIDS, and 34 percent believe that AIDS is caused by a laboratory-created virus. These attitudes have important implications for HIV education and preventive intervention programs in the African American community in which the number of AIDS infections is growing rapidly (Thomas & Quinn, 1991).

HIV and the accident prevention model. HIV infection rates can be high even in people who have adequate knowledge about HIV and risky behaviors. The accident-prevention model suggests additional points for intervention. In addition to having information, individuals must recognize that their risk is almost entirely determined by their own behavioral choices. They need effective skills (e.g., managing relationships, substituting safe behaviors for risky ones), the motivation to use these skills under challenging conditions (temptation by sex or drugs), practice, and the adoption of new norms that both support low-risk behavior and sanction unhealthy behavior (Coates, 1990).

In an accident-prevention approach relevant to most young people, we would recognize that intimacy develops in sequential stages and foster delays in the onset of each stage to reduce risk. One option for teens is to wait until later in adolescence to begin dating, and after that to delay physical intimacy. Later on, the adolescent could lower risk by postponing sex, having sex only if precautions are taken, and remaining sexually monogamous. For intravenous drug users (IDUs), HIV prevention from an accident-prevention perspective can include treatment to reduce or stop IV drug use, providing means for and training in the adoption of safe methods, and education to prevent the initiation of direct injection of drugs in the first place, all of which have had some success (Des Jarlais, Friedman, & Casriel, 1990).

Clean needles and accident prevention. Using a clean needle when taking drugs prevents the transmission of HIV as well as hepatitis. Providing clean needles to addicts as a preventive intervention has proven highly controversial, however. Experiments in Europe have demonstated that providing clean needles to drug addicts can reduce the incidence of HIV and hepatitis infections and does not result in an increase in drug use. An attempt to introduce a similar program in New York City, however, resulted in sustained political controversy. Politicians, ignoring the existing evidence, objected that the program would imply official approval of the use of drugs and would increase drug use. Because of the political controversy, the program was so poorly designed that few addicts used it, and it was stopped. A similar program was mounted successfully elsewhere when the police commissioner supported it, but in another community a volunteer clean needle distributor was arrested; in yet another community, insurance problems delayed implementation. HIV infection and its prevention are not viewed as a technical problem but instead have moral dimensions that are critical for program implementation. This brief history underscores that prevention programs cannot be divorced from the social, political, and moral context in which they are to be implemented (Anderson, 1991).

Small-group Interventions

Face-to-face interventions may be the most effective way to teach and promote the specific skills needed to reduce risk. The best of these interventions are conceptually based and specific to the target group of interest and increase risk-reducing information, motivation, and behavioral skills simultaneously (Fisher & Fisher, 1992). Jemmott, Jemmott, and Fong (1992) provided a single-session, small-group intervention to inner-city African American male adolescents. Compared with those randomly assigned to an intervention dealing with career opportunities, boys in the AIDS risk reduction group showed greater AIDS knowledge and less intention to engage in risky sexual behaviors immediately following the intervention. The gains were sustained at a three-month follow-up, and these boys also reported fewer instances of risky sexual behavior.

Hobfoll and colleagues (Levine et al., 1993) illustrated how HIV prevention can be tailored to a specific gender or ethnic group. They worked with single, pregnant women ages 16 to 29, about half of whom were African American. Their goals were to increase participants' awareness and knowledge regarding HIV prevention and their skills in assertiveness and negotiation with sexual partners. Small groups of women met with a facilitator on four occasions for sessions involving imagery, cognitive rehearsal, role playing, and goal setting. Role-play situations were drawn directly from participants' current experiences. Follow-up results found that women who had been randomly assigned to receive the HIV-focused intervention showed increased knowledge about HIV and lower-risk sexual behavior.

A key component of this intervention was its group format. This process was more comfortable for many women than directive instruction would have been and provided spontaneous opportunities for timely information seeking and support. Participants were relatively homogeneous in their backgrounds, and the group process was based on cultural and gender sensitivity, mutual support, and empowerment. In these respects the intervention resembles mutual help groups, our focus in the next chapter.

Outreach programs. Small-group interventions are labor-intensive and require aggressive outreach. Some high-risk individuals (e.g., runaways, intravenous drug users who are not in treatment and their sexual partners) are hard to reach; others are unresponsive or hostile to intervention efforts. HIV prevention programs can be combined with other outreach efforts towards such groups. Rotheram-Borus et al. (1991) provided a high-intensity intervention to adolescent runaways at a New York City shelter. The intervention provided general HIV knowledge, coping skills to use in high-risk situations, access to health and mental health services, and efforts to reduce attitudinal obstacles to safe-sex behaviors in this population. Adolescents who received the intervention showed less high-risk sexual behavior at three- and six-month follow-ups. The number of sessions may be important. Those adolescents who had fifteen or more sessions of intervention reduced risky behavior more than those who had fewer than fifteen sessions.

School-based programs. Schools are another useful place for prevention. Nearly all adolescents can be reached before they initiate high-risk sexual and drug-related behavior. School-based prevention programs have successfully increased AIDS related knowledge and coping skills while reducing risky behaviors among urban minority youth in New York City (Walter & Vaughn, 1993) and Mississippi (St. Lawrence et al., 1995). In the long run, however, lapses in safe behavior are frequent (Kelly et al., 1991), and here (in contrast to smoking or drinking abusively) a single lapse can prove fatal. In addition to instilling low-risk behavior before adolescents first begin experimenting with sex or drugs, support for safe behavior must be maintained indefinitely. Any intervention should include a strong focus on relapse prevention, such as coping with risk, relapse rehearsal, and self-efficacy in the face of risk (Ekstrand & Coates, 1990). The use of peer educators as positive role models to deliver credible messages and skills has not been adequately studied.

Schools have many responsibilities. They cannot be expected to overcome all the other neighborhood, family, and peer-group risks that many students face. Normative change requires multiple, redundant messages coming from many sources and repeated over time. Think of what was involved in changing Americans' smoking habits or their diet and exercise habits as they affect heart disease.

Changing Social Norms

The scope of HIV infection and the practical limitations of formal programs suggest that efforts built on informal supports and resources will be critical. There is evidence that new norms supporting low-risk behavior can be established for sex (Catania et al., 1991; Ekstrand & Coates, 1990) and for IV drug use (Des Jarlais et al., 1990). Kelly et al. (1992) identified opinion leaders among gay men in three cities where media information campaigns were well established and trained these "trendsetters" to promote risk-reducing behavior change in each gay community. The intervention was introduced in a staggered fashion across the three cities, and postintervention surveys in all three places found gay men reporting significant reductions in risky behavior. Of course, the intervention alone cannot account for the change; knowledge of the risks of AIDS spread rapidly in the gay community when people saw their friends and partners succumb to the disease.

Multiple approaches are necessary. The enormity of the HIV epidemic suggests that multiple approaches to individual change (i.e., media-based, skill-oriented, and norm-focused), combined with policy and environmental modifications, will be necessary to achieve the maximum effect. Basic risk factors are the same across gender, ethnicity, and other groupings, but the nature of optimally effective prevention programs may not be. Different groups vary widely in their expectations and conventions regarding sexual and drug-related behaviors, their access to information and other resources, and their trust in authorities who offer help.

We need to know more about "protective" factors such as the cognitive and social variables that influence motivation to change, the effects of providing opportunities to change (e.g., making condoms or clean needles readily available), the acquisition and use of skills, and support for change (Kelly et al., 1993). In addition, we need to identify the critical ingredients of effective interventions and to concentrate more of our effort on urban, poor, minority populations that face increasing risk. More programs are needed aimed at families, as are programs for use in normative settings like schools and work sites. We also need an adequate infrastructure of risk-reducing services (e.g., treatment programs, distributions of condoms and other devices to control sexually transmitted diseases, bleach sterilization kits, HIV antibody testing, job programs). For all of these reasons, collaborative studies involving investigators and representatives of the indigenous community are important. On the plus side, what is learned about sexual behavior will have implications for efforts to reduce unwanted pregnancy and to control sexually transmitted diseases. The projected impact of prevention efforts on cumulative HIV infection is presented in Figure 8–2.

Prevention is a community issue. Risky behaviors are an individual matter. The necessary scale of change makes HIV prevention a community issue. Community psychology reminds us that in addition to individual competence-building efforts provided by education, the social context (e.g., family stability and support, peer-group norms) is an important aspect of effecting and maintaining change. Given the increasing prevalence of HIV among ethnic minority populations and women, maximizing the involvement and participation of individuals at risk, community leaders, and community-based organizations are especially important. Thomas and Quinn (1991) described how prevention researchers coped

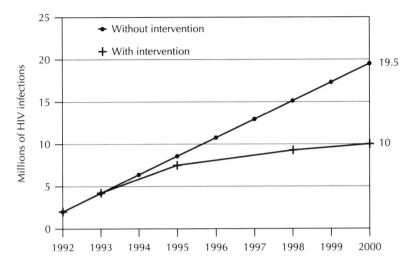

Figure 8-2. Projected impact of prevention interventions on cumulative adult HIV incidence from 1992 to 2000. (From Global Programme on AIDS, World Health Organization)

with the distrust left by the legacy of the Tuskegee experiment by contracting with African American organizations to provide HIV education. In addition, HIV prevention programs may not adequately consider women's realities. Traditional masculine ideology, sex role behavior, and differences in power and status may affect women's ability to take steps to reduce risk. Increasing the social and economic power of women, and prevention methods controlled by women, will help in the long run (Amaro, 1995). Thus far the epidemiological research necessary to guide prevention has been stymied by the political difficulties of doing research on sexual behavior and IV drug use (e.g., needle exchange behavior) and by prejudice against gay men and intravenous drug users.

With adolescents, programs focused explicitly on sexual and drug use behavior are more effective than information-only programs, especially in younger children before they begin experimenting with high-risk behaviors. Yet these interventions are most likely to be resisted by families and communities. Just as with other community interventions, efforts to prevent HIV infection are inseparable from the social and political context in which they occur.

Summary

The metaphors of ecology and vulnerability have led to preventive approaches to behavioral problems. The practice of prevention poses difficult procedural and ethical questions; prevention programs require us to take responsibility in advance for the occurrence of conditions we do not fully understand and to adopt a much more extended outlook on the ultimate success of our efforts.

One intuitively appealing approach, defined as secondary or indicated prevention, involves the early identification and prompt treatment of incipient behavioral maladjustment in individuals. Problems exist with both the accuracy of identification and the treatment procedures currently used in secondary prevention, and efforts to prevent abuses such as domestic violence in people who have already committed such acts have not been very successful. Primary prevention, whose goal is to reduce the incidence of long-term problems, has attracted an extensive following in community psychology. However, its current popularity and appeal are also reason for caution; programs have been launched without evidence of their effectiveness and without adequate provision for evaluation (Weissberg & Elias, 1993). For now authorities emphasize reducing risks and enhancing protective factors and urge the collection of more longitudinal data on such factors across the life span, as well as an increase in the number of experimental studies testing direct causal hypotheses (Mrazek & Haggerty, 1994).

Prevention research is becoming more sophisticated in methodology as well as conceptualization. The most successful prevention programs are those that attempt not just to impart information or new behaviors but to alter life trajectories. They change not only individuals but also their social contexts—families, schools, and community settings. Prevention of social or behavioral problems should not be likened to a one-shot inoculation. Promoting a change in life trajectory requires ongoing support and further skills as new settings and developmental stages are encountered. This makes it difficult to identify the key processes that account for preventive effects in a global intervention like ICPS training, for example, because motivation, skills, and support are all probably important. Programs that work need dissemination and continued evaluation so that the advantages of widespread reductions in incidence and prevalence are realized. Because prevention programs work to lower statistical risk of future difficulties instead of to ameliorate present suffering, their benefits can seem abstract and the concrete cost-benefit advantages claimed for prevention need to be documented where possible.

To maintain our ethical footing, we should remember that prevention is value-driven and subject to analysis from multiple perspectives. Prevention efforts consume resources of the people and settings they involve, and those conducting the intervention should include all who are affected in the planning, implementation, and evaluation of programs. What values are represented in the intervention program and its goals? How do these values mesh with those of other participants? Are outcomes and other effects of the program (including unintended effects) being measured from the relevant perspectives? How has the program altered the settings in which it occurred?

We examined two generic strategies for primary prevention. One, known as competence building, focuses on helping individuals at risk learn specific skills associated with successful adaptations to key settings. We described effective examples of such programs for preschool and middle-school children. The other, which we have termed accident prevention, uses multiple strategies of active behavior change (reducing alcohol use, for example) and passive protection (mandatory use of seat belts) to decrease the likelihood of negative outcomes. We also examined the widely discussed Head Start program, which has had an encouraging impact on the school and community adaptations of disadvantaged children over a respectably long time frame. Finally, there is increasing recognition of the important relationship between psychological and physical health and well-being, and we closed this chapter by reviewing programs to prevent AIDS/HIV.

The field of prevention has seen significant changes in recent decades. The examples discussed in this chapter illustrate current activities in prevention; future activities may change as the field evolves. Prevention is not a panacea for life's problems, and even very dedicated efforts are unlikely to eliminate problems or even affect in the same way every person who is targeted. Many people at risk also have access to important informal resources, and in the next chapter we look closely at a very different alternative for coping with problems—the self-help group.

Notes

1. Seymour Sarason tells the story of what happened when the late Claude Pepper went to heaven. The long-time senator and congressperson from Florida was a hardy and vigorous advocate of health care programs. He took the opportunity to request an audience with God and, when granted his wish, said he had one question he wished the good Lord to answer. That question was whether we would ever achieve health care reform. God pondered a moment and then said, "Yes, but not in my life-time."

2. Similar issues are involved in preventing assaultive violence among young African American men (Hammond & Yung, 1993).

3. In the 1995 murder trial of the former football star O. J. Simpson, some argued that the fact that Simpson had allegedly battered his former wife, Nicole Brown Simpson, could not be taken as evidence of his guilt because of the high false positive problem. On the other hand, reasoning back from the fact that half of murdered women are murdered by batterers, results in a much lower false positive rate.

9

Self-Help Groups

One important response to the "soap opera" of life is the voluntary self-help organization. (Some prefer the term mutual assistance group, and many programs, following the Alcoholics Anonymous (AA) model, are called twelve-step programs.) Self-help groups date back to antiquity and currently are among the fastest-growing forms of assistance, adding substantially to community resources. Any newspaper reader can find regular announcements of self-help or support-group meetings.

Self-help groups are of interest to community psychology because they are an important indigenous resource within the private, nonprofessional segment of the community and because they address the current trend toward greater consumer choice and empowerment (see Chapter 12). Some self-help groups may also serve a clientele different from the young, attractive, verbal, intelligent, successful individual considered the ideal candidate for traditional psychotherapy. One survey, for example, found that the average member of major self-help groups like AA or Parents Without Partners is middle-aged and a homemaker or a blue-collar worker, typically with a high school education (Knight et al., 1980).

Not only are self-help groups important community resources; they are understandable using the same principles we have used in explaining other interventions. In this chapter, we first describe the phenomenon of the self-help group as a source of help and then consider the dynamics of self-help groups, including theoretical explanations of how they apparently facilitate adaptation by vulnerable people. The chapter closes with a discussion of how community psychologists can directly assist individuals at risk by helping create tailor-made self-help groups.

Growth of Self-Help Organizations

The number of self-help groups of all kinds is growing rapidly. Alcoholics Anonymous had about fifty groups in 1942; there are now more than thirty thousand groups with more than six hundred thousand members. Parents Anonymous began in 1969 with one group and two members; by 1975 it had grown to 450 groups with some four thousand members. Today, it claims nearly fifteen hundred chapters. Parents Without Partners had an estimated thirty thousand members in 1966; its national membership grew to more than one hundred thousand, and today it has some twelve hundred chapters. Recovery, Inc., grew from 850 groups in 1973 to more than one thousand groups in 1976; it now claims about 950 chapters. Founded in 1980, Tough Love today has two thousand groups (Tracy & Gussow, 1976; Gartner & Reissman, 1977).

In 1942 there were four national groups in existence. By 1975 there were some two thousand different self-help organizations, many with multiple chapters (Tracy and Gussow, 1976). Obviously, such overall estimates depend upon definitions and sources of information. For example, Katz (1993) estimates there are currently 500,000 to 750,000 groups, with 10 to 15 million members, and uses data from New Jersey to project an annual growth rate of 8 percent. More conservatively, Jacobs and Goodman (1989) estimated that there were 6.25 million self-help group members in 1987 and that groups would experience only a .1 percent growth rate.

Regardless of these different estimates, so many self-help organizations exist today that a National Self-Help Clearinghouse has been formed to disseminate information about the activities of existing groups, the formation of new groups, publications, research findings, funding sources, and ideas and methods for starting new groups (Madara & Meese, 1988; Meissen et al., 1991). In their directory, Madara and Meese (1988) listed approximately six hundred organizations having 1,108,188 chapters, affiliated groups, support groups, or centers. This listing does not include right-to-life groups such as Operation Rescue and its affiliates, local pro-choice organizations, or the thousands of grass-roots environmental groups that Lois Gibbs's Citizens Clearinghouse for Hazardous Waste claims to have contacted. Of the organizations listed in Madara and Meese's directory, 10 percent were founded before 1959, about 40 percent between 1960 and 1979, and 49 percent between 1980 and 1988. Members of self-help groups often cite this growth in numbers as an indication of the need and effectiveness of such groups. In recognition of the growth, the U.S. Surgeon General organized a conference in the mid-1980s on self-help, basically endorsing the groups' usefulness in the health field (Petrakis, 1988).

Self-help is not a new phenomenon on the American scene. When Alexis de Tocqueville visited the United States in 1831, he noted: "Americans of all ages, all conditions and dispositions, constantly form associations . . . of a thousand . . . kinds—religious, moral, serious, futile, enormous or diminutive. . . . If it be proposed to inculcate some truth or foster some feeling by the encouragement of a great example, they form a society" (de Tocqueville, 1835, p. 198). De Tocqueville believed that associations were peculiarly American, a function of a democratic social order.

In 1902 Kropotkin (1972) argued that cooperation is a basic survival mechanism for human beings. He provided many examples throughout history of spontaneously developed cooperative enterprises and associations for purposes of greater mutual protection and productivity. In medieval days, for example, members banded together in guilds to regulate their trades. Guild members constituted a brotherhood. Each guild was responsible not only for maintaining standards for the trade but also for providing fraternal benefits to the membership—aid in the event of illness, aid to widows and orphans, celebrations of births and marriages. Anticipating today's sociobiologists, Kropotkin argued that a social instinct leads people to help each other: "There is the gist of human psychology. Unless men are maddened in the battlefields, they cannot stand it to hear appeals for help, and not to respond to them. . . . The sophisms of the brain cannot resist the mutual aid feeling, because this feeling has been nurtured by thousands of years of pre-human life in societies" (Kropotkin, 1972, p. 234).

Contemporary Reasons for Growth

People have always organized in response to mutual need, whether out of some social instinct, as Kropotkin argued, or as the manifestation of rational coping capacities (Katz & Bender, 1976; Hurvitz, 1976). If people organize in new ways to fulfill social need, existing means of providing support in time of need have evidently proven insufficient.

For our purposes, we can most usefully link the recent spurt of growth of self-help to changes that reflect problems in existing social organizations and the means for providing mutual assistance. Growth in self-help or mutual assistance may reflect changes in other, more traditional groups that might at one time have fulfilled human needs. In Chapter 1 we discussed recent changes in the family, especially the increase in the number of single-parent households. U.S. society is also very mobile. A large number of people change their addresses each year, many moving long distances and loosening their ties with family and old friends, which forces them to readapt by making new ties and becoming a part of new social networks. Geographic mobility puts distinct pressures on the nuclear family, and increasing numbers of working mothers may add to that pressure even as their working alleviates economic difficulties.

A large number of people live alone and may be unable to call upon friends or family for assistance. In still other cases, the resources of friends and family may not be sufficient to aid the individual in coping with problems in living that are foreign to ordinary experience. In a superb book, the late Raoul Naroll (1983) demonstrated on a worldwide basis that ruptures in what he termed "moralnets"—the largest primary or face-to-face group that serves a given person as a normative reference group—are associated with a wide range of mental health and social problems.

Moreover, changing values have produced a decline in the prominence of some traditional organizations that served mutual need. Despite population growth from 1968 to 1975, membership in Greek letter societies, fraternal groups, nationality and ethnic societies, and national religious organizations all declined for several years and then grew slowly from 1980 to 1992 (U.S. Bureau of the Census, 1993). These traditional groups and associations may well have defined a socially shared outlook helpful to members in making sense of contemporary life and in providing social forms through which that outlook could be expressed.

Throughout the 1980s, national nonprofit organizations concerned with social welfare, public affairs, health, and medicine increased in number. From 1980 to 1992 the number of these organizations almost doubled (U.S. Bureau of the Census, 1993). If we include neighborhood associations and block clubs, hundreds of thousands, if not millions, of new groups came to exist across the United States (Perlman, 1976; Wandersman et al., 1987; Wandersman & Florin, in press). Some of these associations are forming coalitions with other groups to extend their influence (Butterforce, Goodman, & Wandersman, 1993). Lois Gibbs's Citizens Clearinghouse for Hazardous Wastes (see Chapter 12) claims to have contact with seven thousand local groups formed spontaneously in response to the perceived threat from toxic dump sites, landfills, radioactive wastes, and incinerators (Wandersman & Hallman, 1993). These groups may well be the successors to community organizations that served similar purposes in another era.

We have already discussed several deficiencies in the medical model of service delivery. Another deficiency of the medical model becomes apparent when we examine Kropotkin's view of charity. Writing from an anarchist viewpoint, Kropotkin (1972) argued that the existence of a centralized state interfered with the mutual assistance that would develop spontaneously in the absence of a state. He extended his argument to organized charitable enterprises as well:

> [W]hile early Christianity, like all other religions, was an appeal to the broadly human feelings of mutual aid and sympathy, the Christian church has aided the State in wrecking all standing institutions of mutual aid and support which were anterior to it, or developed outside of it; and, instead of the *mutual aid* which every savage considers as due to his kinsman, it has preached *charity* which bears a character of inspiration from above, and accordingly implies a certain superiority of the giver upon the receiver. (p 238)

We need not accept Kropotkin's view regarding the role of the church. Drawing an analogy between organized charity and professional services, however, we can argue that the medical model is essentially a "trickle-down" model of assistance. Whatever its other merits, this model limits the possibilities for reciprocity and mutual assistance based on experience with the particular problem in living. Its very professionalism, certainly a strength for many purposes, nonetheless implies the superiority of the giver to the receiver and does not allow for reciprocity in their relationship.

We need not repeat other criticisms of the medical model here, but it is important to reemphasize one. Although a professional may have a great deal to offer, he or she usually does not know in great detail what it means to live with a particular problem or how one copes with it on a day-to-day basis. Our therapeutic philosophies and approaches tell us not to make our clients dependent and not to respond to the plea "Tell me what to do!" Clients live with the problem of coping on a day-by-day basis, however, and most therapists do not focus on those day-by-day coping techniques. Professional therapists often do not transmit practical, gut-level, tried-and-true methods for handling problems. To the degree that all wisdom is seen to reside in the professional, there is a loss of the wisdom that comes from learning to cope on a day-by-day basis. The self-help model addresses that deficiency.

Anyone who reads the daily paper is also aware of the serious and growing problem of the cost of physical and mental health care. Insurance companies, wary of the potential high cost of mental health services and the interminability of some mental health treatments, have imposed limits on both inpatient and outpatient care. If health care reform restricts insurance reimbursement for psychotherapy services, we may expect still further growth in self-help organizations and membership.

For those who pay for care directly, the costs of extended treatment are prohibitive for all but the wealthiest. Public agencies with sliding-fee scales take into account ability to pay, but even their fees can add up to considerable amounts. Moreover, most therapists agree that it is difficult to show an even exchange—that for any unit of fee, a corresponding unit of progress is made. Payment of a fee does not make for an even exchange, nor does it undo the social inequality and lack of reciprocity in the relationship between the client and the professional. Self-help groups do permit equality and reciprocity among members.

Self-help groups provide services indefinitely to substantial numbers of people at very low cost. A telephone survey asking self-help groups in the Buffalo metropolitan area about the typical turnout at meetings revealed that as many as one thousand people a month were being served for little more than coffee money. One thousand people a month was roughly comparable to the caseload of Buffalo's largest mental health center at that time, whose professional mental health services cost millions of dollars per year.

People who attend self-help groups are probably not a representative sample of those in need. Those who responded to our survey estimated that more than two-thirds of the participants in most of the organizations are female. It is also our impression that the vast bulk of participants are white, and there are relatively few examples of interracial groups. Emrick (1987) suggests that other self-selection factors are also important. AA members, for example, may be more sociable and affiliative than the average person. In addition, they may have more severe drinking problems and experience more guilt about their drinking than do alcohol abusers who are not AA members.

Another interesting variation from the medical model is that when more than one chapter of a given self-help group exists, a prospective member can "shop around," facilitating an ecological process of mutual selection that acknowledges the diversity among people and has as its goal the improvement of person-setting fit. We have no data on this point but strongly suspect that tolerance of such "shopping around" by prospective clients is not nearly so great among professionals. Some patients undoubtedly change therapists from time to time. Are such changes always a matter of "resistance," or can they be viewed as attempts by the clients to improve person-environment fit?

Types of Self-Help Groups

So far we have been discussing self-help as if all groups were similar to psychotherapy in their aims and methods. Hurvitz (1976), in fact, termed these organizations "peer psychotherapy" groups. Like psychotherapy, their aim is to assist the individual in coping with the emotions and the dilemmas generated by problems in living. The locus of pathology is within the individual, and the individual is assisted in making a better adaptation to self and to the world.

Sagarin (1969) pointed out that there are two general types of self-help groups. In one,

> individuals seek to reduce their deviant behavior and in this way escape from deviance. . . . Such groups paint deviants as worthwhile individuals, souls to be saved; but they view the deviance itself as immoral, sinful and self-defeating. . . . The second type of deviant group consist[s] of those who are seeking to modify the definition of their conditions as deviant. . . . These groups seek to change the public attitude toward their particular deviance. . . . Groups seeking to change social attitudes thumb their noses at society in order to foster pride in the deviant. (p. 21)

AA is an example of the first type of self-help group. Its aim is to help members overcome their drinking problems through mutual assistance. AA teaches that, for alcoholics, drinking is self-defeating. AA is not a temperance organization—it takes no position about the drinking of others who are not alcoholics, and it takes no public position on legislation related to drinking. It neither favors nor opposes legislation to raise the drinking age or to introduce stiffer penalties against drunk driving. It makes no effort to create sympathy for the alcoholic or to reduce stigmatization or discrimination directed against former alcoholics. It has no interest in changing society's views of alcoholics, except perhaps in furthering the conception that alcoholism is a disease. Even then it does not speak out as an organization, nor does it allow individual members to speak on such issues in the name of the group.

Notable examples of the second type of self-help organization are any of the organizations constituting the civil rights movement. The civil rights movement utilized political and social action and adopted a litigative strategy to help create opportunities for African Americans and other minorities and to instill self-esteem. It also served as a model for other oppressed (read "deviant") groups trying to improve their lives by working to change society's view of and actions toward members of those groups. Milner (1985) described how the mental patients' rights movement (Chamberlin, 1990) used the civil rights movement as a model in working for change through litigation, legislation, and direct social action. Women's consciousness-raising[1] groups of the 1970s also modeled themselves on the civil rights movement. They were concerned not only about helping individual women to adapt in a changing social world but also about changing the larger society's views and treatment of women.

Another case in point is the gay rights movement. Gay activism started in 1969 with a famous incident at the Stonewall Bar in Greenwich Village in New York when a group of gays resisted arrest for nothing more than being in a gay bar. The incident triggered a week-long riot and was a defining episode. Since then, gay groups have been active in attempting to change not homosexuals, except perhaps to instill pride in being gay, but aspects of the larger society (Duberman, 1993). To gay groups, homosexuality is simply an alternative lifestyle that should not be subject to social, economic, or criminal penalties. Gay groups lobby and work for changes in laws that affect their members. They seek to be included in antidiscrimination legislation, and they pursue changes in sodomy laws attaching criminal penalties to sexual acts between consenting adults. Gays do not wish to be barred from having custody of children simply because of their sexual orientations. Some gays want states to legalize gay marriages and are seeking to have partners covered under their health insurance plans and other employment benefits.

Over the years, gay groups have been sufficiently active and persuasive to have homosexuality eliminated as an official psychiatric illness or deviation. All that remains in the current American Psychiatric Association *Diagnostic and Statistical Manual, 4th edition* (*DSM*-IV) is a brief mention of "persistent and marked distress about sexual orientation" as a possible basis for diagnosing a "Sexual Disorder Not Otherwise Specified" (p. 538). This revision in diagnostic practice was the result of social and political action to change the definition of deviance and the world's view of the deviant individual. Other groups have since organized to protest the inclusion of certain conditions in the *DSM*, on the grounds that labeling a condition can be prejudicial to the interests of a particular group (e.g., failing to include abortion as a possible trauma for the diagnosis of posttraumatic stress disorder favors the pro-choice position on abortion) (Kirk & Kutchins, 1992).

None of these goals is achievable simply by helping individuals to cope better with problems in living defined as individual problems. These changes require concerted group action to alter society's views of and actions toward a group commonly defined as deviant and subject to the burdens carried by deviants. The activities of gay organizations would undoubtedly meet Goldenberg's (1978) definition of a social intervention designed to reduce oppression.

This general idea of social and political action to better the lives of certain people suffering with some handicap or feeling some grievance has powered the formation of a large number of groups. Some groups have aims as narrow as raising money to stimulate public interest or research on a given disease. Others form spontaneously in relation to a specific problem. The Love Canal Homeowners Association was formed in 1978 when homeowners living in the neighborhood of a hidden toxic chemical waste dump site believed that they were not getting fair treatment from the state agencies designated to deal with their problem. The homeowners organized and kept fighting for several years, taking their case to the public and in other ways continually making their demands known to public officials. They were successful in seeing their demands met and in the process raised public consciousness about the problems of toxic wastes (Gibbs, 1982; A. Levine, 1982). Their organization also served to alleviate the sense of helplessness experienced by many who felt caught in a severe problem in living that taxed family and community resources (Gibbs, 1983; Stone & Levine, 1985–1986).

The Nature of Self-Help Groups

We have not yet defined self-help groups in any formal sense. This is difficult to do with great precision because we would like to include many different types of organizations, and many of them have mixed characteristics. Sagarin's twofold classification is insufficient to cover the variety of groups that have sufficient characteristics in common to be treated as related phenomena. Many authorities have attempted descriptions and classifications of self-help, but no single attempt seems fully satisfactory (Levy, 1976; Katz & Bender, 1976). We offer our own grouping simply to show the range of different types and their goals for their members.

For convenience of exposition, we list five types of self-help groups. One type of group serves people whose state or condition leads to some disqualification from being "normal." Members of these groups exhibit behavior or have characteristics that subject them to social isolation, stigmatization, scorn, pity, or social punishment. Although the concept of a degraded social identity (Sarbin, 1970) applies more or less here, as does Goldenberg's (1978) concept of oppression, we cannot say that all such people are necessarily limited to ascribed roles. Examples of those with behavioral characteristics that disqualify them from being "normal" are mentally ill people, alcohol abusers, former convicts, gamblers, drug addicts, and gays. Examples of people with physical characteristics or illnesses that make them subject to disqualification are little people (dwarfs), cancer patients, people with colostomies or other physical disabilities (see Hinrichsen, Revenson, & Shinn, 1985), the obese, and people who are elderly. Although not at fault, people who fall into this category are nonetheless subject to varying degrees of social disapprobation and social disqualification. Some are subjected to forms of social discrimination that limit opportunity and may affect self-esteem; African Americans, women, and gays are people subject to discriminatory treatment.

The second type of self-help group is made up of people related to persons with stigmatizing conditions, who themselves may be subject to some secondary stigma or who suffer consequences because of the problems presented by the person related to them. Spouses and children of alcoholics or gamblers or relatives of people with mental illness (Grosser & Vine, 1991) fall into this category, as do children who are charged with the care of elderly relatives. Parents of people with mental retardation, learning disabilities, or autism have much to cope with, as do those in serious conflict with their adolescent children who seek the assistance of the courts to help control their children (York & York, 1980).

A third type of group includes people with common problems that may not be stigmatizing but that do tend to be socially isolating. Other people who do not have the problem may not understand the individual's or the family's situation. Examples of these are widows (Silverman et al., 1974), single parents, parents of diabetic children, or parents of children with cancer (Chesler, Barbarin, & Lego-Stein, 1984).

A fourth type are groups organized along ethnic, religious, or racial lines for mutual assistance. These include fraternal organizations that provide education, recreation, cultural preservation, insurance, prepaid medical care, and similar services. Howe (1976) noted that many of these organizations developed among immigrant groups, and many originated as burial societies. These organizations were very important in the Jewish community; similar groups made and continue to make important contributions to the lives of African Americans. In the recent past, we have seen fewer multipurpose organizations and more groups organized for single functions, such as women's health collectives, cooperative food services, or day care centers organized and run by parents.

A fifth type is organized along quasi-political lines for the preservation of specific interests. These include taxpayers' groups seeking to limit taxation, civic organizations designed to preserve the character of neighborhoods, and organizations concerned with community development. Groups such as these may form whenever a common problem arises. The Love Canal Homeowners Association is an example of a spontaneously appearing organization. Groups opposed to abortion and groups in favor of choice in reproductive matters are additional examples of this type. Men's groups have now organized in response to the women's movement (see *The Liberator*, 1994).

This classification system is difficult to apply because groups rarely fall squarely into any one category. (A dimensional analysis would be more useful than a categorical analysis, but has yet to be developed in a workable form.) Take as an example Equal Rights for Fathers, a relatively new group showing many mixed characteristics. Members of this group of noncustodial parents dealing with the aftermath of divorce are primarily male, but some are new wives or girlfriends and grandparents who wish to maintain ties with grandchildren following a divorce. Equal Rights for Fathers has political aims as well as self-help aims and believes that the legal system is biased against men. Fathers Rights Metro (New York), a related group, has recently filed a class-action lawsuit against the New York Department of Social Services and the New York Office of Court Administration, claiming that men are the victims of gender-biased discrimination by social services agencies and the Family Court (*The Liberator*, 1994). Chapters of this type of group have successfully lobbied to have infant changing stations included in the men's rooms in airports to allow men to care for their infants and young children while traveling.

Members of this group feel stigmatized because some members of the public see them as merely seeking to avoid paying child support. Others feel stigmatized because they feel that their masculinity is questioned when they assert their love for their children and their desire to have or to share custody. Members favor a legal presumption for joint custody. They agree that men should meet their obligations to pay child support but argue that the courts do not show nearly the same vigor in protecting visitation rights as they do in enforcing support orders. Members engage in public information campaigns (broadcasts on public access TV channels, letters to the editor, father's day events designed to capture media attention), share information about the legal system, organize to influence legislation, attempt to educate judges and lawyers, help one another understand what to look for in an attorney, and share information about how to use the time they have with their children effectively. They conduct rap sessions to help one another come to terms with their circumstances and their feelings and attitudes about themselves, their former spouses, the legal system, and many other problems that require adaptation and for which little or no assistance is otherwise available. Members sometimes assist each other outside of the group meetings, and some core members often find themselves intervening in personal crises of other members. Similar functions were served by the women's consciousness-raising groups that grew rapidly in the late 1960s and early 1970s (Levine & Perkins, 1987, Chapter 9).

Dynamics of Self-Help Groups

Describing self-help in theoretical terms may help us understand how self-help works to assist members in adapting. Galanter (1990) compares self-help groups to charismatic religious groups and to cults, such as the Unification Church and Hare Krishna, and finds that they share many similar features that have profound effects on the thinking and behavior of their members. Galanter defines a group as "charismatic" when the members commit to a "fervently espoused, transcendent goal . . . frequently articulated by a charismatic leader" (p. 543). He accepts that participation can relieve some psychopathological symptoms, but he is concerned that participation can also precipitate psychiatric symptoms in some members. His theoretical analysis is consistent with that presented here.

Prospective members of a self-help organization struggle with a problem in living or a life circumstance that departs from some normative ideal. The problem or circumstance will not disappear rapidly no matter what remedies are sought, and as a result the individual faces the problem of adapting over a considerable period of time. Because the core problem represents a departure from a normative ideal, moreover, the individual tends to engage in a process of self-ostracization in perceiving himself or herself as having failed, as abnormal, or as a hapless victim of uncontrollable forces or of fate.

Most important, because the problem is interpreted as a departure from a normative ideal, the individual feels alone, as if his or her problems and feelings and experiences are unique. This feeling of isolation may exist even if the individual is part of a network that is supportive in many other respects. The person's difficulties are often exacerbated because the ordinary agencies of assistance have proved insufficient, inadequate, or even punitive. As a consequence, the individual has not developed a philosophy for viewing the problem or had the opportunity to learn, directly or vicariously, useful strategies for coping with the myriad of everyday issues related to the core problem.

What does participation in a self-help group provide that reduces the vulnerability and/or acute stress affecting a person at risk? Like any significant social support system, a self-help group can profitably be compared with the model of an ideal family. Recall from our discussion of social support that Caplan depicts the ideal family as fulfilling several functions for its members. For example, just as older members of the family collect and disseminate information about the world, providing models for younger members to emulate, so more experienced members of the self-help group provide information about their mutual plight and serve as models for less experienced members.

Women's consciousness-raising groups of the 1970s, for example, worked out ways of thinking about problems such as sharing homemaking and child care responsibilities with husbands, working out the norms of living with partners when not married, and dealing with discrimination in the workplace. Women shared their experiences and their solutions. Eventually members who had been in the movement longer and who seemed to have thought through issues became role models for others who knew they were struggling but didn't know how to think about their situations (Levine & Perkins, 1987).

Self-help groups may also serve as feedback and guidance systems to help members understand their reactions to others and others' reactions to them. Consciousness-raising groups included assigned discussion topics ranging from dress to relationships, assertiveness, and women's lack of self-confidence. In discussing the various topics and in reflecting on their experiences, group members provided a way of interpreting their experiences and a basis for thinking of new ways of responding to others.

Self-help groups provide a philosophy of life, an outlook on the problem condition. Through repeated discussion of concrete situations with other members, the group's philosophy or ideology comes to serve an organizing function in the lives of group members. By applying the tenets of the ideology to everyday problems, the ideology provides, as Caplan puts it, "prescriptions for wise conduct." Women's consciousness-raising groups provided reinforcement for behavior consistent with the groups' objectives and the elimination of undesirable behavior. The groups' ideology promoted action to modify the social environment and provided a rationale, encouragement, and specific methods for dealing with commonplace problems. Similarly, members of local groups of the National Alliance for the Mentally III (NAMI) share experiences, develop a way of looking at mental illness, and engage in political and social action.

Family members share each other's problems, offer each other advice and guidance, assist in finding external sources of aid, and even make arrangements for such assistance. Much analogous learning occurs in self-help groups. Members of the groups share happy occasions as well as problems. In some groups members celebrate birthdays, job promotions, and other successful life changes. In many self-help groups members also extend concrete services and material aid to each other. For example, women in pro-life as well as those in pro-choice groups see each other socially. In the 1970s, members of women's consciousness-raising groups provided assistance to one another during crises, performing baby-sitting or allowing a member to move in temporarily if she decided to seek a divorce and needed a place to stay temporarily.

As a haven for rest and recuperation, the self-help group provides a place where members can be themselves and be assured of understanding and acceptance. There is no need to conceal or to explain the problem to anyone. All understand because all have experienced similar needs and emotions. In many ways, the self-help group also becomes the reference group for its members. For example, in one women's consciousness-raising group, members expressed concern that their bodies did not live up to fashion magazine ideals. Members literally bared their breasts to the group, each woman confessing the feeling that her breasts were inadequate but receiving reassurance from the other members that her breasts were perfectly adequate.

Members feel good when they live up to the codes of the self-help group and presumably feel bad when they fail to live up to its standards. The desire to have the approbation and support of fellow group members motivates the individual to live up to the group's standards. Just as in a family, however, failure to conquer the core problem does not lead to banishment. The sinner, so to speak, may always return to the fold and be welcomed, if not honored, for being willing to try again. In any successful self-help group, members identify with one another and develop a sense of trust and community that promotes belongingess and fellowship, often extending beyond the boundaries of the group.

A foundation for personal identity is established within self-help groups as members share their current problems. In fact, because members are both givers and receivers of help, with the roles changing from moment to moment, sharing of weakness contributes positively to self and to others. An individual member may find himself or herself of value to another simply by sharing a failure. By being of value to another, one may find one's sense of competence and worthwhileness enhanced. Finally, sharing problems and feelings within a family enables members to assist one another with the task of emotional mastery. Sharing problems and feelings within a self-help group comes to fulfill similar functions. For some, participation in the self-help group can become critical, not only for the assistance provided in achieving emotional mastery but also because the individual comes to feel like an integral part of a larger social group. In Naroll's (1983) terms, participation in a mutual-help group may result in an improved condition because of participation in a protective and restorative "moralnet."

How Self-Help Groups Work

While Caplan's model of the ideal family helps us speculate about the important characteristics of self-help groups, psychological research and thinking have expanded our understanding considerably in the past few years. We can identify six aspects of self-help that serve its members' interests. Self-help groups:

(1) Promote the psychological sense of community
(2) Provide an ideology that serves as a philosophical antidote
(3) Provide an opportunity for confession, catharsis, and mutual criticism
(4) Provide role models
(5) Teach effective coping strategies for day-to-day problems
(6) Provide a network of social relationships

Psychological sense of community. Bringing together people who face a common problem overcomes the problem of self-isolation. Another way of putting this is that self-help groups promote a psychological sense of community. Sarason (1974) defines the psychological sense of community as

> [t]he sense that one was part of a readily available, mutually supportive network of relationships upon which one could depend and as a result of which one did not experience sustained feelings of loneliness that impel one to actions or to adopting a style of living masking anxiety and setting the stage for later more destructive anguish. (p. 1)

Discovering that others experience the same problem and feel the same way helps make one's personal crisis a social experience. In Sagarin's terms, the odd man is in. Gay youth who feel isolated and fearful about coming out can find others like them by using the Internet. One said: "When you see people around the world writing the same things, you get the feeling you are not alone. . . . You may be no closer than the modem, but you go, 'Oh my God, that's exactly how I feel' " (Gabriel, 1995). Moreover, for members who feel that their grievances may be attributed to existing social conditions, the personal becomes not only the social but also the political. Members no longer feel isolated, and the group's ideology provides a program for living with and overcoming the core problem. Some groups encourage members to try and change the world or the world's view of their circumstances. This approach was certainly true of many women's consciousness-raising groups, civil rights groups, and gay groups whose aims have included social change as well as personal change.

Ideologies as philosophical (cognitive) antidotes. Self-help groups have more or less articulated ideologies that serve as philosophical or cognitive antidotes to the sense of differentness that haunts members. The dictionary defines ideology as "a system of ideas concerning phenomena, especially those of social life; the manner of thinking characteristic of a class or an individual." Ideologies are based on values that are shared among people and may be used to interpret daily life. An ideology may also be associated with a program of action in keeping with the ideology. Ideologies contribute to a sense of personal identity by defining what an individual should believe, which reduces ambiguity and uncertainty about the world and provides a basis for making choices in everyday life. Many of the articles in *The Liberator* (1994), a newsletter representing aspects of the men's movement, are articulations of a male ideology, developed perhaps in response to the success of the women's movement. The masthead of the newsletter says: "Our definition of men's liberation is freedom *to be* (not from being) men." The articles teach men how to think about themselves and about problems they face as men in a changing world.

Just as every religious group has a body of sacred writings, so many self-help groups have bodies of literature that define the group's beliefs and approach to the common problem. AA's "Twelve Steps" and "Big Book" are primary examples of such core sacred writings. Some groups may not have as precisely delineated a set of beliefs as does AA, but generally speaking such a set of beliefs is identifiable even if not fully detailed (Suler, 1984). Weiss (1987) describes how he developed an ideology for Mothers Against Drunk Driving (MADD) in the form of a therapeutic manual for families who had lost a child to a drunk driver.

Antze (1976) developed a remarkably useful hypothesis about the role of ideologies in self-help. He states that a group's teachings are its very essence and that social scientists have neglected the role of specific self-help group teachings because some teachings seem to contradict others. A group such as AA urges its members to give their problems up to a higher power, arguing that members are powerless to control their situations. On the other hand, a group such as Recovery, Inc., a self-help organization for "nervous people," teaches that members can overcome their problems through an exercise of will power. How can both teachings be correct?

Antze resolves this dilemma by arguing that self-help organizations are specialized. Within this specialization of problem, "It may be possible for a group's ideology to function more precisely, working as a 'cognitive antidote' to basic features of a condition shared by everyone who joins" (p. 327). Given the nature of social organization, anyone having the particular problem is in a

> socially standardized situation. . . . No matter how an individual comes to a given problem, once he arrives he is very much in the same boat with his fellow victims. He comes to cope with life in a similar fashion; he comes to think of himself and others in similar ways; he faces identical problems in trying to change. . . . The ideologies of peer therapy groups may be seen as extremely shrewd and insightful attacks on the most harmful of these stan-

dardized implications. If they have therapeutic value, it is because each manages to break some link in the chain of events maintaining a condition and to provide viable defenses against its renewal. (pp. 328–329)

As examples Antze uses the difference in the core problems of alcoholics and of "nervous" persons such as the members of Recovery, Inc. According to Antze, the core problem of the alcoholic is that:

he exaggerates his own authorship in the events of his life. Sober or drunk, he tends to perceive his world as fashioned mainly by his own acts; somehow he always finds himself at center stage. . . . This group of attitudes adds up to *unrealistic volition.* . . . Problem drinkers have an unusually high need to assert power over people and situations. . . . The alcoholic also feels himself to be sole author of his failures. . . . *To absorb the AA message is to see oneself as much less the author of events in life, the active fighter and doer, and much more as a person with the wisdom to accept limitations and wait for things to come.* (pp. 331–332)

Members of Recovery, Inc., are mental health consumers with complaints of "nervousness." Most experience symptoms that are essentially "ego-alien." In the face of an episode of depression or a panic attack, the person feels he or she is not himself or herself. The symptom appears to come from outside the person, leaving one powerless in the face of it. The ideology of Recovery, Inc., emphasizes the belief that symptoms, no matter how troublesome, are basically within the individual's mind and are therefore capable of being controlled. Members of Recovery, Inc., learn that the one critical faculty, the "Will," can always be utilized to overcome the ego-alien symptom. Recovery, Inc., emphasizes taking specific actions, no matter how small, to exert will against the symptom (Low, 1950); although "the ideologies of AA and Recovery represent mirror images of one another . . . their opposition is explained by an equally marked opposition in the phenomenology of the problems they treat" (p. 337).

Another example of the importance of ideology is provided by the National Alliance for the Mentally Ill (NAMI) groups, whose primary members are families of people with serious mental illness. As a cognitive antidote to problems its members face, the NAMI ideology includes: "(a) belief that family members of a person with mental illness are not pathogenic and dysfunctional themselves, but instead are normal individuals attempting to cope with abnormal events or circumstances; (b) a belief in a biological etiology for schizophrenia and other severe mental illness, plus a rejection of psychogenic theories placing blame on parents and family members; and (c) a belief that clients and family members share with professionals the responsibility for improving services for those with severe mental illness" (Levine, Toro, & Perkins, 1993, p. 540).

Self-help groups develop cultures and specialized languages. Recovery, Inc.'s special language includes procedures for identifying the onset of symptoms (e.g., "spotting" an "angry temper") and taking action to limit the effect of the symptoms (e.g., "swapping thoughts" and "commanding the muscles to relax"). This language is practiced in ritualistic fashion at each meeting, where members are called on to present experiences in which they used the Recovery method to overcome a problem. Other members contribute to the analysis of the experience using the Recovery language. Conceptual tags tied to concrete experiences are thus developed, and the members may take these tags away and use them every day on a minute-by-minute basis.

Al-Anon, an organization for family members of people with alcoholism, follows AA's methods closely. Al-Anon has also developed its own ideas, such as "loving detachment," in which the spouse of the alcoholic is taught to love the alcoholic but not to protect him or her from the consequences of excessive drinking. Al-Anon also teaches its members to "live one day at a time" and to "learn to let go," meaning that the spouse must learn to live his or her own life to recognize and that he or she cannot do anything to control the alcoholic's drinking. These slogans are applied as members discuss their experiences in the group. They take on generalized meaning and may then be used to help the individual decide what to do, if not how to feel, about everyday problems related to the alcoholic spouse and perhaps other problems in living as well. This process can be compared with the way religious sermons use passages from the Bible to show how biblical wisdom can be applied to problems in contemporary life.

Several testable propositions follow from this viewpoint. A member's commitment and understanding of the group's ideology should increase with the length of time in the group. Newer members should have a lesser appreciation of the ideology and use its tenets less often in solving problems in living than veteran members. Using the ideology to help solve other everyday problems results in reduced feelings of hopelessness, increased feelings of self-efficacy, and improved self-esteem.

Data from members of NAMI and of Recovery, Inc., offer support for these propositions. NAMI members who are more involved in their groups and more accepting of the NAMI ideology report reduced feelings of stigma, guilt, and personal responsibility, and more comfortable interactions with mentally ill children (Medvene & Krauss, 1989). Similarly, Galanter (1988) found that the longer a person with mental illness was involved in Recovery, the better was his or her mental health and the less need he or she had for medication and other professional services. Other studies have reported similar results (see a review by Kurtz, 1990). Of course, these results may reflect some self-selection. Those who remained in the groups for longer periods of time may have been stronger persons to begin with or may have found the group, its members, and its procedures more congenial than those who did not stay. Nevertheless, the findings are consistent with theory, and, to the degree that adoption of the ideology correlates with positive coping, the theory's prediction is satisfied.

Confession, catharsis, and mutual criticism. Many groups have a ritualistic format that includes elements of confession, catharsis, and criticism. A sense of group solidarity is developed as members share their feelings and experiences. Members are encouraged to speak of their failures and their problems, experiences that may be associated with lowered self-esteem and guilt. The descriptions of women's consciousness-raising groups provide many examples of confessions of personal inadequacies and quandaries, including honest descriptions of dissatisfaction with sexual relationships and guilt about devoting time to intellectual or professional development instead of to children or husband. By sharing these experiences with others who have "been there," members essentially unload unwanted baggage and find forgiveness. Thoits (1986) hypothesizes that people accept advice or sympathy more readily from someone with whom they can identify. Speaking with and listening to someone who "has been there" may provide more relief than speaking to someone who can only say "I think I know how you feel." Gay youth who used the Internet gay bulletin board seemed to accept counsel from those in similar circumstances where they might not accept help from another source (Gabriel, 1995).

The atmosphere in self-help groups is generally more supportive than that in professionally led therapy groups (Toro et al., 1988), but in some groups, as the feeling of solidarity develops, members feel free to confront each other. This mutual criticism (Levine & Bunker, 1975) is a form of deviance control; it is also a method for enhancing self-esteem. If one lives up to the ideals of the group, by definition one has become a better person. During this experience of sharing, moreover, the group helps the individual learn to use its teachings to overcome the problem. Recovery, Inc., teaches that one need only be "average" and need not be perfect or a superachiever in order to have self-esteem. By adopting that aspect of the ideology, a member can avoid the self-derogation that comes from failing to achieve unattainable goals. Members of consciousness-raising groups help one another let go of the self-imposed demands that they be superwomen and stop trying to excel at the roles of wife, mother, and wage earner to the point of exhaustion.

Role models. Self-help groups create places and roles for individuals. Those who strive to fulfill the group's teachings and are more successful at it become role models for others. Because no formal distinctions exist among members, a new member can easily identify with a more experienced member and say, "If she can overcome this problem, so can I." Even though a given individual may not be able to overcome his or her own problems, for example, that individual understands the difficulty of coping with the problem and is aware of mistakes a person is likely to make. In many instances he or she may be able to give another member the benefit of vicarious learning, transforming something that might have been a matter of shame into an experience of value for the fellow group member. Lois Gibbs serves as a role model for hundreds of people threatened by toxic waste and other pollution problems; she habitually uses examples from her own experiences, including mistakes and her feelings, to instruct others.

The roles of help giver and help receiver are thoroughly interchangeable. Because each member is living with a chronic problem, each will encounter difficulty at one time or another. Even the most successful members may turn to other members of the group for emotional sustenance or support or for help in solving some new problem. Any implication of "inferior" and "superior" positions is reduced because any member may play either role from time to time. Maton (1988) found that those members of self-help groups who both gave and received support had lower levels of depression and higher self-esteem than did those who just received assistance.

Reissman (1965) developed an idea he called the "helper-therapy" principle. It means that the most effective way to learn is to teach and that people who help others may be those who are helped the most. Although not done in a self-help context, research by Li (1989) found that Chinese children randomly selected to teach younger children in preparation for entering the Red Guard, a highly desirable youth group in China, learned public speaking, gained in confidence, and improved their grades in Chinese more than did a control group that lacked the experience of teaching. The effectiveness of this principle can be derived from role theory in that a person playing a role will strive to meet the requirements of that role:

> In effect, as a helper the individual displays mastery over the afflicting condition—plays the role of a nonaddict, for example—and thereby acquires the appropriate skills, attitudes, behaviors and mental set. Having modeled this for others, the individual may see him or herself as behaving in a new way and may, in effect, take on the new role as his or her own. (Gartner & Reissman, 1977, p. 103)

Some persons become active leaders in self-help organizations and build new identities and lifestyles around the membership role. Some women who participated in consciousness-raising groups and political activities associated with the women's movement subsequently changed their dress, their appearance, their demeanor, the language they used, the people with whom they interacted, their activities, and their goals. Members of AA or Al-Anon who engage in twelfth-step work by becoming speakers to other groups illustrate the point; one person in deep difficulty can gain esteem from others by revealing his history in an effort to bring the message to others; a leader in the father's rights movement tells about how his family has learned to share him with the group because he is called on so much by other members.

Coping strategies. By sharing day-by-day experiences, members discover and share proven coping devices. Because the individuals are in a "standardized situation," their problems generally recur, and the solutions that one member passes on to another are pertinent for their respective circumstances. Al-Anon members teach one another not to lie to the spouse's boss to cover up for a spouse who misses work due to a hangover. Members learn to protect their own integrity and learn that their behavior is enabling their spouses' drinking. They can then act without interpreting their actions as "betrayals" of their love for their spouses. Members of the group encourage one another to experiment with new solutions, support one another through any failures, and rejoice even at members' small successes. Members of the Love Canal Homeowners Association who often had to deal with the media learned how to get their major points across to journalists in a few minutes or even seconds by practicing and critiquing one another.

Social relationships. Members provide a network of friends and social relationships not readily available otherwise to the person struggling with social disqualification or with adaptive demands that others who do not share the problem may fail to understand. Members celebrate happy occasions with each other, socialize, have parties, and provide companionship. Salem, Seidman, and Rappaport (1988) reported that GROW, a self-help group for persons with serious mental illness, provided its members with an entire social network. Members of some groups go further and provide concrete help to one another. For example, Reach is a self-help group for relatives of people with mental illness that is sponsored by the Buffalo and Erie County chapter of the National Association for Mental Health. Its members provide respite care for each other; a member who needs a short vacation or rest period may ask another member, experienced in handling the problems of mental illness, to look after the ill family member. Members reciprocate and provide here-and-now assistance for one another. Many groups, including AA, and weight-loss groups, provide new members with sponsors who may be called at any time, day or night, for assistance. Help is delivered when and where it is needed, "on call" so to speak, in the situation where the problem arises.

Self-Help and Ecological Concepts

As we noted in introducing this chapter, self-help groups can also be understood by using the ecological principles and concepts discussed in earlier chapters. Self-help groups represent a broadly applicable mode of intervention, for example, yet they address the ecological fact of diversity among people and their needs by providing relatively precise ideological antidotes that can be tailored to any vulnerable condition. In this respect self-help groups illustrate a point we made about social support in Chapter 7: The specific resources a supportive network provides may be more important to its effectiveness than the size of the group or how it is structured.

Self-help groups are also understandable as ecological settings that improve the degree of behavioral adaptation to the community by improving person-environment fit. In the ideology of self-help groups, improved adaptation follows from concrete, practical changes in behavior. Members of Narcotics Anonymous recognize that former companions provide temptations to use drugs again. They recommend that the recovering addict change his or her "playpen and playmates." Such concrete behaviors can be understood as joint properties of people and settings. We earlier characterized vulnerability as a poor fit between the individual's behavioral repertoire and the demands of settings in his or her life. Participation in new settings enlarges the individual's behavioral repertoire and expands the available community niches, increasing the person's niche breadth. Consumer members of some self-help groups are invited to be members of advisory councils for government agencies; others may testify at public hearings. Members of Al-anon are encouraged to care for themselves by seeking jobs or taking advantage of recreational opportunities.

Two ecological principles of practice are relevant. By what specific mechanisms does participation in a self-help group produce behavior change? How is change maintained? For specific theoretical answers to these questions, recall the three psychological conceptions of Moos, Barker, and Sarbin that were first examined in Chapter 5. In Moos's psychosocial climate conception, for example, one important dimension of a setting is its relationship-oriented qualities. Because membership in most groups is relatively open-ended (the only requirement for membership in AA, for example, is a desire to stop drinking), self-help groups are high in their support and acceptance of participants (Toro, Rappaport, & Seidman, 1987). Support and acceptance serve to reduce self-isolation and to increase the psychological sense of community among members. Relationship-oriented aspects of the climate are also enhanced by a strengthened and expanded network of friendships involving reversible roles, sponsorship, and other activities or contacts outside the meetings.

A second important psychosocial dimension is the degree to which a setting fosters participants' personal development. Important responsibilities, such as those implied by sponsorship and by Reissman's helper-therapy principle, strengthen the personal development dimensions of a self-help group's climate. Clear differences likely exist among groups on specific personal development dimensions, however, reflecting the different directions that personal development ideally takes in different groups (e.g., the importance of taking willful control of one's life in Recovery, Inc., versus the emphasis on acquiring the serenity to accept what one cannot change in AA). Those in groups such as Al-Anon often emphasize that members can come from all walks of life, all socioeconomic and educational backgrounds; yet within the group they still experience a strong sense of equality and mutual understanding. Moos would explain this by suggesting that the social climate, not the specific members as individuals, defines the group experience and accounts for its effects.

In Barker's conception of behavior settings, self-help groups provide alternative settings that the individual can use in structuring his or her time. To a certain extent, group meetings compete with other settings for the person's time, and the standing patterns of behavior they enforce (through the principle of behavior-environment congruence) are risk-reducing in their incompatibility with the maladaptive responses that formerly characterized members' behavior. When a member first begins the AA program, he or she may attend meetings every night in the week, and sometimes during the day as well. The person lives out some portion of his or her life in a new setting.

As behavior settings, moreover, self-help groups instill the specific coping devices and other adaptive responses necessary to cope successfully with the core problem. Recall Barker's description of the person-environment circuits that define all settings. First, goal circuits represent the member's motivation to change (e.g., to stop drinking). The ritualistic procedures in meetings constitute the program circuits. These include confession ("Hi, my name is Jane, and I'm an alcoholic"), catharsis ("here's my story"), and acceptance (applause, handshakes, and hugs). Processes such as confrontation serve a corrective, "deviation-countering" function that may not be present in other settings in the person's life. The chronic nature of the problem situation provides multiple opportunities for learning, rehearsing, and generalizing the new behavioral responses required to improve the vulnerable individual's fit with key community settings.

Unless the individual's repertoire of responses is permanently changed, however, the recurring nature of most problems increases the chance of relapse into the old maladaptive ways. Clinical treatment, being expensive and thus short term, often must be repeated, leading to the "revolving-door" syndrome whereby clients must frequently return for another round of care. Self-help groups, on the other hand, are stable, enduring communities—permanent fixtures in the community habitat. While maladaptation is chronic and recurrent, so are the meetings of self-help groups.

One limitation of self-help groups is that as settings they are bounded in time and space. The existence of a group on paper or in the telephone book does not mean that it is actually available to everyone in need. Given the huge numbers of people at risk implied by the view of life as a soap opera, multiple-setting occasions may be needed weekly in many communities. In this connection, Zimmerman et al. (1991) illustrate how behavior-setting principles can be used to explain the successful proliferation of GROW groups among people with mental illness. Rather than waiting to start a new group only when an existing group had grown too large, GROW organizers exploited contacts with professionals, educational workshops, and the media to establish fledgling groups well in advance of demand from potential members. One result was that these new groups were very "underpopulated" as behavior settings (see Chapter 5), and the resulting pressure on members to occupy more than one role (e.g., help giver as well as help receiver) increased the salience and importance of each individual member and helped to ensure members' commitment to the continuation of their group.

In terms of Sarbin's role theory, self-help groups help structure the various ecologies that surround the vulnerable individual. In the social ecology, a self-help group provides an egalitarian network of peer relationships that reduces isolation and helps to relieve the ambiguity and uncertainty imposed by the real world. Members of the self-help group also respect the individual and help him or her to gain self-respect. The group's ideology also provides a sense of meaningful integrity to the individual's transcendental needs. In cases where other group members provide material aid outside group meetings, such as a place to stay, they enhance even the individual's self-maintenance ecology.

Generally speaking, membership in a self-help group provides important new roles for people otherwise disqualified by some form of stigma. These roles sidestep the negative aspects of the individual's vulnerable condition and instead offer opportunities for responsibility and leadership that are flexible and open-ended in the degrees of involvement they require. Although these factors improve the individual's self-perceptions, the effects of this role enhancement on the public identities of self-help group members are unclear, because membership is usually a private (and often even anonymous) matter.

Are Self-Help Groups Effective?

It is difficult to evaluate the effectiveness of self-help groups because the membership tends to be shifting and because some self-help groups have little interest in cooperating with research on their impact. For the most part we rely on the testimonials of those who are members. Members of self-help groups see themselves as being there to help others with similar problems, not to be research subjects. Leaders point to their personal growth and the growth of the movement as adequate evidence of their effectiveness. We rarely hear about the dropouts from self-help organizations or about their failures. Few if any substantial studies have researched comparable populations served by self-help groups and by professional helpers, so we cannot say that one mode of treatment is more or less effective than another.

Given there are difficult methodological and field problems, a large number of uncontrolled studies have yielded positive results on a variety of criteria. Studies comparing professional help with self-help have generally found that self-help group members improve, and, other than occasional findings that professional care is superior, there is little difference between self-help outcomes and professional outcomes (Levine, Toro, & Perkins, 1993). On the basis of a review of the self-help evaluative literature, Kurtz (1990) concluded that "most involved members report greater life satisfaction, shorter hospital stays if rehospitalized, less dependence on professionals, raised self esteem and improved attitudes [toward life]" (p.110). However, she noted that no one has clearly demonstrated with standardized instruments that self-help membership results in the removal of symptoms and cautioned professionals who refer clients not to expect too much of the group.

The GROW organization, which originated in Australia and uses a modified AA model, received an extensive evaluation when it was established in Illinois. Systematic studies by Rappaport, Seidman, Toro, and their colleagues and students found that the more a member attended GROW meetings, the more positive change the member showed. Moreover, members who attended more frequently also developed more effective coping strategies. Members who attended GROW meetings for at least nine months had a greater number of social relationships, more occupational success, and better mental health functioning than did those who attended for fewer months. Compared to a matched sample of persons with similar psychiatric histories, GROW members were less likely to be rehospitalized. A similar evaluation of GROW has been done in Australia (Young, 1992), and studies of related groups like Recovery, Inc., show comparable results (Galanter, 1988).

As with any heterogeneous group, however, people with mental illness present a diverse spectrum of needs, and any given group is unlikely to meet the needs of all members (Young & Williams, 1988). While GROW apparently helps those who participate, a dropout rate of about 25 percent after the first meeting indicates selection bias and suggests that a select group whose characteristics are not well understood may benefit the most (Levine, Toro, & Perkins, 1993). On the other hand, the dropout rate from self-help groups is probably not terribly different from the dropout rate in psychotherapy.

Self-help group members who have had experience with professional helping services frequently assert that they get something different from the self-help group than they do from professional helpers (Videka-Sherman & Lieberman, 1985). For some, that difference is striking. Some members assert that professional assistance was no help at all and sometimes even made them feel guilty about having the problem for which they sought help; others claim that they get something different from professional assistance than they get from participation in self-help groups and value the opportunity to work problems through on an individual basis.

Many women who participated in consciousness-raising groups were also in psychotherapy. Judging from responses to a survey instrument, women in consciousness-raising groups were dissatisfied with their lives. On standardized scales of depression, anxiety, and other psychological symptoms, they appeared more distressed than a control sample of women who were not in groups. However, they were less distressed than women in outpatient treatment (Videka-Sherman & Lieberman, 1985). Some people who are in self-help groups and who are more distressed may need professional assistance; thus, members of Recovery, Inc., who often take prescribed medication, are encouraged to respect their doctor's authority and to comply with professional advice.

We need not take a black-and-white view of the situation, seeing one form of help as all good and another as all bad or one as superior to the other. Ideally, we should examine each modality carefully to see what each can learn from the other about the therapeutic change process. Some professionals believe that the federal mandate to include patients and their families and representatives of self-help groups on the planning councils of mental health centers helps professional agencies learn to make their services more responsive to the needs of their clients (Segal, Silverman, & Temkin, 1993).

AA and Recovery from Alcoholism

Alcoholism is a devastating disorder that affects tens of millions of Americans (see Chapter 1) and costs the United States an estimated $90 billion per year in expenditures for health care and law enforcement and in its general toll on economic productivity (National Institute on Alcohol Abuse and Alcoholism, 1983). The scope and severity of these problems make alcoholism a major challenge to all help-giving professions. Many professionals freely admit that in the area of alcoholism the effectiveness of their services leaves much to be desired. Perhaps as a result, AA groups are frequently welcomed into hospitals and prisons to recruit members. Although alcoholism is correctly perceived as a relatively intransigent problem and the probability of stable recovery following any given episode of alcoholism is apparently only minimally assisted by formal treatment (Orford & Edwards, 1977; Vaillant, 1983), complete recovery does occur in about half of all cases. Recent evidence suggests that most recovery from alcoholism is attributable to relatively specific "natural healing" processes.

Perhaps the best illustration of this phenomenon comes from the large-scale follow-up studies undertaken by Vaillant (1983). Vaillant's data came from two large cohorts of initially normal males, one upper-middle-class (N = 204) and one working-class (N = 456), each of which was followed from the late 1930s until 1980. Comprehensive and sophisticated measures were taken regarding the incidence of alcoholism and other behavioral characteristics in these samples, and the prospective longitudinal research design enabled Vaillant to untangle specific temporal sequences among many often-related events (for example, the frequent relationship breakups that occurred among alcoholic subjects were more often found to be a consequence of prior heavy drinking than its cause).

Conditions found directly to precede stable recovery from alcoholism included the following specific changes in lifestyle and/or circumstances: (1) development of a *substitute dependency*, such as candy, tranquilizers, heavy smoking, or compulsive work or hobbies; (2) new *constraints* on drinking, either external (e.g., close supervision from a spouse, employer, or judge) or internal (e.g., threats to health, use of Antabuse); (3) increased involvement in religion or some analogous spiritual or ideological experience (such an experience typically helped the alcoholic replace feelings of defeat, worthlessness, helplessness, and guilt with renewed hope, self-esteem, and a powerful new belief system that enabled him to swear off his old maladaptive lifestyle for a new one); and (4) focused *social support*, often in the form of a new (or renewed) love relationship (e.g., with a spouse or other family member or another recovering alcoholic).

Many subjects in Vaillant's samples changed their lives and recovered from alcoholism more or less on their own. Given the specific changes required, however, it is not surprising that the single most effective intervention for alcoholism was AA (see also Polich, Armor, & Braiker, 1981). Although it is certainly no panacea, AA does embody all of the natural recovery processes to an extent that no other contemporary treatment program can. AA facilitates fundamental changes in the alcoholic's belief system, provides an unambiguous conception of the disorder (the disease theory) that is meaningful to the alcoholic, and gives a sense of hope in the possibility of recovery. Thus the alcoholic's previous faith in alcohol as the most dependable source of gratification is turned into a belief in the "curse" of alcohol as the cause of all life's pain, and this new attitude is strongly enforced through adherence to total abstinence as the only acknowledged path to recovery.

The fellowship and support provided by other AA members, both during the actual meetings and when needed at other times and places, are powerful reinforcers in the life of the isolated alcoholic and induce strong tendencies to affiliate and identify. As Edwards et al. (1967) point out:

> Identification is not with any one established member so much as with fragments of a whole series of life histories which are synthesized into identification with the group ideal. . . . Identification assumes particular importance in the leaderless group which must have a clear and firmly established picture of the ideal member. (p. 203)

Identification is easier with other recovering alcoholics than with a professional therapist both because of the obvious similarities among those recovering from the same problem and because of the way psychotherapy is structured asymmetrically (i.e., so that personal disclosure and motivation to change flow only from client to therapist, while effective help and support are assumed to flow only from therapist to client). The social support provided by AA's more reversible roles is clearly expressed in this enthusiastic testimonial from one of Vaillant's upper-middle-class alcoholics:

> Most alcoholics, I believe, grow up in a glass isolation booth which they build for themselves to separate themselves from other people. . . . AA shows us how to dissolve the glass walls around us and realize that there are other people out there, good loving people. . . . I love the AA meetings and love being able to call people up when I feel tense. Occasionally, someone calls me for help and that makes me feel good. I get much more out of this than I got from decades of psychiatry. My relationship with a psychiatrist always seemed to be distressingly cold. I hated the huge bills. For $50 an hour, one doctor kept assuring me that I was nutty to worry about money, and at the time I couldn't keep up my life insurance. I wish there were some form of Alcoholics Anonymous for troubled people who don't drink. We old drunks are lucky. (p. 208)

AA reaches an estimated 650,000 alcoholics in the United States, twice as many as do all hospitals, clinics, and physicians combined (Baekeland et al., 1975). Thousands of AA groups exist in this country, and in a large city it would be rare not to find a group meeting at almost any hour on any day of the week, making AA much more accessible than formal treatment for alcoholism. This ready availability was important to those of Vaillant's subjects who were already flirting with sobriety for one reason or another (e.g., a health problem, a love relationship) and who were able to take advantage of AA's accessibility to help cement the changes in behavior they were already trying to accomplish.

Another important explanation for AA's effectiveness is that the duration of participation in AA is generally much longer than it is in formal treatment; it lasts months, years, or even a lifetime as opposed to a few weeks. One consequence is that the whole meaning of one's relationship to AA is different; one "visits" a treatment clinic, and one "belongs" to AA. The lasting impact of AA's communally shared rituals, performed again and again over months or years of participation, is understandable from Barker's ecological conception, since in that view maintaining continuities in an individual's behavior over time is simply a matter of maintaining continuity in the specific settings in which he or she participates. Although structuring one's time by frequent attendance at AA meetings may become a new "addiction" substituting for time previously spent with alcohol, the risks associated with active alcoholism presumably far outweigh those involved in addiction to AA.

The very question of an addiction to AA reflects the assumptions of the medical model. Operating with the medical model, we feel we ought to be able to cure and discharge the client so that he or she can stand alone, without "crutches." These expectations partly reflect our concern about the cost of treatment and the value that should be returned. AA may reflect another model entirely. We would think it ludicrous if a patient remained in psychoanalysis for an entire adult lifetime, but we might think it admirable if another person remained a member of a church and participated in its activities for an adult lifetime. AA in its underlying model more resembles a church or a fraternal order than it does group therapy. Galanter (1989, 1990) characterizes AA as a charismatic healing group. He recognizes that while AA has features in common with charismatic religious sects and even some cults, it is also differentiated from religious sects along a number of dimensions: AA members relate to the organization because of their common drinking problem; AA makes no demands on how members live their lives, except that they abstain from alcohol; AA's target is the drinking behavior of its members; AA has no interest in proselytizing to transform the beliefs of others.

We noted in Chapter 4 that self-help groups recycle resources more efficiently than do professionally directed programs. Joining AA, for example, involves little cost and puts no burden on health insurance. The member makes voluntary donations and can go to a meeting for little more than coffee money and perhaps the cost of some AA literature. The question of lifetime reliance on AA or similar groups can be examined only in relation to the assumptions that led us to raise the questions in the first place. Are we concerned about lifelong membership because, under medical model assumptions, a healing technology should simply heal and then allow a person to get on with his or her life? If so, we may need to reexamine that assumption from a societal perspective.

These characteristics make AA a clear illustration of the ecological principle that interventions should take a form that can be maintained as a natural part of the community (see Chapter 4). That is, AA begins with a natural resource, indigenous residents of the community, and defines their involvement as participation in a setting entailing nominal cost over an indefinite length of time. Although the most serious conditions of risk are episodic, the members' basic need for this setting is ongoing, and many in the vulnerable population recognize the value of maintaining a relationship with AA similar to the one with their church or fraternal society.

Al-Anon, an offshoot of AA, is a self-help group for spouses or other relatives of alcoholics who are not alcoholic themselves. Al-Anon operates much as AA does. Gillick (1977) conducted a controlled experiment in which wives of patients hospitalized for alcoholism at a VA hospital were randomly assigned to attend an Al-Anon group for six weeks or to do nothing different during that time. More than two-thirds of the spouses of alcoholics attended six or more Al-Anon meetings over the six-week period of the study. Gillick used the Community Adaptation Scale, a 217-item, self-administered measure that evaluates a person's community activities in a number of different spheres: work, family, personal, civic, commercial, professional services (see Roen & Burns, 1968). Gillick used the scale because research on the wives of alcoholics had indicated that they were frequently socially isolated.

After six weeks the group that had attended Al-Anon meetings showed a number of changes compared to the control group. Spouses who attended Al-Anon reported better and more frequent interaction with family and friends and an overall positive change in community adaptation. The control group showed deterioration on some of the scales over the same period. On posttest interviews, fourteen of the fifteen Al-Anon attenders rated the experience "very helpful" or "extremely helpful," and all fifteen were able to describe some benefit from attending meetings. Most often they expressed themselves in terms reflecting Al-Anon's ideology: "I liked the idea of living one day at a time and learning to let go"; "It made me realize there is practically nothing I can do to stop his drinking once he starts." All but two of the fifteen spouses said they planned to continue attending Al-Anon meetings. These short-term results are similar to those claimed for Al-Anon by its long-term members. This controlled experiment demonstrated the systematic benefits of attending the groups beyond those resulting simply from the passage of time and treatment of the alcoholic spouse in the hospital.

Vaillant concludes that at present natural healing processes involved in recovery from alcoholism seem to be far more significant than what formal treatment can provide. About half of alcoholics do recover eventually, and the power of natural healing has long been used by physicians in the treatment of wounds and other conditions where zealous intervention can do more harm than good. Because apparently no amount of formal treatment increases the likelihood of permanent recovery from alcoholism beyond that contributed by natural healing, the most useful role for formal treatment at present is not to pursue increasingly intensive and costly services for a limited number of individual clients but to facilitate the natural healing process in as many alcoholics as possible.

Vaillant's own program, for example, the Cambridge and Somerville Program for Alcohol Rehabilitation (CASPAR), is a comprehensive community-based system set up to lower the incidence and prevalence of alcohol problems by providing an array of medical services, support groups, halfway houses, and educational programs. In a typical year CASPAR receives twenty thousand outpatient visits, conducts twenty-five hundred detoxifications, and adds one thousand new alcoholic clients to its rolls, all at a cost of only about $1 million (Vaillant, 1983). The primary long-term goal of CASPAR is to involve alcoholics with AA.

A potentially important role for existing alcoholism treatment services thus exists if their efforts are part of a comprehensive effort to reduce incidence and prevalence across the entire community. Gillick's study also showed that professionals can cooperate with self-help programs by making referrals and encouraging their clients to participate. Reasoning from the helper-therapy principle, Gartner and Reissman (1977) suggest that one way of overcoming the "numbers problem" in providing help (see Chapter 1) is by finding ways to

transform recipients of help into new dispensers of help, thus reversing their roles, and to structure the situation so that recipients of help will be placed in roles requiring the giving of assistance. The helper-therapy principle operates, of course, in all kinds of peer help situations, in peer counseling in schools, children teaching children or mutual help groups. Therefore, all situations involving human service should be restructured to allow the principle to operate more fully. (p. 106)

Vaillant's research took place before the widespread use of other substances began to complicate treatment for alcoholism. In 1991, fully 26 percent of some 812,000 clients in alcohol and drug abuse treatment units had both alcohol and substance abuse problems (U.S. Bureau of the Census, 1993, Table 207). How the existence of a dual diagnosis complicates the effectiveness of all treatment modalities, including self-help, remains to be seen.

Starting Self-Help Groups. The relationship between professionals and self-help groups has become an important focus of discussion (Katz, 1981). The various alternatives proposed range from essentially no relationship (i.e., where each pursues its helping efforts independently) through some degree of formalized cooperation (e.g., mutual referrals, communication regarding community needs and services) to direct connection and mutual influence.

Self-help groups are sometimes seen as external agents with the potential to "humanize" the professional system of care (Gartner & Reissman, 1977; Segal, Silverman, & Temkin, 1993). More often, however, direct influences probably involve efforts by professionals to create or maintain self-help as one reliable alternative for a particular group at risk. Each chapter of Parents Anonymous, for example, has its own professional sponsor to facilitate the group's functioning. Another option is for professionals simply to stimulate the formation of a group, thereafter leaving its operation largely or entirely in the hands of the members.

The active involvement of professionals can change the character of the group. Professionally led parent groups do not exhibit shared control with members and use a medical model of service delivery. They also engage in little outreach (Cherniss & Cherniss, 1987). Toro et al. (1988) reported that the group atmosphere is different under professional leadership and under member leadership. Segal et al. (1993) believe that consumer-led groups and agencies enhance empowerment of the members and help members to overcome stigma, whereas professionally led agencies may inadvertently support a view that consumers are limited in their abilities to govern themselves. With the exception of AA, survival rates for groups formed with professional assistance are not necessarily higher than for independently established groups, but professionals seem to play an important part in establishing new groups (Leventhal, Maton, & Madara, 1988; Galanter, 1990).

One illustration of this approach of "seeding" the formation of a self-help group is the work of some graduate students and faculty in the department of psychology at the State University of New York at Buffalo who established a self-help group for parents of young diabetic children. Diabetes is a very serious condition when diagnosed in a child under the age of four or five; the child is at greatly increased risk for weight problems, blindness, and early death. The parents in these cases are usually provided with sufficient medical resources and attention, but given the incomplete state of knowledge about the disease, in many communities the only resource available for dealing with sometimes overwhelming emotional and psychological consequences is short-term individual and family psychotherapy. For many parents this option is less than satisfactory, because it requires them to define their problems in personal terms and to accept what some feel is a stigmatizing label and because it does not directly combat the day-to-day feelings of stress and isolation brought on by the child's health crisis.

The Buffalo project began when faculty members contacted the Juvenile Diabetes Foundation of Western New York, an organization made up of parents of diabetics and others interested in helping to raise money, provide information, and generally improve research and treatment efforts for diabetes. The community psychology representatives offered their services as consultants in an open-ended arrangement. In the course of meetings with parents, the group decided that the parents of toddlers newly diagnosed as diabetics presented the most compelling focus for consultation. The parents were contacted through Children's Hospital of Buffalo, which serves all diabetic children in the metropolitan area, and informal group interviews and discussions were arranged.

An interested member of the foundation contacted parents of newly diagnosed young children and invited them to participate in a session with other parents and the student and faculty consultants. The stated purpose of this meeting was to identify parents' common difficulties and to evaluate different strategies for coping with them. The consultants expected that simply providing a forum conducive for parents to bring problems out in the open would reduce their sense of isolation, enable them to establish informal communication links, and indicate the extent of any unmet need for help in the members of this group.

During these informal sessions the consultants took the position that they were interested in gathering information about situations that posed particular difficulties for the parents. What emerged was a list of problems most likely to create psychological stress and exacerbate the new family crisis. One problem area involved managing the child's day-to-day behavior in the context of diabetes (e.g., using the "correct" mix of discipline and flexibility; understanding what normal "monster" behavior is).

Another problem area involved educating other caretakers, such as relatives, baby-sitters, teachers, and other parents about diabetic children's unique dietary needs and restrictions (for example, at birthday parties), their ways of manipulating caretakers regarding the diabetes, and the symptoms of insulin reactions.

Dealing with other children in the family was a third problem common to many parents; coping with the inevitable acute medical crises (for example, severe insulin shock that leaves the child unconscious) was a fourth. A last consistent experience encountered by many families was the so-called predinner crisis, where tensions, fatigue, and irritability among all family members late in the day often build up into more than the usual amount of unwanted conflict and disruption.

The procedure adopted by the consultants for identifying systematic strategies and beliefs to support a viable self-help process was similar to that used by Spivack and Shure (see Chapter 8) in developing the ingredients of a competence-building primary prevention program for preschool children. The key to understanding the ingredients of successful coping was assumed to reside in the specific informational, behavioral, and attitudinal differences that differentiated parents who were handling their predicament well from those who appeared to be experiencing significant distress.

Following Antze's (1976) views, the consultants focused on the differentiation of "pathological" beliefs (i.e., thoughts and feelings that directly led to emotional upsets and maladaptive responses) from the "cognitive antidotes" that might be used explicitly to counteract these beliefs. For example, one pathological cognition identified was the question "Why me?" Some parents asked themselves this repeatedly, and it made even more acute the perceived loss of prior freedoms and other advantages they might have enjoyed. Another of these maladaptive thoughts was the obsessive reminder "I must protect and supervise my child very closely." Taken to extremes, this would make the problem even more disruptive for the child, the parents, and other family members. A third pathological belief was the persistent realization that "There's *so much more* I have to do now," leading the parent to perceive an immense new burden of potentially overwhelming proportions.

As Antze would have predicted, however, for each pathological belief expressed by individuals in this vulnerable condition, a corresponding antidote was provided by other members of the group. For the question "Why me?" the successful copers prescribed accepting the situation for what it is but, more important, wherever possible relabeling powerful feelings such as anxiety or shame in terms of more constructive emotions, such as anger, which better enable parents to advocate for the child and also see to it that their own needs are met. Concerning the intense new responsibilities to protect and supervise the child, these parents recommended allowing the children to be as normal as possible under the circumstances (e.g., to experience normal relationships with other children and with adults), helping them learn to care for themselves where appropriate (e.g., self-administering insulin injections when old enough), and so on. To those overwhelmed by all the new tasks, these parents replied with such useful epigrams as "Some things are easier to let the child do," "It doesn't have to be done in a day," or, when facing others' stupidity or insensitivity, "Ignorance wasn't conquered in a day."

They were even able to point out a few limited but nonetheless useful advantages brought about by their child's diabetes, such as the fact that preparing food for the family that is free of sugar offers a much healthier diet for everyone and is usually more economical as well.

These adaptive beliefs and coping strategies generated by the parents were organized and written up as a preliminary body of "sacred writings," that is, an articulated philosophy, along with additional suggestions regarding general ground rules the group might find useful. Among these ground rules, for example, were recommendations that parents be tolerant of differences among them in parenting styles, ways of expressing feelings, and readiness to disclose personal or otherwise sensitive information and that all information brought out in meetings concerning personal matters be kept strictly confidential to facilitate frank and open discussion.

With a good level of organized feedback, and periodic contacts with a graduate student consultant, the self-help group began holding regular meetings on its own. They continued meetings for about two years. As a result of conflict with the sponsoring organization, some members affiliated with different factions. One of the leaders seemed to have "burned out" and stopped being active; another decided to devote her time to fund-raising activities. Both leaders felt that the group experience had been valuable, however, and they continued to have an affectionate interest in the graduate student consultant.

Involvement of professionals in self-help groups can take different forms and in specific cases is best determined by clear communication and careful planning among all interested parties. Professional efforts on behalf of a variety of chronic or otherwise intransigent conditions may be most helpful when they assist the functioning of self-help alternatives and capitalize on nature's own paths to coping and recovery.

Advocacy Groups

The National Alliance for the Mentally Ill (NAMI) was formed to support the families of people with mental illness and to engage in political and social action to affect the mental health system (Levine, Toro, & Perkins, 1993). NAMI arose in response to the deinsitutionalization movement of the 1960s and 1970s, which greatly increased the burden of care placed on the families of mentally ill people, and on the drive to include consumers on mental health center boards. Increased consumer and citizen involvement put people with similar problems in touch with one another, and in 1979 NAMI was founded with 284 members. By 1989 it had 1050 chapters in all states, with an overall membership of 130,000. In addition to providing mutual support, NAMI has been successful in advocating for better local services (crisis intervention, respite care), lobbying for Social Security disability income and insurance coverage for individuals with severe mental illness, and expanding legal grounds for the involuntary commitment of persons with mental illness. (This last goal is not supported by members of the patients' rights movement, which sees the mental health system as oppressive.)

NAMI has worked to reduce the cost of the drug Clozapine, a medication that is effective with some patients who do not respond to other treatment. NAMI is powerful politically and has influenced the approach to schizophrenia taken by the National Institute of Mental Health in its grant programs. In addition, it has its own research foundation and awards about $1 million per year for research in keeping with its biologically based view of mental illness. The group has also been active in combating the effects of stigma and has worked actively to influence professional training and professionals' views of family members.

Professionals take no leadership positions in NAMI or in its local chapters unless they have mentally ill relatives; they are involved only as consultants or as members of professional advisory groups. The majority of members are relatives of those with mental illnesses, although some current or former patients are also active. Local chapters act as support groups for members, who may share common experiences or organize activities that assist members in coping. For example, some members who have been estranged from children suffering with a mental illness miss celebrating holidays such as Christmas with their children. A local AMI chapter organized Christmas parties for children with disabilities or mental illness, and members participated by hosting parties and giving the children gifts, helping in some small way to make up for a void in their own lives.

Local groups, however, are also organized for grassroots advocacy and attempt to influence state and local officials to improve services. Family members and mental health officials have diverging views about which services are most needed. NAMI members (93 percent) believe that community-based residences certified by the Office of Mental Health are the most desirable living arrangements, but only 21 percent of their mentally ill relatives were living in such a facility (Grosser & Vine, 1991).

NAMI members receive current scientific information about mental illness, medications, rehabilitation services, and alternative ways to understand severe mental illness. They also receive authoritative information about insurance practices. We have already described components of the NAMI ideology, and members absorb that ideology through meetings and literature.

Despite these successes, the organization does face some limitations. It's current membership consists primarily of white, upper-middle-class, well-educated parents of mentally ill adults. The organization is attempting to broaden its base, but it may be difficult to overcome social, economic, and cultural barriers. Sometimes the interests of members who have themselves been hospitalized with mental illness conflict with the interests of parents. A case in point is the organization's emphasis on making involuntary hospitalization less difficult. Parents who worry about their adult children living on the streets or decompensating want the system to be more responsive to their needs and perspectives, making it easier to hospitalize people when necessary. The adult children themselves, the consumers who have had bad experiences with involuntary hospitalization, prefer to retain due-process safeguards that make it more difficult to commit people involuntarily and preserve consumers' rights to request discharge from the hospital.

Starting an Advocacy Group

Thomas Shea is a staff member at People, Inc., of Buffalo, New York, an organization that provides care in community-based group homes and supported apartments for individuals with mental retardation. Shea decided to organize a self-advocacy group among the people with whom he worked. He was influenced by his knowledge of a self-advocacy movement among individuals with mental retardation and also by his reading in community psychology and self-help.

Shea and another counselor invited nine people they knew to an organizational meeting. (We use the term "people" or "persons" because the ideology of the self-advocacy movement objects to terms such as "client," "residents," or "patients," preferring words like "persons," "individuals," or "citizens.") They were introduced to the concepts of self-advocacy through a film developed by the Self-Advocacy Association of New York State, Inc. The film centered on Bernard Carbello, who spent eighteen years of his life in a state institution. Viewers were introduced to the ideas that their opinions have value, people have the power to help bring about changes, and citizens have rights and responsibilities. The film evidently spoke to the interests of members, who applauded and cheered when ideas like improving wages and working conditions in the sheltered workshop were mentioned.

With the help of the two advisers, the group elected officers and assigned responsibilities. All members were encouraged to participate in some way in group projects. The group planned a successful fund-raiser that helped promote group cohesiveness. Over several weekly meetings the group adopted a set of goals, including helping change society's attitudes toward people with disabilities; helping people with disabilities to help themselves and to make decisions collaboratively with agencies and committees that previously had made decisions for them; making an effort to volunteer in the community; attending self-advocacy conventions to meet other people and learn more about self-advocacy; obtaining more jobs for people with disabilities; and raising money to help accomplish these goals. This list of goals was used at subsequent meetings.

Participants were encouraged to discuss their own experiences in relation to the goals. They were exposed to self-advocacy slogans such as "Label jars, not people" and "Don't think that we don't think." Members increasingly discussed their experiences of feeling stigmatized or abused. Members shared problems such as their concern over unfair treatment by a supervisor in the workshop and received advice from others. Members also participated in political decisions that affected their lives. They drafted a letter expressing concern about the threatened shutdown of public transportation and sent it to the county executive and the county legislature. They also drafted and sent a letter to the metropolitan newspaper commenting on the assault of a disabled member of the group on a bus. This letter gave group members the opportunity to express their feelings about wanting to live a normal life, free of fear from the unthinking actions of others, and they used the letter to advertise the existence of their group.

Being a group member enhanced self-esteem as well. One member was quoted as saying, "Now people really know we can do something big because this group is our own." The group obtained some recognition when members were contacted about serving on boards or on committees that affected their lives. Several members expressed confidence that they could serve, whereas before they had been quite reticent and lacking in self-confidence. These activities were in keeping with the self-advocacy credo that persons with mental retardation are citizens, not patients or clients.

The group's advisers were quite active in developing the program but hoped that their role would diminish as group members developed greater competence and confidence. At the time Shea described it, the group had been operating for about four months. It remains to be seen how well the group will function with less input from the organizers and whether it can survive changes in personnel and the inevitable frustrations it will encounter in trying to achieve its aims. Nonetheless, this example suggests that self-advocacy can be stimulated even in a group that many of us might write off because of the nature of the members' limitations. Moreover, processes that were apparent in other self-help groups were also identifiable in this self-advocacy group, suggesting that the self-help conceptualization has considerable generalizability.

The Internet as a Self-Help Resource

The Internet and the widespread availability of home computers will eventually affect our lives in unforeseeable ways. We already read about office workstations in the home and about "telecommuting." These developments will affect where we live as well as the way we live and work. Rapidly proliferating on-line bulletin boards for almost any conceivable interest are already affecting the self-help movement. There are on-line meetings of alcoholics and support groups for parents of terminally ill children.

Gabriel (1995) described bulletin board "chat rooms" and multimedia sites where gay youth can communicate with one another. The Internet is a safe place to express one's concerns about coming out (publicly acknowledging one's homosexuality), a serious problem for gay youth (D'Augelli & Hershberger, 1993). One young man who came out on the Internet received one hundred encouraging e-mail messages, some telling how they coped with the problem of telling their parents. He used these coping devices to come out to his mother. The Internet may be particularly important for people living in smaller places ("Does anyone else feel like you're the only gay guy on the planet, or at least in Arlington, Texas?"). A fifteen-year old gay living in Montana can communicate without revealing himself to those around him who not only are unsympathetic but may reject him or worse. The Internet can also serve as a crisis hot line. One gay teenager logged onto a chat channel and revealed that he had been date-raped but was too fearful to tell his parents or the police. The distraught youth appeared to be on the verge of suicide, but an hour and a half later he calmed down. He logged on the next day to say he was all right.

Some are concerned that the Internet may be used to influence youngsters to become gay or that it may become a vehicle for older gays to prey on younger ones. Current legislation designed to control obscene and pornographic communications on the Internet may have an effect on how the medium can be used. It also remains to be seen whether face-to-face contact is essential for the helping process. The revolutionary potential of this new medium is great. Should self-help research workers monitor and evaluate its potential? Will research create new ethical problems of informed consent? People "lurk" (i.e., tune in but don't actively participate) on networks. Can research workers also "lurk" without telling others what they are doing? Obviously, this new medium will create new ethical problems in the future, but its potential is very exciting. Many years ago, Jacob Moreno, who created psychodrama, envisioned community psychodramas occurring on the stage in huge theaters with an audience of thousands. Perhaps the Internet and the communications revolution will bring his vision to fulfillment on a scale he never dreamed about.

Summary

Over roughly the same period of time that community psychology has existed, the number and use of self-help groups has increased tremendously. The many groups now in existence suggest that they serve a range of important needs. One advantage they offer over professional care is that self-help groups are generally indigenous community resources offering help to vulnerable individuals at little or no cost.

We identified five types of self-help groups, each serving one or more of the following populations: (1) people whose social identities disqualify them from being normal because of a defect in conduct or physical appearance; (2) people who are related to or otherwise involved with those in the first group and who experience increased stress or a restricted range of available coping options; (3) people who are isolated by some social circumstance, such as divorce or widowhood; (4) individuals organized for mutual assistance along ethnic, racial, or religious lines; and (5) people organized on a political basis who seek to preserve certain special interests.

From a conceptual vantage point, self-help groups provide a supportive, relationship-oriented social climate that reduces isolation and self-isolation and promotes a better psychological sense of community. They also function as behavior settings that instill practical, tried-and-true coping techniques through repetitive rehearsal of ritualistic programs and procedures. New roles are provided, allowing members to achieve important opportunities and responsibilities, and all roles are reversible and interchangeable. Most interesting, perhaps, self-help groups apply specific cognitive antidotes to members' problems, tailored precisely to the maladaptive thoughts that make that particular condition of vulnerability so disruptive and distressing. Self-help groups are important, and our increasing conceptual understanding of them may enable us to create self-help alternatives that do not yet exist.

Note

1. The 1987 edition of this book had a chapter on women's consciousness-raising groups of the 1970s. Because the material was dated, and in the interests of space, we eliminated that chapter and incorporated examples in this revised chapter on self-help. The interested reader should consult the earlier edition.

10

The Problem of Change

In the 1960s mental health workers, social activists, lawyers, judges, administrators, social scientists and others who attempted to introduce new programs or to foster change in existing service agencies often encountered system problems (Bennis, 1966). It became apparent very quickly that the "compulsive personality" of the bureaucrat and the symptoms of anxiety felt by those faced with impending change were inadequate to account for those problems.

    Having an insufficient grasp of system problems, many psychologists labeled them politics, threw up their hands, and retreated to the safety of their offices. They failed to appreciate the complexities of social organizations and lacked the conceptual tools needed to understand the problems, estimate the resources necessary for change, or comprehend the time scale of change. In retrospect, they may have wanted too much too quickly. Many efforts were productive and contributed to a theoretical and practical understanding of change. This chapter focuses on some of those efforts to introduce planned change.

Earlier chapters in this book have discussed numerous examples of planned attempts at community change, including Fairweather's lodges for persons with serious mental illness (see Chapter 5), Head Start programs for disadvantaged preschool children (see Chapter 8), and Rochester's Primary Mental Health Project (PMHP), led by Emory Cowen (Cowen et al., 1975) (see Chapter 8). PMHP's creators noted, "Although PMHP evolved in part from a felt need to explore such new approaches [in mental health], the project's rationale was not yet clearly developed when it started" (p. 55). In summarizing the project's early history, and with the benefit of a decade's experience, they were able to say:

> The preceding section is essentially an insider's clinical account of some of the vexing moment-to-moment problems and rooting difficulties associated with implementing a new program in new settings. How true it is, to quote Robbie Burns, that "The best laid schemes o' mice and men gang aft a-gley." Establishing a program is not just a matter of developing a good idea or a sound plan. (p. 97)

Cowen and his associates were anything but naive when they began the project, and their experiences were not idiosyncratic (see Graziano, 1969, 1974). Their success in maintaining and nurturing PMHP over four decades demonstrates that they learned quickly what the system problems were. Cowen and his associates recorded their experiences because they had learned something worthwhile, and their hard-won knowledge was disseminated all over the country through workshops for school and mental health personnel.

If everything is connected to everything else (the principle of interdependence), any attempt at planned change is necessarily influenced by the existing social context. Any social organization that endures has the structures and means to ensure continuity despite environmental vicissitudes. Corporations, for example, have lives that exceed the life of any human being involved with them. They continue to own property even after individual stockholders die. Their contracts bind them no matter who is the chief executive. They cannot be be made to disappear easily.

The same structures and means that provide for the continuity of social organizations also create resistance to change. In principle, the issues are the same for a single agency and for the "community" of agencies.

Sarason's (1990) writing is salient in this era of educational reform. He says that commissions and task forces charged with educational reform are not thinking seriously about what reform entails. The strength of the status quo, "its underlying axioms, its sense of tradition and therefore what seems right, natural and proper—almost automatically rules out options for change in that status quo" (p. 35).

From an ecological perspective, problems of change that arise when a new program or organization is introduced into a community are similar to those that arise when attempts are made to change an existing organization. Change stimulates resistance, although resistance does not necessarily mean that change will be stopped. Anything new that survives will be changed itself by the context, and the context in turn will make some accommodations.

Although these principles seem self-evident now, it took many in the field all a long time to learn them. Experiences in the 1960s and 1970s helped to conceptualize the problem of change. Although the tasks of changing existing organizations and creating new programs involve similar concepts, we will discuss them separately.

The Creation of New Settings

In a major creative contribution to the literature on social organizations, Sarason (1972) identified some core issues in the creation of settings. Claiming that more new settings had been created in the decade of the 1960s than in the entire previous history of the human race,[1] he noted that little thought had been devoted to how settings are created. When new settings turned out to be little different from those they had replaced, participants often believed that it was the vision motivating the new setting that had failed. Sarason's work was dedicated to understanding and neutralizing the issues implicit in the saying "The more things change, the more they remain the same."

Sarason defines a setting as "any instance in which two or more people come together in new relationships over a sustained period of time in order to achieve certain goals" (p. 1). His concepts are applicable to settings as diverse as marriage (probably the most frequent new setting) and revolution, or the creation of a new society. His central interest, however, is the creation of new human service settings.

When two or more people agree on the need for a new setting different from the familiar ones, their agreement is based on either verbal abstractions reflecting their experiences or their vision of the new setting. Agreement on abstract values and strong motivation to succeed are insufficient to guarantee agreement on specific actions that express the abstract values; differences cannot be completely avoided. Sarason describes a common fantasy of participants that a point will be reached when all major goals are accomplished and all conflicts are resolved. This fantasy interferes with coming to terms with the reality that problems and conflicts will always arise.

Agreement on abstract values, strong motivation to succeed, and the fantasy of a problem-free future lead to the neglect of critical issues. Drawing on the experience of the U.S. Constitutional Convention of 1787, he argues that setting creation requires explicit rules by which participants agree to be governed. Some means to resolve the inevitable problems are necessary. If the expectation is that problems will inevitably arise, then settings need to include problem-sensing and problem-resolving devices.

The concept of a universe of alternatives—the recognition that for any problem there is always a range of potential solutions—implies an openness and a social climate conducive to the generation of potential solutions, some of which challenge assumptions that are so much a part of us that we rarely question them. The aim is not to question for its own sake but to allow for the generation of solutions appropriate to the new setting and its context.

Contexts include history; Sarason calls this "the before-the-beginning" (1972, Chapter 2). Settings are not created in vacuums. Something goes on before the creation of the setting. Because the pool of resources is always limited, new settings are always in competition with existing settings for shares of that limited pool. There is frequently ideological competition. The very creation of the new contains an implicit criticism of the old. Creators of new settings often say explicitly that existing settings are not performing well and that a new setting will perform better. Competition for resources and the ideological critique guarantee, if not active conflict with existing settings, a disinclination on the part of existing agencies to be helpful or supportive of the new (see Graziano, 1969, 1974).

By taking into account the mutual interests of the major players and by recognizing a problem that affects all, it is possible to develop a setting with mutual cooperation and without rancor. Officials in Erie County, New York, developed a "one-stop-shopping" advocacy center for sexually abused children and their parents staffed by mental health workers, medical personnel, child protective services workers, and representatives from the police and the prosecutor's offices. Recognizing a mutual interest in serving children and their families, all the departments worked to design a center to meet their needs as well as those of the families. The project emerged out of an experience where major actors identified beforehand the problems that the advocacy center was meant to solve. In that sense, the project's designers "confronted history."

In creating a setting, it is always necessary to confront history. The new setting always develops in a preexisting context of structured relationships that include histories and visions of the future that must be understood and taken into account. Given this history of structured relationships, setting creators have to consider how the context may move the new setting away from the values or concepts that the setting creators intended to implement.

Sarason focuses carefully on the setting leader in the beginning context, but not on the leader's personality. The creation-of-settings game is so structured that, although leaders may deal with the issues differently, all confront the same dilemmas; for example, the pressure to open the new setting according to a timetable while still establishing and negotiating relationships with other leaders and subordinates may result in compromises and undesired changes in the new setting.

Sarason analogizes joining a new setting to entering a relationship based on romantic love. The leader puts the best face on the new venture in order to attract the most desirable people. A new person, often leaving a disappointing situation, is prepared to see only the beauty and to overlook the warts. As Sarason (1972) says, "Time and again I have observed the leader and his core group enter into what is to be an enduring relationship grounded in (if not suffused with) enthusiasm, good will and a problem-free view of their future relationships" (p. 76).

The issues that inevitably lead to differences are predictable. Academics are expected to publish, for example, and all of the differences that can emerge in such a situation—authorship order, share of royalties, ownership of the data, and responsibility for writing and interpreting data—are guaranteed to crop up. Goodwill cannot supplant explicit understandings when active conflict occurs (Fairweather & Tornatzky, 1977).

Predictable problems also occur between the leader and the members of the core group and among the members of the core group, as their relationships to the total enterprise diverge and as members' relationships to the leader change. Such problems are rarely anticipated or discussed, partly because of the tendency for the relationship to begin in an atmosphere of romantic love and partly because we do not have theoretical conceptions that warn us to confront problems before they arise.

Sarason (1972) challenges a core assumption when he asks: "For whom does a setting exist?" He is not satisfied with the obvious answer—that it exists to serve its clients. A service setting should be concerned with its clients' welfare and with "the professional and personal growth and change of its members, and the ways in which their mutuality can enhance this growth and change" (p. 86). He says that clients are better served when the setting provides for the personal development of all its members, including its staff, because burnout and other consequences may be averted. He specifically warns against

> rigidity in function, insularity from changes in the larger society, increased competitiveness for resources within and among settings, decreasing satisfaction in work with a concomitant increase in the need for professional status and money, and the steady loss of the sense of community within the setting. (1972, pp. 124–125)

For Sarason (1974), maintaining the psychological sense of community among staff has a high priority.

At some point, leaders and others become aware that resources are not unlimited. How should the leader convey the limitation on resources to others? Will core group members compete for resources to promote the growth of their departments? Competition for resources will bring out differences in values as each subgroup justifies its call on resources and its version of how things should be done. The choices when allocating resources, including personnel, are critical; values are illuminated in the choices and in their consequences. Bypassing value questions helps defeat the purposes of a setting.

Sarason (1972) summarizes the dilemmas of the leadership position:

> Whereas at the beginning he could dream, savor possibilities, indulge the joys of new-found status and power, and see the future as cloudless, he now knows that he has become (or must become) a "realist," that he has become *dependent* on those whom he has attracted, that the surrounding world tends to be indifferent or demanding, or hostile to his setting, that the problems of today and tomorrow crowd out the future, that there are no isolated problems but rather that everything is potentially related to everything else, and that there is in him a tension between what is and what may be and between his needs and ideas and those of others. (pp. 214–215)

Hargrove and Glidewell (1990) present narratives of adminstrators in public human service agencies that reflect many of the issues Sarason discusses.

Sarason's ideas are complex, subtle, and not easy to summarize. He analyzes commonly recurring dilemmas and the dynamics of creating settings. These issues will be faced by anyone involved in creating settings, a task he views as closer to the work of an artist than that of an engineer. The issues can be sketched but not blueprinted. His concepts are useful; the dilemmas they address are recognizable and replicable because of the common structure that invariably underlies the creation of a new setting. We now illustrate Sarason's concepts using Goldenberg's (1971) book, *Build Me A Mountain*, which describes the Residential Youth Center (RYC), a setting created by following Sarason's concepts.

Box 10–1. The Residential Youth Center (RYC)

Ira Goldenberg was a member of the Yale Psychoeducational Clinic (Sarason, Levine, Goldenberg, Cherlin, & Bennett, 1966), an organization whose activities under Sarason's leadership generated some of the firsthand experiences that gave rise to Sarason's ideas. Goldenberg was a consultant to the work-crew foremen and forewomen of New Haven's pioneer antipoverty agency, Community Progress, Inc. (CPI). The work crews were made up of young men and women ages 16 to 21, unemployable and out of school. They lived at home but received a stipend for working and attending classes at the CPI service center. Crews of five to seven people worked under the direction of a foreperson, an indigenous paraprofessional from the same background as the members. Although none of these forepersons had specialized preparation for their human-service jobs, they were encouraged to develop close working and personal relationships with their charges (Sarason et al., 1966). Goldenberg (1971) described the purposes of the work-crew program: "Within this framework, then, the work crew program could be described more accurately as a therapeutic experience in living—an experience that utilized the world of work as a therapeutic lever to alter, influence, and redirect styles of life that poverty and despair had already warped and misshaped" (p. 21).

Work crews had been in existence for about two years when the federal government announced the Job Corps program, and CPI workers selected urban youths for vocational and educational training in rural Job Corps camps. Many of the New Haven Job Corps youth maintained contact with their work-crew forepersons. After a few months, Goldenberg and a group of forepersons visited their former charges at a Job Corps camp. Disappointed by what they observed, they returned to New Haven with the thought that if they had had the opportunity to set up a Job Corps program, they would have done it better. They all were also dissatisfied with aspects of the work-crew program. The idea that it could be done better and the bonds between the forepersons and Goldenberg represented that combination of strong motivation, dissatisfaction with the past, and a vision of a better future that Sarason described. As Goldenberg (1971) said, "the decision to create a new setting is, in and of itself, a decision born out of the combined feelings of hope and frustration" (p. 43).

The relationship of the new venture created by Goldenberg and the forepersons to CPI, the successful antipoverty program that had sponsored the work crews, added credibility. Funding would be administered by CPI. Goldenberg's proposal for an urban Job Corps received a hostile reception from Job Corps officials, who saw it as an ideological competitor and a criticism of their program. Goldenberg justified his proposal by alleging deficiencies in the existing program, and his funding ended up coming from a rival government agency. He speculated that the rival agency, anticipating potential problems in the Job Corps program, was positioning itself to mount a new, heavily funded initiative should the Job Corps fail.

Other aspects of the "before the beginning" had to be confronted. Once the program was funded, the core group engaged in a two-month planning process. They wanted to find a building suitable for a residence for the participants. CPI officials, then in the process of expanding, were thinking of leasing a large office building. To help cover leasing costs, they wanted the new program, called the Residential Youth Center (RYC) to remodel several floors of the office building. RYC planners wanted a more homelike setting in a real neighborhood. Fortunately, CPI's demand was dropped, but it provides an example of how prehistory can affect a developing program.

Additional prehistory problems emerged. The funding agency, eager to see results, wanted Goldenberg to open quickly before the completion of planning, training, and other preparations. Although he was able to resist this demand, the process did move more quickly. Goldenberg also described problems with existing agencies. The local community mental health center was willing to accept referrals but would not accommodate its services to the RYC clients' cultural characteristics (e.g., the lower importance they placed on punctuality in keeping appointments). Although the mental health center was located at the edge of New Haven's African American ghetto, the psychological distance between the center and the RYC youth was great. Goldenberg also wanted to reach an understanding with the local police. The police were interested in the program, but because many of the youths had had run-ins with the law, a police official proposed placing an undercover agent on the staff or among the residents. Goldenberg declined the offer. Sarason's "before the beginning" phase is richly illustrated by these experiences. The new setting opened in a context that may have shaped it in ways not envisioned or desired by the setting's planners.

The description of the RYC's creation is important to an understanding of how a setting should be organized to support participants doing the setting's work. To enhance the sense of community (see Sarason, 1974), Goldenberg proposed a horizontal organizational structure instead of the more familiar pyramidal one (see Riggio, 1990).

Horizontal structure has several features. Observing that there was an inverse relationship between the time that personnel in hospitals, prisons, or schools for the retarded spent with clients and their decision-making authority, Goldenberg argued this relationship resulted in indifferent treatment and a loss of valuable information, since those in decision-making positions had paper credentials for their jobs but did not necessarily have interpersonal competence. He selected employees from among the paraprofessional staff for their personal characteristics and proposed giving the paraprofessionals decision-making authority to enhance their feelings of responsibility for the welfare of residents.

The group developed a rule that gave workers ultimate decision-making authority over residents for whom they had primary responsibility, with one limitation: If the decision affected other aspects of RYC life, the worker had to consult with all the staff before making a final decision. Decision-making authority was thus placed at the line level with the line group.

To overcome the fragmentation common in settings organized on the basis of separate job descriptions, staff at the RYC had overlapping responsibilities. Many administrative duties were rotated so that all staff obtained some experience with and understanding of administrative problems. All staff took turns at night and weekend duty, no matter what their job description. All workers had primary job responsibilities, but everyone, including the secretary and the cook, had therapeutic responsibilities as well. (Riggio [1990] describes varieties of organizational structures. He would classify this as a "matrix organization.")

Each worker developed a program based on his or her personal interests. Jack, for example, had been a neighborhood worker. (He later became assistant director and then director of a spinoff RYC). His work with youth is best (but perhaps insufficiently) described as case management. A black belt, he developed an evening program in karate. He believed that martial arts training, when accompanied by its philosophy of self-discipline, would be therapeutic. This program gave him a role in the center that enabled him to use a highly valued personal skill. One work-crew foreman offered a carpentry class; another who liked to cook took a role in the kitchen. The horizontal structure and the matrix organization that diffused responsibility also provided the staff with opportunities to develop themselves using skills important to them, no matter their job description, providing them with a great deal of satisfaction, as matrix organizations usually do (Riggio, 1990).

Some inequalities in salary were never resolved because of external bureaucratic considerations. This problem was ameliorated when a new, successful project provided opportunities for advancement for several of the paraprofessionals. RYC's organization thus promoted the development and growth of its members and the fulfillment of their personal ambitions.

To provide for internal self-reflection, self-correction, and an open atmosphere, the core group initiated "sensitivity training" during the planning phase. It also conducted regular group sensitivity sessions in which any staff member was free to bring up any problem concerning the group, specific individuals, or the RYC. Special sensitivity sessions, scheduled at six-month intervals to review where RYC had been and where it was going, were used to work through periodic "crises." These practices resemble both the "Quality Circle" model adopted by some U.S. industries and based on practices observed in Japanese factories (Riggio, 1990) and the mutual criticism practiced in a nineteenth-century religious commune (Levine & Bunker, 1975). The open atmosphere also helped to reduce the leader's isolation.

The problems of leadership succession were confronted from the beginning. Goldenberg was then an assistant professor of psychology at Yale. He was the formal leader of the project for the first six months and then, as planned, became a consultant. The group selected one of the paraprofessionals to succeed him, and another paraprofessional became assistant director. Those arrangements were worked out in anticipation of the need to choose a successor to Goldenberg. The successor was trained within the horizontal and open structure. Confronting the problem of succession ahead of time avoided potentially destructive competition for the post. Later, when an RYC for women opened, the original staff planned it, and one of the paraprofessionals became its director.

The ethos of participation extended to the center's youth. A house council had responsibility for generating house rules and for setting up recreational, educational, and community service programs. The furnishings were built by residents in a woodworking class under the direction of a work-crew foreperson. Youth family members, using materials and instructions provided by the RYC, sewed curtains and other decorations. Some rooms in the house would not pass muster in most public institutions. One room (including the ceiling) was completely painted in a high-gloss black; the shiny black surface was the background and frame for a collage of *Playboy* centerfolds covering most of the ceiling. The room was striking in appearance and reflected its occupant's individuality.

The first residents were recruited from among the most difficult youth served in CPI's neighborhood outreach centers. These youths had extensive records of involvement with the police; some had histories of psychiatric hospitalization and were indeed difficult to work with. Staff had to work through many trying problems to develop an orderly program.

Eventually the program settled down. The six-month evaluation revealed considerable success in helping residents to maintain employment and educational placements, change their attitudes, and reduce their contact with police. Because RYC residents and controls were not assigned at random—the most difficult were selected for treatment—the improved outcomes over time are subject to the technical criticism of regression to the mean. That is, because the worst were selected, there was nothing for them to do but improve. In addition, no long-term follow-up was ever reported, so it is impossible to evaluate the program's long-term effectiveness.

The RYC helped develop its staff members and it provided service to clients who were considered unworkable. Its staff maintained suprisingly high morale over several years. The talents and commitments of individual actors do not tell the whole story. Goldenberg's major achievement was in self-consciously thinking through the organizational conditions that allowed those talents to be used in creative and satisfying ways.

Change in Existing Settings

Pressman and Wildavsky (1979) note that if a change requires positive action by ten independent actors, the a priori probability that everything will go right and the change will be implemented is $1/2^{10}$, or one chance in 1,024! Not much can be left to chance, but how can we think about this problem?

Systems Theory

Open systems theory can be applied to the analysis of change in human service organizations (Schulberg & Baker, 1975). Human service organizations may be viewed as open systems engaging in resource exchanges with their environments. A psychiatric center receives public funds, takes in people in need, helps to solve a community problem, and presumably returns productive citizens to the community. An open system retains some of the resources it receives for its maintenance and growth. Systems that are highly reactive to variations in the exchange process may direct a considerable portion of their resources toward enhancing the exchange. Publicly supported human service organizations obtain resources only indirectly from exchanges, however, and therefore have greater potential for converting resources to the organization's benefit—that is, to use resources to enhance working conditions and rewards for employees rather than to benefit patients. For example, staff members in a specialized child protection team spent 40 percent of their time in paperwork, 29 percent in consultation with colleagues, 20 percent in consultation with other agency staff, and only 11 percent with families (Crittenden, 1992). Ideally there should be no conflict; in practice there is tension between an organization's needs and those of the people it serves. Organizations may not respond readily to the environment because resources do not depend on a direct exchange.

An open system is dependent on its environment for a number of factors: (1) the acquisition of "materials" (e.g., clients); (2) capital (annual program and capital budget allocations); (3) production factors (e.g., services technology, trained employees); (4) labor (e.g., hiring of sufficient personnel with adequate skills, education, or aptitude); and (5) output disposal (release of clients back to a receptive community). The terminology, although useful, is geared to industrial production and inexact when applied to human service organizations.

Open systems respond to "turbulence," by which system theorists mean a change in the relationship between the organization and one or more of the factors on which it depends. Fairweather et al. (1974) noted that little change occurs in mental hospitals without some form of outside intervention. If the turbulence is created by some other agency to which an organization is linked and on whom it is highly dependent (e.g., a legislature that controls its funds), the organization must adapt to the turbulence. In academia, university faculties may be faced with adapting to the demand by cost-conscious citizens and legislators that they spend more time in classroom teaching and less in research, a change university faculty would not make by themselves. Crittenden (1992) describes how an innovation in the practices of a specialized child protection team resulted in a demand from the supervising agency that the team resume its former, demonstrably ineffective approach.

In today's mental health world, turbulence arises from the demands of advocacy groups, from the media, or from legislators with special agendas. Sometimes the demand for change comes from a lawsuit against an institution for violating patient rights (Miller & Iscoe, 1990). The adaptation may be positive, with the organization changing to meet the new demand, or the organization may freeze and fail to adapt. Whether an organization adapts or freezes in relation to environmental turbulence is in turn a function of other variables, such as available resources, knowledge, and leadership.

Types of Change

Watzlawick, Weakland, and Fisch (1974) describe two general classes of change. In one, called first-order change, only a portion of the system is affected; most of the system remains intact. Second-order change is change in the system itself—that is, in the relationships among the component parts. A simple example of first-order change is the addition of something new without taking anything else away, although adding on itself entails complications. For example, an additional faculty member requires office and laboratory space and adds to the demand for services and supplies. It is also possible to effect change by stopping a program entirely by eliminating its budget. Many such changes can have serious ramifications, even if the change appears simple. Michigan eliminated its general assistance (welfare) program, saving money, but the change affected former recipients of the aid who were forced to double up in housing, use shelters, or live on the streets when they lost rent money.

A change requiring the reorganization or reallocation of resources or functions is more complicated. To take staff from one unit and to reassign them to different jobs, for example, may be proscribed by civil service restrictions on "working out of title" or by union rules. As we have noted, if any social organization is to continue, it must have structures that ensure its continuity despite environmental vicissitudes. Structures that provide for organizational continuity also create resistance to change.

Changing materials or tools with little change in relationships among workers or functions may require little more than some in-service education (e.g., the substitution of a new medication for one used previously). However, even apparently simple changes can require extensive training and preparation and changes in related roles. Change from "welfare" to "workfare" or efforts to "reduce welfare fraud" or improve the collection of child support payments is simple in concept but very complex in implementation (Lynn, 1990).

Simple change, even for an ostensibly good purpose, can provoke unexpected and sometimes powerful resistance. Concerned about AIDS, health department officials in San Francisco wanted to close gay bath houses that provided anonymous sex with multiple partners. The mayor, the health commissioner, the courts, and segments of the gay community became locked in conflict over the action. Proposals to exchange intravenous drug users' dirty needles for clean ones or to require AIDS testing of all applicants for marriage licenses have been controversial; even the existence of data supporting the effectivness of needle exchanges in curbing the spread of AIDS and hepatitis has not settled the moral and political conflict about taking public actions that seemed to approve drug use (Lawlor, 1990; Anderson, 1991).

Production and Satisfaction Goals

Change goals may be classified into two types—production and satisfaction. Production goals are related to the manifest purpose of the setting. Achievement test scores, arrest and conviction rates, recidivist rates, the number of patients released from a hospital, and the number of doctoral students graduated from a Ph.D. program are all examples of items of production. In systems theory, items of production are exchanged for resources, but in human service organizations the relationship between items of production and resources is not clear-cut. Administrators have attempted to sharpen this relationship by tying budgets to units of production through contractual arrangements that call for specific numbers of client contact hours or patients discharged from a hospital within a given period of time.[2]

Employees, clients, and other actors interacting with a human service organization all have satisfaction goals. The satisfaction of members of one group is not necessarily positively correlated with the satisfaction of members of the other groups. Production measures and satisfaction measures tend to be orthogonal. It is possible to envision every combination of production achievement and satisfaction level. Workers may be very productive, turning out many items, and still be dissatisfied because they work too hard or are underpaid or because other working conditions are inadequate. A mental hospital may increase "production" by reducing its census, but if the patients still need assistance when discharged to the community, the work has simply been shifted elsewhere. Thus the achievement of a state's production goal, halving the population of its state mental hospitals, will not be greeted with universal acclaim.

Satisfaction goals are more important than we usually acknowledge. Some policies persist even when there is evidence that the policy is harmful. Despite seventy or more years of research showing that it does no good and may do harm to leave children back in school (Levine & Graziano, 1972), from time to time educators back a get-tough nonpromotion policy. Social promotion solutions are unsatisfying to teachers and some citizens who believe that children will not work unless threatened with nonpromotion. Proposals for retaining children in grade rarely include any program for educating the children differently to avoid a repeat of the failure or for dealing with the blow to self-esteem and the stigma of being retained in grade.

Creating the perception that a program is doing good things is a variant of attaining satisfaction. Cowen et al. (1975) pointed out that a decision to allocate funds is determined not by scientific evidence of a program's effectiveness but by its ability to satisfy constituencies who are willing to lobby for it. The satisfied audiences can vary; for a state welfare commissioner, it might be the state's governor or a powerful state legislator (Lynn, 1990).

The Social Context of Change

A program targeted for change always functions in a social context defined by the sets of positions and roles within the organization and by the institutions and constituencies (e.g,. parents of schoolchildren) that make up the external environment. A change may require modification of the relationships among members or groups within the human service agency and among and between members of external groups.

Members of role groups stand to gain or to lose when a change is proposed or implemented. Potential losers will oppose change, either actively or passively, but they may not have the power to defeat or retard the change significantly. Potential gainers will support the change.

The sets of interests that may be affected by change can be categorized in different ways and with many subclassifications. For the sake of exposition, we reduce the sets of interests to seven:

1. Energy (money, work time, amount of work)
2. Power (including status or influence)
3. Culture (beliefs, norms, values)
4. Competence (ability and satisfaction in carrying out work tasks)
5. Relationships (generally, satisfactions in social interaction deriving from work relationships)
6. Legal and administrative considerations
7. Information and communication (knowing what's going on)

We will illustrate each of these dimensions before looking at case studies of change in human service organizations. Because change is usually centered on a single organization and the major actors are the employees, our examples will stress the perspective of employees. The fact that human service agencies have high numbers of professional employees does not change the picture; professionals in organizations are workers, albeit with different statuses, salaries, and privileges than those of blue-collar employees.

1. *Energy.* Workers expend characteristic levels of energy on the job. The amounts of work, time, money, and other benefits are interrelated variables. If a program change requires increased energy output and there is neither a compensating increase in money or other benefits or a decrease in hours spent working, employees will oppose change. The New York City More Effective Schools program was vigorously supported by the teachers' union, in part because it provided additional free periods for teachers and teacher aides to assist with classroom work, despite evidence

that the expensive program had not improved pupil academic achievement (Levine & Graziano, 1972). Researchers have taken budgeted funds to pay teachers for their time after teachers resisted participating in uncompensated research. Under special conditions, as in Goldenberg's RYC, charismatic leadership, a sense of participation in a mission of importance, or hopes for future rewards may provide intangible compensations that sustain support for change. Emotional highs alone, however, cannot substitute for other tangible rewards for very long.

There is an optimal range for the amount of work someone does; changes that require either a marked increase or a marked decrease in work will elicit resistance. A change that removes most functions from a position, even though the person continues to receive full pay, will prove distressing. Most people like to feel that they are earning their money. Some may not work hard or may take extended coffee or restroom breaks, but the illusion of working is maintained. If a person doesn't have enough work, the feeling of being a worthwhile member of society is undermined.

2. *Power.* Power is the ability to issue and enforce a command concerning the use of resources. Power is exercised in the control of resources (allocating physical space, materials, supplies), personnel (hiring, firing, promoting, or determining duties), or territory (granting admission to an institution). Power is generally correlated with both status in a social organization and the expectation of receiving respect or deference from those of lower status. Role incumbents relate to programs and to each other through the exercise of power. An incumbent whose power is increased by a given change will favor that change, while one whose power is decreased will oppose it.

Programmatic efforts to overcome feelings of helplessness and alienation through the sharing of power and the problems of accommodating to power are well documented. The federal law establishing the War on Poverty and community action programs called for the maximum feasible participation of those who were affected. In some cities, these statutory provisions and the availability of resources encouraged independent antipoverty agencies to use the power the legislation gave them, thereby threatening the political power of city officials. New federal legislation was introduced to reduce the independence of the antipoverty agencies from city government (Moynihan, 1969), and power struggles and problems stemming from the fragmentation of local, state, federal, and private-sector agencies resulted in delays and difficulties in the implementation of the Community Mental Health Centers Act (Levine, 1981). Crittenden (1992) describes similar phenomena after a specialized child protection team changed its practices in ways that affected other agencies, the courts, and its funding agency.

Jacobs (1980) notes that prison guards felt that they lost power when courts ruled that inmates could bring suits against prisons. Similarly, hospital personnel lose power to patients when courts recognize a patient's right to refuse treatment. Fairweather et al. (1974) noted that the lodge program (see Chapter 5) encountered resistance because it changed the superordinate-subordinate relationship between professional helper and patient. Prison officials and hospital officials have resisted court-ordered change; their resistance comes from their unwillingness to be told what to do by outsiders, which represents a loss of power.

On the other hand, increasing power for some actors has salutory effects on the change process. Goldenberg's RYC program substantially increased the power of line workers, resulting in great support for the program by employees. In some hospital wards, a similar result was achieved after a change from a hierarchical structure to a therapeutic community with shared power and greater role diffusion (activities shared by those in different roles) (Colarelli & Siegel, 1966).

3. *Culture*. The term "culture" is a convenient shorthand for the set of beliefs, ideologies, values, and norms characteristic of a given group. These concepts suggest what behavior will be acceptable in social relationships. There are rewards for meeting social expectations and sanctions for failing to meet them. Belief systems or ideologies are especially important in institutional change (see Crittenden, 1992).

A change may challenge ideologies. Court orders for change supporting prisoners' rights changed good-guy, bad-guy roles within prisons; whereas guards had thought of themselves as performing a necessary and valuable service, the courts were saying, in the eyes of the guards, that they were oppressors preventing inmates from exercising legitimate constitutional rights (Jacobs, 1980). The *O'Connor* v. *Donaldson* (1975) decision implied that psychiatrists who retain patients who are psychiatrically "sick" but whose behavior does not meet legal standards of dangerousness are not engaging in good psychiatric practice but are violating patient rights. Miller and Iscoe (1990) also observed that employees of mental hospitals were distressed by court findings, in lawsuits filed against institutions, that the employees had not cared sufficiently well for their patients.

Strong commitments to forms of practice (norms) stem from training, cultural conditioning, direct experience, and the need to believe that what is done is right and good. We can appreciate the reaction of physicians told by nineteenth century obstetrician Ignaz Semmelweiss that they carried germs on their hands, causing the deaths of mothers whose deliveries they had attended. Can we be less sympathetic with the schoolteacher's reaction of rage to Kozol's (1967) accusations in *Death at an Early Age* or to mental health workers' decrying the destructiveness of Rosenhan's (1973) demonstration that admitting personnel cannot detect pseudopatients? Psychotherapists, told by critics (e.g., Dawes, 1994) that they do little good, charge high fees, accept for treatment easy, middle-class clients, and could be replaced with paraprofessionals who can do whatever it is they do with a few weeks of training, cannot be expected to react by thanking the critic for providing enlightenment. When a practice to which an individual has a deep commitment is challenged, one cannot expect that individual to say gratefully, "Thank you very much for telling me I have been destroying my clients all these years. I never thought about it that way before, and I am now ready to do everything you say."

Not all resistance is irrational by any means. Sometimes there may be good and sufficient reason to maintain the incumbent's view of what that role and the professional status require. We have to understand what the demand for change means in their contexts and from their perspectives.

All groups involved in a program have beliefs or theories that are as powerful for them as mental health theories are for mental health workers. Such beliefs, learned during professional or occupational socialization, derive from experience or are taken over from authority figures. "Children won't learn unless you make them"; "Inmate self-government will lead to riots or the exploitation of prisoners by each other"; "If high fences or walls around an institution for the retarded are taken down, the residents will wander off"; "Sex education leads to promiscuity and a reduction in the authority and influence of parents"—these are all examples of beliefs held very deeply by some people.

The concepts always reflect the data incompletely, but they often have empirical referents, just as there are some empirical referents for concepts held by professional mental health workers. A change agent, especially one without a great deal of experience in a particular setting, can create resistance by advocating programs that have failed in the past or that discount beliefs about reality that are held by important actors in the social system. A corrections official who has lived through bloody prison riots in the 1930s and who believes that some portion of the troubles then were related to efforts at inmate government is not likely to be receptive to suggestions for inmate self-government proposed by a civil rights attorney or a mental health professional. As another example, school principals who are aware of the difficulty of involving more than a few parents in any program will be wary of a social worker who suggests a program of parental participation as a means of solving school problems, no matter how sound the proposal from the point of view of mental health theory.

In one case, parents of children with mental retardation who were told their children would be moved from an acceptable institution to an open, community-based group home reacted with anger. They opposed the policy, despite the beliefs of mental health workers that the children would be better off (Miller & Iscoe, 1990). Sarason's (1967) observation that receptivity to further innovation is inversely related to the number of previous failed attempts at innovation in that setting is very apt.

Groups responsible for the care of clients have beliefs about their clients'characteristics. Programs for change at variance with those views are greeted with less than good cheer. If prison officials believe that inmates are untrustworthy and likely to manipulate or to exploit each other, they will react poorly to programs that assume the spark of the divine within each inmate. When teachers believe that children will behave chaotically if not controlled, or when managers believe that workers will not work unless closely supervised, they will react poorly to proposals that children or workers be given greater responsibility. Deinstitutionalization was partly justified by labeling theory (see Chapter 6). Proponents claimed that patients in mental hospitals behaved the way they did because of their labels and the institutional regime. Proponents also predicted that the patients would change greatly if the environment changed. Those propositions were not believable to others who had knowledge of the severe disabilities of patients with severe and persistent disorders. We currently have no systematic techniques for determining beliefs about clients prevalent in the various groups concerned with the proposed change; it would be valuable to develop such approaches.

Priorities in the change agent's value system will not necessarily match the value priorities of other concerned groups. Mental health personnel sometimes assume the primacy of mental health values, failing to realize that others may value alternative behaviors and outcomes more. "He may be happier in school, but he is still two years behind in his reading level"; "You can't reward bad kids by giving them special treatment, because it is unfair to good kids"; "You shouldn't use a reward system that rewards children for doing what they should be doing anyway. That's bribery"; "Democratic decision making and participation are all very well, but the result is disrespect for authority"—these familiar statements all reflect value hierarchies. Methods of ascertaining and measuring hierarchies of values are not well developed, and change agents are sometimes insensitive to the issue.

4. *Competence.* Probably the single most important piece of information about an individual in U.S. society is his or her occupational title. Occupation is central to personal identity and to social existence. Beyond the financial and social rewards of an occupation, the mastery and exercise of occupational skills is critical for self-esteem and for individual well-being. People's peak experiences (Maslow, 1962) often arise during the exercise of occupational skills. One enjoys doing what one does well. A psychotherapist in tune with a client, engaging in an inspired intervention, feels good and enjoys recounting the experience to other professionals; the teacher who delivers a compelling lecture, eliciting a positive response from students, is gratified; the police officer takes pride in the ability to elicit an obedient, respectful response to an authoritative, businesslike approach to citizens.

Change may require that an employee no longer exercise skills that provide personal gratification. All of the psychological reactions related to loss may be stimulated by a demand for change. Some teachers, for example, had difficulty adapting to open methods of education because they no longer had the opportunity to perform in front of a large group; others said that they missed the constant feedback of knowing exactly what the children were doing and learning each day. Psychotherapists trained to do long-term therapy with articulate, verbally accessible young people may not feel they are doing anything useful when the patient requires simple support.

A change in program requiring that individuals learn new skills or fulfill new functions may be more threatening to an established worker than to a novice. Crittenden (1992) staffed an innovative child protection team with young, less experienced, but more enthusiastic personnel because experienced professionals refused to participate. Inequalities in a social order are rationalized on the grounds that differential experience and training justify differences in status and related perquisites of office; when individuals having different statuses in the same organization are required to engage in new learning, there is no guarantee that the competence-based order that emerges will match the status order of the original organization. For this reason, shifts to a therapeutic community orientation where employees with different statuses and salaries perform the same jobs have led to considerable embarrassment, because competency on the job does not necessarily match the status structure. Goldenberg's (1971) mixed paraprofessional and professional staff took to using the terms "amateur" and "pro" to describe those who were less and more competent, independent of the individual's professional training and formal credentials.

Learning new skills can be difficult. Conditioned by years of educational experience, we may expect that learning will be painful, that we will be vulnerable to evaluation, and that our self-esteem will be diminished. For all these reasons, the "old dog" may not want to learn new tricks.

We can assume that individuals enter patterns of occupational functioning consistent with their aptitudes, personal styles, and, perhaps, psychological defenses. A change that requires the individual to behave in unfamiliar and uncongenial ways will be threatening. To accept the responsibility of making decisions when one has been in a dependent role, to interact vigorously and relate closely when one has always kept others at a distance, or to face aggression when one has been timid are all extremely difficult. In one case, all the members of a hospital-based child protection team quit when a new program required them to make home visits (Crittenden, 1992).

In order to institute change, not only must persons exercise new competencies; the social organization must support the exercise of these new competencies. For example, teachers trained in methods of life-space interviewing did not use these methods because there was insufficient support from their principals and other teachers in the school who had not been similarly trained. Poythress (1978) demonstrated that he could train attorneys to cross-examine psychiatric expert witnesses, but few attorneys used his methods in the courtroom during commitment hearings, claiming that judges were not interested in vigorous advocacy during routine hearings.

Sometimes clients object to change, and sometimes other staff not directly involved in the change object. In one of our projects, corrections officers being trained as paraprofessional counselors reported that some prisoners resented the activity as an attempt to provide the prisoners with second-class amateur services. Some fellow officers teased them or expressed active hostility because they believed that the counseling approach violated their beliefs about the proper behavior for corrections officers and the proper treatment of inmates.

To change an ongoing service requires us to define required new competencies, assess whether the target populations of the change effort possess those competencies, evaluate the amount of time and training necessary to acquire new competencies (Fairweather et al., 1974), and consider what changes in social organization may be required if the new competencies are to be utilized at all. The problem of change may create a problem of person-environment fit, not only for the clients of a program but also for the employees who will carry out the new program.

5. *Work relationships.* Social relationships on the job can be a great source of satisfaction and a great source of distress. People's emotional states are highly dependent on the state of office politics and rivalries at work. For those who do not have the opportunity or the ambition to be promoted, social relationships on the job are critically important (Kanter, 1977).

In some settings, such as prisons and state mental hospitals located in rural areas, many workers hold second jobs. In other settings, husbands and wives have arrangements for child care that depend on their work shifts. For workers like these, change that affects shift assignments can be critically important because, from the workers' viewpoint, other aspects of their lives will be affected. Crittenden (1992) found that members of a hospital-based child protection team objected to a change requiring that they make home visits at nights and on weekends because the new practice took them away from their families.

A change that requires people to give up attachments to coworkers or to places may well be difficult. When the Harlem Valley, New York, state hospital shifted to outpatient care, workers were reassigned from service to service as needs changed. Although the leaders were sensitive to the issue of shift changes and in their planning took employees' shift preferences into account, line workers reported a great deal of dissatisfaction with the rapid change of assignments and felt unable to accommodate to new supervisors and new coworkers so rapidly. Moreover, they reported less willingness to commit themselves emotionally to their work sites. One indication of this change was that they brought in fewer personal items to decorate offices and wards (Levine, 1980b).

Program changes may require concomitant change in the relationship between supervisors and supervisors, supervisors and agencies, workers and supervisors, workers and workers, workers and clients, and workers and agency and in many other permutations and combinations of people. A change that may be exciting for one person may disrupt many relationships for another. An analysis of relationships that may be affected should probably be undertaken as part of any change effort, taking into account that the change may be a positive factor, as when a conflictful relationship is ended by the change.

6. *Legal and administrative considerations.* Stability in a social organization depends in part on regulations with the force of law and on contractual agreements, as well as on shared expectations.

Examples abound. Laws may restrict or mandate actions. For example, in a mental hospital, only nurses or those attendants who have completed a course of training may by law pass out medications. Problems also arise when clients who may be accused of sexual abuse are referred for treatment; a psychotherapist may have a duty to maintain confidentiality but be mandated by law to violate that confidentiality and report any suspicion of child maltreatment. In some cases union contracts may restrict the degree of freedom to change; a prison superintendent who wanted to institute a weekend recreation program found that he had to change tours of duty of several of his officers; and restrictions in the union contract required prolonged negotiation before he could achieve his aim.

Regulations may be protective and provide a means through which a change effort is carried out. The systematically better conditions that are found in veterans mental hospitals compared to state mental hospitals may be the result of careful regulation and enforcement of standards of patient care. In the Wuori case (discussed later in this chapter; Levine, 1986), reforms achieved through litigation were made permanent when they were written into state statutes and regulations.

Legal or administrative rules and structures may represent barriers to change, or they may be seen as challenges to be met and overcome by risk-taking leaders willing to "bend but not break" the rules to facilitate program implementation (Levine, 1980b; Sarason, 1982). A bureaucratic structure may be an impediment and seem unnecessary, but it is ignored only at the peril of the change effort. Problems that arise because of formal rule-based constraints cannot be ignored.

7. *Information and communication.* Information has psychological importance. People use information to maintain, plan, or reorient their activities or to satisfy their curiosity. They exchange information and opinions on matters of mutual interest, and those "in the know" participate with a sense of belonging. Information in advance of actions prevents surprises and may prevent people from acting at cross-purposes with each other. Moreover, providing information and explanation in advance is a way of showing deference to people's positions and to them as individuals. Not knowing about events may result in a loss of prestige to those who feel they should know about events affecting their domains.

Advance knowledge may facilitate change. However, it may also serve to give the opposition time to organize. From the point of view of the change agent, sometimes a fait accompli is preferable. The issue of whether or not to inform neighbors may be prominent when an agency wishes to open a group home in the community. One school of thought states that neighbors should be brought into the planning in order to win their support for the group home (Miller & Iscoe, 1990). Goldenberg (1971) tells how he made an effort to meet with some concerned citizens and tried to include them in the planning process.

Advance knowledge can lead to active opposition. A local zoning ordinance in Texas required that a group home for retarded youth obtain a permit before it could open, whereas a nursing home for the elderly or a group home for delinquent youngsters did not need one. The U.S. Supreme Court agreed with the group home operator that the decision denying the permit reflected prejudice against those with mental retardation (*Cleburne Living Center, Inc.* v. *City of Cleburne, Texas,* 1985). Opposition to group homes once they open usually dies down, but no one knows how many group homes have not opened because of community opposition (Lubin, Schwartz, Zigman, & Janicki, 1982; Miller & Iscoe, 1990).

In sum, a change in any program occurs in a context consisting of social groups relating to programs and to each other through seven sets of interests. Members of the sets examine the way the proposed changes might affect their interests, and each role representative arrives at a position opposed to or in favor of the change after weighing or balancing those interests. Groups that on balance gain from the changes will support them; groups that on balance lose from the changes will oppose them. The opposition may or may not have the power to block change. Forces in the social context always pull back toward the status quo, however, and those spearheading the change effort must recognize that pull, for it may well result in some modification of the planned change. We have no precise measures of the strength of the existing interests or of their relative weights; the schema we have described is a loose set of guidelines for looking at a problem of change. Within each class of variables it is possible to have a large number of separate dimensions. Given Pressman and Wildavsky's (1979) suggestion that change must touch a large number of "switches" and that all "switches" must be lined up properly, the wonder is not that change efforts fail but that successful change takes place at all. We now turn to an examination of some successful change efforts.

Case Studies of Change in Existing Settings

Changing a State Mental Hospital

In the space of four years the Harlem Valley Psychiatric Center in New York changed from a predominantly custodial institution to a modern psychiatric center (Levine, 1980b). Under the leadership of its director, Yoosuf Haveliwala, its census was reduced rapidly, and it developed an elaborate network of outpatient and aftercare services. The change was accomplished with a declining budget by reallocating, not adding, resources, and patients were served as well as the state of the art permitted. The changes were accomplished following recognizable methods.

On July 1, 1974, the hospital had a census of 2,652 patients, of which 1,826 (69%) were inpatients averaging 19.5 years of hospitalization. The rest were outpatients. Most full-time staff were assigned to inpatient care. A few part-time clinics provided aftercare services. The hospital's orientation was custodial. Staff members had little sense of mission except to keep patients reasonably clean and involved in routine occupational and recreational programs. There was nothing to attract well-trained, ambitious professional personnel. Hospital staff did no research and received only perfunctory in-service training. The community was not involved in hospital programs, and the hospital had no active public relations program.

By 1977, the Joint Commission on the Accreditation of Hospitals (JCAH) had renewed the hospital's accreditation with praise for its progress, for its programs, and for a medical records system it said was a model. The hospital census had been reduced to 590 inpatients, and 2,478 outpatients were being carried on the hospital's rolls. Thirty separate services were located in seven communities offering programs such as individual, group, and family therapy, day care, day hospitalization; crisis intervention; housing and sheltered living; sheltered workshops and work placement; advocacy services to link clients with other community agencies; and outreach, including home visits. Hospital admissions had dropped from about one thousand in 1974 to about 350 in 1977. A vigorous recruiting program had attracted physicians and other mental health professionals, and an extensive in-service education program for professionals and paraprofessionals was in place. Eight psychology interns and twenty students from other disciplines were in training or were doing fieldwork at the hospital.

An extensive new monitoring and evaluation system was a key instrument in the change effort. The monitoring devices produced quantitative data on the status of patients and on the quality of service. In addition, the hospital developed an epidemiological unit to assess the need for care within its catchment area, and new program development was based on its data. The hospital developed a small research department to conduct clinical studies with funds from government agencies and drug companies. Staff members participated in national and international professional meetings.

Community involvement increased strikingly. Community advisory boards were established for each community service by staff who recruited and worked with citizens. Staff were active on community mental health boards and on coordinating councils. Volunteer hours at the hospital increased from 7,530 in 1974 to 36,170 in 1977.

Haveliwala took over as director in July 1974, but there was a "before the beginning." The hospital census had already started to decline in response to New York's deinstitutionalization policy, and its existence was threatened because a rural hospital was no longer needed. (Harlem Valley eventually closed as a psychiatric hospital.) The community depended heavily on the institution, however, and would have suffered economically had it closed in 1974. Staff were motivated by the idea that they could save the hospital by developing innovative programs. Just prior to Haveliwala's tenure, some reorganization had been accomplished. On one service, a group of young professionals discharged patients to communities where they had lived and then sent mobile teams to provide service in their home communities.

Haveliwala was among the first generation of state psychiatric center directors formally trained in the concepts and practices of community mental health. He had gained experience with deinstitutionalization programs as a psychiatric resident and had advanced training in mental health administration and management. He had also been deputy director of a large state facility before he received the appointment as director of Harlem Valley. He was thoroughly familiar with the state system.

Haveliwala had clear plans. He was aware that some strong staff members would follow his lead. He quickly announced his intention to continue to place patients in the community but said that each patient would be placed in accordance with the patient's needs and that excellent care would be provided. He also said that a deinstitutionalization program accompanied by community-based services would preserve jobs. He thus provided the institution with an ideology with which to rationalize change.

Haveliwala reduced the hospital's executive committee (EC) from fifty to fourteen members and changed its composition to give much more representation to the unit chiefs rather than to central staff. His actions were rationally related to his plans and his goals. He gave the unit chiefs more decision-making authority because they were responsible for placing patients and developing community-based services. If they were to be accountable for results, they had to participate in decisions, and they had to be able to deploy personnel as their programs required.

Given civil service and union restrictions, Haveliwala had little power to hire and fire at will. He therefore used peer pressure. The EC became a deliberative and decision-making body, as well as a public forum in which to review each unit chief's success and failure in meeting objectives. Each unit chief consulted with staff and developed a target number of patients for placement in appropriate settings. These targets were discussed in the EC and agreed to by the director. Once objectives were assigned, unit chiefs were responsible for meeting them. A similar approach, called management by objectives, is used in industry (Riggio, 1990).

The program evaluation department produced reports showing each unit's success in meeting targets, and these reports were distributed to all EC members. Some unit chiefs met or exceeded their goals, while others failed, but failure was public, putting competitive pressure on the leaders and their units to meet standards. All the other monitoring devices were used in exactly the same way. Unit chiefs had to explain publicly the reasons for their successes or failures. The director approved high performance; he allocated resources and rewards on the basis of performance. Although workloads and pressure increased, these were offset by rewards, including the prospect of promotion.

Haveliwala intended to create a competency-based organization. He built the organizational chart around staff competence rather than formal civil service titles. He used his authority to create acting titles when the preferred individual did not qualify for a civil service title; sometimes he assigned lower-ranked persons to supervise higher-ranked people because they could do the job. Staff enjoyed the rewards of exercising new competencies. Haveliwala developed a core of competent managers who moved from assignment to assignment as program development required their talents. He used a nonfinancial reward system to recognize effort and success.

He accommodated the interests of physicians who lost some status to nonmedical personnel by providing a line of communication with a physician-supervisor. Their autonomy as physicians was supported even though they were supervised in some aspects of their work by nonphysicians. Lower-level staff did not always feel that their interests were being served. Although jobs were saved and no one was fired, line staff felt that changes were being made at their expense. Their interests were served, however, by unit chiefs who used the same methods of increasing participation and job autonomy and providing opportunity for rapid advancement for those who could produce.

Haveliwala's program assumed that resources should precede the patient into the community. He provided the resources and more by creatively bending rules, although he was always careful not to break the rules, thus taking into account the legal and administrative structure of the institution. Thus, he temporarily overcrowded a few wards to a slight degree, closing a few other wards and releasing the personnel that had staffed the now closed wards to establish community programs.

Later, he used his mastery of the state's budgetary procedure to provide the resources. The state's budget for a hospital is based on a ratio of personnel to the patient population, and that ratio is higher for inpatients than for outpatients. The patient population target for the coming fiscal year and thus the number of personnel allocated are set the previous year. Haveliwala encouraged his staff to release patients to the community rapidly, thus creating an excess of personnel that could be deployed to develop the outpatient services and other new projects. He explored the universe of alternatives and developed some new ways of reaching his goals.

Using a situational theory, he maintained that rehabilitation begins in the community. He argued that preparation for discharge did not predict patient tenure in the community; participation in aftercare programs did. Consequently, he developed resources in the community and devoted little effort to preparing patients to leave the hospital.

Haveliwala and his staff encountered many instances of competititon for resources with existing private and county-based programs, but they sought the proper niche for their programs by taking on services the other agencies were not providing (see also Miller & Iscoe, 1990). Sometimes the new programs adapted to the existing environment of agencies and needs. Where possible, his unit chiefs worked closely with existing agencies and sometimes developed jointly sponsored programs.

Harlem Valley's evaluation research, and our own efforts to review its programs, showed that 72 percent of discharged patients were still in the community one year after discharge. That record is quite good compared to that of other programs. Patients were by and large content with their community placements, and we could find little evidence that current community placements were substandard, although that might not have been true for all of the earlier placements. The outpatient centers maintained contact with almost all inpatients who were discharged, at least for the first few months.

It is striking how little the "state of the art" in downsizing a state mental hospital has changed in the two decades since the Harlem Valley experiment. An adequate quantity and quality of community-based services, such as assertive community treatment (see Chapter 2) and supported living (see Chapter 7), is clearly necessary, as is a mechanism for shifting resources from the state-run facility to community settings, some of which may be privately managed. Perhaps the biggest difference between contemporary practice and the Harlem Valley story is that admission to or discharge from a state hospital in the 1990s is controlled not by the hospital staff but by a community provider (e.g., a mental health center), which must actively manage its use of the hospital to avoid exceeding a fixed number of bed-days per year (see, for example, Rapp & Moore, 1995).

A case study cannot pin down causal factors. In this instance, change followed a design using recognizable tools and methods that were understandable within a systems and social organization perspective. The consistent application of certain principles produced predictable results.[3] This tells us that planned change is possible, even in a bureaucratically organized state hospital. The Harlem Valley story provides concrete proof that static organizations need not remain that way.

Court-Ordered Change in Caring for Persons with Mental Retardation

In the 1970s public-interest lawyers, acting with advocacy organizations, sued some institutions (mental hospitals, institutions for people with mental retardation, prisons) in the federal courts, alleging that they provided a substandard level of care (Chayes, 1976). These highly complex suits brought to the surface the political structure within which human services are embedded and raised issues around the separation of powers (legislative, executive, judicial) and the nature of federalism (state-federal relationships). In the early suits, the violations of standards of care were so egregious that issues of liability (who was responsible) were rarely in dispute. When defendant state agencies lost the suits, they were ordered to remedy the problems, and the courts retained jurisdiction to oversee implementation of the remedies. The cases continued for years; one of the first cases, *Wyatt* v. *Stickney*, was brought in 1972 and remained under the court's supervision into the late 1980s (Levine, 1981). A large body of legal and social science literature reviews court-ordered institutional change (see, for example, D. Levine, 1984; Rosenberg & Phillips, 1981–1982).

Court supervision of change is highly complex. If the defendant state agencies do not or cannot comply with the court's order, the court's prestige and power are challenged. A confrontation between a federal judge and state officials (governors or legislators) can create a political crisis. All parties are involved in a game in which none wish to provoke confrontations testing the limits of each other's power. On the other hand, when a court has ordered change, there is an implicit threat that the court might use its coercive power.

The 1975 case of *Wuori* v. *Zitnay cont'd sub nom Wuori* v. *Concannon* (Levine, 1986)[4] was an unusually successful case. The court gave up active supervision within a relatively few years after finding substantial, if not full, compliance with an expensive, complex, and highly detailed consent decree calling for the improvement of an institution for the retarded and the creation of community facilities and programming.

The case was a class action on behalf of Martti Wuori, a resident of the Pineland Center in Maine, and all others similarly situated, filed by Neville Woodruff, a public interest lawyer. The complaint specified many substandard conditions at Pineland and many instances of poor treatment of residents. Shortly after the suit was initiated, George Zitnay, who had earlier worked with members of the Yale Psychoeducational Clinic (Sarason, Zitnay, & Grossman, 1971), was appointed superintendent of the center. Zitnay, an experienced and gifted administrator, recognized the opportunities provided by the suit. When he testified, he told the truth about the institution, and the state settled out of court.

Shortly afterwards, Zitnay was appointed commissioner of mental health and corrections in Maine. He and Kevin Concannon, then director of the Bureau of Mental Retardation, worked with the plaintiff's attorney to develop a remediation plan. After spending two years developing plans to improve the institution, they came up with a comprehensive remediation plan with the assistance of the Mental Health Law Project, a Washington-based public interest law firm. At Zitnay's and Concannon's recommendation, the state agreed to the plan. U.S. District Court

Judge Edward T. Gignoux, a highly respected jurist, entered the plan as the court's judgment of the court in July 1978.

The plan called for far-reaching changes in the institution and the development of community-based facilities and programming. It included several hundred specifications covering just about every aspect of living and habilitation (treatment) in the institution and in community programs and called for the appointment of a special master, a court-appointed official whose job is to monitor the implementation of the order and to recommend necessary steps to achieve compliance with the decree (Nathan, 1979; D. Levine, 1984).

David Gregory, a law professor with experience in civil rights litigation but none in the care of the retarded, was appointed master for a period of two years. Initially, he thought the monitoring task was straightforward, but he quickly became aware of its organizational and political complexities. Gregory visited the institution and the community services and interviewed staff and residents to educate himself. After the first six months, he realized the need to reach out to other state agencies whose cooperation would be needed to implement the plan fully. (These other agencies were not named as defendants in the suit and were therefore not under the court's jurisdiction.) He also learned that new resources would be required in order to implement the decree. Zitnay and Concannon gave Gregory information about the system's deficiencies, and Gregory encouraged the operators of group homes to press for changes in the overly rigid regulations governing community residences and programming. Gregory concluded that only a vigorous and firm position would move the system to action. His semiannual compliance reports contained graphic descriptions of continued shortcomings and pointedly criticized noncooperating state officials. He also recommended reorganizing the executive branch to give Zitnay greater power over some state programs that were not then within his jurisdiction. Gregory threatened the use of the court's coercive powers if cooperation was not forthcoming. His reports were publicized, to the embarrassment of Maine's public officials; Zitnay and Concannon used the reports with the governor and the state legislature to support their request for increased budgets and other legislative changes.

Zitnay, who had a good working relationship with the governor who had appointed him commissioner of mental health, was unable to sustain that relationship with the next governor. He returned to Pineland as superintendent, and Concannon succeeded him as commissioner. Zitnay now worked closely with Gregory to use the court order to help him improve Pineland. By exercising firm and creative leadership and using the court order to back him when needed, Zitnay quickly managed to turn a backward institution into one that could be shown with pride to any visitor. Even the most disabled residents were clean and well dressed. The living quarters were personalized and attractive. An enthusiastic staff was deployed in creative ways. Good ratios of personnel to residents supported active programming.

At the end of Gregory's two-year tenure, the court order had not yet been fully implemented, and Gregory recommended that the court retain jurisdiction. The state defendants and the plaintiff's attorneys, recognizing that progress had been made, negotiated an agreement to implement the remainder of the court order. The defendants agreed to continue the office of the special master, but they insisted that Gregory be replaced.

Lincoln Clark was named to be the new special master. Clark, a retired professor of marketing, an experienced executive, and a skilled mediator, was Judge Gignoux's close personal friend. Clark concentrated on the Pineland Center first because it was close to compliance with the court order. He conducted many negotiating sessions with Zitnay, Concannon, other state officials, and the plaintiff's attorney to arrive at still more specific agreements about how to meet the remaining points in the order. By July 1981 Zitnay issued a report saying that his institution was in full compliance with the 315 items in the decree. Clark then engaged an experienced consultant to review Zitnay's report, and the consultant confirmed its conclusions after inspecting the institution and its records and interviewing staff and others. When the consultant agreed that the institution was in substantial compliance, Clark recommended that the institution be discharged from the court's supervision.

It took two more years to fulfill the community plan. Concannon provided the leadership. Clark met with all parties to work out plans for correcting the remaining deficiencies in the community-based service system. By then state officials were committed to improving the system of care, but budgetary restraints, bureaucratic inertia, and turf problems between agencies of government slowed progress. Clark used a mediator's skills, but he was well aware that his effectiveness depended on the coercive power of the court in the background. In addition to identifying his actions with the court's wishes, Clark distributed his reports widely to the public, to citizen groups, to state officials, and to state legislators. Clark, who was also head of the state court's mediation service, spoke informally but directly with key officials. His reports encouraged citizen groups to lobby for resources to implement community-based services.

The combination of mediation and pressure moved the state system along. Clark engaged several independent consultants to review progress. By 1983 the consultants issued reports stating that either the standards had been met or working mechanisms had been created to ensure that they would be met. Woodruff, still acting as the plaintiff's attorney, agreed that progress had been made but insisted that permanent and independent monitoring devices be put into place. A consumer's advisory board was given full access to all programs and records related to the care of the retarded and was authorized to hear complaints about any aspect of client care. The state also agreed to public hearings and annual, independent compliance reviews that would be announced publicly, with specific notice being given to advocacy organizations. The auditor's reports would be made public; if they called for corrective action, the commissioner of mental health and mental retardation had to develop and publish a plan for correction.

The monitoring process was put in place. Public hearings to identify problems in the service system, the first step in the reviewing process, took place. The Consumer Advisory Board reorganized itself to handle the work of monitoring compliance with the court order, appointing about 130 "correspondents" to act as friends to those who had no families or who had been abandoned. These correspondents were organized into smaller groups, which reported to a coordinator. The correspondents served as "eyes" on the system, seeing to it that the people they befriended received appropriate care.

Remarkable changes took place. The court's order supplied the blueprint and the leverage for change, and skillful and firm leadership, making use of the opportunity provided by the lawsuit and the court's decree, led to substantial improvement and modernization of the system of care. During litigation and during the implementation phase, Maine changed many of its laws governing the care of the retarded to bring its facilities into compliance with decree requirements, making the changes permanent as a matter of state law. Even though the court eventually stopped its active supervision, the program appeared to be firmly in place. Several years later, the Consumer Advisory Board and some consumers of mental retardation services asked the court to enforce the terms of the 1978 consent decree. (The case report turned on technical, legal issues and did not say which terms of the decree were allegedly being violated.) The court found that the decree continued in force even though there had been no legal action under the decree for eight years (*Consumer Advisory Board* v. *Glover*, 1993). The decree thus continued to provide leverage for advocates seeking to keep the reforms intact.

Litigation was sucessful in this case in achieving the goal of improving the system. Miller and Iscoe (1990), writing from the viewpoint of defendants in institutional reform suits, have a somewhat more jaundiced view of court-ordered change. They argue that some activists' hypercriticism is destructive. Miller and Iscoe say that a minor industry of well-paid, self-serving advocates and special masters has developed and note that if the advocates didn't find anything wrong in the care provided by institutions, they would go out of business.

The change process in *Wouri* was long and complex. The leadership of Zitnay and Concannon was critical, but the special master's role is of particular interest. Although they are quasi-judicial officers, the special masters engaged in indirect lobbying and public relations to create political pressure and public acceptance of the new programs (Miller & Iscoe, 1990), activities that would be highly unusual for a judge. The role of master thus provided a buffer to avoid critical confrontations of power that can lead to political crises.

The change process reveals how much the service system is embedded in our political and governmental system. The disciplines and practices of law, political science, sociology, economics, psychology, medicine, rehabilitation, education, organization and management, mediation and negotiation, evaluation research, and public relations are needed to understand and to produce change.

Summary

If we are to modify existing helping services and implement new program concepts, we must create or modify social organizations to deliver the new services. The principles that guide planned change, be it the creation of a new setting or the modification of an existing service organization, were forged out of difficult experiences in which change failed altogether or failed to fulfill some part of its purpose. These principles help us to understand the problems commonly encountered in creating new settings or changing existing settings.

The creation of new settings requires more than a good idea, agreement on abstract values, and strong motivation to succeed. We illustrated the issues in the creation of settings by showing how the Residential Youth Center was developed.

Changing existing organizations presents other problems. Every new program exists in the context of social groups that have an interest in the program and in each other in relation to the program. We identified seven broad sets of interests: energy, power, culture, competence, relationships, legal and administrative considerations, and information and communication. Members of each of these social groups evaluate proposed changes by examining how the proposed change will affect their interests. Groups that on balance will gain from the changes will support them; groups that on balance stand to lose will oppose the change. Forces in the social context tend to pull new programs or concepts back toward the status quo ante. Change efforts and change agents must recognize and overcome that pull.

We presented two brief case studies of change, one in a mental hospital and one in a state's system for the care of the retarded. In the first case, change was brought about by skillful leadership; in the second, skillful leaders used the power of a court to correct wrongs in the service system.

In the next chapter, we illustrate change brought about on a national scale by examining the racial desegregation of the schools. Once again we will see the interplay among law, social science, and the complexities of introducing widespread change.

Notes

1. Sarason was thinking of the large number of antipoverty programs, community mental health centers, Head Start programs, and the myriad of alternative service settings that emerged in the 1960s and early 1970s. The pace of cre-

ating settings continues today as new problems emerge or new issues capture our attention. Innumerable abortion clinics with attendant counseling facilities sprang up in the wake of *Roe* v. *Wade* protecting a woman's right to an abortion. Rape crisis centers, havens for battered women, and a large number of health maintenance organizations were also formed. Thousands of self-help organizations have been created in recent years; for example, many citizens organizations opposed to burying toxic wastes in landfills near residential neighborhoods and water supplies were formed after the Love Canal revelation raised the nation's consciousness and led to national and state efforts to identify toxic waste dump sites (Gibbs, 1982; A. Levine, 1982).

2. Donald T. Campbell (personal communication), in discussing a critical problem in evaluation research, noted that whenever a program is evaluated by some more or less arbitrary criterion, with political consequences or resource allocation depending on the evaluation, one of two results obtain: Either the process becomes corrupted to satisfy the index or the index becomes corrupted. Thus, if a school program is evaluated by students' achievement test results, the educational process may become corrupted as teachers concentrate on teaching students to perform well on the test. In one notable example, an educational contractor who was to be paid on the basis of achievement test results spent time actually teaching students to do test items that made up the criterion.

The concept of index corruption is undoubtedly familiar to anyone who has ever responded to bureaucratic demands for figures. Many people can attest that the reliability of some of the figures offered is highly suspect. For example, in an academic department that was evaluated by administrators in part on the basis of faculty publication productivity, it was common practice among faculty to include items that were in press in one year and to count the same item again the following year when the piece had been published, effectively doubling output. No doubt readers can multiply the examples from their own experiences.

3. Shortly after the research for the case study of Harlem Valley was completed, Haveliwala left Harlem Valley and took over the directorship of another, larger hospital within the state system. The problems and the task in the new situation were quite different from those at Harlem Valley. Haveliwala encountered great opposition from the state bureaucracy, which accused him of mismanagement. The facts on the public record are unclear, but eventually he resigned his position. Some observers believe he was forced out because he publicly opposed some of the governor's and the commissioner's policies in a letter published in the *New York Times*. At any rate, the circumstances were different at his new post and it is not clear that he could have used the same approach as he had earlier. The lesson is that methods must be adopted to the historical situation and to conditions as they exist. As Sarason (1981a) notes, psychology is peculiarly ahistorical and focused on contextless principles. The case study is a warning that we ignore history and contexts at our peril when applying theoretical principles.

4. The research reported here was completed with support from the National Science Foundation Law and Social Science Program, Grant No. SES-8023954. This section is adapted from a longer report published elsewhere (Levine, 1986).

11

School Desegregation: A Societal-Level Intervention

The desegregation of U.S. society is one of the more profound social changes of our time. We include a discussion of desegregation in part because social scientists played important roles in the desegregation effort (although they were by no means the leaders of the effort to achieve desegregation) and in part because it is a good example of an intervention that affected the entire nation. Moreover, at the level of individual school districts and individual schools, responsible authorities had to institute a process to accommodate change that had been initiated externally.

Another important aspect of desegregation, from the perspective of community psychologists, was that social scientists helped to create a body of knowledge and theory that attributed the plight of African American people in the United States not to their individual characteristics but to the environmental conditions under which they lived—segregation enforced by law. Black and white scholars, literary figures, and social activists developed coherent intellectual rationales to fight racial oppression.

Later, especially with regard to the effort to desegregate the schools, social scientists provided important expert testimony in the courts regarding the detrimental psychological effects of segregation. Social scientists also provided theoretical propositions justifying desegregation remedies.

Although the desegregation of U.S. society was propelled by many forces, it can be described as a massive, planned, societal-level intervention whose purpose was to solve complex moral, social, economic, and psychological problems. Segregation of the races, a social practice enforced by the power of law, was built on an assumption held by the white majority that African Americans were inherently inferior to whites and that the interests of both races would be served by rigidly enforcing racial separation. This assumption rationalized the exploitation of the African American minority, who did not share it and who experienced segregation as oppression. Eventually a body of scholarly opinion developed to support the view that segregation was oppression and was the cause of social, economic, and psychological problems among African Americans. Given that segregation was accepted as the cause of the evils associated with it, attacking the cause by getting rid of the formal barriers to full integration made sense.

The theory that segregation as a social and legal practice was the cause of diverse social, economic, and psychological consequences is a situationally oriented theory. The proposition that removing formal barriers to integration would undo the undesirable consequences is a corollary to the theory. The theory and the intervention were aimed not at changing people but at changing conditions, with the assumption that changes in behavior, attitudes, and self-image would follow.

At the school level, the specific remedy for the evils of segregation—desegregation—was based in part on a set of premises drawn from the psychological study of prejudice. Attempts to change this deeply engrained social pattern has revealed both that we know less than we thought we did and that the underlying phenomena are more complex than we thought. The social science propositions were stated most clearly in relation to public education, and we now have a body of evidence testing their validity. Because documentation is strong in the area of school desegregation, we will concentrate on a discussion of those propositions. The reader should bear in mind the larger context of change in American life, however, and the effects of desegregation on every social institution (Brooks, 1974).

Much has happened in the forty years since *Brown* v. *Board of Education*, the 1954 landmark school desegregation case. Although racial segregation on the basis of law has been eliminated and efforts have been made to desegregate, or integrate, schools, powerful social forces have resulted in the resegregation of many schools because of changing residential patterns and U.S. Supreme Court decisions that limited the options for school desegregation (Orfield, 1993). Out of frustration over the nation's continuing racial problems, some observers have begun to rethink the ideal of integration as a solution to those problems. These changing views remind us that we are always functioning in a social and historical context and that solutions appropriate for one time and one set of circumstances may not be the preferred solutions in another historical period.

Slavery, Segregation, and the Constitution

Slavery and race relations have occupied the attention of Americans from the very beginning of the nation.[1] The contradiction in values is clear between the ringing words of political freedom in the Declaration of Independence—"all men are created equal"—and the section of the Constitution that counted each slave as three-fifths of a person for purposes of taxation and representation.[2] This contradiction was solved for many by viewing African Americans as less than fully human in intellectual, moral, and social characteristics.

Slavery was an issue at every step in the nation's growth before the Civil War. Whether each new state was to be designated a free state or a slave state was a source of political and armed conflict. Eventually that conflict erupted into the Civil War. In the United States, African Americans were viewed and treated as inferior beings and had difficult lives. Slaves had few rights. They did not own their own bodies or labor and were denied an education. Segregation in public accommodations, churches, and schools was common throughout the nonslave states of the North. Before the Civil War, free African Americans were denied the right to vote or had their voting rights drastically restricted.

In 1865, after the Civil War, Lincoln's Emancipation Proclamation became a permanent part of our Constitution as the Thirteenth Amendment, banning involuntary servitude. The Thirteenth Amendment was not sufficient to protect the civil and political rights of newly freed African Americans, however. Many southern states passed black codes designed to restore slavery in fact if not in name. The Fourteenth Amendment (1868) provided all persons, African American and white, with protections against state action that violated the principle of equal protection under the law or that deprived any person of life, liberty, or property without due process of law. Although intended to protect newly freed slaves, the Fourteenth Amendment was written in much broader terms to reflect ideals of political freedom and social equality (tenBroek, 1965). The Fifteenth Amendment, protecting the right to vote, became part of the Constitution in 1870.

For the next thirty years the promise of these amendments was undercut by violence and economic pressure against African Americans and by a U.S. Supreme Court that "interpreted away" the protections of the post–Civil War amendments.[3] Protection became a matter for state law. If the states saw fit to permit private discrimination or if the states did not enforce their laws against violence, citizens had no protection.

In 1890 the Louisiana legislature passed a law calling for separate but equal accommodations for white and "colored" passengers on railroad trains. The phrase "separate but equal" was designed to meet the requirements of the equal-protection clause of the Fourteenth Amendment. The African American citizens of New Orleans, in cooperation with railroad officials who were not pleased with the prospect of having to add extra cars to their trains, tested the law. In 1892 Homer Adolph Plessy, who was seven-eighths Caucasian, boarded a train and refused to move to the segregated car. Arrested and fined, he appealed his conviction, and in 1896 his case reached the U.S. Supreme Court.

The Supreme Court then enunciated its notorious separate-but-equal doctrine. Holding that the equal-protection clause of the Fourteenth Amendment did not abolish all social distinctions and could not require that the races commingle "upon terms unsatisfactory to either," the Court went on to say:

> We consider the underlying fallacy of the plaintiff's argument to consist in the assumption that the enforced separation of the two races stamps the colored race with a badge of inferiority. If this be so, it is not by reason of anything found in the act, but solely because the colored race chooses to put that construction upon it. (*Plessy* v. *Ferguson*, 1896)

In later years, the *Plessy* decision was used to support and sustain discriminatory legislation affecting all American social institutions.[4] The Supreme Court had grounded its decision in *Plessy* on the social psychological proposition that stigma was not inherent in the action of forced segregation because the law itself contained no stigmatizing words. The problem, according to the Court, was in the perceptions of those who were the victims of discrimination. The Court's use of a social psychological proposition was to set the agenda for the next fifty-eight years in the study of race relations. Because the *Plessy* Court used a social psychological concept, the proposition could be challenged with data to show that enforced separation *was* stigmatizing and harmful.

The NAACP and Its Litigative Strategy

The victory for school desegregation in *Brown* v. *Board of Education* (1954) represented the culmination of a planned self-help effort by a private community organization. The National Association for the Advancement of Colored People (NAACP) was formed in 1909, in the shadow of virulent and violent anti–African American sentiment. The organization's major aim was the protection of the rights of African Americans through social, political, and legal action (Hughes, 1962). It settled on litigation as the major means to pursue its aims. After 1929 the Howard University Law School became a center for research on civil rights law, and many of the African American lawyers who carried the fight trained there, including U.S. Supreme Court Justice Thurgood Marshall, the first African American to achieve that position.

The attack on school segregation began as early as 1929, and by 1935 more than one hundred court cases had challenged the legality of school segregation. Direct challenges to segregated schools invariably lost in the courts, however. The administration of the laws, not desegregation itself, seemed a more promising legal target. A review of litigative successes and failures led to a strategy of attacking the myth that, measured objectively (e.g., money spent on schools, quality of school buildings), schools were in fact separate but equal. By insisting that separate schools be equal, the NAACP leadership hoped that segregation would be brought down by the financial weight of maintaining two truly equal school systems.

In the post–World War II period, civil rights litigation attacking segregation extended to housing, labor law, jury service, and voting. Litigation was accompanied by efforts at winning legislative change and by social action that directly confronted segregated institutions (Brooks, 1974).

Thurgood Marshall led the NAACP's legal battles from the late 1930s on. The postwar attack began at graduate and professional schools that were supported by tax money, but that excluded African Americans. With a group of African American lawyers centered at Howard University, and with a few white lawyers, Marshall successfully pursued the strategy of insisting on separate but equal education at the graduate and the professional school levels.[5] These cases resulted in the admission of African American students to formerly all-white schools, since the alternatives were to build equal facilities for blacks or close down the all-white schools. Marshall and the NAACP Legal Defense Fund were also successful in suits seeking equal pay for African American and white teachers.

The struggle against elementary school segregation was renewed in the years after World War II. NAACP legal briefs more and more stressed the stigmatizing and stultifying consequences of segregation, although the basic legal attack continued to center on the inequality of facilities. Although the Supreme Court had struck down segregation barriers in the higher education cases, it had not confronted the argument that separate educational facilities were inherently unequal. The decisions in the higher education cases provided precedents for many lower-courts judges who ordered educational authorities at the posthigh school level to provide truly equal facilities or to admit African Americans to formerly all-white institutions.

Marshall and the NAACP thought carefully about how to mount a direct litigative assault on the assumption that separate could be equal. Not only were the legal grounds uncertain; participation in the cases by African American plaintiffs was perilous both physically and financially. It was also perilous for African American civil rights lawyers to bring cases in the South, where they faced a constant threat of physical violence, but they proceeded with heroic determination. The cultural belief that the low social and economic state of African Americans in society was attributable not to segregation but to blacks' inherent inferiority was at stake. In the years after *Plessy*, scientific literature, scientific in the sense that it was written by men with scholarly credentials and positions, was published that rationalized the belief in racial inferiority.[6] By the late 1920s other social scientists had developed the opposing position that the social environment was the primary cause of African Americans' failure to achieve. The growing social science literature on the effects of racism provided an intellectual rationale for the argument that segregated facilities were inherently unequal because segregation itself caused severe psychological damage.

Kenneth Clark, an African American social psychologist who had been an undergraduate at Howard and later became president of the American Psychological Association, had been experimenting with techniques to show that segregation resulted in impaired self-images in African American children. Although not all of his NAACP legal colleagues agreed, Marshall viewed Clark's studies (conducted in collaboration with Clark's wife, Mamie) as an excellent means of demonstrating that segregation damaged the self-esteem of African American children.

Cases challenging segregation itself as inherently unequal worked their way through the lower courts to the Supreme Court. Clark and other social scientists testified in a number of these cases.[7] Testifying in *Brown* v. *Board of Education of Topeka* (1954), the social science expert Louisa P. Holt influenced the trial court's findings of fact on the ill effects of segregation, and this finding of fact was later cited by the Supreme Court in its decision. At the request of NAACP attorneys, a group of social scientists headed by Isidor Chein, Kenneth Clark, and Stuart Cook prepared a review of the evidence on segregation that was appended to the NAACP brief to the Supreme Court (a footnote now called the Social Science Statement; see the discussion later in this chapter).

When the *Brown* decision was rendered in 1954, the importance of the psychological and sociological premises for the argument were apparent in Chief Justice Earl Warren's opinion for a unanimous Court:

> Segregation of white and colored children in public schools has a detrimental effect upon the colored children. The impact is greater when it has the sanction of law; for the policy of separating the races is usually interpreted as denoting the inferiority of the negro group. A sense of inferiority affects the motivation of the child to learn. Segregation with the sanction of law, therefore, has a tendency to [retard] the educational and mental development of negro children and to deprive them of some of the benefits they would receive in a racial[ly] integrated school system. Whatever may have been the extent of psychological knowledge at the time of *Plessy v. Ferguson*, this finding is amply supported by modern authority.

The court then cited the ample modern evidence for its position, listing social science studies by name and citing their authors in a now famous footnote 11,[8] thus directly contradicting the social psychological assertions made by the Court in *Plessy* and providing an important part of the rationale for overruling the 1896 decision.

Warren's opinion for a unanimous Court declared segregated schools unconstitutional, but the Court waited another year before issuing its word on remedies. The Court offered few guidelines to the federal district courts that were to oversee the implementation of remedies, urging only that desegregation be accomplished "with all deliberate speed." The Court was appropriately cautious, since what would constitute an effective remedy was not clear. No prior decision had affected so many American families and communities directly and personally.

The two *Brown* decisions opposed a few words on paper against two hundred years of history and custom. The words of the Supreme Court were law, however, and all the federal government's power to enforce the law was behind the words. In 1957, when the governor of Arkansas used the National Guard to prevent African American children from entering white schools, President Dwight D. Eisenhower sent federal troops to protect the children's rights (Bickel, 1962). The show of force was not sufficient to end the legal skirmishing, however, as community after community adopted foot-dragging plans. (Constance Baker Motley, an African American woman and a graduate of Columbia University Law School, traveled throughout the South arguing cases for the NAACP to win desegregation orders in different communities. A real novelty, an African American woman lawyer arguing cases in southern courtrooms, she braved hardship, insults, and threats. However, she was determined and regularly won her cases. She was later appointed to the federal bench [Brenner, 1994]).

In legal terms, desegregation meant that African American and white children and African American and white teachers and administrators should work side by side in unitary, racially mixed schools. The remedies— busing within districts, busing across school district lines, pairing schools, and affirmative-action hiring—required a departure from the concept of neighborhood schools and from some hiring practices.[9] Busing was supported by a massive national study showing that African American students in integrated schools performed better than African American students in segregated schools and that the amount of money spent on schools made little difference in performance (Coleman et al., 1966; Ravitch, 1983).

Not only southern schools were segregated. African Americans in northern urban areas also attended segregated schools, partly because of the increasing surbanization of the nation after World War II and the increasing concentration of African Americans in the inner cities. Segregation in northern schools was not only the result of the "succession" of one population by another (see Chapter 4). In many cities, authorities had drawn school district lines or located new schools in such a way as to ensure segregated schools. In 1973 the Supreme Court ruled in *Keyes*

v. *Denver* that if a portion of a school system was segregated as a result of discriminatory practices by school authorities, a systemwide remedy could be imposed even if there was no other history of officially imposed segregation.

Where African American students constituted a majority or near-majority of the school population, integration could not be achieved without busing students across school district lines. In *Milliken* v. *Bradley* (1974) the Court refused to authorize cross-district busing, however, in the absence of evidence that school authorities in the affected suburban districts had acted to cause segregation in the urban district. The Court approved instead the plaintiff's request that resources be allocated to remedy educational deficits and to develop programs that facilitated integration within the urban school district.

The *Milliken* decision limited the possibilities for desegregation to whatever could be accomplished within a given school district, and probably contributed to so-called white flight (the movement of white families out of the cities to avoid busing to integrate the schools), although some have questioned that conclusion (Farley, 1980). Busing undoubtedly contributed to a backlash against integration efforts and to the development of resistance to further efforts at integrating the schools. Moreover, political leaders, sensing the resistance of large numbers of parents to busing programs, articulated those views and turned them into votes (Ravitch, 1983). Although some efforts to impose busing provoked violence (e.g., in the Boston schools; Smith, 1978; Metcalf, 1983), in other places busing and integration proceeded peacefully (Willie, 1984).

Court orders to desegregate affected school districts all over the country. Implementation was monitored by federal judges or special masters reporting to the judges who had issued the order. These cases continued for many years; the Little Rock, Arkansas, case that led President Eisenhower to call out the National Guard is still in the courts. These cases intruded on local prerogatives. For example, the U.S. Supreme Court once upheld a federal judge's order to a local community to increase school taxes to pay for efforts to desegregate the schools. More recently, however, the Supreme Court has been authorizing federal judges to relinquish jurisdiction over school desegregation cases when they find the school district to be in substantial compliance with the court's desegregation order and when new segregation is caused by housing patterns rather than by actions of school officials or legislatures (D. Levine, 1993).

These decisions, along with the decision eliminating busing across school district lines in northern communities, have contributed to the resegregation of the schools (Orfield, 1993). Increasing residential segregation due to population shifts has also made it more difficult to integrate schools racially. In Detroit, for example, 76 percent of the population is now African American. Disappointing experiences in desegregated schools, including ability tracking that effectively resegregated integrated schools, have led some African American leaders to rethink the values of integrated education (Hill, 1993). They question whether integration leading to assimilation into the majority culture is a worthwhile goal even if it is attainable. They argue that self-imposed instead of governmentally imposed separation and an Afrocentric curriculum have value for the development of identity in both male and female African Americans (Cummings, 1993).

Social Science Theory and Integration

The social science testimony given in cases that reached the Supreme Court asserted that segregation was wrong and harmful and that desegregation would undo the harm. It offered little discussion of the specific problems of implementing remedies. Cook (1984), a coauthor of what is now called the Social Science Statement cited in Brown (1954), noted that the legal issue in *Brown* dealt with the effects on children of lifelong de jure (by law) segregation and did not require a detailed discussion of remedies. Nonetheless, social scientists' testimony and position papers contained a set of implicit situational hypotheses.

Stephan (1978) reviewed the testimony in the several cases. He drew a causal model in which white prejudice toward African Americans led to low African American self-esteem and achievement and African American prejudice toward whites. In turn, the same factors looped back to stimulate and maintain white prejudice against African Americans. If enforced segregation, the institutional base for the loop, were to be interrupted, African American self-esteem and achievement should improve, African Americans should develop more positive attitudes toward whites, and whites should have more positive attitudes toward African Americans. Stephan's model implies rapid change but does not include time as a variable. Cook (1984) argues that the Social Science Statement anticipated the gap between African American and white achievement levels and implied that these would be eliminated gradually over an indeterminate number of years.

Stephan (1978) reviewed a large number of studies that tested hypotheses derived from the Social Science Statement. The results are generally equivocal with respect to improving interracial attitudes. An equal number of studies show increases and decreases in African American prejudice toward whites, and more studies show an increase in white prejudice toward African Americans than show a decrease. Methodological problems make it difficult to interpret the results of most studies, but simply placing African Americans and whites in the same physical location is not enough to reduce prejudice, at least not in the short run.

Desegregation has not been shown to have any consistent effect on African American self-esteem. Cook (1984) notes that the studies and the measures lack subtlety, but more likely the original hypothesis that simply removing the barrier and increasing contact would increase self-esteem and reduce prejudice was too simple. Cook (1984) states that, beginning in the mid-1960s, studies showed that African American self-esteem in segregated situations was as high as or higher than the self-esteem of whites. One hypothesis states that widespread cultural change in the 1960s and 1970s—the civil rights movement, black power, the "black is beautiful" slogan, and media attention to prominent African American political, sports, and entertainment figures—contributed to improved self-esteem. This increased attention was associated with the desegregation of U.S. society and the civil rights legislation that followed the *Brown* decision. The changes in African American self-esteem examined by the studies of school desegregation were attributable to many powerful social forces, not just to school desegregation.

The consequences of desegregation for school achievement are also complex. According to Stephan's summary, African American students in integrated schools may do somewhat better than African American students in segregated schools, and white achievement is not adversely affected in desegregated schools. Gerard (1983) finds little evidence of change in African American achievement. Sarason's caveat about giving change a sufficient amount of time to produce an effect is probably relevant here. That is, Cook (1984) argues that the Social Science Statement anticipated favorable effects only over the long run and said nothing about short-term changes in achievement except to predict what was found—that neither African American nor white achievement would be adversely affected by integration.

Gerard (1983) notes that the Social Science Statement specified several conditions under which real integration, and thus the posited effects, could take place. These included:

> (a) firm and consistent endorsement by those in authority; (b) the absence of competition among representatives of different racial groups; (c) the equivalence of positions and functions among all participants in the desegregated setting; and (d) interracial contacts of a type that permitted learning about one another as individuals. (Gerard, 1983, p. 870)

The statement was derived from the existing knowledge about prejudice, extrapolated to the school situation (Cook, 1984). Gerard (1983) notes that the first condition, firm and consistent endorsement by those in authority, required all authority figures, from elected officials to the classroom teacher, to endorse desegregation. In Gerard's view, it was shortsighted to expect such consistency; in any event, pitting busing against the neighborhood school created anything but consistent endorsement. Cook (1984) defends the social science prediction by noting that in other desegregation situations (e.g., the armed forces, industry), forceful leadership overcame the initial disruptions created by integration.

The second condition for successful desegregation was an absence of competition. Gerard reminds his readers that competition is deeply ingrained in American culture, that teachers do not have the skills nor the social characteristics to foster cooperation, and that in any event it was too much to expect of the classroom teacher to homogenize subcultural diversity within the classroom. Cook (1984) responds that there have been many successful experiments in interracial learning teams within the public schools. It was not that it couldn't be done, but that it was not done enough.

The third condition was the equivalence of functions and positions among all participants. Although affirmative-action programs have resulted in greater numbers of African American teachers and administrators within the schools, Gerard claims that the schools have done little to create true equivalence in position or in power.

As for the fourth condition, interracial contact that permits learning about each other as individuals, Gerard notes that self-segregation occurs within the classroom. His sociometric data show very few cross-racial work partnerships or friendship choices. Gerard sums up his argument by saying that teachers would have to have been social engineering geniuses to have put into operation the conditions social scientists said were necessary to induce the positive effects of integration.

Looking back, Gerard concludes that data were not available to warrant the confident predictions that were derived from the Social Science Statement and, moreover, that the social scientists were not fully cognizant of the contexts within which the abstract principles they had culled from the literature would have to be implemented. In effect, he claims, they were unfamiliar with the culture of the schools (see Sarason, 1982). Gerard argues that sufficient *knowledge* was not yet available to legitimize social scientists as "expert witnesses" in school desegregation cases.

Some (e.g., Cahn, 1955) argue that it is an error to rely on empirical outcomes to decide moral questions. Should we be able to argue that because all the postulated benefits of desegregation cannot be demonstrated empirically, we should again allow states to enforce segregation? Although certain benefits were implied for forced busing, if we did not integrate schools and did not integrate faculties, what else could we have done, in Justice William Brennan's words (*Green* v. *County*, 1968), to eliminate discrimination "root and branch"? The social policy of desegregation can rest on premises other than those pressed by social scientists.

Beyond Busing

In hindsight, some observers argue that the premises behind desegregation were flawed. The simple placement of African Americans and whites in the same buildings was insufficient; more profound changes were necessary to equalize the positions of African American and white children.

Substantive change requires the following: an examination of disparate funding levels, a finding of de facto school desegregation [i.e., without the operation of law] as sufficient for an order desegregating suburban school systems, a diverse curriculum, an elimination of testing bias to the extent practicable, and the placement of decisions affecting minority children in the hands of minority parents. Racism is so much a part of the American fabric that every aspect of the school environment must be examined and re-examined to measure its effects on patterns of dominance and exclusion. (Hill, 1993, p. 723)

Some writers prescribe the conditions they believe will enhance the engagement of African American children in the classroom. These writers believe that subtle and not-so-subtle devaluation of African Americans in the larger society and in the classroom result in student disengagement from school and failure to learn. In keeping with the view that emphasizing children's deficits and providing remediation is a form of blaming the victim, Steele (1992) suggests that remedial programs may have the unintended consequence of increasing the African American student's sense of vulnerability. He argues that "wise" teaching—accepting that African American children can learn, creating a classroom atmosphere in which students are valued, and holding out demands for achievement—can be a powerful preventive to the disengagement that leads to failure and dropping out.

Kagan (1990) also believes that classroom settings can alienate students. Drawing on the school dropout and underachievement literature, Kagan believes that some students are systematically labeled early on. These students find other students who, like themselves, experience the classroom as boring if not punishing, helping to create an antischool subculture. The student's identity includes a sense of alienation from the larger society and a belief that the student is an academic failure.

For Kagan, and for Steele, the solutions require a reanalysis of the classroom as a setting that can "coerce" learning and engagement. They would agree with Sarason's (1990) analysis that no school reform can succeed unless it changes student-teacher relationships in the classroom. Steele and Kagan have more integrationist aims and do not believe that "wise" teaching can take place only in racially segregated settings. Kagan wants to reduce alienation by changing classroom practices. Steele (1992, p. 78) wants "to foster in our children a sense of hope and entitlement to mainstream American life and schooling." It is unlikely that successful lawsuits will be brought on the grounds that classrooms are not successful. However, in an attempt to remedy an unsatisfactory condition, community participation in the schools may lead us to a better educational program for all.

Successful Desegregation of the Schools—A Case Study

The organizational changes necessary to support desegregation were not at the forefront of the consciousness of the federal judges who were overseeing desegregation efforts (Kirp & Babcock, 1981).[10] With time, however, judges, plaintiffs, and school board officials did learn to cope with the problems of overseeing desegregation efforts. Although critics of busing have emphasized the difficulties, including the moral questions that attend discriminating on the basis of race even to effect a remedy (e.g., Glazer, 1975), in at least some cases desegregation efforts have produced overall improvements in the schools.

We now turn to a brief case history that describes the successful school desegregation effort in Buffalo, New York. The reader should consider the case material in light of the principles Gerard (1983) says are necessary for a successful program of school integration and in light of our discussion of change in Chapter 10. The reader should also consider values such as decreased alienation from the schools, pride in the schools, and diversified curriculum offerings when evaluating the results of school desegregation.

In 1976, a federal district court judge, John T. Curtin, found that Buffalo city school officials, the Common Council, and the mayor had acted to create or perpetuate segregated schools. The suit, initiated in 1964 by a complaint to the state commissioner of education, ended with findings that the school board had redistricted school zones to maintain segregated schools, allowed whites to transfer out of integrated schools, stopped teaching Polish in a high school with many African American students (thus encouraging whites to enroll in Polish classes in other high schools), placed a junior high school in a neighborhood that guaranteed it would be segregated, and fostered discriminatory policies affecting admission to desirable technical high schools. Moreover, a busing plan ordered by the commissioner of education after the 1964 complaint was found to be inadequate. The Common Council had tried to block a voluntary busing plan and through its fiscal control had refused to support a new building plan that might have relieved segregation.[11] The U.S. Supreme Court had held in *Keyes* (1973) that if any portion of a school system had been segregated as a result of the action of school officials, a systemwide desegregation remedy was in order.

Once the city schools and the city administration had been found responsible for the degree of segregation that existed, it was necessary to prepare a remedy. The school system initiated one, but the plaintiffs and the judge were not satisfied that it would result in sufficient desegregation. Because there had been great fear of violence in the city if two-way busing were to be initiated, African American children were bused into schools in white neighborhoods. Now the judge insisted that a more comprehensive plan be adopted.

White and African American parents were angry, resented the idea of busing for racial balance, and were concerned about their children's safety and their opportunities for a good education. The school system was viewed as poor, and school personnel were not seen as credible. Given ethnic prejudice in the largely blue-collar city and the recent example of disorder in Boston (Smith, 1978), many people, including officials of the U.S. Justice Department, expected violence.

By this time there was sufficient understanding of the problems of integration that school officials, led by school superintendent Eugene Reville, and the plaintiffs agreed on the necessity for developing educational programs of high quality to make the schools attractive to parents, along with instituting busing to achieve integration. Judge Curtin insisted that the integration plans be developed in consultation with the community. Associate superintendent Joseph Murray, who had been a highly effective principal of a secondary school in a difficult neighborhood, played an important role in desegregation planning.

School officials arranged more than forty open meetings with community groups. After one expensive and fruitless attempt, the school administrators, who were responsible for devising and carrying out the integration plan under the supervision of the court, decided not to use outside consultants who did not know the community. Instead, they sent teams of African American and white educators and lawyers into neighborhoods, not only to meet with parents and inform them that desegregation was going to take place, but also to let parents know that this was an opportunity to improve the schools as well. Although parents were outspoken and the meetings were often quite heated, the teams included experienced line educators who were used to working with people in the neighborhoods. The U.S. Justice Department also assisted by sending a staff member from its Division of Community Relations to work with community leaders and to monitor the desegregation program. With the cooperation of the ecumenical Buffalo Area Metropolitan Ministries, clergy were also present when trouble was anticipated. In Buffalo, community leadership was unified behind the desegregation plan.

The meetings were intended to bring forward ideas for regional and citywide "magnet" schools[12] and to organize community groups that would contribute to the development of the desegregation plan. The emphasis on education and educational choice was presented to citizens as a means of avoiding forced busing. The outlines for the plans had been developed by school officials, but citizen participation was well utilized. Many of the meetings resulted in the convening of parent groups to develop constructive plans not only to improve the schools but also to develop schools that reflected diverse educational viewpoints. Much of the strain was relieved once these plans were put into effect, although more work to integrate the schools was still necessary.

The twenty-two regional magnet schools were located in integrated neighborhoods or in inner-city neighborhoods. They were designed to reflect neighborhood interest and to be attractive to white and African American parents whose children would be bused to those schools to keep them integrated. The programs were designed to attract parents to their educational philosophies. One school, for example, operated on Montessori principles. Another was highly structured and traditional. One former alternative school had been developed by white parents and was now taken over by the school system but continued to operate on the same principles of informal and individualized instruction. Still another was located in a new open-plan building suitable for an open-education program. The schools were diverse in emphasis. One had Native American programming, while another emphasized education in English and Spanish. One school specialized in programs for gifted children, while another became a prekindergarten-through-eighth-grade school stressing science in all grades.

Neighborhood leaders were identified and in some instances given paid positions within the school programs they helped design. One grassroots leader, once among the most articulate opponents of busing, subsequently became an advocate of busing. Some might say the school system coopted potential opposition by such a tactic. Be that as it may, active citizen opposition was avoided. Teams of African American and white parents were formed to serve as troubleshooters in schools that were to be integrated.

The magnet schools accepted children from all over the city. In addition to schools at the elementary level, three citywide magnet schools were developed at the high school level, including an academy for visual and performing arts, a traditional high school, and City Honors, a school for academically talented youth.[13] Junior high schools that had been criticized for many reasons were replaced with kindergarten-through-eighth-grade schools. At a later phase, early childhood education programs offering excellent care and education for preschool children accommodated the day care needs of many singe-parent households.

Judge Curtin made himself available on an informal basis to listen to people in the neighborhoods. He received at least his fair share of hate mail, but that did not deter him from his course. Observers say that although he unequivocally supported the integration program, he also was willing to listen to the problems people were experiencing, giving people a feeling that communication was taking place and that plans were not simply being imposed on them from above.

Although they had relinquished some power over public education to the judge and the parents, school administrators became enthusiastic as they realized that the desegregation order now gave them leverage to obtain the financial resources necessary to improve the schools. Judge Curtin backed the city school administrators by ordering the city government, which controlled school finances, to provide funds for desegregation programs when the mayor was reluctant. Moreover, declining enrollments necessitated the closing of some schools. The decision to close a school is always difficult, but the requirements of the desegregation program helped administrators decide which schools to close and helped communities to accept the decisions. Although the positive attitude of school administrators and the school board was critical to the success of the desegregation plan, the plaintiff group stayed active and continually monitored and pressed for full compliance.

The interests of teachers were not ignored. They were allowed to transfer to new schools if the educational philosophy in their current schools clashed with their own. Parents were actively included; for example, when a program required the busing of preschool children, parents were taken to visit the new schools to reassure them and to familiarize them with the new facilities. The school district placed ads in the newspapers and on television supporting the busing and school programs. The press also maintained a favorable stance toward the integration program, and school personnel kept Common Council members informed about its progress. Although an African American candidate was defeated in a three-way race for mayor, it is to the credit of Buffalo politicians that no one overtly exploited feelings about integration for political advantage.

The community was involved at an early date. School superintendent Reville invited the Buffalo Area Metropolitan Ministries to solicit support from the clergy for desegregation programs. In addition, a Citizens Commission on Desegregation was formed with representatives from a variety of constituencies. The Citizens Commission was originally intended as a monitoring group, but it proved ineffective and was disbanded. Beginning in 1978 another citizens' organization, Citizens for Quality Education (C4QE), was funded by the Emergency School Assistance Act and by New York State. This group, under the aegis of the Buffalo Area Metropolitan Ministries, assisted community leadership in desegregating the school system and worked with the school system and the court primarily to develop and assist the grass-roots leadership.

The C4QE project was not central to carrying out the desegregation program, and Judge Curtin, school officials, school board members, and the plaintiffs must be given primary credit for the success of this communitywide effort. The project is worth discussing here, because it provides an example of the way that a professional change agent and citizens can together bring about change in a complex context.

The project was under the direction of Lewis J. Sinatra, an educational administrator. He had been a teacher in the Buffalo schools and formerly headed a Teacher Corps project housed at State University College at Buffalo. Before that he had worked with a new teacher project in the Buffalo schools (Foster, 1974). Sinatra had also served as a consultant for the State Education Department on school desegregation in Buffalo. School officials and community leaders, including Judge Curtin, knew and respected him. A lifelong Buffalo resident and a product of its schools, he knew the local community well.

C4QE set up a citywide advisory council that included representatives from every school board district in the city, as well as a representative from the mayor's office and one from the school board. Most of the members, however, were parent representatives. The organization adopted a strategy of working with specific neighborhood projects, and it worked with a strategy of empowerment. C4QE told parents they had a right to be active and then assisted them in working out their programs. C4QE did the staff work and research but always stayed in the background when it came to any formal presentation to officials. When there was some need to address the school board, project staff assisted community leaders in preparing to present their problems or their plans. C4QE kept Judge Curtin informed about what it was doing, especially because he had indicated that he wanted community input into the desegregation program.

C4QEs staff helped the parents in one school to write a proposal to add a seventh and an eighth grade to the school, prepare a presentation to the school board, and request that the proposal be heard by the committee of the board that recommended changes in school programming. The school's principal was willing to work with and support the parent group. Eventually the Board of Education accepted the core of the parents' plan, added the grades, and kept the school open. The court subsequently approved the plan.

The desegregation program in Buffalo has been hailed as a model program (Winerip, 1985). Desegregation took place in peace and relative harmony and with no significant change in the racial composition of the schools. The white population of the city did not flee but became highly supportive of the schools. Parental involvement and satisfaction with the schools grew. Student achievement scores improved overall, while curriculum options proliferated. Participation by both students and parents in extracurricular school programs increased (see Baud, 1982). The social results are unclear, however. Some observers claim that a level of social interaction between African American and white students takes place that would not have been observed ten years ago. However, in other schools some say that African American and white students do not interact and that their proximity has led to mutual antipathy. In the words of one student, "We're all racists now" (Bissinger, 1994).

One cannot say that Buffalo schools are without problems. In fact, they have many of the problems of any urban school system. The conflicts about school finances between the superintendent of schools and the school board on the one hand and the mayor on the other continue. Some observers claim that schools that are not showcase magnet schools, and thus second-class by definition, do not get as many resources as the system's star schools.

Despite the continuing problems, the same legal mandate to desegregate that led to negative social and educational consequences elsewhere had a more positive impact in Buffalo. We cannot attribute this only to the approach taken to implement the program. In examining that approach, however, we observe that officials responsible for desegregation made sensible use of identifiable community processes to produce change that benefited the entire community.

Summary

The history of efforts to desegregate the schools helps us to understand that the social problem of race relations goes back to the beginning of our nation. We have been struggling with the problem for two hundred years and more, and only in the last thirty years have we approached an open society. The profound social changes that we have seen resulted from a concerted self-help effort. Social scientists participated by developing data and arguments that permitted an attack on the then-conventional wisdom, as embodied in law, that segregation was not only not harmful but was positively beneficial. Social science research and theory provided part of the rationale for the desegregation remedy. We do not know whether the theory that ridding ourselves of formal barriers to integration would have beneficial effects was incorrect or whether instead it was too simply stated.

Events have outrun our ability to control circumstances. The failures of desegregation can be attributed to our oversimplified understanding of the problems and to changes in employment and housing, related socioeconomic issues, and U. S. Supreme Court decisions that limited the available remedies. The schools may in fact be more segregated today than they were twenty years ago. A large majority of African American and Latino students attend schools in which most of the students are members of minority groups and are poor. Students in schools with a large majority of poor families perform less well than minority students in more diverse schools. Even suburban schools in the North have high levels of segregation. Relatively few white students go to school with minority students and, because of housing patterns, minority students in suburban schools tend to be concentrated in a few schools. Some authorities predict that unless that situation changes, inner-city problems will affect suburban schools in the foreseeable future (Orfield, 1993; Bissinger, 1994).

We have not yet learned to balance ethnic pride with mutual respect in a multicultural society. Although it is easy to decry the failures of integration, we cannot overlook the positive changes that have accrued. One of the authors recently had lunch with two young African American professionals in a hotel dining room in Florida. We were all at a professional conference. The conversation turned to the failures of the civil rights movement and the failure of integration. At one point, however, we all acknowledged that not too many years ago, an interracial group like ours would not have been seated together in a hotel dining room in a southern state or in a border state. Our presence together was a visible reminder of the accomplishments of the civil rights movement, accomplishments not to be dismissed lightly.

Clearly, no single discipline's perspective is enough to help us understand a phenomenon as as complex as school desegregation. We will have to take fuller cognizance of the complex historical, social, political, legal, and economic contexts within which we work and live.

One might argue, as Gerard (1983) does, that social scientists do not yet have enough to say and should stay out of public affairs until their disciplines are better developed. On the other hand, social scientists do have analytic methods and concepts and bodies of knowledge with utility for real-world problems. Sarason (1974) issued a call for social scientists not only to engage in relevant research but also to undertake social action as a vehicle for research. In his view, social science would benefit by "messing in a sustained way with the realities of modern society" (p. 261). He argues that social action research with an uncertain disciplinary base is justified when "one does the best one can and relies on the efforts and criticisms of others to do better the next time" (p. 267). In our view, neither social science nor society has suffered by the immersion of social scientists in desegregation efforts, and a strong argument can be made that both have benefited.

In the last two chapters we will deal further with the rationale for participation in social action, with the problems that arise when science is employed in a politicized context, and with the ethics of participation in social action and intervention in the community.

Notes

1. This chapter owes a great deal to Kluger's magnificent book, *Simple Justice* (1976).

2. Article I, Section 2. The Constitution contained two other provisions with respect to slavery. The importation of slaves could not be prohibited by Congress before 1808 (Article I, Section 9), and runaway slaves could be compelled to return to their owners, even if they went to free territory (Article IV, Section 2).

3. *Civil Rights Cases*, 109 U.S. 3 (1883); *U.S.* v. *Cruickshank* 92 U.S. 542 (1875).

4. The U.S. Supreme Court cited *Plessy* when it upheld the decision of a Mississippi school board to send a native-born Chinese girl to a segregated school. The court thus found that the state had the power to segregate its citizens (*Gong Lum* v. *Rice*, 275 U.S. 78, 1927).

5. *Sipuel* v. *Oklahoma State Board of Regents*, 332 U.S. 631 (1948); *McLaurin* v. *Oklahoma State Regents for Higher Education*, 337 U.S. 637 (1950); *Sweatt* v. *Painter*, 339 U.S. 629 (1950).

6. See Myrdal (1944, vol. 2, chap. 28) for a discussion of this literature.

7. See *Briggs* v. *Elliott*, 347 U.S. 497 (1954); *Davis* v. *County School Board of Prince Edward County*, 347 U.S. 483 (1954); *Belton* v. *Gebhart*, 347 U.S. 483 (1954).

8. Since *Brown*, the courts at all levels have paid increasing attention to expert social science testimony in a wide variety of cases, although there are many problems to be resolved (see Levine & Howe, 1985; Monahan & Walker, 1986).

9. *Swann* v. *Charlotte-Mecklenburg Board of Education*, 402 U.S. 1 (1971). Prior to that time the question had been raised whether a remedy that required a state to take into account race would itself be a form of discrimination. The Supreme Court said that to take race into account for purposes of fashioning a remedy was permissible.

10. The information in this section is based on notes taken by Adeline Levine at public lectures given by superintendent Eugene Reville and associate superintendent Joseph Murray, lectures and an interview with Lewis Sinatra conducted by Murray Levine, and Winerip (1985).

11. *Arthur* v. *Nyquist*, 415 F. Supp. 904 (W.D. N.Y. 1976); see Sellers (1979) for a history of ethnic groups and education in Buffalo.

12. The idea here was to create schools so special that students from all parts of the district would be strongly attracted to them (i.e., as if by magnets), even if attending one meant riding a bus.

13. In recent years City Honors has contributed three finalists to the Westinghouse Science Talent Search, bringing national recognition to the city and its schools.

12

Social Action in Community Psychology

Chapter 11, on school desegregation, illustrated the complexity of community change and the need in many real-world settings for action to achieve change, even when our understanding of the process is incomplete. In this chapter, we develop further aspects of this theme in terms of the ecological analogy and other perspectives presented earlier in the book. We focus on two primary modes of action that can relieve powerlessness and that address power disparities that contribute to social problems. One mode is called community development, a strategy that involves consensus and cooperation. The second is social action, a strategy that calls for confrontation and conflict. People who try to change aspects of the social world define problems as having their "cause" in the social world, not in the psychological deficits of people suffering from the problem, whose problem in adaptation is seen as resulting from barriers to access to resources. We begin with issues of problem definition.

The Politics of Problem Definition

Problem definition is basic to how we understand and try to solve problems, but our usual approach may be so grounded in the assumptions of our worldview that we aren't even aware of them. Yet problem definitions are necessarily value-laden. They structure our whole approach to problems, including which among many possible solutions we try to implement and the methods we use to achieve those solutions (Caplan & Nelson, 1973). Our definitions, based as they are on our worldviews, may restrict the universe of alternatives (Sarason, 1972; Levine & Levine, 1992). For example, if we try to understand poverty by studying poor people, we will identify certain person-centered explanations for this problem, such as lack of education or skills, cultural deficits, dysfunctional families, or "laziness," and we will try to correct those flaws. If we define the problem in the context of the overall political and economic system, however, we could just as easily understand poverty by studying rich people. Our explanations would involve capitalism as a system, and solutions such as distributing wealth more equitably might be among our choices.

Humphreys and Rappaport (1993) point out the political and power consequences of different ways of defining problems as they affect the federal government's role in mental illness and substance abuse programs. They characterize the process of defining a problem as staking out a specific "claim" on the way that problem will be understood and dealt with and cite the example of community mental health programs. Federal policy toward behavior disorders in the politically progressive 1960s focused on improving cities and the system of care. Beginning in 1981 the much more conservative Reagan and Bush administrations reallocated considerable federal money from community treatment services to basic biomedical research on mental illness. Humphreys and Rappaport (1993) note that as cutbacks occurred in mental health programs, the Reagan administration substantially increased federal funding for programs that defined substance abuse as a problem of defective individuals. This new claim on the public's understanding of a widely acknowledged problem was backed up with the individually targeted rhetoric of "Just say no" and with sizable funding increases for law enforcement. Redefining the drug problem as one brought about by criminals and defective or weak-willed individuals gave federal policymakers the opportunity to shape the federal role in dealing with disorders of behavior. The definition of drug problems as individual problems also had a substantial impact on federal research funding priorities and therefore on new research, and the new knowledge created in turn affected solutions. Humphreys and Rappaport urge us to recognize our tendency to adopt a one-sided policy analysis because of our values and to combat this tendency by incorporating divergent perspectives into problem definitions right from the start—for example, the view that substance abuse is caused by both individual vulnerabilities and social conditions that put people at risk.

Blaming the Victim

In most people's perception, wealth and power form the obvious metric of successful adaptation in U.S. society. Wealth and power are finite and are not evenly distributed; some people are wealthier and more powerful than others. People, liberals and conservatives alike, who enjoy a disproportionate share of money and power naturally resist attempts to make the distribution more equitable. Because access to wealth and power and control of key community resources is restricted, those without access feel powerless, hopeless, and frustrated—emotions intimately connected to the prevalence of social problems and stressful life circumstances. Given that some degree of vulnerability is present in everyone, events and circumstances in the soap opera of life have more serious implications for those who lack resources. Because most Americans share common values, from time to time many advantaged people become appalled at the existence of poverty, crime, mental disorders, and other social problems and insist that something be changed (Ryan, 1971).

In Ryan's words, one solution is to "blame the victim" by defining the problem in person-centered terms. Primary deviance might be attributed to biological malfunctions understood as "mental illness," which leads to labeling and delimiting the problem at the level of individuals. Thus a problem is contained in a way that does not threaten the existing distribution of power and wealth. Once the problem is defined as a pathological characteristic of certain individuals, the range of relevant solutions naturally becomes restricted to interventions that change those individuals. We can congratulate ourselves that we are a caring society, while at the same time neatly avoiding defining social problems in economic and political terms that have different implications for change. Putting it simply, blaming the victim enables advantaged citizens to reconcile humanitarian values with their own self-interest.

When victims accept the definition of social problems in person-centered terms, they reinforce the process and essentially end up blaming themselves for their predicament. Prior to the U.S. Supreme Court's decision outlawing school segregation, for example, the victim-blaming "separate but equal" doctrine was endorsed, for different reasons, by such influential African American leaders as Booker T. Washington and W. E. B. Du Bois, legitimizing to some degree the implication that inferior performance by African Americans reflected personal deficits in that group. As another example, before the Stonewall riot that initiated the gay rights movement, most gays accepted the then prevailing definition of their condition as a form of deviance based on a psychiatric disorder. As a result, many gays were submissive and concealed their identities, rather than fight openly for their rights and for a definition of themselves as loving human beings who had a different lifestyle (Duberman, 1993).

Blaming the victim is inherent in clinical interventions that may simply encourage victims to feel less distressed about their circumstances. Some prevention programs implicitly blame the victim. Competence-building undertaken with "high-risk" individuals, for example, clearly involves changing these individuals and not the disadvantageous economic and political circumstances that typically surround them. It makes no difference that the alleged deficiency is social or cognitive, not genetic. Victim blaming thus becomes an inevitable by-product of professional activities not directed explicitly at changing circumstances or reallocating resources.

Paradox and Empowerment

One rationale for seeking political solutions to social problems is the limited validity of existing therapeutic and preventive interventions and the recognition that there may not be a perfect solution to many social problems that will allow these problems one day to disappear forever (Sarason, 1978). Rappaport (1981) argues that, far from achieving absolute solutions to social problems, much of what community psychologists have learned leaves us confronting a set of paradoxes—seemingly self-contradictory viewpoints. One paradox, for example, is that professional "experts" with prestigious positions and impressive degrees are still able to learn much about certain behavioral problems from otherwise ordinary people who have managed to overcome those problems, such as members of Alcoholics Anonymous and other self-help groups. Who is really the expert in such cases? Both the professional and the client can make a valid claim to this role, and therein lies the paradox.

Ideological differences can also lead to paradoxes. In the debate over whether people have "needs" or "rights," one issue is this: If people have "needs," they have *deficiencies*, the removal of which makes them "equal" by making them the same as others. If instead they have "rights" they have *strengths*, which if supported make them "equal" by allowing them to be different from others. Rappaport cites the example of the insanity defense in the criminal justice system. On the one hand, we have the traditional position that some defendants are different from others and thus have certain needs requiring that they be treated with special consideration. Szasz (1963) and others, on the other hand, have championed the position that all people have the right to behave as they choose, albeit with specific consequences if they violate a law.

Another paradox concerns the conflict between the creation of "alternative settings" for special populations under a needs model and the movement toward mainstreaming diverse groups from a rights position. In this respect, the Head Start program was a distinctly paradoxical creation inasmuch as it reflected a deficit-oriented needs model implemented in the context of the the War on Poverty's equity-seeking rights policy.

A fourth example of paradox arises from the realization that in trying to help people through identifying and treating "cases" of psychopathology, we may end up harming them through iatrogenic influences such as labeling and its consequence, stigma. Rather than successfully helping people, traditional programs to treat or prevent psychological problems in individuals may represent a kind of paternalistic colonialism by professionals toward society's less powerful members (Rappaport, 1981).

To a large extent, mental health and other human service professionals in effect force the community to accept their goods and services. They hold prestigious jobs and command good salaries for themselves; community residents become dependents unable to determine for themselves how best to live and to attain their own goals. Is professional intervention then helpful to clients, or is it harmful? These perspectives lead to equally valid observations, to potentially different definitions of problems, and to alternative solutions.

Recognition of the paradoxical nature of social problems and their attendant solutions leads to the conclusion that permanent solutions to social problems may not exist (Sarason, 1978); today's "solution" merely sows the seeds for tomorrow's problem, in the way that Moral Treatment, for example, the solution to a problem in its mid-nineteenth-century heyday, itself later became a problem in the form of large custodial mental hospitals (Levine, 1981). Rappaport raises the possibility that social problems, intertwined as they are with basic human differences that may ultimately be irreconcilable, are not "absolute" in nature and in solution but are dialectical—that is, they may best be understood when viewed from more than one perspective. Following Piaget's definition of objectivity, we should assume that phenomena appear different when they are viewed from different perspectives.

One implication of viewing a problem as dialectical is that the solutions should be many and diverse, having in common only that they entail decentralized control and empowerment of citizens at the local level. Decentralization and empowerment are high in Rappaport's value hierarchy. To empower people is to enhance their ability to control their own lives, leaving professionals to function more as a collaborators than as symbolic parents. In this view, professionals have something important to offer, but in a different relationship to their clients than that entailed in the medical model.

The paradoxical status of Head Start within the needs-versus-rights dialectic may be one reason that it has far outlived the rest of the War on Poverty. Head Start was both an educationally oriented prevention program for poverty-stricken preschoolers and a vehicle for empowering disadvantaged communities by creating jobs and fostering parents' sense of control over their lives and those of their children. It is a clear example of a multidimensional solution to poverty.

The concept of the dialectic of social problems is also evident in Cohen and Thompson's (1992) instructive analysis of homelessness among persons with serious and persistent mental illness. What causes homelessness in this population? Are they "crazy" and unable to function, or just poor? Are such people homeless as a direct and inevitable consequence of disabling cognitive or emotional deficits that render them unable to cope outside of institutions, or is their homelessness coincidental with the difficulty they as a vulnerable group, along with others who are not mentally ill—families in crisis, unemployed single parents, disadvantaged ethnic minorities—have had retaining a niche within the ever decreasing supply of low-income housing?

Is the best solution to homelessness among people with mental illness to fund mental health professionals to locate and engage these people in high-intensity psychiatric services, including reinstitutionalization, or would it be better for professionals and others to work collaboratively to improve access to safe, comfortable housing that is well integrated with that of nonmentally ill people and in this way simply help to support people's own coping and problem-solving efforts? The homelessness of people with serious mental illness is another example of an ill-structured, dialectical problem that will respond best to creative, diverse solutions.

To summarize, in Rappaport's judgment community psychologists should clarify paradoxical definitions of social problems and facilitate the proliferation of multiple solutions to those problems. Recognition of the paradoxes and the dialectical nature of problems allows one to see alternatives and exposes one's own basic assumptions to constructive criticism. Neither victim nor environment is blamed. Instead, the focus is on creating settings that empower segments of a community to control their own resources, rather than on solving problems in a once-and-for-all convergent sense.

Competent Communities

One implication of our analysis is that the community psychologist's job is to help build competent communities. How can we understand this task? Adapting to the community level the metaphor of primary prevention through competence building, we might begin by asking what characteristics differentiate more competent from less competent communities. Iscoe (1974) identified three general factors: (1) *power* to generate alternatives and opportunities, (2) *knowledge* of where and how to obtain resources of all kinds, and (3) *self-esteem* in the form of pride, optimism, and motivation. The achievement of these general goals can occur through community development or through social action. Both approaches involve increased participation in decision making by those affected by the decisions, if only to create an independent, critical monitoring of community affairs. However, even these solutions are not without problems. Community participation has not always led to desirable results (Moynihan, 1969).

Community competence building commits us to developing opportunities for self-determination by effecting change through social and political action. Strategies that pursue competence building at the community level can be broadly organized into two general approaches, community development and social action, that differ significantly in their basic assumptions (Heller & Monahan, 1977). Community development techniques assume that the community already has within it the knowledge, resources, and potential for organization and leadership to effect constructive community change through consensus, whereas social action assumes that resources are finite and distributed unequally, that differences among various interests in the community are not easily reconcilable, and that, as a result, the solutions to social problems are explicitly political in nature.

Community Development

Community development is a process designed to create conditions of economic and social progress with the active participation of the whole community and with the fullest possible reliance on the community's initiative (Rothman, 1974). It is based on the theory that the creation of community organizations, housing, businesses, and jobs will improve community life. Much community development is carried out through the vehicle of community development corporations (CDC). Community development may have a preventive effect in two ways—by reducing the probability that stressful life events will result from economic distress and community disorganization and by helping to create resources that promote positive adaptations, provide support, and reduce the demoralization that can itself create psychological and social problems.

An important assumption of community development is that community change will be accomplished most effectively through participation of local citizens in goal determination and in action. The important themes in community development include democratic procedures, voluntary cooperation, self-help, development of indigenous leadership, and education. In order to engage in community development, it is necessary to cooperate with others who control resources. Neighborhoods with high concentrations of people who are "truly disadvantaged" (Wilson, 1987) may be appropriate targets for community development efforts, as are currently stable communities that are subject to succession by poorer groups with fewer resources. The actual units targeted for development can be any size and in urban areas may be as small as individual blocks (Perkins et al., 1990).

Economic development, housing policies, and schools are important community development targets. Leaders work to create community centers and organizations that will help reduce isolation and create a "conspiracy among neighbors" to maintain community standards. From this perspective, maintaining community standards will help to limit crime, violence, drug traffic, child neglect and abuse, despair, and demoralization.

The community development approach assumes that people have potential and will respond to opportunity and that leadership will emerge. Just as crisis theory makes the assumption that people have reserves of coping strength, so this approach assumes that, given resources, people will take advantage of opportunities and participate in social organizations that create roles and settings in which their strengths can blossom.

The impetus for the community development corporation came from the late Robert Kennedy's concerns about the urban riots of the mid- and late 1960s. Kennedy, then a U.S. senator from New York, visited local neighborhoods to try to understand what had gone wrong. The people he spoke with objected to being studied and wanted concrete assistance such as a supermarket or a shopping plaza. In 1966 Kennedy and his fellow senator from New York Jacob Javits successfully amended the antipoverty act to provide for community development projects. The Ford Foundation also contributed through its "gray areas" project. The general movement was founded on the ideas of community participation, and the organizing tactics developed by Alinsky (1971) were useful. Local churches participated, and a combination of private and public funds helped the agency develop and grow.

Peirce and Steinbach (1987) describe a number of CDCs, some of which operate in the most hopeless-appearing neighborhoods. In the mid-1980s there were an estimated three to five thousand CDCs in the United States, located in many states and in rural as well as urban areas. Most had developed during the preceding twenty-five years. CDCs vary in size and in resources but tend to have certain features in common. They operate in distressed city neighborhoods or in rural communities and tend to serve geographically defined low-income target areas. The people who live in that ecosystem niche control the CDC. According to Peirce and Steinbach (1987), CDCs are now the most important suppliers of low-income housing in the country and have a range of other business and service provision activities. Although CDCs serve all ethnic groups, some of the most successful ones serve the African American community, and we will concentrate on those agencies.

Community organizations in the African American community. CDCs did not appear full grown out of thin air; there was a "before the beginning" (Sarason, 1972). Many CDCs in African American communities developed in cooperation with churches and other nonprofit organizations. Taylor (1990) points out that a great strength of the African American community in Buffalo, New York, is the number (about six hundred) and diversity of its social organizations—churches, neighborhood block clubs, cultural groups, youth centers, civil rights organizations, social clubs, fraternal organizations, and formal and informal political organizations. These organizations often provide the base from which CDCs develop. Because members of the majority are generally unaware of the important role such organizations have always played in the life of the African American community, we will discuss some of them briefly.

The church. The church is the African American community's oldest institution, brought into existence by a racism that would not permit integrated churches. The church has been a key to African Americans' survival, an institution within which African American people gain sustenance, grow, and develop. The majority of well-known and effective African American leaders, including Martin Luther King Jr. and Jesse Jackson, emerged from the churches, which provided a niche, a setting, and roles for people who were otherwise blocked from access to resources. A former slave could become president of a congregation, a trustee, a deacon, or a preacher who could speak with authority to his community, and, many times to the majority community as well. These achieved roles all were a source of enhanced self-esteem and leadership experience; they also enabled people to learn organizational skills.

The black church was and is important in unifying its community. It created settings in which people of different social statuses could come to know each other and provided for the social and recreational needs of church members through its many activities (Bryant, 1980). The organization of black churches gave members of the community experience in community development activities; building a church required that people pool resources to buy land or buildings and to construct church buildings (Davis & Nelson, 1980).

Mutual aid organizations. African American churches often developed mutual aid associations and benevolent societies to provide assistance for the sick or disabled, the widows, and fatherless families. African American women's clubs were another important force in community development (Carson, 1993). Some mutual aid organizations that began in the eighteenth and nineteenth centuries developed into insurance companies serving the African American community. Some of these organizations, struggling as they were with the virulent forces of racism that limited access to resources (and sometimes with internal rivalries), didn't always fulfill their promise, but others did.

In the early twentieth century, the National Negro Business League, the National Association for the Advancement of Colored People (NAACP), and the Urban League were organized (Davis & Nelson, 1980). Movements with community development components arose as needs changed. Marcus Garvey promoted a self-help mutual assistance orientation that included the creation of cooperative economic initiatives in his Universal Negro Improvement Association. Father Divine's Peace Mission Movement had as many as 2 million members and owned rental income property, small businesses such as grocery stores, barber shops, produce stands, dry cleaning and tailoring shops, and furriers, and operated hotels and boarding houses. Since the 1930s the Nation of Islam has operated a network of business enterprises. In addition to civil rights organizations, the Opportunities Industrialization Center (OIC), led by the Reverend Leon Sullivan, and the Reverend Jesse Jackson's Operation PUSH continue the tradition of mutual aid and economic development (Davis & Nelson, 1980). African American philanthropic activities remain an important force within the community for stability, direction, problem solving, and individual growth (Carson, 1993).

Political power. Community development requires political support, and for most of its existence the African American community was powerless because so many of its members were barred from voting. The voting rights act of 1964 reduced many of the barriers, however. While there was a negligible number of elected African American officials before passage of this act, by 1988 there were 6,793 black officials at all levels of government, twice the number in 1980 (Fisher, 1992). The presence of black elected officials and the voting power demonstrated by the African American community increased blacks' access to resources for community development projects.

Leadership. The leadership of the new CDCs comes from a wide variety of backgrounds and many different ethnic groups. A great many CDC leaders are women. Some have little professional preparation for their positions, while others, like Brenda Shockley of the Los Angeles Drew Economic Corporation, have outstanding academic credentials and experience. The well-educated Shockley practiced as an attorney in a private law firm and had experience as an administrative assistant to a Los Angeles politician. She also worked in land development and in the Los Angeles City Attorney's office. Her experience in government and business was helpful in appreciating how a community recycles its resources.

Ruby Duncan was a welfare mother who helped organize the Clark County, Colorado, welfare rights organization. She led and participated in demonstrations and other social actions modeled on principles developed by Saul Alinsky. Operation Life, the organization Ruby Duncan and her fellow welfare mothers created, grew into a CDC that built a medical center and housing units and (in an excellent example of the principle of succession) rehabilitated abandoned hotels.

Gary Waldron was a South Bronx native who held a high-level executive position at IBM. His organization, which runs a home for runaway boys, started an herb farm in an advanced-design hydroponic greenhouse on wasteland left over after deteriorated Bronx apartment buildings were torn down. The business has grown, and Waldron's organization now provides consultation to other CDCs that want to develop greenhouses as franchises.

Charles Duff was a Latin teacher with degrees from Amherst and Harvard and training in city planning. His group specializes in real estate development but also operates a "social service conglomerate." Veronica Barcelona grew up in a public housing project in the Hispanic neighborhood in Denver that she now serves. Sandra Phillips, a teacher who obtained a master's degree in urban planning, joined with other citizens on picket lines to protest urban redevelopment plans that in their view didn't take into account community residents' needs. Her group influenced Pittsburgh to engage in a communitywide planning effort, and she became executive director of the organization that emerged from that process. The organization developed condominiums for low-income residents and redesigned an abandoned school to serve as housing, another good example of the principle of succession (Peirce & Steinbach, 1987).

CDCs and the ecological analogy. CDCs provide excellent examples of the ecological principles discussed in Chapter 4 and of the setting and role concepts presented in Chapter 5. First, CDCs provide organizational niches and roles within which people can attain achieved statuses. When a CDC employs people or helps them gain access to better housing through "sweat equity," it is providing resources for improved adaptation. When communities improve and people acquire a stake in them, the new niches facilitate personal development, growth, and satisfaction. People who earn better housing through participation in a community effort may also experience improved self-esteem as a result of perceiving (correctly) that they have done well. With new resources and a stake in the community, residents have the energy to maintain desirable lifestyles for themselves and their children.

Community effects. The factors we have described came together in the Bedford-Stuyvesant Restoration Corporation. Peirce and Steinbach (1987) describe the impact of the corporation on the neighborhood:

> The Bedford-Stuyvesant Restoration Corporation symbolizes the first, grand era of community development corporations. Into Brooklyn's five-mile-square Bed-Stuy section—with 450,000 people the nation's second largest black community—plagued by housing decay, school dropout, junkies, and muggers, comes a flood of investment dollars. Not for the typical poverty-program social services, but for hard investment, a new "business" approach to community development. The federal government and the Ford Foundation pour millions into the Bed-Stuy CDC. Banks and corporations pitch in; IBM opens a major plant in the neighborhood.
> Visit Bed-Stuy twenty years later and there's pride, not depression, the

sights and sounds of an energetic place. There's a Restoration Plaza Commercial Center, a visible central core the community never had before. Within the center are stores and offices, restaurants, two commercial banks, a supermarket, an ice skating rink, the Billie Holiday Theater. The CDC has produced or renovated more than 1,600 units of housing, restored the exteriors of 4,200 homes on 150 blocks, provided mortgage assistance to 1,700 homeowners and loans and technical assistance to 130 local businesses. Some 16,000 jobs have been created. Some summers, the CDC has hired as many as 1,500 young men and women—up on ladders and scaffolds, decked out in hard hats and tee-shirts, refurbishing as many as ten blocks of brownstones in a season. True, social pathologies have not disappeared: now they crop up in such new forms as teenage pregnancies and the drug "crack." Unemployment is still a grave problem. Graffiti stains even some of the CDC's proud new structures. But Bed-Stuy has more: a new middle class. Young professionals have purchased brownstones, deciding to remain or return, becoming vital role models for their community. From restoring housing, then building a commercial core, Restoration has proceeded to the restoration of lives and the re-creation of a viable community. (p. 19)

Peirce and Steinbach (1987) point out that CDCs have not solved all the community's problems, and some of the CDCs have failed. In a few cases they were mismanaged, and in some scandals occurred. There are important limits to what a CDC can accomplish. Developing successful businesses and other enterprises is not easy and requires at least a core of experienced and trained personnel. Some CDCs have managed to build good housing, but because of union rules and other limits the construction jobs did not always stay in the community.

Some enterprises, such as those that provide child care, serve an important community need. Like social services agencies, child care centers may contribute a great deal to community life. But child care work is not well paid and offers few benefits to employees and limited opportunity for advancement. Pitegoff (1993) advises such enterprises to develop closer ties with corporations that value what CDCs and similar agencies have to offer, thus providing access to a variety of resources and reducing dependence on government funding.

Subsequent generations of CDCs have become more sophisticated in their approaches and have developed support networks of organizations. The problem of integrating low and middle income housing and schools so that the schools are improved by the demands of middle income parents for better education is still a difficult one (Orfield, 1981). Such interorganizational integration and change is necessary for the full development of communities (Pitegoff, 1993). Recent efforts to create school-based clinics and community services will also help the process of community development. The CDC movement has really just begun to bring "the opportunities of the American economic system to peoples and neighborhoods long excluded" (Center for the Future of Children, 1992, p. 85).

Social Action

Social action is a strategy used by community groups that do not perceive the government, business leaders, or others who are "in charge" as responsive to their concerns. The members of aggrieved community groups may feel both anger and anxiety, depending on the threat to their interests. Change tactics in the social action approach include conflict, confrontation, and direct action. Saul Alinsky (1971) articulated the "rules" of social action, including mass organizing and the use of pressure tactics to influence those who control resources to share them with those who perceive themselves in need. The sit-ins used by civil rights groups in the 1960s and 1970s to attack racially segregated facilities, the bus boycott initiated by Rosa Parks, who was tired of being told she had to sit at the back of the bus, and the boycotts used to pressure retail organizations to open up jobs to members of minority groups are other examples. Antiabortion groups that use pressure tactics against abortion clinics, against women seeking abortions, and against doctors and other employees of clinics are a current example. Alinsky, however, was opposed to the use of violence and would not have condoned violence such as the shooting of physicians who perform abortions or the fire bombings and vandalism against clinics that have characterized the antiabortion movement. In Alinsky's view, the fundamental tactic is not violence but the exertion of social and political pressure on those who control the resources needed by the aggrieved group.

Social action that empowers people is an ideologically compelling approach to community change. To demonstrate how such an approach actually works, we present as an example the community response to the disaster at the Love Canal in upper New York State.

An Example of Social Action:
The Love Canal Homeowners Association

The Love Canal Homeowners Association (LCHA) developed spontaneously in response to the discovery that toxic waste in an abandoned dump site was leaking into the homeowners' residential neighborhood and imperiling the health of residents living nearby.[1] An announcement by New York State's Commissioner of Health that pregnant women and children under age 2 were being advised to leave came after several months of meetings between New York State Health Department representatives and citizen groups that alerted residents to the possbility of a problem in the area and galvanized the community.

Residents of the affected area had complained from time to time of yawning holes filled with dark, foul-smelling matter on the sixteen-acre site adjoining their property and of fetid materials seeping into their yards and basements, but local officials took no action. Although an elementary school building was located on the filled-in dump site and hundreds of houses surrounded it, little notice was taken of the complaints until 1976. That year, in the course of an investigation of chemical contaminants in Lake Ontario fish, the Love Canal disposal site[2] came to the attention of a local city employee who alerted U.S. Representative John LaFalce, who in turn prevailed on the Environmental Protection Agency (EPA) to investigate the situation.

In 1978 the investigation of the disposal site expanded to involve several state and federal agencies, and local news coverage of the problem increased. At first, Lois Gibbs, then a twenty-five-year-old high-school-educated mother of two children, paid only passing attention to the reports. She lived several blocks away from the dump site and didn't even consider that her life was affected. Shortly after her son started kindergarten at the school built on top of the Love Canal, however, he developed allergies and kidney and neurological symptoms. Gibbs then put two and two together. The more she read, the more she became concerned that chemical contamination of the school property might be responsible. School officials, however, denied her request to transfer her son to a different school. They would not acknowledge that the school might be dangerous.

During the summer of 1978, with encouragement from her brother-in-law, who was a biologist and an environmental activist, Gibbs asked her neighbors to sign a petition asking officials to close the school. As she went door to door during a hot summer, often trailed by her two children, she became aware of the large number and the severity of illnesses in the neighborhood. By this time the homes and the families on streets immediately adjacent to the dump site were under study by the state Health Department and the Department of Environmental Conservation. Some community meetings were held that summer to explain what was happening, but these meetings left Gibbs and her neighbors with more questions than answers.

By now Gibbs was heavily involved and had gained an ally, a high school friend whom she encountered as she went door to door in the Love Canal neighborhood. When the Health Department announced that it would disclose its findings at a meeting in Albany, Lois, her husband, Harry, and her friend Debbie Cerrillo decided to drive the three hundred miles to attend the meeting. There they heard the commissioner announce that pregnant women and young children should move out of the area, but he left the press conference before they could obtain any clarification of the meaning of the announcement.

They drove home despondent, only to find the streets in their neighborhood filled with people who had heard the announcement on television or over the radio. There was no Health Department representative or other official in the area to talk with the frightened, angry people who felt that their health and the lives of their children were being threatened, as well as the value of their homes. Some in the crowd were burning symbolic mortgages and talking of taking drastic action.

Because Lois Gibbs had met many neighborhood people when she was circulating her petition, she was pushed up to the front of the crowd, given a microphone attached to a homemade public address system, and asked to tell what had happened in Albany. Gibbs, self-described as painfully shy, had never addressed an audience before, but she took the microphone and tried to give the people some hope. That evening, plans were announced for a homeowners' group. Within a few days the Love Canal Homeowners Association was organized.

These events of early August 1978 were taking place in the midst of a hotly contested gubernatorial campaign, and because this was the first example of toxic wastes affecting a residential neighborhood and because the Love Canal drained into an international waterway, the Niagara River, the event took on national and international importance. New York Governor Hugh Carey, eager to settle the affair in the most satisfactory way and believing that he had obtained a promise of federal disaster relief support, announced that the state would buy the houses immediately adjacent to the Love Canal site and those across the street from it. At that point all that was known was that toxic wastes were indeed seeping into the basements of the adjacent houses, that toxic substances had been found in the air, and that an excess of miscarriages had occurred among women living in the area nearest to the waste site. Homeowners in the surrounding streets and those who were renting in the low-income project a block away were still left with questions about the safety of their homes.

Within weeks of the original announcement, the state had purchased the first group of houses and the people moved out, with considerable stress to individuals and families. The remaining homeowners were given vague promises that investigations would continue. Gibbs had received a great deal of attention from politicians but quickly concluded that they were interested not so much in what she had to say as in creating the impression that citizens were being allowed to participate in decisions affecting their lives. She also decided that the only way the remaining residents' interests would be taken into consideration was if they remained active and pressed their concerns on officials and rallied public support through the media.

Plans and actions for remedying the leak in the canal were going forward, as were additional health and environmental studies to determine the extent of seepage of chemicals into the surrounding areas. Meetings held from time to time with citizens often became shouting matches as officials gave vague or evasive replies to the remaining neighborhood people, who insisted that they also wanted to get out. These meetings and the emotion they generated often made the television news, and that fact kept pressure on governmental officials.

Gibbs and the group of homemakers who had joined her kept the LCHA informed of changing events. One night, while sitting in her kitchen pondering her next moves, Gibbs hit on the idea of putting pins on a street map to identify the houses where she knew that people had had health problems. When she did that, using her own notes, it seemed that the pins took on a pattern. Illnesses appeared to follow the paths that had been identified by long-time residents as those of underground drainage ditches running off the canal into neighborhoods several blocks away. Gibbs concluded that the underground ditches, called swales, could have provided a preferred path for migration of the chemical leachate. Excited by what she had found, Gibbs took her map to Beverly Paigen, a biologist employed at the Roswell Park Memorial Cancer Research Center in Buffalo. Dr. Paigen had paid attention to the Love Canal situation because she was interested in the interaction of heredity and environment in cancer causation. Roswell Park is funded by the New York State Department of Health, but Paigen was not officially a part of the Health Department team investigating the Love Canal site. She had been warned by her superiors at Roswell Park to limit her involvement in the Love Canal investigation. However, Paigen considered the warning an affront to her academic freedom and continued her involvement.

Paigen trained the Love Canal homemakers to conduct a systematic telephone health survey of the residents in the area. When the survey results were mapped, a concentration of illnesses did appear in what came to be known as "historically wet areas" in the neighborhood. Paigen took her results to Health Department officials, who discounted the research publicly because it was done by "housewives." However, the publicity generated by this home survey forced the Health Department to review its own data. A few months later, in February 1979, the Health Department announced that indeed there was an increased risk of miscarriages in the formerly wet underground drainage areas, and that it would be best if pregnant women and children under 2 who were living on the streets above them left the area at state expense, at least until the corrective work to cap the Canal was completed.

This solution was unsatisfactory to the remaining residents, because it implied that the hazard to unborn children was not a hazard to everyone. Another implication was that it was not safe for young couples to conceive while living in the area. Property values had plummeted by then, and people could neither sell nor afford to leave their houses, which often constituted the bulk of their life savings. Gibbs led the homeowners in a series of actions designed to keep their cause in the newspapers and thus to keep it alive. In addition to general education efforts, speeches to any audience that would listen, and letters to congressional representatives and state legislators, the group's more dramatic actions included leading marches and demonstrations in the Niagara Falls area, taking a child's coffin to Albany to be delivered to the governor, and burning effigies of the governor and the health commissioner. Each of these events received media attention. Gibbs made trips to Albany and to Washington in an effort to persuade state and federal officials to pay attention to the Love Canal situation. The officials repeatedly told her there was no definitive evidence of danger that warranted moving more people.

In the summer of 1979, during remedial construction to cap and partially drain the disposal site, fumes from the canal permeated the neighborhood. Many people reported that they and their children were feeling ill or were subject to asthmatic episodes. As part of an agreement worked out in court between the LCHA and the state, the state agreed to move residents out and to house them at state expense if there was evidence of danger to health during the construction period. More than one hundred families took advantage of this provision and moved into motels, where the state paid the bill for their accommodations and food. This arrangement soon began costing the state several thousand dollars a day, enough to buy many of the houses. After about eight weeks, the state indicated that it would no longer foot the bill. Some of the residents wanted to "sit in" at the motels, but by now some competing groups had emerged, and many people wanted to go home. The residents were no longer united, and many were just sick of motel life. They moved back home.

The homeowners kept up the pressure as much as they could, and the situation continued to draw media attention. The actress and activist Jane Fonda made a highly publicized visit to the area, for example, capped by an emotional plea for help for the Love Canal people. From time to time, governmental agencies released reports that kept the story alive, and residents continued to confront governmental officials whenever they could. One day when Governor Carey visited Buffalo, a Love Canal resident confronted him on the street and managed to get a statement from him that the state would indeed purchase more houses. In fact, a bill went before the state legislature to authorize the use of some existing funds, mandated two decades earlier to "revitalize" neighborhoods, to help buy out the rest of the neighborhood.

Meanwhile, to prepare for an impending lawsuit against the Hooker Chemical Company, which had dumped the toxic chemicals into the canal, the EPA conducted a small pilot study of chromosome damage among Love Canal residents. This study was done without recruiting and testing nonresidents to serve as controls, because the EPA did not wish to spend the money to do a thorough study at that time. In May 1980 this study tentatively reported chromosome damage in a number of Love Canal residents. Leaked to the press, the story made headlines, and soon the area was overrun with television and newspaper reporters from all over the world. The EPA announced that it would assist in the evacuation of residents on the basis of these new data but swiftly backed away from that position, apparently because of pressure from the federal Office of Management and Budget, which was concerned that a precedent was being set for the purchase of houses in "normal" disasters such as floods or tornadoes by the actions being taken in this new and unprecedented type of disaster. Although the chromosome study was criticized severely by some experts, particularly because of its lack of control subjects, it was judged to be scientifically valid by other qualified professionals. At any rate, the inconsistencies frightened and enraged residents, who found themselves learning of matters affecting their health and their families' health from newspaper headlines.

As word spread that the White House had changed its position on evacuating the neighborhood, distressed residents gathered on the lawn in front of the LCHA office. Someone poured gasoline in the form of the letters "EPA" on a lawn across the street and ignited it. Other residents, who in every other way were law-abiding middle-class citizens, stopped cars in the street and in one case began rocking a car, threatening to turn it over. By mid-afternoon Gibbs managed to reach two EPA officials who were in town. They agreed to come to the LCHA office to speak with residents. Someone then got the idea that because the homeowners felt they were being held hostage in the neighborhood, they in turn should hold the federal officials hostage when they arrived. (The event took place during the Iranian hostage crisis.) About one hundred people were gathered on the lawn when the EPA officials entered the office. Lois Gibbs and several others told the two men they couldn't leave because it wasn't safe for them to go outside to face the crowd.

By then the area was crowded with reporters. The telephone in the office was a major link joining the homeowners, the White House, and other government officials. Police officers, a SWAT team, and federal marshals stood by watching the crowd. Early in the evening the FBI called and told the group that they had two minutes to release the hostages. That threat led to the immediate release of the EPA officials, who were escorted through the angry crowd by the police. The residents' point had been made forcefully and was front-page news.

The solution did not emerge immediately. Residents were told that the government was still studying the problem. The 1980 presidential primary campaign was under way, and it was by no means certain that President Jimmy Carter would be renominated or that he would win the primary in New York. Subsequent events took place against this political backdrop. Gibbs and many of the other Love Canal residents who had been told they had chromosome damage were invited to appear on Phil Donahue's talk show to present their problems on national television. Love Canal residents also went to New York City to picket the Democratic nominating convention in the hope of embarrassing the president. In September Gibbs was interviewed on the *Good Morning America* television show, where she blamed Carter for his failure to offer federal help in the crisis. Two weeks later, an announcement came that New York State and the federal government had concluded an agreement to purchase the remaining houses and relocate the residents. President Carter came to Niagara Falls to make the announcement himself. Eventually all of the residents who wished to sell their homes and move out did so. The LCHA had achieved its major goal. It had fought the state and federal government successfully for two years and had finally convinced the government to take action.

Comment

The Love Canal story is important for several reasons. First, it brought the problem of toxic waste disposal to national consciousness. The Love Canal citizens fought for themselves, but by their fight they called attention to the critical national problem of toxic waste disposal. Their efforts resulted in the issuance of long-delayed regulations to implement existing environmental laws, as well as federal legislation creating a "Superfund" to be used to clean up abandoned toxic waste sites.

The Love Canal story has been an inspiration for thousands of citizen groups that have sprung up to protest landfills located too close to homes or schools or that threaten to contaminate water supplies. Industry and some local governments, on the other hand, are concerned that more stringent regulation will increase the costs of waste disposal, and local industries have often used their economic, political, and scientific resources to fight citizen groups. There is still argument about the significance of the scientific data for decision making in a politicized environment (see Box 12–1). Nonetheless, citizens are making their weight felt in decisions affecting their communities.

Second, Lois Gibbs's personal story demonstrates that ordinary citizens can uncover extraordinary abilities during a crisis and can emerge much strengthened. From a shy housewife, concerned primarily with her own home and family, she became a folk heroine and a national figure who dealt with governors, senators, journalists, and governmental officials as an equal. She founded and now heads the Citizens' Clearinghouse for Hazardous Wastes, a Washington, D.C.-based nonprofit corporation, supported largely by private foundation funds, that provides organizing help to local groups faced with toxic waste emergencies in their communities. Others working with Lois Gibbs during the crisis showed similar strength and personal growth. None of them went on to careers based directly on their experiences, but many maintain an active interest in community affairs.

Last, the Love Canal Homeowners Association is an example of a spontaneous organization that developed out of a community crisis and gave people a means of taking vigorous action on their own behalf. It is all the more interesting as an illustration of how traditional, nonpolitical working- and middle-class citizens can take increasingly radical action as their frustration grows. Families in the area were clearly subjected to considerable stress for a prolonged period of time; for many of them the LCHA provided a means of social support and a sense of community that enabled them to cope with the stressful life events that followed their discovery of the problem (Stone & Levine, 1985–1986).

While the homeowners had the benefit of professional assistance from Beverly Paigen (who suffered political reprisals for her participation) and from a few others, the homeowners were always in charge. They were receptive to attention by academics who provided some advice from time to time but who were straightforward about their interest in writing about the Love Canal; the homeowners wanted their story told, were pleased with academic attention, and took the notice as a sign that what they were doing was in fact important. They also were wise to focus their efforts on achieving their narrow goal of relocation. The fact that the story had national significance is a side effect of their efforts; they were concerned with saving themselves, but in struggling in their own interest they contributed to the well-being of all of us.

Box 12–1. *Citizens Clearinghouse for Hazardous Waste and the Dioxin Campaign.*

We include this example of social action to combat an environmental problem because it makes clear the complex interplay among people exposed to risk, government, scientists, and corporate interests. It is of interest to community psychology because its potential consequences for many citizens' sense of well-being and how they live are profound. Our information is drawn from the U.S. Environmental Protection Agency (EPA) *Draft Assessment of Dioxin and Dioxin-Like Compounds, Exposure Assessment Document* (1994), Dwyer and Flesch-Janys (1995), Gladden and Rogan (1995), Schechter, Dai, Thuy et al. (1995), and Gibbs and CCHW (1995). The reader should know that the senior author has chaired the Citizens Clearinghouse for Hazardous Waste (CCHW) board of directors for a number of years, and this presentation may reflect his identification with the organization.

After residents of New York's Love Canal were relocated, Lois Gibbs moved her family to the Washington, D.C. area. She was nationally known by this time and had received thousands of communications asking for help from people facing situations similar to that at Love Canal. She decided to develop an organization to assist grassroots groups struggling with problems of hazardous waste dumps, incinerators, and related threats to their safety and well-being. The CCHW grew out of that vision. Aided by her contacts with citizen advocates like Ralph Nader, who recognized the value of her work, and by her contacts with celebrities interested in the environment, she obtained private foundation support for her work. CCHW has some income from memberships, subscriptions, and sales of its publications, but it accepts no money from government or from industries whose products contribute to pollution.

Founded in 1981, CCHW remains true to its original purpose of helping grassroots organizations with their struggles. It provides technical scientific information, organizing assistance, advice about how to find and use lawyers and technical experts, and leadership training to local groups facing hazardous waste problems. CCHW organizers, including Lois Gibbs, accept invitations to participate in local struggles. Gibbs speaks at meetings; more important, CCHW organizers use such opportunities to energize and strengthen local groups and to encourage coalitions in local areas. CCHW does not testify in Congress for or against particular legislation.

CCHW publishes a regular newsletter, *Everyone's Back Yard* (*EBY*), which educates local groups about environmental issues and legislative and litigation developments and serves as a vehicle to keep grassroots groups in touch with each other. *EBY* also publishes stories concerning the progress being made by groups in different states.

CCHW has been particularly active in the environmental justice movement involving minority and low-income communities. These communities are disproportionately affected by solid waste and hazardous waste dump sites, potentially toxic effluents from incinerator smoke stacks, and waste products released as the by-product of chemical processes, because polluting facilities are often located there.

CCHW has had contact with approximately seven thousand local groups and sponsors a triennial convention of grassroots leaders. As many as one thousand people have come to these three-day meetings, at their own expense or with support from their local organizations. The leaders represent groups in every state, in rural and urban areas, and in white, Native American, African American, and Hispanic communities.

In collaboration with other environmental organizations, CCHW led a very successful campaign to influence fast-food chains like McDonald's to reduce their reliance on foam packaging, in particular one type of packaging that adds fluorocarbons to the atmosphere (Fluorocarbons are believed to contribute to the depletion of protective ozone and have been banned for use in refrigerants). The McToxics campaign, as CCHW called it, partly consisted of dumping discarded foam food containers on the parking lots of McDonald's restaurants. McDonald's and other fast-food chains stopped using foam made from the most offensive substances and also reduced the bulk of nondegradable waste in landfills.

Dioxin. At this writing, CCHW is launching a national campaign against dioxin, which is among the most toxic of chemicals. One of the chemicals found at Love Canal, dioxin is considered dangerous at concentrations in the body as low as 14 parts per trillion per kilogram of body weight. Dioxin, actually a family of substances having similar chemical structures, occurs as a contaminant in industrial production or when organic compounds are burned in the presence of chlorine. (Other families of chemicals, called PCBs and Furans, have similar molecular structures and exert similar physiological effects on the body.)

Dioxin is controversial because it touches so many interests. It is used in the manufacture and disposal of many widely used plastics and pesticides and is formed when chlorine is used to bleach paper or when waste is burned in incinerators. Because it is an important component of pesticides that make their way into the water, air, and soil, dioxin is found everywhere.

Dioxin does not degrade easily. When it is dispersed by winds and water, it enters the food chain and becomes more concentrated as it moves up the food chain. When bigger fish eat smaller fish and humans then eat dioxin-containing fish, the substance accumulates in fat tissues of the body, where it remains for long periods of time. (Because it is fat-soluble, dioxin is also found in meat and dairy products derived from cows exposed to contaminated feed or water.) On the basis of epidemiological studies, the average American appears to have a level of dioxin that is just below the level associated with many adverse health effects. One implication of this statistic is that half the population already carries an excessive amount of dioxin, and another is that any further increase in Americans' ingestion of dioxin could have widespread adverse health effects.

Dioxin is toxic because it interferes with chemical signals and hormones affecting normal cell growth and regulation. The more dioxin in a person's body, the more cells are affected, increasing the risk of disease. Dioxin may also affect the immune system, making people less resistant to many types of diseases, although the precise mechanism of its hypothesized effects on the immune system are unclear.

Epidemiological studies and studies with animals have shown that the relative risks of various cancers are higher in individuals exposed to dioxin than in those with minimal exposure. Dioxin is also implicated in endometriosis, a disorder of the female reproductive system, reduced testosterone and sperm counts in men, and reduced glucose tolerance, a condition that increases the risk of diabetes. Because dioxin accumulates in body fat, infants who are breast-fed may receive heavy doses of it, particularly during their first feedings (after which the concentration of dioxin in breast milk drops). Women who wish to breast-feed may face the choice of pumping their breasts and forgoing early breast-feeding or risking the transmission of a harmful chemical to their newborns. Dioxin-related compounds are also implicated in shortened periods of lactation; the higher the concentration of a dioxin-related compound in the fat content of a mother's milk, the shorter the lactation period. Because dioxin has a hormone-like effect, the early pattern of sexual imprinting in the brain and, consequently, the development of sexuality may also be affected, although this is far from certain.

Economic, social, and scientific complications. Given all of these dire effects, why aren't we making every effort to ban dioxin, remove it from the environment, and prevent its creation in industrial processes and in incinerators? Banning dioxin and related chemicals would have significant economic and social consequences. Dioxin production is important to many industries—plastics, pesticides, and paper—and to waste disposal through incineration. Ironically, medical waste incinerators are among the major sources of dioxin in the environment.

Banning dioxin would require manufacturers and medical facilities to make costly changes in their methods. In some cases reasonably low-cost alternatives are available, but adopting them would mean changing industrial procedures and relationships with suppliers. Incineration, which may destroy substances to the "six-9" level (99.9999 percent destroyed), is a convenient and comparatively inexpensive technology, but many authorities have serious doubts that those levels can be obtained or, if obtained under test conditions, sustained under field conditions. In addition, some incineration processes produce contaminated ash that requires disposal.

Manufacturers and waste disposal companies may be vulnerable to lawsuits for civil damages if it is determined that dioxin they produced has caused illnesses in people exposed to it. Dioxin is an important ingredient in Agent Orange, a herbicide used extensively in Southeast Asia during the Vietnam War, and the question whether soldiers exposed to Agent Orange were harmed and are entitled to medical care and other benefits has been the subject for years of lawsuits and political pressure aimed at affecting Veteran Administration decisions about medical care and compensation.

Companies that produce and dispose of waste, along with the EPA, which regulates these processes, are reluctant to adopt costly procedural changes unless there is clear evidence that dioxin poses a serious health risk to a great many people. We are really dealing with a version of the Type I/Type II error problem in statistical inference. When we emphasize avoiding a Type I error and say we will reject the null hypothesis only when the result is significant at the .05 level, we are saying we will not accept a finding unless it would not have arisen by chance more often than five times in a hundred, the familiar .05 standard. In so doing we are supporting the status quo. Government and industry say the status quo—that is, existing procedures for handling dioxin—should not be changed until we are absolutely sure that harm has occurred or will certainly occur in the very near future. People who are concerned about their welfare and their children's welfare, on the other hand, want to avoid the Type II error of failing to recognize a genuine toxic effect of dioxin amid the "noise" of normal biochemical fluctuations and measurement error; they argue that if there is any chance of harm they should be protected against it.

Risk and benefit/cost analyses have been proposed as aids to resolving these competing interests. The results of such analyses, determining how much will it cost to reduce exposure and how many additional cases of illness will be avoided for each increment in cost, are only as good as the assumptions the analysts make, however, and some assumptions favoring one course of action over another may be hidden or otherwise not readily apparent to affected citizens. Gibbs (1994) challenges the basic assumptions that a reliable threshold of damage can be determined, that regulation can control the release of damaging substances in the environment to less than dangerous levels, and that scientists will recognize the early signs of unanticipated effects in time to stop them. She argues that accepting risk analysis as an approach to solutions deflects attention from the real problem, which is that we are producing too much waste in the first place, and undermines the search for alternatives that would eliminate the waste itself. Her argument represents a different definition of the problem and leads to a different solution.

In cases where chemists can accurately detect the presence of substances in parts-per-trillion concentrations and where the presence of disease can be confirmed by objective means such as laboratory tests, computerized scans, and x-rays, scientific controversy should be limited. Dioxin research, however, has been plagued with controversy. In one example, follow-up studies on workers in West Virginia and in Germany who had accidentally been exposed to chemicals contaminated with dioxin concluded that, aside from the skin disorder chloracne, the workers showed no adverse health effects when compared to nonexposed workers. These 1980 studies were used by the chemical industry to challenge the EPA's regulation of dioxin, which came after animal studies showed that dioxin was a carcinogen. The industry representatives argued that dioxin had different effects in humans than in rats.

The follow-up studies on the workers were themselves challenged several years later, however, in connection with another lawsuit seeking damages from a chemical company after people were exposed to dioxin following a train accident. In the course of this suit the plaintiffs' lawyers discovered that five deaths had been omitted from the dioxin-exposed group and that four exposed workers had inexplicably been placed in the unexposed group. When appropriate corrections were made for these errors, the cancer rate in the exposed group was higher than that in the unexposed group, and the death rate from heart disease was also higher than in the nonexposed group. Evidence uncovered during the discovery phase of the proceedings also showed inexplicable statements claiming that harm was limited to the skin when there was evidence of other symptoms as well. In this second case, the workers didn't believe the company scientists and hired their own consultants to review the data. The independent consultants found that the assignment of people to exposed and unexposed groups had numerous errors; in one case, twenty nonexposed employees had been added to the exposed group. Once these employees were removed from the group, it did show an increased rate of various cancers.

Uncovering the irregularities in these studies helped resolve the lawsuit for damages. However, the studies' flawed conclusions continued to influence the EPA's regulatory decisions and were used by one company to argue that it was not necessary to clean up a contaminated community thoroughly because dioxin was not that dangerous. Another company used unpublished research to claim that dioxin in the environment is caused by any and all forms of combustion. This research had not been published in a journal subject to peer review but had instead been released in a press conference. (It has since been discredited.) Companies worked hard in using science to support their position that dioxin was not as toxic as some researchers were claiming and that its harmful effects did not warrant banning or even very strict regulation.

Agent Orange, the dioxin-containing herbicide, became, as we have noted, a scientific and political football when Vietnam veterans claimed that their exposure to it had caused varied and inexplicable illnesses. Veterans groups, including the American Legion, lobbied Congress to investigate these health problems. After considerable delay some studies were done, although the conclusion that cancer was related to dioxin exposure was discounted because the study design could not link illness directly to dioxin exposure. Later congressional hearings revealed that there were so many errors in the way the studies were conducted and the data were analyzed that no conclusions were possible. An Air Force study, however, did find an increase in skin cancer and other illnesses among exposed veterans, and a study commissioned by the American Legion also found various medical disorders among Vietnam veterans exposed to dioxin. Government and industry representatives disputed these results, and a settlement reached in court precluded any finding of liability. A subsequent study by the Institute of Medicine of the National Academy of Sciences found evidence of a relationship between exposure to herbicides containing dioxin and several different diseases, including some cancers (cited in Gibbs, 1995).

Overall, it appears likely that many disorders are related to dioxin exposure. However, EPA officials are reassessing the scientific literature and holding hearings around the country to help determine what level of dioxin exposure is safe and what kind of regulations are appropriate. At the same time, a panel of outside scientists has criticized some of the EPA's conclusions about dioxin (Stone, 1995).

The dioxin controversy teaches several lessons about the uses and misuses of science. The first is to avoid making sweeping conclusions on the basis of a single study. A second lesson is that publishing studies in peer-reviewed journals and describing methods and procedures accurately and thoroughly allows others to criticize and/or attempt to replicate the results. This "adversarial process," fundamental to scientific research, is a crucial corrective against error and bias (Levine, 1974). In some of the science used by government and corporations in environmental controversies, the data were not subjected to the kind of scrutiny and independent replications that are so critical to separating reliable findings from error or fraud.

People who live close to dump sites, incinerators, or other sources of dioxin pollution often face government science experts, company scientists, and public relations professionals who argue that there is nothing to fear or no evidence of danger. They may base this opinion on only a single study (perhaps a flawed or biased one) that has shown no evidence of risk, or they may mean that no studies have even been done (A. Levine, 1982, Ch. 6). Like the Love Canal residents, people, sometimes advised by scientists sympathetic to their cause, quickly become sensitive to dissembling on the part of authorities. When technical issues are involved, as they so often are, community groups need scientific experts who understand their perspective and on whom they can rely for accurate information. Having one's own trusted consultant partially reintroduces the adversarial structure of scientific research (Levine, 1974).

Many citizens who formerly believed that companies and government officials would do the right thing if they only knew the truth have been disillusioned. They have come to appreciate that truth is difficult to come by and that authority figures cannot necessarily be trusted, that decisions are affected not only by science but also by political and financial considerations. When people in affected communities realize that they are not playing on a level field with corporate officials, they may resort to legal, political, or social action to attain their ends.

Lois Gibbs and CCHW believe that dioxin production will continue and that dioxin in the environment will not be cleaned up adequately simply because the evidence shows that dioxin is dangerous. They believe that change will not occur in the absence of a massive effort by citizens to bring pressure on corporate and government officials to take action. At this writing, they have called for a national campaign against dioxin. Taking advantage of her celebrity, Gibbs went on a national speaking tour promoting the book and the campaign.

Greenpeace, an international environmental organization, has launched an effort to ban the manufacture of chlorine. CCHW is also calling on the large number of grassroots environmental groups with whom it has had contact to join together in concerted, continued action against dioxin. Working with CCHW staff, scientists, and community organizers, Gibbs (1995) has written a book that summarizes and evaluates the evidence showing that dioxin is harmful, reveals the sources of dioxin, and issues a call for action. The book contains information on how to organize community groups and how to obtain information about dioxin sources. It has tips on speaking at public meetings and writing letters to government and corporate officials and on confrontational "actions" designed to capture media attention and keep the issue in the forefront of public attention.

As planned, CCHW's campaign will disseminate persuasive information about the harmful effects of dioxin throughout the population. It recommends that advocates create a one-page fact sheet with information about dioxin, its health effects and dispersion in the environment, and the location and ownership of known sources of pollution. Obviously, a one-page fact sheet cannot include details on the limitations and qualifications of this information and may provide only basic information. Nonetheless, the statements about health—that dioxin causes cancer, affects breast-feeding, and causes infertility and a reduction in sexual potency—appeal to the deepest concerns people have. The educational efforts are intended to create anxiety in the public, with the expectation that that anxiety will result in action. Perhaps the campaign's offer of a set of active coping responses will offset that anxiety.

The information on dioxin may have a number of unintended consequences. The information about protecting oneself against anxiety, for example, suggests that a vegetarian diet will reduce dioxin intake substantially. If many people respond, a change in food habits could affect the market for food, reducing the demand for meat, fish, and chicken, and affecting agriculture and restaurant service. Knowledge that breast-feeding is potentially dangerous may well change breast-feeding practices, especially during the first days after birth. Will mothers pump their breasts to decrease the dioxin load in their bodies? What will be the effect on mother-child bonding if breast-feeding is delayed? How will our understanding of sexual development and functioning change if we come to find out that sexual orientation and sexual functioning are affected by exposure to dioxin? Will our understanding of problems such as learning disorders change if it turns out that dioxin is implicated as a possible cause?

We can also expect strong reactions from large corporations and well-funded groups representing industries, such as the Chemical Manufacturers' Association, whose interests are adversely affected. At a minimum we can expect counterarguments from them asserting that the evidence is inadequate or misinterpreted. These counterarguments may reduce the impact of the dioxin campaign by creating the uncertainty that supports inaction. We will certainly see further controversy about the basic science. Members of advocacy groups will endure the excitement and the stress of participating in an important and hard-fought action. Some activists may lose jobs or go to jail as a result of confrontational "actions" or experience the strongly voiced disapproval of colleagues who fear economic loss for their communities. Because the dioxin campaign touches so many key interests, it illustrates the complexity of community action and the impossibility of conceptualizing or understanding problems from a single perspective.

Summary

An important theme developed in the later chapters of this book is that even though community change is complex and incompletely understood, this is not an excuse for inaction. The starting point for action to accomplish change, as we emphasized in this chapter, is the step of problem definition. Traditional clinical approaches to problem definition are sometimes said to "blame the victim"—that is, they conceptualize the problem as a person-centered characteristic of those individuals who are suffering the most. This approach can create paradoxes, situations in which two or more contradictory interpretations, implying radically different ways of understanding a given problem, both lead to logically convincing and empirically valid solutions—for example, do those at risk need special interventions whose sole purpose is to make them behave the same way others do, or do they instead deserve additional resources sufficient to guarantee their right to behave differently from others?

Community psychology's ecological approach to problem definition assumes that more than one point of view on an issue can be legitimate and that problem definitions and solutions are divergent rather than singular. The ecological metaphor enables us to consider the definition of problems and solutions in terms of situations and systems instead of in terms of individuals. It enlarges the scope of potential directions for change, which helps to resolve paradoxes. An intervention such as Head Start, for example, addresses the serious cognitive and nutritional needs of individual children while at the same time providing employment opportunities to their disadvantaged parents as a fundamental economic right.

Community psychology also assumes that the essential path to change and adaptation is empowerment, in the form of increased access to resources for those at risk. One such resource involves *social organization* (e.g., increased involvement and participation in defining problems and decision making); another is *information*, or substantive knowledge regarding the strategies and resources necessary for adaptation. For the community psychologist, identifying paradoxes and developing strategies of empowerment have the salutary effect of placing in a constructively self-critical light one's own place in the ecological context surrounding a problem.

Community psychology honors a tradition of action outside the established professional system in the service of individual and community adaptation. In this chapter we discussed two examples of community interventions, each most appropriate under relatively specific circumstances. Community development involves identifying and finding new ways to use indigenous community resources, while social action forces a definition (or redefinition) of the problem in terms of an unfair allocation of resources, making the solution the redistribution of those resources.

Many of these points were illustrated by the example of the Love Canal Homeowners Association and its successor organization, the Citizens Clearinghouse for Hazardous Waste. In this case, as in many situations in the soap opera of life, a serious community problem came to be defined in terms of situational circumstances instead of individual weaknesses and was ultimately dealt with ecologically through organization and direct access to public resources, including media publicity.

In the final chapter we will examine the interplay among science, politics, and ethics in community intervention.

Notes

1. The material in this section is drawn largely from A. Levine (1982) and Gibbs (1982).

2. The Love Canal was a short waterway used for recreation for about forty years until 1942, when the Hooker Chemical Company began to dump chemical wastes there. In 1953, when the canal was completely filled, Hooker sold the site for one dollar to the Niagara Falls School Board, which needed land for a new school to accommodate the area's growing population. The deed of sale included a provision that the Hooker Company would be free of responsibility for any injuries or death or damage to property resulting from the chemical waste buried on the site. Deeds of sale to the buyers of the modest, low-priced houses built adjacent to the attractive new school contained no such warning, of course, and citizens never dreamed that government officials would allow a school and houses to be built in such a dangerous location.

13

Science, Politics, and the Ethics of Community Intervention

In previous chapters we have seen how social science research contributed to the development of the school desegregation decision and later became important in the Love Canal controversy. We also observed that political problems can plague scientific research, even when technology is capable of great precision of measurement. In this chapter, we will explore further the relationship among science, politics, ethics, and the social context. We will introduce a model based on the premise that every cultural artifact is a compromise product of its social surroundings, then provide examples of the influence of context on science applied to the solution of social problems, and finally review ethical problems that confront those doing community work.

Ecology and Science

Community psychologists are committed to the belief that applications of scientific approaches to social and psychological problems can contribute to the solution of those problems and to our knowledge of ourselves and our social world. Community psychologists participate in generating the research that defines social problems, and they participate in implementing and evaluating interventions built on that knowledge. The model of a "value-free" science has never fit "pure science," and it is incorrect when we consider the application of scientific approaches to the solution of social problems. Every cultural artifact, in this case scientific research, is a compromise product of its social surroundings. We make this point because the social surroundings of the pure science that most of us learn are different from the social surroundings of science in applied contexts.

A simple model illustrates the point. Films and novels are artistic forms that are shaped by various contexts, including artists, financial sponsors, publishers, critics, and audiences (Huaco, 1965). Analogous roles influence social science research. In pure research the researchers, funding agency officials, journal editors, publishers, critics, and audience all tend to be social scientists who share a common frame of reference. When the research has implications for social issues, however, these roles are filled by people who have different assumptions and different values from those of scientists (see Gardner & Wilcox, 1993). Aside from academic social scientists, the actors may include employees of government agencies, private industry executives, political figures, citizens affected by the particular action, and critics and supporters of a particular position. If a social program is involved, those who are employed in the program also have a stake in it (Levine & Levine, 1977).

We are a rational society. We are unable to say we want something just because we want it and instead must argue on our own behalf by referring to empirical evidence. A political view of this debate sees science as the language of discourse, with the prizes the resources to be redistributed. Scientific studies were used on all sides of the Love Canal conflict, for example, and are central to the current controversy over dioxin.

Pauly (1994) describes how scientific research played a role in the debate over Prohibition and the Eighteenth Amendment, which prohibited "the manufacture, sale, or transportation of intoxicating liquors." Before the enactment of the amendment, lawyers for a major brewer commissioned research by several scientists concerning the effects of low-alcohol beer (about 3 percent by volume) on human adult behavior. Crude studies based on impressionistic judgments of people's conduct suggested that drinking limited amounts of low-alcohol beer did not cause intoxication. Interestingly, one scientist in this group noted that the appropriate conclusions depended on how one defined "intoxication," a term that appeared in the amendment. If intoxication meant impaired cognitive efficiency, then weak beer was indeed intoxicating; if it meant stupefication, then it was not. This expert's findings were discarded by the brewer and not used in its suit to exempt weak beer from the ban on alcoholic drinks.

Those supporting Prohibition had not expected the pro-alcohol advocates to base their arguments on scientific data and for their part relied on moral reasons. They also argued that a law prohibiting all alcoholic beverages would be simpler to enforce. Faced with the brewers' "scientific" approach to influencing policy, however, Prohibition supporters commissioned an elaborate series of experiments by the psychologist Walter Miles. Using relatively precise measurements of mental concentration and psychomotor coordination as his dependent variables, Miles found consistent decrements in performance following consumption of even weak beer. In the end, of course, Prohibition did cover all forms of alcoholic beverage.

By the 1930s the Great Depression had wrought significant changes in the social and political context. Political figures supported the repeal of Prohibition, arguing that legalization would help the struggling economy and reduce the social and economic burden of coping with organized crime. Within this changed context, the liquor industry hired Yandell Henderson, an academic scientist from the Laboratory of Applied Physiology at Yale University who had worked on problems of industrial toxicology and specialized in the safe management of carbon monoxide in mines and factories. He argued that just because a substance was potentially dangerous in high concentrations did not mean that it could not be safely managed at lower doses. (Interestingly, the question of whether any amount of dioxin is safe and whether there is a threshold beyond which exposure to dioxin becomes dangerous is central to that controversy.) This argument was persuasive to millions of Americans, whose experiences as motorists seemed to indicate that regularly ingesting limited amounts of carbon monoxide and other automobile pollutants did them no harm whatsoever.

The United States Brewers' Association then funded another well-known university researcher to replicate Walter Miles's work. This researcher modified Miles's procedures to include a more demographically diverse sample of subjects, lower doses of alcohol, and briefer test trials of subjects' performance. One consequence of these modifications was much greater variation among subjects in their performance, whether drinking or not. This researcher also adopted a more stringent criterion for testing the statistical significance of differences in performance before and after drinking ($p < .01$). Given the greater variance within the drinking and nondrinking conditions and the more stringent statistical criterion, it is not surprising this researcher ended up "proving the null hypothesis" that performance was not significantly different whether subjects had consumed a little alcohol or no alcohol. Although his study was funded by brewers' interests, the researcher claimed that these findings spoke for themselves and were completely objective.

The perceptions of policymakers and many ordinary citizens regarding alcohol changed. Scientific research had helped transform public understanding of alcohol problems from the view that alcohol was an intrinsically dangerous substance to a belief that alcohol problems resided in the excessive drinking of a few individuals. The stage was thus set for the repeal of the Eighteenth Amendment. The solution to dealing with alcohol was seen to be the management of alcohol, whether by individual or by government on behalf of society, instead of the elimination of it. Prohibition was repealed, and funding for alcohol research all but disappeared except for small amounts spent to educate clinicians about the problems of the minority of people who used alcohol to excess.

As this example and others in this chapter illustrate, how a problem gets defined and who defines it determine what gets studied, what data are collected, and how they are interpreted. The process of obtaining knowledge and the policies resulting from the interpretation of the knowledge are all influenced by more than the scientific quest for truth. In fact, research is subject to many different sources of bias in interpretation and content.

Experimental Design

Details of experimental design can favor one group over another by making it easier or more difficult to detect the effects of the experimental variable. The fact that in many situations it is impossible or unfeasible to assign subjects to alternative conditions at random creates such an opportunity. In evaluating a highly politicized experimental school program in New York City during the early 1900s, the evaluator chose to compare experimental schools that had a high density of recent immigrant children to control schools that had a high density of American-born children. This evaluator was employed by the superintendent of schools, who objected to the experimental program, which had been forced on him by school board members who saw features in it that could help the city with its financial problems. Not surprisingly, the results showed that the experimental schools were behind educationally. Even though this study was subjected to intense criticism, it was cited in the debate over the experimental program several years later (Levine & Levine, 1977).

A similar issue of controls affected the Love Canal study. The Health Department research team that studied miscarriages among women living at Love Canal used as a basis for comparison an existing report of miscarriage rates calculated as part of a study whose subjects were women who had previously borne a defective child. The miscarriage rate was based on the women's self-reports. In determining the rate among Love Canal women after exposure to dioxin, however, the Health Department accepted a case of miscarriage only if it had been verified in medical records. The comparison of self-report rates with physician-verified rates biased the study in the direction of minimizing the miscarriage effect among the exposed women. The rate in the Love Canal was still so high that the difference was statistically significant, but Health Department officials and others were able to say that the rate of miscarriage among Love Canal women was "only" one and one-half times the control rate when, if it had been compared with a proper control sample, it might actually have been three or four times the control rate (A. Levine, 1982).

Type I and Type II Error

Other issues that we take for granted in research also have important implications when decision making is involved. In pure science we generally try to avoid the Type I error, that is, rejecting the null hypothesis when it should not be rejected. In simple terms, this means avoiding the conclusion that the evidence shows that something has happened when it has not actually happened. In the alcohol example, when the investigator changed the standard for rejecting the null hypothesis from .05 to .01, he made it less likely that the results would demonstrate that something had happened. Of course, in avoiding the Type I error by changing the decision standard, an arbitrary matter in any event, this researcher also made it *more* likely that he would commit a Type II error, mistakenly concluding that nothing had happened when in fact there had been an effect. He therefore concluded that low doses of alcohol had no effects on behavior when in fact they probably did.

In the Love Canal situation much of the dispute between health department scientists and citizens concerned a tradeoff between Type I and Type II errors. Health Department officials, concerned that a decision that the area was unhealthy would result in costly relocation of many people, wanted to avoid the Type I error. They adopted the usual scientific standard, demanding strong evidence before they concluded that there was an inordinate amount of illness in the area. On the other hand, residents wanted to avoid the Type II error. They took the position that if there was any chance of danger they should be moved out of harm's way, whether or not compelling proof of the danger was present. Whereas a journal editor might want data indicating an increase in fetal morbidity and mortality significant at the .05 level before publishing an article, a pregnant woman would more likely be interested in being relieved of anxiety over the possibility that her baby might be harmed, regardless of whether there was absolute proof that the chemicals buried in the Love Canal were the cause of the harm.

In this case the adoption of the usual scientific decision standard proved to be very favorable to the government's position that it wanted to avoid wholesale buyouts of homes. The Love Canal residents, eager to have the government buy their homes, were very suspicious of the state health department's "neutrality," a position unfavorable to the residents who wished to avoid any avoidable risk (A. Levine, 1982).

The Written Report

An evaluation report and its interpretation may also reflect systematic biases of the investigators or their sponsors. We have already noted that the characterization of the fetal abnormality rate at Love Canal as being "only" one and one-half times the normal rate was intended to minimize the implications of what was in fact a statistically significant difference. It is not unusual for reports to be shaped to meet their sponsor's views or needs. In the Gary, Indiana, schools program, an administrator who wrote a descriptive report based on a site visit to a Gary school was forced by members of the school board to rewrite the report so that it came out more favorable to the program under review (Levine & Levine, 1977). While the assertion of naked power in the writing of a report may be unusual, authors of research reports, particularly evaluation reports, probably do take into consideration the positions and sensibilities of their audiences and patrons. Adams (1985) provides a short course in "gamesmanship" for program evaluators who must deal with the ethical quandaries posed by research reports that have significance for the allocation of resources.

The integrity of a scientific effort is not guaranteed by the names and scientific reputations of the participants. We have all heard of instances in which reputable senior researchers had their names on papers that proved to be fraudulent. In many laboratories, the senior scientist is named as a coauthor even if he or she had very little to do with the research. Senior people are also subject to a variety of powerful nonscientific influences. In the Love Canal situation, the governor of New York appointed a commission of highly reputable medical scientists to review all research done to that time on the Love Canal. All but one of the five participants in this commission were administrators in medical facilities regulated by the New York Department of Health. (Among its other powers, the Health Department sets reimbursement rates for hospital beds, decides how much money is allotted in the rates for teaching costs, and approves certificates for building or remodeling medical facilities, including laboratories.) Although we have no "smoking gun" showing that commission participants were directly influenced by such considerations, the appearance of a potential conflict of interest leads one to look with skepticism on their conclusions that there was no evidence of major systemic disorders present among residents of the Love Canal area (A. Levine, 1982).

Timing the Release of Reports

The timing of the release of reports is still another matter. In the Gary school situation, there is some reason to believe that the release of a negative report was delayed until after a mayoral election in order not to embarrass the incumbent mayor, who had supported the program (Levine & Levine, 1977). We have already seen how a leaked report in the Love Canal situation led to turmoil that resulted in the eventual relocation of the citizens. If the report had not been leaked, the results might have been buried; if officially released, the results might have been accompanied by criticism carefully designed to mute their effect.

Impact on the Research Worker

Research results may affect the researcher. Beverly Paigen's employers subjected her to harrassment for her work with the Love Canal residents. She eventually left New York State for employment elsewhere (A. Levine, 1982). In the Gary school situation, the office of the researcher who issued the negative findings was subject to reprisal by school board officials. The school administrator who took responsibility for implementing the Gary program in New York had difficulty gaining reappointment to his position, apparently in retaliation for his participation in the Gary experiment (Levine & Levine, 1977).

Impact on Those Affected by the Research

Research can also have direct and indirect effects on those who are the subjects of the research. In the early 1900s a body of scholarly opinion developed that purported to show the inherent inferiority of African Americans. That research was used to support segregationist practices and to justify the low social status of African Americans in the United States. It required another body of scholarly opinion to assert the opposite position in order to rally efforts to attack segregation. Arthur Jensen's (1969) assertions that most of the variance in intelligence is due to heredity and that the learning styles of blacks and whites are fundamentally different were used politically to justify cutting off aid to education. It is not clear whether renewed arguments of this sort by Herrnstein and Murray (1994) will affect current debates over educational policy. In human terms, consider the impact on children and youth's motivation to achieve and on their self-esteem when they learn that scientific studies show they are less intelligent or less well able to learn (Steele, 1993).

Research Bias

Because the stakes are high, the actors diverse, and the points of potential influence many, we should recognize that the error is not in having "biased" research but in believing that research can ever be completely unbiased. The closed character of the logical system underlying our concepts of research design may be inappropriate when applied to practical arguments about the real world (Toulmin, 1958). The social context modifies and influences the research procedures, the inferential process, the report, the participants, and the varied uses to which research may be put. Donald Campbell identifies and discusses many of the problems in evaluation research and suggested many creative "social inventions" designed to cope with these problems (Campbell, 1969, 1979; Campbell & Kimmel, 1985). It is an important problem in evaluation research that we do not have a self-critical scientific community whose members critique and replicate each other's work. Too often, a single study is commissioned, and that study constitutes the sole evidence for a political decision about resource allocation.

We need to recognize in this field that we are as much concerned with fairness as with accuracy and that any approach to research has to be deemed fair by those it affects. We also need to recognize that, given even the best of intentions, many research efforts yield ambiguous or disputable results and that, in the end, decisions are often made on the basis of power, politics, and related values, despite any wishes we may have as social scientists that decisions be grounded entirely on hard evidence.

The Ethics of Community Intervention

Clinical psychologists have an ethical code that largely defines proper relationships between professionals and clients and between professionals and the public (American Psychological Association, 1992). The professionally trained individual who lays claim to the mantle of science and enters the difficult field of social intervention has no such guidelines but does have special problems. One question is simply: "Who asked you?" By what authority does a community psychologist or any other social scientist try to influence other people's lives? In the medical model, a client seeks out a professional who offers a defined treatment under specific terms. In the community model, the development of policies and the allocation of resources are political questions. Elected officials or their appointees decide the policies they will pursue, and these may be shaped by advice from social scientists.

When a professional person enters this field and claims some special knowledge or expertise, what obligations does he or she have to the community at large and to his or her professional discipline? Is it enough simply to report data? Does the professional person have an obligation to acknowledge openly his or her own values? After all, data depend on how the question was framed initially and on what interpretations were made.

O'Neill (1989) provides a case study in which a community psychologist's slanting of her interpretation of data to support a sponsor's agenda had unforeseen consequences. The psychologist was working with a women's group that wanted to expand a battered women's transition house. The group needed data to convince the government officials who would be funding the project that the expansion was economically viable and invited the psychologist to conduct a needs assessment to determine how many people, with what needs, might use such an expanded center. Because it was not feasible to do a random sampling survey, the psychologist sought information from key informants, people with experience who might be able to offer reasonable estimates. The information was ambiguous. If taken from any single source, the number of physically battered women in that community was too small to justify the center's expansion. If the psychologist assumed that there was no overlap in the cases described by key informants, however, then the number did justify the project. Despite her reservations about the numbers and about assuming that every identified women would use the service, the researcher concluded that there was probably enough need to justify the cost.

The center was funded, but very few clients came and it was seriously underused. Eventually, the center was filled, but few of the clients were physically battered. The center's staff had redefined "battering" to include "emotional battering," and many of the clients were women who had separated from their husbands. The psychologist knew that the funders' intent was to serve physically battered women, and she knew that the staff had concealed the change in objective from the funders, reporting only the large number of women and children who used the service and collecting the per diem stipend from the funders to operate the service.

The psychologist was faced with a dilemma. What was her responsibility in the situation? She spoke to the center's administrator, who justified the actions by saying that the house was performing a valuable service and without the funds couldn't be kept open. If it closed, the few physically battered women who did use it would have no place to go. The psychologist thus fulfilled one ethical duty by calling the attention of responsible people to the unethical conduct. But the administrator hadn't responded. Did the psychologist have an ethical duty to go further and inform the founders of what was going on? O'Neill didn't say but went on to discuss the ethical principles that might govern the situation. Things are never simple when it is necessary to balance competing values of loyalty to the funder, to the client, and to the people in need.

What if a community psychologist disagrees with positions held by consultees or accepts an assignment while hiding a professional agenda to move an agency to another position or pursues a personal agenda about who should be served, how, and by whom (O'Neill, 1989; Heller, 1989)? Given the limits of knowledge, what obligation does the professional have to be forthcoming about the limits of expertise in a given field or about the limits of knowledge for decision making? Does the professional person have a right to "invade" institutions in order to study them or change them, sometimes surreptitiously (Heller, 1989)? What if the mode of intervening in the institutions is experimental and unproved?

One answer is that all such interventions ought to be undertaken collaboratively, in the interests of all those who participate in the particular setting. Such a simple answer fails to recognize the diverse constituencies and the conflicting interests that are usually represented in any setting. None of the complex issues originating in the context of community intervention is well understood. Ethical discussion is still rare. (For welcome exceptions see O'Neill's [1989] case vignettes and comments by the psychologists Kenneth Pope, Clayton Alderfer, Meg Bond, Alexander Tymchuk, Kenneth Heller, Stephanie Riger, Willam S. Davidson II, and Shulamit Reinharz in that same journal.)

We have saved formal consideration of the ethical implications of community intervention until this point so that we could base our discussion of ethics on a comprehensive understanding of community psychology concepts and practices. Our discussion relies heavily on Bermant, Kelman, and Warwick (1978) and on O'Neill (1989) and commentary on his paper. Certain characteristics peculiar to community interventions create different problems from those that obtain in clinical interventions. Professional ethical codes are written in general terms and do not always offer precise guidelines for specific situations. Moreover, professional ethical guidelines such as those promulgated by the American Psychological Association (1992) are directed to defining and protecting the fiduciary relationship between a professional and a client and may not have much to say about the complex contexts in which the professional's contract and obligations are unclear or subject to shifting with circumstances.

Bermant, Kelman, and Warwick (1978) say that important ethical considerations affect several aspects of community intervention. Implicit in their discussion is the question of whether the professional accepts an invitation to intervene. Each invitation and each issue must be judged against the psychologist's personal and professional values, although the issues may not become clear until a consulting relationship is well along. The psychologist is then faced with an ethical and personal decision about how to proceed when his or her initial assumptions have not been borne out and the interests of the client may be adversely affected by the psychologist's subsequent actions. Should the psychologist become a whistle-blower when he or she observes problems in a setting?

The first decision in an intervention is the choice of *goals*, or what we choose to change—individuals or relationships among elements of society. The choice is by no means obvious or routine. Scientists must be able to recognize and question their own ideologies and paradigms if they are to be in a position to contribute to solving large-scale problems and to communicate those goals to those who might be most affected.

A second issue is the definition of *targets*—the "victims" themselves or some other point of entry into the problem (visible need doesn't always provide the most effective point of intervention). We have previously pointed to the dilemma posed by the potential stigmatization of persons recruited for primary or secondary prevention programs. The important ethical questions, however, are whether the cumulative damage to the individual's mental health from labeling outweighs the benefit of the preventive intervention itself and who is to make that decision.

A third issue is the means of *intervention*. What desirable effects does it have? what undesirable or side effects? Will participation be compulsory or voluntary? What if we have reason to believe at the outset that the community interventions will at best have a weak effect? In seeking informed consent under those circumstances, can we describe direct or indirect benefits of participation, especially in relation to any risks that the subjects may face, such as loss of privacy or potential labeling? Given the doubtful empirical status of any cause-and-effect hypothesis in community intervention, any expectation of direct benefit given to participants may be equivalent to false advertising (Campbell & Kimmel, 1985). How can we participate responsibly when we can't confidently predict the results of our efforts? Is there a place for "responsible chutzpah," a place for trying to solve a problem in the absence of reliable data?

A final issue is our assessment of *consequences.* Our choice of outcome variables and measures will define the nature of our results, including the unanticipated consequences. The principle of interdependence tells us that what we do may well have radiating effects. As a matter of ethics, we should always be alert to the possibility of unintended negative as well as positive consequences and to our responsibilities should these arise. Some long-term longitudinal studies of preventive interventions have shown that adverse effects are a likely outcome for some participants even when there are also direct positive effects (Campbell & Kimmel, 1985). Such effects, even if iatrogenic, provide important information about the processes underlying our interventions. They will never even be observed, however, unless investigators are conceptually and methodologically prepared to observe them and feel ethically obligated to search for them.

How do the activities we described in this chapter and the ethical position outlined here differ from those of the ordinary "good citizen" participating in his or her community? In part, the answer is that they do not differ, and so here we confront yet another paradox of professional activity. Every citizen has the obligation to remain informed about whatever affects the community. The professional community psychologist has the obligation to learn about the community from many vantage points and to disseminate that knowledge in many community forums. In doing our best to promote understanding from many different perspectives, perhaps we can contribute to the development and maintenance of the sense of community that is so important to all of us. Sarason (1976a) reminds us that the community psychologist necessarily views problems and solutions from a specific position in time and in social space but that his or her actions should be "more consciously and expertly applied" (p. 328) than are those of "Mr. Everyman." The community psychologist thus has a responsibility to conform to the ethics and the best practices of his or her professional discipline that is different from the responsibility of the ordinary citizen, and in the end we are left with the reassuring if still somewhat paradoxical conclusion that the community psychologist is both similar to *and* different from every other member of the community.

Epilogue: Community Psychology and the Contract with America

The midterm U.S. elections in 1994 initiated what could become a profound change in the relationship of government to the people. At least in rhetoric, the U.S. Congress, taking as its program the Republican party's election platform, dubbed the Contract with America, introduced legislation to limit federal authority, return authority to the states, limit government regulation that interfered with the private use of property, and reduce taxation in order to allow people to keep more of their own money on the assumption that their spending decisions would be wiser than those made by distant bureaucrats. The welfare system was to be restructured under the rationale that it oppressed poor people by keeping them dependent and encouraging out-of-wedlock births. The theoreticians of the new movement argued that if the oppressive system were eliminated, the natural inclination of people to work for their own and their families' benefits would surface.

The new conservatives speak the language of empowerment and advocate reducing government interference in the lives of people and giving people more authority to order their own lives. Government closest to the people, they believe, is the best government.

Let's look at some representative rhetoric:

- It is our belief that the concept of the whole person is violated by the legal division of responsibility for the care of people into pieces that follow arbitrary lines laid down by accidents of history, by a legal rather than a human view of the way people live, and by the exigencies of a political climate that permit one program but not another. However they grew, current practices in many instances do not serve human needs, and urgently require re-evaluation from the point of view of human needs.

- The central state (and its governmental apparatus), by its very nature and dynamics, inevitably becomes a force alien to the interests of its people, and the stronger the state becomes, the more it enslaves people in the sense that they are required, they are forced, to do things they do not want to do: i.e., there is a dilution in personal autonomy. The rhetoric of the state is one thing; its actual operations are something else again.

  The more powerful the state becomes, the more people look to it as the fount of initiative and succor, the more is the psychological sense of community diluted. That is to say, the more the lives of people are a consequence of decisions made by Kafkaesque officialdom, the more they are robbed of those communal bonds and responsibility upon which the sense of rootedness is built.

- By empowerment I mean that our aim should be to enhance the possibilities for people to control their own lives. If this is our aim then we will necessarily find ourselves questioning both our public policy and our role relationship to dependent people. We will not be able to settle for a public policy which limits us to programs we design, operate or package for social agencies to use on people, because it will require that the form and the meta communications as well as the content be consistent with empowerment.

- The mental health professions also exercise a great deal of social control. The institutional system serves the function of removing and holding the deviant and the repulsive. The publicly supported mental health service system serves as an arm to implement the police powers of the state.

Whose rhetoric is quoted here? The first statement comes from Sarason, Levine, et al., 1966, p. 269; the second is from Sarason, 1976b, p.

251; the third is from Rappaport, 1981, p. 15; and the fourth is from Levine, 1981, p. 169. These positions have been adopted over the years by community psychologists. We quote these individuals, not because they are sympathetic with or have contributed directly to the new conservative revolution, but because their words, ideas, and research, and those of many others, have contributed to the development and justification of the now dominant ideology. Will the beliefs of many community psychologists in the efficacy of self-help and the promotion of autonomy now be tested in the new political environment?

Paradoxically, rhetoric calling for a return to an earlier time, particularly in the welfare and human services field, ignores the earlier history. The community mental health movement was powered by scandals in mental hospitals and in institutions for the mentally retarded when these facilities were under state, not federal, control. Care in colonial times, when it was largely a function of the family or local poorhouses and jails, was equally bad. State hospitals grew as a response to those inadequacies; welfare systems under local control were never kindly to their charges, and the poorhouse was a scandal as late as the 1950s (Levine, 1981). Social Security was partly a federal response to the powerful Townsend movement of the 1930s, when thousands of the elderly without adequate pensions from the states or their employers organized into hundreds of clubs and flooded Washington with their demands for a federal pension system (Witte, 1963; Altmeyer, 1966).

For decades, states' rights was a code term for an appeal to allow states to continue to subjugate their minority populations. Under local control, the nation's air and water were polluted, and toxic wastes were disposed of in the cheapest way instead of the safest way. Occupational health and safety were ignored. Left to their own devices, communities prevented African Americans from voting, and individuals wrote restrictive covenants to prevent Jews, Italians, or other "undesirables" from living in certain communities. Banks and real estate agents could freely discriminate in their activities, restricting minorities' opportunities for home ownership. A woman, a Jew, an African American, a Latino, or an Asian could be denied a job, or an education, or admission to public accommodations; the person had no recourse.

In short, the governmental policies about which some Americans now complain were once conceived as good-faith solutions to underlying problems. Attacking the solutions without understanding that the underlying problems are still there will result only in a reemergence of the problems. Benign neglect may be useful for some problems, but if the solution to a problem requires resources, benign neglect may become malignant, as the residents of institutions for the mentally ill and the mentally retarded discovered. Benign neglect may leave the public schools in shambles, to the detriment of those in the next generation who cannot afford to choose private schools.[1]

We should not look at every change negatively. Block granting to the states, an emphasis on privatization, and the involvement of churches and volunteers in charitable work may well yield diverse solutions to the problems of those citizens who are unable to care for themselves. Historical experience with similar solutions in the past should, however, raise questions. Professional social work grew out of the inadequacies of private charitable enterprise and church-based services. The private solution as a whole was inadequate in its time. In addition to resource limitations, private charity often exposed recipients to demeaning conditions, and recipients resented the "Lady Bountifuls." As a result, part-time volunteerism gave way to full-time workers who, seeking greater effectiveness and eventual recognition as a profession, adopted "scientific charity." Religiously based volunteerism was simply inadequate to the tasks it faced (Katz, 1986; Levine & Levine, 1992).

Limited resources may result in unintentional empowerment of those in need as they seek their own solutions. This diversity may well prove helpful in many cases. Julian Rappaport's (1981) insight that we can learn from this diversity if we keep our minds open may be extraordinarily useful in appreciating new developments.

It may also be that there exists a sufficient infrastructure of advocacy groups so that the worst excesses of government action or, more likely, inaction will be brought to public attention. Social scientists will probably not be at the forefront of tracking and evaluating new developments; scandals are more likely to be revealed by investigative reporters who are less constrained by strictures of method and who do not need to seek permission or informed consent from their subjects to gather data (Levine, 1980, 1981). Professionals who do keep their minds, their eyes, and their sources of information open may, however, be extremely useful as conceptualizers and in tracking and assessing new developments.

Do community psychologists have a role to play in these watershed developments? Yes. Many community psychologists do work with community agencies and volunteer organizations. Under the empowerment ideology the professional can lend expertise but must respect the people with whom he or she works: "Prevention suggests professional experts; empowerment suggests collaborators" (Rappaport, 1981, p. 16). Moreover, in Rappaport's view, complex problems lend themselves to diverse and sometimes seemingly contradictory solutions. A professional operating in an environment of diverse solutions needs to be open to diversity.

The most extreme rhetoric nothwithstanding, there will continue to exist public agencies that for the foreseeable future will command the lion's share of the resources, even if these funds are inadequate to remedy the conditions the agencies are charged with ameliorating. Professionals will have roles in program development and in evaluation. The Dohrenwend model and other perspectives discussed in this book suggest many possibilities for intervention. In a time of fiscal cutbacks, newer solutions such as the resource exchange network (Sarason et al., 1977;

Sarason & Lorentz, 1979) can be described and brought to the attention of public agencies who are struggling with the consequences of diminished resources.

The professional risks capture by the realities of working within government (Sarason, 1976b), thereby losing sight of the mission. In Chapter 10 we raised the question of what organizational arrangements effectively support the accomplishment of given tasks. We might well ask the same question about the relationship between professional and government or government-funded private-sector agencies. What relationship between agency and consumer, agency and citizens at large, and agencies and government will permit the exploration of the universe of alternatives? How can we contribute to agency functioning in a way that addresses the necessity of providing for the development of agency employees as well as clients (Sarason, 1972)? Professionals can raise these questions and contribute concepts that may facilitate locally beneficial solutions.

In the beginning of this book, we described the aims of community psychologists. It is worth repeating them here:

> It [is] their mission to help create or change service organizations and other institutions . . . to achieve the goals of providing humane, effective care and less stigmatizing services to those in need, and of enhancing human growth and development.

We all have those duties as participants in a community, as citizens, and as professionals.

Note

1. The benign neglect of government may also lead to the "Balkanization" of our communities. People with similar ethnic, racial, and age characteristics and people with common religious or political philosophies may create enclaves. These may provide a sense of community for those within them, but they may destroy the overall sense of community. We already have neighborhoods reflecting specific ethnic, religious, and socioeconomic characteristics. The degree to which the separations reflect individual choice is the degree to which we can think of people as creating environments within which they can seek fulfillment for themselves and their families. To the degree that separation is imposed and maintained by the view that the others are not Americans, or are some lesser form of humanity, however, we risk "ethnic cleansing" in our country.

References

Adams, K. A. (1985). Gamesmanship for internal evaluators: Knowing when to "hold 'em" and when to "fold 'em". *Evaluation and Program Planning, 8,* 53–57.

Addams, J. (1910). *Twenty years at Hull House.* New York: Macmillan.

Adler, N. E., Boyce, T., Chesney, M. A., Cohen, S., Folkman, S., Kahn, R. L., & Syme, S. L. (1994). Socioeconomic status and health: The challenge of the gradient. *American Psychologist, 49,* 15–24.

Albee, B. W. (1995). Ann and Me. *Journal of Primary Prevention, 15,* 331–349.

Albee, G. W. (1986). Toward a just society: Lessons from observations on the primary prevention of psychopathology. *American Psychologist, 41,* 891–898.

Albee, G. W. (1959). *Mental health manpower trends.* New York: Basic Books.

Albers, D. A., Pasewark, R. A., & Smith, T. C. (1976). Involuntary hospitalization: The social construction of danger. *American Journal of Community Psychology, 4,* 129–132.

Alinksy, S. (1971). *Rules for radicals.* New York: Vantage Press.

Alley, S., Blanton, J., Feldman, R.E., Hunter, G.D., & Rolfson, M. (1979). *Case studies of mental health paraprofessionals. Twelve effective programs.* New York: Human Sciences Press.

Altmeyer, A J. (1966). *The formative years of Social Security.* Madison, WI: University of Wisconsin Press.

Alvarez, J., & Jason, L. A. (1993). The effectiveness of legislation, education, and loaners for child safety in automobiles. *Journal of Community Psychology, 21,* 280–284.

Amaro, H. (1995). Love, sex, and power. Considering women's realities in HIV prevention. *American Psychologist, 50*, 437–447.

American Bar Association. (1984). Standing Committee on Association Standards for Criminal Justice. Proposed Criminal Justice Mental Health Standards. Washington, DC: American Bar Association.

American Psychiatric Assocation. (1994). *Diagnostic and Statistical Manual of Mental Disorders, 4th Ed.* Washington, DC: Author.

American Psychiatric Association. (1964). *Planning psychiatric services for children in the community mental health program.* Washington, DC: Author.

American Psychological Association (1992). Ethical principles of psychologists and code of conduct. *American Psychologist, 47*, 1597–1611.

American Psychological Association Task Force on the Victims of Crime and Violence (1984). *Final report.* Washington, DC: American Psychological Association.

American Public Health Association. (1991). Large percent of Americans exposed to alcoholism in the family. *Nation's Health, 11*, 1–24.

Anderson, W. (1991). The New York needle trial: The politics of public health in the age of AIDS. *American Journal of Public Health, 81*, 1506–1517.

Anthony, W. A., Cohen, M. R., & Cohen, E. F. (1983). Philosophy, treatment process, and principles of the psychiatric rehabilitation approach. In L. L. Bachrach (Ed.), *Deinstitutionalization. New Directions for Mental Health Services, No. 17.* San Francisco: Jossey-Bass.

Anthony, W. A., Cohen, M. R., & Vitalo, R. (1978). The measurement of rehabilitation outcome. *Schizophrenia Bulletin, 4*, 365–383.

Antze, P. (1976). The role of ideologies in peer psychotherapy organizations: Some theoretical considerations and three case studies. *Journal of Applied Behavioral Science, 12*, 323–346.

Arnhoff, F. N. (1975). Social consequences of policy toward mental illness. *Science, 188*, 1277–81.

Arthur v. *Nyquist*, 415 F. Supp. 904 (W. D. NY 1976).

Atkinson, R. M., et al. (1984). Diagnosis of posttraumatic stress disorder in Vietnam veterans: Preliminary findings. *American Journal of Psychiatry, 141*, 694–696.

Auerbach, J. S. (1976). *Unequal justice.* New York: Oxford University Press.

Bachrach, L. L. (1984). The homeless mentally ill and mental health services. An analytical review of the literature. In H. R. Lamb (Ed.), *The homeless mentally ill.* Washington, DC: American Psychiatric Association.

Bachrach, L. L. (1975). *Deinstitutionalization: An analytical review and sociological perspective.* DHEW Publication No. (ADM) 76–351. Washington DC: U.S. Government Printing Office.

Baekeland, F., Lundwall, L., & Kissin, B. (1975). Methods for the treatment of chronic alcoholism: A critical appraisal. In R. Gibbons et al. (Eds.), *Research advances in alcohol and drug problems*, vol. 2. New York: Wiley.

Barker, R. G. (1965). Explorations in ecological psychology. *American Psychologist, 20*, 1–14.

Barker, R. G. (1968). *Ecological psychology: Concepts and methods for studying the environment of human behavior.* Stanford, CA: Stanford University Press.

Barker R. G. (1978). *Habitats, environments, and human behavior.* San Francisco: Jossey-Bass.

Barker, R. G., & Gump, P. V. (1964). *Big school, small school; High school size and student behavior.* Stanford, CA: Stanford University Press.

Barker, R. G., & Schoggen, P. (1973). *Qualities of community life: Methods of measuring environment and behavior applied to an American and an English town.* San Francisco: Jossey-Bass.

Barker, R. G., & Wright, H. F. (1955). *Midwest and its children.* New York: Harper & Row.

Barnes, G. M. (1984). *Alcohol use among secondary school students in New York State.* Buffalo, NY: New York State Research Institute on Alcoholism.

Barnett, W. S. (1993). Benefit-cost analysis of preschool education: Findings from a 25-year follow-up. *American Journal of Orthopsychiatry, 63,* 500–508.

Barrera, M., Jr. (1982). Raza populations. In L. R. Snowden (Ed.), *Reaching the underserved: Mental health needs of neglected populations.* Beverly Hills, CA: Sage.

Barrera, M., Jr. (1986). Distinctions between social support concepts, measures and models. *American Journal of Community Psychology, 14,* 413–445.

Bass, E., & Davis, L. (1988). *The courage to heal.* New York: Harper and Row.

Baud, R. K. (Ed.), (1982). *Parent power: A handbook for Buffalo public school parents.* Buffalo, NY: Citizens for Quality Education.

Baum, C., Kennedy, D. L., & Knapp, D. G. (1988). Prescription drug use in 1984 and changes over time. *Medical Care, 26,* 105–114.

Bauman, L. J., Stein, R. E. K., & Ireys, H. T. (1991). Reinventing fidelity: the transfer of social technology among settings. *American Journal of Community Psychology, 19,* 619–639.

Baxter, S., Chodorkoff, B., & Underhill, R. (1968). Psychiatric emergencies: Dispositional determinants and the validity of the decision to admit. *American Journal of Psychiatry, 124,* 1542–1548.

Baxtrom v. *Herald,* 383 US 107 (1966).

Beachler, M. (1990). The mental health services program for youth. *Journal of Mental Health Administration, 17,* 115–121.

Bechtel, R. B. (1977). *Enclosing behavior.* Stroudsburg, PA: Dowden, Hutchinson & Ross.

Beiser, M., Shore, J.H., Peters, R., & Tatum, E. (1985). Does community care for the mentally ill make a difference? A tale of two cities. *American Journal of Psychiatry, 142,* 1047–1052.

Belsky, J. (1980). Child maltreatment: An ecological integration. *American Psychologist, 35,* 320–335.

Belton v. *Gebhart,* 347 US 483 (1954).

Bennett, C. C., Anderson, L. S., Cooper, S., Hassol, L., Klein, D. C., & Rosenblum, G. (1966). *Community psychology. A report on the Boston conference on the education of psychologists for community mental health.* Boston: Department of Psychology, Boston University.

Bennis, W. G. (1966). *Changing organizations.* New York: McGraw Hill.

Benson, P. R., Milazzo-Sayre, L. J., Rosenstein, M. J., Johnson, W. E., & Manderscheid, R. W. (1992). *Clients/patients with a principal diagnosis of affective disorder served in inpatient, outpatient and partial care programs of specialty mental health organizations, United States, 1986.* DHHS Publication No. (ADM) 92–187. Washington DC: Alcohol, Drug Abuse, and Mental Health Administration.

Berger, R. S. (1985). The psychiatric expert as due process decision maker. *Buffalo Law Review, 33,* 681–727.

Bergin, A. E. (1971). The evaluation of therapeutic outcomes. In A. E. Bergin and S. L. Garfield (Eds.), *Handbook of psychotherapy and behavior change: An empirical analysis.* New York: Wiley.

Bermant, G., Kelman, H. C., & Warwick, D. P. (1978). *The ethics of social intervention.* New York: Halstead Press.

Berrueta-Clement, J. R., Schweinhart, L. J., Barnett, W. S., Epstein, A. S., & Weikart, D. P. (1984). *Changed lives. The effects of the Perry preschool program on youths through age 19.* Ypsilanti, MI: High/Scope Press.

Bickel, A. M. (1962). *The least dangerous branch: The Supreme Court at the bar of politics.* Indianapolis: Bobbs-Merrill.

Bissinger, H. G. (1994). "We're all racists now." *New York Times Magazine,* May 29, 27–33, 43, 50, 53–56.

Blatt, B., & Kaplan, F. (1966). *Christmas in purgatory.* Boston: Allyn & Bacon.

Blazer, D. G. (1982). Social support and mortality in an elderly community population. *American Journal of Epidemiology, 115,* 684–694.

Bloch, A. (1984). Twenty-year follow-up of pupils in a special class for the mentally retarded: A study of a complete school community. *American Journal of Orthopsychiatry, 54,* 436–443.

Bloom, B. L. (1979). Prevention of mental disorders: Recent advances in theory and practice. *Community Mental Health Journal, 15,* 179–191.

Bloom, B. L. (1984). *Community mental health. a general introduction.* 2nd Ed. Monterey, CA: Brooks/Cole.

Bloom, B. L., Asher, S. J., & White, S. W. (1978). Marital disruption as a stressor: A review and analysis. *Psychological Bulletin, 85,* 867–894.

Bloom, B. L., & Hodges, W. F. (1988). The Colorado separation and divorce program: A preventive intervention for newly separated persons. In R. H. Price, E. L. Cowen, R. P. Lorion, & J. Ramos-McKay. *14 Ounces of prevention.* Washington, DC: American Psychological Association.

Bloom, B. L., Hodges, W. F., & Caldwell, R. A. (1982). A preventive intervention program for the newly separated: Initial evaluation. *American Journal of Community Psychology, 10,* 251–264.

Blouch, R. G. (1982). Rural people. In L. R. Snowden (Ed.), *Reaching the underserved: Mental health needs of neglected populations.* Beverly Hills: Sage.

Bond, G. R. (1992). Vocational rehabilitation. In R. Liberman (Ed.), *Handbook of psychiatric rehabilitation* (pp. 244–275). New York: MacMillan.

Bond, G. R., Miller, L. D., Krumweid, R. D., & Ward, R. S. (1988). Assertive case management in three CMHCs: A controlled study. *Hospital and Community Psychiatry, 39,* 411–417.

Bond, G. R., Witheridge, T. F., Dincin, J., & Wasmer, D. (1990). Assertive Community Treatment for frequent users of psychiatric hospitals in a large city: A controlled study. *American Journal of Community Psychology, 18,* 865–891.

Bouchard, T. J. (1994). Genes, environment, and personality. *Science, 264,* 1700–1701.

Braginsky, B. M., Braginsky, D. D., & Ring, K. (1969). *The mental hospital as a last resort.* New York: Holt, Rinehart & Winston.

Brand, R. C., Jr., & Claiborn, W. L. (1976). Two studies of comparative stigma: Employer attitudes and practices toward rehabilitated convicts, mental and tuberculosis patients. *Community Mental Health Journal, 12,* 168–175.

Brenner, M. (1994). Judge Motley's verdict. *The New Yorker,* May 16, 65–71.

Breslau, N., & Prabucki, K. (1987). Siblings of disabled children: Effects of chronic stress in the family. *Archives of General Psychiatry, 44,* 1040–1046.

Briggs v. *Elliott,* 347 US 497 (1954).

Broadhead, W. E. et al. (1983). The epidemiologic evidence for a relationship between social support and health. *American Journal of Epidemiology, 117,* 521–537.

Brockman, J., D'Arcy, C., & Edmonds, L. (1979). Facts or artifacts? Changing public attitudes toward the mentally ill. *Social Science and Medicine, 13,* 673–682.

Broman, C. L., Hamilton, V. L., & Hoffman, W. S. (1990). Unemployment and its effect on families: Evidence from a plant closing study. *American Journal of Community Psychology, 18,* 643–659.

Bronfenbrenner, U. (1979). *The ecology of human development.* Cambridge, MA: Harvard University Press.

Brooks, T. R. (1974). *Walls come tumbling down.* Englewood Cliffs, NJ: Prentice-Hall.

Brown v. *Board of Education of Topeka,* 349 US 294 (1955).

Brown v. *Board of Education,* 347 US 483 (1954).

Brown, B. B., & Perkins, D. D. (1992). Disruptions in place attachment. In I. Altman & S. Low (Eds.), *Place attachment* (pp. 279–304). New York: Plenum.

Browne, A. (1993). Violence against women by male partners: Prevalence, outcomes, and policy implications. *American Psychologist, 48,* 1077–1087.

Browne, A., & Finkelhor, D. (1985). Impact of child sexual abuse: A review of research. *Psychological Bulletin, 99,* 66–77.

Browne, K. (1993). Home visitation and child abuse: The British experience. *ASPA Advisor, 6,* 11–2, 28–31.

Bryant, J. R. (1980). The black church as the unifier of the black community. In L. S. Yearwood (Ed.), *Black organizations: Issues on survival techniques* (pp 5–8). Lanham, MD: University Press of America.

Bui, K-V. T., & Takeuchi, D. T. (1992). Ethnic minority adolescents and the use of community mental health care services. *American Journal of Community Psychology, 20,* 403–417.

Burgess, A. W., & Holmstrom, L. L. (1979). Rape: Sexual disruption and recovery. *American Journal of Orthopsychiatry, 49,* 648–657.

Buss, T. F., Redburn, F. S., & Waldron, J. (1983). *Mass unemployment. Plant closings and community mental health.* Beverly Hills, CA: Sage.

Butterforce, F. D., Goodman, R. M., & Wandersman, A. (1993). Community coalitions for prevention and health promotion. *Health Education Research, Theory and Practice, 8,* 315–330.

Byrne, D., Kelley, K., & Fisher, W. A. (1993). Unwanted teenage pregnancies: Incidence, interpretation, and intervention. *Applied and Preventive Psychology, 2,* 101–113.

Cahn, E. (1955). Jurisprudence. *NYU Law Review, 30,* 150–169.

Caldwell, R. A., Bogat, G. A., & Davidson, W. S. II (1988). The assessment of child abuse potential and the prevention of child abuse and neglect: A policy analysis. *American Journal of Community Psychology, 16,* 608–624.

Campbell, D. T. (1969). Reforms as experiments. *American Psychologist, 24,* 409–429.

Campbell, D. T. (1979). Assessing the impact of planned social change. *Evaluation and Program Planning, 2,* 67–90.

Campbell, D. T., & Kimmel, H. (1985). *Guiding preventive intervention research centers for research validity.* Unpublished manuscript, Department of Social Relations, Lehigh University, Bethlehem, PA.

Caplan, G. (1959). *Concepts of mental health and consultation: Their application in public health social work.* Washington, DC: Social and Rehabilitation Service, Children's Bureau.

Caplan, G. (1964). *Principles of preventive psychiatry.* New York: Basic Books.

Caplan, G. (1970). *The theory and practice of mental health consultation.* New York: Basic Books.

Caplan, G. (1976). The family as a support system. In G. Caplan & M. Killilea (Eds.), *Support systems and mutual help.* New York: Grune & Stratton.

Caplan, N., & Nelson, S. D. (1973). On being useful: The nature and consequences of psychological research on social problems. *American Psychologist, 28,* 199–211.

Caplan, R. D., Vinokur, A. D., Price, R. H., & van Ryn, M. (1989). Job seeking, reemployment, and mental health: A randomized field experiment in coping with job loss. *Journal of Applied Psychology, 74,* 759–769.

Carling, P. J. (1990). Major mental illness, housing, and supports: The promise of community integration. *American Psychologist, 45,* 969–975.

Carling, P. J. (1993). Housing and supports for persons with mental illness: Emerging approaches to research and practice. *Hospital and Community Psychiatry, 44,* 439–449.

Carper, L. (1970). The Negro family and the Moynihan report. In P. I. Rose (Ed.), *Slavery and its aftermath.* New York: Atherton.

Carson, E. D. (1993). *A hand up. Black philanthropy and self-help in America.* Washington, DC: Joint Center for Political and Economic Studies Press.

Catania, J. A., et al. (1991). Changes in condom use among homosexual men in San Francisco. *Health Psychology, 10,* 190–199.

Center for the Future of Children (1992). *The future of children. School linked services.* 2 (1) (Whole Issue).

Centers for Disease Control (1995). Update: Aquired Immunodeficiency Syndrome—United States, 1994. *Morbidity and Mortality Weekly Report, 44* (February 3), 64–67.

Chamberlin, J. (1990). The ex-patient's movement: Where we've been and where we're going. *Journal of Mind and Behavior, 11,* 323–336.

Chayes, A. (1976). The role of the judge in public law litigation. *Harvard Law Review, 89,* 1281–1316.

Cheng, S.-T. (1993). The social context of Hong Kong's booming elderly home industry. *American Journal of Community Psychology, 21,* 449–467.

Cherniss, C. (1980). *Professional burnout in human service organizations.* New York: Praeger.

Cherniss, C., & Cherniss, D. S. (1987). Professional involvement in self-help groups for parents of high-risk newborns. *American Journal of Community Psychology, 15,* 435–444.

Chesler, M., Barbarin, O., & Lego-Stein, J. (1984). Patterns of participation in a self–help group for parents of children with cancer. *Journal of Psychosocial Oncology, 2,* 41–64.

Children's Defense Fund. (1974). *Children out of school in America.* Washington, DC: Author.

Children's Defense Fund. (1978). *Children without homes.* Washington, DC: Author.

Cicirelli, V. G. (1969). *The impact of Head Start: An evaluation of the effects of Head Start on children's cognitive and affective development.* Washington, DC: National Bureau of Standards, Institute for Applied Technology.

City of Cleburne, Texas v. *Cleburne Living Center,* 473 US 432 (1985).

Civil Rights Cases 109 US 3 (1883).

Clausen, J. A. (1981). Stigma and mental disorder: Phenomena and terminology. *Psychiatry, 44,* 287–296.

Clingempeel, W. G., & Reppucci, N. D. (1982). Joint custody after divorce: Major issues and goals for research. *Psychological Bulletin, 91,* 102–127.

Cloward, R., & Piven, F. F. (1971). *Regulating the poor: The function of public welfare in America.* New York: Random House.

Coates, T. J. (1990). Strategies for modifying sexual behavior for primary and secondary prevention of HIV disease. *Journal of Consulting and Clinical Psychology, 58,* 57–69.

Cohen, C. I., & Thompson, K. S. (1992). Homeless mentally ill or mentally ill homeless? *American Journal of Psychiatry, 149,* 816–823.

Cohen, N. D. (Ed.). (1990). *Psychiatry takes to the streets: Outreach and crisis intervention for the mentally ill.* New York: Guilford.

Cohen, S., & Wills, T. A. (1985). Stress, social support, and the buffering hypothesis. *Psychological Bulletin, 98,* 310–357.

Coie, J. D., Watt, N. F., West, S. G., et al. (1993). The science of prevention: A conceptual framework and some directions for a national research program. *American Psychologist, 48,* 1013–1022.

Colarelli, N. J., & Siegel, S. M. (1966). *Ward H. An adventure in innovation.* Princeton, NJ: Van Nostrand

Cole, N. J., McDonald, B. W. Jr., & Branch, C. H. H. (1968). A two-year follow-up study of the work performance of former psychiatric patients. *American Journal of Psychiatry, 124,* 1070–1075.

Coleman, J. S., Campbell, E. Q., Hobson, C. J., McPartland, J., Mood, A. M., Weinfeld, F. D., & York, R. L. (1966). *Equality of educational opportunity.* Washington, DC: U.S. Government Printing Office.

Coleman, L. (1990). False accusations of sexual abuse: Psychiatry's latest reign of error. *Journal of Mind and Behavior, 11,* 545–556.

Coll, B. D. (1969). *Perspectives in public welfare: A history.* Washington, DC: U.S. Department of Health, Education, and Welfare.

Collins, N. L., Dunkel-Schetter, C., Lobel, M., & Scrimshaw, S. C. M. (1993). Social support in pregnancy: Psychosocial correlates of birth outcomes and postpartum depression. *Journal of Personality and Social Psychology, 65,* 1243–1258.

Comptroller General of the United States. (1977). Report to Congress. *Returning the mentally disabled to the community: Government needs to do more.* Washington, DC: Author.

Consumer Advisory Board v. *Glover,* 989 F. 2d 65 (1st Cir 1993).

Cowen, E. L. (1973). Social and community interventions. *Annual Review of Psychology, 24,* 423–472.

Cowen, E. L. (1977). Baby steps toward primary prevention. *American Journal of Community Psychology, 5,* 1–22.

Cowen, E. L. (1982). Help is where you find it: Four informal helping groups. *American Psychologist, 37,* 385–395.

Cowen, E. L. (1983). Primary prevention in mental health: Past, present, and future. In R. Felner et al. (Eds.), *Preventive psychology.* (pp. 11–25). New York: Plenum.

Cowen, E. L., & Hightower, A. D. (1989). The Primary Mental Health Project: Thirty years after. *Prevention in Human Services, 6,* 225–257.

Cowen, E. L., Izzo, L. D., Miles, H., Telschow, E. F., Trost, M. A., & Zax, M. (1963). A mental health program in the school setting: Description and evaluation. *Journal of Psychology, 56,* 307–356.

Cowen, E. L., Pederson, A., Babigian, H., Izzo, L. D., & Trost, M. A. (1973). Long-term follow-up of early detected vulnerable children. *Journal of Consulting and Clinical Psychology, 41,* 438–446.

Cowen, E. L., Trost, M. A., Izzo, L. D., Lorion, R. P., Dorr, D., & Isaacson, R. V. (1975). *New ways in school mental health.* New York: Human Sciences Press.

Cowen, E. L., Zax, M., Izzo, L. D., & Trost, M. A. (1966). The prevention of emotional disorders in the school setting: A further investigation. *Journal of Consulting Psychology, 30,* 381–387.

Coyne, J. C., Kessler, R. S., Tal, M. Turnbull, J., Wortman, C. B., & Greden, J. F. (1987). Living with a depressed person. *Journal of Consulting and Clinical Psychology, 55,* 347–352.

Crawford, I., et al. (1990). A multimedia-based approach to increasing communication and the level of AIDS knowledge within families. *Journal of Community Psychology, 18*, 361–373.

Crittenden, P. M. (1992). The social ecology of treatment: Case study of a service system for maltreated children. *American Journal of Orthopsychiatry, 62*, 22–34.

Cronon, W. (1991). *Nature's metropolis: Chicago and the Great West.* New York: Norton.

Cullison v. *Califano*, 613 F. 2d 55 (4th Cir. 1980).

Cummings, J. (1983, November 20). Breakup of black family imperils gains of decades. *New York Times*, pp. 1, 56.

Cummings, R. (1993). All-male black schools: Equal protection, the new separatism and *Brown v. Board of Education. Hastings Constitutional Law Quarterly, 20*, 725–782.

Darlington, R. B., Royce, J. M., Snipper, A. S., Murray, H. W., & Lazar, I. (1980). Preschool programs and later school competence of children from low-income families. *Science, 208*, 202–204.

D'Augelli, A. R. (1982). Historical synthesis of consultation and education. In D. R. Ritter (Ed.), *Consultation, education and prevention in community mental health.* Springfield, IL: Charles C. Thomas.

D'Augelli, A. (1983). Social support networks in mental health. In J. Whittaker & J. Garbarino (Eds.), *Social support networks: Informal helping in the human services.* Hawthorne, NY: Aldine.

D'Augelli, A. R., & Hershberger, S. L. (1993). Lesbian, gay, and bisexual youth in community settings: Personal challenges and mental health problems. *American Journal of Community Psychology, 21*, 421–448.

Davis v. *County School Board of Prince Edward County*, 347 US 483 (1954).

Davis, L. G., & Nelson, W. E. (1980). The politics of black self-help in the United States: A historical overview. In L. S. Yearwood (Ed.), *Black organizations: Issues on survival techniques: A historical overview.* (pp 37–50). Lanham, MD: University Press of America.

Davis, R. C., Brickman, E., & Baker, T. (1991). Supportive and unsupportive responses of others to rape victims: Effects on concurrent victim adjustment. *American Journal of Community Psychology, 19*, 443–451.

Dawes, R. M. (1994). *House of cards: Psychology and psychotherapy built on myth.* New York: Free Press.

Dear, M. J., & Wolch, J. R. (1987). *Landscapes of despair.* Princeton, NJ: Princeton University Press.

DeGrazia, S. (1962). *Of time, work and leisure.* New York: Twentieth Century Fund.

Department of Health, Education, & Welfare (1979). *Promoting health, preventing disease. Objectives for the nation.* Washington, DC: Author.

Des Jarlais, D. C., Friedman, S. R., & Casriel, C. (1990). Target groups for preventing AIDS among intravenous drug users: 2. The "hard" data studies. *Journal of Consulting and Clinical Psychology, 58*, 50–56.

De Tocqueville, A. (1956). *Democracy in America*. New York: Mentor Books.

DeYoung, A. (1977). Classroom climate and class success: A case study at the university level. *Journal of Educational Research, 70,* 252–257.

Dincin, J. (1990). Assertive case management. *Psychiatric Quarterly, 61,* 49–55.

Dohrenwend, B. P., & Dohrenwend, B. S. (1969). *Social status and psychological disorder*. New York: Wiley.

Dohrenwend, B. P., Levav, I., Shrout, P. E., Schwartz, S., Naveh, G., Link, B. G., Skodol, A. E., & Steueve, A. (1992). Socioeconomic status and psychiatric disorders: The causation-selection issue. *Science, 255,* 946–952.

Dohrenwend, B. S. (1978). Social stress and community psychology. *American Journal of Community Psychology, 6,* 1–14.

Dolan, L. W., & Wolpert, J. (1982). *Long term neighborhood property impacts of group homes for mentally retarded people*. Unpublished report. Woodrow Wilson School of Public and International Affairs, Princeton University, Princeton, NJ.

Dooley, D., Catalano, R., & Wilson, G. (1994). Depression and unemployment: Panel findings from the epidemiological catchment area study. *American Journal of Community Psychology, 22,* 745–765.

Dowart, R. A., & Hoover, C. W. (1994). A national study of transitional hospital services in mental health. *American Journal of Public Health, 84,* 1229–1234.

Downs, M. W., & Fox, J. C. (1993). Social environments of adult homes. *Community Mental Health Journal, 29,* 15–23.

Dressler, W. W. (1991). *Stress and adaptation in the context of culture*. Albany, NY: State University of New York Press.

Du Bois, W. E. B. (1903). *The souls of black folk*. Chicago: McClung.

Duberman, M. (1993). *Stonewall*. New York: Dutton.

Dunford, F. W. (1990). System-initiated warrants for suspects of misdemeanor domestic assault: A pilot study. *Justice Quarterly, 7,* 631–653.

Dunham, H. W. (1965). Community psychiatry: The newest therapeutic bandwagon. *Archives of General Psychiatry, 12,* 303–313.

Dunn, B. (1993). Growing up with a psychotic mother: A retrospective study. *American Journal of Orthopsychiatry, 63,* 177–189.

Durlak, J. A. (1983). Social problem-solving as a primary prevention strategy. In R. Felner et al. (Eds.), *Preventive psychology*. (pp. 31–480). New York: Plenum.

Dwyer, J. H., & Flesch-Janys, D. (1995). Editorial: Agent Orange in Viet Nam. *American Journal of Public Health, 85,* 476–478.

Edelstein, M. R. (1988). *Contaminated communities. The social and psychological impacts of residential toxic exposure*. Boulder, CO: Westview.

Edwards, G., Hensman, C., Hawker, A., & Williamson, V. (1967). Alcoholics Anonymous: The anatomy of a self-help group. *Social Psychiatry, 1,* 195–204.

Egolf, B., Lasker, J., Wolf, S., & Potvin, L. (1992). The Roseto effect: A fifty-year comparison of mortality rates. *American Journal of Public Health, 82,* 1089–1092.

Ekstrand, M. L., & Coates, T. J. (1990). Maintenance of safer sexual behaviors and predictors of risky sex: The San Franciso Men's Health study. *American Journal of Public Health, 80,* 973–977.

Elias, M. J., Gara, M., Ubriaco, M., Rothbaum, P. A., Clabby, J. F., & Schuyler, T. (1986). Impact of a preventive social problem solving intervention on children's coping with middle school stressors. *American Journal of Community Psychology, 14,* 259–275.

Elias, M. J., Gara, M. A., Schuyler, T. F., et al. (1991). The promotion of social competence: Longitudinal study of a preventive school-based program. *American Journal of Orthopsychiatry, 61,* 409–417.

Elias, M. J., & Weissberg, R. P. (1990). School-based social competence promotion as a primary prevention strategy: A tale of two projects. *Prevention in Human Services, 7,* 177–200.

Ellis, T. E. (1986). Toward a cognitive therapy for suicidal individuals. *Professional Psychology: Research and Practice, 17,* 125–130.

Ellison, R. (1947). *Invisible man.* New York: Random House.

Ellsworth, R. B., Foster, L., Childers, B., Arthur G., & Kroeker, D. (1968). *Journal of Consulting and Clinical Psychology Monograph Supplement, 32* (Part 2), 1–41.

Emery, R. E. (1982). Interparental conflict and the children of discord and divorce. *Psychological Bulletin, 92,* 310–330.

Emrick, C. D. (1987). Alcoholics Anonymous: Affiliation processes and effectiveness as treatment. *Alcoholism: Clinical and Experimental Research, 11,* 416–423.

Ennis, B. J., & Litwack, T. R. (1974). Psychiatry and the presumption of expertise: Flipping coins in the courtroom. *California Law Review, 62,* 693–752.

Ennis, B. J., & Siegel, L. (1973). *The rights of mental patients.* New York: Avon Press.

Epstein, S. S., Brown, L. O., & Pope, C. (1982). *Hazardous waste in America.* San Francisco: Sierra Club Books.

Erikson, E. H. (1950). *Childhood and society.* New York: Norton.

Ewing, C. P. (1978). *Crisis intervention as psychotherapy.* New York: Oxford University Press.

Eysenck, H. J. (1952). The effects of psychotherapy: An evaluation. *Journal of Consulting Psychology, 16,* 319–324.

Eysenck, H. J. (1961). The effects of psychotherapy. In H. J. Eysenck (Ed.), *Handbook of abnormal psychology.* New York: Basic Books.

Ezorsky, G. (1991). *Racism and justice: The case for affirmative action.* Ithaca, NY: Cornell University Press.

Fairweather, G. W. (1980). *The Fairweather lodge: A twenty-five year retrospective.* San Francisco: Jossey-Bass.

Fairweather, G. W., & Fergus, E. O. (1993). *Empowering the mentally ill.* Austin, TX: Fairweather Publishing.

Fairweather, G. W., Sanders, D. H., Maynard, H., & Cressler, D. L. (1969). *Community life for the mentally ill.* Chicago: Aldine.

Fairweather, G. W., Sanders, D. H., & Tornatzky, L. G. (1974). *Creating change in mental health organizations.* New York: Pergamon.

Fairweather, G. W., & Tornatzky, L. G. (1977). *Experimental methods for social policy research.* New York: Pergamon.

False Memory Syndrome Foundation Newsletter, 1992, 1993, 1994.

Farber, B. A. (Ed.). (1983). *Stress and burnout in the human service professions.* New York: Pergamon.

Farkas, M. D., & Anthony, W. A. (1989). *Psychiatric rehabilitation programs: Putting theory into practice.* Baltimore: Johns Hopkins University Press.

Farley, R. (1980). School desegregation and white flight: An investigation of competing models and their discrepant findings. *Sociology of Education, 53,* 123–139.

Felner, R. D., & Adan, A. M. (1988). The School Transitional Environment Project: An ecological intervention and evaluation. In Price, R. H., Cowen, E. L., Lorion, R. P., & Ramos-McKay, J., *14 ounces of prevention: A casebook for practicioners* (pp. 111–122). Washington, DC: American Psychological Association.

Felner, R. D., Brand, S., Adan, A. M., et al. (1993). Restructuring the ecology of the school as an approach to prevention during school transitions. *Prevention in Human Services, 10,* 103–136.

Felner, R. D., Ginter, M., & Primavera, J. (1982). Primary prevention during school transitions: Social support and environmental structure. *American Journal of Community Psychology, 10,* 277–290.

Felton, B. J., & Shinn, M. (1992). Social integration and social support: Moving "social support" beyond the individual level. *Journal of Community Psychology, 20,* 103–115.

Finch, J. F., Okun, M. A., Barrerra, M. Jr., Zautra, A. I., & Reich, J. W. (1989). Positive and negative social ties among older adults: Measurement models and the prediction of psychological distress and well-being. *American Journal of Community Psychology, 17,* 585–605.

Finkel, N. J. (1974). Strens and traumas: An attempt at categorization. *American Journal of Community Psychology, 2,* 265–273.

Finkel, N. J. (1975). Strens, traumas, and trauma resolution. *American Journal of Community Psychology, 3,* 173–178.

Finkel, N. J., & Jacobsen, C. A. (1977). Significant life experiences in an adult sample. *American Journal of Community Psychology, 5,* 165–177.

Finkelhor, D., & Dziuba-Leatherman, J. (1994). Victimization of children. *American Psychologist, 49,* 173–183.

Fischer, P. J., & Breakey, W. R. (1991). The epidemiology of alcohol, drug, and mental disorders among homeless persons. *American Psychologist, 46,* 1115–1128.

Fisher, J. D., & Fisher, W. A. (1992). Changing AIDS-risk behavior. *Psychological Bulletin, 111,* 455–474.

Fisher, S. (1992). *From margin to mainstream. The social progress of Black Americans.* 2d ed. Lanham, MD: Rowman and Littlefield.

Folkman, S. (1984). Personal control and stress and coping processes: A theoretical analysis. *Journal of Personality and Social Psychology, 46,* 839–852.

Folkman, S., & Lazarus, R. S. (1980). An analysis of coping in a middle-aged sample. *Journal of Health and Social Behavior, 21,* 219–239.

Folkman, S., & Lazarus, R. S. (1988). Coping as a mediator of emotion. *Journal of Personality and Social Psychology, 54,* 466–475.

Foster, H. L. (1974). *Ribbin', jivin' and playin' the dozens.* Cambridge, MA: Ballinger.

Frankl, V. E. (1963). *Man's search for meaning.* New York: Washington Square Press.

French, S. L., Knox, V. J., & Gekoski, W. L. (1992). Confounding as a problem in relating life events to health status in elderly individuals. *American Journal of Community Psychology, 20,* 243–252.

Friedman, R. M., & Duchnowski, A. J. (1990). Service trends in the children's mental health system: implications for the training of psychologists. In R. R. Magrab and P. Wohlford (Eds.), *Improving psychological services for children and adolescents with severe mental disorders: Clinical training in psychology.* Washington, DC: American Psychological Association.

Fuchs, V. R. (1968). *The service economy.* New York: National Bureau of Economic Research.

Furstenberg, F. F., Jr., Moore, K. A., & Peterson, J. L. (1985). Sex education and sexual experience among adolescents. *American Journal of Public Health, 75,* 1331–1332.

Gabriel, T. (1995). Some on-line discoveries give gay youth a path to themselves. *New York Times,* July 2, A–1, 16.

Galanter, M. (1988). Zealous self-help groups as adjuncts to psychiatric treatment: A study of Recovery, Inc. *American Journal of Psychiatry, 145,* 1248–1253.

Galanter, M. (1989). *Cults. Faith, healing, and coercion.* New York: Oxford University Press.

Galanter, M. (1990). Cults and zealous self-help movements: A psychiatric perspective. *American Journal of Psychiatry, 147,* 543–551.

Galbraith, J. K. (1958). *The affluent society.* Boston: Houghton-Mifflin.

Garbarino, J., Kostelny, K., & Dubrow, N. (1991). *No place to be a child: growing up in a war zone.* Lexington, MA: Lexington Books.

Gardner, W., & Wilcox, B. L. (1993). Political intervention in scientific peer review: Research on adolescent sexual behavior. *American Psychologist, 48,* 972–983.

Garland, A. F., & Zigler, E. (1993). Adolescent suicide prevention: Current research and social policy implications. *American Psychologist, 48,* 169–182.

Garrett, B., & Posey, T. (1993). Involuntary commitment: A consumer perspective. *Innovations & Research, 2,* 39–41.

Gartner, A., & Reissman, F. (1977). *Self-help in the human services.* San Francisco: Jossey-Bass.

Gebhard, C., & Levine, M. (1985). Does membership in Alcoholics Anonymous reduce the stigma of alcoholism? Paper presented at the annual meeting of the Eastern Psychological Association, Boston, MA, March 22.

Geller, J. L. (1993). On being "committed" to treatment in the community. *Innovations & Research, 2,* 23–27.

Geller, J. L., & Fisher, W. H. (1993). The linear continuum of transitional residences: Debunking the myth. *American Journal of Psychiatry, 150,* 1070–1076.

Gerard, H. B. (1983). School desegregaton: The social science role. *American Psychologist, 38,* 869–877.

Gesten, E. L., Rains, M. H., Rapkin, B. D., Weissberg, R. P., de Apocada, R. F., Cowen, E. L., & Bowen, R. (1982). Training children in social problem-solving competencies: A first and second look. *American Journal of Community Psychology, 10,* 95–115.

Gibbs, L. (1994). Risk assessments from a community perspective. *Environmental Impact Assessment Review, 14,* 327–335.

Gibbs, L. M. (1982). *Love Canal: My story.* Albany: State University of New York Press.

Gibbs, L. M. (1983). Community response to an emergency situation: Psychological destruction and the Love Canal. *American Journal of Community Psychology, 11,* 116–125.

Gibbs, L. and Citizens Clearinghouse for Hazardous Waste (1995). *Dying from dioxin. A citizen's guide to reclaiming our health and rebuilding democracy.* Boston, MA: South End Press.

Gillick, J. (1977). *Al-Anon: A self-help group for co-alcoholics.* Unpublished doctoral dissertation, Department of Psychology, State University of New York at Buffalo.

Gilman, S. R., & Diamond, R. J. (1985). Economic analysis in community treatment of the chronically mentally ill. In L. Stein & M. A. Test (Eds.), *The Training in Community Living model: A decade of experience* (New Directions for Mental Health Services, No. 26, pp. 77–84). San Francisco: Jossey-Bass.

Giordano, J., & Giordano, G. P. (1976). Ethnicity and community mental health. *Community Mental Health Review, 1,* No. 3.

Gist, R., & Stolz, S. (1982). Mental health promotion and the media: Community response to the Kansas City hotel disaster. *American Psychologist, 37,* 1136–1139.

Gladden, B. C., & Rogan, W. J. (1995). DDT and shortened duration of lactation in a northern Mexican town. *American Journal of Public Health, 85,* 504–508.

Goffman, E. (1961). *Asylums.* New York: Doubleday.

Goffman, E. (1963). *Stigma.* Englewood Cliffs, NJ: Prentice-Hall.

Golan, N. (1978). *Treatment in crisis situations.* New York: Free Press.

Goldberg, E. L., & Comstock, G. W. (1980). Epidemiology of life events: Frequency in general populations. *American Journal of Epidemiology, 111,* 736–752.

Goldberg, L. R. (1993). The structure of phenotypic personality traits. *American Psychologist, 48,* 26–34.

Goldenberg, I. I. (1971). *Build me a mountain. Youth, poverty and the creation of new settings.* Cambridge, MA: MIT Press.

Goldenberg, I. I. (1978). *Oppression and social intervention.* Chicago: Nelson-Hall.

Goldsmith, J. M. (1984). *Final report of the Governor's Select Commission on the Future of the State-Local Mental Health System.* Albany, NY: Governor's Select Commission.

Gong Lum v. *Rice*, 275 US 78 (1927).

Gordon, J. S. (1978). Final report to the President's Commission on Mental Health of the special study on alternative mental health services. *Task Panel Reports Submitted to the President's Commission on Mental Health*, Appendix, Vol 2. Washington, DC: U.S. Government Printing Office.

Gordon, M. (1982). *Attitudes toward mental illness held by two disadvantaged inner-city ethnic groups.* Unpublished doctoral dissertation, Department of Psychology, SUNY at Buffalo.

Gottesman, I. I. (1991). *Schizophrenia genesis.* New York: Freeman.

Gottlieb, B. (1981). *Social networks and social support in community mental health.* Beverly Hills: Sage.

Gottlieb, B. H. (1983). Social support as a focus for integrative research in psychology. *American Psychologist, 38,* 278–287.

Gove, W. R. (1976). Adult sex roles and mental illness. In F. Denmark & R. Wesner (Eds.). *Women* (Vol. 1). New York: Psychological Dimensions.

Gove, W. R. (Ed.). (1980). *The labelling of deviance.* 2nd Ed. Beverly Hills, CA: Sage.

Gove, W. R. (Ed.). (1982). *Deviance and mental illness.* Beverly Hills, CA: Sage.

Gralnick, A. (1985). Build a better state hospital: Deinstitutionalization has failed. *Hospital and Community Psychiatry, 36,* 738–741.

Graziano, A. (1969). Clinical innovation and the mental health power structure: A social case history. *American Psychologist, 24,* 10–18.

Graziano, A. M. (1974). *Child without tomorrow.* New York: Pergamon.

Graziano, A. M. (1977). Parents as behavior therapists. *Progress in Behavior Modification, 4,* 251–298.

Graziano, A. M., & Fink, R. (1973). Second-order effects in mental health treatment. *Journal of Consulting and Clinical Psychology, 40,* 356–364.

Graziano, A. M., & Mooney, K. C. (1984). *Children and behavior therapy.* New York: Aldine.

Green v. *County School Board*, 391, US 430 (1968).

Grob, G. N. (1994). *The mad among us: A history of the care of America's mentally ill.* New York: Free Press.

Grosser, R. C. , & Vine, P. (1991). Families as advocates for the mentally ill: A survey of characteristics and service needs. *American Journal of Orthopsychiatry, 61,* 282–290.

Grunebaum, L., & Gammeltoft, M. (1993). Young children of schizophrenic mothers: Difficulties of intervention. *American Journal of Orthopsychiatry, 63,* 16–27.

Guerin, D., & MacKinnon, D. P. (1985). An assessment of the California child passenger restraint requirement. *American Journal of Public Health, 75,* 142–144.

Gupta, R. K. (1971). New York's Mental Health Information Service: An experiment in due process. *Rutgers Law Review, 25,* 405–435.

Guttentag, M., Salasin, S., Legge, W. W., Bray, M., Dewhirst, J., Goldman, N., Phegley, T., & Weiss, S. (1974). *Sex differences in the utilization of publicly supported mental health facilities: The puzzle of depression.* Final Report, Collaborative Grant, Mental Health Services Branch, NIMH, MH26523-02.

Hammen, C. (1992). Life events and depression: The plot thickens. *American Journal of Community Psychology, 20,* 179–193.

Hammond, W. R., & Yung, B. (1993). Psychology's role in the public health response to assaultive violence among young African-American men. *American Psychologist, 48,* 142–154.

Handler, J. F., & Satz, J. (Eds.) (1982). *Neither angels nor thieves: Studies in deinstitutionalization of status offenders.* Washington, DC: National Academy Press.

Hankin, J. R., & Locke, B. Z. (1982). The persistence of depressive symptomatology among prepaid group practice enrollees: An exploratory study. *American Journal of Public Health, 72,* 1000–1007.

Hansell, N. (1974). *Enhancing adaptational work during service.* Paper presented at Conference on State Hospitals and Emerging Alternatives, Human Resources Institute of Boston, Newton, MA, January 17–19.

Hargrove, E. C., & Glidewell, J. C. (1990). *Impossible jobs in public management.* Lawrence: University Press of Kansas.

Harloff, H. J., Gump, P. V., & Campbell, D. E. (1981). The public life of communities: Environmental change as a result of the intrusion of a flood control, conservation, and recreational reservoir. *Environment and Behavior, 13,* 685–706.

Harrington, M. (1962). *The other America: Poverty in the United States.* New York: Macmillan.

Harrington, M. (1984). *The new American poverty.* New York: Holt Rinehart & Winston.

Harrison, S. I., McDermott, J. F., Wilson, P. T., & Schrager, J. (1965). Social class and mental illness in children: Choice of treatment. *Archives of General Psychiatry, 13,* 411–417.

Hatfield, A. (1993). Involuntary commitment: A consumer perspective. *Innovations & Research, 2,* 43–46.

Hathaway, W. L., & Pargament, K. I. (1991). The religious dimensions of coping: Implications for prevention and promotion. *Prevention in Human Services, 9*(2), 65–92.

Hayes, L. M. (1983). And darkness closes in . . . A national study of jail suicides. *Criminal Justice and Behavior, 10,* 461–484.

Health: United States, 1975. (1976). (DHEW Publication No. [HRA] 76-1232.) Washington, DC: Department of Health, Education, and Welfare.

Heller, K. (1989). Ethical dilemmas in community intervention. *American Journal of Community Psychology, 17*, 367–378.

Heller, K., & Monahan, J. (1977). *Psychology and community change.* Homewood, IL: Dorsey Press.

Heller, K., Price, R. H., & Sher, K. J. (1980). Research and evaluation in primary prevention: Issues and guidelines. In R. Price, R. Ketterer, B. Bader, & J. Monahan (Eds.), *Prevention in mental health.* Beverly Hills, CA: Sage.

Heller, K., & Swindle, R. W. (1983). Social networks, perceived social support and coping with stress. In R. Felner, L. Jason, J. Moritsugu & S. Farber (Eds.), *Preventive psychology: Theory, research and practice in community intervention.* New York: Pergamon.

Heller, K., Thompson, M. G., Trueba, P. E., Hogg, J. R., & Vlachos-Weber, I. (1991). Peer support dyads for elderly women: Was this the wrong intervention? *American Journal of Community Psychology, 19*, 53–74.

Henggleer, S. W., Broudin, C. M., Melton, G., Mann, B. J., Smith, L. A., et al. (1991). Effects of multisystemic therapy on drug use and abuse in serious juvenile offenders: A progress report from two outcome studies. *Family Dynamics of Addiction Quarterly, 1*, 40–51.

Herrenkohl, E. C., Herrenkohl, R. C., & Egolf, B. (1994). Resilient early school-age children from maltreating homes: Outcomes in late adolescence. *American Journal of Orthopsychiatry, 64*, 301–309.

Herrnstein, R. J., & Murray, C. (1994). *The bell curve: Intelligence and class structure in American life.* New York: Free Press.

Herz, M. I., & Melville, C. (1980). Relapse in schizophrenia. *American Journal of Psychiatry, 137*, 801–805.

Hiday, V. A. (1977). Reformed commitment procedures: An empirical study of the courtroom. *Law & Society Review, 11*, 651–656.

Hill, D. D. (1993). Afrocentric movements in education: Examining equity, culture, and power relations in the public schools. *Hastings Constitutional Law Quarterly, 20*, 681–724.

Hilts, P. J. (1992). Mentally ill jailed on no charges, survey says. *New York Times,* Thursday, September 10, A18.

Hinrichsen, G. A., Revenson, T. A., & Shinn, M. (1985). Does self-help help? An empirical investigation of scoliosis peer support groups. *Journal of Social Issues, 41*, 65–87.

Hoffman, F. L., & Mastrianni, X. (1992). The hospitalized young adult: New directions for psychiatric treatment. *American Journal of Orthopsychiatry, 62*, 297–302.

Hogarty, G. E., Dennis, H., Guy, W., & Gross, G. M. (1968). Who goes there? Critical evaluation of admission to a day hospital. *American Journal of Psychiatry, 124*, 939–944.

Hoge, S. K., Lidz, C., Mulvey, E., Roth, L., Bennett, N., Siminoff, L., Arnold, R., & Monhaan, J. (1993). Patient, family, and staff perceptions of coercion in mental hospital admission: an exploratory study. *Behavioral Sciences and the Law, 11*, 281–293.

Hollingshead, A. B., & Redlich, F. C. (1958). *Social class and mental illness.* New York: Wiley.

Holmes, T. H., & Rahe, R. H. (1967). The Social Readjustment Rating Scale. *Journal of Psychosomatic Research, 11,* 213–218.

Holmes-Eber, P., & Riger, S. (1990). Hospitalization and the composition of mental patients' social networks. *Schizophrenia Bulletin, 16,* 157–164.

Holtzworth-Munroe, A., Markman, H., O'Leary, K. D., Neidig, P., Leber, D., Heyman, R. D., Hulbert, D., & Smutzler, N. (1995). The need for marital violence prevention efforts: A behavioral-cognitive secondary prevention program for engaged and newly married couples. *Applied & Preventive Psychology, 4,* 77–88.

Horan, S., Kang, G., Levine, M., Duax, C., Luntz, B., & Tasca, C. (1993). Empirical studies on foster care: Review and assessment. *Journal of Sociology and Social Welfare, 20,* 131–154.

Hotaling, G. T., & Sugarman, D. B. (1986). An analysis of risk markers in husband to wife violence: The current state of knowledge. *Violence and Victims, 1,* 101–124.

House, J. S., Landis, K. R., & Umberson, D. (1988). Social relationships and health. *Science, 241,* 540–545.

Howard, M., & McCabe, J. B. (1990). Helping teenagers postpone sexual involvement. *Family Planning Perspectives, 22,* 21–26.

Howe, I. (1976). *World of our fathers.* New York: Simon & Schuster.

Huaco, G. (1965). *The sociology of film art.* New York: Basic Books.

Hughes, L. (1962). *Fight for freedom: The story of the NAACP.* New York: Norton.

Humphreys, K., & Rappaport, J. (1993). From the community mental health movement to the war on drugs: A study in the definition of social problems. *American Psychologist, 48,* 892–901.

Hunt, J. McV. (1968). Toward the prevention of incompetence. In J. Carter (Ed.), *Research contributions from psychology to community mental health.* New York: Behavioral Publications.

Hurvitz, N. (1976). The origins of the peer self-help psychotherapy group movement. *Journal of Applied Behavioral Science, 12,* 283–294.

Hyman, I. A. (1995). Corporal punishment, psychological mlatreatment, violence, and punitiveness in America: Research advocacy, and public policy. *Applied & Preventive Psychology, 4,* 113–130.

In re Gault 387 US 1 (1967).

Indiana Division of Mental Health (1992). *The Hoosier Assurance Plan.* Indianapolis: Author.

Innovations & Research (1993). Special section: Mental illness and the law. *Innovations & Research, 2,* 3–54.

Institute of Medicine. (1989). *Research on children & adolescents with mental, behavioral & developmental disorders.* Washington, DC: National Academy Press.

Iscoe, I. (1974). Community psychology and the competent community. *American Psychologist, 29,* 607–613.

Iscoe, I., Bloom, B., & Spielberger, C.D. (1977). *Community psychology in transition*. New York: Halsted Press.

Iscoe, I., & Harris, L. C. (1984). Social and community interventions. *Annual Review of Psychology, 35,* 333–360.

Iscoe, I., & Spielberger, C.D. (Eds.). (1970). *Community psychology: Perspectives in training and research*. New York: Appleton-Century-Crofts.

Jackson, D. N. (1965). *Personality Research Form*. Goshen, NY: Research Psychologists Press.

Jackson v. Indiana, 406 US 715 (1972).

Jacob, H. (1989). Another look at no-fault divorce and the post-divorce finances of women. *Law & Society Review, 23,* 95–115.

Jacobs, J. B. (1980). The prisoners' rights movement and its impacts, 1960–1980. In N. Morris & M. Tonry, (Eds.). *Crime, and justice: An annual review of research.* Chicago: University of Chicago Press.

Jacobs, M. K., & Goodman, G. (1989). Psychology and self–help groups: Predictions on a partnership. *American Psychologist, 44,* 536–545.

Jacobson, N. S., & Addis, M. E. (1993). Research on couples and couple therapy: What do we know? Where are we going? *Journal of Consulting and Clinical Psychology, 61,* 85–93.

Jacoby, J. E. (1983). Securing compliance of mental health professionals to changing commitment laws. Paper presented at the meeting of the Society for the Study of Social Problems, Detroit, MI, August.

Janis, I. L. (1983). The role of social support in adherence to stressful life decisions. *American Psychologist, 38,* 143–160.

Jason, L. A., & Rose T. (1984). Influencing the passage of child passenger restraint legislation. *American Journal of Community Psychology, 12,* 485–495.

Jemmott, J. B., Jemmott, L. S., & Fong, G. T. (1992). Reductions in HIV risk-associated sexual behaviors among black male adolescents: Effects of an AIDS prevention intervention. *American Journal of Public Health, 82,* 372–377.

Jensen, A. R. (1969). How much can we boost I. Q. And scholastic achievement? *Harvard Educational Review, 39,* 1–123.

Johnston, L. D., O'Malley, P. M., & Bachman, J. G. (in preparation). *National survey results on drug use from Monitoring the Future study, 1975–1994,* volume 1. Rockville, MD: National Institute on Drug Abuse.

Joint Commission on Mental Illness and Health. (1961). *Action for mental health.* New York: Basic Books.

Joint Commission on the Mental Health of Children. (1969). *Crisis in child mental health: Challenge for the 1970's.* New York: Harper & Row.

Jones, E. E., & Matsumoto, D. R. (1982). Psychotherapy with the underserved: Recent developments. In L. R. Snowden (Ed.), *Reaching the underserved: Mental health needs of neglected populations.* Beverly Hills, CA: Sage.

Kadushin, A. (1980). *Child welfare services.* 3rd Ed. New York: Macmillan.

Kagan, D. M. (1990). How schools alienate students at risk: A model for examining proximal classroom variables. *Educational Psychologist, 25,* 105–125.

Kaminer, W. (1992). *I'm dysfunctional, you're dysfunctional: The recovery movement and other self-help fashions.* Reading, MA: Addison-Wesley.

Kanter, R. M. (1977). *Men and women of the corporation.* New York: Basic Books.

Katz, A. H. (1993). *Self-help in America: A social movement perspective.* NY: Maxwell Macmillan International.

Katz, A. H. (1981). Self-help and mutual aid: An emerging social movement? *Annual Review of Sociology, 7,* 129–155.

Katz, A. H., & Bender, E. I. (Eds.). (1976). *The strength in us: Self-help groups in the modern world.* New York: New Viewpoints.

Katz, D., & Kahn, R. L. (1966). *The social psychology of organizations.* New York: Wiley.

Katz, M. B. (1986). *In the shadow of the poorhouse. A social history of welfare in America.* New York: Basic Books.

Kazdin, A. E. (1993). Adolescent mental health: Prevention and treatment programs. *American Psychologist, 48,* 127–141.

Keefe, F. J., Caldwell, D. S., Queen, K. T. Gil, K. M., Martinez, S., Crisson, J. E., Ogden, W., & Nunley, J. (1987). Pain coping strategies in osteoarthritis patients. *Journal of Consulting and Clinical Psychology, 55,* 208–212.

Keil, T. J., Usui, W. M., & Busch, J. A. (1983). Repeat admissions for perceived problem drinking: A social resources perpsective. *Journal of Studies on Alcohol, 44,* 95–108.

Kellam, S. G., Branch, J. D., Agrawal, K. C., & Grabill, M. E. (1972). Woodlawn Mental Health Center: An evolving strategy for planning in community mental health. In S. E. Golann & C. Eisdorfer (Eds.), *Handbook of community mental health.* New York: Appleton-Century-Crofts.

Kelly, J. A., Kalichman, S. C., Kauth, M. R., et al. (1991). Situational factors associated with AIDS risk behavior lapses and coping strategies used by gay men who successfully avoid lapses. *American Journal of Public Health, 81,* 1335–1338.

Kelly, J. A., Murphy, D. A., Sikkema, K. J., & Kalichman, S. C. (1993). Psychological interventions to prevent HIV infection are urgently needed. *American Psychologist, 48,* 1023–1034.

Kelly, J. A., St. Lawrence, J. S., Stevenson, L. Y., et al. (1992). Community AIDS/HIV risk reduction: The effects of endorsements by popular people in three cities. *American Journal of Public Health, 82,* 1483–1489.

Kelly, J. G. (1966). Ecological constraints on mental health services. *American Psychologist, 21,* 535–539.

Kelly, J. G. (1979). *Adolescent boys in high school: A psychological study of coping and adaptation.* Hillsdale, NJ: Erlbaum.

Kelly, J. G. (1990). The Midwest Psychological Field Station: Some legacies. *Environment and Behavior, 22,* 514–517.

Kelly, J. G., Edwards, D. W., Fatke, R., Gordon, T. A., McClintock, S. K., McGee, D. P., Newman, B. M., Rice, R. R., Roistacher, R. C., & Todd, D. M. (1971). The coping process in varied high school environments. In M. J. Feldman (Ed.), *Buffalo Studies in Psychotherapy and Behavior Change.* No. 2, Theory and Research in Community Mental Health. Buffalo: State University of New York at Buffalo.

Kennedy, J. F. (1963). Mental illness and mental retardation. Message from the President of the United States relative to mental illness and mental retardation. House of Representatives, 88th Congress, 1st Session, Document No. 58, February 5.

Kerr, P. (1991). Mental hospital chains accused of much cheating on insurance. *New York Times*, November 24, pp. A–1, 28.

Kessler, M., & Albee, G. W. (1975). Primary prevention. *Annual Review of Psychology, 26*, 557–591.

Kessler, R., Price, R. H., & Wortman, C. (1985). Social factors in psychopathology: Stress, social support, and coping processes. *Annual Review of Psychology, 36*, 531–572.

Kessler, R. C., Turner, J. B., & House, J. S. (1987). Intervening processes in the relationship between unemployment and health. *Psychological Medicine, 17*, 949–961.

Keyes v. *Denver School District, No. 1*, 413 US 189 (1973).

Kiernan, M., Toro, P. A., Rappaport, J., & Seidman, E. (1989). Economic predictors of mental health service utilization: A time series analysis. *American Journal of Community Psychology, 17*, 801–820.

Kiesler, C. A. (1982). Public and professional myths about mental hospitalization. An empirical reassessment of policy-related beliefs. *American Psychologist, 37*, 1323–1339.

Kiesler, C. A. (1992). U.S. mental health policy: Doomed to fail. *American Psychologist, 47*, 1077–1082.

Kiesler, C. A., & Simkins, C. (1991). The de facto system of psychiatric inpatient care. Piecing together the national puzzle. *American Psychologist, 46*, 579–584.

Kiesler, C. A., Simpkins, C. G., & Morton, T. L. (1989). The psychiatric inpatient treatment of children and youth in general hospitals. *American Journal of Community Psychology, 17*, 821–830.

Killian, T. M., & Killian, L. T. (1990). Sociological investigations of mental illness: A review. *Hospital and Community Psychiatry, 41*, 902–911.

Kilpatrick, D. G., Best, C. L., Veronen, L. J., Amick, A. E., Velleponteaux, L. A., & Ruff, G. A. (1985). Mental health correlates of criminal victimization: A random community survey. *Journal of Consulting and Clinical Psychology, 53*, 866–873.

Kilpatrick, D. G., Veronen, J. J., & Resick, P. A. (1979). The aftermath of rape: Recent empirical findings. *American Journal of Orthopsychiatry, 49*, 658–669.

Kinney, J., Haapala, D., & Booth, C. (1991). *Keeping families together: The Homebuilders Model*. Hawthorne, NY: Aldine de Gruyter.

Kiritz, S., & Moos, R. H. (1974). Physiological effects of social environments. *Psychosomatic Medicine, 36*, 96–114.

Kirk, M. O. (1995). When surviving just isn't enough when seeking reemployment. *New York Times*, June 25, Sec. 3, p. 11.

Kirk, S. A., & Kutchins, H. (1992). *The selling of DSM: The rhetoric of science in psychiatry*. Hawthorne, NY: Aldine de Gruyter.

Kirkby, R. J. (1994). Changes in premenstrual symptoms and irrational thinking following cognitive-behavioral coping skills training. *Journal of Consulting and Clinical Psychology, 62,* 1026–1032.

Kirp, D. L., & Babcock, G. (1981). Judge and company: Court-appointed masters, school desegregation, and institutional reform. *Alabama Law Review, 32,* 313–397.

Kittrie, N. N. (1971). *The right to be different. Deviance and enforced therapy.* Baltimore, MD: Johns Hopkins Press.

Klaus, P. A. (1994). The costs of crime to victims. *Crime Data Brief.* Washington, DC: Department of Justice.

Klerman, G. L. (1982). The psychiatric revolution of the past twenty-five years. In W. R. Gove, (Ed.), *Deviance and mental illness.* Beverly Hills, CA: Sage.

Kluger, R. (1976). *Simple justice.* New York: Knopf.

Knight, B., Wollert, R. W., Levy, L. H., Frame, C. L., & Padgett, V. P. (1980). Self-help groups: The members' perspectives. *American Journal of Community Psychology, 8,* 53–65.

Knitzer, J. (1984). Mental health services to children and adolescents: A national view of public policies. *American Psychologist, 39,* 905–911.

Knitzer, J., Steinberg, Z., & Fleisch, B. (1990). *At the schoolhouse door.* New York: Bank Street College of Education.

Knobloch, H., & Pasamanick, B. (1961). Some thoughts on the inheritance of intelligence. *American Journal of Orthopsychiatry, 31,* 454–73.

Kobasa, S. C. (1979). Stressful life events, personality, and health: An inquiry into hardiness. *Journal of Personality and Social Psychology, 37,* 1–11.

Kobasa, S. C. O., & Puccetti, M. C. (1983). Personality and social resources in stress resistance. *Journal of Personality and Social Psychology, 45,* 839–850.

Koss, M. P., Goodman, L. A., Browne, A., Fitzgerald, L. F., Keita, G. P., & Russo, N. F. (1994). *No safe haven: Male violence against women at home, at work, and in the community.* Washington, DC: American Psychological Association.

Kraft, S. P., & DeMaio, T. J. (1982). An ecological intervention with adolescents in low-income families. *American Journal of Orthopsychiatry, 52,* 131–140.

Kraus, S. (1981). *A multidimensional approach to the assessment of social support.* Unpublished doctoral dissertation, Department of Psychology, State University of New York at Buffalo.

Kriechman, A. M. (1985). A school-based program of mental health services. *Hospital and Community Psychiatry, 36,* 876–878.

Krizan, L. (1982). *A descriptive study of the Niagara Falls Christian Fellowship from a social intervention perspective.* Unpublished manuscript, Department of Psychology, State University of New York at Buffalo.

Kropotkin, P. (1972). *Mutual aid. A factor of evolution.* New York: New York University Press (originally published 1902).

Kruzich, J. M., & Berg, W. (1985). Predictors of self–sufficiency for the mentally ill in long-term care. *Community Mental Health Journal, 21,* 198–207.

Kubler-Ross, E. (1969). *On death and dying.* New York: Macmillan.

Kuhn, T. S. (1970). *The structure of scientific revolutions.* (2nd ed.) Chicago: University of Chicago Press.

Kurtz, L. F. (1990). The self-help movement: Review of the past decade of research. *Social Work with Groups, 13,* 101–115.

Labrecque, M. S., Peak, T., & Toseland, R. W. (1992). Long-term effectiveness of a group program for caregivers of frail elderly veterans. *American Journal of Orthopsychiatry, 62,* 575–588.

Lamb, H. R. (Ed.), (1984). *The homeless mentally ill.* Washington, DC: American Psychiatric Association.

Lamb, H. R., & Grant, R. W. (1981). The mentally ill in an urban county jail. *Archives of General Psychiatry, 39,* 17–22.

Lamb, H. R., & Zusman, J. (1979). Primary prevention in perspective. *American Journal of Psychiatry, 136,* 12–17.

Lambert, M. J., & Bergin, A. E. (1994). The effectiveness of psychotherapy. In A. Bergin & S. Garfield (Eds.), *Handbook of psychotherapy and behavior change* (4th Ed.). New York: Wiley.

Langer, E. (1983). *The psychology of control.* Beverly Hills, CA: Sage.

Langer, E. J., & Abelson, R. P. (1974). A patient by any other name. . . . Clinician group differences in labeling bias. *Journal of Consulting and Clinical Psychology, 42,* 4–9.

Lavelle, J. M., Hovell, M. F., West, M. P., & Wahlgren, D. R. (1992). Promoting law enforcement for child protection: A community analysis. *Journal of Applied Behavior Analysis, 25,* 885–892.

Lawlor, E. F. (1990). When a possible job becomes impossible: Politics, public health and the management of the AIDS epidemic. In E. C. Hargrove & J. C. Glidewell (Eds.), *Impossible jobs in public management.* Lawrence: University Press of Kansas.

Lazar, I., Darlington, R. B., Levenstein, P., Miller, L., Palmer, F., Weikart, D., Woolman, M., Zigler, E., Beller, K., Deutsch, C., Deutsch, M., Gordon, I., Gray, S., & Karnes, M. (1978). *Lasting effects after preschool.* Washington, DC: Office of Human Development Services, Administration for Children, Youth and Families. DHEW Publication No. (OHDS) 79–30178.

Lazarus, R. S. (1966). *Psychological stress and the coping process.* New York: McGraw-Hill.

Lazarus, R. S. (1990). Theory-based stress management. *Psychological Inquiry, 1,* 3–13.

Lazarus, R. S. (1991). *Emotion and adaptation.* New York: Oxford University Press.

Lazarus, R. S., Delongis, A., Folkman, S., & Gruen, R. (1985). Stress and adaptational outcomes: The problem of confounded measures. *American Psychologist, 40,* 770–779.

Leavy, R. L. (1983). Social support and psychological disorder. *Journal of Community Psychology, 11,* 3–21.

Leichter, H. M. (1991). *Free to be foolish: Politics and health promotion in the United States and Great Britain.* Princeton, NJ: Princeton University Press.

Leighton, D. C., Harding, J. S., Macklin, D. B., Macmillan, A. M., & Leighton,

A. H. (1963). *The character of danger: Psychiatric symptoms in selected communities*. New York: Basic Books.

Lemann, N. (1991). *The promised land. The great black migration and how it changed America*. New York: Knopf.

Lemke, S., & Moos, R. H. (1987). Measuring the social climate of congregate residences for older people: Sheltered Care Environment Scale. *Psychology and Aging, 2*, 20–29.

Lepore, S. T., Evans, G. W., & Schneider, M. L. (1991). Dynamic role of social support in the link between chronic stress and psychological distress. *Journal of Personality and Social Psychology, 61*, 899–909.

Leventhal, G. S., Maton, K. I., & Madara, E. J. (1988). Systematic organizational support for self-help groups. *American Journal of Orthopsychiatry, 58*, 592–603.

Levine, A. (1982). *Love Canal: Science, politics and people*. Lexington, MA: Heath.

Levine, A. G. (1977). Women at work in America: History, status and prospects. In H. Kaplan (Ed.), *American minorities and economic opportunity*. Itasca, IL: Peacock.

Levine, A., & Levine, M. (1977). The social context of evaluative research: A case study. *Evaluation Quarterly, 1*, 515–542.

Levine, D. I. (1984). The authority for the appointment of remedial special masters in federal institutional reform litigation: The history reconsidered. *U.C. Davis Law Review, 17*, 753–805.

Levine, D. I. (1993). The latter stages of enforcement of equitable decrees: The course of institutional reform cases after *Dowell, Rufo* and *Freeman. Hastings Constitutional Law Quarterly, 20*, 579–648.

Levine, I. S., & Rog, D. J. (1990). Mental health services for homeless mentally ill persons: Federal initiatives and current service trends. *American Psychologist, 45*, 963–968.

Levine, M. (1966). Residential change and school adjustment. *Community Mental Health Journal, 2*, 61–69.

Levine, M. (1969). Some postulates of community psychology practice. In F. Kaplan & S. B. Sarason (Eds.), *The Psycho-Educational Clinic papers and research studies*. Springfield, MA: Department of Mental Health.

Levine, M. (1972). The practice of mental health consultation. Some definitions from social theory. In J. Zusman & D. L. Davidson (Eds.), *Practical aspects of mental health consultation*. Springfield, IL: Charles C. Thomas.

Levine, M. (1973). Problems of entry in light of some postulates of practice in community psychology. In I. I. Goldenberg (Ed.), *Clinical psychologists in the world of work*. New York: Heath.

Levine, M. (1974). Scientific method and the adversary model: Some preliminary thoughts. *American Psychologist, 29*, 661–677.

Levine, M. (1979). Congress (and evaluators) ought to pay more attention to history. *American Journal of Community Psychology, 7*, 1–17.

Levine, M. (1980a). Investigative reporting as a research method. An analysis of Bernstein and Woodward's *All the President's Men. American Psychologist, 35*, 626–638.

Levine, M. (1980b). *From state hospital to psychiatric center: The implementation of planned organizational change.* Lexington, MA: Lexington Books.

Levine, M. (1981). *The history and politics of community mental health.* New York: Oxford University Press.

Levine, M. (1982). Method or madness: On the alienation of the professional. *Journal of Community Psychology, 10,* 3–14.

Levine, M. (1985). The adversary process and social science in the courts: *Barefoot* v. *Estelle. Journal of Psychiatry and Law, 12,* 147–181.

Levine, M. (1986). The role of special master in institutional reform litigation: A case study. *Law & Policy, 8,* 275–321.

Levine, M., & Bunker, G. (Eds.). (1975). *Mutual criticism.* Syracuse, NY: Syracuse University Press.

Levine, M., Compaan, C., & Freeman, J. (1994). Maltreatment-related fatalities: Issues of policy and prevention. *Law & Policy, 16,* 449–471.

Levine, M., & Doherty, E. (1991). The Fifth Amendment and therapeutic requirements to admit abuse. *Criminal Justice and Behavior, 18,* 98–112.

Levine, M., Doueck, H. J., & associates. (1995). *The impact of mandated reporting on the therapeutic process. Picking up the pieces.* Thousand Oaks, CA: Sage.

Levine, M., & Graziano, A. M. (1972). Intervention programs in elementary schools. In S. E. Golann & C. Eisdorfer (Eds.), *Handbook of community mental health* (pp. 541–573). New York: Appleton-Century-Crofts.

Levine, M., & Howe, B. (1985). The penetration of social science into legal culture. *Law & Policy, 7,* 173–198.

Levine, M., & Levine, A. (1992). *Helping children: A social history.* New York: Oxford University Press.

Levine, M., & Perkins, D. V. (1980a). Tailor-making a life events scale. In D. Perkins (Chair), *New developments in research on life stress and social support.* Symposium presented at the American Psychological Association Convention, Montreal.

Levine, M., & Perkins, D. V. (1980b). Social setting interventions and primary prevention: Comments on the Report of the Task Panel on Prevention to the President's Commission on Mental Health. *American Journal of Community Psychology, 8,* 147–158.

Levine, M., & Perkins, D. V. (1987). *Principles of community psychology.* New York: Oxford University Press.

Levine, M., Reppucci, N. D., & Weinstein, R. S. (1990). Learning from Seymour Sarason. *American Journal of Community Psychology, 18,* 343–351.

Levine, M., Toro, P. A., & Perkins, D. V. (1993). Social and community interventions. *Annual Review of Psychology, 44,* 525–588.

Levine, O. H., Britton, P. J., James, T. C., Jackson, A. P., & Hobfoll, S. E. (1993). The empowerment of women: A key to HIV prevention. *Journal of Community Psychology, 21,* 320–334.

Levitan, S. A. (1969). *The Great Society's poor law.* Baltimore: Johns Hopkins Press.

Levitan, S. A., & Taggart, R. III. (1971). *Social experimentation and manpower policy.* Baltimore: Johns Hopkins Press.

Levitt, E. E. (1957). The results of psychotherapy with children: An evaluation. *Journal of Consulting Psychology, 21*, 189–196.

Levy, L. H. (1976). Self-help groups: Types and psychological processes. *Journal of Applied Behavioral Science, 12*, 310–322.

Lewin, K. (1935). *Principles of topological psychology.* New York: McGraw-Hill.

Lewis, D. A., Goetz, E., Schoenfield, M., Gordon, A. C., & Griffin, E. (1984). The negotiation of involuntary civil commitment. *Law & Society Review, 18*, 629–649.

Lewis, M. S., Gottesman, D., & Gutstein, S. (1979). The course and duration of crisis. *Journal of Consulting and Clinical Psychology, 47*, 128–134.

Li, D. (1989). The effect of role change on intellectual ability and on the ability self-concept in Chinese children. *American Journal of Community Psychology, 17*, 73–81.

Libow, J. A., & Doty, D. W. (1979). An exploratory approach to self-blame and self derogation by rape victims. *American Journal of Orthopsychiatry, 49*, 670–679.

Lidz, C. W., Mulvey, E. P., Arnold, R. P., Bennett, N. S., & Kirsch, B. L. (1993). Coercive interactions in a psychiatric emergency room. *Behavioral Sciences & the Law, 11*, 269–280.

Light, D. W. (1982). Learning to label: The social construction of psychiatrists. In W. R. Gove (Ed.), *Deviance and mental illness.* Beverly Hills, CA: Sage.

Lindemann, E. (1944). Symptomatology and management of acute grief. *American Journal of Psychiatry, 101*, 141–148.

Lindsay, W. R. (1982). The effects of labelling: Blind and nonblind ratings of social skills on schizophrenic and nonschizophrenic control subjects. *American Journal of Psychiatry, 139*, 216–219.

Lipton, H., & Kaden, S. E. (1965). Predicting the posthospital work adjustment of married male schizophrenics. *Journal of Consulting Psychology, 29*, 93.

Loftus, E. E. (1993). The reality of repressed memories. *American Psychologist, 48*, 518–537.

Lorion, R. P., & Ross, J. G. (Eds.). (1992). Programs for Change: Office of Substance Abuse Prevention demonstration models. *Journal of Community Psychology,* OSAP Special Issue.

Low, A. A. (1952). *Mental health through will-training.* 2d Ed. North Quincy, MA: The Christopher Publishing House.

Lubin, R. A., Janicki, M. P., Zigman, W., & Ross, R. (1982). *The likelihood of police contacts with developmentally disabled persons in community residences.* Unpublished report. Institute for Basic Research in Developmental Disabilities, Staten Island, New York.

Lubin, R. A., Schwartz, A. A., Zigman, W. B., & Janicki, M. P. (1982). Community acceptance of residential programs for developmentally disabled persons. *Applied Research in Mental Retardation, 3*, 191–200.

Luepnitz, D. (1982). *Child custody.* Lexington, MA: Heath.

Luke, D. A., Rappaport, J., & Seidman, E. (1991). Setting phenotypes in a mutual help organization: Expanding behavior setting theory. *American Journal of Community Psychology, 19*, 147–167.

Luntz, B. K., & Widom, C. S. (1994). Antisocial personality disorder in abused and neglected children grown up. *American Journal of Psychiatry, 151,* 670–674.

Lustig, J. L., Wolchick, S. A., & Braver, S. L. (1992). Social support in chumships and adjustment in children of divorce. *American Journal of Community Psychology, 20,* 309–332.

Luthar, S. S., & Zigler, E. (1991). Vulnerability and competence: A review of research on resilience in childhood. *American Journal of Orthopsychiatry, 61,* 6–22.

Lynn, L. E. Jr. (1990). Managing the social safety net: The job of social welfare executive. In E. C. Hargrove & J. C. Glidewell (Eds.), *Impossible jobs in public management.* Lawrence: University Press of Kansas.

Madara, E. J., & Meese, A. (1988). *The self-help sourcebook. Finding and forming mutual aid self-help groups.* Denville, NJ: St. Clares-Riverside Medical Center.

Malloy, M. (1995). *Mental illness and managed care: A primer for families and consumers.* Arlington, VA: National Alliance for the Mentally Ill.

Mangellsdorf, A. D. (1985). Lessons learned and forgotten: The need for prevention and mental health interventions in disaster preparedness. *Journal of Community Psychology, 13,* 239–257.

Mann, P. A. (1978). *Community psychology: Concepts and applications.* New York: Free Press.

Manson, S. M., & Trimble, J. E. (1982). American Indian and Alaska native communities: Past efforts, future inquiries. In L. R. Snowden (Ed.), *Reaching the underserved: Mental health needs of neglected populations.* Beverly Hills, CA: Sage.

Markman, H. J., Renick, M. J., Floyd, F. J., Stanley, S. M., & Clements, M. (1993). Preventing marital distress through communication and conflict management training: A 4- and 5-year follow-up. *Journal of Consulting and Clinical Psychology, 61,* 70–77.

Maslow, A. H. (1962). *Toward a psychology of being.* Princeton, NJ: Van Nostrand.

Masterpasqua, F. (1989). A competence paradigm for psychological practice. *American Psychologist, 44,* 1366–1371.

Maton, K. I. (1988). Social support, organizational characteristics, psychological well-being, and group appraisal in three self-help groups. *American Journal of Community Psychology, 16,* 53–77.

McCarroll, J. E., Ursano, R. J., Wright, K. M., & Fullerton, C. S. (1993). Handling bodies after violent death: Strategies for coping. *American Journal of Orthopsychiatry, 63,* 209–214.

McCord, J. (1978). A thirty-year follow-up of treatment effects. *American Psychologist, 33,* 284–289.

McCurdy, K., & Daro, D. (1993). Current trends in child abuse reporting and fatalities: The results of the 1992 annual fifty state survey. Working Paper No. 808, National Committee for the Prevention of Child Abuse, Chicago, IL.

McGaughey, W. H., & Whalon, M. E. (1992). Managing insect resistance to *Bacillus thuringiensis* toxins. *Science, 258,* 1451–1455.

McGee, R. K. (1974). *Crisis intervention in the community*. Baltimore: University Park Press.

McLarin, K. J. (1995). Slaying of Connecticut infant shifts policy on child abuse. *New York Times*, July 30, I–1.

McLaurin v. *Oklahoma State Regents for Higher Education*, 337 US 637 (1950).

McLindon, J. B. (1989). Separate but unequal: The economic disaster of divorce for women and children. *Family Law Quarterly, 21,* 351–409.

Medvene, L. J., & Krauss, D. H. (1989). Causal attributions and parent-child relationships in a self-help group for families of the mentally ill. *Journal of Applied Social Psychology, 19,* 1413–1430.

Meehl, P. E. (1954). *Clinical versus statistical prediction*. Minneapolis: University of Minnesota Press.

Meichenbaum, D., & Jaremko, M. E. (1983). *Stress reduction and prevention*. New York: Plenum.

Meissen, G. J., Gleason, D. F., & Embree, M. G. (1991). An assessment of the needs of mutual help groups. *American Journal of Community Psychology, 19,* 427–442.

Melton, G. B. (1984). Family and mental hospital as myths: Civil commitment of minors. In N. D. Reppucci, L. A. Weithorn, E. P. Mulvey & J. Monahan (Eds.) *Children, mental health and the law*. Beverly Hills, CA: Sage.

Metcalf, G. R. (1983). *From Little Rock to Boston. The history of school desegregation*. Westport, CT: Greenwood Press.

Miller, G. E., & Iscoe, I. (1990). A state mental health commissioner and the politics of mental illness. In E. C. Hargrove & J. C. Glidewell (Eds.), *Impossible jobs in public management*. Lawrence: University Press of Kansas.

Miller, H. L., Coombs, D. W., Leeper, J. D., & Barton, S. N. (1984). An analysis of the effects of suicide prevention facilities on suicide rates in the United States. *American Journal of Public Health, 74,* 340–343.

Miller, K. S. (1976). *The case against civil commitment*. New York: Free Press.

Milliken v. *Bradley,* 418 US 717 (1974).

Milner, N. (1985). *Viewing and assessing the mental health patient rights movement*. Paper presented at the meeting of the Law and Society Association, San Diego, CA.

Mincy, R. B., Sawhill, I. V., & Wolf, D. A. (1990). The underclass: Definition and measurement. *Science, 248,* 450–452.

Mirowsky, J., & Ross, C. E. (1989). *Social causes of psychological distress*. Hawthorne, NY: Aldine de Gruyter.

Mischel, W. (1973). Toward a cognitive social learning reconceptualization of personality. *Psychological Review, 80,* 252–283.

Monahan, J. (1976). The prevention of violence. In J. Monahan (Ed.), *Community mental health and the criminal justice system*. New York: Pergamon.

Monahan, J., & Walker, L. (1986). Social authority: Obtaining, evaluating and establishing social science in law. *University of Pennsylvania Law Review, 134,* 477–517.

Monroe, S. M., & Steiner, S. C. (1986). Social support and psychopathology: Interrelations with preexisting disorder, stress and personality. *Journal of Abnormal Psychology, 95*, 29–39.

Moore, M. H., & Trojanowicz, R. C. (1988). Policing and fear of crime. *Perspectives on Policing. National Institute of Justice, 3*, 1–7.

Moore, T. (1982). Blacks: Rethinking service. In L. R. Snowden (Ed.), *Reaching the underserved. Mental health needs of neglected populations.* Beverly Hills, CA: Sage.

Moos, R. H. (1973). Conceptualizations of human environments. *American Psychologist, 28*, 652–665.

Moos, R. H. (1976). *The human context: Environmental determinants of behavior.* New York: Wiley.

Moos, R. H. (1979). Social climate measurement and feedback. In R. Munoz, L. Snowden, & J. Kelly (Eds.), *Social and psychological research in community settings.* San Francisco: Jossey-Bass.

Moos, R. H. (1987). Person-environment congruence in work, school, and health care settings. *Journal of Vocational Behavior, 31*, 231–247.

Moos, R. H., & Insel, P. (1974). *Issues in social ecology.* Palo Alto, CA: National Press Books.

Moos, R. H., & Van Dort, B. (1979). Student physical symptoms and the social climate of college living groups. *American Journal of Community Psychology, 7*, 31–43.

Morell, M. A., Levine, M., & Perkins, D. V. (1982). Study of behavioral factors associated with psychiatric rehospitalization. *Community Mental Health Journal, 18*, 190–199.

Morse, S. J. (1978). Crazy behavior, morals and science: An analysis of mental health law. *Southern California Law Review, 51*, 527–564.

Mowbray, C. T., Greenfield, A., & Freddolino, P. P. (1992). An analysis of treatment services provided in group homes for adults labeled mentally ill. *Journal of Nervous and Mental Disease, 180*, 551–559.

Moxley, D. P., Mowbray, C. T., & Brown, K. S. (1993). Supported education. In R. Flexer & P. Solomon (Eds.), *Psychiatric rehabilitation in practice* (pp. 137–153). New York: Butterworth.

Moynihan, D. P. (1965). *The Negro family: The case for national action.* Washington, DC: Office of Planning and Research, U.S. Department of Labor.

Moynihan, D. P. (1969). *Maximum feasible misunderstanding. Community action in the War on Poverty.* New York: Free Press.

Mrazek, P. J., & Haggerty, R. J. (Eds.). (1994). *Reducing risks for mental disorders: Frontiers for preventive intervention research.* Washington, DC: National Academy Press.

Mulvey, E. P., Geller, J. L., & Roth, L. H. (1987). The promise and peril of involuntary outpatient commitment. *American Psychologist, 42*, 571–584.

Mumford, E., Schlesinger, H. J., & Glass, G. V. (1982). The effects of psychological intervention on recovery from surgery and heart attacks: An analysis of the literature. *American Journal of Public Health, 72*, 141–151.

Murphy, J. M. (1964). Psychotherapeutic aspects of shamanism on St. Lawrence Island, Alaska. In A. Kiev (Ed.), *Magic, faith and healing.* New York: Free Press of Glencoe.

Murphy, J. M. (1976). Psychiatric labelling in cross-cultural perpsective. *Science, 191,* 1019–1028.

Murphy, J. M. (1982). Cultural shaping and mental disorders. In W. R. Gove (Ed.), *Deviance and mental illness.* Beverly Hills, CA: Sage.

Murray, H. A. (1938). *Explorations in personality.* New York: Oxford University Press.

Murray J. P. (Ed.). (1983). *Status offenders. A sourcebook.* Boys Town, NE: Boys Town Center.

Myers, J. K., Weissman, M. M., Tischler, G. L., et al. (1984). Six-month prevalence of psychiatric disorders in three communities: 1980–1982. *Archives of General Psychiatry, 41,* 959–967.

Myrdal, G. (1944). *An American dilemma* (2 Vols). New York: Harper & Row.

Namir, S., & Weinstein, R. S. (1982). Children: Facilitating new directions. In L. R. Snowden (Ed.), *Reaching the underserved: Mental health needs of neglected populations.* Beverly Hills, CA: Sage.

Naroll, R. (1983). *The moral order. An introduction to the human situation.* Beverly Hills, CA: Sage Publications.

Narrow, W. E., Regier, D. A., Rae, D. S., Manderscheid, R. W., & Locke, B. Z. (1993). Use of services by persons with mental and addictive disorders: Findings from the National Institute of Mental Health Epidemiological Catchment Area program. *Archives of General Psychiatry, 50,* 95–107.

Nathan, V. M. (1979). The use of masters in institutional reform litigation. *Toledo Law Review, 10,* 419–464.

National Academy of Sciences. (1984). *Bereavement: Reactions, consequences, and care.* Washington, DC: National Academy Press.

National Advisory Mental Health Council (1990). *National plan for research on child and adolescent mental disorders.* DHHS Publication No. (ADM) 90–1683. Washington, DC: Alcohol, Drug Abuse, and Mental Health Administration.

National Alliance for the Mentally Ill Staff, & Public Citizen Health Research Group Staff (1992). *Criminalizing the seriously mentally ill: The abuse of jails as mental hospitals.* Washington, DC: Public Citizen, Inc.

National Alliance for the Mentally Ill. (1993). 'Critical need' cited for employment data. *NAMI Advocate, 14,* 1.

National Center for Health Statistics. (1993). *Vital statistics of the United States, 1989: Volume II—Mortality (Part A).* Hyattsville, MD: U.S. Department of Health and Human Services.

National Institute of Mental Health (1970). *Volunteers in community mental health.* Washington, DC: U.S. Government Printing Office.

National Institute on Alcohol Abuse and Alcoholism. (1983). *Fifth special report to the U.S. Congress on alcohol and health.* Washington, DC: U.S. Government Printing Office.

National Research Council. (1993). *Understanding child abuse and neglect.* Washington, DC: National Academy Press.

Neighbors, H. W. (1985). Seeking professional help for personal problems: Black Americans' use of health and mental health services. *Community Mental Health Journal, 21,* 156–166.

Nelson, B. J. (1984). *Making an issue of child abuse.* Chicago: University of Chicago Press.

Nikkel, R. E., Smith, G., & Edwards, D. (1992). A consumer-operated case management project. *Hospital and Community Psychology, 43,* 577–579.

Novaco, R. W., Kliewer, W., & Broquet, A. (1991). Home environment consequences of commuter travel impedence. *American Journal of Community Psychology, 19,* 881–909.

O'Connor v. *Donaldson,* 422 US 563 (1975).

Odum, E. P. (1963). *Ecology.* New York: Holt, Rinehart, & Winston.

Office of Mental Health (1992). *At the crossroads: expanding community-based care for children and families: New York State Plan for Children and Families Mental Health Services.* Albany, NY: Office of Mental Health.

Office of Technology Assessment. (1983a). *The effectiveness and costs of alcoholism treatment.* Washington, DC: U.S. Congress.

Office of Technology Assessment. (1983b). *Technologies and management strategies for hazardous waste control.* Washington, DC: U.S. Congress.

Olfson, M. (1990). Assertive Community Treatment: An evaluation of the experimental evidence. *Hospital and Community Psychiatry, 41,* 634–641.

Olshansky, S. (1968). Some assumptions challenged. *Community Mental Health Journal, 4,* 152–156.

Oltman, J. E., & Friedman, S. (1965). Trends in admissions to a state hospital, 1942–1964. *Archives of General Psychiatry, 13,* 544–551.

O'Neill, P. O. (1989). Responsible to whom? Responsible for what? Some ethical issues in community intervention. *American Journal of Community Psychology, 17,* 323–341.

Orfield, G. (1981). *Toward a strategy for urban integration.* New York: Ford Foundation.

Orfield, G. (1993). *The growth of segregation in American schools: Changing patterns of separation and poverty since 1968.* Cambridge, MA: Harvard Project on School Desegregation.

Orford, J. (1992). *Community psychology: Theory and practice.* Chichester, England: Wiley.

Orford, J., & Edwards, G. (1977). *Alcoholism.* New York: Oxford University Press.

Osipow, S. H., & Fitzgerald, L. F. (1993). Unemployment and mental health: A neglected relationship. *Applied and Preventive Psychology, 2,* 59–64.

O'Sullivan, M. J., Peterson, P. D., Cox, G. B., & Kirkeby, J. (1989). Ethnic populations: Community mental health centers ten years later. *American Journal of Community Psychology, 17,* 17–30.

Page, R. (1992). *Data reference book.* San Francisco: California Commission on the Future of the Courts.

Page, S. (1977). Effects of the mental illness label in attempts to obtain accommodations. *Canadian Journal of Behavioural Science, 9*, 85–90.

Page, S. (1983). Psychiatric stigma: Two studies of behaviour when the chips are down. *Canadian Journal of Community Mental Health, 2*, 13–19.

Pakenham, K. I., Dadds, M. R., & Terry, J. (1994). Relationships between adjustment to HIV and both social support and coping. *Journal of Consulting and Clinical Psychology, 62*, 1194–1203.

Parad, H. J. (1965). *Crisis intervention: Selected readings*. New York: Family Service Association of America.

Pargament, K. I., Ensing, D. S., Falgout, K., Olsen, H., Reilly, B., Van Haitsman, K., & Warren, R. (1990). God help me (I): Religious coping efforts as predictors of the outcomes to significant life events. *American Journal of Community Psychology, 18*, 793–824.

Parham v *J.R. and J.L.*, 442 US 584 (1979).

Pauly, P. J. (1994). Is liquor intoxicating? Scientists, Prohibition, and the normalization of drinking. *American Journal of Public Health, 84*, 305–313.

Payton, B. F. (1970). New trends in civil rights. In P. I. Rose (Ed.), *Slavery and its aftermath*. New York: Atherton.

Pearl, A., & Reissman, F. (1965). *New careers for the poor: The nonprofessional in human services*. New York: Free Press.

Pearlin, L. I., & Schooler, C. (1978). The structure of coping. *Journal of Health and Social Behavior, 19*, 2–21.

Peirce, N. R., & Steinbach, C. F. (1987). *Corrective capitalism. The Rise of American's Community Development Corporations*. New York: Ford Foundation.

Perkins, C. A., Stephan, J. J., & Beck, A. J. (1995). Jails and jail inmates, 1993–1994. Bureau of Justice Statistics Bulletin, April.

Perkins, D. D., Florin, P., Rich, R. C., Wandersman, A., & Chavis, D. M. (1990). Participation and the social and physical environment of residential blocks: Crime and community context. *American Journal of Community Psychology, 18*, 83–115.

Perkins, D. D., Meeks, J. W., & Taylor, R. B. (1992). The physical environment of street blocks and resident perceptions of crime and disorder: Implications for theory and measurement. *Journal of Environmental Psychology, 12*, 21–34.

Perkins, D. V. (1982). The assessment of stress using life events scales. In L. Goldberger & S. Breznitz (Eds.), *Handbook of stress*. New York: Free Press.

Perkins, D. V., & Baker, F. (1991). A behavior setting assessment for community programs and residences. *Community Mental Health Journal, 27*, 313–325.

Perkins, D. V., Burns, T. F., Perry, J. C., & Nielsen, K. P. (1988). Behavior setting theory and community psychology: An analysis and critique. *Journal of Community Psychology, 16*, 355–372.

Perkins, D. V., Kraus, S. Levine, M., & Perrotta, P. (1980). Characteristics of stressful life events and help-seeking among college students. Paper read at the meeting of the Eastern Psychological Association, Hartford, CT.

Perkins, D. V., & Perry, J. C. (1985). Dimensional analysis of behavior setting demands in a community residence for chronically mentally ill women. *Journal of Community Psychology, 13*, 350–359.

Perkins, D. V., Tebes, J. A., Joss, R. H., Lacy, O. W., & Levine, M. (1982). Big schools, small schools: Characteristics of life stress and help-seeking at three contrasting colleges. Paper read at the meeting of the Eastern Psychological Association, Baltimore, MD.

Perlman, J. E. (1976). Grassrooting the system. *Social Policy, 7,* 4–20.

Perrotta, P. (1982). *The experience of caring for an elderly family member.* Unpublished doctoral dissertation, Department of Psychology, State University of New York at Buffalo.

Perrow, C. (1984). *Normal accidents: Living with high-risk technologies.* New York: Basic Books.

Peterson, L., & Mori, L. (1985). Prevention of child injury: An overview of targets, methods, and tactics for psychologists. *Journal of Consulting and Clinical Psychology, 53,* 586–594.

Petrakis, P. L. (1988). *The Surgeon General's workshop on Self-Help and Public Health.* Washington, DC: U.S. Government Printing Office.

Pianta, R., Egeland, B., & Erickson, M. F. (1989). The antecedents of maltreatment: Results of the Mother-Child Interaction Research Project. In D. Cicchetti & V. Carlson (Eds.), *Child maltreatment: Theory and research on the causes and consequences of child abuse and neglect* (pp. 203–253). New York: Cambridge University Press.

Pillow, D. R., Sandler, I. N., Braver, S. L., Wolchik, S. A., & Gersten, J. C. (1991). Theory-based screening for prevention: Focusing on mediating processes in children of divorce. *American Journal of Community Psychology, 19,* 809–836.

Pitegoff, P. (1993). Child care enterprise, community development, and work. *Georgetown Law Journal, 81,* 1897–1943.

Plessy v. *Ferguson,* 163 US 537 (1896).

Polich, J. M., Armor, D. J., & Braiker, H. B. (1981). *The course of alcoholism.* New York: John Wiley & Sons Inc.

Poythress, N. G. (1978). Psychiatric expertise in civil commitment: Training attorneys to cope with expert testimony. *Law and Human Behavior, 2,* 1–24.

President's Commission on Mental Health. (1978). *Report to the President from the President's Commission on Mental Health.* Washington, DC: US Government Printing Office.

Pressman, J. L., & Wildavsky, A. (1979). *Implementation* (2d Ed.). Berkeley: University of California Press.

Price, R. H. (1990). [Review of P. Schoggen, *Behavior settings.*] *Environment and Behavior, 22,* 538–544.

Price, R. H. (1992). Psychosocial impact of job loss on individuals and families. *Current Directions in Psychological Science, 1,* 9–11.

Price, R. H., & Moos, R. H. (1975). Toward a taxonomy of inpatient treatment environments. *Journal of Abnormal Psychology, 84,* 181–188.

Price, R. H., van Ryn, M., & Vinokur, A. D. (1992). Impact of a preventive job search intervention on the likelihood of depression among the unemployed. *Journal of Health and Social Behavior, 33,* 158–167.

Psychosocial Rehabilitation Journal (1992), *16*, No. 2, October.

Rabkin, J. G., & Streuning, E. L. (1976). Life events, stress and illness. *Science, 194*, 1013–1020.

Rapp, C. A., & Moore, T. D. (1995). The first 18 months of mental health reform in Kansas. *Psychiatric Services, 46*, 580–585.

Rappaport, J. (1977). *Community psychology: Values, research, and action.* New York: Holt, Rinehart, & Winston.

Rappaport, J. (1981). In praise of paradox: A social policy of empowerment over prevention. *American Journal of Community Psychology, 9*, 1–26.

Rappaport, J. (1992). The dilemma of primary prevention in mental health services: Rationalize the status quo or bite the hand that feeds you. *Journal of Community and Applied Social Psychology, 2*, 95–99.

Ravitch, D. (1983). *The troubled crusade: American education, 1945–1980.* New York: Basic Books.

Redick, R. W., Witkin, M. J., Amy, J. E., & Manderscheid, R. W. (1992). *Patient care episodes in mental health organizations, United States: Selected years from 1955 to 1988.* Washington, DC: NIMH Division of Applied and Services Research.

Regier, D. A., Hirschfeld, R. M. A., Goodwin, F. K., et al. (1988). The NIMH Depression Awareness, Recognition, and Treatment program: Structure, aims, and scientific basis. *American Journal of Psychiatry, 145*, 1351–1357.

Regier, D. A., Narrow, W. E., Rae, D. S., Manderscheid, R. W., Locke, B. Z., & Goodwin, F. K. (1993). The de facto U.S. mental and addictive disorders service system: Epidemiological Catchment Area prospective 1-year prevalence rates of disorders and services. *Archives of General Psychiatry, 50*, 85–94.

Reich, C. A. (1970). *The greening of America.* New York: Random House.

Reiss, B. F., & Brandt, L. W. (1965). What happens to applicants for psychotherapy? *Community Mental Health Journal, 1*, 175–180.

Reissman, F. (1965). The 'helper-therapy' principle. *Social Work, 10*, 27–32.

Richart, R. H., & Milner, L. M. (1968). Factors influencing admission to a community mental health center. *Community Mental Health Journal, 4*, 27–35.

Richmond, J. B., Stipek, D. J., & Zigler, E. (1979). A decade of Head Start. In E. Zigler & J. Valentine (Eds.), *Project Head Start: A legacy of the War on Poverty* (Chapter 4). New York: Free Press.

Riger, S. (1985). Crime as an environmental stressor. *Journal of Community Psychology, 13*, 270–280.

Riggio, R. E. (1990). *Introduction to industrial/organizational psychology.* Glenview, IL: Scott, Foresman/Little, Brown.

Robins, L. N. (1974). *Deviant children grown up.* Huntington, NY: Krieger.

Roe v. *Wade*, 410 US 113 (1973).

Roen, S. R., & Burnes, A. J. (1968). *The community adaptation schedule: Preliminary manual.* New York: Behavioral Publications.

Rogers, A. (1993). Coercion and "voluntary" admission: An examination of psychiatric patient views. *Behavioral Sciences & the Law, 11*, 259–267.

Rogler, L. (1994). International migrations: A framework for directing research. *American Psychologist, 49,* 701–708.

Roosens, E. (1979). *Mental patients in town life. Geel—Europe's first therapeutic community.* Beverly Hills, CA: Sage.

Rosenberg, J., & Phillips, W. R. F. (1981–1982). The institutionalization of conflict in the reform of the schools: A case study of the PARC decree. *Indiana Law Journal, 57,* 425–449.

Rosenberg, M. S., & Reppucci, N. D. (1985). Primary prevention of child abuse. *Journal of Consulting and Clinical Psychology, 53,* 576–585.

Rosenhan, D. L. (1973). On being sane in insane places. *Science, 179,* 250–258.

Rossman, M. (1976). Self-help marketplace. *Social Policy, 7,* 86–91.

Roszak, T. (1969). *The making of a counter culture.* New York: Doubleday.

Rotheram-Borus, M. J., Koopman, C., Haignere, C., & Davies, M. (1991). Reducing HIV sexual risk behaviors among runaway adolescents. *Journal of the American Medical Association, 266,* 1237–1241.

Rothman, D. J. (1971). *The discovery of the asylum.* Boston: Little, Brown.

Rothman, D. J. (1982). The courts and social reform: A postprogressive outlook. *Law and Human Behavior, 6,* 113–19.

Rothman, J. (1974). Three models of community organization practice. In F. Cox, J. Erlich, J. Rothman, & J. Tropman (Eds.), *Strategies of community organization: A book of readings* (2d Ed.). Itasca, IL: Peacock.

Rowlinson, R. T., & Felner, R. D. (1988). Major life events, hassles, and adaptation in adolescence: Confounding in the conceptualization and measurement of life stress and adjustment revisited. *Journal of Personality and Social Psychology, 55,* 432–444.

Ryan, R. (1971). *Blaming the victim.* New York: Random House.

Ryan, W. (1969). *Distress in the city.* Cleveland: Press of Case Western Reserve University.

Sagan, L. A. (1987). *The health of nations.* New York: Basic Books.

Sagarin, E. (1969). *Odd man in: Societies of deviants in America.* Chicago: Quadrangle Books.

Salem, D. A., Seidman, E., & Rappaport, J. (1988). Community treatment of the mentally ill: The promise of self-help organizations. *Social Work, 33,* 403–410.

Sarason, I. G., & Sarason, B. R. (1981). Teaching cognitive and social skills to high school students. *Journal of Consulting and Clinical Psychology, 49,* 908–918.

Sarason, S. B. (1967). Toward a psychology of change and innovation. *American Psychologist, 22,* 227–233.

Sarason, S. B. (1972). *The creation of settings and the future societies.* San Francisco: Jossey-Bass.

Sarason, S. B. (1974). *The psychological sense of community: Prospects for a community psychology.* San Francisco: Jossey-Bass.

Sarason, S. B. (1976a). Community psychology, networks, and Mr. Everyman. *American Psychologist, 31,* 317–328.

Sarason, S. B. (1976b). Community psychology and the anarchist insight. *American Journal of Community Psychology*, 4, 243–261.

Sarason, S. B. (1978). The nature of problem solving in social action. *American Psychologist*, 33, 370–380.

Sarason, S. B. (1981a). *Psychology misdirected.* New York: Free Press.

Sarason, S. B. (1981b). An asocial psychology and a misdirected clinical psychology. *American Psychologist*, 36, 827–836.

Sarason, S. B. (1982a). *Psychology and social action: Selected papers.* New York: Praeger.

Sarason, S. B. (1982b). *The culture of the school and the problem of change.* 2d Ed. Boston: Allyn & Bacon.

Sarason, S. B. (1990). *The predictible failure of educational reform.* San Francisco: Jossey-Bass.

Sarason, S. B., Carroll, C. F., Maton, K., Cohen, S., & Lorentz, E. (1977). *Human services and resource networks.* San Francisco: Jossey-Bass.

Sarason, S. B., & Doris. J. (1969). *Psychological problems in mental deficiency.* (4th Ed.). New York: Harper & Row.

Sarason, S. B., & Klaber, M. (1985). The school as a social situation. *Annual Review of Psychology*, 36, 115–140.

Sarason, S. B., Levine, M., Goldenberg, I. I., Cherlin, D. L., & Bennett, E. M. (1966). *Psychology in community settings.* New York: Wiley.

Sarason, S. B., & Lorentz, E. (1979). *The challenge of the resource exchange network.* San Francisco: Jossey-Bass.

Sarason, S. B., Zitnay, G., & Grossman, F. K. (1971). *The creation of a community setting.* Syracuse, NY: Syracuse University Division of Special Education and Rehabilitation and the Center on Human Policy.

Sarbin, T. R. (1970). A role theory perspective for community psychology: The structure of social identity. In D. Adelson & B. Kalis (Eds.), *Community psychology and mental health: Perspectives and challenges.* Scranton, PA: Chandler.

Schechter, A., Dai, L. C., Thuy, L. T. B., Quynh, H. T., Minh, D. Q., Cau, H. D., Phiet, P. H., Phuong, N. T. N., Constable, J. D., Baughman, R., Papke, O., Ryan, J.J., Furst, P., and Raisanen, S. (1995). Agent Orange and the Vietnamese: The persistence of elevated dioxin levels in human tissues. *American Journal of Public Health*, 85, 516–522.

Scheff, T. J. (1966). *Being mentally ill: A sociological perspective.* Chicago: Aldine.

Scheff, T. J. (Ed.). (1975). *Labelling madness.* Englewood Cliffs, NJ: Prentice-Hall.

Scheff, T. J. (1984). *Being mentally ill. A sociological theory.* 2nd ed. Chicago: Aldine.

Schoggen, P. (1989). *Behavior settings: A revision and extension of Roger G. Barker's Ecological psychology.* Stanford, CA: Stanford University Press.

Schulberg, H. C., & Baker, F. (1975). *The mental hospital and human services.* New York: Behavioral Publications.

Schulz, R., & Hanusa, B. H. (1978). Long-term effects of control and predictability-enhancing interventions: Findings and ethical issues. *Journal of Personality and Social Psychology, 36,* 1194–1201.

Schuster, T. I., Kessler, R. C., & Aseltine, R. H., Jr., (1990). Supportive interactions, negative interactions, and depressed mood. *American Journal of Community Psychology, 18,* 423–438.

Schwartz, C. E., & Rogers, M. (1994). Designing a psychosocial intervention to teach coping flexibility. *Rehabilitation Psychology, 39,* 57–72.

Schwebel, M., & Schwebel, B. (1981). Children's reactions to the threat of nuclear plant accidents. *American Journal of Orthopsychiatry, 51,* 260–270.

Schweinhart, L. J., & Weikart, D. B. (1988). The High/Scope Perry Preschool Program. In R. Price et al. (Eds.), *14 Ounces of prevention* (pp. 53–66). Washington, DC: American Psychological Association.

Scull, A. T. (1977). *Decarceration: Community treatment and the deviant—A radical view.* Englewood Cliffs, NJ: Prentice-Hall.

Sedgwick, P. (1982). Antipsychiatry from the sixties to the eighties. In W. R. Gove (Ed.), *Deviance and mental illness.* Beverly Hills, CA: Sage.

Seekins, T., et al. (1988). Experimental evaluation of public policy: The case of state legislation for child passenger safety. *Journal of Applied Behavior Analysis, 21,* 233–243.

Segal, S. P., & Baumol, J. (1982). The new chronic patient: The creation of an underserved population. In L. R. Snowden (Ed.), *Reaching the underserved: Mental health needs of neglected populations.* Beverly Hills, CA: Sage.

Segal, S. P., Silverman, C., & Temkin, T. (1993). Empowerment and self-help agency practice for people with mental disabilities. *Social Work, 38,* 705–712.

Select Committee on Children, Youth and Families, U.S. House of Representatives (1990). *No place to call home: Discarded children in America.* Washington, DC: U.S. Government Printing Office.

Seller, M. S. (1979). *Ethnic communities and education in Buffalo, New York: Politics, power and group identity 1838–1979* (Occasional paper #1). Buffalo Community Studies Graduate Group. Buffalo: State University of New York at Buffalo.

Selye, H. (1956). *The stress of life.* New York: McGraw-Hill.

Sermabeikian, P. (1994). Our clients, ourselves: The spiritual perspective and social work practice. *Social Work, 39,* 178–183.

Sexton, P. C. (1961). *Education and income.* New York: Viking.

Shapiro, S., Skinner, E. A., et al. (1984). Utilization of health and mental health services. *Archives of General Psychiatry, 41,* 971–978.

Sherman, L. W. (1992). *Policing domestic violence: Experiments and dilemmas.* New York: Free Press.

Sherman, L. W., & Berk, R. A. (1984). The specific deterrent effects of arrest for domestic assault. *American Sociological Review, 49,* 261–272.

Sherman, P. S., & Porter, R. (1991). Mental health consumers as case management aides. *Hospital and Community Psychiatry, 42,* 494–498.

Shinn, M. (1992). Homelessness: What is a psychologist to do? *American Journal of Community Psychology, 20,* 1–24.

Shinn, M., & Felton, B. J. (Eds.). (1981). Institutions and alternatives. *Journal of Social Issues, 37*, 1–176.

Silverman, D. C. (1978). Sharing the crisis of rape: Counseling the mates and families of victims. *American Journal of Orthopsychiatry, 48*, 166–173.

Silverman, P. R., et al. (Eds.). (1974). *Helping each other in widowhood.* New York: Health Sciences.

Sipuel v. *Oklahoma State Board of Regents*, 332 US 631 (1948).

Skinner, L. J., Berry, K. K., Griffith, S. E., & Byers, B. (1995). Generalizability and specificity of the stigma associated with the mental illness label: A reconsideration twenty-five years later. *Journal of Community Psychology, 23*, 3–17.

Slaikeu, K. A. (1984). *Crisis intervention: A handbook for practice and research.* Boston: Allyn and Bacon.

Slater, P. (1970). *The pursuit of loneliness.* Boston: Beacon Press.

Slotnick, R. S., Jeger, A. M., & Trickett, E. J. (Eds.). (1980). Social ecology in community psychology. *Division of Community Psychology Newsletter, 13*, 1–19.

Smith, R. E., Johnson, J. H., & Sarason, I. G. (1978). Life change, the sensation seeking motive, and psychological distress. *Journal of Consulting and Clinical Psychology, 46*, 348–349.

Smith, R. R. (1978). Two centuries and twenty-four months: A chronicle of the struggle to desegregate the Boston public schools. In H. Kalodner & J. J. Fishman (Eds.), *Limits of justice: The courts' role in school desegregation.* Cambridge, Mass.: Ballinger.

Snell, T. L., & Morton, D. C. (1994). *Women in prison.* Bureau of Justice Statistics Special Report. Washington, DC: U.S. Department of Justice.

Snowden, L. R. (Ed.), (1982). *Reaching the underserved: Mental health needs of neglected populations.* Beverly Hills, CA: Sage.

Snowden, L. R. (1993). Emerging trends in organizing and financing human services: Unexamined consequences for ethnic minority populations. *American Journal of Community Psychology, 21*, 1–13.

Sobey, F. (1970). *The nonprofessional revolution in mental health.* New York: Columbia University Press.

Socall, D. W., & Holtgraves, T. (1992). Attitudes toward the mentally ill: The effects of labels and beliefs. *Sociological Quarterly, 33*, 3, 435–445.

Sommer, R., & Wicker, A. W. (1991). Gas station psychology: The case for specialization in ecological psychology. *Environment and Behavior, 23*, 131–149.

Spaulding, J., & Balch, P. (1983). A brief history of primary prevention in the twentieth century: 1908 to 1980. *American Journal of Community Psychology, 11*, 59–80.

Special Populations Subpanel on Mental Health of Black Americans. (1978). *Task Panel Reports Submitted to the President's Commission on Mental Health* (Appendix, Vol 3). Washington, DC: U.S. Government Printing Office.

Spitzer, R. L., & Williams, J. B. W. (1982). The definition and diagnosis of mental disorder. In W. R. Gove (Ed.), *Deviance and mental illness.* Beverly Hills, CA: Sage.

Spivack, G., Platt, J. J., & Shure, M. B. (1976). *The problem-solving approach to adjustment.* San Francisco: Jossey-Bass.

Spivack, G., & Shure, M. (1974). *Social adjustment of young children.* San Francisco: Jossey-Bass.

Spivack G., & Shure, M. B. (1985). ICPS and beyond: Centripetal and centrifugal forces. *American Journal of Community Psychology, 13,* 226–243.

Spivack, G., & Shure, M. B. (1989). Interpersonal Cognitive Problem Solving (ICPS): A competence-building primary prevention program. *Prevention in Human Services, 6,* 151–178.

Srebnik, D. S., & Elias, M. J. (1993). An ecological, interpersonal skills approach to drop-out prevention. *American Journal of Orthopsychiatry, 63,* 526–535.

Srole, L., Langner, T. S., Michael, S. T., Opler, M. K., & Rennie, T. A. C. (1962). *Mental health in the metropolis: The midtown Manhattan study.* New York: McGraw-Hill.

St. Lawrence, J. S., Brasfield, T. L., Jefferson, K. W., et al. (1995). Cognitive-behavioral intervention to reduce African American adolescents' risk for HIV infection. *Journal of Consulting and Clinical Psychology, 63,* 221–237.

Stack, L. C., Lannon, P. B., & Miley, A. D. (1983). Accuracy of clinicians' expectancies for psychiatric rehospitalization. *American Journal of Community Psychology, 11,* 99–113.

Steele, C. M. (1992). Race and the schooling of black Americans. *The Atlantic Monthly,* April, 68–78.

Stein, L. I., & Test, M. A. (1985). *The Training in Community Living model: A decade of experience.* (New Directions for Mental Health Services, No. 26). San Francisco: Jossey-Bass.

Stephan, W. G. (1978). School desegregation: An evaluation of predictions made in *Brown v. Board of Education. Psychological Bulletin, 85,* 217–238.

Stone, R. (1995). Panel slams EPA's dioxin analysis. *Science, 268,* 1124.

Stone, R. A., & Levine, A. G. (1985–1986). Reactions to collective stress: Correlates of active citizen participation at Love Canal. *Prevention in Human Services, 4,* 153–177.

Stott, M. W. R., Gaier, E. L., & Thomas, K. B. (1984). Supervised access: A judicial alternative to noncompliance with visitation arrangements following divorce. *Children and Youth Services Review, 6,* 207–217.

Stroul, B. A. (1986). *Models of community support services: Approaches to helping persons with long-term mental illness.* Boston: Center for Psychiatric Rehabilitation.

Suler, J. (1984). The role of ideology in self-help groups. *Social Policy, 14,* 29–36.

Sunshine, J. H., Witkin, M. J., Atay, J. E., & Manderscheid, R. W. (1991). Residential treatment centers and other organized mental health care for children and youth: United States, 1988. *Mental Health Statistical Note No. 198.* Rockville, MD: National Institute of Mental Health.

Surles, R., Blanch, A., Shern, D., & Donahue, S. (1992). Case management as a strategy for systems change. *Health Affairs, 11,* 151–163.

Sutherland, S., & Scherl, D. J. (1970). Patterns of response among victims of rape. *American Journal of Orthopsychiatry, 40,* 503–511.

Swann v. *Charlotte-Mecklenburg Board of Education*, 402 US 1 (1971).

Sweatt v. *Painter*, 339 US 629 (1950).

Szasz, T. S. (1961). *The myth of mental illness.* New York: Dell.

Szasz, T. S. (1963). *Law, liberty and psychiatry.* New York: Macmillan.

Task Panel. (1978). Report of the Task Panel on the nature and scope of the problems. *Task Panel Reports Submitted to the President's Commission on Mental Health.* Vol 2. Appendix. Washington, DC: U.S. Government Printing Office.

Task Panel on Prevention. (1978). Report of the Task Panel on Prevention. *Task Panel Reports Submitted to the President's Commission on Mental Health.* Vol 4. Washington, DC: U.S. Government Printing Office.

Taube, C. A., Burns, B. J., & Kessler, L. (1984). Patients of psychiatrists and psychologists in office-based practice: 1980. *American Psychologist, 39,* 1435–1447.

Taube, C. A., Morlock, L., Burns, B. J., & Santos, A. B. (1990). New directions in research on Assertive Community Treatment. *Hospital and Community Psychiatry, 41,* 642–646.

Taylor, B. R. (1991). *Affirmative action at work: Law, politics, and ethics.* Pittsburgh, PA: University of Pittsburgh Press.

Taylor, H. L. Jr. (1990). *African Americans and the rise of Buffalo's post-industrial city, 1940 to present. Volume 1: An introduction to a research report.* Buffalo, NY: Buffalo Urban League.

Taylor, S. E. (1983). Adjustment to threatening events: A theory of cognitive adaptation. *American Psychologist, 38,* 1161–1173.

Tebes, J. A. (1983). *Stigma and mental disorder: A review and analysis.* Unpublished doctoral qualifying paper, Department of Psychology, State University of New York at Buffalo.

Tebes, J. A., & Perkins, D. V. (1984). *Converting stress to positive mental health: Evidence from students coping with parental death.* Paper presented at the Eastern Psychological Association Convention, Baltimore.

Tebes, J. K., & Kraemer, D. T. (1991). Quantitative and qualitative knowing in mutual support research: Some lessons from the recent history of psychology. *American Journal of Community Psychology, 19,* 739–756.

Telch, C. F., & Telch, M. J. (1986). Group coping skills instruction and supportive group therapy for cancer patients: A comparison of strategies. *Journal of Consulting and Clinical Psychology, 54,* 802–808.

TenBroek, J. (1965). *Equal under law.* London: Collier.

Teplin, L. A. (1983). The criminalization of the mentally ill: Speculation in search of data. *Psychological Bulletin, 94,* 54–67.

Teplin, L. A. (1984). Criminalizing mental disorder: The comparative arrest rate of the mentally disordered. *American Psychologist, 39,* 794–803.

Test, M. A. (1991). The Training in Community Living Model: Delivering treatment and rehabilitation services through a continuous treatment team. In R. Liberman (Ed.), *Handbook of psychiatric rehabilitation.* New York: Pergamon.

The Liberator, Defender of Men. (1994). *21.*

The Spokeswoman. (1977, August 15). *8,* No. 2.

Thoits, P. A. (1986). Social support as coping assistance. *Journal of Consulting and Clinical Psychology, 54,* 416–423.

Thomas, D., & Veno, A. (1992). *Psychology and social change.* Palmerston, NZ: Dunmore.

Thomas, S. B., & Quinn, S. C. (1991). The Tuskegee syphillis study, 1932 to 1972: Implications for HIV education and AIDS risk education programs in the Black community. *American Journal of Public Health, 81,* 1498–1505.

Thompson, C. M. (1985). Characteristics associated with outcome in a community mental health partial hospitalization program. *Community Mental Health Journal, 21,* 179–188.

Timko, C., & Moos, R. H. (1991). A typology of social climates in group residential facilities for older people. *Journal of Gerontology, 46,* S160–169.

Tischler, G. L. (1966). Decision making in the emergency room. *Archives of General Psychiatry, 14,* 69–78.

Tomkins, A. J., Steinman, M., Kenning, M. K., Mohamed, S., & Afrank, J. (1992). Children who witness woman battering. *Law & Policy, 14,* 169–184.

Toro, P. A. (1990). Evaluating professionally operated and self-help programs for the seriously mentally ill. *American Journal of Community Psychology, 18,* 903–908.

Toro, P. A., & Wall, D. D. (1991). Research on homeless persons: diagnostic comparisons and practice implications. *Professional Psychology: Research and Practice, 22,* 479–488.

Toro, P. A., Rappaport, J., & Seidman, E. (1987). Social climate comparison of mutual help and psychotherapy groups. *Journal of Consulting and Clinical Psychology, 55,* 430–431.

Toro, P. A., Reischl, T. M., Zimmerman, M. A., Rappaport, J., Seidman, E., Luke, D. A., & Roberts, L. J. (1988). Professionals in mutual help groups: Impact on social climate and members' behavior. *Journal of Consulting and Clinical Psychology, 56,* 631–632.

Torrey, E. F. (1990). Economic barriers to widespread implementation of model programs for the seriously mentally ill. *Hospital and Community Psychiatry, 41,* 526–531.

Torrey, E. F., Bowler, A., Taylor, E., & Gottesman, I. (1994). *Schizophrenia and manic-depressive disorder.* New York: Basic Books.

Torrey, E. F., Wolfe, S. M., & Flynn, L. M. (1988). *Care of the seriously mentally ill: A rating of state programs* (2d Ed.). Arlington, VA: National Alliance for the Mentally Ill and Public Citizen Health Research Group.

Toulmin, S. (1958). *The uses of argument.* London: Cambridge University Press.

Tracy, G. S., & Gussow, Z. (1976). Self-help health groups: A grass-roots response to a need for services. *Journal of Applied Behavioral Science, 12,* 381–396.

Trickett, E. J. (1978). Toward a social-ecological conception of adolescent socialization: Normative data on contrasting types of public school classrooms. *Child Development, 49,* 408–414.

Trickett, E. J., & Moos, R. H. (1974). Personal correlates of contrasting environments: Student satisfactions in high school classrooms. *American Journal of Community Psychology, 2,* 1–12.

Trickett, E. J., Kelly, J. G., & Vincent, T. A. (1985). The spirit of ecological inquiry in community research. In E. C. Susskind & D. C. Klein (Eds.), *Community research: Methods, paradigms, and applications* (pp. 283–333). New York: Praeger.

Tuckman, J., & Lavell, M. (1962). Patients discharged with or against medical advice. *Journal of Clinical Psychology, 13,* 177–180.

Tuckman, J., & Lavell, M. (1959). Attrition in psychiatric clinics for children. *Public Health Reports, Public Health Service, 74,* 309–315.

Tumin, M. M. (1970). Some social consequences of research on racial relations. In P. I. Rose (Ed.), *Slavery and its aftermath.* New York: Atherton.

Uhl, G., & Levine, M. (1990). Group homes and crime. *Hospital and Community Psychiatry, 41,* 1028.

Unger, D.G., & Wandersman, A. (1985). The importance of neighbors: The social, cognitive, and affective components of neighboring. *American Journal of Community Psychology, 13,* 139–169.

U.S. Advisory Board on Child Abuse and Neglect. (1990). *Child abuse and neglect: Critical first steps to a national emergency.* Washington, DC: Office of Human Development Services.

U.S. Advisory Board on Child Abuse and Neglect. (1993). *Neighbors helping neighbors: A new national strategy for the protection of children.* Washington, DC: Administration for Children and Families.

U.S. Advisory Board on Child Abuse and Neglect. (1995). *A nation's shame: Fatal child abuse and neglect in the United States.* Washington, DC: Administration for Children and Families.

U.S. Bureau of the Census. (1981). *Statistical abstract of the United States, 1981* (102d Ed.). Washington, DC: U.S. Department of Commerce.

U.S. Bureau of the Census. (1991). *Statistical abstract of the United States, 1991* (111th Ed.). Washington, DC: U.S. Department of Commerce.

U.S. Bureau of the Census. (1993). *Statistical abstract of the United States, 1993* (113th Ed.). Washington, DC: U.S. Department of Commerce.

U.S. Bureau of Justice Statistics. (1985). *The crime of rape.* Washington, DC: U.S. Department of Justice.

U.S. Bureau of Justice Statistics. (1990). *Jail inmates.* Washington, DC: U.S. Department of Justice.

U.S. Bureau of Justice Statistics. (1994). *Criminal victimization in the United States, 1992.* Washington, DC: U.S. Department of Justice.

U.S. Department of Education. (1990). *12th annual report to Congress on the implementation of the Education of the Handicapped Act.* Washington, DC: U.S. Department of Education.

U.S. Department of Health, Education and Welfare. (1979). *Promoting health, preventing disease. Objectives for the nation.* Washington, DC: Author.

U.S. Department of Health, Education and Welfare. (1976). *Health: United States, 1975.* DHEW Publication No. (HRA) 76–1232. Washington, DC: Author.

U.S. Department of Justice. (1989). *Children in custody, 1975–1985. Census of public and private juvenile detention, correctional and shelter facilities.* Washington, DC: U.S. Department of Justice.

U.S. Environmental Protection Agency. (1994). *Draft reassessment of dioxin and dioxin-like compounds, Exposure Assessment Document.* Washington, DC: Author.

U.S. General Accounting Office. (1993). *Foster care. Services to prevent out-of-home placements are limited by funding barriers.* Washington, DC: Author.

U.S. House of Representatives Select Committee on Children, Youth and Families. (1990). *No place to call home: Discarded children in America.* Washington, DC: U.S. Government Printing Office.

U.S. Office of Special Education and Rehabilitative Services. (1990). *"To assure the free appropriate education of all handicapped children."* 12th Annual Report to Congress on the Implementation of the Education of the Handicapped Act. Washington, DC: U.S. Department of Education.

U.S. v. Cruickshank, 92 US 542 (1875).

Vaillant, G. E. (1983). *The natural history of alcoholism.* Cambridge, Mass.: Harvard University Press.

Valerio, A. M. (1985). *Sex education program evaluations: A review and analysis.* Unpublished doctoral preliminary paper, Department of Psychology, State University of New York at Buffalo.

van Ryn, M., & Vinokur, A. D. (1992). How did it work? An examination of the mechanisms through which an intervention for the unemployed promoted job-search behavior. *American Journal of Community Psychology, 20,* 577–597.

Videka-Sherman, L., & Lieberman, M. (1985). The effects of self-help and psychotherapy on child loss: The limits of recovery. *American Journal of Orthopsychiatry, 55,* 70–82.

Vincent, T. A., & Trickett, E. J. (1983). Preventive interventions and the human context: Ecological approaches to environmental assessment and change. In R. Felner, L. Jason, J. Moritsugu, & S. Farber (Eds.), *Preventive psychology.* New York: Pergamon.

Vinokur, A. D., van Ryn, M., Gramlich, E. M., & Price, R. H. (1991). Longer-term follow-up and benefit-cost analysis of the Jobs Program: A preventive intervention for the unemployed. *Journal of Applied Psychology, 76,* 213–219.

Vivian, D., & O'Leary, K. D. (1990). Physical aggression in marriage. In F. D. Fincham & T. N. Bradbury (Eds.), *The psychology of marriage: Basic issues and applications* (pp. 323–348). New York: Guilford Press.

Vogel, W. (1991). A personal memoir of the state hospitals of the 1950s. *Hospital and Community Psychiatry, 42,* 593–597.

Vyner, H. M. (1988). *Invisible trauma: The psychosocial effects of the invisible environmental contaminants.* Lexington, MA: Lexington Books.

Walker, K. N., MacBride, A., & Vachon, M. L. S. (1977). Social support networks and the crisis of bereavement. *Social Science and Medicine, 11,* 35–41.

Walter, H. J., & Vaughn, R. D. (1993). AIDS risk reduction among a multiethnic sample of urban high school students. *Journal of the American Medical Association, 270,* 725–730.

Wandersman, A., & Florin, P. (Eds.). (1990). Citizen participation, voluntary organizations and community development: Insights for empowerment through research (Special Section). *American Journal of Community Psychology, 18*, 41–177.

Wandersman, A., & Florin, P. (in press). Citizen participation in community organizations. In J. Rappaport & E. Seidman (Eds.), *Handbook of community psychology*. New York: Plenum Press.

Wandersman, A., Florin, P., Friedmann, R., & Meier, R. (1987). Who participates, who does not, and why? An analysis of volunatry neighborhood associations in the United States and Israel. *Sociological Forum, 2*, 534–555.

Wandersman, A. H., & Hallman, W. K. (1993). Are people acting irrationally? Understanding public concerns about environmental threats. *American Psychologist, 48*, 681–686.

Warr, P. (1987). *Work, unemployment, and mental health*. Oxford: Clarendon.

Warren, C. B. (1977). Involuntary commitment for mental disorder: The application of California's Lanerman-Petris-Short Act. *Law & Society Review, 11*, 629–650.

Watzlawick, P., Weakland, J. H., & Fisch, R. (1974). *Change: Principles of problem formation and problem resolution*. New York: Norton.

Weiss, R. S. (1987). Principles underlying a manual for parents whose children were killed by a drunk driver. *American Journal of Orthopsychiatry, 57*, 431–440.

Weissberg, R. P., & Elias, M. J. (1993). Enhancing young people's social competence and health behavior: An important challenge for educators, scientists, policymakers, and funders. *Applied & Preventive Psychology, 2*, 179–190.

Weithorn, L. A. (1988). Mental hospitalization of troublesome youth: An analysis of skyrocketing admission rates. *Stanford Law Review, 40*, 773–838.

Weitzman, L. J. (1985). *The divorce revolution*. New York: Free Press.

Wenger, D. L., & Fletcher, C. R. (1969). The effect of legal counsel on admissions to a state mental hospital: A confrontation of professions. *Journal of Health and Social Behavior, 10*, 66–72.

Whitaker, C. J., & Bastian, L. D. (1991). *Teenage victims. A National Crime Survey report*. NCJ-128129. Washington, DC: U.S. Department of Justice.

White, M. A., & Harris, M. W. (1961). *The school psychologist*. New York: Harper & Row.

Whitehead, B. D. (1994). The failure of sex education. *The Atlantic Monthly* (October). Reprinted in *American Educator, 18*, 22–29, 46–52.

Whitt, H., & Meile, R. (1985). Alignment, magnification, and snowballing: Processes in the definition of "symptoms of mental illness." *Social Forces, 63*, 682–697.

Whyte, W. H. (1980). *The social life of small urban spaces*. Washington, DC: Conservation Foundation.

Wicker, A. W. (1972). Processes which mediate behavior-environment congruence. *Behavioral Science, 17*, 365–277.

Wicker, A. W. (1979). *An introduction to ecological psychology*. Monterey, CA: Brooks-Cole.

Widom, C. S. (1989). The cycle of violence. *Science, 244,* 160–166.

Wilensky, H. L., & Lebeaux, C. N. (1965). *Industrial society and social welfare.* New York: Free Press.

Willer, B., & Intagliata, J. (1984). An overview of the social policy of deinstitutionalization. *International Review of Research in Mental Retardation, 12,* 1–23.

Willie, C. V. (1984). *School desegregation plans that work.* Westport, CT: Greenwood Press.

Wilson, W. J. (1987). *The truly disadvantaged: The inner city, the underclass, and public policy.* Chicago: University of Chicago Press.

Winerip, M. (1985). School integration in Buffalo is hailed as a model for U.S. *New York Times,* May 13, pp. A1, B4.

Witheridge, T. F., & Dincin, J. (1985). The Bridge: An assertive outreach program in an urban setting. In L. Stein & M. A. Test (Eds.), *The Training in Community Living model: A decade of experience.* (New Directions for Mental Health Services, No. 26, pp. 65–76). San Francisco: Jossey-Bass.

Witte, E. E. (1963). *The development of the social security act.* Madison: University of Wisconsin Press.

Wohlford, P. (1990). National responsiblities to improve training for psychological services for children, youth and families in the 1990s. In P. R. Magrab and P. Wohlford (Eds.), *Improving psychological services for children and adolescents with severe mental disorders: Clinical training in psychology.* Washington, DC: American Psychological Association.

Wolchik, S. A., Ruehlman, L. S., Braver, S. L., & Sandler, I. N. (1989). Social support of children of divorce: Direct and stress buffering effects. *American Journal of Community Psychology, 17,* 485–501.

Wolchik, S. A., West, S. G., Westover, S., Sandler, I. N., Martin, A., Lustig, J., Jenn-Yun Tein, & Fisher, J. (1993). The Children of Divorce parenting intervention: Outcome evaluation of an empirically based program. *American Journal of Community Psychology, 21,* 293–332.

Wong, H. Z. (1982). Asian and Pacific Americans. In L. R. Snowden (Ed.), *Reaching the underserved: Mental health needs of neglected populations.* Beverly Hills, CA: Sage.

Woodward, B., & Bernstein, C. (1976). *The final days.* New York: Simon & Schuster.

Wyatt, G. E., & Powell, G. J. (Eds.). (1988). *Lasting effects of child sexual abuse.* Newbury Park, CA: Sage.

York, P., & York, D. (1980). *Toughlove.* Sellersville, PA: Community Service Foundation.

Young, J. (1992). An evaluation of the mutual help organisation, GROW. In D. Thomas and A. Veno (Eds.), *Psychology and Social Change.* Palmerston North, New Zealand: Dunmore Press.

Young, J., & Williams, C. L. (1988). Whom do mutual-help groups help? A typology of members. *Hospital and Community Psychiatry, 39,* 1178–1182.

Zahner, G. E. P., Kasl, S. V., White, M., & Will, J. C. (1985). Psychological consequences of infestation of the dwelling unit. *American Journal of Public Health*, *75*, 1303–1307.

Zane, N., Sue, S., Castro, F. G., & George, W. (1982). Service system models for ethnic minorities. In L. R. Snowden (Ed.), *Reaching the underserved: Mental health needs of neglected populations*. Beverly Hills, CA: Sage.

Zapata, B. C., Rebolledo, A., Atalah, E., Newman, B., & King, M.C. (1992). The influence of social and political violence on the risk of pregnancy complications. *American Journal of Public Health*, *82*, 685–690.

Zax, M., & Spector, G. A. (1974). *An introduction to community psychology*. New York: Wiley.

Zigler, E., & Muenchow, S. (1992). *Head Start: The inside story of America's most successful educational experiment*. New York: Basic Books.

Zigler, E., & Styfco, S. J. (Eds.). (1993). *Head Start and beyond*. New Haven, CT: Yale University Press.

Zimmerman, M. A., Reischl, T. M., Seidman, E., Rappaport, J., Toro, P. A., & Salem, D. A. (1991). Expansion strategies of a mutual help organization. *American Journal of Community Psychology*, *19*, 251–278.

Zorc, J. J., Larson, D. B., Lyons, J. S., & Beardsley, R. S. (1991). Expenditures for psychotropic medications in the United States in 1985. *American Journal of Psychiatry*, *148*, 644–647.

Zusman, J. (1967). Some explanations of the changing appearance of psychotic patients. *International Journal of Psychiatry*, *3*, 216–237.

Zusman, J., & Simon, J. (1983). Differences in repeated psychiatric examinations of litigants to a law suit. *American Journal of Psychiatry*, *140*, 1300–1304.

Name Index

Subject Index